INTERNATIONAL TRADE

About the Authors

Bud Harmon

Robert C. Feenstra and **Alan M. Taylor** are Professors of Economics at the University of California, Davis. They each began their studies abroad: Feenstra received his B.A. in 1977 from the University of British Columbia, in Canada, and Taylor received his B.A. in 1987 from King's College, Cambridge, in England. They trained as professional economists in the United States, where Feenstra earned his Ph.D. in economics from MIT in 1981 and Taylor earned his Ph.D. in economics from Harvard University in 1992. Feenstra has been teaching international trade at the undergraduate and graduate levels at the University of California, Davis, since 1986, where he holds the C. Bryan Cameron Distinguished Chair in International Economics. Taylor teaches international finance and macroeconomics at the University of California, Davis, where he also holds appointments as Director of the Center for the Evolution of the Global Economy and Professor of Finance in the Graduate School of Management.

Both Feenstra and Taylor are active in research and policy discussions in international economics. They are research associates of the National Bureau of Economic Research, where Feenstra directed the International Trade and Investment research program from 1992 to 2016. They have published monographs in international economics: *Offshoring in the Global Economy* and *Product Variety and the Gains from International Trade* (MIT Press, 2010) by Robert C. Feenstra, and *Global Capital Markets: Integration, Crisis, and Growth* (Cambridge University Press, 2004) by Maurice Obstfeld and Alan M. Taylor. Feenstra received the Bernhard Harms Prize from the Institute for World Economics, Kiel, Germany, in 2006, and he delivered the Ohlin Lectures at the Stockholm School of Economics in 2008. Taylor was awarded a Guggenheim Fellowship in 2004 and was a Houblon-Norman/George Fellow at the Bank of England in 2009–10.

Feenstra lives in Davis, California, with his wife, Gail. They have two grown children, Heather and Evan, and two grandchildren, Grant and Lily. Taylor also lives in Davis, with his wife, Claire, and their two children, Olivia and Sebastian.

Brief Contents

INTERNATIONAL TRADE

Preface

A Course That's More Important Than Ever

As the writing of this book draws to a close in April 2020, the world economy is experiencing what is likely to be its biggest adverse macroeconomic shock since World War II. The 2019–20 coronavirus pandemic has already tipped most countries into recession—starting in China, where the virus originated, and then spreading outwards to East Asia, Australasia, Europe, the United States, and beyond. This event is unfolding barely a decade after what was the previous largest postwar economic shock, the Global Financial Crisis of 2008. Both crises caused great damage to aggregate economic activity—contracting output, trade, investment, and consumption and causing the levels of unemployment around the world to rapidly increase. The damage was only slowly repaired after 2008, and we might be in for an equally slow recovery after this latest shock.

These two recent crises, and the patchy economic recovery that fell between them, illustrate the importance of international linkages in today's globalized world. Obviously, the transmission of a virus pays no heed to international borders, absent intervention measures to limit travel or impose quarantines. But economic transactions also cross borders, and those links have served for decades, or even centuries, as ways for events in faraway places to cause sudden disruptions to our own economic conditions at home. In 2008, the global economy was tied together by financial transactions, some of which fell under suspicion of being very risky; countries were also connected via trade flows, which often collapsed as trouble in an importing country spilled over into reduced demand for the products of the exporting country, government debts dramatically expanded, central banks made extraordinary interventions, and currency values moved this way and that with every piece of news. After the crisis, growth took new forms and different trade patterns emerged. Some groups in society fared better or worse than others, amplifying distributional concerns, and protectionist trade policies caused further disruption in the global economy, particularly so under U.S. president Donald Trump. Many of the same tensions continue to simmer and could well flare up again.

We saw huge shocks and policy responses emerge and propagate throughout the global economy a decade ago, and we see similar phenomena yet again today. The magnitude of the economic, political, and social impacts is hard to overstate, and they are felt across the entire globe, from the richest advanced economies to the upcoming emerging markets and the poorest developing nations. Arguably, looking at this fraught landscape, it has never been clearer that a sound grasp of international economics is essential knowledge if we are to better understand the world we inhabit.

Why Our Book?

Since the first edition of our text, it has been our goal to present the theories of international economics and bring its models alive through applications that draw on world events. All students want to understand the events they see described on their mobile screens, and our book helps them do just that. We draw on the very latest research—presented at a level appropriate to undergraduate students—to put solid numbers on the models we discuss. Our applications deal not only with the economics behind world events but also with the political economy underlying policy decisions.

Emphasis on Applications

How do you bring theories and models to life? You pair them with real life stories, so most of our chapters include a story, either told directly or taken from a media report. Examples include the tumult at the beginning stages of the coronavirus pandemic (Chapter 1), tariffs used by U.S. presidents (including and before President Trump, Chapter 8), the influence of the Swedish teenager and environmental activist Greta Thunberg (Chapter 11), the suffering in Iceland during the Great Recession (Chapter 12), or in contrast the successful policy followed by Chile (Chapter 17). In each case, the story is meant to draw the student into the theme of the chapter by using a current or historical event. But it's not just these stories that will engage the students: our textbook is unique in that it integrates empirical applications throughout the chapters. Students are asked to think critically about the theory and how it holds up in reality by applying it to historical and current examples. We accomplish these goals by integrating special features throughout:

Applications are integrated into the main text because they are an essential part of our approach to seamlessly blend theory and empirical data with real-world policies, events, and evidence.

Headlines present excerpts from current and historic media stories that further illustrate how topics in the main text relate directly to media coverage of the global economy.

Side Bars illuminate topics that, while not essential, nonetheless provide deeper understanding of the issues under discussion.

To see all Applications, Headlines, and Side Bars, please go to the Detailed Table of Contents.

Emphasis on Empirical Studies

In addition to expanding our coverage to include up-to-date theory and policy applications, our other major goal is to present all the material—both new and old—in the most teachable way. To do this, we ensure that all of the material presented rests on firm and up-to-the-minute empirical evidence. We believe this approach is the right way to study economics, and it is our experience, shared by many instructors, that teaching is more effective and more enlivened when students can see not just an elegant derivation in theory but, right next to it, some persuasive evidence of the economic mechanisms under investigation.

Balanced Coverage of Emerging and Advanced Economies

In our view, emerging markets and developing countries deserve more attention in the curriculum because of their substantial and growing importance in the global economy. For example, in the sections on international trade we discuss in detail the evolving factor endowments in China, including both capital and human capital, the effect of free trade within North America on Mexico, and the migration flows into the United States from Mexico and neighboring countries to the south. In the sections on international macroeconomics, we examine fixed exchange rates in Peru and Argentina, austerity in Poland and Latvia, sudden stops in emerging markets, and the importance of foreign aid in developing countries.

Broadening Learning with Practice

Each chapter concludes with exercises that ask students to think critically about the core concepts in each chapter.

- **Discovering Data** problems at the end of each chapter ask students to seek out, analyze, and interpret real-world data related to chapter topics.

- **Work It Out** problems at the end of each chapter provide students with step-by-step assistance, thus helping develop analytical skills. Each of these problems has a live, online counterpart in *Achieve*, Macmillan's new digital platform, available with this edition.

Introducing *Achieve*: Engage Every Student

Achieve is a comprehensive set of interconnected teaching and assessment tools. It incorporates the most effective elements from Macmillan's market-leading solutions into a single, easy-to-use platform.

Everything Your Students Need in a Single Learning Path

Achieve supports students and instructors at every step, from the first point of contact with new content to demonstrating mastery of concepts and skills. Powerful multimedia resources with an integrated e-book, robust homework, and a variety of interactivities create an extraordinary learning resource for students. *LearningCurve* is adaptive quizzing with a game-like interface, offering students a low-stakes way to brush up on concepts and help identify knowledge gaps. LearningCurve's design nudges students to reference the e-book, providing both the incentive to read and a framework for an efficient reading experience. In addition to *Discovering Data* and *Work It Out* problems, each chapter includes curated *End of Chapter* problems. These multistep questions are adapted from problems found in the text. Each problem is paired with rich feedback for incorrect and correct responses that guide students through the process of problem solving. These questions also feature graphing problems designed so that the student's entire focus is on shading the correct areas or moving the appropriate curves in the correct directions, virtually eliminating grading issues for instructors.

The best place for pricing and bundle options is the Macmillan Learning Online Student Store.

Everything Instructors Need

Achieve's Instructor's Resource Section includes the following:

Instructor's Resource Manual provides summaries and teaching tips for the text's content, along with suggested in-class problems and answers.

Solutions Manual includes answers to end-of-chapter questions.

Test Bank includes expansive multiple-choice and essay-assessment questions.

Lecture Slides include chapter notes and figures, as well as clicker questions and data exercises that can be used in class.

Multiple Formats Support Classroom Needs

The International Economics course is sometimes taught as two separate courses, so this text is issued in multiple formats to allow instructors to tailor the content to their needs and keep costs down for their students:

- A combined edition (*International Economics*)
- Two split editions (*International Trade* and *International Macroeconomics*)

What's New in This Edition (Combined and Split Versions)

Below is a brief list including some of the major updates made to this edition of the text:

A new opening example in **Chapter 1, Trade in the Global Economy**, covers the effects of the coronavirus pandemic on international trade.

Chapter 2, Trade and Technology: The Ricardian Model, includes a heavily revised application on "Labor Productivity and Wages" and a new figure showing the impact of different deflators for real wages in the United States.

Chapter 3, Gains and Losses from Trade in the Specific-Factors Model, features two new applications, both of which include new figures. "The 'China Shock' and Employment in the United States" examines whether jobs lost within import-competing industries are made up for by jobs gained in export industries, as the international trade models typically assume. "Can Losses to Factors of Production Be Offset?" discusses policies that encourage the movement of factors of production between sectors when changing international prices cause losses in a given sector.

Chapter 4, Trade and Resources: The Heckscher–Ohlin Model, includes several new sections and a heavily revised section now titled "Evolution of Factor Endowments in China and the United States." The new coverage looks at "effective" endowments in China and in the United States over several years and tells an interesting story about growth in China as compared with the United States.

Chapter 5, Movement of Labor and Capital Between Countries, contains a new application, "The Political Economy of Migration," that discusses extensively the economics of and policies concerning immigrants in the United States and Europe.

Chapter 6, Increasing Returns to Scale and Monopolistic Competition, contains new extensive coverage of the differences between NAFTA and USMCA.

The chapters dealing with trade policy, including **Chapter 8 (Import Tariffs and Quotas Under Perfect Competition)**, **Chapter 9 (Import Tariffs and Quotas Under Imperfect Competition)**, and **Chapter 10 (Export Policies in Resource-Based and High-Technology Industries)**, have been thoroughly revised. All chapters have extensive new coverage of President Trump's tariffs applied on imports from China and other countries, as well as retaliatory tariffs against the United States, and also the U.S. attempt to compensate its farmers.

Chapter 11, International Agreements on Trade and the Environment, has been thoroughly revised to reflect recent events, including the U.S. withdrawal from the Trans-Pacific Partnership, the trade war with China, Brexit, the USMCA, and the Green Deal.

Chapter 12 (Chapter 1), The Global Macroeconomy, contains a new introduction about the post-coronavirus pandemic international macroeconomic environment.

Chapter 17 (Chapter 6), Balance of Payments I: The Gains from Financial Globalization, is redesigned and now contains a chapter appendix titled "Can Poor Countries Gain from Financial Globalization?"

Chapter 18 (Chapter 7), Balance of Payments II: Output, Exchange Rates, and Macroeconomic Policies in the Short Run, has a new application about monetary policy at the zero lower bound after the Global Financial Crisis and the coronavirus pandemic recession.

Chapter 21 (Chapter 10), The Euro: Economics and Politics, has been updated thoroughly to reflect the most recent changes in the EU and the Eurozone, including Brexit, and includes a new figure (21-8) showing how often EU members violate the fiscal rules.

Topics and Approaches

The hundreds of instructors using our book have enthusiastically supported the topics we have included and the approach we have taken in our presentation. Topics covered in international trade (Chapters 1–11 in *International Economics* and in the *International Trade* split volume) include the offshoring of goods and services (Chapter 6); tariffs and quotas under imperfect competition (Chapter 9); and international agreements on trade and the environment (Chapter 11). These topics are in addition to core chapters on the Ricardian model (Chapter 2), the specific-factors model (Chapter 3), the Heckscher–Ohlin model (Chapter 4), trade with increasing returns to scale and imperfect competition (Chapter 6), import tariffs and quotas under perfect competition (Chapter 8), and export subsidies (Chapter 10).

Topics covered in international macroeconomics (Chapters 12–21 in *International Economics* and Chapters 1–10 in the *International Macroeconomics* split volume) include the gains from financial globalization (Chapter 17/Chapter 6), fixed versus floating regimes (Chapter 19/Chapter 8), exchange rate crises (Chapter 20/Chapter 9), and the euro (Chapter 21/Chapter 10). These topics are in addition to core chapters on foreign exchange markets and exchange rates in the short run and the long run (Chapters 13–15/Chapters 2–4), the national and international accounts (Chapter 16/Chapter 5), and the open economy IS–LM model (Chapter 18/Chapter 7). In addition, an online chapter, Topics in International Macroeconomics, covers applied topics of current interest (Exchange Rates in the Long Run: Deviations from Purchasing Power Parity; Exchange Rates in the Short Run: Deviations from Uncovered Interest Parity; Debt and Default; and Case Study: The Global Macroeconomy and the Global Financial Crisis).

In writing our chapters we have made every effort to link them analytically. For example, although immigration and foreign direct investment are sometimes treated as an afterthought in international economics books, we integrate these topics into the discussion of the trade models by covering the movement of labor and capital between countries in Chapter 5. Specifically, we analyze the movement of labor and capital between countries in the short run using the specific-factors model, and we explore the long-run implications using the Heckscher–Ohlin model. Chapter 5 therefore builds on the models that the student has learned in Chapters 3 and 4 and applies them to issues at the forefront of policy discussion.

In the macroeconomics section, this analytical linking is seen in the parallel development of fixed and floating exchange rate regimes, from the opening introductory tour in Chapter 12/Chapter 1, through the workings of exchange rates in Chapters 13–15/ Chapters 2–4 and the discussion of policy in the IS–LM model of Chapter 18/ Chapter 7, to the discussion of regime choice in Chapter 19/Chapter 8. Many textbooks discuss fixed and floating regimes separately, with fixed regimes often treated as an afterthought. But given the widespread use of fixed rates in many countries, the rising macro weight of fixed regimes, and the collapse of fixed rates during crises, we think it is more helpful for the student to grapple with the different workings and cost-benefit trade-offs of the two regimes by studying them side by side. This approach also allows us to address numerous policy issues, such as the implications of the trilemma and the optimal choice of exchange rate regime.

Acknowledgments

A book like this would not be possible without the assistance of many people, whom we gratefully acknowledge.

First, the renowned team at Worth has spared no effort to help us; their experience and skill in publishing economics textbooks were invaluable. Numerous individuals have been involved with this project, but we must give special mention to a few: the project has been continually and imaginatively guided by program manager Carolyn Merrill, program director Shani Fisher, and development editor Valerie Raymond. The online portion of the book has been brought to fruition by Lindsay Neff, senior media editor, and Kristyn Brown, assessment editor. Through it all, the manuscript was improved endlessly by our primary development editor, Jane Tufts. We would also like to thank our content project manager, Edgar Doolan, who worked tirelessly on this edition. We are greatly in their debt.

We have also relied on the assistance of a number of graduate students in collecting data for applications, preparing problems, and proofreading material. We would like to thank Leticia Arroyo Abad, Felipe Benguria, Chang Hong, Anna Ignatenko, David Jacks, Joseph Kopecky, Alyson Ma, Ahmed Rahman, Seema Sangita, Radek Szulga, and Yingying Xu for their assistance.

We are grateful to Benjamin Mandel, who worked on many of the international trade chapters in the first edition; Philip Luck, who worked on all the chapters in the second edition; Mingzhi Xu and Joseph Kopecky, who worked on the trade and the macro chapters, respectively, in the fourth edition; and especially to Charles Liao, who worked on the trade chapters in the fourth and fifth editions. Thanks for advice on the fifth and earlier editions also go to Christian Broda, Colin Carter, Michele Cavallo, Menzie Chinn, Sebastian Edwards, Ann Harrison, Mervyn King, Philip Lane, Judith Lavin, Karen Lewis, Christopher Meissner, Gian Maria Milesi-Ferretti, Michael Pakko, Ugo Panizza, Giovanni Peri, Eswar Prasad, Andrés Rodríguez-Clare, Katheryn Russ, Jay Shambaugh, Deborah Swenson, and Martin Wolf, many of whom provided data used in applications and examples.

We have taught the chapters of this book ourselves many times and have benefited from the feedback of colleagues. For this fifth edition, we received valuable input from the following instructors:

Adina Ardelean—Santa Clara University

Brian Bethune—Tufts University

Geoffrey Carliner—Boston University, Boston

Xiaofen Chen—Truman State University

Jonathan Conning—CUNY, Hunter College

Anthony Delmond—The University of Tennessee, Martin

Kacey Douglas—Arizona State University, Tempe

Stefania Garetto—Boston University, Boston

William Hauk—University of South Carolina, Columbia

Denise Hazlett—Whitman College

Ralf Hepp—Fordham University, Bronx

Aldo Sandoval Hernandez—University of Western Ontario

Alex Hohmann—Rutgers University, New Brunswick

Jason Jones—Furman University

Young Cheol Jung—Mount Royal University

Ayse Kabukcuoglu Dur—North Carolina State University

Evan Kraft—American University, Washington

Moshe Lander—Concordia University, Montreal, Sir G. William Campus

Xuepeng Liu—Kennesaw State University

Beyza Ural Marchand—University of Alberta, Edmonton

Sandeep Mazumder—Wake Forest University, Winston-Salem

Karl Pinno—University of British Columbia, Kelowna

Jennifer Poole—American University, Washington

Pau Pujolas—McMaster University, Hamilton

Carlos Pulido—Arizona State University, Tempe

Dhimitri Qirjo—SUNY College, Plattsburgh

Dina Rady—George Washington University

Mark Scanlan—Stephen F. Austin State University

Krishnakali SenGupta—McMaster University, Hamilton

Arjun Sondhi—Bloomsburg University of Pennsylvania

Richard Stahl—Louisiana State University and A&M College

Andrey Stoyanov—York University, North York

Bedassa Tadesse—University of Minnesota, Duluth

Mark Tendall—Stanford University

Kasaundra Tomlin—Oakland University

Russell Triplett—University of North Florida

Michael Vaney—University of British Columbia, Vancouver

Mary Jane Waples—Memorial University, St. John's

Pinar Cebi Wilber—Georgetown University

George Zestos—Christopher Newport University

Kevin Zhang—Illinois State University

For the fourth edition, we benefited from the suggestions of the following instructors:

Bradley Andrew—Juniata College

Damir Cosic—Brooklyn College

Lane Eckis—Troy University

Gerald Fox—High Point University

Fuad Hasanov—Georgetown University

Viktoria Hnatkovska—University of British Columbia

Kathy Kelly—University of Texas at Arlington

Paul Kubik—DePaul University

James McDermott—George Mason University

Thomas Mondschean—DePaul University

Braimoh Oseghale—Fairleigh Dickinson University

Masha Rahnama—Texas Tech University

Stefania Scandizzo—University of Maryland, College Park

Brandon Sheridan—North Central College

Till Schreiber—College of William & Mary

Scott Siegel—San Francisco State

Edward Stuart—Loyola University of Chicago

Miao Wang—Marquette University

Yanling Wang—Carleton University

Derrill Watson—Tarleton State University

Diana Weymark—Vanderbilt University

Janice Yee—Worcester State University

For the third edition, we benefited from the suggestions of the following instructors:

Basil Al-Hashimi—Mesa Community College

Sam Andoh—Southern Connecticut State University

Adina Ardelean—Santa Clara University

Joel Auerbach—Florida Atlantic University

Mohsen Bahmani-Oskooee—University of Wisconsin, Milwaukee

Jeremy Baker—Owens Community College

Rita Balaban—University of North Carolina, Chapel Hill

Jim Bruehler—Eastern Illinois University

Thomas Chaney—Toulouse School of Economics

John Chilton—Virginia Commonwealth University

Reid Click—George Washington University

Catherine Co—University of Nebraska at Omaha

Antoinette Criss—University of South Florida

Judith Dean—Brandeis University

James Devault—Lafayette College

Asif Dowla—St. Mary's College of Maryland

Justin Dubas—Texas Lutheran University

Lee Erickson—Taylor University

Xin Fang—Hawaii Pacific University

Stephen Grubaugh—Bentley University

Ronald Gunderson—Northern Arizona University

Chang Hong—Clark University

Carl Jensen—Rutgers University

Jeff Konz—University of North Carolina, Asheville

Robert Krol—California State University, Northridge

Dave LaRivee—United States Air Force Academy

Daniel Lee—Shippensburg University

Yu-Feng (Winnie) Lee—New Mexico State University

James Lehman—Pitzer College

Carlos Liard-Muriente—Central Connecticut State University

Rita Madarassy—Santa Clara University

Margaret Malixi—California State University, Bakersfield

Diego Mendez-Carbajo—Illinois Wesleyan University

Kathleen Odell—Dominican University

Kerry Pannell—DePauw University

Elizabeth Perry-Sizemore—Randolph College

Diep Phan—Beloit College

Reza Ramazani—Saint Michael's College

Artatrana Ratha—St. Cloud State University

Raymond Riezman—University of Iowa

Helen Roberts—University of Illinois, Chicago

Mari L. Robertson—University of Cincinnati

Margaretha Rudstrom—University of Minnesota, Crookston

Fred Ruppel—Eastern Kentucky University

Farhad Saboori—Albright College

Jeff Sarbaum—University of North Carolina, Greensboro

Mark Scanlan—Stephen F. Austin State University

Katherine Schmeiser—Mount Holyoke College

Annie Voy—Gonzaga University

Linda Wilcox Young—Southern Oregon University

Zhen Zhu—University of Central Oklahoma

James C. Hall

Sixth-grade class with their teacher in La Carreta #2 school in Ciudad Darío, Nicaragua.

We would also like to thank our families, especially Gail and Claire, for their sustained support during the time we have devoted to writing this book.

Finally, you will see an accompanying picture of children in Ciudad Darío, Nicaragua, with their teacher in the classroom of a small schoolhouse that was built for them by Seeds of Learning (www.seedsoflearning.org), a nonprofit organization dedicated to improving educational opportunities in rural Latin America. A portion of the royalties from this book go toward supporting the work of Seeds of Learning.

ROBERT C. FEENSTRA

ALAN M. TAYLOR
Davis, California
April 2020

Contents

INTERNATIONAL TRADE

1

Trade in the Global Economy

Since this [coronavirus] is necessarily a global war, we need to organize the production of basic weaponry—testing kits, cleansing chemicals, masks, protective clothing, ventilators—across the world.

Raghuram Rajan, former Chief Economist at the International Monetary Fund and former Governor of the Reserve Bank of India, 2020[1]

The emergence of China, India, and the former communist-bloc countries implies that the greater part of the earth's population is now engaged, at least potentially, in the global economy. There are no historical antecedents for this development.

Ben Bernanke, former chairman of the U.S. Federal Reserve, 2006

The main losers in today's very unequal world are not those who are too much exposed to globalization. They are those who have been left out.

Kofi Annan, former secretary general of the United Nations, 2000

Questions to Consider

1 How does international trade today differ from trade in the past?

2 How does the United States' recent use of tariffs compare with the past?

3 How does the movement of companies and people around the world compare with the movement of goods and services?

On Thursday, March 12th, 2020, the U.S. stock market fell by more than it had since the crash of 1987. The next day, on Friday, March 13th, it rose by more than it had for a decade. Then on Monday, March 16th, it fell again by even more than it had the week before. And, by the following week, it rose again by more than it had since 1933. What caused these enormous fluctuations in the U.S. and global stock markets? The novel strain of coronavirus, which led to the coronavirus disease starting in 2019, or COVID-19.

The day before the stock market plummeted on Thursday, March 12th, the World Health Organization declared coronavirus a global pandemic. At that time, the virus had already created national health care crises in China, Iran, Italy, Japan, Singapore, and South Korea. The announcement by the World Health Organization led many other governments around the world to realize that no country would be spared, and that emergency measures would be needed to slow the spread of the virus. The fluctuations in the stock market occurred as governments grappled with the appropriate economic policy response.

What was the impact of coronavirus on **international trade**, by which we mean the buying and selling of goods and services across countries? One immediate impact was that many factories in China were temporarily closed. The city of Wuhan, where the virus was first reported, has a number of factories that make displays for televisions and laptops, and it is located the province of Hubei, a center for the production of fiber-optic

---

[1] Raghuram Rajan, 2020, "Rich Countries Cannot Win the War Alone," *Financial Times*, March 22, p. 7.

cables and components for smartphones. These factories were producing goods mainly for **export**, meaning that their goods were sold to other countries, whose purchases are called **imports**. The closure of these factories quickly reduced those exports from China and imports by other countries. In addition to its effect on the international trade in goods, coronavirus had a dramatic impact on international trade in services. Airline travel between countries is a service export from the country whose companies own the airlines, and it is a service import of the countries whose citizens are passengers. Many flights between countries were cancelled to prevent the spread of coronavirus, which reduced international trade in services. Since airfreight is carried in the cargo hold of passenger aircraft, the cancellation of flights further restricted international trade in goods.

Still, international trade in some items increased because of the virus. The demand for medical equipment rose across the world, as indicated in the first quote at the start of the chapter from the economist Raghuram Rajan. The areas of the world initially hit by coronavirus—in Asia, Europe, and North America—included many industrialized countries. But, Professor Rajan argues that we should not forget the developing countries—often with dense populations—that have more limited medical resources. The scale of the pandemic in these countries could be even worse and will surely require a large-scale flow of medical goods and personnel to them. This flow of goods between countries is an example of the gains from trade. As indicated by the other quotes at the start of the chapter, the gains from international trade are meant to apply to *all* countries, especially those that have been historically left out of the globalization process.

In this book, we will learn the economic forces that determine what international trade looks like: what products are traded, who trades them, at what quantities and prices they are traded, and what the benefits and costs of trade are. We will also learn about the policies that governments use to shape trade patterns among countries. President Trump applied many **import tariffs**, taxes on goods being imported into the United States. As we discuss in this chapter and later in the book (Chapter 8), those tariffs were applied especially against imports from China. The tariff on medical equipment imported from China, however, was reduced in March 2020 to allow U.S. companies to purchase more of that equipment. At the same time, other countries restricted their exports of medical equipment so as to keep those goods for emergency use at home. That action is an example of an **export quota**, a trade policy that restricts the amount exported.

The second international trade topic that we study in this book is **migration**, the movement of people across borders to live elsewhere. People entering a country to live there are **immigrants**, and persons leaving a county to live elsewhere are **emigrants**. Until about 2014, most emigration from Mexico into the United States was by Mexican citizens who wanted to earn higher wages in the United States. They would stay in the United States temporarily (as with seasonal farm workers) or permanently and would often send a portion of the money that they earned back home. But since 2012, more and more persons attempting to cross from Mexico into the United States have been citizens of Guatemala, Honduras and El Salvador, trying to escape poverty and violence in those countries. Since 2017, caravans of these persons—often coming as families that include young children—have traveled north through Mexico to the United States border. Such migrants are called **refugees** if their safety is endangered in their home country, and under international law, refugees cannot be forced to return home. The closure of the U.S. border with Mexico to nonessential travel during the coronavirus pandemic delayed the processing of migrants seeking refugee status.

The United States is not alone in facing a wave of migrants who seek refugee status. In Europe, migrants from Africa and Asia attempt to cross into northern Europe in numbers much greater than those migrating from Central to North America. Persons facing hardship in their home countries who desire to migrate create a political challenge for the countries they seek to enter. Both President Trump and President Obama (in 2014) tried to address this challenge by having Mexico place more security personnel at its southern border. Only President Trump, however, used an import tariff as a threat to ensure that these security personnel were actually added.

The third facet of international trade that we study is **foreign direct investment (FDI)**, which occurs when a firm in one country owns some or all of a firm located in another country. When factories were temporarily closed in China to prevent the spread of coronavirus, some of those factories—especially in the automobile industry—were owned by American, European, and Japanese firms producing for Chinese consumers and for export. The closure of those factories contributed to a fall in trade, as we have discussed. But the opening of factories in China as the coronavirus moderated helped offset the closing of factories owned by those companies elsewhere in the world. For example, in late March 2020, production at the Telsa car factory in Fremont, California, and its solar panel plant in Buffalo, New York, were suspended. The production of the Model 3 and Model Y cars could be shifted from Tesla's Fremont factory to its Shanghai factory, which had already reopened after a 10-day closure.

Because international trade is the flow of goods and services across borders, while migration is the flow of people across borders, we sometimes loosely refer to FDI as the flow of capital across borders, by which we mean the ownership of physical capital (including machines and structures and also land).

All three types of flow between countries—of products (goods and services), people, and capital—are so common today that we take them for granted. Why are these international flows so common? What are the consequences of these flows for the countries involved? And what actions do governments take to make their countries more or less open to trade, migration, and FDI? These are the questions we'll address.

1 International Trade

Why should we care about international trade? Many people believe that international trade creates opportunities for countries to grow and thrive. The manufacturing of goods exported from China, for example, creates employment for many millions of workers there. The same is true for exports from the United States and European countries. It is not just large countries that potentially benefit from trade; smaller countries, too, are affected. The quote at the beginning of the chapter from Kofi Annan, former secretary general of the United Nations, suggests that countries that are left out of the globalization process are likely to suffer as a consequence.

This section begins our study of international economics by defining some important terms and summarizing the overall trends in world trade.

The Basics of World Trade

Let's begin by looking at a very broad picture of international trade. What country was the world's largest exporter of goods in 2018? If you guessed China, you are right. In 2018 China sold around $2.5 trillion in goods to other countries, far ahead of the $1.7 trillion exported by the second-place country, the United States. The third-largest exporting country in 2018 was Germany, which exported $1.6 trillion in goods.

These numbers reveal only part of the trade picture, however, because in addition to exporting goods, countries export services. In 2018, the United States exported $0.8 trillion in services (including movies, business services, education of foreign students, travel by foreigners, and so forth). If we combine exports in goods and services, then the United States exported $2.5 trillion in 2018, but China is still slightly ahead because its service exports were $0.2 trillion, giving it a combined export total of $2.7 trillion in goods and services. These two countries are followed by Germany, the United Kingdom, and Japan as the top exporters of goods and services.

Nations trade goods for many reasons, but the primary reason is that they can obtain products from abroad that are cheaper or of higher quality than those they can produce at home. China, for example, can produce goods more cheaply than can most industrial countries because of its abundant supply of labor. The United States, on the other hand, is able to produce high-quality manufactured goods because of its high levels of education and technological knowledge, and it is able to produce agricultural goods very cheaply because of its abundant land resources.

A country's **trade balance** is the difference between its total value of exports and its total value of imports (usually including both goods and services). Countries that export more than they import, such as China, run a **trade surplus**, whereas countries that import more than they export, such as the United States, run a **trade deficit**. In addition to keeping track of the overall trade balance for a country with the rest of the world, media often reports the **bilateral trade balance**, meaning the difference between exports and imports between two countries. The U.S. bilateral trade balance with China, for example, has been a trade deficit of more than $200 billion every year between 2005 and the present.

In the models developed to understand international trade, we are not concerned with whether a country has a trade deficit or surplus, but we just assume that each country has balanced trade, with exports equal to imports. There are two reasons why we make this assumption. First, economists believe that an overall trade deficit or surplus arises from macroeconomic conditions, such as the overall levels of spending and savings in an economy—countries with high spending and low savings will run a trade deficit. (See **Side Bar: The Macroeconomics of the Trade Balance**.)

SIDE BAR

The Macroeconomics of the Trade Balance

The gross domestic product (GDP) of a country is the value of all final goods produced in a year. From your introductory macroeconomics class, you learned an identity that shows how to measure GDP:

$$Y = C + I + G + EX - IM$$

In this equation, Y is GDP; C is "consumption," and it equals total spending by private households on final goods and services; I is "investment," and it equals total spending by firms (and households) on machinery and buildings (including housing) that add to the economy's capital stock; G is "government spending," and it equals total spending by the government on final goods and services; EX equals the value of goods and services that are exported; and IM equals the value of goods and services that are imported.

The difference between the value of exports and imports, $EX - IM$, is the trade balance of the economy. If the value of exports exceeds the value of imports, then $EX - IM > 0$ and the trade balance is in surplus; if the value of exports is less than the value of imports, then $EX - IM < 0$ and the trade balance is in deficit.

What determines the trade balance for an economy? We give a simplified answer by rearranging the terms in the above GDP identity to define $EX - IM$.[2] First, subtract from both sides of the equation the total value of taxes T that are paid by households to the government. We also move consumption C and investment I from the right-hand side to the left-hand side of the equation, to get:

$$(Y - T - C) - I = G - T + EX - IM$$

The first two terms on the left, $Y - T$, are the income that is earned by households minus the taxes that are paid, which equals *disposable income*. When we subtract household consumption C from disposable income, we obtain the *private saving* of the households, which equals $S_p = (Y - T - C)$.

The final step is to move the terms $G - T$ from the right-hand side to the left-hand side of the equation, so that the trade balance will equal:

$$(S_p - I) + (T - G) = EX - IM.$$

The first two terms on the left, $(S_p - I)$, equal the difference between private saving and investment in the economy. If private saving is less than investment, as it has been in the United States since the early 1980s, then $(S_p - I) < 0$. The next two terms on the left, $(T - G)$, equal total taxes collected by the government minus its expenditures, and this difference is sometimes called *public saving*. If the government is running a budget deficit, then $(T - G) < 0$, as was the case in the United States from the early 1980s until about 1995, and again since 2000.

When both $(S_p - I) < 0$ and $(T - G) < 0$, then the equation shows that $EX - IM < 0$, so that the trade balance *must be* in deficit. That deficit reflects the low saving in the economy, either by households (with $S_p < I$) or by the government through running a deficit (with $T < G$). This result shows how the trade balance of the economy is determined by the macroeconomic saving behavior of the households and the government.

---

[2] Our answer is simplified because we do not make the distinction between GDP of the economy and a closely related concept called *gross national disposable income* (GNDI). That distinction is explained in the international macroeconomics chapters that accompany this textbook.

Second, the interpretation of a trade deficit or surplus is problematic when we focus on the bilateral trade balance between two countries, such as the United States and China. To see what the problem is, think about the U.S. import of a particular good from China, such as the iPhone. An Apple iPhone 11 64GB sold for $699 in the United States in 2019, and much of its assembly occurs in China. To understand how much assembly occurs in China, we can use a study of the earlier iPhone 5 16GB, which was valued at about $227 when it was shipped from China to the United States in 2013 and sold for about $650 in the United States. However, only $8 of that amount reflects the value of Chinese labor used in the assembly.[3] The rest of the $219 export value was very likely imported into China from other countries, including: $65 for the flash memory, display module, and touch screen, typically imported from Toshiba in Japan; $24 for the processor chip and sensors, typically imported from Samsung in Korea; $57 for the camera and transmitting and receiving devices, typically imported from Infineon in Germany; and so on. Nevertheless, the entire $227 is counted as an export from China to the United States.

Products like the Apple iPhone are often assembled in China from components made in many other countries.

Christoph Dernbach/dpa/AGE Fotostock

This example shows that the bilateral trade deficit or surplus between countries is a slippery concept. It doesn't really make sense to count the entire $227 iPhone as a Chinese export to the United States, as is done in official trade statistics, when only $8 is the **value-added** in China: that is, the difference between the value of the iPhone when it leaves China and the cost of parts and materials purchased in China and imported from other countries. That shortcoming of official statistics gives us a good reason to not focus on the bilateral trade deficit or surplus between countries, even though that number is often reported in the media.

The iPhone example illustrates how the manufacturing required for a single final product is often spread across many countries. That so many countries can be involved in manufacturing a final product and its components is a new phenomenon that illustrates the drop in transportation and communication costs in the modern world economy. In the past, trade occurred in more standardized goods (such as raw materials) that were shipped long distances but were not shipped back and forth between countries during the manufacturing process. This new feature of world trade and production, often called **offshoring**, is discussed in Chapter 7; here, we present the idea by looking at how trade patterns have changed over time.

APPLICATION

Is Trade Today Different from the Past?

Is the type of trade today different from that in the past? The answer to this question is *yes*. Not only is there more international trade today than in the past, but the type of trade has also changed. We can see the changes in the type of trade by organizing imports and exports into four categories, depending on their use in the economy: (1) foods, feeds, and beverages; (2) industrial supplies and materials (which include raw materials like chemicals and petroleum and basic processed goods such as steel, paper, and textiles); (3) capital goods (durable goods such as aircraft, cars, computers,

---

[3] See Yuqing Xing and Neal Detert, "How the iPhone Widens the United States Trade Deficit with the People's Republic of China," Asian Development Bank Institute, Working Paper no. 257, December 2010 (revised May 2011). The estimates in this paragraph are drawn from Joshua Sherman, "Spendy but Indispensable: Breaking Down the Full $650 Cost of the iPhone 5," digitaltrends.com, July 26, 2013.

FIGURE 1-1

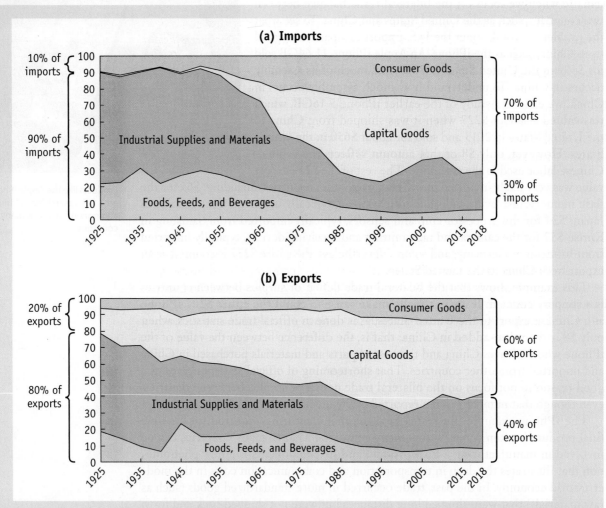

The Changing Face of U.S. Import and Export Industries, 1925–2018
The types of goods imported and exported by the United States have changed drastically over the past century. Foods, feeds, and beverages and industrial supplies were 90% of imports in 1925, but represented only 30% in 2018. These categories' shares of exports have also fallen from 80% in 1925 to 40% in 2018. Capital plus consumer goods plus automobiles have increased from 10% of imports in 1925 to 70% of imports in 2018. Exports of these goods have likewise increased from 20% in 1925 to 60% in 2018.
Data from: Bureau of Economic Analysis.

and machinery); and (4) finished consumer goods (all finished household goods except durable goods like cars and computers, but including the iPhone). The percentage of U.S. imports and exports accounted for by these four categories from 1925 to 2018 is shown in Figure 1-1, with U.S. imports in panel (a) and exports in panel (b).

In Figure 1-1(a), we see that U.S. trade has shifted away from agriculture and raw materials and toward manufactured goods, as shown by the declining shares of foods, feeds, and beverages and of industrial supplies and materials. Together, these two categories of traded goods accounted for 90% of imports in 1925 but only 30% in 2018. Figure 1-1(b) shows that the export share of these same categories also fell from 80% to 40% over that time. These changes have occurred because in 1925 the relative size of agriculture, mining, and basic industries like steel in the U.S. economy, which provide food, feed, and industrial supplies, was much larger than it is today, so those were the types of goods that were exported from the United States. These sectors were also a larger part of economies in the rest of the world, and other countries provided foods (like tea) or industrial supplies (like certain minerals) that were different from those in the United States. So these types of goods were also imported into the United States.

Figure 1-1(a) also shows that the imports of capital goods plus consumer goods have increased from 10% in 1925 to 70% in 2018. In Figure 1-1(b), we see that the export of capital plus consumer goods has likewise increased from about 20% of exports in 1925 to 60% of exports in 2018. These changes have occurred because as the relative importance of agriculture, mining, and basic industries has fallen, these sectors have been replaced by more sophisticated goods and services, like aircraft, cars, and consumer electronics, as well as the needed parts and semi-finished versions of these products as they are shipped between countries. It is these capital goods and consumer products that make up the bulk of world trade today, which is why trade has changed greatly from the past.

Map of World Trade

To show the flow of exports and imports around the world, we use the map in Figure 1-2, which shows trade in billions of dollars for 2018. That year about $21.1 trillion in goods crossed international borders. (Because trade in services is harder to measure between countries, we do not include it in Figure 1-2.) The amount of trade in goods is illustrated by the width of the lines, with the largest trade flows having the heaviest lines and the smallest having dashed lines. When the trade flows in each direction between two regions are dissimilar, we draw two lines of different widths; but when the trade flows are

FIGURE 1-2

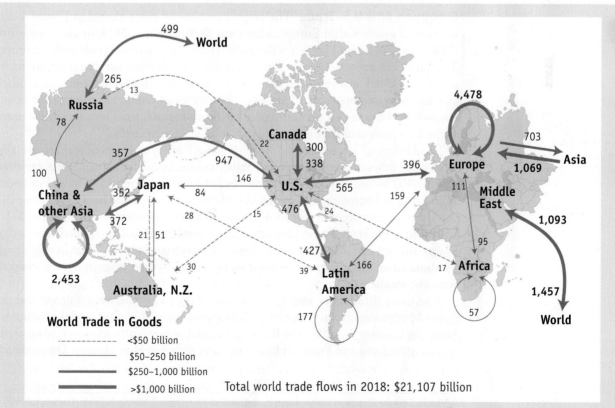

World Trade in Goods, 2018 ($ billions) This figure shows the trade in merchandise goods between selected countries and regions of the world for 2018 in billions of dollars. The amount of trade in goods is illustrated by the width of the lines, with the largest trade flows having the heaviest lines and the smallest having dashed lines.
Data from: United Nations trade data.

TABLE 1-1

Shares of World Trade, Accounted for by Selected Regions, 2018 This table shows the share of trade within each region, or the share of exports from each region, as a percentage of total world trade in 2018. Europe and the Americas combined account for about one-half (49%) of world exports, and Asia accounts for nearly one-third (29%) of world exports.

	Share of World Trade (%)		Share of World Trade (%)
Europe (internal trade)	21	Asia (exports)	29
Europe (internal) plus trade with the United States	26	Middle East and Russia (exports)	9
Americas (internal trade)	8	Africa (exports)	2
Europe and the Americas (exports)	49	Australia and New Zealand (exports)	2

Note: The shares of world trade are calculated from Figure 1-2, as explained in the text. The Americas includes North, Central, and South America and the Caribbean. Exports for the Middle East and Russia also include exports for the Commonwealth of Independent States, which consists of Azerbaijan, Armenia, Belarus, Georgia, Kazakhstan, Kyrgyzstan, Moldova, Russia, Tajikistan, Turkmenistan, Uzbekistan, and Ukraine.

Data from: United Nations trade data.

of similar size, we draw a single line, with the amount of the trade flows shown on each arrow. The trade flows within certain regions, such as Europe, are described by a circle, with the total amount of trade shown.

European and U.S. Trade The largest amount of trade shown in Figure 1-2 is the flow of goods within Europe, which was $4.5 trillion in 2018, or about one-fifth (21%) of trade. This fact is shown in Table 1-1 as internal trade within Europe. The European countries trade a great deal with one another because there are many countries located near to each other, so it is easy to ship from one country to another, and also because import tariffs are low. The European Union is a group of 28 countries within Europe that do not impose tariffs on imports from one another, so most of the European countries trade with one another at zero tariffs.[4]

In addition to large trade flows among the European countries, there are also large trade flows between the United States and Europe. The United States exported nearly $400 billion of goods to Europe in 2018 and imported $565 billion of goods from Europe. Therefore, the combined trade within Europe and between Europe and the United States accounts for $5.4 trillion, or about one-quarter (26%) of the $21.1 trillion in world trade flows. This fact is also recorded in Table 1-1, which shows that a large amount of world trade occurs between countries that are similar in their levels of advanced industrialization and great wealth. Why do these countries trade so much with one another?

The many differences among European countries and between Europe and the United States explain, in part, the trade between them. The first model of trade we study (in Chapter 2), called the Ricardian model, was initially used to explain trade between England and Portugal based on their differences in climate. Despite such

---

[4] Prior to 2004 the European Union countries consisted of 15 countries: Austria, Belgium, Denmark, Finland, France, Germany, Greece, Ireland, Italy, Luxembourg, the Netherlands, Portugal, Spain, Sweden, and the United Kingdom. Since that time another 13 countries have joined: Bulgaria, Croatia, Republic of Cyprus, Czech Republic, Estonia, Hungary, Latvia, Lithuania, Malta, Poland, Romania, Slovakia, and Slovenia. In addition to zero tariffs, countries within the European Union have many common economic regulations, and some of them share a currency (the euro). In 2016 the United Kingdom voted in favor of exiting from the European Union, which is referred to as *Brexit*, as will be discussed later in the chapter.

differences, however, high-income countries like the United Kingdom and the United States have many similarities in their consumption patterns and in their ability to produce goods and services. Why, then, do "similar" countries trade so much with one another? We try to answer that question in Chapter 6, by arguing that even similar countries have enough variety in the goods they produce (such as different models of cars or types of cheese) that it is natural for them to trade with one another.

Trade in the Americas There is also a large amount of trade recorded within the Americas (North, Central, and South America, and the Caribbean). If we add together all the trade flows between the countries in these regions, we find that total trade in goods within the Americas in 2018 was $1.7 trillion, about 8% of world trade. That percentage seems small compared to trade within Europe (which accounts for 21% of world trade), but that is because we are not counting all the *intra-national* trade that occurs *within* the United States and other countries in the Americas.

The vast majority of international trade within the Americas is between Canada, the United States, and Mexico. Since 1994, those three countries have belonged to the North American Free Trade Agreement (NAFTA). A **free-trade area** is a group of countries that do not impose import tariffs on goods and services traded between them. President Trump wanted to replace NAFTA with a new deal among the three countries, and in September 2018, negotiators from the United States, Mexico, and Canada reached an agreement on the United States–Mexico–Canada Agreement (USMCA), which is also a free-trade area. The USMCA was ratified by the government of Mexico in 2019, and by the governments of Canada and the United States in 2020, and it took effect that year.

If we add the trade flows within the Americas to those within Europe and include all other exports of these two regions to the rest of the world, we find that these combined regions account for $10.3 trillion in exports, or about one-half (49%) of the $21.1 trillion in world trade. This finding is also recorded in Table 1-1.

Trade with Asia Figure 1-2 also shows very large trade flows to and from Asia. All the exports from Asia totaled about $6.1 trillion in 2018, or nearly one-third (29%) of world trade, as shown in Table 1-1. Remember that this total includes only trade in goods and omits trade in services, which is becoming increasingly important. India, for example, performs a wide range of services such as accounting, customer support, computer programming, and research and development for firms in the United States and Europe. Because these services are performed for U.S. and European firms in another country, they are considered service exports from the country in which the services are performed. In the quote at the beginning of the chapter, Ben Bernanke, the former chairman of the U.S. Federal Reserve, points out that the entrance of China, India, and the former Communist-bloc countries into the world economy has led to a level of globalization that exceeded anything we had seen in the past.

Why does Asia trade so much with the rest of the world? There are many answers to this question. One answer is that wages in many Asian countries are much lower than in high-income countries. China's low wages allow it to produce goods cheaply and then export them. But why are Chinese wages so low? One explanation is that Chinese workers are less productive (the Ricardian model presented in the next chapter explains wages in that way). Low wages cannot explain why Japan exports so much, however. Japan's wages are very high because its workers are very productive; its exports to Europe and the United States are large because its highly skilled workforce and large amount of capital (factories and machines) make it possible for Japan to produce high-quality goods in abundance. Conversely, its scarcity of raw materials explains why it imports those goods from resource-rich countries such as Australia, Canada, and the United States. Trade patterns based on the amounts of labor, capital, and natural resources found in each country are explained by the Heckscher–Ohlin trade model, the topic of Chapter 4.

Other Regions The Middle East sells oil to many countries, earning $1.5 trillion in export revenues and spending $1.1 trillion on imports. Like the Middle East, Russia also has reserves of oil and natural gas, which it exports to countries in Europe. These exports are an important source of revenue for Russia. The exports of the Middle East and Russia combined (together with countries around Russia like Azerbaijan, Kazakhstan, Kyrgyzstan, Uzbekistan, Tajikistan, and Turkmenistan) total $1.9 trillion, or 9% of world trade, as shown in Table 1-1.

More than one-half of Russian exports and imports are with European countries. In contrast, Russia trades a surprisingly small amount with the United States, exporting only $22 billion to the United States and importing only $13 billion from there. This fact reflects, in part, a legacy of the Cold War—the period from 1945 to about 1990 when the United States and the Soviet Union were political adversaries. The Cold War ended with the breakup of the Soviet Union in 1991, but there are still political tensions between Russia and the United States that affect trade between them. In 2014, for example, a separatist movement in the Ukraine was supported by Russia but opposed by the United States and the European Union. The opposing countries applied **sanctions** against Russian companies and individuals that limited their ability to travel and do business in the West. Russia responded with sanctions of its own that restricted the travel of specific individuals from the West, and it banned food imports from the European Union, the United States, Norway, Canada, Australia, and other countries.[5] These sanctions are an example of a **trade embargo**, which means a complete elimination of imports. In this case, however, the embargo applied only to food products. The embargo has hit farmers in countries that border Russia particularly hard, such as dairy farmers in Latvia, Lithuania, and Estonia, who had relied on the large Russian market for their sales. The embargo has also reduced agricultural exports from the United States and the European Union to Russia, adversely affecting farmers in those regions too.

And then there is Africa. Africa has the closest trade links with the European nations, reflecting both its proximity to Europe and the former colonial status of many African countries. For this reason, Europe has greater exports and imports with Africa than the United States has with Africa, though in both cases the amount of trade is small. Internal trade within Africa is also small: only $57 billion in 2018. Adding up all its exports, the continent of Africa accounts for only 2% of world trade, a very small number given that Africa accounts for 20% the Earth's land mass and 17% of its population.

In the quote at the start of the chapter, Kofi Annan, former secretary general of the United Nations, expresses the view that Africa's growth out of poverty will depend on its developing greater linkages with the world economy through trade. A thorough treatment of the difficulties faced by African and other least-developed countries is beyond the scope of this book, and we recommend that the interested reader consult a textbook on development economics. The lessons we draw from our examination of international trade and trade policy also hold for the African countries, even though they have low incomes and account for only a small part of world trade.

The export percentages shown in Table 1-1 add up to 100% (being careful not to add Europe and the Americas twice), once we include the trade of Australia and New Zealand, which export and import less than 2% of the world totals. You do not need to know all the specific percentages shown in Table 1-1, but an understanding of the broad picture (such as which regions trade the most) will be useful as we undertake our study of international trade.

---

[5] That import ban is in effect until the end of 2019, but it could be extended further.

Trade Compared with GDP

So far, we have discussed the dollar amounts of trade crossing international borders. But trade can also be measured as a ratio of a country's trade to its **gross domestic product (GDP)**, the value of all final goods produced in a year. For the United States, the average value of imports and exports (for goods and services) expressed relative to GDP was 16% in 2018. Most other countries have a higher ratio of trade to GDP, as shown in Table 1-2.

At the top of the list are Hong Kong and Singapore, where the amount of trade exceeds their GDP![6] These two regions are important shipping and processing

TABLE 1-2

Trade/GDP Ratio in 2018 This table shows the ratio of total trade to GDP for selected countries, where trade includes both merchandise goods and services and is calculated as (Imports + Exports)/2. Countries with the highest ratios of trade to GDP tend to be small in economic size and are often important centers for shipping goods, like Hong Kong (China) and Singapore. Countries with the lowest ratios of trade to GDP tend to be very large in economic size, like China, Japan, and the United States, or are not very open to trade because of their distance from other countries, like Argentina and Brazil, or because of trade barriers, like Pakistan.

Country	Trade/GDP (%)	GDP ($ billions)
Hong Kong (China)	188%	$332
Singapore	163	377
Hungary	84	185
Malaysia	66	438
Thailand	62	507
Switzerland	59	771
Austria	53	511
Denmark	52	419
Sweden	45	669
Germany	44	4,524
Mexico	40	1,505
Greece	36	290
Norway	35	562
Spain	33	2,435
Canada	33	2,186
France	32	3,359
United Kingdom	31	3,282
Italy	31	2,456
Turkey	30	1,421
South Africa	30	493
Russian Federation	26	1,978
India	22	3,269
Indonesia	22	1,317
China	19	1,779
Japan	18	7,109
United States	16	20,494
Argentina	15	513
Brazil	15	2,653
Pakistan	14	292

Data from: World Development Indicators, World Bank.

[6] Hong Kong (China) has been a part of the People's Republic of China since July 1, 1997, but its trade statistics are measured separately, so we list Hong Kong in Table 1-2 as a distinct region.

centers, so they are importing goods, processing them, and then exporting the final products to other countries. As in our iPhone example, the value-added involved in the exports ($8 for each iPhone) can be much less than the total value of exports ($227). That explains how the total amount that countries trade can be greater than their GDP. At the bottom of the list are China, Japan, and the United States, which are very large in economic size; Argentina and Brazil, which are relatively far away from their trading partners; and Pakistan, which has high trade barriers with its neighbor, India.

So even though the United States and China are among the world's largest exporters and importers, they are nearly the smallest trading nations when trade is measured as a percent of a country's GDP. What is the reason for this inverse relationship? Very large countries tend to have a lot of trade among states or provinces *within* their borders, but that trade is not counted as part of international trade. Other countries that are not quite as large as the United States or China, but are close to their major trading partners, such as Germany, France, Italy, Spain, and the United Kingdom, along with Mexico, Canada, and Russia, tend to appear in the middle of the list in Table 1-2. Smaller countries with close neighbors, such as Hong Kong, Singapore, Malaysia, and Thailand, as well as the smaller European nations, will have more trade spilling across their borders and have the highest ratios of trade to GDP.

Barriers to Trade

Table 1-2 shows the differences among countries in the amount of trade relative to GDP, but this ratio changes over time. There are many reasons, aside from country size, for the amount of trade to change. Those reasons include import tariffs; transportation costs of shipping from one country to another; events, such as wars and natural disasters, that lead to reduced trade; and so on. The term **trade barriers** refers to all factors that influence the amount of goods and services shipped across international borders. To see how these trade barriers have changed over time, Figure 1-3 graphs the ratio of trade in goods and services to GDP for a selection of countries for which historical data are available: Australia, Canada, Japan, the United Kingdom, the United States, and an average of countries in continental Europe (Denmark, France, Germany, Italy, Norway, and Sweden).[7]

"First Golden Age" of Trade

The period from 1890 until World War I (1914–1918) is sometimes called a "golden age" of international trade. Those years saw dramatic improvements in transportation, such as the steamship and the railroad, which allowed for a great increase in the amount of international trade. Figure 1-3 shows this increase in the ratio of trade to GDP between 1890 and World War I. The United Kingdom reached the highest ratio of trade to GDP in 1913 (30%), while Australia and the average of European countries reached peaks of 20% that year. Canada reached a ratio of 17% in 1913, while Japan reached 12.5% in that year. In contrast, the ratio of trade to GDP was lowest for the United States, which achieved 6% in 1913.

Political Economy of Tariffs

The low ratio of trade to GDP for the United States in 1913 and today is expected for a large country. In addition, trade was low for the United States because it had higher tariffs than many other countries in the period before World War I. This can

---

[7] Because historical data on trade in services are not available, in Figure 1-3 we include trade in services starting in 1950.

FIGURE 1-3

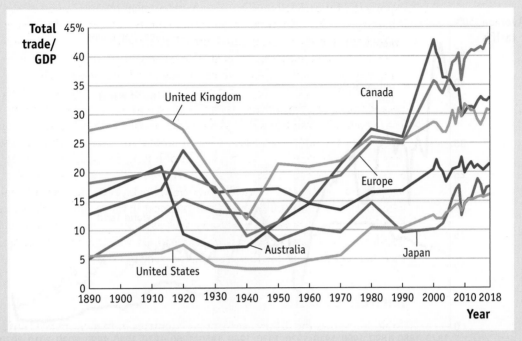

Trade in Goods and Services Relative to GDP, 1890–2018 This diagram shows total trade in merchandise goods and services for each country (i.e., the average of imports and exports) divided by gross domestic product (GDP), from 1890 to 2018. There was a considerable increase in the ratio of trade to GDP between 1890 and 1913. This trend ended with World War I and the Great Depression, and it took many years to regain the same level of trade. Most of the industrial countries shown did not reach the level of trade prevailing in 1913 until the 1970s. Certain countries—such as Australia and the United Kingdom—did not reach their earlier levels until the end of the twentieth century. The financial crisis in 2008–09 led to a fall in trade relative to GDP for most countries, with recovery in trade relative to GDP since that time.

Data from: Updated from Robert C. Feenstra, Fall 1998, "Integration of Trade and Disintegration of Production in the Global Economy," Journal of Economic Perspectives, *31–50.*

be seen in Figure 1-4, where we show the average tariff applied by the United States between 1865 and 2019, along with the average worldwide tariffs over 35 countries (including the United States) for 1865–2017.

In 1865 the United States had high tariffs to raise revenue during the U.S. Civil War (1861–1865), and these tariffs were much higher than the average worldwide tariffs. Those U.S. tariffs erratically rose and fell in the decades leading up to World War I, but they still remained much higher than in the rest of the world. Why were U.S. tariffs so high in this period? Later in this book we will carefully explain who gains and who loses from tariffs and discuss whether tariffs can ever be in the national interest. The *economic* reasons for tariffs are also reflected in *political* reasons because groups that gain from tariffs will vote for parties that support the tariffs, whereas groups that lose will vote for parties that support free trade. Explanations for tariffs and other policy actions that combine both economic and political reasoning are referred to as **political economy**, and these explanations will be an important theme throughout this book.

U.S. Tariffs After the Civil War in the United States, tensions between the North and the South remained strong. The industrial North tended to vote Republican and the agricultural South tended to vote Democrat. In the 1888 election, the Democrat and incumbent president, Grover Cleveland, was defeated by the Republican candidate Benjamin Harrison in a close election.[8] President Cleveland supported a large

---

[8] The 1888 election was the third of only five times that the U.S. president has been elected with a majority of the Electoral College votes without winning a majority of the popular vote.

FIGURE 1-4

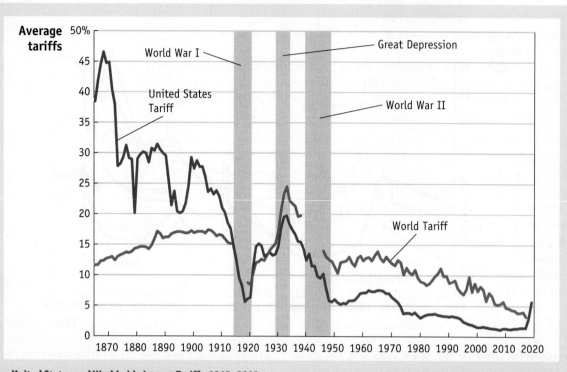

Average United States and Worldwide Import Tariffs, 1865–2019
This diagram shows the average tariff applied by the United States from 1865 to 2019 and the worldwide average tariff applied by 35 countries for 1865–2017. Some world tariffs are not available during World War I and World War II. The average tariff in the United States was higher than in the other countries before 1910 and lower than in the other countries after World War II. In 1933, during the Great Depression, the average tariff rose sharply to 20% to 25% because of the Smoot–Hawley Tariff Act enacted in the United States and

the reaction to it by other countries. Since the end of World War II in 1945, tariffs generally fell, but tariffs increased in 2018 and 2019 in the United States under President Trump.

Data from: U.S. average tariff updated from Douglas Irwin, 2017, Clashing over Commerce: A History of U.S. Trade Policy (Chicago: University of Chicago Press), using Mary Amiti, Stephen J. Redding, and David Weinstein, "The Impact of the 2018 Trade War on U.S. Prices and Welfare," Journal of Economic Perspectives, 2019, 33(4), 187–210, and authors' calculations. Worldwide average tariff updated from Michael A. Clemens and Jeffrey G. Williamson, 2004, "Why Did the Tariff-Growth Correlation Change After 1950?" Journal of Economic Growth, 9(1), 5–46.

reduction in tariffs as a way to benefit U.S. consumers, whereas President Harrison supported higher tariffs as a way to protect U.S. industries that were mainly located in the North. President Harrison prevailed, and his administration included Congressman William McKinley, who was chairman of the House Ways and Means Committee and who could therefore push legislation on tariffs. The Tariff Act of 1890, also known as the McKinley Tariff, substantially raised U.S. tariffs. In Figure 1-4, U.S. tariffs are higher in that year than they had been just before or after.

The high tariffs in 1890 did not last, however. Even the industrialists in the North were not in agreement over whether they supported the tariffs. While those producing final goods might support tariffs as a way to protect the U.S. market, other industries that relied on import goods did not support tariffs. The tariff on wool imports, for example, benefited the sheep herder by raising the price of wool, but it hurt the textile industry that relied on wool as an intermediate input.[9] This disagreement over tariffs led the Republicans to lose their majority in the House of Representatives in 1890, and it also started to influence McKinley's views. He was elected as president

---

[9] This example is provided by Professor Douglas Irwin, cited in: Zach Wichter, "President McKinley Was First 'Tariff Man,' but His Policy Evolved," *New York Times*, December 6, 2018, p. B-4, from which this paragraph draws.

in 1896 and pushed through another tariff act in 1897, when we again see a rise in U.S. tariffs in Figure 1-4. But by that time, President McKinley was changing his views and recognized that high tariffs were not an end in themselves but could be used to negotiate an overall lowering of tariffs with trade partners.

These ideas about tariffs from more than a century ago have come back recently in the tariffs used by President Trump. Under his administration there is a noticeable rise in import tariffs (especially against China), as seen in Figure 1-4 by the increase in the average U.S. tariff in 2018 and 2019. We describe these recent U.S. tariffs after completing our historical discussion.

Interwar Period After World War I, the ratio of trade to GDP was higher in some countries and lower in others than before the war, but this ratio declined in all countries during the Great Depression, which began in 1929, and during World War II, which began in Europe in 1939. In the Great Depression, the United States adopted high tariffs called the Smoot–Hawley tariffs, named after Senator Reed Smoot from Utah and Representative Willis C. Hawley from Oregon. Signed into law in June 1930, the Smoot–Hawley Tariff Act raised tariffs to as high as 60% on some categories of imports.

While the United States applied tariffs as high as 60% on some imports, the *average* tariff over *all* imported goods (including those goods with zero tariffs) peaked at about 20% in 1933. The tariffs were meant to protect farmers and other industries, but they backfired by causing other countries to retaliate. Canada retaliated by applying high tariffs of its own against the United States; France used **import quotas**, which are a limit on the quantity of an imported good allowed into a country, to restrict imports from the United States; Britain gave preferences to goods available from its former colonies; and other countries reacted, too. As described by one economic historian:[10]

> A groundswell of resentment spread around the world and quickly led to retaliation. Italy objected to duties on hats and bonnets of straw, wool-felt hats, and olive oil; Spain reacted sharply to increases on cork and onions; Canada took umbrage at increases on maple sugar and syrup, potatoes, cream, butter, buttermilk, and skimmed milk. Switzerland was moved to boycott American typewriters, fountain pens, motor cars, and films because of increased duties on watches, clocks, embroidery, cheese and shoes. . . . Retaliation was begun long before the [Smoot–Hawley] bill was enacted into law in June 1930.

The response of these countries, initially against the United States and then against one another, led to a dramatic increase in worldwide tariffs during the interwar period, as shown in Figure 1-4. This sort of tariff increase, as countries retaliate against the actions of one another, is called a **trade war**. The average worldwide tariff for 35 countries peaked at 25% in 1933, which shows that the Smoot–Hawley tariffs adopted by the United States were matched by import tariffs in many other countries. The high tariffs led to a dramatic fall in world trade in the interwar period, with large costs to the United States and the world economy. These costs are one reason that the Allied countries met together after World War II to develop international agreements, such as the World Trade Organization (formerly known as the General Agreement on Tariffs and Trade), to keep tariffs low. Later in this book we study tariffs and other trade policies in more detail and discuss the international institutions that govern their use.

---

[10] Charles Kindleberger, 1989, "Commercial Policy Between the Wars," in P. Mathias and S. Pollard, eds., *The Cambridge Economic History of Europe*, vol. 8 (Cambridge, UK: Cambridge University Press), p. 170.

BananaStock/Jupiter Images

A fully loaded container ship can carry thousands of containers.

"Second Golden Age" of Trade

It took many years for the world economy to regain the same level of global integration that existed before World War I. From Figure 1-3, we can see that some countries (the United Kingdom, Europe, and Australia) began increasing trade immediately after the end of World War II in 1945, so their ratio of trade to GDP was much higher in 1950 than it was in 1940. Some countries did not show an increase until after 1950, and others not until after 1960. In addition to the end of World War II and tariff reductions under the General Agreement on Tariffs and Trade, lower transportation costs contributed to the growth in trade. The shipping container, invented in 1956, allowed goods to be moved by ship, rail, and truck more cheaply than before. You have no doubt seen these containers piled high on ships and in docks, as well as on trains and trucks. As a result of all these factors, world trade grew steadily after 1950 in dollar terms and as a ratio to GDP. For this reason, the period after 1950 is called the "second golden age" of trade and globalization.

Many of the countries shown in Figure 1-3 have substantially exceeded the peak levels of trade relative to GDP that prevailed just before or after World War I. Canada's trade ratio grew from 24% in 1920 to 43% by 2000, and then dropped back down to 31% in 2013 (due to reduced exports of oil and natural gas). The average trade ratio of European countries increased from 20% in 1913 to 40% in 2013. Likewise, the U.S. trade ratio grew from 7.5% in 1920 to 15% by 2013. A few countries, such as Australia and the United Kingdom, have only recently achieved the level of trade relative to GDP that they had prior to World War I and are now in a position to surpass that level. For the world as a whole, the ratio of trade to GDP in 2013 was about 30%, up from 20% in 1980 and 12% in 1970.

There is an abrupt fall in the ratios of trade to GDP from 2008 to 2009 for most countries in Figure 1-3. What happened to cause this slowdown in trade? In the fall of 2008 there was a financial crisis in the United States that quickly spread to other countries, becoming a Global Financial Crisis (also called the Great Recession). The crisis had a substantial impact on the amount of international trade because it sent many countries into recessions that led to a fall in both exports and imports. This drop in the ratios of trade to GDP from 2008 to 2009 can be seen for most countries in Figure 1-3. Since then, the trade ratios have recovered (except in Canada), as the world economy has bounced back from the Global Financial Crisis.

In 2019, the world economy was in its 10th year of recovery from the Global Financial Crisis of 2008–2009. Now that many countries have attained the highest ratio of trade to GDP they have ever experienced, what can we expect for the future of trade? Are there factors that will allow for the continued growth of trade between countries, or is this growth at risk?

The U.S.–China Trade War

The spread of coronavirus in 2020 led to a downturn in the global economy. As consumers stayed at home to limit their exposure to the virus, the demand for services (such as restaurant meals, entertainment, and travel) collapsed, leading to layoffs and further reductions in spending through a multiplier effect. As discussed at the beginning of the chapter, international trade in goods and services also fell dramatically. At the time of writing, it is not known how long it will take the global economy to recover from this shock. Even when it does, international trade may not return to its former high level because of the tariffs that have been enacted by the United States and other countries.

In January 2018, President Trump imposed tariffs on U.S. imports of solar panels and washing machines from all countries importing those products into the United States, and later that year he applied tariffs against imports of steel from all countries, too. Tariffs had previously been applied by other U.S. presidents against solar panels, as we will discuss in Chapter 8, so these new tariffs on solar panels and washing machines were not that different from the past. Tariffs had also been applied by other U.S. presidents against steel, though the new tariffs were a bit different because they were initially applied against all countries including Canada and Mexico, even though those two countries had a free-trade agreement with the United States (NAFTA). Later, the steel tariffs against Canada and Mexico were removed in the hopes that the governments in all three countries would ratify the new U.S.–Mexico–Canada Agreement (USMCA).

But starting in July 2018, President Trump applied import tariffs against China that were very different from those imposed by other modern U.S. presidents because the tariffs were applied *only against* China and at *high levels*, and they have been extended to apply to more and more imports from that country. By September 1, 2019, the tariffs applied to nearly all U.S. imports from China. In Figure 1-5, we show the average U.S. tariff against imports from China, which rose from 3.1% in January 2018 to 12% in December 2018 to 21% in September 2019. Each time the United States announced tariffs on more Chinese imports, China responded in kind by applying tariffs against more imports from the United States. The average Chinese tariff on U.S. imports rose from 8% in January 2018 to 21.8% in September 1, 2019, which covered about two-thirds of China's imports from the United States. You can see that these tariffs have increased nearly one-for-one with each other in this trade war, as the United States initiated the tariff increases and China responded likewise.

FIGURE 1-5

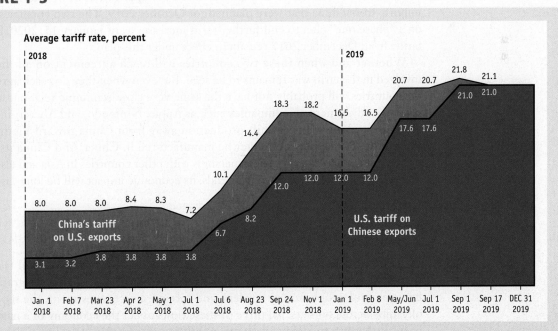

The U.S.–China Trade War, 2018–2019 This diagram shows the average tariff charged by the United States on imports from China from January 2018 to December 2019 and the average tariff charged by China on its imports from the United States during the same time period. As the United States applied tariffs against more imports from China, China responded by applying tariffs against more imports from the United States. The average tariff charged by the United States on Chinese imports was 21% as of September 1, 2019, and the average tariff charged by China on its U.S. imports was 21.1% as of September 17, 2019. Tariffs remained at that level during 2019 and into 2020 as a "phase one" plan to end further tariff increases was agreed upon.

From: Chad Bown, Petersen Institute for International Economics, https://www.piie.com/research/piie-charts/trade-war-suddenly-getting-worse.

It is not uncommon to see tariffs of 20% or 25% on an individual product for a limited period of time, but it is very unusual to see a tariff this high applied against *all imports* from a country. Comparing Figure 1-5 with Figure 1-4, we can see that the U.S. import tariff on China of 21% on September 1, 2019 was slightly larger than the average U.S. tariff in the early 1930s, which was 20%. An important difference between the current tariffs and those during the Great Depression, however, is that the 20% tariff applied in the early 1930s was the average U.S. tariff against *all importing countries*, whereas the 21% tariff is *only applied against China*. When we take the average U.S. tariff *over all countries*, including China, it was slightly above 3% in December 2018 and by September 1, 2019 it was slightly above 5%, as shown in Figure 1-4.

Why did President Trump impose these tariffs against China? The reason is that he hoped to gain concessions from China in negotiating with the Chinese over their own trade barriers. As we mentioned earlier when discussing the historical McKinley tariff, high tariffs are often not a goal in themselves but can serve as a bargaining tactic to get a trade partner to reduce its trade barriers. In the case of China, the United States would like to see it reduce import tariffs on products such as automobiles and other consumer goods, increase its purchases of U.S. agricultural goods, be more open to the entry of foreign firms, and more strongly enforce its protection for intellectual property (meaning that counterfeit goods made in China should not be allowed to undercut the market for brand-name U.S. goods that are imported). Countries in Europe are also concerned over China's treatment of foreign firms and intellectual property protection.

On September 17, 2019, the trade war between the United States and China showed the first sign of ending. On that day, China lowered its tariffs on a relatively small amount of U.S. imports, resulting in a drop in its average tariff from 21.8% to 21.1%, in what was likely a gesture meant to signal its willingness to resume negotiations. President Trump then delayed the application of new tariffs on U.S. imports from China that were planned for October 2019. The two countries agreed on a "phase one" plan to end further tariff increases as of January 15, 2020. Existing tariffs from December 2019 remain in effect under this plan.

Whether and when these two countries will reach agreement on all the issues involved in the tariff war remains to be seen. But even when they do reach agreement, the countries will probably not have the same very close economic relations as in the past. Already, American companies such as Apple, Nintendo, and Abercrombie and Fitch are making plans to shift production away from China toward Vietnam and India. The iPhone may no longer be manufactured in China. And China itself may decide to forge stronger trade partnerships with other countries in Asia and elsewhere. So regardless of when the tariff war ends, its economic impact will be long-lasting.

2 Migration and Foreign Direct Investment

In addition to examining the reasons for and the effects of international trade (the flow of goods and services between countries), we will also analyze migration, the movement of people across borders, and foreign direct investment, the movement of capital across borders. All three of these flows affect the economy of a nation that opens its borders to interact with other nations.

Map of Migration

In Figure 1-6, we show a map of the number of migrants around the world. The values shown are the number of people in 2017 who were living (legally or illegally) in a country other than the one in which they were born. For this map, we combine two

FIGURE 1-6

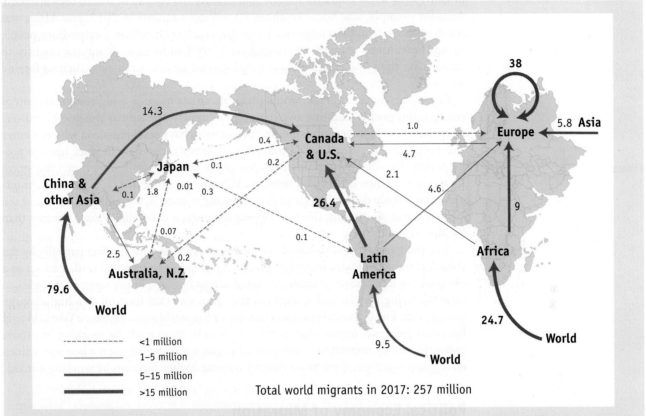

Foreign-Born Migrants, 2017 (millions) This figure shows the number of foreign-born migrants living in selected countries and regions of the world for 2017 in millions of people. The level of migration is illustrated by the width of the lines, with the largest migrant numbers having the heaviest lines and the smallest having dashed lines.
Data from: OECD and UN migration data.

different sources of data: (1) the movement of people from one country to another, reported for just the Organisation for Economic Co-operation and Development (OECD) countries and shown by arrows from one country to another,[11] and (2) the number of foreign-born people located in each region (but without data on their country of origin), shown by the bold arrows from World into Asia, Africa, and Latin America.

In 2017 there were 135 million foreign-born people living in the OECD countries. That was 53% of the total 257 million foreign-born people worldwide. In contrast, only 58 million people from the OECD countries live in another country, which is 23% of the total number of foreign-born people worldwide. These figures show that most migration occurs from countries *outside* the OECD, with more than one-half of migrants moving to countries *within* the OECD.

Comparing the map of immigration in Figure 1-6 with that of international trade in Figure 1-2, we see that there is a big difference: while most trade arrows point in both directions (countries both import from and export to their trading partners), the immigration arrows often point in one direction only, from lower-income countries toward higher-income countries. Exceptions to that rule occur with two-way

---

[11] The Organisation for Economic Co-operation and Development (OECD) consists of 34 member countries, including most European countries as well as Australia, Canada, Chile, Japan, Mexico, South Korea, and the United States. See the complete list of countries at oecd.org.

migration between higher-income countries, such as the United States with Canada or Europe, or when migrants are not able to leave the continent where they are born. Asia, for example, was home to about 80 million migrants in 2017, and Africa was home to about 25 million migrants. Latin America has 10 million foreign-born people living there. Many of these migrants have likely had to move from one country to another on the same continent for employment or other reasons, such as famine and war.

Given the choice, migrants would probably rather move to a high-wage, industrial country. But people cannot move to another country as easily as the goods and services that move in international trade. All countries have restrictions on who can enter and work there. In many OECD countries, these restrictions are in place because policy makers fear that immigrants from low-wage countries will drive down the wages for a country's own less-skilled workers. Whether or not that fear is justified, immigration is a hotly debated political issue in many countries, including Europe and the United States. As a result, the flow of people between countries is *much less* free than the flow of goods.

The limitation on migration out of the low-wage countries is offset partially by the ability of these countries to export products instead. International trade can act as a *substitute* for movements of labor or capital across borders, in the sense that trade can raise the living standard of workers in the same way that moving to a higher-wage country can. The increased openness to trade in the world economy since World War II has provided opportunities for workers to benefit from trade by working in export industries and by importing less-expensive goods from abroad, even when restrictions on migration prevent them from directly earning higher incomes by working abroad.

Political Economy of Migration

We have just learned that restrictions on migration, especially into the wealthier countries, limit the movement of people between countries. Let us see how such restrictions are reflected in recent policy actions in two regions: the European Union and the United States.

Migration in the EU Prior to 2004 the European Union (EU) consisted of 15 countries in western Europe, and labor mobility between them was very open.[12] On May 1, 2004, 10 more countries of central Europe were added: Cyprus, the Czech Republic, Estonia, Hungary, Latvia, Lithuania, Malta, Poland, Slovakia, and Slovenia; and since that time Bulgaria, Croatia, and Romania have joined, bringing the total number of countries in the EU to 28. These new countries had per capita incomes that were only about one-quarter of the average per capita incomes in those western European countries that were already EU members. This large difference in wages created a strong incentive for labor migration from low-wage to high-wage countries. As shown in Figure 1-6, in 2017 there were 38 million people from Europe living in an EU country in which they were not born. Fear of this movement of labor led to policy disagreements among the countries involved.

Germany and Austria, which border some of the new member countries, originally argued for a seven-year moratorium on allowing labor mobility from new members, if desired by the host countries. Ultimately, however, free labor mobility was adopted for all countries within the EU, except for the United Kingdom and Ireland. The other 26 countries in the EU agreed to have open borders between themselves, in what is known as the Schengen Area. That agreement is now being put to the test, however, by another type of migration: refugees coming from Africa and Asia who are

---

[12] These 15 countries are detailed in footnote 4.

streaming into Europe in unprecedented numbers. These refugees are fleeing wars and economic hardships in their home countries and have created a controversy in Europe over which countries should take them in and whether they can then move to other countries. We discuss this European immigration crisis in Chapter 5.

The concern over migration in Europe played a role in the 2016 vote in the United Kingdom to leave the European Union. By a vote of 51.9% in favor, citizens of the United Kingdom (which includes Great Britain and Northern Ireland) approved exiting from the European Union, an action that has come to be called *Brexit*. But the details of how to break ties with the European Union remained to be worked out, and those details have created further political upheaval and even changes in the U.K. government. Prime Minister Theresa May tried to negotiate the terms of withdrawal, but she was unsuccessful and lost her position as prime minister in July 2019. She was replaced by Prime Minister Boris Johnson, who vowed to leave the European Union by October 31, 2019. The United Kingdom was not able to leave the European Union under this strict deadline, which was extended into 2020.

Migration in the United States The political concern over migration is equally important in the United States. As shown in Figure 1-6, there were 26 million people from Latin America living in the United States and Canada in 2017, and the largest group of these migrants was composed of Mexicans living in the United States. It is estimated that there are about 11 million Mexicans living in the United States, and slightly less than one-half of these (5 million) are undocumented immigrants. The concern that immigration will drive down wages applies to Mexican migration to the United States and is amplified by the high number of undocumented immigrants. It is no surprise, then, that immigration policy is a frequent topic of debate in the United States. That debate becomes especially heated during a presidential election.

During the 2016 election in the United States, the candidate and future president Donald Trump promised to "build a wall" between the United States and Mexico. While the funds to build that wall have not been approved by the U.S. Congress, portions of the wall are being built by diverting money away from defense spending. As we mentioned at the beginning of the chapter, the recent increase in persons trying to cross the U.S.–Mexico border comes not from Mexican citizens, but rather from citizens of Guatemala, Honduras, and El Salvador who first cross the southern border of Mexico and then travel north. This flow of immigrants is smaller in number than the flow in Europe, but similar in that for both America and Europe, the immigrants are increasingly composed of families who are seeking refugee status. The challenges faced by the United States in deciding whether to absorb these refugees are the same as those faced by the European countries, and some of the policies being used to limit this flow of immigrants (other than building a wall) are also the same, as we discuss in Chapter 5.

Map of Foreign Direct Investment

As mentioned earlier in the chapter, foreign direct investment (FDI) occurs when a firm in one country owns (in part or in whole) a company or property in another country. There are two ways to measure FDI: either by the *new* ownership each year acquired by firms from one country investing in other countries, which is the "flow" of FDI; or by the *total* ownership (adding up over all years) by firms from one country investing in other countries, which is the "stock" of FDI. Figure 1-7 shows the principal stocks of FDI in 2018, with the magnitude of the stocks illustrated by the width of the lines. As we did for migration, we again combine two sources of information: (1) stocks of FDI found in the OECD countries that are owned by another country, shown by arrows from the country of ownership to the country of location, and (2) FDI stocks from anywhere in the world found in Africa, Asia, Europe, and Latin America.

FIGURE 1-7

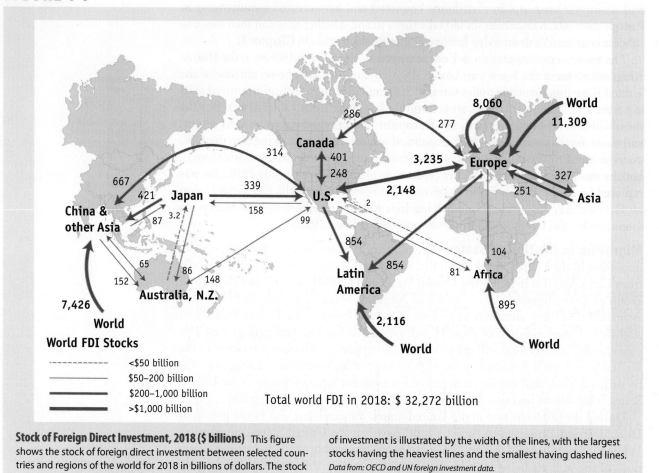

Stock of Foreign Direct Investment, 2018 ($ billions) This figure shows the stock of foreign direct investment between selected countries and regions of the world for 2018 in billions of dollars. The stock of investment is illustrated by the width of the lines, with the largest stocks having the heaviest lines and the smallest having dashed lines. *Data from: OECD and UN foreign investment data.*

In 2018 the total value of FDI stocks worldwide was $32.3 trillion, as shown in Figure 1-7. Comparing the arrows in that figure with the arrows indicating the flows of international trade in Figure 1-2, we can see some similarities. Both figures have very heavy "rings" of trade and FDI within Europe. For international trade, the trade within Europe was 21% of world trade (see Table 1-1). For FDI, the stocks that are both owned by and located in European countries are even greater: there is $8.1 trillion of FDI within Europe, or 25% of the world FDI.

Glancing at Figures 1-2 and 1-7, we can also see that there is a considerable amount of trade and FDI between Europe and the United States. An example of a European direct investment in the United States is the merger of the German company Daimler-Benz (which produces the Mercedes-Benz car) and Chrysler Corporation in 1998, resulting in the firm DaimlerChrysler. That deal lasted for fewer than 10 years, however, and in 2007 DaimlerChrysler sold the Chrysler firm back to an American financial company, Cerberus Capital Management, so Chrysler returned to American ownership. Then, in 2009, Chrysler was again sold to a European automobile firm, Fiat. An example of American direct investment in Europe is Ford Motor Company's acquisitions of the British firm Jaguar (in 1989) and the Swedish firm Volvo (in 1999), though both of these companies were later sold again, as we discuss below.

Including the trade and FDI that occur within Europe and between Europe and the United States, then, trade was 26% of the world total (see Table 1-1), while that amount of FDI is $13.4 trillion or 42% of the world FDI. So we see that there is even more FDI than international trade between high-income countries like those in Europe and the United States.

This is a surprising finding, because the traditional view of FDI is that it should flow from rich countries into poor countries, or from industrial countries to developing countries. Those flows are expected to occur because the poor countries are lacking in the physical capital (meaning factories and machines) to build up their industries, and that is what makes them poor. The ability to fund these investments comes from rich countries, and so capital should flow from there into poor countries. Some developing countries restrict the inflow of foreign investment because they are worried that the foreign companies will earn high profits and exert too much influence in their economies. China, for example, requires approval of all foreign investments and until recently required that foreign firms have a local partner.

There is some truth to the traditional view that capital flows from rich to poor countries. If we look at China and other Asia countries in Figure 1-7 (which excludes wealthy Japan), then there are $7.4 trillion of FDI stocks from the world, or 23% of the total. That is a considerable inflow of investment into China and other Asian countries, which we can think of as a middle-income and low-income region. But to put this amount of FDI into perspective, we can compare it to the total trade from Asia, which is even higher at 29% of world exports (Table 1-1). So while the inflow of investment into Asia is high, it does not reach the percentage of trade that comes from this region. From these comparisons, we must conclude that the traditional view of FDI as mainly flowing from rich to poor countries is not very realistic. There is even more FDI than trade between high-income countries of the world, and there is less FDI than trade between high-income and middle- or low-income countries. To capture the complexity of what happens in the world, we need to introduce a more nuanced view of FDI.

We can describe FDI in two different ways: horizontal and vertical.

Horizontal FDI As we have already seen, a great deal of FDI occurs between high-income countries, when a firm from one industrial country owns a company in another industrial country. We refer to these flows between industrial countries as **horizontal FDI**. The purchase of automobile companies between the United States and Europe, which we already described, is a good example of horizontal FDI. Another example is the 2014 purchase of Tim Hortons—a Canadian fast-food chain specializing in coffee and donuts—by the American company Burger King.

There are many reasons why companies want to acquire firms in another industrial country. The first reason is to avoid or to minimize taxes. In the merger of Burger King and Tim Hortons, the headquarters moved from the United States to Canada, where the corporate income tax is lower. Even in cases where the headquarters does not move, taxes in the form of import tariffs can be reduced. For example, as early as the 1950s and 1960s, American auto manufacturers produced and sold cars in Europe to avoid having to pay any tariffs to enter that market. In the 1980s and 1990s many Japanese auto firms opened plants in the United States to avoid U.S. import quotas (restrictions on the amount imported). Today, more Japanese cars are built in the United States than are imported from Japan.

Second, having a foreign subsidiary abroad also provides improved access to that country because the local firms will have better facilities and information for marketing products. Burger King had more than 7,000 outlets in the United States and another 6,000 outside of North America, but fewer than 300 in Canada. Tim Hortons, however, had about 3,500 outlets in Canada but only 900 in the United States. The combined chain will be able to expand its business against competitors (such as McDonald's and Dunkin' Donuts) in both countries, by combining the expertise that Tim Hortons has in coffee and breakfast items with the established strengths of

Burger King. The importance of having a retail presence extends beyond the restaurant industry and applies to manufacturing firms, too. For example, Toyota Motor Sales U.S.A. is a wholly owned subsidiary of Japan's Toyota Motor Corporation, and it markets Toyota cars and trucks in the United States. Many other foreign firms selling in the United States have similar local retail firms.

Third, an alliance between the production divisions of firms allows technical expertise to be shared and avoids possible duplication of products. We have already noted that Burger King and Tim Hortons expect to learn from each other. In another example, the American and Canadian divisions of General Motors, Ford, and Chrysler have operated plants specializing in different vehicles on both sides of the border (in Detroit, Michigan, and Windsor, Ontario) for decades. There are many reasons for horizontal FDI, which is really just a way for a firm to expand its business across international borders.

Vertical FDI The other form of FDI occurs when a firm from an industrial country owns a plant in a developing country, which we call **vertical FDI**. Low wages are the principal reason that firms shift production abroad to developing countries. In the traditional view of FDI, firms from industrial economies use their technological expertise and combine this with inexpensive labor in developing countries to produce goods for the world market. This is a reasonable view of FDI into China, although, as we have already seen, much of worldwide FDI does not fit this traditional view because it is between industrial countries.

In addition to taking advantage of low wages, firms have entered the Chinese market to avoid tariffs and acquire local partners to sell there. For example, China formerly had high tariffs on automobile imports, so many auto producers from the United States, Germany, and Japan established plants there, always with a Chinese partner, enabling them to sell more easily in that market. China joined the World Trade Organization in 2001, which means that it has reduced its tariffs on nearly all imports, including automobiles. Nevertheless, the foreign automobile firms are planning to remain and are now beginning to export cars from China.

Notice in Figure 1-7 that Asia also has $314 billion of direct investment into the United States, or what we might call "reverse-vertical FDI." Contrary to the traditional view of FDI, companies from developing countries also buy firms in industrial countries. Obviously, these companies are not going after low wages in the industrial countries; instead, they are acquiring the technological knowledge of those firms, which they can combine with low wages in their home countries. An early and widely publicized example was the 2005 purchase of IBM's personal computer division by Lenovo, a Chinese firm, and then Lenovo's announcement in 2014 that it would also buy IBM's low-end server business. What expertise did Lenovo acquire from these purchases? According to media reports, Lenovo acquired the management and international expertise of IBM and even hired IBM executives to run the business. Instead of using FDI to acquire inexpensive labor, Lenovo has engaged in FDI to acquire expensive and highly skilled labor, which is what it needs to succeed in the computer industry.

Other examples of reverse-vertical FDI are the 2008 purchase of Jaguar (formerly a British company) by the Indian automaker Tata and the 2010 purchase of Volvo (formerly a Swedish company) by the Chinese automaker Geely, both purchased from Ford Motor Company. In a later chapter, we discuss how automobile companies from the United States, Europe, and Japan entered the automobile industry in China by buying partial ownership in Chinese firms, which allowed the Chinese firms to learn from their foreign partners. That process of learning the best technology continues in the case of Geely purchasing Volvo from Ford, but in this case it is the Chinese firm that is doing the buying rather than the American, European, or Japanese firms.

The automobile industry relies on many other firms to provide automobile parts, and these Chinese firms are also entering the U.S. market through reverse-vertical FDI. A Netflix movie, *American Factory*, has been made about one such company, Fuyao Glass America, which provides automobile glass to companies like General Motors, Ford, BMW, Honda, and more. We describe the experience of this company in **Application: An American Factory**.

APPLICATION

An American Factory

In 2013, the Chinese company Fuyao Glass Industry Group purchased a shut-down General Motors plant in Dayton, Ohio. The General Motors plant had been used to manufacture cars but was closed in 2008 and the workers were laid off. The goal of Fuyao Glass was to redesign the plant to produce automobile glass, which it began doing in 2015. Fuyao brought in workers from China and also hired local U.S. workers with the goal of making this American plant as profitable as Fuyao's operations in China, even though wages in the United States are much higher than wages in China.

How could the Fuyao Glass America plant be profitable? First, while high wages had been paid to the former workers at the General Motors plant, the American automobile industry had since lowered the wages it paid to all entry-level workers in the United States. Thus, the American workers at Fuyao Glass were paid much less than the workers who had formerly worked at the General Motors plant before it was shut down.

Second, to be profitable, the plant had to achieve a high level of automobile glass production each day. American managers employed by Fuyao Glass were brought to China to observe how the factory and workers there were organized to achieve high production levels. Some of the production practices in China could not automatically be used in the United States because of safety hazards as well as differences in the cultures of the two countries, so adjustments had to be made.

A third challenging issue occurred when the workers in the Fuyao Glass America plant were invited to join a union. That was a situation that the Chinese owners and managers were not familiar with, and they resisted the presence of a union. The ability of workers in America to organize into a union is guaranteed by law, provided that the workers vote in favor of it. A vote was taken among the workers in the Fuyao Glass America plant to see whether they wished to be unionized, but that vote narrowly failed.

By 2018, the Fuyao Glass America plant was profitable, but not for the reasons that you might expect. To achieve profitability, robots were introduced to perform certain manual tasks. That meant that the employees who formerly did those jobs were laid off. Still, there were many more American workers than Chinese workers at the plant, and wages had been increased slightly from their initial level in 2015.

Netflix's documentary, *American Factory*, is about the experience at Fuyao Glass America. If you have access to Netflix, you will learn something—and probably be surprised—by watching this movie.[13] Not everyone who sees this movie will feel that it gives an accurate picture of Chinese-owned factories in the United States. An alternative point of view is presented in **Headlines: Don't Think That All Chinese Factories Are like the One in *American Factory***, which you are encouraged to read.

---

[13] Problem 5 in this chapter has questions to think about while you are watching the film.

HEADLINES

Don't Think That All Chinese Factories Are like the One in *American Factory*

In September 2019, Netflix released the documentary American Factory. It is thought-provoking and sometimes disturbing, and it does not leave you with an easy answer about whether a Chinese-owned factory can be profitable in the United States. This op-ed article written by Madeline Janis, an executive director at the nonprofit group Jobs to Move America, argues that the experience of other Chinese companies investing in the United States may be different from that of Fuyao Glass.

Netflix subscribers and theatergoers can now watch *American Factory*, a powerful new documentary about what happens when a manufacturing plant opens in a job-deprived town but the plant's owners are callous to workers, hostile to unions, and obsessed with profits at any cost. It is a story that has played out in towns and cities throughout the country for decades. Over a lifetime of advocacy on behalf of workers, I have dealt with numerous company owners who have insisted on their "right" to pay workers poverty wages, bust unions, and pollute the environment, just like the owners in *American Factory*.

... *American Factory* tells an important and compelling story. But I worry that for some viewers the takeaway will be that this is how Chinese companies operate when they set up shop in the United States. I've seen a lot of manufacturing companies that share many of the worst traits exhibited by Fuyao in the film, and most of them were owned by U.S., Canadian, or European companies.

On the other hand, I've also worked closely with a Chinese-owned manufacturing company that couldn't be more different from the one in *American Factory*. Like Fuyao, BYD is a Chinese company that opened a plant in the United States—in its case, in the city of Lancaster in northern Los Angeles County's Antelope Valley. BYD builds environmentally friendly buses for city fleets all over the world, including Los Angeles'. The new plant has delivered on its promise of jobs that are beneficial not just to local workers but for all of us living on a rapidly warming planet.

... When it comes to the treatment of workers and the protection of the environment, any company anywhere can choose to be a good actor or a bad one—and left unchecked, they often choose the latter. In my experience, nine times out of 10, the key factor determining their choice is whether public officials, workers, and local residents have organized effectively to hold the company accountable to fair standards of treatment of workers on the job and protection of the environment. This lesson ... should guide public discussion generated by this important film.

Source: Excerpted from Madeline Janis, "Sure, Watch 'American Factory.' But Don't Think That All Chinese Factories Are like the One in the Film," LA Times, August 21, 2019.

Chinese firms have also been actively investing in foreign companies whose products are needed to meet the growing demand of China's 1.4 billion people. For example, in 2013, the Chinese firm Shuanghui International purchased the American firm Smithfield Foods, one of the largest producers of pork in the United States. Rising incomes in China have led to increased demand for pork, exceeding that country's own ability to supply it. This example illustrates the more general trend of Chinese companies investing in natural resource and infrastructure projects around the world.

As China continues to industrialize, which will raise the income of its consumers and the ability of its firms to invest overseas, we can expect that its firms and government will continue to look beyond its borders to provide for the needs of its population.

3 Conclusions

Globalization means many things: the flow of goods and services across borders, the movement of people and firms, the spread of culture and ideas among countries, and the tight integration of financial markets around the world. Although it might seem that such globalization is new, international trade and the integration of financial markets were also very strong in the period before World War I. That war and the Great Depression disrupted these global linkages. Since World War II, world trade has grown rapidly again, even faster than the growth in world GDP, so that the ratio of trade to world GDP has risen steadily. International institutions established after World War II have promoted the growth in trade: the General Agreement on Tariffs and Trade (now known as the World Trade Organization), the International Monetary Fund, the United Nations, and the World Bank were all established in the postwar years to promote freer trade and economic development.

The view of these international organizations that trade should be free was challenged by President Donald Trump in the United States, who has been willing to use import tariffs as a way to achieve political objectives at home and abroad. One example of this action was in May 2018, when President Trump threatened to apply a tariff against U.S. imports from Mexico unless that country placed more security personnel on its southern border to limit the flow of migrants traveling north to the United States. In general, migration across countries is not as free as international trade, and all countries have restrictions on immigration because of the fear that the inflow of workers will drive down wages. That fear is not necessarily justified. We argue in a later chapter that immigrants can sometimes be absorbed into a country with no change in wages.

FDI is largely unrestricted in its flows between high-income countries but sometimes faces some restrictions in developing countries. The traditional view of FDI is that firms invest in developing countries to take advantage of lower wages in those countries. But there are large flows of FDI between high-income countries, and China is increasingly investing in plants in both high-income areas (such as the United States and Europe) and low-income areas (such as Africa). Migration and FDI are further aspects of the globalization that has become so widespread today.

KEY POINTS

1. The trade balance of a country is the difference between the value of its exports and the value of its imports, and it is determined by macroeconomic conditions in the country.

2. The type of goods being traded between countries has changed from the period before World War I, when standardized goods (raw materials and basic processed goods like steel) were predominant. Today, the majority of trade occurs in highly processed consumer and capital goods, which might cross borders several times during the manufacturing process.

3. A large portion of international trade takes place between industrial countries. Trade within Europe and trade between Europe and the United States account for roughly one-quarter of total world trade.

4. Many of the trade models we study emphasize the differences between countries, but it is also possible to explain trade between countries that are similar. Similar countries will trade different varieties of goods with each other.

5. Larger countries tend to have smaller shares of trade relative to GDP because so much of their trade occurs internally. Hong Kong (China) and Singapore have ratios of trade to GDP that exceed 100%, whereas the United States' ratio of trade to GDP is 16%.

6. Trade wars occur when countries respond to the tariffs of one country by applying higher tariffs themselves. There was a global trade war during the Great Depression, and there was a U.S.–China trade war in 2018–19.

7. The majority of world migration comes from developing countries, and, when possible, the migrants prefer to enter wealthier, industrial countries.

8. International trade in goods and services acts as a substitute for migration and allows workers to improve their standard of living through working in export industries, even when they cannot migrate to earn higher incomes.

9. There is even more FDI than international trade between high-income countries like those in Europe and the United States, and there is less FDI than trade between high-income and middle- or low-income countries.

international trade, p. 1

export, p. 2

imports, p. 2

import tariffs, p. 2

export quota, p. 2

migration, p. 2

immigrants, p. 2

emigrants, p. 2

refugees, p. 2

foreign direct investment (FDI), p. 3

trade balance, p. 4

trade surplus, p. 4

trade deficit, p. 4

bilateral trade balance, p. 4

value-added, p. 5

offshoring, p. 5

free-trade area, p. 9

sanctions, p. 10

trade embargo, p. 10

gross domestic product (GDP), p. 11

trade barriers, p. 12

political economy, p. 13

import quotas, p. 15

trade war, p. 15

horizontal FDI, p. 23

vertical FDI, p. 24

PROBLEMS

1. **Discovering Data** In this question, you are asked to update the numbers for world trade shown in Table 1-1.

   Go to the World Trade Organization's website at wto.org, and under "Documents, data and resources," look for "Statistics" and "WTO Data Portal"; you can also find this site directly by going to data.wto.org. In the Indicators menu, choose "International trade statistics," where you will expand the menu and choose only "Merchandise trade values" and expand it to choose "Merchandise exports by product group and destination – annual (million U.S. dollars)." (*Hint:* You can use the Deselect All button to eliminate choices that you do not want, and then choose only the variables that you do want.) In the menus for Reporting Economy and Partner Economy, choose the following regions: World; Africa; Asia; Australia and New Zealand; Commonwealth of Independent States; Europe; Middle East; North America; and South and Central America and the Caribbean. In the menu for Product/Sector, expand it to choose only "Total Merchandise." Finally, choose the most recent year for which trade data are available. Then click "Apply" on the right screen to show the values of these trade flows between regions, which you can download to Excel if you wish, and answer the following questions:

   a. What is the value of World exports to the World? (Even if you choose 2018, you will not get the same total as in Figure 1-2, because the sources of the data are different.)

   b. What is the total amount of trade within Europe? What percentage of total world trade is this?

   c. What is the total amount of trade (in either direction) between Europe and North America? Add that to the total trade within Europe, and calculate the percentage of this total to the world total.

   d. What is the total amount of trade within the Americas (i.e., between North America, Central America, South America, and within each of these regions)? What percentage of total world trade is this?

   e. What is the total value of exports from Europe and the Americas, and what percentage of the world total is this?

   f. What is the total value of exports from Asia, and what percentage of the world total is this?

   g. What is the total value of exports from the Middle East and the Commonwealth of Independent States,[14] and what percentage of the world total is this?

   h. What is the total value of exports from Africa, and what percentage of the world total is this?

   i. How do your answers to (b) through (h) compare with the shares of worldwide trade shown in Table 1-1?

---

[14] The Commonwealth of Independent States consists of Azerbaijan, Armenia, Belarus, Georgia, Kazakhstan, Kyrgyzstan, Moldova, Russia, Tajikistan, Turkmenistan, Uzbekistan, and Ukraine.

2. The quotation from former Federal Reserve chairman Ben Bernanke at the beginning of the chapter is from a speech that he delivered in Jackson Hole, Wyoming, on August 25, 2006, titled "Global Economic Integration: What's New and What's Not?" The full transcript of the speech is available at http://www.federalreserve.gov/newsevents/speech/bernanke20060825a.htm. Read this speech and answer the following questions:

   a. List three ways in which international trade today does not differ from the trade that occurred before World War I.

   b. List three ways in which international trade today differs from the trade that occurred before World War I.

3. Explain what each of the following terms means, and describe one example from this chapter in which each term is used.

   a. Bilateral trade balance

   b. Trade embargo

   c. Free-trade area

   d. Import quota

   e. Offshoring

   f. Trade war

4. Find online press reports dealing with immigration issues in Europe and in the United States. Summarize the issues being discussed in each case.

5. If you watch the Netflix film *American Factory*, answer the following questions:

   a. What is the very first scene of the movie? Did that scene surprise you, and why? Later, are there any scenes that occur in China that surprise you, and why?

   b. In the middle of the movie, a new Chinese manager starts at the plant. What personal story does he tell about himself as one reason for him to be the manager?

   c. What hourly wages were paid to the workers in the General Motors plant before it closed? What wages are paid to workers in the Fuyao Glass America plant when it first opens? Later, by how much do wages increase? What reason does the boss give for the wage increase? What is another reason (that is not said) for the wage increase?

   d. During the movie, a person is escorted out of the plant for walking through with a sign to promote a workers' union. When he is interviewed outside, he says, "Sometimes, you gotta be Sally Field." What is he talking about? (*Hint:* Look up the 1979 movie *Norma Rae*.)

   e. About how many Chinese workers and how many American workers are employed in the plant in 2018?

   f. Was the Fuyao Glass America plant profitable in the first year that it opened? Is the plant profitable when the movie ends, in 2018? Why did this change occur?

   g. Is there any American worker or manager that you admire in the movie, and why?

   h. Is there any Chinese worker or manager that you admire in the movie, and why?

2

Trade and Technology: The Ricardian Model

England exported cloth in exchange for wine, because, by so doing her industry was rendered more productive to her; she had more cloth and wine than if she had manufactured both for herself; and Portugal imported cloth and exported wine, because the industry of Portugal could be more beneficially employed for both countries in producing wine. . . . It would therefore be advantageous for [Portugal] to export wine in exchange for cloth. This exchange might even take place, notwithstanding that the commodity imported by Portugal could be produced there with less labour than in England.

David Ricardo, *On the Principles of Political Economy and Taxation*, 1821

Comparative advantage is the best example of an economic principle that is undeniably true yet not obvious to intelligent people.

Paul Samuelson, "The Way of an Economist," 1969[1]

Questions to Consider

1 What are reasons for countries to trade?

2 Will the country that is best at producing a good always export it?

3 How can countries compete with low-wage exporters, like China?

Pick any manufactured product and you will most likely find that it is traded among a number of countries. Let's choose snowboards as an example. In 2018 the United States **imported** (i.e., purchased from other countries) $28.5 million of snowboards from 19 different countries; Table 2-1 identifies the 12 countries with the highest dollar amount of snowboard sales to the United States.

At the top of the list in Table 2-1 is China, **exporting** (i.e., selling to another country) $12.7 million worth of snowboards to the United States. The second-largest exporter to the United States is Austria, selling $6.9 million in 2018. The next six countries on the list are the United Arab Emirates ($5 million), Taiwan ($2.5 million), Tunisia, a country on the north coast of Africa (about $450,000), Canada (about $380,000), and Australia (about $100,000).

The remaining European and Asian countries sold less than $100,000 worth of snowboards to the United States. This rather long list of countries raises a question: With all the manufacturing capability in the United States, why does it purchase snowboards from these countries at all instead of producing them domestically?

[1] Samuelson, Paul A. 1969. "The Way of an Economist." In *International Economic Relations: Proceedings of the Third Congress of the International Economic Association*, edited by Paul A. Samuelson (London: Macmillan), pp. 1–11.

TABLE 2-1

U.S. Imports of Snowboards, 2018

Rank	Country	Value of Imports ($ thousands)	Quantity of Snowboards (thousands)	Average Price ($/board)
1	China	$12,664	224,018	$57
2	Austria	6,940	53,318	130
3	United Arab Emirates	5,028	40,232	125
4	Taiwan	2,547	36,393	70
5	Tunisia	454	3,729	122
6	Canada	381	3,667	104
7	Australia	98	710	139
8	Poland	91	274	331
9	Switzerland	70	435	161
10	Netherlands	55	563	97
11	Japan	34	168	205
12	Hong Kong	27	871	31
13–19	All other countries	75	1,711	44
	Total	28,463	366,089	78

Data from: U.S. Department of Commerce and the U.S. International Trade Commission.

Cloe Kim won the gold in the Snowboard Half Pipe at the 2018 Olympics. Where did her snowboard come from?

The first chapters of this book look at various reasons why countries trade goods with one another. These reasons include:

- Differences in the **technology** used in each country (i.e., differences in each country's ability to manufacture products)

- Differences in the total amount of **resources** (including labor, capital, and land) found in each country

- Differences in the costs of **offshoring** (i.e., producing the various parts of a good in different countries and then assembling them into the finished product in a final location)

- The **proximity** of countries to one another (i.e., how close they are to one another)

In this chapter, we focus on the first of these reasons—technology differences across countries—as an explanation for trade. This explanation is often called the **Ricardian model** because it was proposed by the nineteenth-century economist David Ricardo. This model explains how the level of a country's technology affects the wages paid to labor, such that countries with better technologies have higher wages. This, in turn, helps to explain how a country's technology affects its **trade pattern**, the products that it imports and exports.

1 Reasons for Trade

Besides technology differences across countries, which is the focus of the Ricardian model, there are many other reasons why countries trade goods. Before we get into the details of the Ricardian model, let's briefly explore the other reasons for trade.

Proximity

The proximity of countries is a reason for trade primarily because it affects the costs of transportation. Countries that are near each other will usually have lower shipping costs added to the cost of their traded goods. The proximity of countries helps to explain why Canada is among the top 12 exporters of snowboards to the United States and why Canada and Mexico are both among the top three trading partners of the United States (the third being China). There are many other examples of how the physical closeness of countries affects trade partners. The largest trading partner of many European countries is another European country, and the largest trading partner of many Asian countries is Japan or China. Sometimes neighboring countries take advantage of their proximity by joining into a **free-trade area**, in which the countries have no restrictions on trade between them.

Resources

Proximity is only a partial explanation for trade patterns. As you can see in Table 2-1, Austria sells nearly 20 times the value of snowboards to the United States as does Canada, despite being farther away. What characteristics do Austria and Canada share that makes them good locations for the production and export of snowboards? They both have cold climates and mountains, both of which support winter sports, including snowboarding. In many cases, the local production of (and expertise in) ski and snowboard equipment develops as a result of being in a place where snow sports are common. This local production occurs because of the high demand for equipment and the ready supply of a complementary good (such as a snowy mountain).

This is an example of how the geography of a country (mountains and climate, in this case) affects its exports. Mountains that support snowboarding can be found near most of the other 19 countries selling snowboards to the United States, but there are some obvious exceptions on the list, such as the United Arab Emirates, Tunisia, and Hong Kong, which are too warm, and the Netherlands, which is too flat. So there must be other reasons for these countries to export snowboards.

Geography includes the **natural resources** (such as land and minerals) found in a country, as well as its **labor resources** (labor of various education and skill levels) and **capital** (machinery and structures). A country's resources—the land, labor, and capital used to produce goods and services—are often collectively called its **factors of production**. In the next two chapters, we study how a country's resources influence its trade patterns and how trade leads to economic gains or losses for different factors of production.

In some cases, a country can export a good without having any advantage in the natural resources needed to produce it. The United Arab Emirates was the third-largest exporter of snowboards to the United States in 2018, but it has no natural snow at all, so what explains its exports of snowboards? In 2006, the United Arab Emirates opened an indoor ski center at Ski Dubai, and since then it has started to manufacture and export snowboards. The Netherlands has Europe's largest indoor ski facility. These indoor ski areas are an example of creating comparative advantage. The United Arab Emirates and the Netherlands specialize in medium- to high-quality snowboards, as can be seen from the relatively high wholesale price: a snowboard purchased by the United States from the United Arab Emirates costs $125 and from the Netherlands costs $97 (Table 2-1), prices that are similar to some other countries listed: Tunisia ($122), Austria ($130), Canada ($104), and Australia ($139).

There are also some countries with lower wholesale prices for snowboards exported to the United States, such as China ($57), Taiwan ($70), and Hong Kong ($31), and some with higher prices, such as Poland ($331), Switzerland ($161), and Japan ($205). Low prices indicate that the snowboards these countries sell to the United States are either lower-quality or unfinished boards imported for further processing. That is especially true for the very low price per board from Hong Kong ($31). Hong Kong serves as a center for arranging to have unfinished goods shipped in, further processed in manufacturing facilities in China, and then shipped out again in unfinished or completed form. This type of trade in unfinished goods is an example of *offshoring*, a process in which a company spreads its production activities across several countries. The snowboards exported from Tunisia are produced by the company Meditech (standing for "Mediterranean technology") in an offshore factory of the Swiss company Nidecker, which produces high-quality boards.[2] The manufacturing of the iPhone that was discussed in Chapter 1, which occurs in many countries including China, is another example of offshoring. We study this phenomenon in Chapter 7.

Absolute Advantage

We've now explained some possible reasons for many countries to export snowboards to the United States, but we haven't yet explained the imports from China, the largest exporter of snowboards to the United States. The wholesale price for those snowboards is $57 (Table 2-1), indicating that they are of lower quality. In comparison with the second-largest exporter, Austria, the Chinese factories are mass-producing snowboards using a technology that is not the best in the world. The Austrian companies, in contrast, use world-class technologies that have been recognized for their energy efficiency, and they produce snowboards for many other European companies.[3]

When a country has the best technology for producing a good, it has an **absolute advantage** in the production of that good. Based on its superior technology, we can say that Austria has absolute advantage in the production of snowboards. Why does the United States import so many more snowboards from China, which is using a less-advanced technology to produce snowboards and other goods? Furthermore, while Austria uses the most advanced technology in snowboards, so does the United States in many products. So why should the United States import snowboards from Austria or China at all? Why doesn't it just produce all the snowboards it needs with U.S. technology and factors of production?

Comparative Advantage

These questions indicate that absolute advantage is not, in fact, a good explanation for trade patterns, and this is one of the key lessons from this chapter. Instead, **comparative advantage** is the primary explanation for trade among countries. To get an idea of what comparative advantage means, let us consider the example of trade between Portugal and England, as described by David Ricardo (see **Side Bar: David Ricardo and Mercantilism**).

To keep things simple, Ricardo considered just two commodities: wine and cloth. Ricardo allowed Portugal to have an absolute advantage in the production of both goods. Portugal's absolute advantage may reflect, for example, its more favorable climate for growing grapes and raising sheep. Even though Portugal can produce wine and cloth more easily than England, England is still able to produce both cloth and wine, but it is *relatively more difficult* to produce wine than cloth in England because England lacks the steady sunshine needed to produce good grapes. Based on these assumptions, Ricardo argued that England would have a comparative advantage in

---

[2] See http://www.boardsportsource.com/2013/10/17/global-snowboard-production-trouble-ahead/ for a description of global production and offshoring in snowboards.
[3] One Austrian factory producing CAPiTA boards that has won awards for its energy efficiency is described at https://www.capitasnowboarding.com/mothership.

David Ricardo and Mercantilism

David Ricardo (1772–1823) was one of the great classical economists, and the first model we study in this book is named after him. At the time that Ricardo was writing, there was a school of economic thought known as *mercantilism*. Mercantilists believed that exporting (selling goods to other countries) was good because it generated gold and silver for the national treasury and that importing (buying goods from other countries) was bad because it drained gold and silver from the national treasury. To ensure that a country exported a lot and imported only a little, the mercantilists were in favor of high *tariffs* (taxes that must be paid at the border when a good is imported). The mercantilist school of thought was discredited shortly after the time that Ricardo wrote, but some of these old ideas are still advocated today. For example, the United States sometimes insists that other countries should buy more from its companies and sometimes restricts import purchases from other countries; proponents of these ideas are called "mercantilists."

Ricardo was interested in showing that countries could benefit from international trade without having to use tariffs and without requiring exports to be higher than imports. He considered a case that contrasted sharply with what mercantilists believed to be best for a nation: in his writings about trade, Ricardo assumed that the value of exports equaled the value of imports (a situation called *balanced trade*) and that countries

David Ricardo

engaged in *free trade*, with no tariffs or other restrictions to limit the flow of goods across borders. Under these assumptions, can international trade benefit every country? Ricardo showed that it could. All countries gain from trade by exporting the goods in which they have comparative advantage.

Ricardo's ideas are so important that it will take some time to explain how and why they work. It is no exaggeration to say that many of the major international institutions in the world today, including the United Nations, the World Bank, and the World Trade Organization, are founded at least in part on the idea that free trade between countries brings gains for all trading partners. This idea comes from the writings of David Ricardo (and Adam Smith, a great classical economist of the eighteenth century).

producing cloth and would export cloth to Portugal, whereas Portugal would have a comparative advantage in producing wine and would export wine to England.

From this example, we can see that a country has comparative advantage in producing those goods that it produces best *compared with* how well it produces other goods. That is, Portugal is better at producing wine than cloth, and England is better at producing cloth than wine, even though Portugal is better than England at producing both goods. This is the idea behind the quotation from Ricardo at the start of the chapter—it is advantageous for Portugal to import cloth from England because England has a comparative advantage in cloth. In our snowboard example, we would expect that China has a disadvantage compared with Austria or the United States in producing many manufactured goods, but it is still better at producing snowboards than some other goods, so it is able to export snowboards to the United States.

It will take us most of the chapter to explain the concept of comparative advantage and why it works as an explanation for trade patterns. As indicated by the other quotation at the beginning of the chapter, from Nobel laureate Paul Samuelson, this concept is far from obvious, and students who master it will have come a long way in their understanding of international trade.

2 Ricardian Model of Trade

In developing the Ricardian model of trade, we will work with an example similar to that used by Ricardo; instead of wine and cloth, however, the two goods will be wheat and cloth. Wheat and other grains (including barley, rice, and so on) are major exports of the United States and Europe, while many types of cloth are imported into these countries. In our example, the home country (we will call it just "Home") will end up with the trade pattern of exporting wheat and importing cloth.

The Home Country

To simplify our example, we will ignore the role of land and capital and suppose that both goods are produced with labor alone. In Home, one worker can produce 4 bushels of wheat or 2 yards of cloth. This production can be expressed in terms of the **marginal product of labor (MPL)** for each good. Recall from your study of microeconomics that the marginal product of labor is the extra output obtained by using one more unit of labor.[4] In Home, one worker produces 4 bushels of wheat, so $MPL_W = 4$. Alternatively, one worker can produce 2 yards of cloth, so $MPL_C = 2$.

one worker for MPL

Home Production Possibilities Frontier Using the marginal products for producing wheat and cloth, we can graph Home's **production possibilities frontier (PPF)**. Suppose there are $\overline{L} = 25$ workers in Home (the bar over the letter L indicates our assumption that the amount of labor in Home stays constant). If all these workers were employed in wheat, they could produce $Q_W = MPL_W \cdot \overline{L} = 4 \cdot 25 = 100$ bushels. Alternatively, if they were all employed in cloth, they could produce $Q_C = MPL_C \cdot \overline{L} = 2 \cdot 25 = 50$ yards. The production possibilities frontier is a straight line between these two points at the corners, as shown in Figure 2-1. The straight-line PPF, a special feature of the Ricardian model, follows from the assumption that the marginal products of labor are *constant*. That is, regardless of how much wheat or cloth is already being produced, one extra worker yields an additional 4 bushels of wheat or 2 yards of cloth. There are *no diminishing returns* in the Ricardian model because it ignores the role of land and capital.

FIGURE 2-1

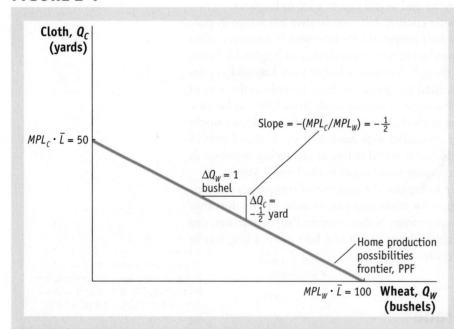

Home Production Possibilities Frontier
The Home PPF is a straight line between 50 yards of cloth and 100 bushels of wheat. The slope of the PPF equals the negative of the opportunity cost of wheat, that is, the amount of cloth that must be given up ($\frac{1}{2}$ yard) to obtain 1 more bushel of wheat. Equivalently, the magnitude of the slope can be expressed as the ratio of the marginal products of labor for the two goods.

---

[4] A special assumption of the Ricardian model is that there are no diminishing returns to labor, so the marginal product of labor is constant. That assumption will no longer be made in the next chapter, when we introduce capital and land, along with labor, as factors of production.

Given this property, the slope of the PPF in Figure 2-1 can be calculated as the ratio of the quantity of cloth produced to the quantity of wheat produced at the corners, as follows:

$$\text{Slope of PPF} = -\frac{50}{100} = -\frac{MPL_C \cdot \bar{L}}{MPL_W \cdot \bar{L}} = -\frac{MPL_C}{MPL_W} = -\frac{1}{2}$$

Ignoring the minus sign, the slope equals the ratio of marginal products of the two goods. The slope is also the **opportunity cost** of wheat, the amount of cloth that must be given up to obtain one more unit of wheat.[5] To see this, suppose that Q_W is increased by 1 bushel. It takes one worker to produce 4 bushels of wheat, so increasing Q_W by 1 bushel means that one-quarter of a worker's time must be withdrawn from the cloth industry and shifted into wheat production. This shift would reduce cloth output by $\frac{1}{2}$ yard, the amount of cloth that could have been produced by one-quarter of a worker's time. Thus, $\frac{1}{2}$ yard of cloth is the opportunity cost of obtaining 1 more bushel of wheat and is the slope of the PPF.

Home Indifference Curve With this production possibilities frontier, what combination of wheat and cloth will Home actually produce? The answer depends on the country's demand for each of the two goods. There are several ways to represent demand in the Home economy, but we will start by using **indifference curves.** Each indifference curve shows the combinations of two goods, such as wheat and cloth, that a person or economy can consume and be equally satisfied.

In Figure 2-2, the consumer is indifferent between points A and B, for example. Both of these points lie on an indifference curve U_1 associated with a given level of satisfaction, or **utility.** Point C lies on a higher indifference curve U_2, indicating that it gives a higher level of utility, whereas point D lies on a lower indifference curve U_0, indicating that it gives a lower level of utility. It is common to use indifference curves to reflect the utility that an individual consumer receives from various consumption

$L = \frac{1}{3} \cdot Q_C + \frac{1}{2} \cdot Q_T$

$L - \frac{1}{2} Q_T = \frac{1}{3} Q_C \cdot 3$

$3\left(L - \frac{1}{2} Q_T\right) = Q_C$

FIGURE 2-2

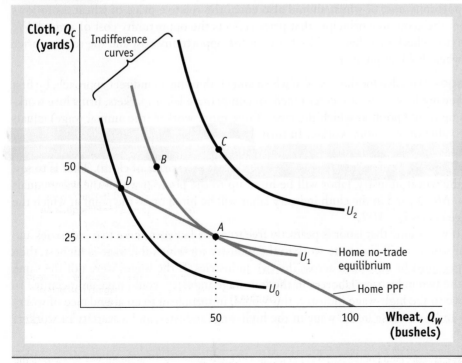

Home Equilibrium with No Trade
Points A and B lie on the same indifference curve and give the Home consumers the level of utility, U_1. The highest level of Home utility on the PPF is obtained at point A, which is the no-trade equilibrium. Point D is also on the PPF but would give lower utility. Point C represents a higher utility level but is off of the PPF, so it is not attainable in the absence of international trade.

---

[5] Notice that the slope of the PPF is the opportunity cost of the good on the horizontal axis—wheat, in this case.

points. In Figure 2-2, we go a step further, however, and apply this idea to an entire country. That is, the indifference curves in Figure 2-2 show the preferences of an entire country. The combinations of wheat and cloth on U_0 give consumers in the country lower utility than the combinations on indifference curve U_1, which in turn gives lower utility than the combinations of wheat and cloth on U_2.

Home Equilibrium In the absence of international trade, the production possibilities frontier acts like a budget constraint for the country, and with perfectly competitive markets, the economy will produce at the point of highest utility subject to the limits imposed by its PPF. The point of highest utility is at point A in Figure 2-2, where Home consumes 25 yards of cloth and 50 bushels of wheat. This bundle of goods gives Home the highest level of utility possible (indifference curve U_1) given the limits of its PPF. Notice that Home could produce at other points such as point D, but this point would give a lower level of utility than point A (i.e., point D would offer lower utility because U_0 is lower than U_1). Other consumption points, such as C, would give higher levels of utility than point A but cannot be obtained in the absence of international trade because they lie outside of Home's PPF.

We will refer to point A as the "no-trade" or the "pre-trade" equilibrium for Home.[6] What we really mean by this phrase is "no *international* trade." Home is able to reach point A by having its own firms produce wheat and cloth and sell these goods to its own consumers. We are assuming that there are many firms in each of the wheat and cloth industries, so the firms act under perfect competition and take the market prices for wheat and cloth as given. The idea that perfectly competitive markets lead to the highest level of well-being for consumers—as illustrated by the highest level of utility at point A—is an example of the "invisible hand" that Adam Smith (1723–1790) wrote about in his famous book *The Wealth of Nations*. Like an invisible hand, competitive markets lead firms to produce the amount of goods that results in the highest level of well-being for consumers.

Opportunity Cost and Prices Whereas the slope of the PPF reflects the opportunity cost of producing one more bushel of wheat, under perfect competition the opportunity cost of wheat should also equal the relative price of wheat, as follows from the economic principle that price reflects the opportunity cost of a good. We can now check that this equality between the opportunity cost and the relative price of wheat holds at point A.

Wages We solve for the prices of wheat and cloth using an indirect approach, by first reviewing how wages are determined. In competitive labor markets, firms hire workers up to the point at which the cost of one more worker (the annual wage) equals the value of one more worker. In turn, the value of one worker equals the amount of goods produced by that worker (the marginal product of labor) times the price of the good (P_W for the price of wheat and P_C for the price of cloth). That is to say, in the wheat industry, labor will be hired up to the point at which the wage equals $P_W \cdot MPL_W$, and in the cloth industry labor will be hired up to the point at which the wage equals $P_C \cdot MPL_C$.

If we assume that labor is perfectly free to move between these two industries and that workers will choose to work in the industry for which the wage is highest, then wages must be equalized across the two industries. If the wages were not the same in the two industries, laborers in the low-wage industry would have an incentive to move to the high-wage industry; this would, in turn, lead to an abundance of workers and a decrease in the wage in the high-wage industry, and a scarcity of workers

---

[6] We also refer to point A as the "autarky equilibrium," because "autarky" means a situation in which the country does not engage in international trade.

and an increase in the wage in the low-wage industry. This movement of labor would continue until wages are equalized between the two industries.

We can use the equality of the wage across industries to obtain the following equation:

$$P_W \cdot MPL_W = P_C \cdot MPL_C$$

By rearranging terms, we see that

$$P_W/P_C = MPL_C/MPL_W$$

The right-hand side of this equation is the slope of the production possibilities frontier (the opportunity cost of obtaining one more bushel of wheat) and the left-hand side of the equation is the **relative price** of wheat, as we will explain in the next paragraph. This equation says that the relative price of wheat (on the left) and the opportunity cost of wheat (on the right) must be equal in the no-trade equilibrium at point A.

To understand why we measure the relative price of wheat as the ratio P_W/P_C, suppose that a bushel of wheat costs \$3 and a yard of cloth costs \$6. Then \$3/\$6 = $\frac{1}{2}$, which shows that the relative price of wheat is $\frac{1}{2}$; that is, $\frac{1}{2}$ of a yard of cloth (or half of \$6) must be given up to obtain 1 bushel of wheat (the price of which is \$3). A price ratio like P_W/P_C always denotes the relative price of the good in the numerator (wheat, in this case), measured in terms of how much of the good in the denominator (cloth) must be given up. In Figure 2-2, the slope of the PPF equals the relative price of wheat, the good on the *horizontal axis*.

The Foreign Country

Now let's introduce another country, Foreign, into the model. We will assume that Foreign's technology is inferior to Home's so that it has an absolute *disadvantage* in producing both wheat and cloth as compared with Home. Nevertheless, once we introduce international trade, we will still find that Foreign will trade with Home.

Foreign Production Possibilities Frontier   Suppose that one worker in Foreign can produce 1 bushel of wheat ($MPL_W^* = 1$) or 1 yard of cloth ($MPL_C^* = 1$), whereas recall that a worker in Home can produce 4 bushels of wheat or 2 yards of cloth. Suppose that there are $\bar{L}^* = 100$ workers available in Foreign. If all these workers were employed in wheat, they could produce $MPL_W^* \cdot \bar{L}^* = 100$ bushels, and if they were all employed in cloth, they could produce $MPL_C^* \cdot \bar{L}^* = 100$ yards. Foreign's production possibilities frontier is thus a straight line between these two points, with a slope of -1, as shown in Figure 2-3.

You might find it helpful to think of Home in our example as the United States or Europe and Foreign as the "rest of the world." Empirical evidence supports the idea that the United States and Europe have the leading technologies in many goods and an absolute advantage in the production of both wheat and cloth. Nevertheless, they import much of their clothing and textiles from abroad, especially from Asia and Latin America. Why does the United States or Europe import these goods from abroad when it has superior technology at home? To answer this question, we want to focus on the *comparative advantage* of Home and Foreign in producing the two goods.

Comparative Advantage   In Foreign, it takes one worker to produce 1 bushel of wheat or 1 yard of cloth. Therefore, the opportunity cost of producing 1 yard of cloth is 1 bushel of wheat. In Home, one worker produces 2 yards of cloth or 4 bushels of wheat. Therefore, Home's opportunity cost of a bushel of wheat is $\frac{1}{2}$ a yard of cloth, and its opportunity cost of a yard of cloth is 2 bushels of wheat. Based on this comparison, Foreign has a *comparative advantage in producing cloth* because its opportunity cost

FIGURE 2-3

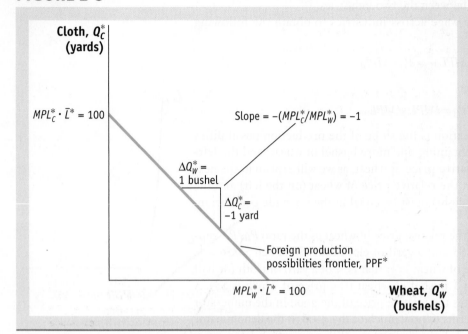

Foreign Production Possibilities Frontier The Foreign PPF is a straight line between 100 yards of cloth and 100 bushels of wheat. The slope of the PPF equals the negative of the opportunity cost of wheat, that is, the amount of cloth that must be given up (1 yard) to obtain 1 more bushel of wheat.

of cloth (which is 1 bushel of wheat) is *lower* than Home's opportunity cost of cloth (which is 2 bushels of wheat). Conversely, Home has a *comparative advantage in producing wheat* because Home's opportunity cost of wheat (which is $\frac{1}{2}$ yard of cloth) is lower than Foreign's (1 yard of cloth). In general, a country has a comparative advantage in a good when it has a lower opportunity cost of producing it than does the other country. Notice that Foreign has a comparative advantage in cloth even though it has an absolute disadvantage in both goods.

As before, we can represent Foreign's preferences for wheat and cloth with indifference curves like those shown in Figure 2-4. With competitive markets, the economy will produce at the point of highest utility for the country, point A^*, which is the no-trade equilibrium in Foreign. The slope of the PPF, which equals the opportunity cost of wheat, also equals the relative price of wheat.[7] Therefore, in Figure 2-4, Foreign's no-trade relative price of wheat is $P_W^*/P_C^* = 1$. Notice that this relative price *exceeds* Home's no-trade relative price of wheat, which is $P_W/P_C = \frac{1}{2}$. This difference in these relative prices reflects the comparative advantage that Home has in the production of wheat.[8]

APPLICATION

Comparative Advantage in Apparel, Textiles, and Wheat

The U.S. textile and apparel industries face intense import competition, especially from Asia and Latin America. Employment in these industries in the United States fell from about 1.7 million people in 1990 to 670,000 in 2005 to 340,000 in December 2017. An example of this import competition can be seen in one U.S. fabric manufacturer,

---

[7] Remember that the slope of the PPF (ignoring the minus sign) equals the relative price of the good on the horizontal axis—wheat in Figure 2-4. Foreign has a steeper PPF than Home as shown in Figure 2-2, so Foreign's relative price of wheat is higher than Home's. The inverse of the relative price of wheat is the relative price of cloth, which is lower in Foreign.

[8] Taking the reciprocal of the relative price of wheat in each country, we also see that Foreign's no-trade relative price of cloth is $P_C^*/P_W^* = 1$, which is less than Home's no-trade relative price of cloth, $P_C/P_W = 2$. Therefore, Foreign has a comparative advantage in cloth.

FIGURE 2-4

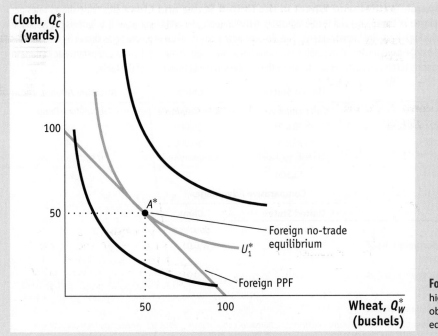

Foreign Equilibrium with No Trade The highest level of Foreign utility on the PPF is obtained at point A^*, which is the no-trade equilibrium.

Burlington Industries, which announced in January 1999 that it would reduce its production capacity by 25% because of increased imports from Asia. Burlington closed seven plants and laid off 2,900 people, approximately 17% of its domestic force. After the layoffs, Burlington Industries employed 17,400 people in the United States. Despite these reductions in employment, textiles and apparel remain an important industry in some cities, especially Los Angeles and New York. The "Made in USA" label can still be found, and it attracts customers.

The average sales total per employee for all U.S. apparel producers was $58,000 in 2018, as shown in Table 2-2. The textile industry, producing the fabric and material inputs for apparel, is even more productive, with annual sales per employee of $135,000 in the United States. In comparison, the average employee in China produces $35,000 of sales per year in the apparel industry and $34,000 in the textile industry. Thus, an employee in the United States produces $58,000/\$35,000 = 1.7$ times more apparel sales than an employee in China and $135,000/\$34,000 = 4$ times more textile sales. This ratio is shown in Table 2-2 in the column labeled "Absolute Advantage." It illustrates how much more productive U.S. labor is in these industries relative to Chinese labor. The United States clearly has an absolute advantage in both these industries, so why does it import so much of its textiles and apparel from Asia, including China?

The answer can be seen by also comparing the productivities in the wheat industry. The typical wheat farm in the United States grows 13,500 bushels of wheat per worker (by which we mean either the farmer or an employee). In comparison, the typical wheat farm in China produces only 450 bushels of wheat per worker, so the U.S. farm is $13,500/450 = 30$ times more productive! The United States clearly has an *absolute advantage* in the textile and apparel and wheat industries.

But China has the *comparative advantage* in both apparel and textiles, as illustrated by the columns labeled "Comparative Advantage." To determine comparative advantage, we compute the *opportunity cost* of apparel and of textiles. In the United States, shifting one worker from wheat to apparel production will lower wheat output by 13,500 bushels

TABLE 2-2

Apparel, Textiles, and Wheat in the United States and China This table shows sales per employee for the apparel and textile industries in the United States and China, as well as bushels per worker in producing wheat. The United States has an absolute advantage in all these products (as shown by the numbers in the right-hand column of the table). But China has a lower opportunity cost and a comparative advantage in producing textiles and apparel (as shown by the numbers in the bottom rows of the table).

	United States	China	Absolute Advantage
	Sales/Employee	*Sales/Employee*	*U.S./China Ratio*
Apparel	$58,000	$35,000	1.7
Textiles	$135,000	$34,000	4
	Bushels/Worker	*Bushels/Worker*	*U.S./China Ratio*
Wheat	13,500	450	30

Comparative Advantage		
	United States	China
	Bushels/$	*Bushels/$*
Opportunity cost of apparel	0.23	0.01
Opportunity cost of textiles	0.10	0.01

Note: Data are for 2018.

Data from: U.S. apparel and textile data from U.S. Bureau of Labor Statistics, 2018. U.S. wheat data from USDA Wheat Yearbook 2018. All China data from China Statistical Yearbook 2018.

and raise apparel sales by $58,000. The ratio of these numbers is $13,500/\$58,000 = 0.23$ bushels/\$, indicating that 0.23 bushels of wheat must be foregone to obtain an extra dollar of sales in apparel. In textiles, the U.S. ratio is $13,500/\$135,000 = 0.10$ bushels/\$, so that 0.10 bushels of wheat must be foregone to obtain an extra dollar in textile sales. These ratios are much smaller in China: only $450/\$35,000$ or $450/\$34,000 \approx 0.01$ bushels of wheat must be foregone to obtain $1 of extra sales in either textiles or apparel. As a result, China has a lower opportunity cost of both textiles and apparel than the United States, which explains why it has a comparative advantage in and exports those goods, while the United States exports wheat, just as predicted by the Ricardian model.

3 Determining the Pattern of International Trade

Now that we have examined each country in the absence of trade, we can start to analyze what happens when goods are traded between them. We will see that a country's no-trade relative price determines which product it will export and which it will import when trade is opened. Earlier, we saw that the no-trade relative price in each country equals its opportunity cost of producing that good. Therefore, the pattern of exports and imports is determined by the opportunity costs of production in each country, or by each country's pattern of comparative advantage. This section examines why this is the case and details each country's choice of how much to produce, consume, and trade of each good.

International Trade Equilibrium

The differences in no-trade prices across the countries create an opportunity for international trade between them. In particular, producers of cloth in Foreign, where the relative price of cloth is $P_C^*/P_W^* = 1$, would want to export cloth to Home, where the relative price, $P_C/P_W = 2$, is higher. Conversely, producers of wheat in Home, where the relative price of wheat is $P_W/P_C = \frac{1}{2}$, would want to export wheat to Foreign, where the relative price of $P_W^*/P_C^* = 1$ is higher. The trade pattern that we expect to arise, then, is that *Home will export wheat*, and *Foreign will export cloth*. Notice that both countries export the good in which they have a comparative advantage, which is what the Ricardian model predicts.

To solidify our understanding of this trade pattern, let's be more careful about explaining where the two countries would produce on their PPFs under international trade and where they would consume. As Home exports wheat, the quantity of wheat sold in Home falls, and this condition bids up the price of wheat in the Home market. As the exported wheat arrives in Foreign's wheat market, more wheat is sold there, and the price of wheat in Foreign's market falls. Likewise, as Foreign exports cloth, the price of cloth in Foreign will be bid up and the price of cloth in Home will fall. The two countries are in an **international trade equilibrium,** or just "trade equilibrium," for short, when the relative price of wheat is the same in the two countries, which means that the relative price of cloth is also the same in both countries.[9]

To fully understand the international trade equilibrium, we are interested in two issues: (1) determining the relative price of wheat (or cloth) in the trade equilibrium, and (2) seeing how the shift from the no-trade equilibrium to the trade equilibrium affects production and consumption in both Home and Foreign. Addressing the first issue requires some additional graphs, so let's delay this discussion for a moment and suppose for now that the relative price of wheat in the trade equilibrium is established at a level between the pre-trade prices in the two countries. This assumption is consistent with the bidding up of export prices and bidding down of import prices, as discussed previously. Since the no-trade prices were $P_W/P_C = \frac{1}{2}$ in Home and $P_W^*/P_C^* = 1$ in Foreign, let's suppose that the world relative price of wheat is between these two values, say, at $\frac{2}{3}$. Given the change in relative prices from their pre-trade level to the international trade equilibrium, what happens to production and consumption in each of the two countries?

Change in Production and Consumption The world relative price of wheat that we have chosen for this example is higher than Home's pre-trade price $\left(\frac{2}{3} > \frac{1}{2}\right)$. This relationship between the pre-trade and world relative prices means that Home producers of wheat can earn more than the opportunity cost of wheat (which is $\frac{1}{2}$) by selling their wheat to Foreign. For this reason, Home will shift its labor resources toward the production of wheat and produce more wheat than it did in the pre-trade equilibrium (point A in Figure 2-5). To check that this intuition is correct, let us explore the incentives for labor to work in each of Home's industries.

Recall that Home wages paid in the wheat industry equal $P_W \cdot MPL_W$, and wages paid in the cloth industry equal $P_C \cdot MPL_C$. We know that the relative price of wheat in the trade equilibrium is $P_W/P_C = \frac{2}{3}$, that the marginal product of labor in the Home wheat industry is $MPL_W = 4$, and that the marginal product of labor in the Home cloth industry is $MPL_C = 2$. We can plug these numbers into the formulas for wages to compute the *ratio* of wages in the two industries as

$$\frac{P_W \cdot MPL_W}{P_C \cdot MPL_C} = \left(\frac{2}{3}\right)\left(\frac{4}{2}\right) = \frac{8}{6} > 1, \text{ so that } P_W \cdot MPL_W > P_C \cdot MPL_C$$

This formula tells us that with the world relative price of wheat, wages paid in Home's wheat industry ($P_W \cdot MPL_W$) are greater than those paid in its cloth industry ($P_C \cdot MPL_C$). Accordingly, all of Home's workers will want to work in the wheat

---

[9] Notice that if the relative price of wheat P_W/P_C is the same in the two countries, then the relative price of cloth, which is just its inverse (P_C/P_W), is also the same.

FIGURE 2-5

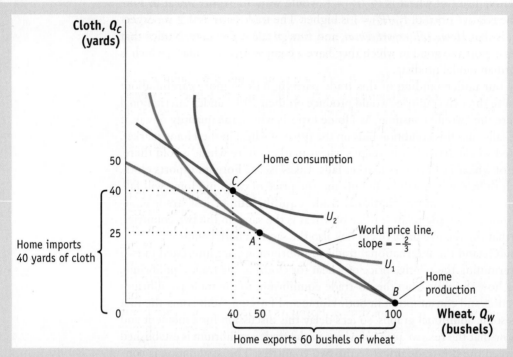

Home Equilibrium with Trade With a world relative price of wheat of $\frac{2}{3}$, Home production will occur at point B. Through international trade, Home is able to export each bushel of wheat it produces in exchange for $\frac{2}{3}$ yard of cloth. As wheat is exported, Home moves up the world price line, BC. Home consumption occurs at point C, at the tangent intersection with the indifference curve, U_2, since this is the highest possible utility curve on the world price line. Given these levels of production and consumption, we can see that total exports are 60 bushels of wheat in exchange for imports of 40 yards of cloth and also that Home consumes 10 fewer bushels of wheat and 15 more yards of cloth relative to its pre-trade levels.

industry, and no cloth will be produced. With trade, the Home economy will be fully specialized in wheat production, as occurs at production point B in Figure 2-5.[10]

International Trade Starting at the production point B, Home can export wheat at a relative price of $\frac{2}{3}$. This means that for 1 bushel of wheat exported to Foreign, it receives $\frac{2}{3}$ yard of cloth in exchange. In Figure 2-5, we can trace out its international trades by starting at point B and then exchanging 1 bushel of wheat for $\frac{2}{3}$ yard of cloth, another bushel of wheat for $\frac{2}{3}$ yard of cloth, and so on. From point B, this traces out the line toward point C, with slope $-\frac{2}{3}$. We will call the line starting at point B (the production point), and with a slope equal to the negative of the world relative price of wheat, the **world price line,** as shown by BC. The world price line shows the range of *consumption possibilities* that a country can achieve by specializing in one good (wheat, in Home's case) and engaging in international trade (exporting wheat and importing cloth). We can think of the world price line as a new budget constraint for the country under international trade.

Notice that this budget constraint (the line BC) lies *above* Home's original PPF. The ability to engage in international trade creates consumption possibilities for Home that were not available in the absence of trade when the consumption point had to be on Home's PPF. Now, Home can choose to consume at any point on the world price line, and utility is maximized at the point corresponding to the intersection with

---

[10] The fully specialized economy (producing only wheat) is a special feature of the Ricardian model because of its straight-line production possibilities frontier.

the highest indifference curve, labeled C with a utility of U_2. Home obtains a higher utility with international trade than in the absence of international trade (U_2 is higher than U_1); the finding that Home's utility increases with trade is our first demonstration of the **gains from trade,** by which we mean the ability of a country to obtain higher utility for its citizens under free trade than with no trade.

Pattern of Trade and Gains from Trade Comparing production point B with consumption point C, we see that Home is exporting $100 - 40 = 60$ bushels of wheat, in exchange for 40 yards of cloth imported from Foreign. If we value the wheat at its international price of $\frac{2}{3}$, then the value of the exported wheat is $\frac{2}{3} \cdot 60 = 40$ yards of cloth, and the value of the imported cloth is also 40 yards of cloth. Because Home's exports equal its imports, this outcome shows that Home's trade is balanced.

What happens in Foreign when trade occurs? Foreign's production and consumption points are shown in Figure 2-6. The world relative price of wheat $\left(\frac{2}{3}\right)$ is less than Foreign's pre-trade relative price of wheat (which is 1). This difference in relative prices causes workers to leave wheat production and move into the cloth industry. Foreign specializes in cloth production at point B^*, and from there, it trades along the world price line with a slope of (negative) $\frac{2}{3}$, which is the relative price of wheat. That is, Foreign exchanges $\frac{2}{3}$ yard of cloth for 1 bushel of wheat, then $\frac{2}{3}$ yard of cloth for another 1 bushel of wheat, and so on repeatedly, as it moves down the world price line B^*C^*. The consumption point that maximizes Foreign's utility is C^*, at which point 60 units of each good are consumed and utility is U_2^*. Foreign's utility is greater than it was in the absence of international trade (U_2^* is a higher indifference curve than U_1^*), as is true for Home. Therefore, both countries gain from trade.

Foreign produces 100 yards of cloth at point B^*: it consumes 60 yards itself and exports $100 - 60 = 40$ yards of cloth in exchange for 60 bushels of wheat imported from Home.

FIGURE 2-6

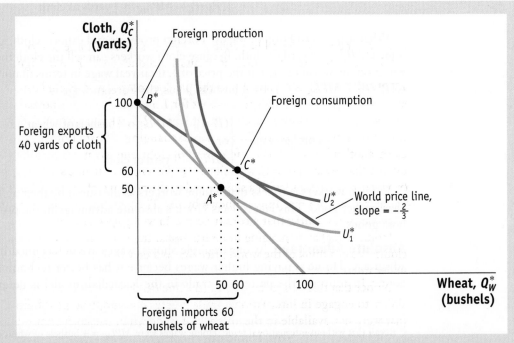

Foreign Equilibrium with Trade With a world relative price of wheat of $\frac{2}{3}$, Foreign production will occur at point B^*. Through international trade, Foreign is able to export $\frac{2}{3}$ yard of cloth in exchange for 1 bushel of wheat, moving down the world price line, B^*C^*. Foreign consumption occurs at point C^*, and total exports are 40 yards of cloth in exchange for imports of 60 bushels of wheat. Relative to its pre-trade wheat and cloth consumption (point A^*), Foreign consumes 10 more bushels of wheat and 10 more yards of cloth.

This trade pattern is exactly the opposite of Home's, as must be the case. In our two-country world, everything leaving one country must arrive in the other. We see that Home is exporting wheat, in which it has a comparative advantage (Home's opportunity cost of wheat production is $\frac{1}{2}$ yard of cloth compared with 1 yard in Foreign). Furthermore, Foreign is exporting cloth, in which it has a comparative advantage (Foreign's opportunity cost of cloth production is 1 bushel of wheat compared with 2 bushels in Home). This outcome confirms that *the pattern of trade is determined by comparative advantage*, which is the first lesson of the Ricardian model. We have also established that there are *gains from trade for both countries*, which is the second lesson.

These two conclusions are often where the Ricardian model stops in its analysis of trade between countries, but the story is incomplete because we have not yet determined the level of wages across countries. We have seen that with trade, the relative price of each good converges to a single equilibrium price in both countries. Does the same occur with wages? As we now show, this is not the case. Wage levels differ across countries with trade, and wages are determined by *absolute* advantage, not *comparative* advantage. This is a third, less-emphasized lesson from the Ricardian model, which we explore next.

Solving for Wages Across Countries To understand how wages are determined, we go back to microeconomics. In competitive labor markets, firms will pay workers the value of their marginal product. Home produces and exports wheat, so we can think of Home workers being paid in terms of that good: their real wage is $MPL_W = 4$ bushels of wheat. We refer to this payment as a "real" wage because it is measured in terms of a good that workers consume and not in terms of money. The workers can then sell the wheat they earn on the world market at the relative price of $P_W/P_C = \frac{2}{3}$. Thus, their real wage in terms of units of cloth is $(P_W/P_C) \cdot MPL_W = \frac{2}{3} \cdot 4 = \frac{8}{3}$ yard. Summing up, the Home wage is[11]

$$\text{Home wage} = \begin{cases} MPL_W = 4 \text{ bushels of wheat} \\ \text{or} \\ (P_W/P_C) \cdot MPL_W = \frac{8}{3} \text{ yards of cloth} \end{cases}$$

What happens to Foreign wages? Foreign produces and exports cloth, and the real wage is $MPL_C^* = 1$ yard of cloth. Because cloth workers can sell the cloth they earn for wheat on the world market at the price of $\frac{3}{2}$, their real wage in terms of units of wheat is $(P_C^*/P_W^*) \cdot MPL_C^* = (\frac{3}{2}) \cdot 1 = \frac{3}{2}$ bushels. Thus, the Foreign wage is[12]

$$\text{Foreign wage} = \begin{cases} (P_C^*/P_W^*) \cdot MPL_C^* = \frac{3}{2} \text{ bushels of wheat} \\ \text{or} \\ MPL_C^* = 1 \text{ yard of cloth} \end{cases}$$

Foreign workers earn less than Home workers as measured by their ability to purchase either good. This fact reflects Home's absolute advantage in the production of both goods.

Absolute Advantage As our example shows, wages are determined by absolute advantage: Home is paying higher wages because it has better technology in both goods. In contrast, the pattern of trade in the Ricardian model is determined by

---

[11] Recall that without international trade, Home wages were $MPL_W = 4$ bushels of wheat or $MPL_C = 2$ yards of cloth. Home workers are clearly better off with trade because they can afford to buy the same amount of wheat as before (4 bushels) but more cloth ($\frac{8}{3}$ yards instead of 2 yards). This is another way of demonstrating the gains from trade.

[12] Without international trade, Foreign wages were $MPL_W^* = 1$ bushel of wheat or $MPL_C^* = 1$ yard of cloth. Foreign workers are also better off with trade because they can afford to buy the same amount of cloth (1 yard) but more wheat ($\frac{3}{2}$ bushels instead of 1 bushel).

comparative advantage. Indeed, these two results go hand in hand—the only way that a country with poor technology can export at a price others are willing to pay is by having low wages.

This statement might sound like a pessimistic assessment of the ability of less-developed countries to pay reasonable wages, but it carries with it a silver lining: as a country develops its technology, its wages will correspondingly rise. In the Ricardian model, a logical consequence of technological progress is that workers will become better off through receiving higher wages. In addition, as countries engage in international trade, the Ricardian model predicts that their real wages will rise.[13] We do not have to look very hard to see examples of this outcome in the world. Per capita income in China in 1977, just as that nation began to open up to international trade, is estimated to have been about $1,600, whereas 40 years later in 2017, per capita income in China had risen by more than eight times to $13,100. These estimates mean that the real income that Chinese consumers had available to spend doubled every 13 years. For India, per capita income increased by more than four times from $1,300 in 1977 to $6,300 in 2017, so that real income doubled every 18 years.[14] Many people believe that the opportunity for these countries to engage in international trade has been crucial in raising their standard of living. As our study of international trade proceeds, we will try to identify the conditions that have allowed China, India, and many other developing countries to improve their standards of living through trade.

APPLICATION

Labor Productivity and Wages

The close connection between wages and labor productivity is evident by looking at data across countries. Labor productivity can be measured by the *real value-added per hour* in manufacturing. Value-added is the difference between sales revenue in an industry and the costs of intermediate inputs (e.g., the difference between the value of a car and the cost of all the parts used to build it). Value-added then equals the payments to labor and capital in an industry. In the Ricardian model, we ignore capital, so we can measure labor productivity as value-added divided by the number of hours worked, or value-added per hour. We don't want productivity to change just because of inflation, so in this calculation we measure sales revenue and the cost of intermediate inputs in real terms, that is, by dividing each amount by the price of output and a price index of intermediate inputs. The difference between these two is real value-added, and dividing that by the number of hours worked, we get labor productivity.

In Figure 2-7, we show the real value-added per hour in manufacturing in 2012 for several different countries. The United States has the highest level of productivity, and Taiwan has the lowest of the countries shown. Figure 2-7 also shows the real wages per hour in manufacturing for each country, which equals the hourly wage divided by an index of consumer prices. These real wages are less than real value-added per hour in most cases because value-added is also used to pay capital. Notice that Sweden and France have higher real wages than the United States, and Japan and Italy have real wages nearly equal to the United States, despite these countries all having lower productivity. That is because the wage being used includes the *benefits* received by workers, in

---

[13] That result is shown by comparing real wages in the trade equilibrium with the no-trade equilibrium in each country, as is done in the previous two footnotes.

[14] These values are expressed in 2011 dollars and are taken from the Penn World Table version 9.1, https://www.rug.nl/ggdc/productivity/pwt/. For comparison, over the same period 1977–2017, real per capita income in the United States roughly doubled from $27,500 to $56,200.

FIGURE 2-7

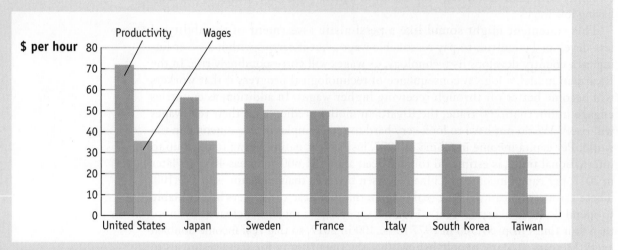

Labor Productivity and Real Wages, 2012 Labor productivity is measured by real value-added per hour of work and can be compared with the real wages paid in manufacturing in various countries. The general ranking of countries in terms of labor productivity—from highest to lowest—is the same as the ranking in terms of wages: countries with higher labor productivity generally pay higher wages, just as the Ricardian model predicts.

Data from: U.S. Department of Labor, Bureau of Labor Statistics.

the form of medical benefits, Social Security, and so on. Many European countries and Japan have higher social benefits than the United States. Although including benefits distorts the comparison between wages and productivity, we still see from Figure 2-7 that higher productivity countries tend to have higher real wages, broadly speaking, as the Ricardian model predicts.

The connection between labor productivity and real wages is also evident if we look at countries over time. Figure 2-8 shows that the general upward movement in labor productivity during 1973–2012 is matched by upward movement in real wages, as the Ricardian model predicts. In some countries, however, such as the United States, Japan, South Korea, and Taiwan, the connection between labor productivity and real wages seems to work better in the earlier years: up to about 1994, in the middle of the years shown. After that, productivity continues to grow in these countries but real wages do not grow as fast. In France and Italy, too, real wages experience a dip after 1994. What can explain the looser connection between labor productivity and real wages after 1994?

To explain this puzzle, we focus on just one country, the United States. For that country, we will broaden our focus from the manufacturing sector, which was used in Figures 2-7 and 2-8, to consider the entire business sector of the economy, that is, the production of both goods and services. In Figure 2-9 we show labor productivity in the business sector, which is again measured by real value-added per hour worked. We also show two different measures of real wages. The first is real wages that are measured by dividing the wage by the consumer price index (CPI). This measure of real wages grows more slowly than labor productivity, so there is a noticeable gap between the two by 2012 in Figure 2-9, just as we found for the manufacturing sector in the United States in Figure 2-8.

Then in Figure 2-9, we measure real wages by dividing the wage by an index of prices in the overall business sector. That is similar to the prices we used to measure real value-added in Figure 2-9, where we divided the sales of each industry by its own price and the intermediate inputs by their prices, in order to obtain real value-added and labor productivity. In this case, we see that real wages measured relative to the business sector prices grow at nearly the same rate as labor productivity.

FIGURE 2-8

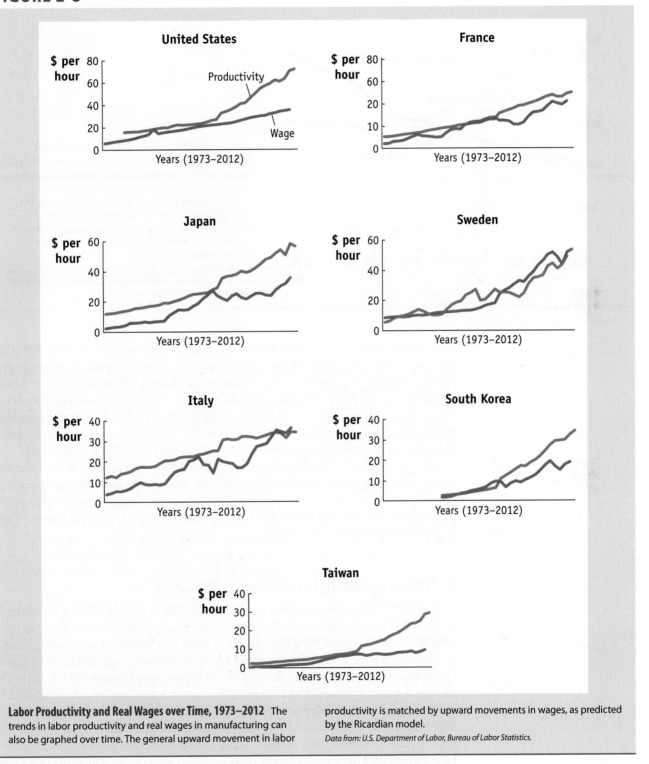

Labor Productivity and Real Wages over Time, 1973–2012 The trends in labor productivity and real wages in manufacturing can also be graphed over time. The general upward movement in labor productivity is matched by upward movements in wages, as predicted by the Ricardian model.

Data from: U.S. Department of Labor, Bureau of Labor Statistics.

How should we interpret the two different measures of real wages in Figure 2-9? Dividing wages by the CPI is the normal way to measure the well-being of consumers, because as consumer prices rise (with no change in income) consumers cannot afford to buy as much. As the price of housing goes up, for example, people may have to downsize their house or apartment. Housing plays a major role in the CPI, and housing prices

FIGURE 2-9

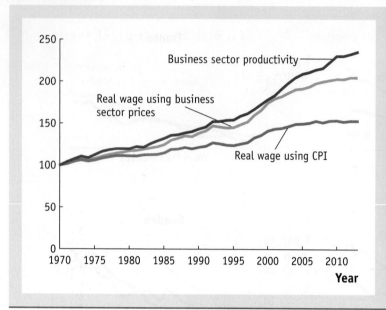

Labor Productivity and Real Wages in the United States, 1970–2012 The trends in labor productivity and real wages are shown for the business sector, including the production of goods and services, in the United States. When the real wage is measured relative to the consumer price index (CPI), it grows more slowly than labor productivity. But when the real wage is measured relative to the business sector prices, then its growth is similar to labor productivity.

Data from: Robert Z. Lawrence, June 2015, "Recent Declines in Labor's Share in US Income: A Preliminary Neoclassical Account," Working Paper 15-10, Peterson Institute for International Economics.

have usually gone up faster than the overall rate of inflation since the mid-1990s. In contrast, housing prices *do not* play a significant role in overall business sector prices, because these prices include the construction of new homes but not the prices of homes sold after they are built. The reason for the difference in the two real wages shown in Figure 2-9 is the *more rapid* rise in housing prices in the CPI, which leads to a *slower* rise in real wages measured relative to the CPI than the rise in real wages measured relative to business sector prices (which grow at nearly the same rate as labor productivity).

Thus, it is the rise in housing prices—which is not taken into account in the Ricardian model—that leads to the difference between labor productivity and real wages measured relative to the CPI. When we instead measure real wages relative to business sector prices, in which housing prices are less important, we find that real wages follow U.S. labor productivity more closely.

4 Solving for International Prices

In Figures 2-5 and 2-6, we assumed that the world relative price of wheat was $\frac{2}{3}$ and that at this level Home's exports of wheat just equaled Foreign's imports of wheat (and vice versa for cloth). Now let's dig a little deeper to show how the world price is determined.

To determine the world relative price of wheat, we will use supply and demand curves. Home exports wheat, so we will derive a Home **export supply curve,** which shows the amount it wants to export at various relative prices. Foreign imports wheat, so we will derive a Foreign **import demand curve,** which shows the amount of wheat that it will import at various relative prices. The international trade equilibrium is the quantity and relative price at which Home's exports equal Foreign's imports of wheat. This equality occurs where the Home export supply curve intersects the Foreign import demand curve.

Home Export Supply Curve

In panel (a) of Figure 2-10, we repeat Figure 2-5, which shows the trade equilibrium for Home with production at point *B* and consumption at point *C*. At the world relative price of $P_W/P_C = \frac{2}{3}$, Home exports 60 bushels of wheat

FIGURE 2-10

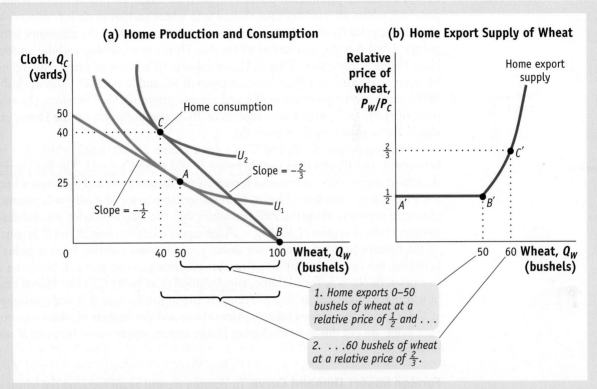

(a) Home Production and Consumption

(b) Home Export Supply of Wheat

Cloth, Q_C (yards)

Home consumption

U_2

Slope = $-\frac{2}{3}$

Slope = $-\frac{1}{2}$

U_1

Relative price of wheat, P_W/P_C

Home export supply

50
40
25

C
A
B

$\frac{2}{3}$
$\frac{1}{2}$

C'
A' B'

0   40 50   100 **Wheat, Q_W (bushels)**

50 60 **Wheat, Q_W (bushels)**

1. Home exports 0–50 bushels of wheat at a relative price of $\frac{1}{2}$ and ...

2. ...60 bushels of wheat at a relative price of $\frac{2}{3}$.

Home Export Supply Panel (a) repeats Figure 2-5, showing the trade equilibrium for Home with production at point B and consumption at point C. Panel (b) shows Home's export supply of wheat. When the relative price of wheat is $\frac{1}{2}$, Home will export any amount of wheat between 0 and 50 bushels, along the segment $A'B'$ of the Home export supply curve. For relative prices above $\frac{1}{2}$, Home exports more than 50 bushels, along the segment $B'C'$. For example, at the relative price of $\frac{2}{3}$, Home exports 60 bushels of wheat.

(the difference between wheat production of 100 and consumption of 40). We can use these numbers to construct a new graph, the Home export supply curve of wheat, shown in panel (b). The vertical axis in panel (b) measures the relative price of wheat and the horizontal axis measures the exports of wheat. The points B and C in panel (a), with the relative price of $P_W/P_C = \frac{2}{3}$ and Home exports of 60 bushels of wheat, now appear as point C' in panel (b), with $P_W/P_C = \frac{2}{3}$ on the vertical axis and Home wheat exports of 60 bushels on the horizontal axis. This is our first point on the Home export supply curve.

To derive other points on the export supply curve, consider the no-trade equilibrium in panel (a), which is shown by production and consumption at point A. The no-trade relative price of wheat is $\frac{1}{2}$ (the slope of Home's PPF), and Home exports of wheat are zero because there is no international trade. So the point A in panel (a) can be graphed at point A' in panel (b), with a relative price of $P_W/P_C = \frac{1}{2}$ and zero Home exports of wheat. This gives us a second point on the Home export supply curve.

To get a third point, let us keep the relative price of wheat at $P_W/P_C = \frac{1}{2}$, as in the no-trade equilibrium, but now allow Home to export some wheat in exchange for cloth at this price. Home consumption remains at point A in panel (a), but production can shift from that point. The reason that production can shift to another point on the PPF is that, with the relative price $P_W/P_C = \frac{1}{2}$, the wages of workers are equal in wheat and cloth. This result was shown in our earlier discussion. With wages equal in the two industries, workers are willing to shift between them, so any point on the PPF is a possible production point. Consider, for example, production at point B in panel (a), where all workers have shifted into wheat and no cloth is produced. With the relative price $P_W/P_C = \frac{1}{2}$, consumption is still at point A, so the difference between points A and B is the amount of wheat that Home is exporting and the amount of cloth Home is importing. That is, Home exports 50 bushels of wheat (the difference between production of 100 and consumption of 50) and imports 25 yards of cloth (the difference between production of 0 and consumption of 25). Therefore, the relative price of $P_W/P_C = \frac{1}{2}$, with wheat exports of 50, is another point on the Home export supply curve, shown by B' in panel (b).

Joining up points A', B', and C', we get a Home export supply curve that is flat between A' and B', and then rises between B' and C' and beyond. The flat portion of the export supply curve is a special feature of the Ricardian model that occurs because the PPF is a straight line. That is, with the relative price of $P_W/P_C = \frac{1}{2}$, production can occur anywhere along the PPF as workers shift between industries; meanwhile, consumption is fixed at point A, leading to all the export levels between A' and B' in panel (b). As the relative price of wheat rises above $\frac{1}{2}$, production remains fixed at point B in panel (a), but the consumption point changes, rising above point A. With the relative price $P_W/P_C = \frac{2}{3}$, for example, consumption is at point C. Then Home exports of wheat are calculated as the difference between production at B and consumption at C. Graphing the various relative prices above and the bushels of wheat exported at each price, we get the upward-sloping Home export supply curve between B' and C' in panel (b).

Foreign Import Demand Curve In Foreign we will again focus on the wheat market and construct an import demand curve for wheat. In panel (a) of Figure 2-11, we repeat Figure 2-6, which shows the Foreign trade equilibrium with production at point B^* and consumption at point C^*. At the world relative price of $P_W/P_C = \frac{2}{3}$, Foreign imports 60 bushels of wheat (the difference between wheat consumption of 60 and production of 0). These numbers are graphed as point $C^{*\prime}$ in panel (b), where we have the relative price of wheat on the vertical axis and the Foreign imports of wheat on the horizontal axis.

Other points on Foreign's import demand curve can be obtained in much the same way as we did for Home. For example, the no-trade equilibrium in Foreign is shown by production and consumption at point A^* in panel (a), with the relative price of wheat equal to 1 (the slope of Foreign's PPF) and zero imports (since there is no international trade). This no-trade equilibrium is graphed as point $A^{*\prime}$ in panel (b). Keeping the relative price of wheat fixed at 1 in Foreign, production can shift away from point A^* in panel (a). This can occur because, as we argued for Home, wages are the same in Foreign's wheat and cloth industries when the relative price is at its no-trade level, so workers are willing to move between industries. Keeping Foreign consumption fixed at point A^* in panel (a), suppose that all workers shift into the cloth industry, so that production is at point B^*. Then Foreign imports of wheat are 50 bushels (the difference between Foreign consumption of 50 and production of zero), as shown by point $B^{*\prime}$ in panel (b).

Joining up points $A^{*\prime}$, $B^{*\prime}$, and $C^{*\prime}$, we get an import demand curve that is flat between $A^{*\prime}$ and $B^{*\prime}$ and then falls between $B^{*\prime}$ and $C^{*\prime}$ and beyond. The flat portion of the Foreign import demand curve is once again a special feature of the Ricardian model that occurs because the PPF is a straight line. As we investigate other trade models in the following chapters, in which the production possibilities frontiers are curved rather than straight lines, the export supply and import demand curves will no longer have the flat portions. A general feature of these export supply and import demand curves is that they begin at the no-trade relative price for each country and then slope up (for export supply) or down (for import demand).

FIGURE 2-11

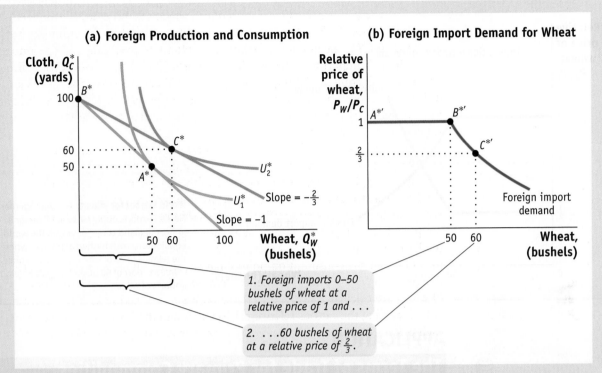

(a) Foreign Production and Consumption

Cloth, Q_C^* (yards)

Slope = $-\frac{2}{3}$

Slope = -1

Wheat, Q_W^* (bushels)

(b) Foreign Import Demand for Wheat

Relative price of wheat, P_W/P_C

Foreign import demand

Wheat, (bushels)

1. Foreign imports 0–50 bushels of wheat at a relative price of 1 and . . .

2. . . .60 bushels of wheat at a relative price of $\frac{2}{3}$.

Foreign Import Demand Panel (a) repeats Figure 2-6, showing the Foreign trade equilibrium with production at point B^* and consumption at point C^*. Panel (b) shows Foreign's import demand for wheat. When the relative price of wheat is 1, Foreign will import any amount of wheat between 0 and 50 bushels, along the segment $A^{*'}B^{*'}$ of Foreign's import demand curve. For relative prices below 1, Foreign imports more than 50 bushels, along the segment $B^{*'}C^{*'}$. For example, at the relative price of $\frac{2}{3}$, Foreign imports 60 bushels of wheat.

International Trade Equilibrium

Now that we have derived the Home export supply curve and the Foreign import demand curve, we can put them together in a single diagram, shown in Figure 2-12. The intersection of these two curves at point C' gives the international trade equilibrium, the equilibrium relative price of wheat at which the quantity of Home exports just equals Foreign imports. In Figure 2-12, the equilibrium relative price of wheat is $P_W/P_C = \frac{2}{3}$. This graph looks just like the supply = demand equilibria that you have seen in other economics classes, except that Figure 2-12 now refers to the *world* market for wheat rather than the market in a single country. That is, Home's export supply of wheat is the *excess* of the total Home supply over the quantity demanded by Home consumers, whereas Foreign import demand is the excess of total Foreign demand over the quantity supplied by Foreign suppliers. The intersection of these excess supply and demand curves, or export supply and import demand curves in Figure 2-12, determines the relative price of wheat that clears the world market, that is, at which the desired sales of Home equal the desired purchases by Foreign.

The Terms of Trade The price of a country's exports divided by the price of its imports is called the **terms of trade**. Because Home exports wheat, (P_W/P_C) is its terms of trade. Notice that an increase in the price of wheat (Home's export) or a fall in the price of cloth (Home's import) would both *raise* its terms of trade. Generally, an increase in the terms of trade is good for a country because it is earning more for its exports or paying less for its imports, thus making it better off. Foreign exports cloth, so (P_C/P_W) is its terms of trade. In this case, having a higher price for cloth (Foreign's export) or a lower price for wheat (Foreign's import) would make Foreign better off.

FIGURE 2-12

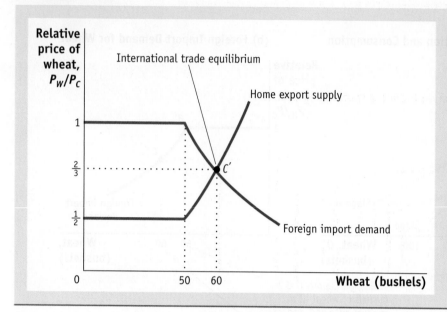

World Market for Wheat Putting together Home's export supply curve and Foreign's import demand curve for wheat, the world equilibrium is established at point *C*, where the relative price of wheat is $\frac{2}{3}$. At this price, Home's export of 60 bushels equals Foreign's imports of wheat.

APPLICATION

The Terms of Trade for Primary Commodities

What has happened over time to the terms of trade? Writing in the 1950s, the Latin American economist Raúl Prebisch and the British economist Hans Singer each put forward the hypothesis that the price of *primary commodities* (i.e., agricultural products and minerals) would decline over time relative to the price of manufactured goods. Because primary commodities are often exported by developing countries, this would mean that the terms of trade in developing countries would decline over time.

There are several reasons why the Prebisch–Singer hypothesis may be true. First, it is well known that as people or countries become richer, they spend a smaller share of their income on food.[15] This means that as world income grows, the demand for food will decline relative to the demand for manufactured goods. Therefore, the price of agricultural products can also be expected to decline relative to manufactured goods. Second, for mineral products, it may be that industrialized countries continually find substitutes for the use of minerals in their production of manufactured products. For example, much less steel is used in cars today because automobile producers have shifted toward the use of plastic and aluminum in the body and frame. We can think of the substitution away from mineral products as a form of technological progress, and as it proceeds, it can lead to a fall in the price of raw minerals.

However, there are also several reasons why the Prebisch–Singer hypothesis may not be true. First, technological progress in manufactured goods can certainly lead to a fall in the price of these goods as they become easier to produce (e.g., think of the reduction in prices of many electronic goods, such as laptop computers). This is a fall in the terms of trade for industrialized countries rather than developing countries. Second, at least in the case of oil exports, the Organization of Petroleum Exporting Countries (OPEC) has managed to keep oil prices high by restricting supplies on the world market. This has resulted in an increase in the terms of trade for oil-exporting countries, which includes developing and industrialized nations.

---

[15] This relationship is known as Engel's law, after the nineteenth-century German statistician Ernst Engel. It is certainly true for purchases of food eaten at home but might not hold for dining out. As your income rises, you might spend a constant or even increasing share of your budget on restaurant food.

Data on the relative price of primary commodities are shown in Figure 2-13.[16] This study considered 24 primary commodities from 1900 to 1998 and measured their

FIGURE 2-13

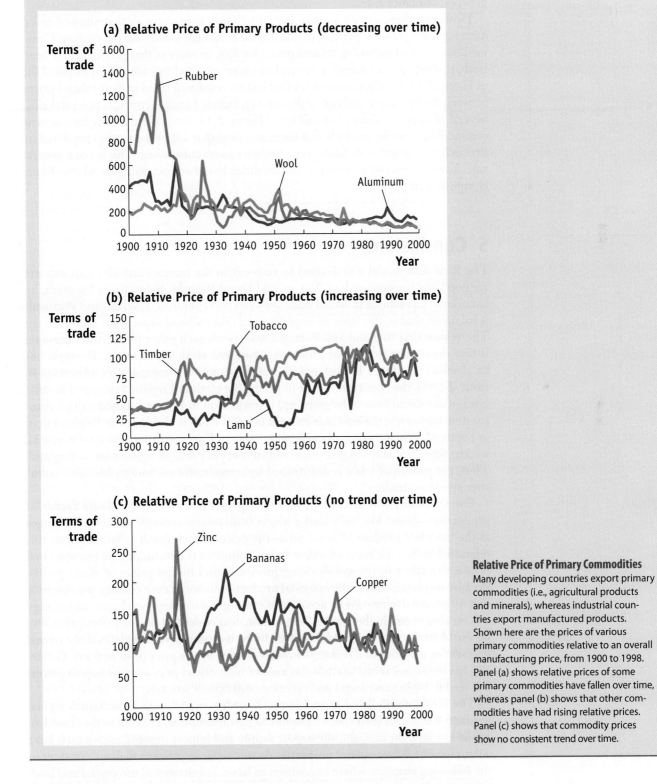

Relative Price of Primary Commodities Many developing countries export primary commodities (i.e., agricultural products and minerals), whereas industrial countries export manufactured products. Shown here are the prices of various primary commodities relative to an overall manufacturing price, from 1900 to 1998. Panel (a) shows relative prices of some primary commodities have fallen over time, whereas panel (b) shows that other commodities have had rising relative prices. Panel (c) shows that commodity prices show no consistent trend over time.

[16] These results are provided by Neil Kellard and Mark E. Wohar, 2006, "Trends and Persistence in Primary Commodity Prices," *Journal of Development Economics*, 79(1), February, 146–167.

world price relative to the overall price of manufactured goods. Of the 24 commodities, one-half of them showed a decline in their relative price for 50% or more of that period, including aluminum, cotton, hides, palm oil, rice, sugar, rubber, wheat, and wool. This evidence provides some support for the Prebisch–Singer hypothesis. Several examples of these commodities, with declining relative prices, are shown in panel (a) of Figure 2-13.

However, there are also a number of primary commodities that showed price increases for significant periods, or showed no consistent trend over the century. Commodities that had increasing relative prices for 50% or more of that period include beef, lamb, timber, tin, and tobacco. Several of these commodities are shown in panel (b) of Figure 2-13. Finally, commodities that had no consistent trend in their relative prices between the beginning and end of the century include bananas, coffee, copper, and zinc. Several of these are shown in panel (c) of Figure 2-13. From these results for different commodities, we can conclude that there are some that follow the pattern predicted by Prebisch and Singer, with falling prices relative to manufacturing. This is not a general rule, however, and other primary commodities have had increasing or no consistent change in their prices.

5 Conclusions

The Ricardian model was devised to respond to the mercantilist idea that exports are good and imports are bad. Not so, said David Ricardo, and to prove his point, he considered an example in which trade between two countries (England and Portugal) is balanced; that is, the value of imports equals the value of exports for each country. The reason that England and Portugal trade with each other in Ricardo's example is that their technologies for producing wine and cloth are different. Portugal has an absolute advantage in both goods, but England has a comparative advantage in cloth. That is, the opportunity cost of producing cloth in England (measured by how much wine would have to be given up) is lower than in Portugal. Based on this comparative advantage, the no-trade relative price of cloth is also lower in England than in Portugal. When trade is opened, merchants in England export cloth to Portugal, where they can obtain a higher price, and vintners in Portugal export wine to England. Thus, the pattern of trade is determined by comparative advantage, and both countries gain from trade.

For simplicity, the Ricardian model is presented with just a single factor of production—labor. We have used a lesson from microeconomics to solve for wages as the marginal product of labor times the price of each good. It follows from this relationship that the ratio of wages across countries is determined by the marginal product of labor in the goods being produced and by the prices of those goods. Because wages depend on the marginal products of labor in each country, we conclude that wages are determined by absolute advantage—a country with better technology will be able to pay higher wages. In addition, wages depend on the prices prevailing on world markets for the goods exported by each country. We have defined the "terms of trade" as the price of a country's exports divided by the price of its imports. Generally, having higher terms of trade (because of high export prices or low import prices) will lead to higher real wages and therefore will benefit workers.

The fact that only labor is used in the Ricardian model, with a constant marginal product of labor, makes it special. Because of this assumption, the PPF in the Ricardian model is a straight line, and the export supply and import demand curves each have a flat segment. These special properties do not occur in other models we consider in the following chapters, where in addition to labor, industries will use capital and land. Once we allow for the more realistic assumption of several factors of production, the gains from trade become more complicated. Even when there are overall gains for a country, some factors of production will gain as other factors of production lose due to the opening up of trade. That is the topic we explore in the next chapter.

KEY POINTS

1. A country has a comparative advantage in producing a good when the country's opportunity cost of producing the good is lower than the opportunity cost of producing the good in another country.

2. The pattern of trade between countries is determined by comparative advantage. This means that even countries with poor technologies can export the goods in which they have a comparative advantage.

3. All countries experience gains from trade. That is, the utility of an importing or exporting country is at least as high as it would be in the absence of international trade.

4. The level of wages in each country is determined by its absolute advantage, that is, by the amount the country can produce with its labor. This result explains why countries with poor technologies are still able to export: their low wages allow them to overcome their low productivity.

5. The equilibrium price of a good on the world market is determined at the point where the export supply of one country equals the import demand of the other country.

6. A country's terms of trade equal the price of its export good divided by the price of its import good. A rise in a country's terms of trade makes it better off because it is exporting at higher prices or importing at lower prices.

KEY TERMS

import, p. 31
export, p. 31
technology, p. 32
resources, p. 32
offshoring, p. 32
proximity, p. 32
Ricardian model, p. 32
trade pattern, p. 32
free-trade area, p. 33
natural resources, p. 33

labor resources, p. 33
capital, p. 33
factors of production, p. 33
absolute advantage, p. 34
comparative advantage, p. 34
marginal product of labor (MPL), p. 36
production possibilities frontier (PPF), p. 36
opportunity cost, p. 37

indifference curves, p. 37
utility, p. 37
relative price, p. 39
international trade equilibrium, p. 43
world price line, p. 44
gains from trade, p. 45
export supply curve, p. 50
import demand curve, p. 50
terms of trade, p. 53

PROBLEMS

1. **Discovering Data** In this problem you will use the World Development Indicators (WDI) database from the World Bank to compute the comparative advantage of two countries in the major sectors of gross domestic product (GDP): agriculture, industry (which includes manufacturing, mining, construction, electricity, and gas), and services. Go to the WDI database at http://wdi.worldbank.org/tables, where you will be choosing separately the sections on "People" and on the "Economy."

a. In the "People" section, start by choosing "Labor force structure." Choose two countries that you would like to compare, and for a recent year write down their total labor force (in millions) and the percentage of the labor force that is female. Then calculate the number of the labor force (in millions) who are male and the number who are female.

b. Again using the "People" section of the WDI, go to the "Employment by sector" table. For the same two countries that you chose in part (a) and for roughly the same year, write down the percentage of male employment and the percentage of female employment in each of the three sectors of GDP: agriculture, industry, and services. (If the data are missing in this table for the countries that you chose in part (a), choose different countries.)

Use these percentages along with your answer to part (a) to calculate the number of male workers and the number of female workers in each sector. Add together the number of male and female workers to find the total labor force in each sector.

c. In the "Economy" section, go to the table "Structure of output." There you will find GDP (in $ billions) and the % of GDP in each of the three sectors: agriculture, industry, and services. For the same two countries and the same year that you chose in part (a), write down their GDP (in $ billions) and the percentage of their GDP accounted for by agriculture, by industry, and by services. Multiply GDP by the percentages to obtain the dollar amount of GDP coming from each of these sectors, which is interpreted as the *value-added* in each sector, that is, the dollar amount that is sold in each sector minus the cost of materials (not including the cost of labor or capital) used in production.

d. Using your results from parts (b) and (c), divide the GDP from each sector by the labor force in each sector to obtain the *value-added per worker in each sector*. Arrange these numbers in the same way as the "Sales/Employee" and "Bushels/Worker" shown in Table 2-2. Then compute the absolute advantage of one country relative to the other in each sector, as shown on the right-hand side of Table 2-2. Interpret your results. Also compute the comparative advantage of agriculture/industry and agriculture/services (in the same way as shown at the bottom of Table 2-2) and the comparative advantage of industry/services.

Based on your results, what should be the trade pattern of these two countries if they were only trading with each other?

2. At the beginning of the chapter, there is a brief quotation from David Ricardo; here is a longer version of what Ricardo wrote:

"England may be so circumstanced, that to produce the cloth may require the labour of 100 men for one year; and if she attempted to make

the wine, it might require the labour of 120 men for the same time. . . . To produce the wine in Portugal, might require only the labour of 80 men for one year, and to produce the cloth in the same country, might require the labour of 90 men for the same time. It would therefore be advantageous for her to export wine in exchange for cloth. This exchange might even take place, notwithstanding that the commodity imported by Portugal could be produced there with less labour than in England."

Suppose that the amount of labor Ricardo describes can produce 1,000 yards of cloth or 2,000 bottles of wine in either country. Then answer the following:

a. What is England's marginal product of labor in cloth and in wine, and what is Portugal's marginal product of labor in cloth and in wine? Which country has an absolute advantage in cloth, and in wine, and why?

b. Use the formula $P_W/P_C = MPL_C/MPL_W$ to compute the no-trade relative price of wine in each country. Which country has a comparative advantage in wine, and why?

3. Suppose that each worker in Home can produce two cars or three TVs. Assume that Home has four workers.

a. Graph the production possibilities frontier for Home.

b. What is the no-trade relative price of cars in Home?

4. Suppose that each worker in Foreign can produce three cars or two TVs. Assume that Foreign also has four workers.

a. Graph the production possibilities frontier for Foreign.

b. What is the no-trade relative price of cars in Foreign?

c. Using the information provided in Problem 3 regarding Home, in which good does Foreign have a comparative advantage, and why?

5. Suppose that in the absence of trade, Home consumes two cars and nine TVs, while Foreign consumes nine cars and two TVs. Add the indifference curve for each country to the figures in Problems 3 and 4. Label the production possibilities frontier (PPF), indifference curve (U_1), and the no-trade equilibrium consumption and production for each country.

6. Now suppose the world relative price of cars is $P_C/P_{TV} = 1$.

   a. In what good will each country specialize? Briefly explain why.

   b. Graph the new world price line for each country in the figures in Problem 5, and add a new indifference curve (U_2) for each country in the trade equilibrium.

   c. Label the exports and imports for each country. How does the amount of Home exports compare with Foreign imports?

   d. Does each country gain from trade? Briefly explain why or why not.

WORK IT OUT   ≈ Achieve | interactive activity

7. Answer the following questions using the information given by the accompanying table:

	Home	Foreign	Absolute Advantage
Number of bicycles produced per worker	4	6	?
Number of snowboards produced per worker	6	8	?
Comparative advantage	?	?	

   a. Complete the table for this problem in the same manner as Table 2-2.

   b. Which country has an absolute advantage in the production of bicycles? Which country has an absolute advantage in the production of snowboards?

   c. What is the opportunity cost of bicycles in terms of snowboards in Home? What is the opportunity cost of bicycles in terms of snowboards in Foreign?

   d. Which product will Home export, and which product does Foreign export? Briefly explain why.

8. Assume that Home and Foreign produce two goods, TVs and cars, and use the information below to answer the following questions:

In the No-Trade Equilibrium

Home		Foreign	
$Wage_{TV} = 12$	$Wage_C = ?$	$Wage^*_{TV} = ?$	$Wage^*_C = 6$
$MPL_{TV} = 4$	$MPL_C = ?$	$MPL^*_{TV} = ?$	$MPL^*_C = 1$
$P_{TV} = ?$	$P_C = 4$	$P^*_{TV} = 8$	$P^*_C = ?$

   a. What is the marginal product of labor for TVs and cars in Home? What is the no-trade relative price of TVs in Home?

   b. What is the marginal product of labor for TVs and cars in Foreign? What is the no-trade relative price of TVs in Foreign?

   c. Suppose the world relative price of TVs in the trade equilibrium is $P_C/P_{TV} = 1$. Which good will each country export? Briefly explain why.

   d. In the trade equilibrium, what is the real wage in Home in terms of cars and in terms of TVs? How do these values compare with the real wage in terms of either good in the no-trade equilibrium?

   e. In the trade equilibrium, what is the real wage in Foreign in terms of TVs and in terms of cars? How do these values compare with the real wage in terms of either good in the no-trade equilibrium?

   f. In the trade equilibrium, do Foreign's workers earn more or less than Home's workers, measured in terms of their ability to purchase goods? Explain why.

9. Why do some low-wage countries, such as China, pose a threat to manufacturers in industrial countries, such as the United States, whereas other low-wage countries, such as Haiti, do not?

Answer Problems 10 to 12 using the chapter information for Home and Foreign.

10. a. Suppose that the number of workers doubles in Home. What happens to the Home PPF, and what happens to the no-trade relative price of wheat?

    b. Suppose that there is technological progress in the wheat industry such that Home can produce more wheat with the same amount of labor. What happens to the Home PPF, and what happens to the relative price of wheat? Describe what would happen if a similar change occurred in the cloth industry.

11. a. Using Figure 2-5, show that an increase in the relative price of wheat from its world relative price of $\frac{2}{3}$ will raise Home's utility.

    b. Using Figure 2-6, show that an increase in the relative price of wheat from its world relative price of $\frac{2}{3}$ will lower Foreign's utility. What is Foreign's utility when the world relative price reaches 1, and what happens in Foreign when the world relative price of wheat rises above that level?

12. (*This is a harder question.*) Suppose that Home is much larger than Foreign. For example, suppose we double the number of workers in Home from 25 to 50. Then, suppose that Home is willing to export up to 100 bushels of wheat at its no-trade price of $P_W/P_C = \frac{1}{2}$ rather than the 50 bushels of wheat as shown in Figure 2-12. In the following figure, we draw a new version of Figure 2-12, with the larger Home.

   a. From this figure, what is the new world relative price of wheat (at point *D*)?

   b. Using this new world equilibrium price, draw a new version of the trade equilibrium in Home and in Foreign, and show the production point and consumption point in each country.

   c. Are there gains from trade in both countries? Explain why or why not.

13. Using the results from Problem 12, explain why the Ricardian model predicts that Mexico would gain more than the United States when the two countries signed the North American Free Trade Agreement, establishing free trade between them.

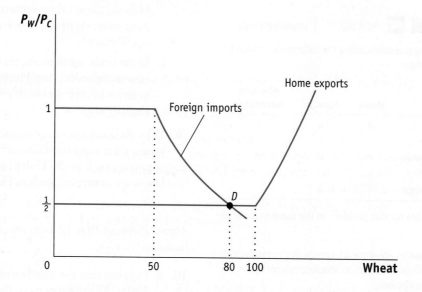

3

Gains and Losses from Trade in the Specific-Factors Model

The time has come, the awaited day, a historic day in which Bolivia retakes absolute control of our natural resources.

Evo Morales, President of Bolivia, 2006[1]

We estimate that import competition from China, which surged after 2000, was a major force behind both recent reductions in US manufacturing employment and . . . weak overall US job growth. Our central estimates suggest job losses from rising Chinese import competition over 1999–2011 in the range of 2.0–2.4 million.

Daron Acemoglu et al., "Import Competition and the Great US Employment Sag of the 2000s," 2016[2]

Questions to Consider

1 Do you personally gain from inexpensive imported goods?

2 Besides you, who gains and who loses from trade?

3 What government policies can help firms and workers that lose from trade?

For nearly 14 years, Evo Morales was the president of Bolivia. First elected in December 2005 and taking office in January 2006, he was the first Aymara Indian elected to president in Bolivia's 180-year history. In May 2006 he nationalized the gas industry, which meant that all natural gas resources were placed under the control of the state-owned energy company. With this policy change, foreign investors lost their majority ownership claims to the gas fields, pipelines, and refineries that they had built, and they also lost a significant portion of the profits from the sales of Bolivian natural gas. This drastic step, which was criticized heavily by foreign governments, was supported by the majority of Bolivians. By nationalizing the gas industry, President Morales ensured that these profits would go to the people of Bolivia.

A new constitution in 2009 gave indigenous peoples control over natural resources in their territories. Companies from Japan and Europe made deals with the Morales government to extract this resource, but the government ensured that the gains flowed to the local population through poverty-reduction programs. Since 2009, Bolivia experienced high economic growth, averaging at least 4% per year

---

[1] Speech from the San Alberto field operated by Petrobras, "Bolivia Nationalizes Natural Gas Industry," *USA Today*, May 1, 2006.
[2] Daron Acemoglu, David Autor, David Dorn, Gordon H. Hanson, and Brendan Price, 2016, "Import Competition and the Great US Employment Sag of the 2000s," *Journal of Labor Economics*, 34(S1), S141–S198.

up to 2018, and millions of people—especially from indigenous rural areas—were pulled out of poverty. There was substantial migration from rural areas to cities such as El Alto, which was the site of violent protests before the election of Evo Morales but then became host to thriving small businesses owned by both men and women.[3]

According to the new constitution, any president can serve for only two terms, but the first term served by Morales occurred before the constitution in 2009, so Evo Morales was reelected twice more—in 2009 and in 2014. He wanted to continue as president and in 2016 a public referendum was held that would allow him to run for another term. The referendum was narrowly defeated. Dissatisfied with this outcome, Morales persuaded the Bolivian Supreme Court to grant him the right to run again. So in the election of October 2019, President Morales was a candidate and at first it appeared that he had won the election. But then evidence of irregularities in the voting were reported, and violent demonstrations broke out in Bolivia once again. President Morales resigned his position and fled to Mexico. In November 2019, a provisional government was set up in Bolivia, which promised to hold new elections on May 3, 2020. It remains to be seen what the future holds for the Bolivian government and for the continuation of the policies started under President Morales.

The Bolivian experience illustrates the difficulty of ensuring that all people within a country share in the gains from trade. Despite the abundant natural gas resources, along with other minerals such as silver, tin, and lithium (used to make car batteries), many of the local population remained in poverty. The difficulty of sharing these gains among Bolivia's citizenry made the export of gas a contentious issue. Although the export of natural gas clearly generated gains for the foreign-owned and state-owned companies that sold the resources, the indigenous peoples did not historically share in those gains. President Morales was able to correct that historic injustice so the indigenous peoples shared in the gains, but he did not ensure that these gains would necessarily continue through a stable transfer of power to the next president.

A key lesson from this chapter is that in most cases, opening a country to trade generates winners *and* losers. In general, the gains of those who benefit from trade exceed the losses of those who are harmed, and in this sense there are overall gains from trade. That was a lesson from the Ricardian model in the last chapter. But our argument in the last chapter that trade generates gains for *all* workers was too simple because, in the Ricardian model, labor is the only factor of production. Once we make the more realistic assumption that capital and land are also factors of production, then trade generates gains for some factors and losses for others. Our goal in this chapter is to determine who gains and who loses from trade and under what circumstances.

The concern for those who are not gaining from trade arises not only in developing countries like Bolivia but also in all countries of the world. At the beginning of the chapter we included a quote from a research study by economists in the United States. They refer to the surge in China's imports to the United States following China's entry into the World Trade Organization (WTO) in 2001. All WTO members must maintain low tariffs on imports, so these lower U.S. tariffs benefitted China.[4] According to the

---

[3] You can read more about this case in Simon Romero, "In Bolivia, Untapped Bounty Meets Nationalism," *New York Times*, February 3, 2009, and in Sara Shahriari, "The Booming World: Bolivia," *The Guardian*, December 20, 2012, from which this paragraph is drawn.

[4] The tariffs that President Trump has imposed against China and other countries, discussed in Chapter 1, are all exceptions to these WTO rules. In Chapter 8 we will explain why these exceptions can be made, so that under specific circumstances, WTO members can apply tariffs against other WTO members.

study, after China joined the WTO, its rising imports into the United States led to a substantial loss of jobs in U.S. import industries, so the factory owners and workers in those industries did not gain from trade. Balanced against these losses, however, we should take into account the gains for farmers, factory owners, and workers in U.S. *export* industries. An important lesson of this chapter is that while there are losses in import industries, there will be gains in export industries, and that on balance there are gains overall.

The model we use to analyze the role of international trade in determining the earnings of labor, land, and capital assumes that one industry (agriculture) uses labor and land and the other industry (manufacturing) uses labor and capital. This model is sometimes called the **specific-factors model** because land is *specific* to the agriculture sector and capital is *specific* to the manufacturing sector; labor is used in both sectors, so it is not specific to either one. The idea that land is specific to agriculture and that capital is specific to manufacturing may be true in the short run but does not really hold in the long run. In later chapters, we develop a long-run model, in which capital and other resources can be shifted from use in one industry to use in another. But for now we focus on the short-run specific-factors model, which offers many new insights about the gains from trade beyond those obtained from the Ricardian model.

1 Specific-Factors Model

We address the following question in the specific-factors model: How does trade affect the earnings of labor, land, and capital? We have already seen from our study of the Ricardian model that when a country is opened to free trade, the relative price of exports rises and the relative price of imports falls. Thus, the question of how trade affects factor earnings is really a question of how changes in *relative prices* affect the earnings of labor, land, and capital. The idea we develop in this section is that the earnings of *specific factors*, or *fixed factors* (such as capital and land), rise or fall primarily because of changes in relative prices (i.e., specific-factor earnings are the most sensitive to relative price changes) because in the short run they are "stuck" in a sector and cannot be employed in other sectors. In contrast, mobile factors (such as labor) can offset their losses somewhat by seeking employment in other industries.

As in our study of international trade in Chapter 2, we look at two countries, called Home and Foreign. We first discuss the Home country.

The Home Country

Let us call the two industries in the specific-factors model "manufacturing" and "agriculture." Manufacturing uses labor and capital, whereas agriculture uses labor and land. In each industry, increases in the amount of labor used are subject to **diminishing returns**; that is, the marginal product of labor declines as the amount of labor used in the industry increases. Figure 3-1(a) plots output against the amount of labor used in production, and it shows diminishing returns for the manufacturing industry. As more labor is used, the output of manufacturing goes up, but it does so at a diminishing rate. The slope of the curve in Figure 3-1(a) measures the marginal product of labor, which declines as labor increases.

Figure 3-1(b) graphs MPL_M, the marginal product of labor in manufacturing, against the labor used in manufacturing L_M. This curve slopes downward because of diminishing returns. Likewise, in the agriculture sector (not drawn), the marginal

FIGURE 3-1

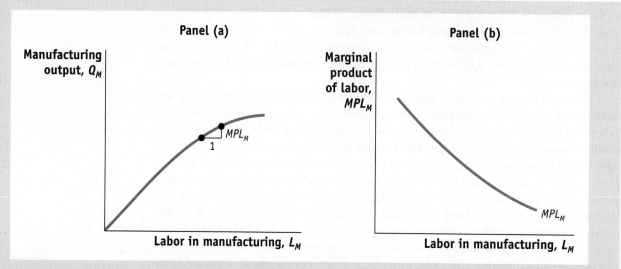

Panel (a)

Panel (b)

Panel (a) Manufacturing Output As more labor is used, manufacturing output increases, but it does so at a diminishing rate. The slope of the curve measures the marginal product of labor, which declines as the quantity of labor used in manufacturing increases.

Panel (b) Diminishing Marginal Product of Labor An increase in the amount of labor used in manufacturing lowers the marginal product of labor.

product of labor MPL_A also diminishes as the amount of labor used in agriculture L_A increases.

Production Possibilities Frontier Combining the output for the two industries, manufacturing and agriculture, we obtain the production possibilities frontier (PPF) for the economy (Figure 3-2). Because of the diminishing returns to labor in both sectors, the PPF is *bowed out*, or concave, with respect to the graph's origin. (You may recognize this familiar shape from your introductory economics class.)

By using the marginal products of labor in each sector, we can determine the slope of the PPF. Starting at point A in Figure 3-2, suppose that one unit of labor leaves agriculture and enters manufacturing so that the economy's new output is at point B. The drop in agricultural output is MPL_A, and the increase in manufacturing output is MPL_M. The slope of the PPF between points A and B is the negative of the ratio of marginal products, or $-MPL_A/MPL_M$. This ratio can be interpreted as the opportunity cost of producing one unit of manufacturing, the cost of one unit of manufacturing in terms of the amount of food (the agricultural good) that would need to be given up to produce it.

Opportunity Cost and Prices As in the Ricardian model, the slope of the PPF, which is the opportunity cost of manufacturing, also equals the relative price of manufacturing. To understand why this is so, recall that in competitive markets, firms hire labor up to the point at which the cost of one more worker (the wage) equals the value of one more worker in terms of output. In turn, the value of one more worker equals the amount of goods produced by that person (the marginal product of labor) times the price of the good. In manufacturing, labor will be hired to the point at which the wage W equals the price of manufacturing P_M times the marginal product of labor in manufacturing MPL_M.

$$W = P_M \cdot MPL_M$$

FIGURE 3-2

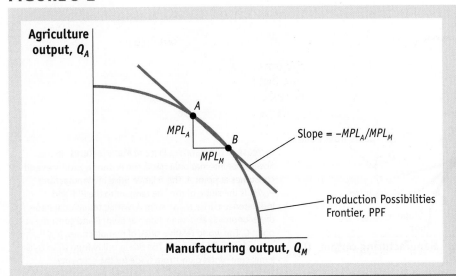

Production Possibilities Frontier
The production possibilities frontier shows the amount of agricultural and manufacturing outputs that can be produced in the economy with labor. Its slope equals $-MPL_A/MPL_M$, the ratio of the marginal products of labor in the two industries. The slope of the PPF can be interpreted as the opportunity cost of the manufacturing output—it is the amount of the agricultural good that would need to be given up to obtain one more unit of output in the manufacturing sector.

Similarly, in agriculture, labor will be hired to the point at which the wage W equals the price of agriculture P_A times the marginal product of labor in agriculture MPL_A.

$$W = P_A \cdot MPL_A$$

Because we are assuming that labor is free to move between sectors, the wages in these two equations must be equal. If the wages were not the same in both sectors, labor would move to the sector with the higher wage. This movement would continue until the increase in the amount of labor in the high-wage sector drove down the wage, and the decrease in the amount of labor in the low-wage sector drove up the wage, until the wages were equal. By setting the two wage equations equal, we obtain $P_M \cdot MPL_M = P_A \cdot MPL_A$, and by rearranging terms, we get

$$(P_M/P_A) = (MPL_A/MPL_M)$$

This equation shows that the relative price of manufacturing (P_M/P_A) equals the opportunity cost of manufacturing (MPL_A/MPL_M), the slope of the production possibilities frontier. These relative prices also reflect the value that Home's consumers put on manufacturing versus food. In the absence of international trade, the equilibrium for the Home economy is at point A in Figure 3-3, where the relative price of manufacturing (P_M/P_A) equals the slope of the PPF as well as the slope of the indifference curve for a representative consumer with utility of U_1. The intuition for the no-trade equilibrium is exactly the same as for the Ricardian model in Chapter 2: equilibrium occurs at the tangency of the PPF and the consumer's indifference curve. This point on the PPF corresponds to the highest possible level of utility for the consumer.

The Foreign Country

In this chapter, we do not discuss the Foreign country in any detail. Instead, we simply assume that the no-trade relative price of manufacturing in Foreign (P_M^*/P_A^*) differs from the no-trade price (P_M/P_A) in Home. There are several reasons why these prices can differ. In the previous chapter, we showed how differences in productivities across countries cause the no-trade relative prices to differ across countries. That is the key assumption, or starting point, of the Ricardian model. Another reason for relative prices to differ, which we have not yet investigated, is that the amounts of labor,

FIGURE 3-3

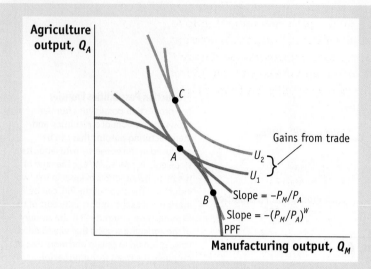

Increase in the Relative Price of Manufactures In the absence of international trade, the economy produces and consumes at point A. The relative price of manufactures, P_M/P_A, is the slope of the line tangent to the PPF and indifference curve, U_1, at point A. With international trade, the economy is able to produce at point B and consume at point C. The world relative price of manufactures, $(P_M/P_A)^W$, is the slope of the line BC. The rise in utility from U_1 to U_2 is a measure of the gains from trade for the economy.

capital, or land found in the two countries are different. (That will be the key assumption of the Heckscher–Ohlin model, which we discuss in the next chapter.)

For now, we will not explain why the no-trade relative prices differ across countries but will take it for granted that this is not unusual. For the sake of focusing on one case, let us assume that the Home no-trade relative price of manufacturing is *lower* than the Foreign relative price, $(P_M/P_A) < (P_M^*/P_A^*)$. This assumption means that Home can produce manufactured goods relatively more cheaply than Foreign, or, equivalently, that Home has a comparative advantage in manufacturing.

Overall Gains from Trade

Starting at the no-trade equilibrium point *A* in Figure 3-3, suppose that Home opens up to international trade with Foreign. Once trade is opened, we expect that the world equilibrium relative price—that is, the relative price in *all* countries $(P_M/P_A)^W$—will lie between the no-trade relative prices in the two countries, so

$$(P_M/P_A) < (P_M/P_A)^W < (P_M^*/P_A^*)$$

This equation shows us that when Home opens to trade, the relative price of manufacturing will *rise*, from (P_M/P_A) to $(P_M/P_A)^W$; conversely, for Foreign, the relative price of manufacturing will *fall*, from (P_M^*/P_A^*) to $(P_M/P_A)^W$. With trade, the world relative price $(P_M/P_A)^W$ is represented by a line that is tangent to Home's PPF, line *BC* in Figure 3-3. The increase in the Home relative price of manufactured goods is shown by the steeper slope of the world relative price line as compared with the Home no-trade price line (through point *A*).

What is the effect of this increase in (P_M/P_A) in Home? The higher relative price of the manufactured good in Home attracts more workers into that sector, which now produces at point *B* rather than *A*. As before, production takes place at the point along the Home PPF tangent to the relative price line, where equality of wages across industries is attained. The country can then export manufactured goods and import agricultural products along the international price line *BC*, and it reaches its highest level of utility, U_2, at point *C*. The difference in utility between U_2 and U_1 is a measure of the country's overall gains from trade. (These overall gains would be zero if the relative prices with trade equaled the no-trade relative prices, but they can never be negative—a country can never be made worse off by opening to trade.)

Notice that the good whose relative price goes up (manufacturing, for Home) is exported and the good whose relative price goes down (agriculture, for Home) is imported. By exporting manufactured goods at a higher price and importing food at a lower price, Home is better off than it was in the absence of trade. To measure the gains from trade, economists rely on the price increases for exports and the price decreases for imports to determine how much extra consumption a country can afford. The following application considers the magnitude of the overall gains from trade in historical cases in which the gains have been measured.

APPLICATION

How Large Are the Gains from Trade?

How large are the overall gains from trade? There are a few historical examples of countries that have moved from **autarky** (i.e., no trade) to free trade, or vice versa, quickly enough that we can use the years before and after this shift to estimate the gains from trade.

One such episode in the United States occurred between December 1807 and March 1809, when the U.S. Congress imposed a nearly complete halt to international trade at the request of President Thomas Jefferson. A complete stop to all trade is called a **trade embargo**. The United States imposed its embargo because Britain was at war with Napoleon, and Britain wanted to prevent ships from arriving in France that might be carrying supplies or munitions. As a result, Britain patrolled the eastern coast of the United States and seized U.S. ships that were bound across the Atlantic. To safeguard its own ships and possibly inflict economic losses on Britain, the United States declared a trade embargo for 14 months from 1807 to 1809. The embargo was not complete, however; the United States still traded with some countries, such as Canada and Mexico, that didn't have to be reached by ship.

As you might expect, U.S. trade fell dramatically during this period. Exports (such as cotton, flour, tobacco, and rice) fell from about $49 million in 1807 to $9 million in 1809. The drop in the value of exports reflects both a drop in the quantity exported and a drop in the price of exports. Recall that in Chapter 2 we defined the terms of trade of a country as the price of its export goods divided by the price of its import goods, so a drop in the price of U.S. exports is a fall in its terms of trade, which is a loss for the United States. According to one study, the cost of the trade embargo to the United States was about 5% of gross domestic product (GDP). That is, U.S. GDP was 5% lower than it would have been without the trade embargo. The cost of the embargo was offset somewhat because trade was not completely eliminated and because some U.S. producers were able to shift their efforts to producing goods (such as cloth and glass) that had previously been imported. Thus, we can take 5% of GDP as a lower estimate of what the gains from trade for the United States would have been relative to a situation with no trade.

Another historical case was Japan's rapid opening to the world economy in 1854, after 200 years of self-imposed autarky. In this case, military action by Commodore Matthew Perry of the United States forced Japan to open up its borders so that the United States could establish commercial ties. When trade was opened, the prices of Japanese exports to the United States (such as silk and tea) increased, and the prices of U.S. imports (such as woolens) decreased. These price movements were a terms-of-trade gain for Japan. According to one estimate, Japan's gains from trade after its opening were 4% to 5% of GDP.[5] The gains were not one-sided, however; Japan's trading partners—such as the United States—also gained from being able to trade in the newly opened markets.

There are no recent examples of industrial countries suddenly opening or closing to trade. Instead, we can rely on the theory of international trade to infer what the gains from trade are. In Figure 3-3, the extent to which the consumption point C is lifted off

[5] Daniel M. Bernhofen and John C. Brown, March 2005, "Estimating the Comparative Advantage Gains from Trade," *American Economic Review*, 95(1), 208–225.

TABLE 3-1

Gains from Trade, 2007 This table shows the ratio of total trade to GDP for selected countries, calculated as (Imports + Exports)/2, and two estimates of the gains from trade. The first estimate is the gains from trade from imported final goods used by consumers. The second estimate reflects imported intermediate inputs that are used by firms, and it includes services, which are treated as a nontraded sector. Countries with the highest ratios of trade to GDP tend to have the highest gains from trade.

Country	Trade/GDP (%)	Gains from Trade (%)	Adjusted Gains (%)
Malaysia	116%	74%	219%
Hungary	81	87	166
Thailand	75	51	89
Switzerland	65	135	111
Austria	56	104	96
Denmark	54	79	75
Sweden	50	58	55
Germany	44	46	40
Norway	38	63	51
South Africa	37	31	42
Canada	33	54	44
China	33	13	30
United Kingdom	30	45	32
Indonesia	29	25	36
Italy	29	33	38
Mexico	29	45	34
Spain	29	52	53
Greece	28	73	122
France	28	39	35
Turkey	26	38	41
Russian Federation	26	25	35
Venezuela	25	28	41
India	25	14	21
Argentina	23	28	32
Pakistan	18	37	62
Japan	16	26	21
United States	15	19	14
Brazil	14	10	10
Average	38	48	59

Note: Trade is calculated as (Imports + Exports)/2, including merchandise goods and services, with data for the year 2008.
Data from: World Development Indicators, The World Bank, and Ralph Ossa, 2015, "Why Trade Matters After All," Journal of International Economics, 97(2), 266–277.

the production possibilities frontier will depend on how much trade there is. If there is very little trade, then point C will be close to the autarky consumption point A, and the gains from trade are small. If there is a lot of trade, then the consumption point C will differ from the production point B, and so C is lifted off the PPF by more and the gains from trade are large. This means that we can use the amount of imports or exports that a country has (measured as a share of GDP) to infer its gains from trade. In addition, because countries often import goods that are different from those they produce at home, calculating the gains from trade requires knowing the value that consumers place on the imported goods as compared to the domestic substitutes for these imports.

With this approach, the gains from trade for a number of countries in the world are shown in Table 3-1 for the year 2007.[6] These estimates are based on trade in merchandise

---

[6] This is the most recent year for which these estimates of the gains from trade are available.

goods only (that is, manufacturing, agriculture, and mining) and do not include services trade. We show the ratio of trade to GDP in the first column, which is the highest for Malaysia and the lowest for Brazil. Then we provide two estimates of the gains from trade, both measured as a percentage of GDP. The first estimate is the gains from trade from imported *final goods* that are used by consumers. The second, adjusted estimate of the gains also includes imported *intermediate inputs* that are used by firms, as well as services, which are treated as a nontraded sector.

Generally, countries with the highest ratios of trade to GDP tend to have the highest gains from trade. Malaysia, for example, has the highest ratio of trade to GDP (116%) and among the highest estimates of the gains from trade (between 74% and 219%). Brazil, on the other hand, has the lowest ratio of trade to GDP (14%) and the lowest estimate of the gains from trade (10%). We see that the United States is just above Brazil and that Japan is just above the United States: both those countries have very large economies, and as we discussed in Chapter 1, very large economies tend to have lower ratios of trade to GDP because we do not count the *internal* trade that happens within a country. For the same reason, the estimates of the gains from international trade are lower for large economies. Still, the average size of the gains from trade is quite large: between 48% and 59%, as shown at the bottom of Table 3-1.

2 Earnings of Labor

Because there are overall gains from trade, *someone* in the economy must be better off, but not *everyone* is better off. The goal of this chapter is to explore how a change in relative prices, such as that shown in Figure 3-3, feeds back into the earnings of workers, landowners, and capital owners. We begin our study of the specific-factors model by looking at what happens to the wages earned by labor when there is an increase in the relative price of manufactures.

Determination of Wages

To determine wages, it is convenient to take the marginal product of labor in manufacturing (MPL_M), which was shown in Figure 3-1(b), and the marginal product of labor in agriculture (MPL_A), and put them in one diagram.

First, we add the amount of labor used in manufacturing L_M and the amount used in agriculture L_A to give us the total amount of labor in the economy $\bar{L}$:

$$L_M + L_A = \bar{L}$$

Figure 3-4 shows the total amount of labor $\bar{L}$ on the horizontal axis. The amount of labor used in manufacturing L_M is measured from left (0_M) to right, while the amount of labor used in agriculture L_A is measured from right (0_A) to left. Each point on the horizontal axis indicates how much labor is used in manufacturing (measured from left to right) and how much labor is used in agriculture (measured from right to left). For example, point L indicates that $0_M L$ units of labor are used in manufacturing and $0_A L$ units of labor are used in agriculture, which adds up to $\bar{L}$ units of labor in total.

The second step in determining wages is to multiply the marginal product of labor in each sector by the price of the good in that sector (P_M or P_A). As we discussed earlier, in competitive markets, firms will hire labor up to the point at which the cost of one more worker (the wage) equals the value of one worker in production, which is the marginal product of labor times the price of the good. In each industry, then, labor will be hired until

$$W = P_M \cdot MPL_M \text{ in manufacturing}$$
$$W = P_A \cdot MPL_A \text{ in agriculture}$$

FIGURE 3-4

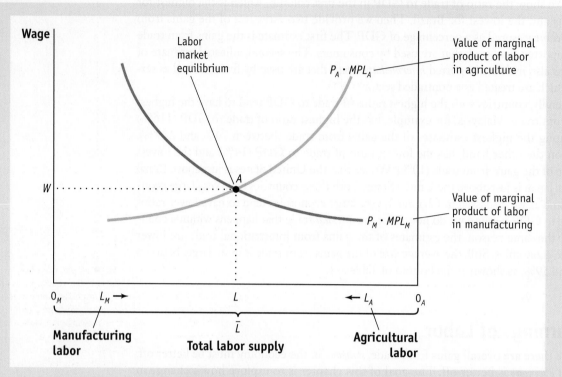

Allocation of Labor Between Manufacturing and Agriculture The amount of labor used in manufacturing is measured from left to right along the horizontal axis, and the amount of labor used in agriculture is measured from right to left. Labor market equilibrium is at point A. At the equilibrium wage of W, manufacturing uses 0_ML units of labor and agriculture uses 0_AL units.

In Figure 3-4, we draw the graph of $P_M \cdot MPL_M$ as downward sloping. This curve is basically the same as the marginal product of labor MPL_M curve in Figure 3-1(b), except that it is now multiplied by the price of the manufactured good. When we draw the graph of $P_A \cdot MPL_A$ for agriculture, however, it slopes upward. This is because we are measuring the labor used in agriculture L_A from *right to left* in the diagram: the marginal product of labor in agriculture falls as the amount of labor increases (moving from right to left).

Equilibrium Wage The equilibrium wage is found at point A, the intersection of the curves $P_M \cdot MPL_M$ and $P_A \cdot MPL_A$ in Figure 3-4. At this point, 0_ML units of labor are used in manufacturing, and firms in that industry are willing to pay the wage $W = P_M \cdot MPL_M$. In addition, 0_AL units of labor are used in agriculture, and farmers are willing to pay the wage $W = P_A \cdot MPL_A$. Because wages are equal in the two sectors, there is no reason for labor to move, and the labor market is in equilibrium.

Change in Relative Price of Manufactures

Now that we have shown how the wage is determined in the specific-factors model, we want to ask how the wage *changes* in response to an increase in the relative price of manufactures. That is, as the relative price of manufactures rises (shown in Figure 3-3), and the economy shifts from its no-trade equilibrium at point A to its trade equilibrium with production and consumption at points B and C, what is the effect on the earnings of each factor of production? In particular, what are the changes

FIGURE 3-5

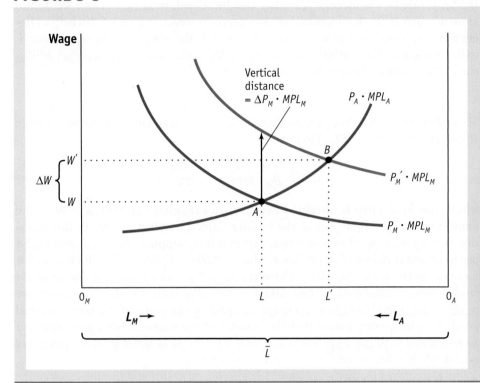

Increase in the Price of Manufactured Goods With an increase in the price of the manufactured good, the curve $P_M \cdot MPL_M$ shifts up to $P_M' \cdot MPL_M$ and the equilibrium shifts from point A to point B. The amount of labor used in manufacturing rises from $0_M L$ to $0_M L'$, and the amount of labor used in agriculture falls from $0_A L$ to $0_A L'$ The wage increases from W to W', but this increase is less than the upward shift $\Delta P_M \cdot MPL_M$.

in the wage, and in the earnings of capital owners in manufacturing and landowners in agriculture?

Effect on the Wage An increase in the relative price of manufacturing P_M/P_A can occur due to either an increase in P_M or a decrease in P_A. Both these price movements will have the same effect on the **real wage,** that is, on the amount of manufactures and food that a worker can afford to buy. For convenience, let us suppose that the price of manufacturing P_M rises, while the price of agriculture P_A does not change.

When P_M rises, the curve $P_M \cdot MPL_M$ shifts up to $P_M' \cdot MPL_M$, as shown in Figure 3-5. The vertical rise in this curve is exactly $\Delta P_M \cdot MPL_M$, as illustrated in the diagram. (We use the symbol Δ, delta, to stand for the *change* in a variable.) The new intersection of the two curves occurs at point B, where the wage is W' and the allocation of labor between the two sectors is identified by point L'. The equilibrium wage has risen from W to W', the amount of labor used in the manufacturing sector has increased from $0_M L$ to $0_M L'$, and the amount of labor used in agriculture has fallen from $0_A L$ to $0_A L'$.

Effect on Real Wages The fact that the wage has risen does not really tell us whether workers are better off or worse off in terms of the amount of food and manufactured goods they can buy. To determine this, we have to take into account any change in the prices of these goods. For instance, the amount of food that a worker can afford to buy with their hourly wage is W/P_A.[7] Because W has increased from W to W' and we have assumed that P_A has not changed, workers can afford to buy more food. In other words, the real wage has increased in terms of food.

---

[7] For example, suppose that you earn $12 per hour, and your favorite snack costs $3. Then you could afford to buy $12/$3 = 4 of these snacks after working for one hour.

The amount of the manufactured good that a worker can buy is measured by W/P_M. While W has increased, P_M has also increased, so at first glance we do not know whether W/P_M has increased or decreased. However, Figure 3-5 can help us figure this out. Notice that as we've drawn Figure 3-5, the increase in the wage from W to W' is less than the vertical increase $\Delta P_M \cdot MPL_M$ that occurred in the $P_M \cdot MPL_M$ curve. We can write this condition as

$$\Delta W < \Delta P_M \cdot MPL_M$$

To see how W/P_M has changed, divide both sides of this equation by the initial wage W (which equals $P_M \cdot MPL_M$) to obtain

$$\frac{\Delta W}{W} < \frac{\Delta P_M \cdot MPL_M}{P_M \cdot MPL_M} = \frac{\Delta P_M}{P_M}$$

where the final ratio is obtained because we canceled out MPL_M in both the numerator and denominator of the middle ratio. The term $\Delta W/W$ in this equation is the *percentage change in wages*. For example, suppose the initial wage is $8 per hour and it rises to $10 per hour. Then $\Delta W/W = \$2/\$8 = 0.25$, which is a 25% increase in the wage. Similarly, the term $\Delta P_M/P_M$ is the *percentage change in the price of manufactured goods*. When $\Delta W/W < \Delta P_M/P_M$, then the percentage increase in the wage is *less than* the percentage increase in the price of the manufactured good. This inequality means that the amount of the manufactured good that can be purchased with the wage has fallen, so the *real wage in terms of the manufactured good W/P_M* has decreased.[8]

Overall Impact on Labor We have now determined that as a result of our assumption of an increase in the relative price of manufactured goods, the *real wage in terms of food has increased and the real wage in terms of the manufactured good has decreased*. In this case, we assumed that the increase in relative price was caused by an increase in the price of manufactures with a constant price of agriculture. Notice, though, that if we had assumed a constant price of manufactures and a decrease in the price of agriculture (taken together, an increase in the relative price of manufactures), then we would have arrived at the same effects on the real wage in terms of both products.

Is labor better off or worse off after the price increase? We cannot tell. People who spend most of their income on manufactured goods are worse off because they can buy fewer manufactured goods, but those who spend most of their income on food are better off because more food is affordable. Who spends most of their income on food? It is well established that poor individuals spend a greater share of their income than rich individuals on food: this finding is called **Engel's Law**. Thus, if food prices are falling due to trade, then poorer people will be gaining from the price fall more than rich people. We discuss whether this finding holds when looking across many countries in **Side Bar: Do Poor or Rich Consumers Gain the Most from Trade?** The bottom line is that in the specific-factors model, the increase in the price of the manufactured good has an ambiguous effect on the real wage and therefore an ambiguous effect on the well-being of workers, depending on which goods they consume the most.

The conclusion that we cannot tell whether workers are better off or worse off from the opening of trade in the specific-factors model might seem wishy-washy to you, but it is important for several reasons. First, this result is different from what we found in the Ricardian model of Chapter 2, in which the real wage increases with the opening of trade so that workers are always unambiguously better off than they

---

[8] For example, suppose that the manufactured good is memory sticks, which initially cost $9 and then rise in price to $12. The increase in the price of memory sticks is $3, and so the percentage increase in their price is $\Delta P_M/P_M = \$3/\$9 = 0.33 = 33\%$. Suppose also that the wage has increased from $10 to $12 per hour, or 20%, which is less than the percentage increase in the price of a memory stick. Using the initial prices, by working one hour, you could afford to buy $W/P_M = \$10/\$9 = 1.1$, or *more than* one memory stick. Using the new prices, by working one hour, you can afford to buy $W/P_M = \$12/\$12 = 1$, or exactly one memory stick. So, your real wage measured in terms of memory sticks has gone down.

Do Poor or Rich Consumers Gain the Most from Trade?

Trade lowers the relative price of imported goods in each country and raises the relative price of exported goods. It follows that consumers who spend a greater portion of their income on imported goods will tend to gain, and consumers who spend a greater portion of their income on exported goods will tend to lose. The gains for each individual also depend on their sources of income. In the idealized model of this chapter, all workers earn the same wage and therefore have the same income. In reality, individuals earn different wages because of their differing levels of education and skills, and they also have earnings from owning capital and land, so they can have very different incomes.

It follows that there are two channels by which changes in prices due to international trade affect individuals: through the change in the prices of goods that they buy, and through the change in the income that they earn. Let us call the first channel the *spending channel* and the second channel the *earnings channel*. How do these channels affect poor versus rich individuals around the world?

Let us start with the spending channel. If the prices of food tend to fall due to international trade, then that will benefit poor consumers the most, because they spend a greater share of their income on food. This conclusion is supported by a detailed study of international trade and consumption across many countries.[9] Food and other necessities that are demanded more by low-income individuals are imported into many countries, so these poor individuals gain the most from purchasing those imports. It follows that the spending channel tends to benefit poor consumers the most.

There are exceptions to this rule. Not all countries are importers of food. The United States, for example, exports many agricultural goods and has roughly balanced trade in food. The share of food imports within the budgets of U.S. households falls slightly as income rises, but not by as much. Furthermore, imported luxury goods are demanded more by rich households in the United States: those goods include cars—and richer individuals prefer foreign brands—and consumer electronics like computers. Looking across all goods, the effects of falling import shares in food and rising import shares in luxury goods tend to cancel out, and so there is no systematic relationship between the budget share devoted to imports overall and consumer's income. This means that the spending channel does not favor the poor versus the rich in the United States.[10]

What about the earnings channel? How do changing prices affect the incomes of poor versus rich individuals? As we will discuss in Chapter 7, international trade has tended to raise the incomes of higher-skilled individuals in the United States as compared to those with fewer skills. Thus, the earnings channel tends to favor richer individuals in the United States. Does this conclusion hold in the rest of the world? We explore this challenging question in later chapters.

[9] Pablo Fajgelbaum and Amit Khandelwal, 2016, "Measuring the Unequal Gains from Trade," *Quarterly Journal of Economics*, 131, 1113–1180.

[10] Kirill Borusyak and Xavier Jaravel, 2018, "The Distributional Effects of Trade: Theory and Evidence from the United States," Working Paper, University College London and London School of Economics.

are in the absence of trade.[11] In the specific-factors model, that is no longer the case; the opening of trade and the shift in relative prices raise the real wage in terms of one good but lower it in terms of the other good. Second, our results for the specific-factors model serve as a warning against making unqualified statements about the effect of trade on workers, such as "Trade is bad for workers" or "Trade is good for workers." Even in the specific-factors model, which is simplified by considering only two industries and not allowing capital or land to move between them, we have found that the effects of opening trade on the real wage are complicated. In reality, the effect of trade on real wages is more complex still.

Unemployment in the Specific-Factors Model We have ignored one significant, realistic feature in the specific-factors model: unemployment. You may often see news stories about workers who are laid off because of import competition and who then face a period of unemployment. Despite this outcome, most economists do not believe that trade necessarily harms workers overall. It is true that we have ignored unemployment in the specific-factors model: the labor employed in manufacturing L_M plus the labor employed in agriculture L_A always sums to the total labor supply $\overline{L}$, which means that there is no unemployment. One of the reasons we ignore unemployment in this model is that it is usually treated as a macroeconomic phenomenon, caused by business cycles, and it is hard to combine business cycle models with international trade models to isolate the effects of trade on workers. But the other, simpler

[11] The only situation in which workers do not gain from trade in the Ricardian model is if Home is very large, as discussed in Problem 11 of Chapter 2, such that the international relative price equals the no-trade relative price. In that case, Home workers are no better off from international trade but also no worse off.

reason is that even when people are laid off because of import competition, many of them find new jobs within a reasonable period, and sometimes they find jobs with *higher* wages, as shown in the next application. Therefore, even if we take into account spells of unemployment, once we recognize that workers can find new jobs—possibly in export industries that are expanding—then we still cannot conclude that trade is necessarily good or bad for workers.

In the two applications that follow, we look at some evidence from the United States on employment in the manufacturing sector, as well as on the amount of time it takes to find new jobs and on the wages earned. We also investigate the **"China shock,"** the impact on the U.S. labor market of China joining the WTO in 2001.

APPLICATION

Manufacturing and Services in the United States: Employment and Wages Across Sectors

Although the specific-factors model emphasizes manufacturing and agriculture, the amount of labor devoted to agriculture in most industrialized countries is small. A larger sector in industrialized countries is that of **services**, which includes wholesale and retail trade, finance, law, education, information technology, software engineering, consulting, and medical and government services. In the United States and most industrial countries, the service sector is larger than the manufacturing sector and much larger than the agriculture sector.

In Figure 3-6, we show employment in the manufacturing sector of the United States, both in terms of the number of workers employed in it and as a percentage of total employment in the economy. Using either measure, employment in manufacturing has been falling over time; given zero or negative employment growth in the agriculture sector, this indicates that the service sector has been growing. As we mentioned at the beginning of the chapter, China joined the WTO in 2001, and the employment decline in Figure 3-6 appears to accelerate after 2001, as we discuss in the next Application.

FIGURE 3-6

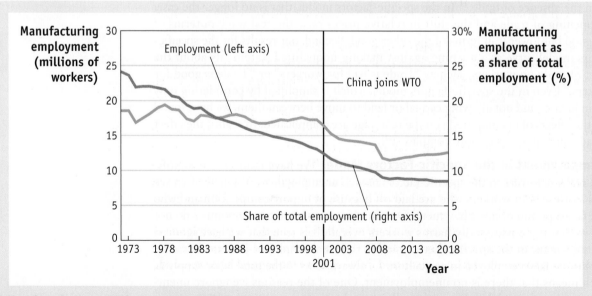

U.S. Manufacturing Sector Employment, 1973–2018 Employment in the U.S. manufacturing sector is shown on the left axis, and the share of manufacturing employment in total U.S. employment is shown on the right axis. Both manufacturing employment and its share in total employment have been falling over time, indicating that the service sector has been growing. The decline in manufacturing employment accelerated after China joined the WTO in 2001.

Data from: U.S. Department of Labor, Bureau of Labor Statistics.

FIGURE 3-7

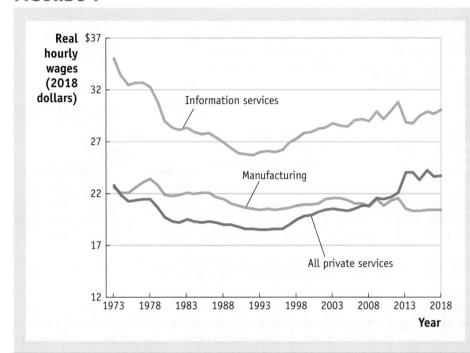

Real Hourly Earnings of Production Workers, 1973–2018 This chart shows the real wages (in constant 2018 dollars) earned by production workers in U.S. manufacturing, in all private services, and in information services (a subset of all private services). Although wages were slightly higher in manufacturing than in all private services from 1973 through 2007, all private service wages have been higher since 2008. This change is due in part to the effect of wages in the information service industry, which are substantially higher than those in manufacturing. Real wages for production workers in manufacturing have tended to fall since about 1986, whereas real wages in the service sector fell until about 1996 but have been rising since then. Real wages in information services have been growing since about 1993.

Data from: U.S. Department of Labor, Bureau of Labor Statistics.

Figure 3-7 shows the real wages earned by production, or blue-collar, workers in manufacturing, in all private services, and in information services (a subset of private services).[12] Although wages were slightly higher in manufacturing than in private services from 1973 through 2007, all private service wages have been higher since 2008. This change is due in part to the effect of wages in the *information service* industry, which are substantially higher than those in manufacturing. For example, average hourly earnings in all private services were $23.66 per hour in 2018 and lower—$20.44 per hour—in manufacturing overall. But in information services, average wages were much higher—$30.07 per hour.

In both manufacturing and services, many workers are *displaced* or laid off each year and need to look for other jobs. In the three years from January 2015 to December 2017, for example, about 479,000 workers were displaced in manufacturing and 2.2 million in all service industries, as shown in Table 3-2. Of those laid off in manufacturing, 65% were reemployed by January 2018. Slightly more than one-half (53%) of these workers earned less in their new jobs, and slightly less than one-half (47%) earned the same or more. For services, 69% of workers were reemployed by January 2018, with the same percentages earning less or more in their new jobs. The total economy also includes workers in agriculture, mining, and government positions, and two-thirds (66%) of all displaced workers were reemployed by January 2018, nearly evenly split between those who earned less and those who earned the same or more in their new jobs.

There are four lessons that we can take away from this comparison of employment and wages in manufacturing and services. First, wages differ across different sectors in the economy, so our theoretical assumption that wages are the same in agriculture and

---

[12] The real wages shown in Figure 3-7 are measured relative to consumer prices in 2018 and represent the average hourly earnings for *production* workers, those workers involved in the assembly of services or products. Production workers are sometimes called "blue-collar" workers and typically earn hourly wages. The other category of workers, *nonproduction* workers, includes managers and all those who work at a desk. They are sometimes called "white-collar" workers and typically earn annual salaries instead of hourly wages.

TABLE 3-2

Job Losses in Manufacturing and Service Industries, 2015–2017 This table shows the number of displaced workers in manufacturing and service industries from 2015 to 2017. A total of 65% of the manufacturing workers displaced from 2015 to 2017 were reemployed by January 2018, with 53% earning less in their new jobs in manufacturing and 47% earning the same or more. The numbers are nearly the same in service industries, with 69% of workers finding work by January 2018.

Industry	Total Displaced Workers (thousands) Jan 2015–Dec 2017	PERCENTAGES		
		Workers Reemployed by Jan 2018	Of the Workers Reemployed:	
			Earn Less in New Job	Earn Same or More in New Job
Total	2,981	66%	51%	49%
Manufacturing industries	479	65%	53%	47%
Service industries	2,239	69%	53%	47%

Data from: U.S. Bureau of Labor Statistics.

manufacturing is a simplification. Second, many workers are displaced each year and must find jobs elsewhere. Some of these workers may be laid off because of competition from imports, but there are other reasons, too—for instance, popular products go out of fashion, firms reorganize as computers and other technological advances become available, and businesses change locations. Third, about two-thirds of displaced workers find a new job within two or three years but not necessarily at the same wage. Typically, older workers (aged 45 to 64 years) experience earnings losses when shifting between jobs, whereas younger workers (aged 25 to 44 years) are often able to find a new job with the same or higher wages. Finally, when we measure wages in real terms by adjusting for inflation in the price of consumer goods, we see that real wages for all production workers fell in most years between 1979 and 1995 (we examine the reasons for that fall in later chapters). The real wages for production workers in manufacturing have risen only slightly and then fallen again since then, while the real wages for workers in services have risen by much more, so that workers in services now have higher earnings than those in manufacturing on average (especially so for workers in information services).

APPLICATION

The "China Shock" and Employment in the United States

In the specific-factors model, we assumed that the workers leaving one industry could be absorbed freely into the other. In reality, when there is a very large change in prices, it can take more than 10 years for enough jobs to be created in export industries to balance the losses in import industries. This application examines what has happened since China joined the WTO.

After China joined the WTO in 2001, it could expect to receive the same low tariffs in the United States and other countries as those enjoyed by other WTO members. The higher import tariffs that President Trump applied against China in 2018–2019 are an exception to this rule, as we discuss in Chapter 8. Still, from 2001 to 2017 China received the low WTO tariffs in the United States, and those lower tariffs encouraged investment by existing and new Chinese firms in the production of goods for the U.S. market. As a result, U.S. imports from China grew rapidly after 2001, as is shown in Figure 3-8.

FIGURE 3-8

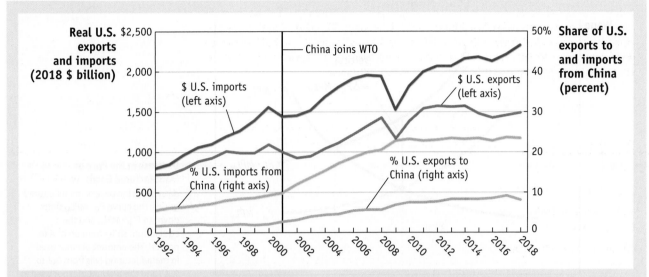

Real U.S. Imports and Exports and the China Share, 1992–2018

Real values (in 2018 dollars) of U.S. nonpetroleum imports (the red line) and exports (the green line) to the world are shown on the left axis. The share of U.S. imports coming from China (the orange line) and the share of U.S. exports going to China (the light green line) are shown on the right axis. Real imports roughly tripled over this period and real exports roughly doubled. The share of U.S. imports coming from China grew noticeably faster after China's entry to the WTO in 2001, and it more than doubled, from 10% that year to 23% in 2009 through 2018. In comparison, the share of U.S. exports going to China is fairly small; it grew from 3% in 2001 to 8% in 2018.

Data from: U.S. Department of the Census, Foreign Trade Division.

During the period 1992–2018, the real value of U.S. nonpetroleum imports from the world roughly tripled. A substantial amount of that growth was accounted for by increased imports from China. In Figure 3-8, we see that the share of U.S. imports from China grew noticeably faster after its entry to the WTO in 2001. That share more than doubled from 10% in 2001 to 23% in 2009, and it remained at that high level through 2018.

China is less important as a destination for U.S. exports than as a source of imports. Despite the fairly small percentage of U.S. exports going to China, the real value of U.S. nonpetroleum exports to the world still grew rapidly, more than doubling from 1992 to 2018.

Several research studies have examined the impact of growing U.S. imports from China on employment in manufacturing industries. The large increase in the share of U.S. imports coming from China and its impact on employment in manufacturing are called the "China shock."[13] These studies have found that 2 million jobs or more were lost in U.S. manufacturing industries, as summarized in the quotation at the beginning of the chapter.

We can interpret these job losses using the specific-factors model. Instead of an increase in the price of manufactured goods, as we looked at earlier in the chapter, we now suppose that inexpensive imports from China led to a decrease in the price of manufactured goods. In Figure 3-9, we start at equilibrium A and then experience a fall in the manufacturing price. When P_M falls, the curve $P_M \cdot MPL_M$ shifts down to $P'_M \cdot MPL_M$,

---

[13] David Autor, David Dorn, and Gordon H. Hanson, 2013, "The China Syndrome: Local Labor Markets Effects of Import Competition in the United States," *American Economic Review*, 103(6), 2121–2168; Daron Acemoglu, David Autor, David Dorn, Gordon H. Hanson, and Brendan Price, 2016, "Import Competition and the Great US Employment Sag of the 2000s," *Journal of Labor Economics*, 34(S1), S141–S198.

FIGURE 3-9

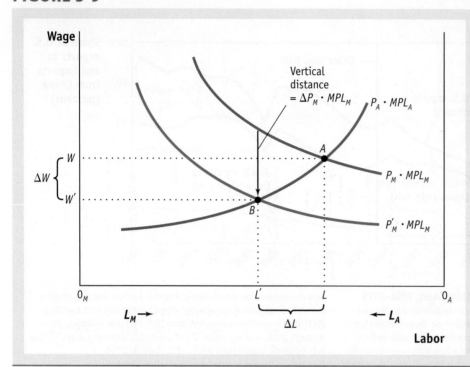

Decrease in the Price of Manufactured Goods With a decrease in the price of manufactured goods, the curve $P_M \cdot MPL_M$ shifts down to $P'_M \cdot MPL_M$ and the equilibrium shifts from point A to point B. The amount of labor used in manufacturing falls from $0_M L$ to $0_M L'$, and the amount of labor used in agriculture rises from $0_A L$ to $0_A L'$. So the amount of labor ΔL is transferred from manufacturing to agriculture. The wage falls by the amount by the amount ΔW, from W to W'.

as shown in Figure 3-9. The vertical fall in this curve is exactly $\Delta P_M \cdot MPL_M$. The new intersection of the two curves occurs at point B, where the wage is W' and the allocation of labor between the two sectors is identified by point L'. The equilibrium wage has fallen from W to W', the amount of labor used in the manufacturing sector has fallen from $0_M L$ to $0_M L'$, and the amount of labor used in agriculture has increased from $0_A L$ to $0_A L'$.

We label the total shift in labor from the manufacturing sectors to the agriculture sector by the amount ΔL. From research studies, about 2 million workers were shifted out of the U.S. manufacturing sector due to rising imports from China. In Figure 3-9, this amount of labor ΔL is quickly absorbed into "agriculture," which we should think of in reality as any industry in manufacturing or agriculture that is exported by the United States. To compare our diagram to the actual U.S. economy, we need to ask whether or not these workers really find employment in export industries.

To answer this question, we start by looking at U.S. job gains and losses in various manufacturing industries during the decade before China joined the WTO (1991–1999).[14] Figure 3-10 shows the estimated job gains in the United States due to rising exports to the world (in green), and the estimated job losses due to rising U.S. imports from the world (in orange), over 1991–1999. In this period, U.S. industries such as electronics, transportation, and machinery experienced the greatest job gains, while the largest job losses were in leather, furniture, and miscellaneous industries. The number of industries that gained jobs due to rising U.S. exports exceeded the number of industries that experienced job losses from rising imports.

After China joined the WTO in 2001, however, the picture changed completely. Figure 3-10 also shows the estimated job gains due to rising U.S. exports to the world (in blue), and the estimated job losses due to rising U.S. imports from the world (in red), over 1999–2011.[15] Many industries such as electronics, transportation, and machinery

---

[14] We have omitted the job changes in certain industries (like paper, printing, and tobacco) because these changes were small.
[15] The employment data are not available to study the job gains and losses for the year 2001, when China joined the WTO.

FIGURE 3-10

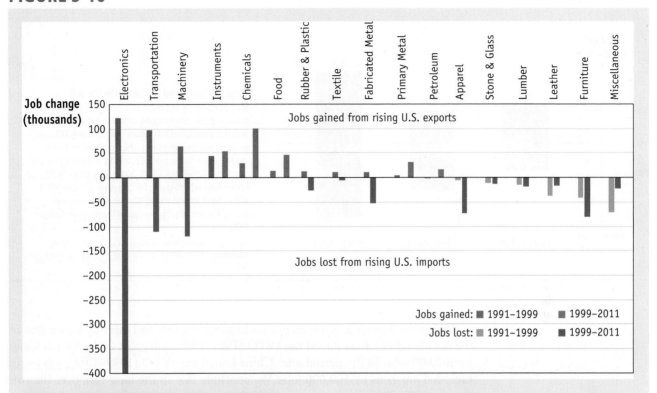

Job Gains and Job Losses in U.S. Manufacturing Industries, 1991–1999 and 1999–2011 For the period 1991–1999, estimated job gains due to rising U.S. exports are shown in green, and the estimated job losses due to rising U.S. imports are shown in orange. In this period, U.S. industries such as electronics, transportation, and machinery experienced the greatest job gains. For the period 1999–2011, estimated job gains due to rising U.S. exports are shown in blue, and the estimated job losses due to rising

U.S. imports are shown in red. In this period, industries such as electronics, transportation, and machinery (which had experienced the greatest job gains over 1991–1999) now faced import competition, especially from China, and experienced job losses. Only a small number of industries such as chemicals, instruments, and food experienced job gains.

Data from: Robert C. Feenstra, Hong Ma, and Yuan Xu, 2019, "US Exports and Employment," Journal of International Economics, 120, 46–58.

that had experienced the greatest job gains over 1991–1999 now faced import competition, especially from China, and, as a result, experienced job losses in 1999–2011. Only a small number of industries such as instruments, chemicals, and food experienced job gains.

Figure 3-11 summarizes the results from the first period, 1991–1999, the second period, 1999–2011, and the entire two decades, 1991–2011. For each period we add up the job gains from rising exports and the job losses from rising imports.[16] As a result of rising imports, there were about 1 million jobs lost before China joined the WTO, in 1991–1999. That number grew to about 1.7 million jobs lost in the decade 1999–2011, after China joined the WTO in 2001. Over both periods, the total number of jobs lost was 2.7 million. Those job losses reflect the impact of imports from *all countries*, but imports from China, which grew particularly rapidly, account for the majority of the job losses.

Balancing out these job losses were jobs created by rising exports: about 1.4 million jobs in 1991–1999, and 1.2 million jobs in 1999–2011. Over both periods, the total number of jobs created was 2.6 million. The U.S. exports to China explain only a small part of these job gains, which are primarily due to U.S. exports to the rest of world.

---

[16] The job gains and losses shown in Figure 3-11 include additional jobs gained and lost outside of manufacturing. That is why the totals in Figure 3-11 exceed what we get if we add up the job gains and losses from Figure 3-10.

FIGURE 3-11

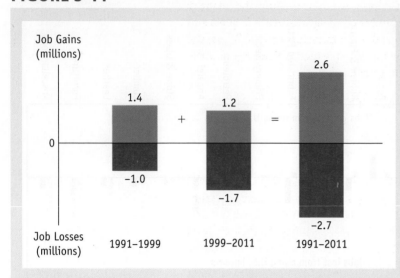

Total Job Gains and Job Losses in the U.S. Manufacturing Sector, 1991–2011 The estimated job gains due to rising exports are shown in green, and the estimated job losses due to rising U.S. imports are shown in red. These job gains and losses are the total for all manufacturing industries for the periods 1991–1999, 1999–2011, and 1991–2011. Job losses exceed job gains for the period 1999–2011 after China joined the WTO, but the losses are nearly balanced with the gains for the two decades 1991–2011.

Data from: Robert C. Feenstra, Hong Ma, and Yuan Xu, 2019, "US Exports and Employment," Journal of International Economics, 120, 46–58.

Taking the difference between our findings for imports and exports, we see that in the decade *before* China joined the WTO (1991–1999), job gains exceeded job losses by 400,000 jobs. In the period *after* China joined the WTO (1999–2011), job losses exceeded job gains by 500,000 jobs. We conclude that in the long run, over the two decades 1991–2011, job losses exceeded job gains by only 100,000, so that these gains and losses are close to being balanced. In the specific-factors model, we assumed that the workers leaving one industry could be absorbed freely into the other. In reality, we see that with a very large change in prices (as occurred with the "China shock"), it takes more than one decade for enough jobs to be created in export industries to balance the losses in import industries.

3 Earnings of Capital and Land

Let us now return to the specific-factors model. We have found that with the opening of trade and an increase in the relative price of manufactures, there are overall gains for the country, but labor does not necessarily gain. What about the gains to the other factors of production, either the capital used in manufacturing or the land used in agriculture? Capital and land are the two specific factors of production that cannot shift between the two industries; let us now look at the effect of the increase in the relative price of manufactures on the earnings of these specific factors.

Determining the Payments to Capital and Land

In each industry, capital and land earn what is left over from sales revenue after paying labor. Labor (L_M and L_A) earns the wage W, so total payments to labor in manufacturing are $W \cdot L_M$ and in agriculture are $W \cdot L_A$. By subtracting the payments to labor from the sales revenue earned in each industry, we end up with the payments to capital and to land. If Q_M is the output in manufacturing and Q_A is the output in agriculture, the revenue earned in each industry is $P_M \cdot Q_M$ and $P_A \cdot Q_A$, and the payments to capital and to land are

$$\text{Payments to capital} = P_M \cdot Q_M - W \cdot L_M$$
$$\text{Payments to land} = P_A \cdot Q_A - W \cdot L_A$$

It will be useful to take these payments one step further and break them down into the earnings of each unit of capital and land. To do so, we need to know the quantity of capital and land. We denote the quantity of land used in agriculture as T acres and the quantity of capital (number of machines) used in manufacturing as K. Thus, the earnings of one unit of capital (a machine, for instance), which we call R_K, and the earnings of an acre of land, which we call R_T, are calculated as

$$R_K = \frac{\text{Payments to capital}}{K} = \frac{P_M \cdot Q_M - W \cdot L_M}{K}$$

$$R_T = \frac{\text{Payments to land}}{T} = \frac{P_A \cdot Q_A - W \cdot L_A}{T}$$

Economists call R_K the **rental on capital** and R_T the **rental on land**. The use of the term "rental" does not mean that the factory owners or farmers rent their machines or land from someone else, although they could. Instead, the rental on machines and land reflects what these factors of production earn during a period when they are used in manufacturing and agriculture. Alternatively, the rental is the amount these factors *could* earn if they were rented to someone else over that same time.

There is a second way to calculate the rentals, which will look similar to the formula we have used for wages. In each industry, wages reflect the marginal product of labor multiplied by the price of the good, $W = P_M \cdot MPL_M = P_A \cdot MPL_A$. Similarly, capital and land rentals can be calculated as

$$R_K = P_M \cdot MPK_M \text{ and } R_T = P_A \cdot MPT_A$$

where MPK_M is the marginal product of capital in manufacturing, and MPT_A is the marginal product of land in agriculture. These marginal product formulas give the same values for the rentals as first calculating the payments to capital and land, as we just did, and then dividing by the quantity of capital and land. We will use both approaches to obtain rental values, depending on which is easiest.

Change in the Real Rental on Capital Now that we understand how the rentals on capital and land are determined, we can look at what happens to them when the price of the manufactured good P_M rises, holding constant the price in agriculture P_A. From Figure 3-5, we know that the wage rises throughout the economy and that labor shifts from agriculture into manufacturing. As more labor is used in manufacturing, the marginal product of capital rises because each machine has more labor to work it. In addition, as labor leaves agriculture, the marginal product of land falls because each acre of land has fewer laborers to work it. The general conclusion is that *an increase in the quantity of labor used in an industry will raise the marginal product of the factor specific to that industry, and a decrease in labor will lower the marginal product of the specific factor.* This outcome does not contradict the law of diminishing returns, which states that an increase in labor will lower the marginal product *of labor* because now we are talking about how a change in labor affects the marginal product of *another factor*.

Using the preceding formulas for the rentals, we can summarize the results so far with

$$P_M \uparrow \Rightarrow \begin{cases} L_M \uparrow, \text{ so that } MPK_M = R_K/P_M \uparrow \\ L_A \downarrow, \text{ so that } MPK_A = R_T/P_A \downarrow \end{cases}$$

That is, the increase in the marginal product of capital in manufacturing means that R_K/P_M also increases. Because R_K is the rental for capital, R_K/P_M is the amount of the manufactured good that can be purchased with this rent. Thus, the fact that R_K/P_M increases means that the real rental on capital in terms of the manufactured good has gone up. For the increase in the real rental on capital to occur even though the price of the manufactured good has also gone up, the percentage increase in R_K must be greater than the percentage increase in P_M.[17]

The amount of food that can be purchased by capital owners is R_K/P_A. Because R_K has increased, and P_A is fixed, R_K/P_A must also increase; in other words, the real rental on capital in terms of food has also gone up. Because capital owners can afford to buy more of both goods, they are clearly better off when the price of the manufactured good rises. Unlike labor, whose real wage increased in terms of one good but fell in terms of the other, capital owners clearly gain from the rise in the relative price of manufactured goods.

Change in the Real Rental on Land Let us now consider what happens to the landowners. With labor leaving agriculture, the marginal product of each acre falls, so R_T/P_A also falls. Because R_T is the rental on land, R_T/P_A is the amount of food that can be purchased with this rent. The fact that R_T/P_A falls means that the real rental on land in terms of food has gone down, so landowners cannot afford to buy as much food. Because the price of food is unchanged while the price of the manufactured good has gone up, landowners will not be able to afford to buy as much of the manufactured good either. Thus, landowners are clearly worse off from the rise in the price of the manufactured good because they can afford to buy less of both goods.

Summary The real earnings of capital owners and landowners move in opposite directions, an outcome that illustrates a general conclusion: *an increase in the relative price of an industry's output will increase the real rental earned by the factor specific to that industry but will decrease the real rental of factors specific to other industries*. This conclusion means that the specific factors used in export industries will generally gain as trade is opened and the relative price of exports rises, but the specific factors used in import industries will generally lose as trade is opened and the relative price of imports falls.

Numerical Example

We have come a long way in our study of the specific-factors model and conclude by presenting a numerical example of how an increase in the relative price of manufactures affects the earnings of labor, capital, and land. This example uses convenient numbers to review the results we have obtained so far. Suppose that the manufacturing industry has the following payments to labor and capital:

$$\textit{Manufacturing: Sales revenue} = P_M \cdot Q_M = \$100$$
$$\text{Payments to labor} = W \cdot L_M = \$60$$
$$\text{Payments to capital} = R_K \cdot K = \$40$$

Notice that 60% of sales revenue in manufacturing goes to labor, and 40% goes to capital.

In agriculture, suppose that the payments to labor and land are as follows:

$$\textit{Agriculture: Sales revenue} = P_A \cdot Q_A = \$100$$
$$\text{Payments to labor} = W \cdot L_A = \$50$$
$$\text{Payments to capital} = R_T \cdot T = \$50$$

In the agriculture industry, we assume that land and labor each earn 50% of the sales revenue.

An increase in the relative price of manufactures P_M/P_A can be caused by an increase in P_M or a decrease in P_A. To be specific, suppose that the price of manufactures P_M rises by 10%, whereas the price of agriculture P_A does not change at all. We have

---

[17] For example, if the price of manufactured goods rises by 6% and the rental on capital rises by 10%, then owners of capital can afford to buy 4% more of the manufactured good.

found in our earlier discussion that $\Delta W/W$, the percentage change in the wage, will be between the percentage change in these two industry prices. So let us suppose that $\Delta W/W$ is 5%. We summarize these output and factor price changes as follows:

Manufacturing: Percentage increase in price = $\Delta P_M/P_M = 10\%$

Agriculture: Percentage increase in price = $\Delta P_A/P_A = 0\%$

Both industries: Percentage increase in the wage = $\Delta W/W = 5\%$

Notice that the increase in the wage applies in both industries because wages are always equalized across sectors.

Change in the Rental on Capital   Our goal is to use the preceding data for manufacturing and agriculture to compute the change in the rental on capital and the change in the rental on land. Let's start with the equation for the rental on capital, which was computed by subtracting wage payments from sales revenue and then dividing by the amount of capital:

$$R_K = \frac{\text{Payments to capital}}{K} = \frac{P_M \cdot Q_M - W \cdot L_M}{K}$$

If the price of manufactured goods rises by $\Delta P_M > 0$, holding constant the price in agriculture, then the change in the rental is

$$\Delta R_K = \frac{\Delta P_M \cdot Q_M - \Delta W \cdot L_M}{K}$$

We want to rewrite this equation using percentage changes, like $\Delta P_M/P_M$, $\Delta W/W$, and $\Delta R_K/R_K$. To achieve this, divide both sides by R_K and rewrite the equation as

$$\frac{\Delta R_K}{R_K} = \frac{(\Delta P_M/P_M) \cdot P_M \cdot Q_M - (\Delta W/W) \cdot W \cdot L_M}{R_K \cdot K}$$

You can cancel terms in this equation to check that it is the same as before.

The term $\Delta P_M/P_M$ in this equation is the percentage change in the price of manufacturing, whereas $\Delta W/W$ is the percentage change in the wage. Given this information, along with the preceding data on the payments to labor, capital, and sales revenue, we can compute the percentage change in the rental on capital:

$$\frac{\Delta R_K}{R_K} = \frac{(10\% \cdot 100 - 5\% \cdot 60)}{40} = 17.5\%$$

We see that the percentage increase in the rental on capital, 17.5%, *exceeds* the percentage increase in the relative price of manufacturing, 10% (so $\Delta R_K/R_K > \Delta P_M/P_M > 0$). This outcome holds no matter what numbers are used in the preceding formula, provided that the percentage increase in the wage is less than the percentage increase in the price of the manufactured good (as proved in Figure 3-5).

Change in the Rental on Land   We can use the same approach to examine the change in the rental on land. Continuing to assume that the price of the manufactured good rises while the price in agriculture stays the same ($\Delta P_A = 0$), the change in the land rental is

$$\Delta R_T = \frac{0 \cdot Q_A - \Delta W \cdot L_A}{T}$$

Because the wage is increasing $\Delta W > 0$, it follows immediately that the *rental on land is falling*, $\Delta R_T < 0$. The percentage amount by which it falls can be calculated by rewriting the above equation as

$$\frac{\Delta R_T}{R_T} = -\frac{\Delta W}{W}\left(\frac{W \cdot L_A}{R_T \cdot T}\right)$$

Using these earlier data for agriculture in this formula, we get

$$\frac{\Delta R_T}{R_T} = -5\% \left(\frac{50}{50} \right) = -5\%$$

In this case, the land rent falls by the same percentage amount that the wage increases. This equality occurs because we assumed that labor and land receive the same share of sales revenue in agriculture (50% each). If labor receives a higher share of revenue than land, then the rent on land will fall even more; if it receives a lower share, then the rent on land won't fall as much.

General Equation for the Change in Factor Prices By summarizing our results in a single equation, we can see how all the changes in factor and industry prices are related. Under the assumption that the price of the manufactured good increased but the price of the agricultural good did not change, we have shown the following:

$$\underbrace{\Delta R_T/R_T < 0}_{\substack{\text{Real rental} \\ \text{on land falls}}} < \underbrace{\Delta W/W < \Delta P_M/P_M}_{\substack{\text{Change in the real} \\ \text{wage is ambiguous}}} < \underbrace{\Delta R_K/R_K}_{\substack{\text{Real rental} \\ \text{on capital rises}}}, \text{ for an increase in } P_M$$

In other words, wages rise but not as much as the percentage increase in the price of the manufactured good; the rental on capital (which is specific to the manufacturing sector) rises by more than the manufacturing price, so capital owners are better off; and the rental on land (which is the specific factor in the other sector) falls, so landowners are worse off.

What happens if the price of the manufactured good falls? Then the inequalities are reversed, and the equation becomes

$$\underbrace{\Delta R_K/R_K}_{\substack{\text{Real rental} \\ \text{on capital falls}}} < \underbrace{\Delta P_M/P_M < \Delta W/W}_{\substack{\text{Change in the real} \\ \text{wage is ambiguous}}} < 0 < \underbrace{\Delta R_T/R_T}_{\substack{\text{Real rental} \\ \text{on land rises}}}, \text{ for a decrease in } P_M$$

In this case, wages fall but by less than the percentage decrease in the manufactured good; the rental on capital (which is specific to the manufacturing sector) falls by more than the manufacturing price, so capital owners are worse off; and the rental on land (which is the specific factor in the other sector) rises, so landowners are better off.

What happens if the *price of the agricultural good rises*? You can probably guess, based on the previous example, that this change will benefit land and harm capital. The equation summarizing the changes in all three factor earnings becomes

$$\underbrace{\Delta R_K/R_K < 0}_{\substack{\text{Real rental} \\ \text{on capital falls}}} < \underbrace{\Delta W/W < \Delta P_A/P_A}_{\substack{\text{Change in the real} \\ \text{wage is ambiguous}}} < \underbrace{\Delta R_T/R_T}_{\substack{\text{Real rental} \\ \text{on land rises}}}, \text{ for an increase in } P_A$$

Note that it is the specific factor in the agricultural sector that gains and the specific factor in manufacturing that loses. The general result of these summary equations is that *the specific factor in the sector whose relative price has increased gains, the specific factor in the other sector loses, and labor is "caught in the middle," with its real wage increasing in terms of one good but falling in terms of the other*. These equations summarize the response of all three factor prices in the short run, when capital and land are specific to each sector but labor is mobile.

What It All Means

Our results from the specific-factors model show that the earnings of *specific factors* change the most from changes in relative prices due to international trade. Regardless of which good's price changes, the earnings of capital and land show the most extreme changes in their rentals, whereas the changes in the wages paid to labor are in the middle. Intuitively, these extreme changes in factor prices occur because in the short run the specific factors are not able to leave their sectors and find employment elsewhere. In contrast, labor is able to move between sectors, and so the changes in the wage are not so extreme.

These results suggest that we ought to be able to find real-world examples in which a change in international prices leads to losses for either owners of capital or landowners. For labor, the key to avoiding falling wages is the ability to shift between sectors. Is it possible to design policies that encourage the movement of factors like labor? And for a specific factor like land, is it possible to offset the losses that can occur due to changing prices? In the next application we discuss several policies of this type.

APPLICATION

Can Losses to Factors of Production Be Offset?

Earnings of Labor Should the government step in to compensate workers who are looking for jobs or who do not find them in a reasonable period? The unemployment insurance program in the United States provides some compensation, regardless of the reason for the layoff. Moreover, the **Trade Adjustment Assistance (TAA)** program offers additional unemployment insurance payments and health insurance to workers who are laid off because of import competition. To receive this assistance, workers must enroll in a retraining program that will enable them to find a job in another industry. Recent economic studies have shown that the TAA program is effective in moving workers into industries with greater chances of lasting employment and higher earnings: about $50,000 cumulative extra earnings over 10 years.[18]

This program was started in the United States under President Kennedy in 1962. He believed that this program was needed to compensate those Americans who lost their jobs because of international trade. Since 1993 there was also a special TAA program under the North American Free Trade Agreement (NAFTA) for workers who were laid off as a result of import competition from Mexico or Canada. The TAA program was extended again in 2009, to allow workers outside of the manufacturing sector—in the service sector and also in agriculture—who lose their jobs because of trade to also apply for TAA benefits. The entire TAA program was reauthorized in 2015. Countries in Europe and elsewhere also have programs of this type.

Earnings of Capital The United States also has a TAA program for firms that face strong competition from imports. For example, this program provides firms with matching funds to hire consultants, engineers, and other industry experts to assist in redesigning a manufacturing plant to make it more competitive. There are many instances in which these federal funds have helped a firm to survive.[19]

Earnings of Land Farmers often face changing prices on world markets, and when those prices fall, the real earnings of their land will fall even more, as our specific-factors model shows. Faced with declining real earnings in the agriculture sector, governments and other groups often take actions to prevent the incomes of farmers from falling.

An example of an agricultural commodity with particularly volatile prices is coffee. The price of coffee on world markets fluctuates a great deal from year to year because of weather and the entry of new suppliers in coffee-producing countries like Brazil and Vietnam. According to the specific-factors model, big fluctuations in coffee prices are extremely disruptive to the real earnings of landowners in coffee-exporting developing countries, many of whom are small farmers and their families.

---

[18] Benjamin G. Hyman, 2018, "Can Displaced Labor Be Retrained? Evidence from Quasi-Random Assignment to Trade Adjustment Assistance," University of Chicago.
[19] You are asked to investigate the TAA program for firms in Problem 1 at the end of the chapter.

FIGURE 3-12

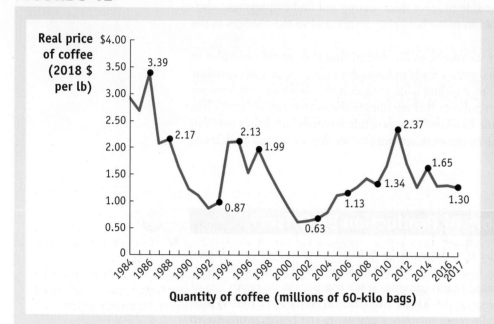

Real price of coffee (2018 $ per lb)

Quantity of coffee (millions of 60-kilo bags)

World Coffee Market, 1984–2017
Real wholesale prices for coffee fluctuate greatly on world markets. Prices (in 2018 dollars) reached a high of $3.39 per pound in 1986, a low of $0.63 per pound in 2001, and in 2017 were at $1.30. These erratic price movements are due to short-term fluctuations in the weather and longer-term fluctuations in supply as countries expand their production.

Data from: International Coffee Organization, http://www.ico.org.

The movements in the real wholesale price of coffee (measured in 2018 dollars) are shown in Figure 3-12. Wholesale prices hit a high of $3.39 per pound in 1986 and fluctuated a lot over the next 30 plus years. In 2017, coffee prices were at $1.30 per pound. These dramatic fluctuations in prices create equally large movements in the real incomes of farmers, making it difficult for them to sustain a living. The very low price of $0.63 per pound in 2001 created a crisis in the coffee-growing regions of Central America, requiring humanitarian aid for farmers and their families. The governments of coffee-growing regions in Central America and Asia cannot afford to protect their coffee farmers by propping up prices, as the industrial countries can (and do).

One idea that is gaining appeal as a way to help coffee farmers weather the kind of boom-and-bust cycles that occur regularly in coffee markets is to sell coffee from developing countries directly to consumers in industrial countries. By avoiding the middlemen (such as local buyers, millers, exporters, shippers, and importers), such an approach can ensure that farmers receive a higher price for their coffee. In addition, such programs help ensure a *more stable* price for farmers by guaranteeing them a minimum price, even if the market price falls lower.

You may have seen "fair-trade" coffee at your favorite coffeehouse. This coffee first appeared in the United States in 1999, imported by a group called TransFair USA—now called Fair Trade USA—that is committed to passing more of the profits back to the growers. Fair Trade USA is an example of a nongovernmental organization that is trying to help farmers by raising prices and allowing the consumer to choose whether to purchase this higher-priced product. Fair Trade USA also applies its Fair Trade label to imports of tea, cocoa, sugar, spices, honey, grains, wine, and other products.

Between 2004 and 2005, world coffee prices rose from $0.81 per pound to $1.13 per pound. When prices rose, groups like Fair Trade USA faced a dilemma because the fair-trade prices that they had guaranteed to farmers were actually lower than the world

Harvesting Fair Trade coffee in Jaltenango, Chiapas, Mexico.

Jutta Ulmer/mauritius images GmbH/Alamy

HEADLINES

Rise in Coffee Prices—Great for Farmers, Tough on Co-ops

TransFair USA – now called Fair Trade USA – guarantees a minimum purchase price for coffee farmers, acting as insurance against a falling market price. But during periods when the market price is rising, it is challenging to ensure that farmers deliver their coffee. Such a rise in coffee prices occurred the drought in 2005, when the price of the Fair Trade contracts fell below the market price.

During winter and spring of the 2005 harvest, a dilemma surfaced in rural areas of Central America and Mexico. Fairtrade cooperative managers found it increasingly difficult to get members to deliver coffee to their own organization at fair-trade prices. The co-op managers were holding contracts that were set months before at fixed fair-trade prices ..., but now the world coffee price was higher. Growers were seeing some of the highest prices paid in five years, and the temptation was great to sell their coffee to the highest local bidder, instead of delivering it as promised to their own co-ops.

In most cases, the co-ops' leaders were able to convince farmers to deliver coffee, but often based on arguments of loyalty, as the fair-trade fixed price was now lower than the premium prices being offered by the local middleman. It was not the model that the founders of fair-trade coffee pricing had envisioned when they created the program.

"It's worth noting that we were pleased to see prices rise in late 2004," says Christopher Himes, TransFair USA's Director of Certification and Finance. "This price rise, in conjunction with the impact fair trade was already having, increased the income and living standards of coffee farmers around the world. The most challenging thing during this time for TransFair USA was the speed with which the local differentials [between the fair-trade price and the world price] rose in Indonesia. They quickly skyrocketed to 80 cents [per pound] or higher, making the market value of farmers' coffee higher than that of some of the . . . fair-trade contracts."

Source: David Griswold, http://www.FreshCup.com, June 2005.

---

price of coffee. The accompanying article **Headlines: Rise in Coffee Prices—Great for Farmers, Tough on Co-ops** describes how some farmers were tempted to break their contracts with local co-ops (at fixed, fair-trade prices) to deliver coffee to local middlemen at prevailing world prices. Fair Trade USA and similar organizations purchase coffee at higher than the market price when the market price is low, but in other years, they purchase coffee at lower than the market price when the market price is high. Essentially, Fair Trade USA is offering farmers a form of *insurance* whereby the fair-trade prices of coffee will not fluctuate too much. Farmers are thus protected against the highs and lows of fluctuating prices and are able to enjoy greater gains from trade by exporting their coffee. So when you consider buying a cup of fair-trade coffee at your favorite coffeehouse, you are supporting coffee farmers who rely on the efforts of groups like Fair Trade USA to raise their incomes, and you are applying the logic of the specific-factors model, all at the same time!

4 Conclusions

In the Ricardian model of Chapter 2, we showed that free trade could never make a country worse off, and in most cases free trade would make it better off. This result remains true for all factors of production: labor, land, and capital. As long as the relative price with international trade differs from the no-trade relative price, a country will gain from international trade. This conclusion does not mean, however, that each and every factor of production gains. On the contrary, we have shown in this chapter that the change in relative prices due to the opening of trade creates winners and losers. Some factors of production gain in real terms, and other factors of production lose. To demonstrate this result, we have used a short-run model, in which labor is mobile between sectors but land and capital are each specific to their sectors.

Classical economists believed that, in the short run, factors of production that could not move between industries would lose the most from trade. We have found that this is true for the factor that is specific to the import-competing industry. That industry suffers a drop in its relative price because of international trade, which leads to a fall in the real rental on the specific factor in that industry. On the other hand, the specific factor in the export industry—whose relative price rises with the opening of trade—enjoys an increase in its real rental. Labor is mobile between the two industries, which allows it to avoid such extreme changes in wage: real wages rise in terms of one good but fall in terms of the other good, so we cannot tell whether workers are better off or worse off after a country opens to trade.

Economists have carefully proved that, in theory, the gains of individuals as a result of opening trade exceed the losses. This means that, in principle, the government should be able to tax the winners and use the additional tax revenue to compensate the losers so that everyone is better off because of trade. Sharing the gains from trade is very challenging in practice, however. In our opening story about Bolivia, it took a change in the country's government, which then took over the industry producing natural gas, to ensure that the gains were widely shared. In other countries, governments often use policies such as import tariffs and quotas that limit the amount of imports and that are intended to protect individuals from the effect of price changes resulting from international trade. We examine these policies later in the book.

KEY POINTS

1. Opening a country to international trade leads to overall gains, but in a model with several factors of production, some factors of production will lose.

2. The fact that some people are harmed because of trade sometimes creates social tensions that may be strong enough to topple governments. A recent example is Bolivia, where the citizens in the early 2000s could not agree on how to share the gains from exporting natural gas.

3. In the specific-factors model, factors of production that cannot move between industries will gain or lose the most when a country is opened to trade. The factor of production that is specific to the import industry will lose in real terms, as the relative price of the import good falls. The factor of production that is specific to the export industry will gain in real terms, as the relative price of the export good rises.

4. In the specific-factors model, labor can move between the industries and earns the same wage in each. When the relative price of either good changes, then the real wage rises when measured in terms of one good but falls when measured in terms of the other good. Without knowing how much of each good workers prefer to consume, we cannot say whether workers are better off or worse off because of trade.

5. Economists do not normally count the costs of unemployment as a loss from trade because people are often able to find new jobs. In the United States, for example, about two-thirds of people who are laid off from manufacturing or services companies find new jobs within three years, about one-half at lower wages and one-half at the same or higher wages.

6. The "China shock" refers to the impact on the U.S. labor market of China joining the WTO in 2001. Over 1999–2011, this shock led to a reduction in jobs within import and related industries of about 1.7 million workers in the United States. But over the longer period 1991–2011, the job losses in imports are nearly balanced with job gains in exports.

7. Even when many people are employed in export activities, such as those involved in coffee export from certain developing countries, fluctuations in the world market price can lead to large changes in income for workers in that industry.

KEY TERMS

specific-factors model, p. 63
diminishing returns, p. 63
autarky, p. 67
trade embargo, p. 67

real wage, p. 71
Engel's Law, p. 72
"China shock," p. 74
services, p. 74

rental on capital, p. 81
rental on land, p. 81
Trade Adjustment Assistance (TAA), p. 85

PROBLEMS

1. **Discovering Data** In this chapter, we learned that workers displaced by import competition are eligible for compensation through the Trade Adjustment Assistance (TAA) program. Firms are also eligible for support through Trade Adjustment Assistance for Firms, a federal program that provides financial assistance to manufacturers affected by import competition. Go to taacenters.org to read about this program, and then answer the following questions:

   a. Describe the criteria a firm has to meet to qualify for benefits.

   b. What amount of money is provided to firms, and for what purpose? Describe one of the "success stories," in which a firm used financial assistance to improve its performance.

   c. Provide an argument for and an argument against the continued funding of this federal program.

2. Why is the specific-factors model referred to as a short-run model?

3. Figure 3-7 presents wages in the manufacturing and services sectors for the period 1973 to 2018. Is the difference in wages across sectors consistent with either the Ricardian model studied in Chapter 2 or the specific-factors model? Explain why or why not.

4. In the gains from trade diagram in Figure 3-3, suppose that instead of having a rise in the relative price of manufactures, there is instead a fall in that relative price.

   a. Starting at the no-trade point A in Figure 3-3, show what would happen to production and consumption.

   b. Which good is exported and which is imported?

   c. Explain why the overall gains from trade are still positive.

5. Starting from equilibrium in the specific-factors model, suppose the price of manufactured goods falls so that wages fall from W' to W in Figure 3-5.

   a. Show that the percentage fall in wages is less than the percentage fall in the price of manufacturing so that the real wage of labor in terms of manufactured goods goes up.

   b. What happens to the real wage of labor in terms of agriculture?

   c. Are workers better off, are they worse off, or is the outcome ambiguous?

WORK IT OUT   Achieve | interactive activity

6. Use the information given here to answer the following questions:
   Manufacturing:

   Sales revenue $= P_M \cdot Q_M = 150$

   Payments to labor $= W \cdot L_M = 100$

   Payments to capital $= R_K \cdot K = 50$

   Agriculture:

   Sales revenue $= P_A \cdot Q_A = 150$

   Payments to labor $= W \cdot L_A = 50$

   Payments to land $= R_T \cdot T = 100$

   Holding the price of manufacturing constant, suppose the increase in the price of agriculture is 20% and the increase in the wage is 10%.

   a. Determine the impact of the increase in the price of agriculture on the rental on land and the rental on capital.

   b. Explain what has happened to the real rental on land and the real rental on capital.

7. If instead of the situation given in Problem 6, suppose that the price of manufacturing were to fall by 20% and the wage declined by 10%. Then would landowners or capital owners be better off? Explain. How would the decrease in the price of manufacturing affect the real wage? Explain.

8. Read the article by Grant Aldonas, Robert Lawrence, and Matthew Slaughter, available online at: hks.harvard.edu/fs/rlawrence/fsf_adjustment_assistance_plan.pdf. Then answer the following questions.

   a. What is the name of the new program that these authors propose, and from what three programs in the United States would it combine elements?

   b. What is the authors' specific proposal for wage-loss insurance?

   c. What is their specific proposal for health insurance?

   d. What is their specific proposal for giving workers access to savings?

   e. Would the program they propose depend on a worker losing their job because of trade competition or a shift of production facilities overseas?

   f. What would their proposed program cost annually, and how does that compare with the annual cost of the Trade Adjustment Assistance program?

9. In the specific-factors model, assume that the price of agricultural goods decreases while the price of manufactured goods is unchanged ($\Delta P_A/P_A < 0$ and $\Delta P_M/P_M = 0$). Arrange the following terms in ascending order:

   $$\Delta R_T/R_T \quad \Delta R_K/R_K \quad \Delta P_A/P_A \quad \Delta P_M/P_M \quad \Delta W/W$$

   Hint: Try starting with a diagram like Figure 3-5, but change the price of agricultural goods instead.

10. Suppose two countries, Canada and Mexico, produce two goods: lumber and televisions. Assume that land is specific to lumber, capital is specific to televisions, and labor is free to move between the two industries. When Canada and Mexico engage in free trade, the relative price of televisions falls in Canada and the relative price of lumber falls in Mexico.

    a. In a graph similar to Figure 3-5, show how the wage changes in Canada due to a fall in the price of televisions, holding constant the price of lumber. Can we predict that change in the real wage?

    b. What is the impact of opening trade on the rentals on capital and land in Canada? Can we predict that change in the real rentals on capital and land?

    c. What is the impact of opening trade on the rentals on capital and land in Mexico? Can we predict that change in the real rentals on capital and land?

    d. In each country, has the specific factor in the export industry gained or lost, and has the specific factor in the import industry gained or lost?

11. Home produces two goods, computers and wheat, for which capital is specific to computers, land is specific to wheat, and labor is mobile between the two industries. Home has 100 workers and 100 units of capital but only 10 units of land.

    a. Draw a graph similar to Figure 3-1(a) with the output of wheat on the vertical axis and the labor used in wheat on the horizontal axis. What is the relationship between the output of wheat and the marginal product of labor in the wheat industry as more labor is used?

    b. Draw the production possibilities frontier for Home with wheat on the horizontal axis and computers on the vertical axis.

    c. Explain how the price of wheat relative to computers is determined in the absence of trade.

    d. Reproduce Figure 3-4 with the amount of labor used in wheat, measuring from left to right along the horizontal axis, and the amount of labor used in computers, moving in the reverse direction.

    e. Assume that as a result of international trade, the price of wheat rises. Analyze the effect of the increase in the price of wheat on the allocation of labor between the two sectors.

12. Similar to Home in Problem 11, Foreign also produces computers and wheat using capital, which is specific to computers; land, which is specific to wheat; and labor, which is mobile between the two sectors. Foreign has 100 workers and 100 units of land but only 10 units of capital. It has the same production functions as Home.

    a. Will the no-trade relative price of wheat be higher in Home or in Foreign? Explain why you expect this outcome.

    b. When trade is opened, what happens to the relative price of wheat in Foreign and to the relative price of wheat in Home?

    c. Based on your answer to (b), predict the effect of opening trade on the rental on land in each country, which is specific to wheat. What about the rental on capital, which is specific to computers?

4

Trade and Resources: The Heckscher–Ohlin Model

God did not bestow all products upon all parts of the earth, but distributed His gifts over different regions, to the end that men might cultivate a social relationship because one would have need of the help of another. And so He called commerce into being, that all men might be able to have common enjoyment of the fruits of the earth, no matter where produced.

Libanius (AD 314–393), *Orations* (III)

Nature, by giving a diversity of geniuses, climates, and soils, to different nations, has secured their mutual intercourse and commerce. . . . The industry of the nations, from whom they import, receives encouragement: Their own is also [i]ncreased, by the sale of the commodities which they give in exchange.

David Hume, *Essays, Moral, Political, and Literary*, 1752,
Part II, Essay VI, "On the Jealousy of Trade"

Questions to Consider

1 Why does the United States export agricultural products and airplanes?

2 What country has the most capital (i.e., factories) as compared with its GDP?

3 How does trade affect the earnings of labor and capital?

In Chapter 2, we examined U.S. imports of snowboards. We argued there that the resources found in a country would influence its pattern of international trade. Canada's export of snowboards to the United States reflects its mountains and cold climate, as do the exports of snowboards to the United States from Austria, Switzerland, and other countries bordering the Alps. Because each country's resources are different and because resources are spread unevenly around the world, countries have a reason to trade the goods made with these resources. This is an old idea, as shown by the quotations at the beginning of this chapter; the first is from the fourth-century Greek scholar Libanius, and the second is from the eighteenth-century philosopher David Hume.

In this chapter, we outline the **Heckscher–Ohlin model**, a model that assumes that trade occurs because countries have different resources. This model contrasts with the Ricardian model, which assumed that trade occurs because countries use their technological comparative advantage to specialize in the production of different goods. The model is named after the Swedish economists Eli Heckscher, who wrote about his views of international trade in a 1919 article, and his student Bertil Ohlin, who further developed these ideas in his 1924 dissertation.

The Heckscher–Ohlin model was developed at the end of a "golden age" of international trade (as described in Chapter 1) that lasted from about 1890 until 1914, when World War I started. Those years saw dramatic improvements in transportation: the steamship and the railroad allowed for a great increase in the amount of international trade. For these reasons, there was a considerable increase in the ratio of trade to GDP between 1890 and 1914. It is not surprising, then, that Heckscher and Ohlin would want to explain the large increase in trade that they had witnessed in their own lifetimes. The ability to transport machines across borders meant that they did not look to differences in technologies across countries as the reason for trade, as Ricardo had done. Instead, they assumed that technologies were the same across countries, and they used the uneven distribution of resources across countries to explain trade patterns.

Even today, there are many examples of international trade driven by the land, labor, and capital resources found in each country. Canada, for example, has a large amount of land and therefore exports agricultural and forestry products, as well as petroleum; the United States, western Europe, and Japan have many highly skilled workers and much capital, and these countries export sophisticated services and manufactured goods; China has a large amount of capital and workers who are rapidly increasing their skills, so it is competing with the United States, Japan, and Europe; and other Asian countries have a large number of workers and moderate but growing amounts of capital and they export less sophisticated manufactured goods. We study these and other examples of international trade in this chapter.

Our first goal is to describe the Heckscher–Ohlin model of trade. The specific-factors model that we studied in the previous chapter was a short-run model because capital and land could not move between the two industries we looked at. In contrast, the Heckscher–Ohlin model is a long-run model because all factors of production can move between industries. It is difficult to deal with three factors of production (labor, capital, and land) in two industries, so we assume that there are just two factors (labor and capital).

After predicting the long-run pattern of trade between countries using the Heckscher–Ohlin model, our second goal is to examine the empirical evidence on the Heckscher–Ohlin model. Although you might think it is obvious that a country's exports will be based on the resources the country has in abundance, it turns out that this prediction does not always hold true in practice. To obtain better predictions from the Heckscher–Ohlin model, we extend it in several directions, first by allowing for more than two factors of production and second by allowing countries to differ in their technologies, as in the Ricardian model. Both extensions make the predictions from the Heckscher–Ohlin model match more closely the trade patterns we see in the world economy today.

The third goal of the chapter is to investigate how the opening of trade between the two countries affects the payments to labor and to capital in each of them. We use the Heckscher–Ohlin model to predict which factors gain when international trade begins and which factors lose.

1 Heckscher–Ohlin Model

In building the Heckscher–Ohlin model, we assume two countries, Home and Foreign, each of which produces two goods, computers and shoes, using two factors of production, labor and capital. Using symbols for capital (K) and labor (L), we can add up the resources used in each industry to get the total for the economy. For example, the amount of capital Home uses in shoes K_S, plus the amount of capital used in computers K_C, adds up to the total capital available in the economy $\overline{K}$, so that $K_C + K_S = \overline{K}$. The same applies for Foreign: $K_C^* + K_S^* = \overline{K}^*$. Similarly, the amount of labor Home uses in shoes L_S, and the amount of labor used in computers L_C, add up to the total labor in the economy $\overline{L}$, so that $L_C + L_S = \overline{L}$. The same applies for Foreign: $L_C^* + L_S^* = \overline{L}^*$.

Assumptions of the Heckscher–Ohlin Model

Because the Heckscher–Ohlin (HO) model describes the economy in the long run, its assumptions differ from those in the short-run specific-factors model of Chapter 3:

Assumption 1: Both factors can move freely between the industries.

This assumption implies that if both industries are actually producing, then capital must earn the same rental R in each of them. The reason for this result is that if capital earned a higher rental in one industry than the other, then all capital would move to the industry with the higher rental and the other industry would shut down. This result differs from the specific-factors model, in which capital in manufacturing and land in agriculture earned different rentals in their respective industries. But like the specific-factors model, if both industries are producing, then all labor earns the same wage W in each of them.

Our second assumption concerns how the factors are combined to make shoes and computers:

Assumption 2: Shoe production is labor-intensive; that is, it requires more labor per unit of capital to produce shoes than computers, so that $L_S/K_S > L_C/K_C$.

Another way to state this assumption is to say that computer production is capital-intensive; that is, more capital per worker is used to produce computers than to produce shoes, so that $K_C/L_C > K_S/L_S$. The idea that shoes use more labor per unit of capital, and computers use more capital per worker, matches how most of us think about the technologies used in these two industries.

In Figure 4-1, the demands for labor relative to capital in each industry (L_C/K_C and L_S/K_S) are graphed against the wage relative to the rental on capital, W/R (or the wage–rental ratio). These two curves slope down just like regular demand curves: as W/R falls, the quantity of labor demanded relative to the quantity of capital demanded rises As we work through the HO model, remember that these are *relative* demand curves for labor; the "quantity" on the horizontal axis is the ratio of labor to capital used in production, and the "price" is the ratio of the labor wage to the capital rental. Assumption 2 says that the relative demand curve in shoes, L_S/K_S in Figure 4-1, lies to the right of the relative demand curve in computers L_C/K_C, because shoe production is more labor-intensive.

Whereas the preceding assumptions have focused on the production process within each country, the HO model requires assumptions that apply across countries as well. Our next assumption is that the amounts of labor and capital found in Home and Foreign are different:

Assumption 3: Foreign is labor-abundant, by which we mean that the labor–capital ratio in Foreign exceeds that in Home, $\overline{L}^*/\overline{K}^* > \overline{L}/\overline{K}$. Equivalently, Home is capital-abundant, so that $\overline{K}/\overline{L} > \overline{K}^*/\overline{L}^*$.

There are many reasons for labor, capital, and other resources to differ across countries: countries differ in their geographic size and populations, previous waves of immigration or emigration may have changed a country's population, countries are at different stages of development and so have differing amounts of capital, and so on. If we are considering land in the HO model, Home and Foreign will have different amounts of usable land because of their different border shapes, topography, and climate. In building the HO model, we do not consider why the amounts of labor, capital, or land differ across countries but simply accept these differences as important determinants of why countries engage in international trade.

Assumption 3 focuses on a particular case, in which Foreign is labor-abundant and Home is capital-abundant. This assumption is true, for example, if Foreign has a larger workforce than Home ($\overline{L}^* > \overline{L}$) and Foreign and Home have equal amounts of capital, $\overline{K}^* = \overline{K}$. Under these circumstances, $\overline{L}^*/\overline{K}^* > \overline{L}/\overline{K}$, so Foreign is labor-abundant.

FIGURE 4-1

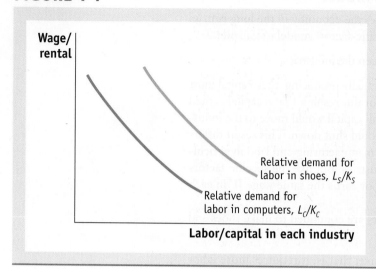

Labor Intensity of Each Industry The demand for labor relative to capital is assumed to be higher in shoes than in computers, $L_S/K_S > L_C/K_C$. These two curves slope down just like regular demand curves, but in this case, they are *relative* demand curves for labor (i.e., demand for labor divided by demand for capital).

Conversely, the capital–labor ratio in Home exceeds that in Foreign, $\overline{K}/\overline{L} > \overline{K}^*/\overline{L}^*$, so the Home country is capital-abundant.

Assumption 4: The final outputs, shoes and computers, can be traded freely (i.e., without any restrictions) between nations, but labor and capital do not move between countries. In this chapter, we do not allow labor or capital to move between countries. We relax this assumption in the next chapter, in which we investigate the movement of labor between countries through immigration as well as the movement of capital between countries through foreign direct investment.

Our final two assumptions involve the technologies of firms and tastes of consumers across countries:

Assumption 5: The technologies used to produce the two goods are identical across the countries.

This assumption is the opposite of that made in the Ricardian model (Chapter 2), which assumes that technological differences across countries are the reason for trade. It is not realistic to assume that technologies are the same across countries because, often, the technologies used in rich countries versus poor countries are quite different (as described in the following application). Although assumption 5 is not very realistic, it allows us to focus on a single reason for trade: the different amounts of labor and capital found in each country. Later in this chapter, we use data to test the validity of the HO model and find that the model performs better when assumption 5 is not used.

Our final assumption is as follows:

Assumption 6: Consumer tastes are the same across countries, and preferences for computers and shoes do not vary with a country's level of income.

That is, we suppose that a poorer country will buy fewer shoes and computers, but will buy them in the same ratio as a wealthier country facing the same prices. Again, this assumption is not very realistic: consumers in poor countries do spend more of their income on shoes, clothing, and other basic goods than on computers, whereas in rich countries a higher share of income can be spent on computers and other electronic goods than on footwear and clothing. Assumption 6 is another simplifying assumption that again allows us to focus attention on the differences in resources as the sole reason for trade.

APPLICATION

Are Factor Intensities the Same Across Countries?

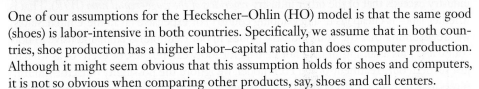

One of our assumptions for the Heckscher–Ohlin (HO) model is that the same good (shoes) is labor-intensive in both countries. Specifically, we assume that in both countries, shoe production has a higher labor–capital ratio than does computer production. Although it might seem obvious that this assumption holds for shoes and computers, it is not so obvious when comparing other products, say, shoes and call centers.

In principle, all countries have access to the same technologies for making footwear. In practice, however, the machines used in the United States are different from those used in Asia and elsewhere. While much of the footwear in the world is produced in developing nations, the United States retains a small number of shoe factories. New Balance, which manufactures sneakers, has five plants in the New England states, and 25% of the shoes it sells in North America are produced in the United States. One of their plants is in Norridgewock, Maine, where employees operate computerized equipment that allows one person to do the work of six.[1] This is a far cry from the plants in Asia that produce shoes for Nike, Reebok, and other U.S. producers. Because Asian plants use older technology (such as individual sewing machines), they use more workers to operate less productive machines.

In call centers, on the other hand, technologies (and, therefore, factor intensities) are similar across countries. Each employee works with a telephone and a personal computer, so call centers in the United States and India are similar in terms of the amount of capital per worker that they require. The telephone and personal computer, which cost several thousand dollars, are much less expensive than the automated manufacturing machines in the New Balance plant in the United States, which cost tens or hundreds of thousands of dollars. So the manufacture of footwear in the New Balance plant is capital-intensive as compared with a U.S. call center. In India, by contrast, the sewing machine used to produce footwear is cheaper than the computer used in the call center. So footwear production in India is labor-intensive as compared with the call center, which is the opposite of what holds in the United States. This example illustrates a **reversal of factor intensities** between the two countries.

There are many examples of factor intensity reversals in other industries. The San Francisco–based company American Giant makes all of its clothing, including its popular hooded sweatshirt, in the United States. Its plants are highly capital-intensive as compared with a call center in the United States,[2] whereas clothing production in Asia or Mexico is often labor-intensive.

A final example uses a very high-technology product: artificial intelligence (AI). You would think that creating the hardware and software to support AI would require more capital (i.e., computers) and more highly skilled labor than a call center. But there is a catch: in order for AI to learn a task such as recognizing objects, the software first needs to process many examples from humans who describe the content of pictures. After learning with the help of millions of such pictures, the AI algorithms can make very fast inferences about what a picture is showing. These algorithms require both capital and highly skilled labor. But the initial activity of explaining what a picture shows is no more capital- or skill-intensive than a call center: it requires that workers have a moderate level of education and work with a personal computer. China has

Despite its nineteenth-century exterior, this New Balance factory in Maine houses advanced shoe-manufacturing technology.

---

[1] This description of the New Balance plant is drawn from Aaron Bernstein, "Low-Skilled Jobs: Do They Have to Move?" *BusinessWeek*, February 26, 2001, 94–95.
[2] See the description of the American Giant plant in Stephanie Clifford, "Textile Plants Humming, but Not with Workers," *New York Times*, September 20, 2013, A1.

an especially large population to draw on for such workers, so the development of AI in China is more labor-intensive than when this activity is done in other countries.[3]

In assumption 2 and Figure 4-1, we assume that the labor–capital ratio (L/K) of one industry exceeds that of the other industry *regardless of the wage–rental ratio* (W/R). That is, whether labor is cheap (as in a developing country) or expensive (as in the United States), we are assuming that the same industry (shoes, in our example) is labor-intensive in both countries. This assumption may not be true for footwear, textiles, or even AI, as we have just seen. In our treatment of the HO model, we ignore the possibility of factor-intensity reversals. The reason for ignoring these is to get a definite prediction from the model about the pattern of trade between countries so that we can see what happens to the price of goods and the earnings of factors when countries trade with each other.

No-Trade Equilibrium

In assumption 3, we outlined the difference in the amount of labor and capital found in Home and in Foreign. Our goal is to use these differences in resources to predict the pattern of trade. To do this, we begin by studying the equilibrium in each country in the absence of trade.

Production Possibilities Frontiers To determine the no-trade equilibria in Home and Foreign, we start by drawing the production possibilities frontiers (PPFs) in each country as shown in Figure 4-2. Under our assumptions that Home is capital-abundant and that computer production is capital-intensive, Home has greater capacity to produce computers than shoes. The Home PPF drawn in panel (a) is skewed in the direction of computers to reflect Home's greater capability to produce

FIGURE 4-2

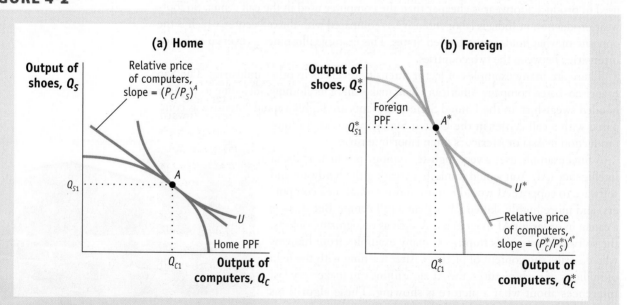

No-Trade Equilibria in Home and Foreign The Home production possibilities frontier (PPF) is shown in panel (a), and the Foreign PPF is shown in panel (b). Because Home is capital-abundant and computers are capital-intensive, the Home PPF is skewed toward computers. Home preferences are summarized by the indifference curve, U, and the Home no-trade (or autarky) equilibrium is at point A, with a low relative price of computers, as indicated by the flat slope of $(P_C/P_S)^A$. Foreign is labor-abundant and shoes are labor-intensive, so the Foreign PPF is skewed toward shoes. Foreign preferences are summarized by the indifference curve, U^*, and the Foreign no-trade equilibrium is at point A^*, with a higher relative price of computers, as indicated by the steeper slope of $(P_C^*/P_S^*)^{A^*}$.

---

[3] See Li Yuan, "Doing Time on the AI Assembly Line," *New York Times*, November 26, 2018, B1.

computers. Similarly, because Foreign is labor-abundant and shoe production is labor-intensive, the Foreign PPF shown in panel (b) is skewed in the direction of shoes, reflecting Foreign's greater capability to produce shoes. These particular shapes for the PPFs are reasonable given the assumptions we have made. When we continue our study of the Heckscher–Ohlin (HO) model in Chapter 5, we prove that the PPFs must take this shape.[4] For now, we'll accept these shapes of the PPF and use them as the starting point for our study of the HO model.

Indifference Curves Another assumption of the HO model (assumption 6) is that consumer tastes are the same across countries. As we did in the Ricardian model, we graph consumer tastes using indifference curves. Two of these curves are shown in Figure 4-2 (U and U^* for Home and Foreign, respectively); one is tangent to Home's PPF, and the other is tangent to Foreign's PPF. Notice that these indifference curves are the same shape in both countries, as required by assumption 6. They are tangent to the PPFs at different points because of the distinct shapes of the PPFs just described.

The slope of an indifference curve equals the amount that consumers are willing to pay for computers measured in terms of shoes rather than dollars. The slope of the PPF equals the opportunity cost of producing one more computer in terms of shoes given up. When the slope of an indifference curve equals the slope of a PPF, the relative price that consumers are willing to pay for computers equals the opportunity cost of producing them, so this point is the no-trade equilibrium.[5] The common slope of the indifference curve and PPF at their tangency equals the relative price of computers (P_C/P_S). A steeply sloped price line implies a high relative price of computers, whereas a flat price line implies a low relative price for computers.

No-Trade Equilibrium Price Given the differently shaped PPFs, the indifference curves of each country will be tangent to the PPFs at different production points, corresponding to different relative price lines across the two countries. In Home the no-trade or autarky equilibrium is shown by point A, at which Home produces Q_{C1} of computers and Q_{S1} of shoes at the relative price of $(P_C/P_S)^A$. Because the Home PPF is skewed toward computers, the slope of the Home price line $(P_C/P_S)^A$ is quite flat, indicating a low relative price of computers. In Foreign, the no-trade or autarky equilibrium is shown by point A^*, at which Foreign produces Q_{C1}^* of computers and Q_{S1}^* of shoes at the relative price of $(P_C^*/P_S^*)^{A^*}$. Because the Foreign PPF is skewed toward shoes, the slope of the Foreign price line $(P_C^*/P_S^*)^{A^*}$ is quite steep, indicating a high relative price of computers. Therefore, the result from comparing the no-trade equilibria in Figure 4-2 is that the *no-trade relative price of computers in Home is lower than in Foreign.* (Equivalently, we can say that the no-trade relative price of shoes in Home is higher than in Foreign.)

These comparisons of the no-trade prices reflect the differing amounts of labor found in the two countries: the Foreign country has abundant labor, and shoe production is labor-intensive, so the no-trade relative price of shoes is lower in Foreign than in Home. That Foreigners are willing to give up more shoes for one computer reflects the fact that Foreign resources are more suited to making shoes. The same logic applies to Home, which is relatively abundant in capital. Because computer production is capital-intensive, Home has a lower no-trade relative price of computers than Foreign. Thus, Home residents need to give up fewer shoes to obtain one computer, reflecting the fact that their resources are more suited to making computers.

---

[4] See Problem 8 in Chapter 5.
[5] Remember that the slope of an indifference curve or PPF reflects the relative price of the good on the *horizontal* axis, which is computers in Figure 4-2.

Free-Trade Equilibrium

We are now in a position to determine the pattern of trade between the countries. To do so, we proceed in several steps. First, we consider what happens when the world relative price of computers is *above* the no-trade relative price of computers in Home, and trace out the Home export supply of computers. Second, we consider what happens when the world relative price is *below* the no-trade relative price of computers in Foreign, and trace out the Foreign import demand for computers. Finally, we put together the Home export supply and Foreign import demand to determine the equilibrium relative price of computers with international trade.

Home Equilibrium with Free Trade The first step is displayed in Figure 4-3. We have already seen in Figure 4-2 that the no-trade relative price of computers is lower in Home than in Foreign. Under free trade, we expect the equilibrium relative price of computers to lie between the no-trade relative prices in each country (as we already found in the Ricardian model in Chapter 2). Because the no-trade relative price of computers is lower in Home, the free-trade equilibrium price will be above the no-trade price in Home. Therefore, panel (a) of Figure 4-3 shows the Home PPF with a free-trade or world relative price of computers, $(P_C/P_S)^W$, higher than the no-trade Home relative price, $(P_C/P_S)^A$, shown in panel (a) of Figure 4-2.

The no-trade equilibrium in Home, point A, has the quantities (Q_{C1}, Q_{S1}) for computers and shoes, shown in Figure 4-2. At the higher world relative price of computers, Home production moves from point A, (Q_{C1}, Q_{S1}), to point B in Figure 4-3, (Q_{C2}, Q_{S2}), with more computers and fewer shoes. Thus, with free trade, Home produces fewer shoes and specializes further in computers to take advantage of higher world relative prices of computers. Because Home can now engage in trade at the world relative price, Home's consumption can now lie on any point along the world price

FIGURE 4-3

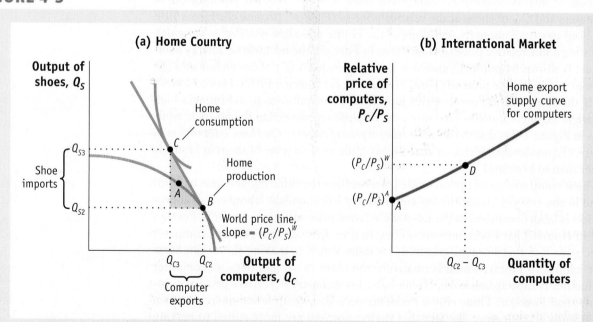

International Free-Trade Equilibrium in Home At the free-trade world relative price of computers, $(P_C/P_S)^W$, Home produces at point B in panel (a) and consumes at point C, exporting computers and importing shoes. (Point A is the no-trade equilibrium.) The "trade triangle" has a base equal to the Home exports of computers (the difference between the amount produced and the amount consumed with trade, $Q_{C2} - Q_{C3}$). The height of this triangle is the Home imports of shoes (the difference between the amount consumed of shoes and the amount produced with trade, $Q_{S3} - Q_{S2}$). In panel (b), we show Home exports of computers equal to zero at the no-trade relative price, $(P_C/P_S)^A$, and equal to $(Q_{C2} - Q_{C3})$ at the free-trade relative price, $(P_C/P_S)^W$.

line through B with slope $(P_C/P_S)^W$. The highest Home utility is obtained at point C, which is tangent to the world price line $(P_C/P_S)^W$ and has the quantities consumed (Q_{C3}, Q_{S3}).

We can now define the Home "trade triangle," which is the triangle connecting points B and C, shown in panel (a) of Figure 4-3. Point B is where Home is producing and point C is where it is consuming, and the line connecting the two points represents the amount of trade at the world relative price. The base of this triangle is the Home exports of computers (the difference between the amount produced and the amount consumed with trade, or $Q_{C2} - Q_{C3}$). The height of this triangle is the Home imports of shoes (the difference between the amount consumed of shoes and the amount produced with trade, or $Q_{S3} - Q_{S2}$).

In panel (b) of Figure 4-3, we graph the Home exports of computers against their relative price. In the no-trade equilibrium, the Home relative price of computers was $(P_C/P_S)^A$, and exports of computers were zero. This no-trade equilibrium is shown by point A in panel (b). Under free trade, the relative price of computers is $(P_C/P_S)^W$, and exports of computers are the difference between the amount produced and amount consumed with trade, or $(Q_{C2} - Q_{C3})$. This free-trade equilibrium is shown by point D in panel (b). Joining up points A and D, we obtain the Home export supply curve of computers. It is upward-sloping because at higher relative prices as compared with the no-trade price, Home is willing to specialize further in computers to export more of them.

Foreign Equilibrium with Free Trade We proceed in a similar fashion for the Foreign country. In panel (b) of Figure 4-2, the Foreign no-trade equilibrium is at point A^*, (Q_{C1}^*, Q_{S1}^*), with the high equilibrium relative price of computers $(P_C^*/P_S^*)^{A^*}$. Because the Foreign no-trade relative price was higher than in Home, and we expect the free-trade relative price to lie between, it follows that the free-trade or world equilibrium price of computers $(P_C/P_S)^W$, shown in panel (a) of Figure 4-4, is lower than the no-trade Foreign price $(P_C^*/P_S^*)^{A^*}$.

At the world relative price, Foreign production moves from point A^* in panel (a) of Figure 4-4 to point B^*, (Q_{C2}^*, Q_{S2}^*), with more shoes and fewer computers. Thus, with free trade, Foreign specializes further in shoes and produces fewer computers. Because Foreign can now engage in trade at the world relative price, Foreign's consumption can now lie on any point along the world price line through B^* with slope $(P_C/P_S)^W$. The highest Foreign utility is obtained at point C^*, which is tangent to the world price line $(P_C/P_S)^W$ and has the quantities consumed (Q_{C3}^*, Q_{S3}^*). Once again, we can connect points B^* and C^* to form a trade triangle. The base of this triangle is Foreign imports of computers (the difference between consumption of computers and production with trade, or $Q_{C3}^* - Q_{C2}^*$), and the height is Foreign exports of shoes (the difference between production and consumption with trade, or $Q_{S2}^* - Q_{S3}^*$).

In panel (b) of Figure 4-4, we graph Foreign's imports of computers against its relative price. In the no-trade equilibrium, the Foreign relative price of computers was $(P_C^*/P_S^*)^{A^*}$, and imports of computers were zero. This no-trade equilibrium is shown by the point A^* in panel (b). Under free trade, the relative price of computers is $(P_C/P_S)^W$, and imports of computers are the difference between the amount produced and amount consumed with trade, or $(Q_{C3}^* - Q_{C2}^*)$. This free-trade equilibrium is shown by the point D^* in panel (b). Joining up points A^* and D^*, we obtain the Foreign import demand curve for computers. It is downward-sloping because at lower relative prices as compared with no trade, Foreign specializes more in shoes and exports those in exchange for computers.

Equilibrium Price with Free Trade As we see in Figure 4-5, the equilibrium relative price of computers with free trade is determined by the intersection of the Home export supply and Foreign import demand curves, at point D (the same as point D in Figure 4-3 or D^* in Figure 4-4). At that relative price, the quantity of computers that the Home country wants to export equals the quantity of computers that Foreign wants to import; that is,

FIGURE 4-4

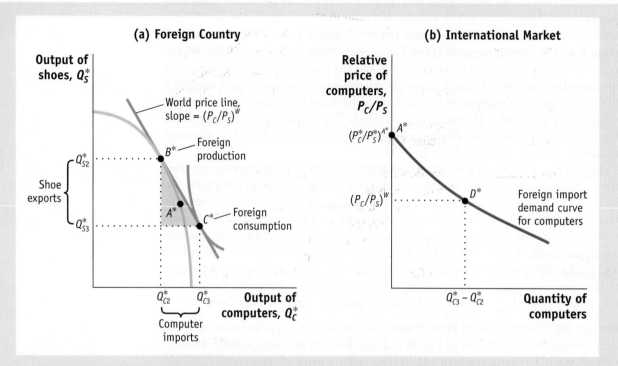

(a) Foreign Country

(b) International Market

International Free-Trade Equilibrium in Foreign At the free-trade world relative price of computers, $(P_C/P_S)^W$, Foreign produces at point B^* in panel (a) and consumes at point C^*, importing computers and exporting shoes. (Point A^* is the no-trade equilibrium.) The "trade triangle" has a base equal to Foreign imports of computers (the difference between the consumption of computers and the amount produced

with trade, $Q_{C3}^* - Q_{C2}^*$). The height of this triangle is Foreign exports of shoes (the difference between the production of shoes and the amount consumed with trade, $Q_{S2}^* - Q_{S3}^*$). In panel (b), we show Foreign imports of computers equal to zero at the no-trade relative price, $(P_C^*/P_S^*)^{A^*}$, and equal to $(Q_{C3}^* - Q_{C2}^*)$ at the free-trade relative price, $(P_C/P_S)^W$.

$(Q_{C2} - Q_{C3}) = (Q_{C3}^* - Q_{C2}^*)$. Because exports equal imports, there is no reason for the relative price to change and so this is a **free-trade equilibrium**. Another way to see the equilibrium graphically is to notice that in panel (a) of Figures 4-3 and 4-4, the trade triangles of the two countries are identical in size—the quantity of computers one country wants to sell is the same as the quantity the other country wants to buy.

FIGURE 4-5

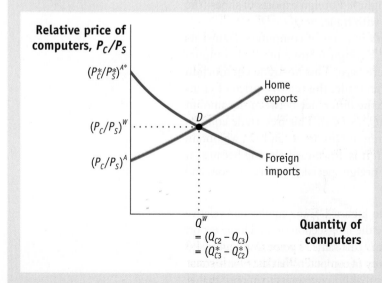

Determination of the Free-Trade World Equilibrium Price The world relative price of computers in the free-trade equilibrium is determined at the intersection of the Home export supply and Foreign import demand, at point D. At this relative price, the quantity of computers that Home wants to export, $(Q_{C2} - Q_{C3})$, just equals the quantity of computers that Foreign wants to import, $(Q_{C3}^* - Q_{C2}^*)$.

Pattern of Trade Using the free-trade equilibrium, we have determined the pattern of trade between the two countries. Home exports computers, the good that uses intensively the factor of production (capital) found in abundance in Home. Foreign exports shoes, the good that uses intensively the factor of production (labor) found in abundance there. This important result is called the **Heckscher–Ohlin theorem**.

Heckscher–Ohlin Theorem: With two goods and two factors, each country will export the good that uses intensively the factor of production it has in abundance and will import the other good.

It is useful to review the assumptions we made at the beginning of the chapter to see how they have led to the Heckscher–Ohlin theorem.

Assumption 1: Labor and capital flow freely between the industries.
Assumption 2: The production of shoes is labor-intensive as compared with computer production, which is capital-intensive.
Assumption 3: The amounts of labor and capital found in the two countries differ, with labor abundant in Foreign and capital abundant in Home.
Assumption 4: There is free international trade in goods.
Assumption 5: The technologies for producing shoes and computers are the same across countries.
Assumption 6: Tastes are the same across countries.

Assumptions 1 to 3 allowed us to draw the PPFs of the two countries as illustrated in Figure 4-2, and in conjunction with assumptions 5 and 6, they allowed us to determine that the no-trade relative price of computers in Home was lower than the no-trade relative price of computers in Foreign; that is, $(P_C/P_S)^A$ was less than $(P_C^*/P_S^*)^{A^*}$. This key result enabled us to determine the starting points for the Home export supply curve for computers (point A) and the Foreign import demand curve for computers (point A^*) in panel (b) of Figures 4-3 and 4-4. Using those starting points, we put together the upward-sloping Home export supply curve and downward-sloping foreign import demand curve. We see from Figure 4-5 that the relative price of computers in the free-trade equilibrium lies between the no-trade relative prices (which confirms the expectation we had when drawing Figures 4-3 and 4-4).

Therefore, when Home opens to trade, its relative price of computers rises from the no-trade equilibrium relative price $(P_C/P_S)^A$ to the free-trade equilibrium price $(P_C/P_S)^W$, giving Home firms an incentive to export computers. That is, higher prices give Home an incentive to produce more computers than it wants to consume and export the difference. Similarly, when Foreign opens to trade, its relative price of computers falls from the no-trade equilibrium price $(P_C^*/P_S^*)^{A^*}$, to the trade equilibrium price $(P_C/P_S)^W$, encouraging Foreign consumers to import computers from Home. That is, lower prices give Foreign an incentive to consume more computers than it wants to produce and import the difference.

You might think that the Heckscher–Ohlin theorem is somewhat obvious. It makes sense that countries will export goods that are produced easily because the factors of production are found in abundance. It turns out, however, that this prediction does not always work in practice, as we discuss in the next section.

2 Testing the Heckscher–Ohlin Model

The first test of the Heckscher–Ohlin theorem was performed by economist Wassily Leontief in 1953, using data for the United States from 1947. We describe his test in the next section and show that he reached a surprising conclusion, which is called

Leontief's paradox. After that, we discuss more recent data for many countries that can be used to test the Heckscher–Ohlin model.

Leontief's Paradox

To test the Heckscher–Ohlin theorem, Leontief measured the amounts of labor and capital used in all industries needed to produce $1 million of U.S. exports and to produce $1 million of imports into the United States. His results are shown in Table 4-1.

Leontief first measured the amount of capital and labor required in the production of $1 million worth of U.S. exports. To arrive at these figures, Leontief measured the labor and capital used *directly* in the production of final good exports in each industry. He also measured the labor and capital used *indirectly* in the industries that produced the intermediate inputs used in making the exports. From the first row of Table 4-1, we see that $2.55 million worth of capital was used to produce $1 million of exports. This amount of capital seems much too high, until we recognize that what is being measured is the *stock* of capital in the United States that will be used to produce $1 million of exports for many years, which is larger than the part of the capital stock that was *used up* to produce exports that year: the capital used up that year to produce $1 million of exports would be measured by the *depreciation* on the capital stock. For labor, 182 person-years were used to produce the exports. Taking the ratio of these, we find that each person employed (directly or indirectly) in producing exports was working with $14,000 worth of capital.

Turning to the import side of the calculation, Leontief immediately ran into a problem—he could not measure the amount of labor and capital used to produce imports because he didn't have data on foreign technologies. To get around this difficulty, Leontief did what many researchers have done since—he simply used the data on U.S. technology to calculate estimated amounts of labor and capital used in imports from abroad. Does this approach invalidate Leontief's test of the Heckscher–Ohlin model? Not really, because the Heckscher–Ohlin model assumes that technologies are the same across countries, so Leontief is building this assumption into the calculations needed to test the theorem.

Using U.S. technology to measure the labor and capital used directly and indirectly in producing imports, Leontief arrived at the estimates in the last column of Table 4-1: $3.1 million of capital and 170 person-years were used in the production of $1 million worth of U.S. imports, so the capital–labor ratio for imports was $18,200 per worker. Notice that this amount *exceeds* the capital–labor ratio for exports of $14,000 per worker, so the United States is importing the capital-intensive good. This result

---

TABLE 4-1

Leontief's Test Leontief used the numbers in this table to test the Heckscher–Ohlin theorem. Each column shows the amount of capital or labor needed to produce $1 million worth of exports from, or imports into, the United States in 1947. As shown in the last row, the capital–labor ratio for exports was less than the capital–labor ratio for imports, which is a paradoxical finding because it shows that the United States is importing rather than exporting capital-intensive goods.

	Exports	Imports
Capital ($ millions)	2.55	3.1
Labor (person-years)	182	170
Capital/labor ($/person)	14,000	18,200

Data from: Wassily Leontief, 1953, "Domestic Production and Foreign Trade: The American Capital Position Re-examined," Proceedings of the American Philosophical Society, 97, September, 332–349. Reprinted in Richard Caves and Harry G. Johnson, eds., 1968, Readings in International Economics *(Homewood, IL: Irwin).*

presented Leontief with a paradox: if we assume that the United States was abundant in capital in 1947, then the Heckscher–Ohlin theorem predicts that the United States should be *exporting* capital-intensive goods, whereas the results in Table 4-1 show that the United States was *importing* capital-intensive goods.

Given the devastation of the capital stock in Europe and Japan due to World War II, Leontief supposed that in 1947 the United States was abundant in capital relative to the rest of the world. Thus, from the Heckscher–Ohlin theorem, Leontief expected that the United States would export capital-intensive goods and import labor-intensive goods. What Leontief actually found, however, was just the opposite: the capital–labor ratio for U.S. imports was *higher* than the capital–labor ratio found for U.S. exports, indicating that the United States was importing rather than exporting the capital-intensive goods. This finding contradicted the Heckscher–Ohlin theorem and came to be called Leontief's paradox.

Explanations Many explanations have been offered for Leontief's paradox, including the following:

- U.S. and foreign technologies were not the same, in contrast to what the Heckscher–Ohlin theorem and Leontief assumed.

- By focusing only on labor and capital, Leontief ignored land abundance in the United States.

- Leontief should have distinguished between high-skilled and low-skilled labor (because it would not be surprising to find that U.S. exports are intensive in high-skilled labor).

- The data for 1947 may be unusual because World War II had ended just two years earlier, and so trade patterns may have been unusual.

- Because of import tariffs between countries, the United States was not engaged in completely free trade, as the Heckscher–Ohlin theorem assumes.

Several additional possible explanations for the Leontief paradox depend on having more than two factors of production. The United States is abundant in land, for example, and that might explain why in 1947 it was exporting labor-intensive products: these might have been agricultural products, which use land intensively and, in 1947, might also have used labor intensively. By ignoring land, Leontief was therefore not performing an accurate test of the Heckscher–Ohlin theorem. Alternatively, it might be that the United States was mainly exporting goods that used skilled labor. This is certainly true today, with the United States being a leading exporter of high-technology products, and was probably also true in 1947. By not distinguishing between high-skilled versus low-skilled labor, Leontief was again giving an inaccurate picture of the factors of production used in U.S. trade.

Research in later years aimed to redo the test that Leontief performed, while taking into account land, high-skilled versus low-skilled labor, checking whether the Heckscher–Ohlin theorem holds in other years, and so on. We now discuss the data that can be used to test the Heckscher–Ohlin theorem in a more recent year—2017.

Factor Endowments in 2017

In Figure 4-6, we show the country shares of six factors of production and world GDP in 2017, broken down by select countries (the United States, China, Japan, India, Germany, the United Kingdom, France, and Canada) and then the rest of the world. To determine whether a country is abundant in a certain factor, we compare the country's share of that factor with its share of world GDP. If its share of a factor exceeds its share of world GDP, then we conclude that the country is **abundant in that factor**, and if its share in a certain factor is less than its share of world GDP, then

FIGURE 4-6

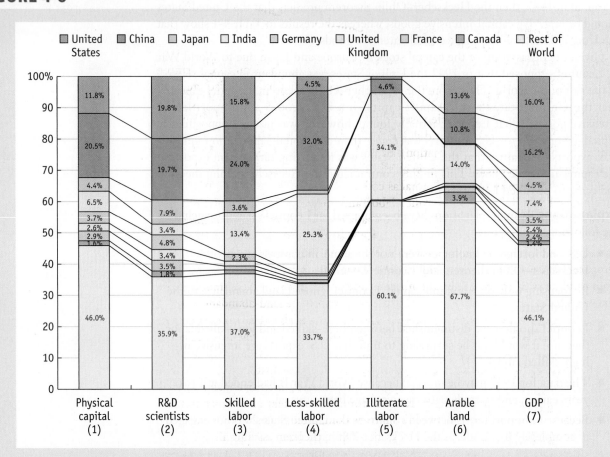

Country Factor Endowments, 2017 Shown here are country shares of six factors of production and GDP in the year 2017, for eight selected countries and the rest of the world. In the first bar graph, we see that 11.8% of the world's physical capital in 2017 was located in the United States, with 20.5% located in China, 4.4% located in Japan, and so on. In the final bar graph, we see that in 2017 the United States had 16.0% of world GDP, China had 16.2%, Japan had 4.5%, and so on. When a country's factor share is larger than its share of GDP, then the country is abundant in that factor, and when a country's factor share is less than its share of GDP, then the country is scarce in that factor.

Data from:
1) *PWT (Penn World Trade) version 9.1 (University of Groningen and University of California, Davis).*
2) *The product of R&D researchers per million and total population (World Bank, World Development Indicators).*
3) *Labor force with tertiary education (World Bank, World Development Indicators).*
4) *Labor force with primary and/or secondary education (World Bank, World Development Indicators).*
5) *The product of one minus the adult literacy rate and the adult population (World Bank, World Development Indicators).*
6) *Hectares of arable land (World Bank, World Development Indicators).*
7) *Gross domestic product converted to 2017 dollars using purchasing power parity rates (PWT version 9.1, University of Groningen and University of California, Davis).*

we conclude that the country is **scarce in that factor**. This definition allows us to calculate factor abundance in a setting with as many factors and countries as we want.

Capital Abundance In the first bar of Figure 4-6, we see that in 2017, 11.8% of the world's physical capital was located in the United States, with 20.5% located in China, 4.4% in Japan, 6.5% in India, 3.7% in Germany, and so on. When we compare these numbers with the final bar in the graph, which shows each country's percentage of world GDP, we see that in 2017 the United States had 16.0% of world GDP, China had 16.2%, Japan 4.5%, India 7.4%, Germany 3.5%, and so on. Because the United States had 11.8% of the world's capital and 16.0% of world GDP, we can conclude that the United States was scarce in physical capital in 2017. China, on the other hand, was abundant in physical capital: it had 20.5% of the world's capital and produced 16.2% of the world's GDP. Japan had 4.4% of the world's capital and 4.5% of world GDP in 2017, so it was slightly scarce in capital, while India had 6.5% of the world's capital and 7.4% of world GDP, so it was clearly scarce in capital. Germany, the United Kingdom, France, and Canada were all slightly abundant in capital, while the group of countries in the rest of the world were slightly scarce. In many of these cases, however, the differences between their capital shares and GDP shares are so slight that they are nearly neutral in capital.

Labor and Land Abundance We can use a similar comparison to determine whether each country is abundant in R&D scientists, in types of labor distinguished by skill, in arable land, or any other factor of production. For example, the United States was abundant in R&D scientists in 2017 (with 19.8% of the world's total as compared with 16.0% of the world's GDP), slightly scarce in skilled labor (workers with more than a high school education), and very scarce in less-skilled labor (workers with a high school education or less) and illiterate labor. India was scarce in R&D scientists (with 3.4% of the world's total as compared with 7.4% of the world's GDP) but abundant in skilled labor, less-skilled labor, and illiterate labor (with shares of the world's total that exceed its GDP share). Canada was abundant in arable land (with 3.9% of the world's total as compared with 1.4% of the world's GDP), as we would expect. But the United States was scarce in arable land (13.6% of the world's total as compared with 16.0% of the world's GDP). That is a surprising result because we often think of the United States as a major exporter of agricultural commodities, so from the Heckscher–Ohlin theorem, we would expect it to be land-abundant.

Another surprising result in Figure 4-6 is that China was abundant in research and development (R&D) scientists: it had 19.7% of the world's R&D scientists, as compared with 16.2% of the world's GDP in 2017. This finding also seems to contradict the Heckscher–Ohlin theorem, because we think of China as historically exporting greater quantities of basic manufactured goods than research-intensive manufactured goods. That historical trade pattern follows from China's clear abundance in less-skilled labor, with 32.0% of the world's share as compared to 16.2% of the world's GDP. For the past decade or two, however, China has been rapidly investing in research capabilities at its universities, state-owned companies, and private companies. It could be that these investments have allowed China to become abundant in R&D scientists, and if so, we should ask when this factor abundance first occurred. In addition, we should ask whether the facilities available to these R&D scientists in China are comparable to those in United States, so that scientists in the two countries have the same productivities.

To answer these questions, we need to compare the factor endowments in 2017 to earlier years and consider whether an R&D scientist or an acre of arable land has the same productivity in all countries. If it does not have the same productivity, then our measures of factor abundance are misleading: if an R&D scientist in the United States is more productive than their counterpart in China, then it does not make sense to just compare each country's share of these scientists with each country's share of GDP. Similarly, if an acre of arable land is more productive in the United States than in other countries, then we should not compare the share of land in each country with each country's share of GDP. Instead, we need to make some adjustment for the differing productivities of R&D scientists and land across countries and over time. In other words, we need to abandon the original Heckscher–Ohlin assumption (assumption 5) that technologies are identical in all countries.

Evolution of Factor Endowments in China and the United States

Leontief himself suggested that we should abandon the assumption that technologies are the same across countries and instead allow for differing productivities, as in the Ricardian model. Remember that in the original formulation of the paradox, Leontief had found that the United States was exporting labor-intensive products even though it was capital-abundant at that time. One explanation for this outcome would be that labor is highly productive in the United States and less productive in the rest of the world. If that is the case, then the **effective labor force** in the United States, which equals the labor force times its productivity (which measures how much output the labor force can produce), is much larger than it appears to be when we just count people. If labor is more productive in the United States, then the United States is abundant in *skilled* labor (like R&D scientists), and it should be no surprise that it is exporting labor-intensive products.

We now explore how differing productivities can be introduced into the Heckscher–Ohlin model. In addition to allowing labor productivity to differ across countries, we can also allow the productivity of land and other factors of production to differ across countries.

Revisiting How to Measure Factor Abundance To allow factors of production to differ in their productivities across countries, we define the **effective factor endowment** as the actual amount of a factor found in a country times its productivity:

Effective factor endowment = Actual factor endowment · Factor productivity

The amount of an effective factor found in the world is obtained by adding up the effective factor endowments across all countries. Then to determine whether a country is abundant in a certain factor, we compare the country's share of that *effective* factor with its share of world GDP. If its share of an effective factor exceeds its share of world GDP, then we conclude that the country is **abundant in that effective factor**; if its share of an effective factor is less than its share of world GDP, then we conclude that the country is **scarce in that effective factor**. We can illustrate this approach to measuring effective factor endowments using two examples: R&D scientists and arable land.

Effective R&D Scientists The productivity of an R&D scientist depends on the laboratory equipment, computers, and other types of material with which the scientist has to work. R&D scientists working in different countries will not necessarily have the same productivities because the equipment they have available to them differs. A simple way to measure the equipment they have available is to look at a country's *R&D spending per scientist*. If a country has more R&D spending per scientist, then its productivity will be higher, but if there is less R&D spending per scientist, then its productivity will be lower. To measure the effective number of R&D scientists in each country, we take the total number of scientists and multiply that by the R&D spending per scientist:

Effective R&D scientists = Actual number of R&D scientists · R&D spending per scientist

Using the R&D spending per scientist in this way to obtain effective R&D scientists is one method to correct for differences in the productivity of scientists across countries. It is not the only way to make such a correction because there are other measures that could be used for the productivity of scientists (e.g., we could use scientific publications available in a country, or the number of research universities). The advantage of using R&D spending per scientist is that this information is collected annually for many countries, so using this method to obtain a measure of effective R&D scientists means that we can easily compare the share of each country with the world total.[6]

Effective Arable Land As we did for R&D scientists, we also need to correct arable land for its differing productivity across countries. To make this correction, we use a

---

[6] Notice that by correcting the number of R&D scientists by the R&D spending per scientist, we end up with the total R&D spending in each country: Effective R&D scientists = Actual R&D scientists · R&D spending per scientist = Total R&D spending. So a country's share of effective R&D scientists equals its share of world R&D spending.

measure of agricultural productivity in each country. Then the effective amount of arable land found in a country is

Effective arable land = Actual arable land · Productivity in agriculture

We will not discuss here the exact method for measuring productivity in agriculture, except to say that it compares the output in each country with the inputs of labor, capital, and land: countries with higher output as compared with inputs are the more productive, and countries with lower output as compared with inputs are the less productive. The United States has very high productivity in agriculture, whereas China has lower productivity.

The Evolution of Capital in China In Figure 4-7, we show the actual and the "effective" factor endowments for China. We begin by looking at the capital endowment, even though that factor of production is not corrected for productivity. In the first bar, we report the share of the world capital stock that is found in China, in the years 2000, 2010, 2013, and 2017. China's share of the world capital stock has more

FIGURE 4-7

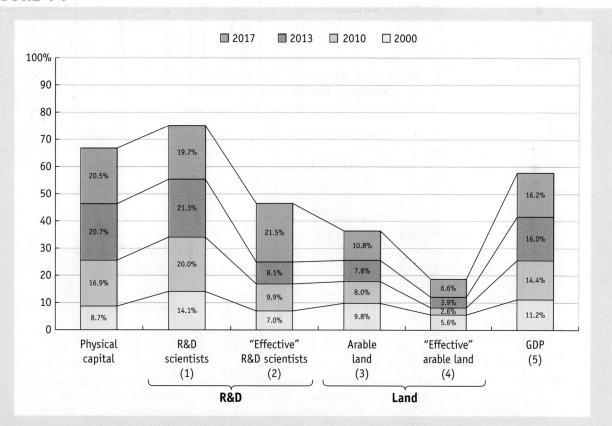

Actual and Effective Factor Endowments, China, 2000–2017 Shown here are the actual endowments in capital, R&D scientists, and arable land for China, as well as the effective factor endowments in R&D scientists and arable land for China, in selected years from 2000 to 2017. Also shown is China's share of world GDP. China's share of the world capital endowment has more than doubled, from 8.7% in 2000 to 20.5% in 2017 (the same share seen in Figure 4-6). Its share of R&D scientists has been at about 20% since 2010, but its *effective* share of R&D scientists has been at that level only since 2017. So China's abundance in R&D scientists is a recent phenomenon.

We also see here that China is very scarce in effective arable land.

Data from: In addition to the notes in Table 4-6, the data sources are:
1) The product of R&D researchers per million and total population (World Bank, World Development Indicators).
2) R&D expenditure in units of purchasing power parity (World Bank, World Development Indicators, and PWT version 9.1, University of Groningen).
3) Hectares of arable land (World Bank, World Development Indicators).
4) Productivity adjustment based on agriculture TFP (Total Factor Productivity) estimation.
5) Gross domestic product converted to 2011 dollars using purchasing power parity rates (PWT version 9.0, University of Groningen).

than doubled from 2000 to 2017. China's share of the world capital stock was less than its share of world GDP in 2000, but then exceeded its share of world GDP in 2010 and later years. So China was scarce in capital in 2000, but it has been abundant in capital since 2010.

Is China Really Abundant in R&D Scientists? In the second bar of Figure 4-7, we show China's share of R&D scientists. That share has been at about 20% since 2010. In 2017, China's share of effective R&D scientists was even a bit higher (21.5%), which exceeded its share of world GDP. So China really was abundant in R&D scientists in 2017! But that is a very recent phenomenon. China's share of effective R&D scientists was much smaller than its actual share in 2000, 2010, and 2013: only 7% to 10% in those years, which was less than its share of GDP. Thus, China was scarce in effective R&D scientists in those earlier years. The high amount of spending on research and development in recent years in China has paid off in moving it from being scarce to abundant in R&D scientists.

How does China's effective endowment of R&D scientists compare with the United States? In Figure 4-8, we show the actual and the effective factor endowments for the United States. This figure is organized the same way as Figure 4-7. The first bar shows the share of the world capital stock found in United States; the second bar shows the share of actual R&D scientists in the United States; and the third bar shows the share of effective

FIGURE 4-8

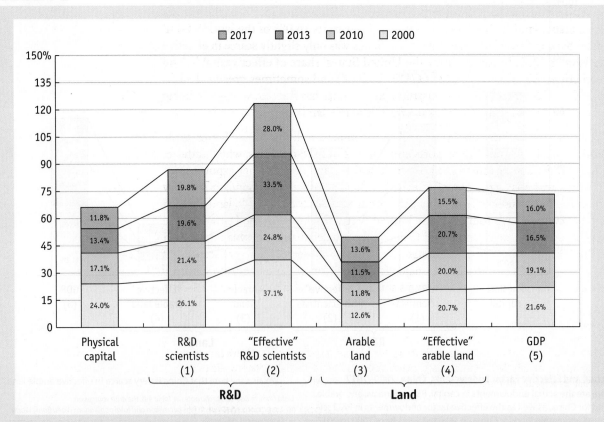

Actual and Effective Factor Endowments, United States, 2000–2017 Shown here are the actual endowments in capital, R&D scientists, and land, as well as the effective factor endowments for R&D scientists and land, in selected years from 2000 to 2017. The United States' share of the world capital endowment has fallen over time, as other countries have grown in capital. Its shares of effective R&D scientists and effective arable land have always exceeded its shares of actual R&D scientists and arable land. Comparing the United States' share of effective arable land with its share of GDP, it has fluctuated between being scarce and abundant.

Notes: See Table 4-7.

R&D scientists found in the United States. In all years, the United States' share of effective R&D scientists greatly exceeded its share of actual R&D scientists. That was never the case in China, except in 2017, when China's effective share of R&D scientists was slightly greater than its actual share. Because the United States' share of effective R&D scientists is so much greater than its actual share, we can conclude that the spending on each R&D scientist is much higher in the United States than in China. Still, both countries were abundant in that effective factor in 2017, so we can expect that they will be competing to produce the same types of high-technology goods.

The Evolution of Capital in the United States In the first bar of Figure 4-8, we report the share of the world capital stock found in United States. In 2000, the United States was abundant in capital because its share of the world capital stock (24.0%) exceeded its share of world GDP (21.6%). In 2010 and later years, however, the United States was scarce in capital. Remember that between the years 2000 and 2010, China went from scarce to abundant in capital. These two findings for China and for the United States are linked: the United States' share of the world capital endowment has fallen over time as China's has grown. That linkage occurs because as China accumulates more capital, the world total increases, and so the United States has a smaller share of that total.

Is the United States Scarce in Arable Land? Let us turn now to the question of whether the United States is scarce in arable land. In the fourth bar of Figure 4-8, we show the United States' share of actual arable land in 2017 as 13.6%, as also shown in Figure 4-6. In the fifth bar, we show the United States' share of effective arable land, corrected for productivity differences. The United States had 15.5% of the world's effective arable land in 2017, which is much closer to its 16.0% of the world's GDP (the final bar). We conclude that the United States was only slightly scarce in effective arable land in 2017. In earlier years, the United States' share of effective arable land was sometimes less than its share of GDP (in 2000) and sometimes greater than its share of GDP (2010 and 2013). Thus, the United States has fluctuated between being slightly scarce and slightly abundant in effective arable land.

U.S. Trade in Food How does this conclusion compare with the United States' trade pattern? Table 4-2 shows U.S. exports and imports of food products, which indicate that U.S. food trade has fluctuated between positive and negative net exports since 2000. This pattern is suggestive of an exporter that is neither very abundant nor very scarce in the factor used intensively in the production of food—arable land—which is exactly what we have found for the United States. Included in food products are exports of soybeans, for example, and China is the top destination for this export item from the United States. So even though the United States is neither very scarce nor abundant in arable land, it is still a major food exporter to China because China is very scarce in arable land (as shown by its small shares of arable land in Figure 4-7).

TABLE 4-2

U.S. Food Trade, 2000–2017 This table shows that U.S. food trade has fluctuated between positive and negative net exports since 2000. This is consistent with our finding that the United States is neither very abundant nor very scarce in arable land.

	U.S. FOOD TRADE (BILLIONS U.S.$)						
	2000	**2003**	**2006**	**2009**	**2012**	**2015**	**2017**
Exports	47.9	55.0	66.0	93.9	133.0	127.7	132.7
Imports	46.5	56.5	76.1	82.9	111.1	128.8	138.8
Net exports	1.4	−1.2	−10.1	11.0	21.9	−1.0	−6.1

Data from: U.S. food trade data, Bureau of Economic Analysis.

Leontief's Paradox Once Again

Our discussion of factor endowments in 2017 and earlier years shows that it is possible for countries to be abundant in more than one factor of production: China, for example, was abundant in capital, effective R&D scientists, skilled labor, and less-skilled labor in 2017 (see Figure 4-6). We have also found that it is sometimes important to correct the actual amount of a factor of production for its productivity, obtaining the effective factor endowment. Now we can apply these ideas to the United States in 1947 to reexamine the Leontief paradox.

A sample of 30 countries for which GDP information is available for 1947 has shown that the U.S. share of those countries' GDP was 37%. That estimate of the U.S. share of "world" GDP is shown in the last bar of Figure 4-9. To determine whether the United States was abundant in physical capital or labor, we need to estimate its share of the world endowments of these factors.

Capital Abundance It is hard to estimate the U.S. share of the world capital stock in the postwar years. But given the devastation of the capital stock in Europe and Japan due to World War II, we can presume that the U.S. share of world capital was more than 37%. That estimate (or really a "guesstimate") means that the U.S. share of world capital exceeds the U.S. share of world GDP, so that the United States was abundant in capital in 1947.

Labor Abundance What about the abundance of labor for the United States? If we do not correct labor for productivity differences across countries, then the population of each country is a rough measure of its labor force. The U.S. share of population for the sample of 30 countries in 1947 was very small, as shown in the first bar of Figure 4-9. This estimate of labor abundance is much less than the U.S. share of GDP. According to that comparison, then, the United States was scarce in labor (its share of that factor was less than its share of GDP).

FIGURE 4-9

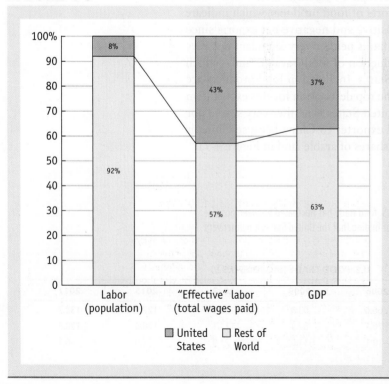

Labor Endowment and GDP for the United States and Rest of World, 1947 Shown here are the share of labor, "effective" labor, and GDP of the United States and the rest of the world (measured by 30 countries for which data are available) in 1947. The United States had only 8% of the world's population, as compared with 37% of the world's GDP, so it was very scarce in labor. If we measure effective labor by the total wages paid in each country, however, then the United States had 43% of the world's effective labor as compared with 37% of GDP, so it was abundant in effective labor.

Data from: Author's own calculations.

Labor Productivity Using the U.S. share of population is not the right way to measure the U.S. labor endowment, however, because it does not correct for differences in the productivity of labor across countries. A good way to make that correction is to use wages paid to workers as a measure of their productivity. To illustrate why this is a good approach, in Figure 4-10 we plot the wages of workers in various countries and the estimated productivity of workers in 1990. The vertical axis in Figure 4-10 measures wages earned across a sample of 33 countries relative to (i.e., as a percentage of) the United States. Only one country—Canada—has wages higher than those in the United States (probably reflecting greater union presence in that country). All other countries have lower wages.

The horizontal axis in Figure 4-10 measures labor productivity in various countries relative to that in the United States and shows that in 1990, productivity in all these countries was less than that in the United States. Notice that the labor productivities (on the horizontal axis) and wages (on the vertical axis) are highly correlated across countries: the points in Figure 4-10 line up approximately along the 45-degree line. This close connection between wages and labor productivity holds for the data in

FIGURE 4-10

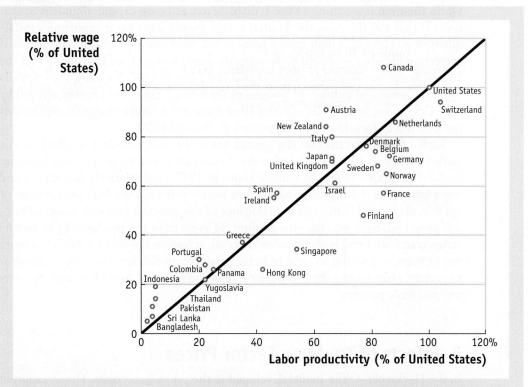

Labor Wages and Productivity in 1990 Shown here are estimated wages (vertical axis) and labor productivities (horizontal axis) across countries, relative to the United States. Only one country—Canada—had wages higher than those in the United States. All other countries had lower wages, ranging from Austria and Switzerland with wages that were about 95% of the U.S. wage; to Ireland, France, and Finland, with wages at about 50% of the U.S. level; to Bangladesh and Sri Lanka, with wages at about 5% of the U.S. level. Labor productivity in Canada was 80% of that in the United States; labor productivity in Austria and New Zealand was about 60% of that in the United States; and labor productivity in Indonesia, Thailand, Pakistan, Sri Lanka, and Bangladesh was about 5% of that in the United States. Notice that labor and wages were highly correlated across countries: the points roughly line up along the 45-degree line.

Data from: Daniel Trefler, 1993, "International Factor Price Differences: Leontief Was Right!" Journal of Political Economy, 101(6), December, 961–987.

1990; we expect that it also held in 1947, so that we can use wages to adjust for labor productivity in explaining the Leontief paradox.

Effective Labor Abundance As suggested by Figure 4-10, wages across countries are strongly correlated with labor productivity. Going back to the data for 1947 that Leontief used, if we use the wages earned by labor to measure the productivity of labor in each country, then the *effective* amount of labor found in each country equals the actual amount of labor times the wage. By multiplying the amount of labor in each country by average wages, we obtain total wages paid to labor. That information is available for 30 countries in 1947, and we have already found that the United States accounted for 37% of the GDP of these countries, as shown in the final bar in Figure 4-9. Adding up total wages paid to labor across the 30 countries and comparing it with the United States, we find that the United States accounted for 43% of wages paid to labor in these 30 countries, as shown in the bar labeled "effective" labor. By comparing this estimate with the United States' share of world GDP of 37% in 1947, we see that the United States was abundant in effective labor. So not only was the United States abundant in capital, it was also abundant in effective—or skilled—labor in 1947!

Summary When Leontief tested the Heckscher–Ohlin theorem, he found that the capital–labor ratio for exports from the United States in 1947 was less than the capital–labor ratio for imports. That finding seemed to contradict the Heckscher–Ohlin theorem if we think of the United States as being capital-abundant at that time: if that *was* the case, the United States should have been exporting capital-intensive goods (with a high capital–labor ratio). After examining additional data (and correcting for labor productivity by using its wage), however, we have found that the United States was abundant in *both* capital and labor in 1947. Basically, the relatively low population and number of workers in the United States are boosted upward by high U.S. wages, making the effective labor force much larger—large enough so that the U.S. share of worldwide wages exceeds its share of GDP.

Such a finding means that the United States was *also* abundant in effective—or skilled—labor in 1947. Armed with this finding, it is not surprising that Leontief found that exports from the United States in 1947 used relatively less capital and more labor than did imports: that pattern simply reflected the high productivity of labor in the United States and its abundance of this effective factor. As Leontief himself proposed, once we take into account differences in the productivity of factors across countries, there is no "paradox" after all, at least in the data for 1947. For more recent years, too, taking account of factor productivity differences across countries is important when testing the Heckscher–Ohlin theorem and using it to explain international trade patterns.

3 Effects of Trade on Factor Prices

In the Heckscher–Ohlin model developed in the previous sections, Home exported computers and Foreign exported shoes. Furthermore, we found in our model that the relative price of computers *rose* in Home from the no-trade equilibrium to the trade equilibrium (this higher relative price with trade is why computers are exported). Conversely, the relative price of computers *fell* in Foreign from the no-trade equilibrium to the trade equilibrium (this lower relative price with trade is why computers are imported abroad). The question we ask now is how the changes in the relative prices of goods affect the wage paid to labor in each country and the rental earned by capital. We begin by showing how the wage and rental are determined, focusing on Home.

Effect of Trade on the Wage and Rental of Home

To determine the wage and rental, we go back to Figure 4-1, which showed that the quantity of labor demanded relative to the quantity of capital demanded in each industry in Home depends on the relative wage in Home W/R. We can use these relative demands for labor in each industry to derive an economy-wide relative demand for labor, which can then be compared with the economy-wide relative supply of labor $\overline{L}/\overline{K}$. By comparing the economy-wide relative demand and supply, just as we do in any supply and demand context, we can determine Home's relative wage. Moreover, we can evaluate what happens to the relative wage when the Home relative price of computers rises after Home starts trading.

Economy-Wide Relative Demand for Labor To derive an economy-wide relative demand for labor, we use the conditions that the quantities of labor and capital used in each industry add up to the total available labor and capital: $L_C + L_S = \overline{L}$ and $K_C + K_S = \overline{K}$. We can divide total labor by total capital to get

$$\underbrace{\frac{\overline{L}}{\overline{K}}}_{\substack{\text{Relative} \\ \text{supply}}} = \frac{L_C + L_S}{\overline{K}} = \underbrace{\frac{L_C}{K_C} \cdot \left(\frac{K_C}{\overline{K}}\right) + \frac{L_S}{K_S} \cdot \left(\frac{K_S}{\overline{K}}\right)}_{\substack{\text{Relative} \\ \text{demand}}}$$

The left-hand side of this equation is the economy-wide supply of labor relative to capital, or relative supply. The right-hand side is the economy-wide demand for labor relative to capital, or relative demand. The relative demand is a weighted average of the labor–capital ratio in each industry. This weighted average is obtained by multiplying the labor–capital ratio for each industry, L_C/K_C and L_S/K_S, by the terms $K_C/\overline{K}$ and $K_S/\overline{K}$, the shares of total capital employed in each industry. These two terms must add up to 1, $(K_C/\overline{K}) + (K_S/\overline{K}) = 1$, because capital must be employed in one industry or the other.

The determination of Home's equilibrium relative wage is shown in Figure 4-11 as the intersection of the relative supply and relative demand curves. The supply of labor relative to the supply of capital, the relative supply $(\overline{L}/\overline{K})$, is shown as a vertical line because the total amounts of labor and capital do not depend on the relative wage; they are fixed by the total amount of factor resources in each country. Because the relative demand (the RD curve in the graph) is an average of the L_C/K_C and L_S/K_S curves from Figure 4-1, it therefore lies *between* these two curves. The point at which relative

FIGURE 4-11

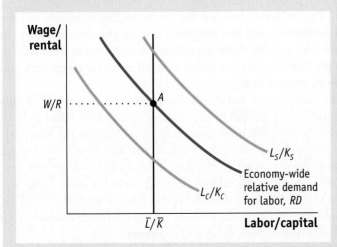

Determination of Home Wage/Rental The economy-wide relative demand for labor, *RD*, is an average of the L_C/K_C and L_S/K_S curves and lies between these curves. The relative supply, $\overline{L}/\overline{K}$, is shown by a vertical line because the total amount of resources in Home is fixed. The equilibrium point *A*, at which relative demand *RD* intersects relative supply $\overline{L}/\overline{K}$, determines the wage relative to the rental, *W/R*.

FIGURE 4-12

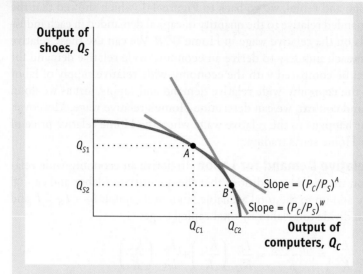

Increase in the Price of Computers Initially, Home is at a no-trade equilibrium at point *A* with a relative price of computers of $(P_C/P_S)^A$. An increase in the relative price of computers to the world price, as illustrated by the steeper world price line, $(P_C/P_S)^W$, shifts production from point *A* to *B*. At point *B*, there is a higher output of computers and a lower output of shoes, $Q_{C2} > Q_{C1}$ and $Q_{S2} < Q_{S1}$.

demand intersects relative supply, point *A*, tells us that the wage relative to the rental is *W/R* (from the vertical axis). Point *A* describes an equilibrium in the labor and capital markets and combines these two markets into a single diagram by showing relative supply equal to relative demand.

Increase in the Relative Price of Computers When Home opens itself to trade, it faces a higher relative price of computers; that is, P_C/P_S increases in Home. We illustrate this higher relative price using Home's production possibilities frontier in Figure 4-12. At the no-trade or autarky equilibrium, point *A*, the relative price of computers is $(P_C/P_S)^A$ and the computer industry produces Q_{C1}, while the shoe industry produces Q_{S1}. With a rise in the relative price of computers to $(P_C/P_S)^W$, the computer industry increases its output to Q_{C2}, and the shoe industry decreases its output to Q_{S2}. With this shift in production, labor and capital both move from shoe production to computer production. What is the effect of these resource movements on the relative supply and relative demand for labor?

The effects are shown in Figure 4-13. Relative supply $\overline{L}/\overline{K}$ is the same as before because the total amounts of labor and capital available in Home have not changed. The relative demand for labor changes, however, because capital has shifted to the computer industry. This shift affects the terms used in the weighted average: $(K_C/\overline{K})$ rises and $(K_S/\overline{K})$ falls. The relative demand for labor in the economy is now more weighted toward computers and less weighted toward the shoe industry. In Figure 4-13, the change in the weights shifts the relative demand curve from RD_1 to RD_2. The curve shifts in the direction of the relative demand curve for computers, and the equilibrium moves from point *A* to *B*.

The impacts on all the variables are as follows. First, the relative wage *W/R* falls from $(W/R)_1$ to $(W/R)_2$, reflecting the fall in the relative demand for labor as both factors move into computer production from shoe production. Second, the lower relative wage induces *both* industries to hire more workers per unit of capital (a move down along their relative demand curves). In the shoe industry, for instance, the new, lower relative wage $(W/R)_2$ intersects the relative demand curve for labor L_S/K_S at a point corresponding to a higher *L/K* level than the initial relative wage $(W/R)_1$. That is, $(L_S/K_S)_2 > (L_S/K_S)_1$, and the same argument holds for the computer industry. As a result, the labor–capital ratio rises in both shoes and computers.

How is it possible for the labor–capital ratio to rise in both industries when the amount of labor and capital available in total is fixed? The answer is that more labor per unit of

FIGURE 4-13

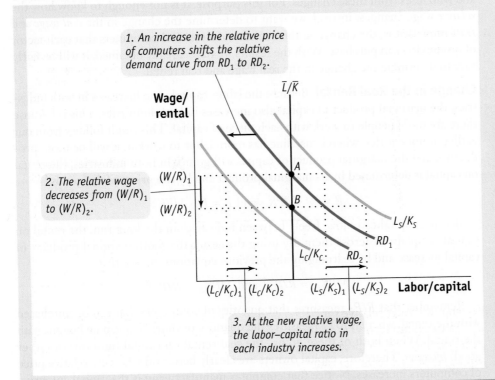

1. An increase in the relative price of computers shifts the relative demand curve from RD_1 to RD_2.

2. The relative wage decreases from $(W/R)_1$ to $(W/R)_2$.

3. At the new relative wage, the labor–capital ratio in each industry increases.

Effect of a Higher Relative Price of Computers on Wage/Rental An increase in the relative price of computers shifts the economy-wide relative demand for labor, RD_1, toward the relative demand for labor in the computer industry, L_C/K_C. The new relative demand curve, RD_2, intersects the relative supply curve for labor at a lower relative wage, $(W/R)_2$. As a result, the wage relative to the rental falls from $(W/R)_1$ to $(W/R)_2$. The lower relative wage causes both industries to increase their labor–capital ratios, as illustrated by the increase in both L_C/K_C and L_S/K_S at the new relative wage.

capital is released from shoes than is needed to operate that capital in computers (because computers require fewer workers per machine). As the relative price of computers rises, computer output rises while shoe output falls, and labor is "freed up" to be used more in both industries. In terms of our earlier equation for relative supply and relative demand, the changes in response to the increase in the relative price of computers P_C/P_S are

$$
\underbrace{\frac{\overline{L}}{\overline{K}}}_{\substack{\text{Relative supply} \\ \text{No change}}} = \underbrace{\frac{L_C}{K_C} \cdot \left(\frac{K_C}{\overline{K}}\right) + \frac{L_S}{K_S} \cdot \left(\frac{K_S}{\overline{K}}\right)}_{\substack{\text{Relative demand} \\ \text{No change in total}}}
$$

$$\uparrow \qquad \uparrow \qquad \uparrow \qquad \downarrow$$

The relative supply of labor has not changed, so relative demand for labor cannot change overall. Because some of the individual components of relative demand have increased, other components must decrease to keep the overall relative demand the same. After the rise in the price of computers, even more capital will be used in the computer industry ($K_C/\overline{K}$ rises while $K_S/\overline{K}$ falls) because the output of computers rises and the output of shoes falls. This shift in weights on the right-hand side pulls down the overall relative demand for labor (this is necessarily true since $L_C/K_C < L_S/K_S$ by assumption). But because the relative supply on the left-hand side doesn't change, another feature must increase the relative demand for labor: this feature is the increased labor–capital ratios in *both* industries. In this way, relative demand continues to equal relative supply at point B, and at the same time, the labor–capital ratios have risen in both industries.

Determination of the Real Wage and Real Rental

To summarize, we have found that an increase in the relative price of computers—which are capital-intensive—leads to a fall in the relative wage (W/R). In turn, the decrease in the relative wage leads to an increase in the labor–capital ratio used in each industry (L_C/K_C and L_S/K_S). Our goal in this section is to determine who gains and who loses from these changes. For this purpose, it is not enough to know how the *relative* wage changes; instead, we want to determine the change in the *real wage* and *real rental:* that is, the change in the quantity of shoes and computers that each factor of production can purchase. With the results we have already obtained, it will be fairly easy to determine the change in the real wage and real rental.

Change in the Real Rental Because the labor–capital ratio increases in both industries, the marginal product of capital also increases in both industries. This is because there are more people to work with each piece of capital. This result follows from our earlier argument that when a machine has more labor to work it, it will be more productive, and the marginal product of capital will go up. In both industries, the rental on capital is determined by its marginal product and by the prices of the goods:

$$R = P_C \cdot MPK_C \text{ and } R = P_S \cdot MPK_S$$

Because capital can move freely between industries in the long run, the rental on capital is equalized across them. By using the result that both marginal products of capital increase and by rearranging the previous equations, we see that

$$MPK_C = R/P_C \uparrow \text{ and } MPK_S = R/P_S \uparrow$$

Remember that R/P_C measures that quantity of computers that can be purchased with the rental, whereas R/P_S measures the quantity of shoes that can be bought with the rental. When both of these go up, the real rental on capital (in terms of either good) *increases.* Therefore, capital owners are clearly better off when the relative price of computers increases. Notice that computer manufacturing is the capital-intensive industry, so the more general result is that *an increase in the relative price of a good will benefit the factor of production used intensively in producing that good.*

Change in the Real Wage To understand what happens to the real wage when the relative price of computers rises, we again use the result that the labor–capital ratio increases in *both* industries. The law of diminishing returns tells us that the marginal product of labor must fall in both industries (since there are more workers on each machine). In both industries, the wage is determined by the marginal product of labor and the prices of the goods:

$$W = P_C \cdot MPL_C \text{ and } W = P_S \cdot MPL_S$$

Using the result that the marginal product of labor falls in both industries, we see that

$$MPL_C = W/P_C \downarrow \text{ and } MPL_S = W/P_S \downarrow$$

Therefore, the quantity of computers that can be purchased with the wage (W/P_C) and the quantity of shoes that can be purchased with the wage (W/P_S) both fall. These decreases mean that the real wage (in terms of either good) is *reduced*, and labor is clearly worse off because of the increase in the relative price of computers.

We can summarize our results with the following theorem, first derived by economists Wolfgang Stolper and Paul Samuelson.

Stolper–Samuelson Theorem: In the long run, when all factors are mobile, an increase in the relative price of a good will increase the real earnings of the factor used intensively in the production of that good and decrease the real earnings of the other factor.

For our example, the **Stolper–Samuelson theorem** predicts that when Home opens to trade and faces a higher relative price of computers, the real rental on capital in Home rises and the real wage in Home falls. In Foreign, the changes in real factor prices are just the reverse. When Foreign opens to trade and faces a lower relative price of computers, the real rental falls and the real wage rises. Remember that Foreign is abundant in labor, so our finding that labor is better off there, but worse off in Home, means that workers in

SIDE BAR

Does International Trade Reduce Poverty and Income Inequality?

We have found that in the Heckscher–Ohlin model, the abundant factor gains from trade, and the scarce factor loses from trade. As an example, suppose that the abundant factor is low-skilled labor and the scarce factor is high-skilled labor. Then the Heckscher–Ohlin model predicts that trade will lead to a rise in the earnings of low-skilled labor. If some of those workers were in poverty, then a rise in their wage means a *reduction in poverty*. In addition, the Heckscher–Ohlin model predicts that trade will lead to a fall in the earnings of high-skilled labor. That change means that the earnings of low- and high-skilled workers will become more similar, so that *income inequality will be reduced*. Moving from this example to the real world, how has international trade affected poverty and income inequality?

The example in which low-skilled labor is the abundant factor and high-skilled labor is the scarce factor applies to China up until the year 2013. In that year, China had 13.9% of the world's skilled labor and 39.8% of the world's less-skilled labor, as compared to 16.0% of the world GDP, so it was scarce in high-skilled labor and abundant in less-skilled labor. The same pattern holds for China in earlier years. According to the Heckscher–Ohlin model, less-skilled labor in China will gain from trade, which reduces poverty for those workers. Because the population of China is so large, raising the income of the poorest workers in China is enough to reduce poverty on a global basis. That is the conclusion of the *Economist*, which reports that the number of people in extreme poverty in the world—meaning those who live on less than $1.25 per day—was cut by about one-half over the past 20 years, from 43% of the world's population in 1990 to 21% in 2010. *the Economist* attributes much of this achievement to China:

China is responsible for about three-quarters of the achievement. Its economy has been growing so fast that, even though income inequality is rising fast, extreme poverty is disappearing. China pulled 680 million people out of misery in 1981–2010, and reduced its extreme-poverty rate from 84% to 10%. . . . [T]he biggest poverty-reduction measure of all is liberalizing markets to let poor people get richer. That means free trade between countries and within them (China's real great leap forward occurred because it allowed private business to grow).[7]

This evidence from China shows that global poverty has fallen due to free trade. But what about income inequality *within* countries? The above quotation from the *Economist* points out that within China, income inequality has actually been increasing: those with higher incomes are gaining more than those with lower incomes. The same is true in the United States.[8] So in both countries, high-skilled workers have been gaining more than low-skilled workers. That result is not what we expect from the Heckscher–Ohlin model, which predicts that skilled labor, which was scarce in China up until 2013, would lose from trade, but it has not. In the United States, skilled labor is the abundant factor, so the Heckscher–Ohlin model predicts that it should gain from trade, as it has. In Chapter 7, we develop a different model of trade in which high-skilled workers gain more than low-skilled workers in both countries, an outcome that is consistent with rising inequality of income in both China and the United States. Despite that rise in inequality within countries, global poverty has been reduced worldwide because of China's opening to trade.

---

[7] Republished with permission of the *Economist*. From "Towards the End of Poverty," *Economist*, June 1, 2013. Permission conveyed through Copyright Clearance Center, Inc.

[8] In 2016, the real incomes of those in the highest 1% in the United States had more than tripled since 1979, while the real income of those in the middle 20% had increased by only 41% "Elizabeth's Warren's Many Plans Would Reshape American Capitalism," *Economist*, Print edition, October 24, 2019.

---

the labor-abundant country gain from trade but workers in the capital-abundant country lose. In addition, capital in the capital-abundant country (Home) gains, and capital in the labor-abundant country loses. These results are sometimes summarized by saying that in the Heckscher–Ohlin model, *the abundant factor gains from trade, and the scarce factor loses from trade*. Some evidence on this prediction is discussed in **Side Bar: Does International Trade Reduce Poverty and Income Inequality?**

Changes in the Real Wage and Rental: A Numerical Example

To illustrate the Stolper–Samuelson theorem, we use a numerical example to show how much the real wage and rental can change in response to a change in price. Suppose that the computer and shoe industries have the following data:

Computers: Sales revenue = $P_C \cdot Q_C = 100$

Earnings of labor = $W \cdot L_C = 50$

Earnings of capital = $R \cdot K_C = 50$

Shoes: Sales revenue $= P_S \cdot Q_S = 100$

Earnings of labor $= W \cdot L_S = 60$

Earnings of capital $= R \cdot K_S = 40$

Notice that shoes are more labor-intensive than computers: the share of total revenue paid to labor in shoes (60/100 = 60%) is more than that share in computers (50/100 = 50%).

When Home and Foreign undertake trade, the relative price of computers rises. For simplicity we assume that this occurs because the price of computers P_C rises while the price of shoes P_S does not change:

Computers: Percentage increase in price $= \Delta P_C / P_C = 10\%$

Shoes: Percentage increase in price $= \Delta P_S / P_S = 0\%$

Our goal is to see how the increase in the relative price of computers translates into long-run changes in the wage W paid to labor and the rental on capital R. Remember that the rental on capital can be calculated by taking total sales revenue in each industry, subtracting the payments to labor, and dividing by the amount of capital. This calculation gives us the following formulas for the rental in each industry:[9]

$$R = \frac{P_C \cdot Q_C - W \cdot L_C}{K_C}, \text{ for computers}$$

$$R = \frac{P_S \cdot Q_S - W \cdot L_S}{K_S}, \text{ for shoes}$$

The price of computers has risen, so $\Delta P_C > 0$, holding fixed the price of shoes, $\Delta P_S = 0$. We can trace through how this affects the rental by changing P_C and W in the previous two equations:

$$\Delta R = \frac{\Delta P_C \cdot Q_C - \Delta W \cdot L_C}{K_C}, \text{ for computers}$$

$$\Delta R = \frac{0 \cdot Q_C - \Delta W \cdot L_S}{K_S}, \text{ for shoes}$$

It is convenient to work with percentage changes in the variables. For computers, $\Delta P_C / P_C$ is the percentage change in price. Similarly, $\Delta W / W$ is the percentage change in the wage, and $\Delta R / R$ is the percentage change in the rental of capital. We can introduce these terms into the preceding formulas by rewriting them as

$$\frac{\Delta R}{R} = \left(\frac{\Delta P_C}{P_C}\right)\left(\frac{P_C \cdot Q_C}{R \cdot K_C}\right) - \left(\frac{\Delta W}{W}\right)\left(\frac{W \cdot L_C}{R \cdot K_C}\right), \text{ for computers}$$

$$\frac{\Delta R}{R} = -\left(\frac{\Delta W}{W}\right)\left(\frac{W \cdot L_S}{R \cdot K_S}\right), \text{ for shoes}$$

(You should cancel terms in these equations to check that they are the same as before.)

Now we'll plug the above data for shoes and computers into these formulas:

$$\frac{\Delta R}{R} = 10\% \cdot \left(\frac{100}{50}\right) - \left(\frac{\Delta W}{W}\right)\left(\frac{50}{50}\right), \text{ for computers}$$

$$\frac{\Delta R}{R} = -\left(\frac{\Delta W}{W}\right)\left(\frac{60}{40}\right), \text{ for shoes}$$

---

[9] Remember that because of factor mobility, the rental is the same in each industry, but it is helpful here to derive two separate equations for the percentage change in rental by industry.

Our goal is to find out by how much rentals and wages change given changes in the relative price of the final goods, so we are trying to solve for two unknowns ($\Delta R/R$ and $\Delta W/W$) from the two equations given here. A good way to do this is to reduce the two equations with two unknowns into a single equation with one unknown. This can be done by subtracting one equation from the other, as follows:

$$\frac{\Delta R}{R} = 10\% \cdot \left(\frac{100}{50}\right) - \left(\frac{\Delta W}{W}\right)\left(\frac{50}{50}\right), \text{ for computers}$$

$$\text{Minus: } \frac{\Delta R}{R} = 0 - \left(\frac{\Delta W}{W}\right)\left(\frac{60}{40}\right), \text{ for shoes}$$

$$\text{Equals: } 0 = 10\% \cdot \left(\frac{100}{50}\right) + \left(\frac{\Delta W}{W}\right)\left(\frac{20}{40}\right)$$

Simplifying the last equation, we get $0 = 20\% + \left(\frac{\Delta W}{W}\right)\left(\frac{1}{2}\right)$, so that

$$\left(\frac{\Delta W}{W}\right) = \frac{-20\%}{\left(\frac{1}{2}\right)} = -40\%, \text{ is the change in wages}$$

So when the price of computers increases by 10%, the wage falls by 40%. With the wage falling, labor can no longer afford to buy as many computers (W/P_C has fallen since W is falling and P_C has increased) or as many pairs of shoes (W/P_S has fallen since W is falling and P_S has not changed). In other words, the *real wage* measured in terms of either good has *fallen*, so labor is clearly worse off.

To find the change in the rental paid to capital ($\Delta R/R$), we can take our solution for $\Delta W/W = -40\%$, and plug it into the equation for the change in the rental in the shoes sector:[10]

$$\frac{\Delta R}{R} = -\left(\frac{\Delta W}{W}\right)\left(\frac{60}{40}\right) = 40\% \cdot \left(\frac{60}{40}\right) = 60\%, \text{ change in rental}$$

The rental on capital increases by 60% when the price of computers rises by 10%, so the rental increases even more (in percentage terms) than the price. Because the rental increases by more than the price of computers in percentage terms, it follows that (R/P_C) rises: owners of capital can afford to buy more computers, even though their price has gone up. In addition, they can afford to buy more shoes (R/P_S also rises, since R rises and P_S is constant). Thus, the real rental measured in terms of either good has *gone up*, and capital owners are clearly better off.

General Equation for the Long-Run Change in Factor Prices The long-run results of a change in factor prices can be summarized in the following equation:

$$\underbrace{\Delta W/W < 0}_{\substack{\text{Real wage} \\ \text{falls}}} \underbrace{< \Delta P_C/P_C < \Delta R/R}_{\substack{\text{Real rental} \\ \text{increases}}}, \text{ for an increase in } P_C$$

That is, the increase in the price of computers (10%) leads to an even larger increase in the rental on capital (60%) and a decrease in the wage (–40%). If, instead, the price of computers falls, then these inequalities are reversed, and we get

$$\underbrace{\Delta R/R < \Delta P_C/P_C < 0}_{\substack{\text{Real rental} \\ \text{falls}}} \underbrace{< \Delta W/W}_{\substack{\text{Real wage} \\ \text{increases}}}, \text{ for a decrease in } P_C$$

What happens if the relative price of shoes increases? From the Stolper–Samuelson theorem, we know that this change will benefit labor, which is used intensively in shoe

[10] You should check that you get the same answer if instead you plug the change in the wage into the formula for the change in the rental in the computer sector.

production, and will harm capital. The equation summarizing the changes in factor earnings when the price of shoes increases is

$$\underbrace{\Delta R/R < 0}_{\substack{\text{Real rental} \\ \text{falls}}} < \Delta P_S/P_S < \underbrace{\Delta W/W}_{\substack{\text{Real wage} \\ \text{increases}}}, \text{ for an increase in } P_S$$

These equations relating the changes in product prices to changes in factor prices are sometimes called the "magnification effect" because they show how changes in the prices of goods have *magnified effects* on the earnings of factors: even a modest fluctuation in the relative prices of goods on world markets can lead to exaggerated changes in the long-run earnings of both factors. This result tells us that some groups—those employed intensively in export industries—can be expected to support opening an economy to trade because an increase in export prices increases their real earnings. But other groups—those employed intensively in import industries—can be expected to oppose free trade because the decrease in import prices decreases their real earnings.

4 Conclusions

The Heckscher–Ohlin model is one of the most widely used models in explaining trade patterns. This framework isolates the effect of different factor endowments across countries and determines the impact of these differences on trade patterns, relative prices of goods between countries, and factor returns. The Heckscher–Ohlin model predicts that countries export the goods that use their abundant factor intensively. This approach is a major departure from the Ricardian model's view that technology differences determine trade patterns and is also a departure from the short-run specific-factors model that we studied in Chapter 3, which focused on factor returns in the short run rather than on trade patterns.

In this chapter, we have investigated some empirical tests of the Heckscher–Ohlin theorem, that is, tests to determine whether countries actually export the goods that use their abundant factor intensively. The body of literature testing the theorem originates in Leontief's puzzling finding that U.S. exports just after World War II were relatively labor-intensive. Although the original formulation of his test did not seem to support the Heckscher–Ohlin theorem, later research has reformulated the test to measure the effective endowments of labor, capital, and other factors found in each country. Using this approach, we found that the United States was abundant in effective labor in 1947. It is therefore not surprising that the United States was exporting goods that had a higher labor–capital ratio than goods that it was importing. Thus once we define factors as effective factors by taking into account the productivity of those factors, the trade patterns we observe are consistent with both the Heckscher–Ohlin predictions and Leontief's findings, so there was really no "paradox" after all.

In the present time, adjusting factors of production for their productivity is important when we measure countries' abundance or scarcity in effective factors. We have found that between 2000 and 2017 the United States was sometimes slightly abundant in effective arable land and sometimes slightly scarce. The change from being abundant to scarce has occurred because the rest of the world has improved the productivity of its land, so that the United States' share of the world's effective arable land has fallen slightly. Consistent with this finding, over these years the United States has sometimes been a net exporter of food and sometimes a net importer of food.

Adjusting the stock of R&D scientists for their productivity (which we measured by the country's spending on the equipment used by each R&D scientist) is also very important. From 2000 to 2013, China was scarce in effective R&D scientists because

China's spending on R&D equipment did not keep up with the spending of other countries. That finding changed in 2017, however, when China was abundant in effective R&D scientists. The United States still has a greater share of the world's effective R&D scientists than does China, but the gap between these two countries in this factor of production is shrinking. From the Heckscher–Ohlin theorem, we would therefore expect that the United States will face increasing competition from China in high-technology products that use R&D scientists intensively.

By focusing on the factor intensities among goods (i.e., the relative amount of labor and capital used in production), the Heckscher–Ohlin (HO) model also explains who gains and who loses from the opening of trade. In the specific-factors model, an increase in the relative price of a good leads to real gains for the specific factor used in that industry, losses for the other specific factor, and an ambiguous change in the real wage for labor. In contrast, the HO model predicts real gains for the factor used intensively in the export good, whose relative price goes up with the opening of trade, and real losses for the other factor. Having just two factors, both of which are fully mobile between the industries, leads to a very clear prediction about who gains and who loses from trade in the long run.

KEY POINTS

1. In the Heckscher–Ohlin model, we assume that the technologies are the same across countries and that countries trade because the available resources (labor, capital, and land) differ across countries.

2. Unlike the short-run specific-factors model, in which capital and land resources cannot move between industries, the Heckscher–Ohlin model is a long-run framework that assumes that labor, capital, and other resources can move freely between the industries.

3. With two goods, two factors, and two countries, the Heckscher–Ohlin model predicts that a country will export the good that uses its abundant factor intensively and import the other good.

4. The first test of the Heckscher–Ohlin model was made by Leontief using U.S. data for 1947. He found that U.S. exports were less capital-intensive and more labor-intensive than U.S. imports. This was a paradoxical finding because the United States was abundant in capital.

5. The assumption of identical technologies used in the Heckscher–Ohlin model does not hold in practice. Current research has extended the empirical tests of the Heckscher–Ohlin model to allow for many factors and countries, along with differing productivities of factors across countries. When we allow for different productivities of labor in 1947, we find that the United States is abundant in effective—or skilled—labor, which explains the Leontief paradox.

6. According to the Stolper–Samuelson theorem, an increase in the relative price of a good will cause the real earnings of labor and capital to move in opposite directions: the factor used intensively in the industry that makes the good whose relative price goes up will find its earnings increased, and the real earnings of the other factor will fall.

7. Putting together the Heckscher–Ohlin theorem and the Stolper–Samuelson theorem, we conclude that a country's abundant factor gains from the opening of trade (because the relative price of exports goes up), and its scarce factor loses from the opening of trade.

KEY TERMS

Heckscher–Ohlin model, p. 91
reversal of factor intensities, p. 95
free-trade equilibrium, p. 100
Heckscher–Ohlin theorem, p. 101
Leontief's paradox, p. 102

abundant in that factor, p. 103
scarce in that factor, p. 104
effective labor force, p. 106
effective factor endowment,
  p. 106

abundant in that effective factor,
  p. 106
scarce in that effective factor, p. 106
Stolper–Samuelson theorem, p. 116

PROBLEMS

1. **Discovering Data** In this problem you will learn how to download data for U.S. exports and imports for highly disaggregated products. Suppose that you are hired by a company that wants to start exporting the product it already sells in the United States. You are asked to find out how much is already sold abroad by other U.S. firms and to which countries. To answer this question, you can access the "Trade Stats Express" database at the International Trade Administration, U.S. Department of Commerce.

a. Access the U.S. TradeStats Express website at tse.export.gov/tse/tsehome.aspx. Click on "National Trade Data" and then "Product Profiles of U.S. Merchandise Trade with a Selected Market." You will be asked to select a "Trade Partner", which can be a "Geographic region"; and to select a "Product" along with its "flow" (Exports, Imports, or Trade Balance) and "item" with a Change button. Click this Change button and you will find several methods of keeping track of items, one of which is called the Harmonized System (HS).

U.S. Exports and Imports for 2018

HS Code	Product	Region or Country	Export ($ thousands)	Import ($ thousands)
09	Coffee, Tea, Mate, and Spices	Africa	6,206	875,990
0901	Coffee, Coffee Husks, etc.	Africa	778	284,422
0902	Tea, Whether or Not Flavored	Africa	867	33,894
0903	Mate	Africa	6	0
0904	Pepper, Genus Piper, etc.	Africa	562	4,130
0905	Vanilla Beans	Africa	1,754	531,170
0906	Cinnamon and Tree Flowers	Africa	45	41
0907	Cloves (Whole Fruit, etc.)	Africa	0	2,636
0908	Nutmeg, Mace, and Cardamoms	Africa	85	40
0909	Seeds: Anise, Badian, Fennel, Coriander, etc.; Juniper Berries	Africa	53	10,952
0910	Ginger, Saffron, Turmeric, Thyme, Bay Leaves, etc.	Africa	2,054	8,702

Choose any two-digit HS code that you like, from HS 01 to HS 99. For the product you have selected, choose a region of the world and a recent year, and write down in a table the U.S. exports to that region of the two-digit and detailed four-digit products that are shown (see an example for HS 09 in the table).

b. Repeat the same exercise for the imports to the United States from that region for the HS products that are shown (see table).

c. Now from the Trade Partner menu, choose at least one specific country in the region that you have chosen, and write down the U.S. exports and imports for the same HS products.

d. Do you think that the U.S. exports and imports for the region/country/products you have chosen support the predictions of the Heckscher–Ohlin theorem? Explain why or why not. Do you think that there is potential for the U.S.

firm that hired you to begin exporting these products? Explain.

2. This problem uses the Heckscher–Ohlin model to predict the direction of trade. Consider the production of handmade rugs and assembly-line robots in Canada and India.

a. Which country would you expect to be relatively labor-abundant, and which is capital-abundant? Why?

b. Which industry would you expect to be relatively labor-intensive, and which is capital-intensive? Why?

c. Given your answers to parts (a) and (b), draw production possibilities frontiers for each country. Assuming that consumer preferences are the same in both countries, add indifference curves and relative price lines (without trade) to your PPF graphs. What do the slopes of the price lines tell you about the direction of trade?

d. Allowing for trade between countries, redraw the graphs and include a "trade triangle" for each country. Identify and label the vertical and horizontal sides of the triangles as either imports or exports.

e. Using the PPF graphs from part (c) and relative prices under autarky and trade, explain how both countries gain from trade.

3. Leontief's paradox is an example of testing a trade model using actual data observations. If Leontief had observed that the amount of labor needed per $1 million of U.S. exports was 100 person-years instead of 182, would he have reached the same conclusion? Explain.

WORK IT OUT   ⚡ Achieve | interactive activity

4. Suppose there are drastic technological improvements in shoe production in Home such that shoe factories can operate almost completely with computer-aided machines. Consider the following data for the Home country:

Computers: Sales revenue = $P_C Q_C = 100$

Payments to labor = $WL_C = 50$

Payments to capital = $RK_C = 50$

Percentage increase in the price = $\Delta P_C / P_C = 0\%$

Shoes: Sales revenue = $P_S Q_S = 100$

Payments to labor = $WL_S = 10$

Payments to capital = $RK_S = 90$

Percentage increase in the price = $\Delta P_S / P_S = 40\%$

a. Which industry is capital-intensive? Is this a reasonable question, given that some industries are capital-intensive in some countries and labor-intensive in others?

b. Given the percentage changes in output prices in the data provided, calculate the percentage change in the rental on capital.

c. How does the magnitude of this change compare with that of labor?

d. Which factor gains in real terms, and which factor loses? Are these results consistent with the Stolper–Samuelson theorem?

5. Using the information in the chapter, suppose Home doubles in size, while Foreign remains the same size. Show that an equal proportional increase in capital and labor in Home will change

the relative price of computers, wage, rental on capital, and the amount traded but not the pattern of trade.

6. In this chapter, we learned that China is abundant in less-skilled labor. Over time, it has changed from being scarce in physical capital to being abundant in physical capital, and it has also changed from being scarce in R&D scientists to being abundant in R&D scientists. To relate these changes to our two-good, two-factor model, suppose that labor represents less-skilled labor, which is used intensively in shoes, and capital represents physical capital or human capital (like R&D scientists), which is used intensively in computers. China starts off being abundant in labor and scarce in capital, whereas the United States starts off being scarce in labor and abundant in capital. Therefore, the United States is exporting computers and China is importing computers.

a. Suppose that China accumulates more capital. Show what happens to its production possibility frontier between computers and shoes. Based on this shift, what happens to its no-trade relative price of computers?

b. Treat China as the Foreign country in Figure 4-5, and based on your answer to part (a), show what happens to China's import demand curve for computers. Therefore, what happens to the equilibrium world relative price of computers with free trade?

c. Based on your answer to part (b), show how this change in the world relative price of computers affects production and consumption in the United States. Determine if utility in the United States goes up or down, and explain why. (*Hint*: the United States is exporting computers, so the world relative price of computers is the "terms of trade" for the United States. What has happened to its terms of trade?)

d. Instead of China accumulating capital in part (a), suppose that it raises its endowment of less-skilled labor (by moving less-skilled workers from the countryside into manufacturing, for example). Then redo parts (a), (b), and (c), starting with the increase in China's endowment of labor and no change in its endowment of capital.

7. Using a diagram similar to Figure 4-13, show the effect of a decrease in the relative price of computers, like what happens to Foreign in the chapter. What happens to the wage relative to the rental? Is there an increase in the labor–capital ratio in each industry? Explain.

8. Suppose that when Japan opens to trade, it imports rice, a labor-intensive good.

   a. According to the Heckscher–Ohlin theorem, is Japan capital-abundant or labor-abundant? Briefly explain.

   b. What is the impact of opening trade on the real wage in Japan?

   c. What is the impact of opening trade on the real rental on capital?

   d. Which group (capital owner or labor) would support policies to limit free trade? Briefly explain.

9. In Figure 4-3, we show how the movement from the no-trade equilibrium point A to a trade equilibrium at a higher relative price of computers leads to an upward-sloping export supply, from points A to D in panel (b).

   a. Suppose that the relative price of computers rises further in panel (a), and label the production and consumption points at several higher prices.

   b. In panel (b), extend the export supply curve to show the quantity of exports at the higher relative prices of computers.

   c. What happens to the export supply curve when the price of computers is high enough? Can you explain why this happens? (*Hint*: An increase in the relative price of a country's export good means that the country is richer because its terms of trade have improved.) Explain how that can lead to fewer exports as their price rises.

10. Following are data for soybean yield, production, and trade for 2010–2011. Suppose that the countries listed in the table are engaged in free trade and that soybean production is land-intensive. Answer the following:

    a. In which countries does land benefit from free trade in soybeans? Explain.

    b. In which countries does land lose from free trade in soybeans? Explain.

    c. In which countries does the move to free trade in soybeans have little or no effect on the land rental? Explain.

Country	Yield (metric tons/ hectare)	Production (100,000 metric tons)	Exports (100,000 metric tons)	Imports (100,000 metric tons)
Australia	1.71	0.29	0.025	0.007
Brazil	3.12	748.2	258	1.18
Canada	2.75	42.5	27.8	2.42
China	1.89	144	1.64	570
France	2.95	1.23	0.24	5.42
Japan	1.60	2.19	0.0006	34.6
Mexico	1.32	2.05	0.001	37.7
Russian Federation	1.48	17.6	0.008	10.7
United States	2.79	831	423	4.45

Data from: Food and Agriculture Organization.

11. According to the Heckscher–Ohlin model, two countries can equalize wage differences by either engaging in international trade in goods or allowing high-skilled and low-skilled labor to freely move between the two countries. Discuss whether this is true or false, and explain why.

12. According to the standard Heckscher–Ohlin model with two factors (capital and labor) and two goods, the movement of Turkish migrants to Germany would decrease the amount of capital-intensive products produced in Germany. Discuss whether this is true or false, and explain why.

5

Movement of Labor and Capital Between Countries

Amidst growing dissent, housing and job shortages as well as a plummeting economy, Cuban Premier Fidel Castro withdrew his guards from the Peruvian embassy in Havana on April 4, 1980. . . . Less than 48 hours after the guards were removed, throngs of Cubans crowded into the lushly landscaped gardens at the embassy, requesting asylum. . . . By mid-April, [U.S. president] Carter issued a Presidential Memorandum allowing up to 3,500 refugees sanctuary in the U.S. . . . But the Carter Administration was taken by surprise when on April 21, refugees started arriving on Florida's shores—their numbers would eventually reach 125,000.

"Memories of Mariel, 20 Years Later"[1]

The Guatemalan border with Chiapas [Mexico] is now our [the United States'] southern border.

Alan Bersin, U.S. Department of Homeland Security, 2011

If Europe fails on the question of refugees, then it won't be the Europe we wished for.

German Chancellor Angela Merkel, August 31, 2015

From May to September 1980, boatloads of refugees from Cuba arrived in Miami, Florida. For political reasons, Fidel Castro had allowed them to leave freely from the port of Mariel, Cuba, during that brief period. Known as "the Mariel boat lift," this influx of about 125,000 refugees to Miami increased the city's Cuban population by 20% and its overall population by about 7%. The widespread unemployment of many of the refugees during the summer of 1980 led many people to expect that the wages of other workers in Miami would be held down by the Mariel immigrants.

Not surprisingly, the refugees were less skilled than the other workers in Miami, as is confirmed by looking at their wages: the immigrants initially earned about one-third less than other Cubans in Miami. What is surprising, however, is that this influx of low-skilled immigrants does not appear to have pulled down the wages of

---

[1] Judy L. Silverstein, "Memories of Mariel, 20 Years Later," *U.S. Coast Guard Reservist*, 47(3), April/May 2000, electronic edition.

Cuban refugees sailing for
Miami, 1980.

other less-skilled workers in Miami.[2] The wages for low-skilled workers in Miami essentially followed national trends over this period, despite the large inflow of workers from Cuba. This finding seems to contradict the prediction of basic supply and demand theory—that a higher supply of workers should bid down their wage and that restricting immigration will raise the wages for local workers. The fact that wages in Miami did not respond to the inflow of Mariel refugees calls for an explanation, which is one goal of this chapter.

A similar sudden migration outcome occurred after 1989, when the Soviet Union relaxed its restrictions on the emigration of Russian Jews to Israel. From late 1989 to 1996, some 670,000 Russian Jews immigrated to Israel, which increased Israel's population by 11% and its workforce by 14%. This wave of immigration was especially notable because the Russian immigrants were more highly skilled than the existing Israeli population. But despite this large influx of immigrants, the relative wages of high-skilled workers in Israel actually *rose* during the 1990s. Careful studies of this episode can find little or no negative impact of the Russian immigrants on the wages of other high-skilled workers.[3]

These emigrations were of different types of workers—the Cuban emigrants were low-skilled and the Russian emigrants high-skilled—but they share the finding that large inflows of workers need not depress wages in the areas where they settle. In other cases of large-scale migration—such as occurred from Europe to America during the 1800s and 1900s—wages did indeed fall because of the inflow of immigrants. So the Mariel boat lift and Russian immigration to Israel should be seen as special cases in which the economic principles of supply and demand do not at first glance work as we would expect them to.

In this chapter, we begin our study of the movement of labor across countries by explaining the case in which immigration leads to a fall in wages, as we normally expect. The model we use is the **specific-factors model**, the short-run model introduced in Chapter 3. That model allows labor to move between industries but keeps capital and land specific to each industry. To study migration, we allow labor to move between countries as well as industries, while still keeping capital and land specific to each industry in each country.

Next, we use the long-run Heckscher–Ohlin model, from Chapter 4, in which capital can also move between industries in each country. In the long run, an increase in labor *will not* lower the wage, as illustrated by the Mariel boat lift to Miami and the Russian immigration to Israel. This outcome occurs because industries have more time to respond to the inflow of workers by adjusting their outputs. It turns out that by adjusting industry output enough, the economy can absorb the new workers without changing the wage for existing workers. The explanation for this surprising outcome relies on the assumption that industries are able to sell their outputs on international markets.

To give a brief idea of how this long-run explanation will work, think about the highly skilled scientists and engineers emigrating from Russia to Israel. The only

[2] See David Card, 1990, "The Impact of the Mariel Boatlift on the Miami Labor Market," *Industrial Labor Relations Review*, 43(2), 245–257; Giovanni Peri and Vasil Yasenov, 2019, "The Labor Market Effects of a Refugee Wave: Synthetic Control Method Meets the Mariel Boatlift," *The Journal of Human Resources*, 54(2), 267–309.
[3] See Neil Gandal, Gordon Hanson, and Matthew Slaughter, 2004, "Technology, Trade and Adjustment to Immigration in Israel," *European Economic Review*, 48(2), 403–428.

way to employ the large number of these workers at the going wages would be to increase the number of scientific and engineering projects in which Israeli companies are engaged. Where does the demand for these new projects come from? It is unlikely this demand would be generated in Israel alone, and more likely that it would come from Israeli *exports* to the rest of the world. We see then that the ability of Israel to export products making use of the highly skilled immigrants is essential to our explanation: with international demand, it is possible for the Russian immigrants to be fully employed in export activities in Israel without lowering wages. Likewise, with the influx of low-skilled Cuban immigrants to Miami, many of whom could work in the textile and apparel industry or in agriculture, it was the ability of Florida to export those products that allowed the workers to be employed at the going wages.

The effect of immigration on wages can be quite different in the short run and in the long run. In this chapter we demonstrate that difference, and discuss government policies related to immigration. Policies to restrict or to allow immigration are an important part of government regulation in every country. The United States and many countries in Europe have been struggling with a surge of immigrants who are often coming as **refugees**, meaning that they emigrate because they face persecution in their home countries. Some of the U.S. immigrants are coming from countries south of Mexico—from Guatemala, Honduras, and El Salvador—while some of the European immigrants have been coming from the Middle East and Africa. The challenge of accommodating this surge in refugees was anticipated in 2011 by an official at the U.S. Department of Homeland Security in the quote at the start of the chapter, as well as by German chancellor Angela Merkel in the quote from 2015.

After studying what happens when labor moves across countries, we study the effects of foreign direct investment (FDI), the movement of capital across countries. FDI occurs when a company from one country owns a company in another country. We conclude the chapter by discussing the gains to the source and destination countries, and to the world, from the movement of labor or capital between countries.

1 Movement of Labor Between Countries: Migration

Consider the examples of labor migration described earlier: the Mariel boat lift and the Russian migration to Israel. We can think of each migration as a movement of labor from the Foreign country to the Home country. What is the impact of this movement of labor on wages paid in Home? To answer this question, we make use of our work in Chapter 3, in which we studied how the wages paid to labor and the rentals paid to capital and land are determined by the prices of the goods produced. The prices of goods themselves are determined by supply and demand in world markets. In the analysis that follows, we treat the prices of goods as fixed and ask how the Home wage and the rentals paid to capital and land change as labor moves between countries.

Effects of Immigration in the Short Run: Specific-Factors Model

We begin our study of the effect of factor movements between countries by using the specific-factors model we learned in Chapter 3 to analyze the *short run*, when labor is mobile among Home industries but land and capital are fixed. After that, we consider the *long run*, when all factors are mobile among industries in Home.

Determining the Wage Figure 5-1 shows a diagram that we used in Chapter 3 to determine the equilibrium wage paid to labor. The horizontal axis measures the total amount of labor in the economy, $\overline{L}$, which consists of the labor used in manufacturing L_M and the amount used in agriculture L_A:

$$L_M + L_A = \overline{L}$$

In Figure 5-1, the amount of labor used in manufacturing L_M is measured from left (0_M) to right, and the amount of labor used in agriculture L_A is measured from right (0_A) to left.

The two curves in Figure 5-1 take the marginal product of labor in each sector and multiply it by the price (P_M or P_A) in that sector. The graph of $P_M \cdot MPL_M$ is downward-sloping because as more labor is used in manufacturing, the marginal product of labor in that industry declines, and wages fall. The graph of $P_A \cdot MPL_A$ for agriculture is upward-sloping because we are measuring the labor used in agriculture L_A from *right to left* in the diagram: as more labor is used in agriculture (moving from right to left), the marginal product of labor in agriculture falls, and wages fall.

The equilibrium wage is at point A, the intersection of the marginal product curves $P_M \cdot MPL_M$ and $P_A \cdot MPL_A$ in Figure 5-1. At this point, $0_M L$ units of labor are used in manufacturing, and firms in that industry are willing to pay the wage $W = P_M \cdot MPL_M$. In addition, $0_A L$ units of labor are used in agriculture, and farmers are willing to pay the wage $W = P_A \cdot MPL_A$. Because wages are equal in the two sectors, there is no reason for labor to move between them, and the Home labor market is in equilibrium.

In the Foreign country, a similar diagram applies. We do not draw this but assume that the equilibrium wage abroad W^* is less than W in Home. This assumption would apply to the Cuban refugees, for example, who moved to Miami and to the Russian emigrants who moved to Israel to earn higher wages as well as to enjoy more freedom. As a result of this difference in wages, workers from Foreign would want to immigrate to Home and the Home workforce would increase by an amount ΔL, reflecting the number of immigrants.

FIGURE 5-1

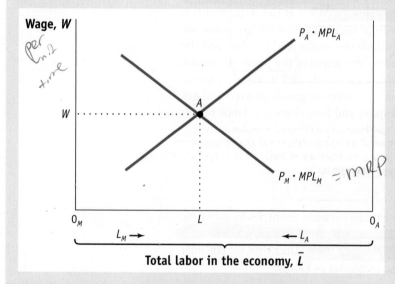

Home Labor Market The Home wage is determined at point A, the intersection of the marginal product of labor curves $P_M \cdot MPL_M$ and $P_A \cdot MPL_A$ in manufacturing and agriculture, respectively. The amount of labor used in manufacturing is measured from left to right, starting at the origin 0_M, and the amount of labor used in agriculture is measured from right to left, starting at the origin 0_A. At point A, $0_M L$ units of labor are used in manufacturing and $0_A L$ units of labor are used in agriculture.

Effect of Immigration on the Wage in Home The effects of immigration are shown in Figure 5-2. Because the number of workers in Home has grown by ΔL, we expand the size of the horizontal axis from $\overline{L}$ to $\overline{L}' = \overline{L} + \Delta L$. The right-most point on the horizontal axis, which is the origin 0_A for the agriculture industry, shifts to the right by the amount ΔL. As this origin moves rightward, it carries along with it the marginal product curve $P_A \cdot MPL_A$ for the agriculture industry (because the marginal product of labor curve is graphed relative to its origin). That curve shifts to the right by exactly the amount ΔL, the increase in the Home workforce. There is no shift in the marginal product curve $P_M \cdot MPL_M$ for the manufacturing industry because the origin 0_M for manufacturing has not changed.[4]

The new equilibrium Home wage is at point B, the intersection of the marginal product curves. At the new equilibrium, the wage is lower. Notice that the extra workers ΔL arriving in Home are shared between the agriculture and manufacturing industries: the number of workers employed in manufacturing is now $0_M L'$, which is higher than $0_M L$, and the number of workers employed in agriculture is $0_A' L'$, which is also higher than $0_A L$.[5] Because both industries have more workers but fixed amounts of capital and land, the wage in both industries declines due to the diminishing marginal product of labor.

FIGURE 5-2

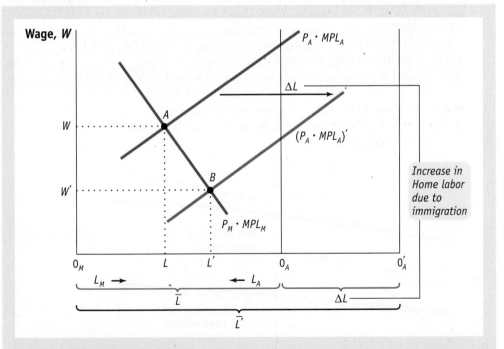

Increase in Home Labor When the amount of labor in Home increases by the amount ΔL, the origin for agriculture shifts to the right by that amount, from $0A$ to $0'A$. The marginal product of labor curve in agriculture also shifts right by the amount ΔL.

Equilibrium in the Home labor market is now at point B: wages have fallen to W' and the amount of labor has increased in manufacturing (to $0_M L'$) and in agriculture (to $0_A' L'$).

---

[4] If, instead, we had added labor to the left-hand side of the graph, the origin and marginal product curve for manufacturing would have shifted and those of agriculture would have remained the same, yielding the same final results as in Figure 5-2—the wage falls and both industries use more labor.
[5] We know that the number of workers employed in agriculture rises because the increase in workers in manufacturing, from $0_M L$ to $0_M L'$, is less than the total increase in labor ΔL.

We see, then, that the specific-factors model predicts that an inflow of labor will lower wages in the country in which the workers are arriving. This prediction has been confirmed in numerous episodes of large-scale immigration, as described in the applications that follow.

APPLICATION

Immigration to the New World

Between 1870 and 1913, some 30 million Europeans left their homes in the "Old World" to immigrate to the "New World" of North and South America and Australia. The population of Argentina rose by 60% because of immigration, and Australia and Canada gained 30% more people. The population of the United States increased by 17% as a result of immigration (and it absorbed the largest number of people, more than 15 million). The migrants left the Old World for the opportunities present in the New and, most important, for the higher real wages. In Figure 5-3, we show an index of average real wages in European countries and in the New World (an average of the United States, Canada, and Australia).[6] In 1870 real wages were nearly three times higher in the New World than in Europe—120 as compared with 40.

Real wages in both locations grew over time as capital accumulated and raised the marginal product of labor. But because of the large-scale immigration to the New World, wages grew more slowly there. By 1913, just before the onset of World War I, the wage index in the New World was at 160, so real wages had grown by $(160 - 120)/120 = 33\%$ over 43 years. In Europe, however, the wage index reached 75 by 1913, an increase of $(75 - 40)/40 = 88\%$ over 43 years. In 1870 real wages in the New World were three times as high as those in Europe, but by 1913 this wage gap was substantially reduced, and wages in the New World were only about twice as high as those in Europe. Large-scale migration therefore contributed to a "convergence" of real wages across the continents.

FIGURE 5-3

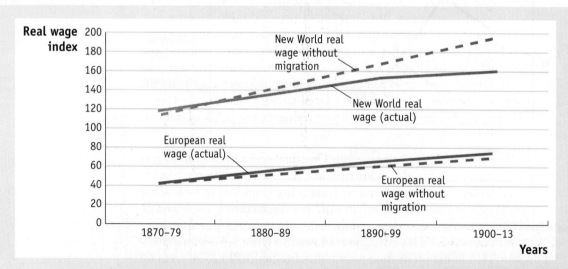

Wages in Europe and the New World Large-scale migration from Europe to the New World in America and Australia closed the wage gap between the two locations. In 1870 wages in the New World were almost three times as high as wages in Europe, whereas in 1910 they were about twice as high. Migration also slowed the growth of wages in the New World relative to what they would have been without migration and allowed for slightly faster growth of wages in Europe.

Data from: Alan M. Taylor and Jeffrey G. Williamson, 1997, "Convergence in the Age of Mass Migration," European Review of Economic History, 1, April, 27–63.

---

[6] From Alan M. Taylor and Jeffrey G. Williamson, 1997, "Convergence in the Age of Mass Migration," *European Review of Economic History*, 1, April, 27–63.

In Figure 5-3, we also show estimates of what real wages would have been if migration had not occurred. Those estimates are obtained by calculating how the marginal product of labor would have grown with capital accumulation but without the immigration. Comparing the actual real wages with the no-migration estimates, we see that the growth of wages in the New World was slowed by immigration (workers arriving), while wages in Europe grew slightly faster because of emigration (workers leaving).

Other Effects of Immigration in the Short Run

The United States and Europe have both welcomed foreign workers into specific industries, such as agriculture and the high-tech industry, even though these workers compete with domestic workers in those industries. This observation suggests that there must be benefits to the industries involved. We can measure the potential benefits by the payments to capital and land, which we refer to as "rentals." We saw in Chapter 3 that there are two ways to compute the rentals: either as the earnings left over in the industry after paying labor or as the marginal product of capital or land times the price of the good produced in each industry. Under either method, the owners of capital and land benefit from the reduction in wages due to immigration.

Rentals on Capital and Land Under the first method for computing the rentals, we take the revenue earned in either manufacturing or agriculture and subtract the payments to labor. If wages fall, then there is more left over as earnings of capital and land, so these rentals are higher. Under the second method for computing rentals, capital and land earn their marginal product in each industry times the price of the industry's good. As more labor is hired in each industry (because wages are lower), the marginal products of capital and land both increase. The increase in the marginal product occurs because each machine or acre of land has more workers available to it, and that machine or acre of land is therefore more productive. So under the second method, too, the marginal products of capital and land rise and so do their rentals.

From this line of reasoning, we should not be surprised that owners of capital and land often support more open borders, which provide them with foreign workers who can be employed in their industries. The restriction on immigration in a country should therefore be seen as a compromise between entrepreneurs and landowners who might welcome the foreign labor; local unions and workers who view migrants as a potential source of competition leading to lower wages; and the immigrant groups themselves, who if they are large enough (such as the Cuban population in Miami) might also have the ability to influence the political outcome on immigration policy.

Effect of Immigration on Industry Output One final effect of labor immigration is its effect on the output of the industries. In Figure 5-2, the increase in the labor force due to immigration led to more workers being employed in each of the industries: employment increased from $0_M L$ to $0_M L'$ in manufacturing and from $0_A L$ to $0'_A L'$ in agriculture. With more workers and the same amount of capital or land, the output of both industries rises. This outcome is shown in Figure 5-4—immigration leads to an outward shift in the production possibilities frontier (PPF). With constant prices of goods (as we assumed earlier, because prices are determined by world supply and demand), the output of the industries rises from point A to point B.

Although it may seem obvious that having more labor in an economy will increase the output of both industries, it turns out that this result depends on the short-run nature of the specific-factors model, when capital and land in each industry are fixed. If instead these resources can move between the industries, as would occur in the long run, then the output of one industry will increase but that of the other industry will decline, as we explain in the next section.

FIGURE 5-4

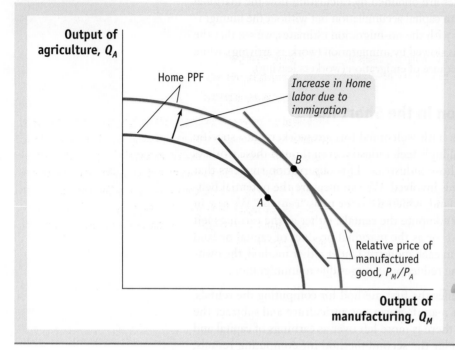

Shift in Home Production Possibilities Curve With the increase in labor in Home from immigration, the production possibilities frontier shifts outward and the output of both industries increases, from point *A* to point *B*. Output in both industries increases because of the short-run nature of the specific-factors model; in the short run, land and capital do not move between the industries, and the extra labor in the economy is shared between both industries.

APPLICATION

The Political Economy of Migration

Immigration into the United States In 1980, the year of the Mariel boat lift, the percentage of foreign-born people in the U.S. population was 6.2%. The percentage grew to 9.1% in 1990 and then to 13.0% in 2005, so there was slightly more than a doubling of foreign-born people in 25 years, from 1980 to 2005. That period saw the greatest recent increase in foreign-born people in the United States, and by 2017 the percentage had grown only slightly more, to 13.7%. See the explanation of who is foreign-born in **Side Bar: Who Is a Foreign-born Person?**

While most foreign-born people living in the United States are either citizens, permanent residents, or temporary residents, it is estimated that there are about 10.5 million undocumented migrants in the United States, and about one-half of these are Mexican citizens. Gaining control over U.S. borders is one goal of immigration policy, but focusing on that goal alone obscures the fact that the majority of immigrants who enter the United States each year are legal. Persons seeking to legally enter the United States sometimes must wait a very long time, because under current U.S. law, migrants from any one foreign country cannot number more than 7% of the green cards that are granted each year to those seeking to enter the United States permanently.

The potential competition that immigrants create for U.S. workers with the same educational level is illustrated in Figure 5-5. On the vertical axis we show the share of immigrants (legal and undocumented) as a percentage of the total workforce in the United States with that educational level. For example, the first bar shows that immigrants account for close to 40% of the total number of workers in the United States who do not have a high school education (the remaining 60%

Who Is a Foreign-born Person?

In the United States, the U.S. Census Bureau uses the following definitions of native-born and foreign-born persons. A native-born person is anyone who is a U.S. citizen at birth, which means that they are either:

- Born in the United States
- Born in Puerto Rico
- Born in a U.S. Island Area (for example, Guam)
- Born abroad of U.S. citizen parent(s)

A foreign-born person is anyone who *is not* a U.S. citizen at birth but who is living in the United States, which means that they are either:

- Naturalized U.S. citizens
- Legal permanent residents

- Temporary migrants
- Humanitarian migrants
- Unauthorized migrants

Naturalized U.S. citizens are entitled to hold a U.S. passport and to vote. Legal permanent residents are often referred to as *green card* holders, because that is the name of the document that they hold instead of a U.S. passport. Temporary migrants include those who are on student visas, temporary worker visas (such as the H-1B and H-2A), or other visa programs. Humanitarian migrants are also called *refugees*. Finally, unauthorized migrants are those that are in the United States without legal documentation; these people are also called undocumented migrants.

FIGURE 5-5

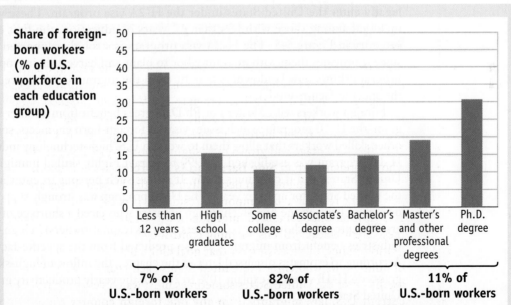

Share of Foreign-Born Workers in U.S. Workforce, 2017 This figure shows the share of foreign-born workers in the U.S. workforce, categorized by educational level. For example, among workers with 0 to 11 years of education, close to 40% were foreign-born. At the other end of the spectrum, the foreign-born make up nearly 20% of workers with Master's and professional degrees, and slightly more than 30% of those with Ph.D.'s. In the middle educational levels (high school and college graduates), there are much smaller shares of foreign-born workers, ranging from 10% to 15%. On the horizontal axis, we show the share of U.S.-born workers in each educational group. Only 7% of U.S.-born workers do not graduate from high school, while 11% obtain Master's, professional, or Ph.D. degrees; most U.S.-born workers are either high school graduates or college graduates.

Data from: 2017 American Community Survey, U.S. Census Bureau.

are U.S. born). Many of those immigrants without a high school education are undocumented, but we do not know the exact number. We do know, however, that the share of high school dropouts in the U.S.-born workforce is small: only 7% of workers born in the United States do not have a high school education. That percentage is shown on the horizontal axis of Figure 5-5. So, even though the topic of illegal immigration attracts much attention in the U.S. debate over immigration, those immigrants with less than high school education are competing with only a small share (7%) of U.S.-born workers.

As we move to the next bars in Figure 5-5, the story changes. A large portion of U.S.-born workers—81%, as shown on the horizontal axis—have completed high school, may have started college, or have graduated with an Associate's or Bachelor's degree. The shares of these educational groups that are composed of immigrants are small, ranging between 10% and 15% (the remainder being U.S.-born workers). So in these middle levels of education, immigrants are not numerous enough to create a significant amount of competition with U.S.-born workers for jobs.

At the other end of the spectrum, 11% of U.S.-born workers have Master's degrees or Ph.D.'s. Within this high-education group, foreign-born Master's-degree holders make up nearly 20% of the U.S. workforce, and foreign-born Ph.D.'s make up slightly more than 30% of the U.S. workforce. To summarize, Figure 5-5 shows that immigrants into the United States compete primarily with workers at the lowest and highest ends of the educational levels and much less with the majority of U.S.-born workers with mid-levels of education.

Special visa programs in the United States allow for workers to enter specific industries for certain periods. Some seasonal agricultural workers, for example, legally enter the United States under the H-2A visa program. These workers are included among those with less than 12 years of education, the first educational category in Figure 5-5. The H-2A visa program is strongly supported by farmers since it provides them with migrant labor to plant and harvest their crops. This visa program shows how landowners benefit from the migrants, just as predicted from the specific-factors model.

Foreign workers with Master's or Ph.D. degrees benefit from another special program, the H-1B program, which issues visas to foreign-born engineers, scientists, and other skilled workers that allow them to work in U.S. high-technology industries. The H-1B program was established in 1990 to attract highly skilled immigrants to the United States, and it continues today. It allows such persons to enter and work in the United States for up to six years. The H-1B program was strongly supported by the owners of firms in the high-technology industry who faced a shortage of U.S. workers. This program shows how the owners of firms (capital-owners) in high-technology industries benefit from migrants, as also predicted from the specific-factors model. According to estimates discussed later in the chapter, the inflow of high-skilled immigrants on H-1B visas can explain 10% to 20% of the yearly productivity growth in the United States.[7]

Illegal Immigration into the United States   As we pointed out earlier, the lowest educational group in Figure 5-5, workers with less than 12 years of education, has the greatest number of undocumented migrants, and about one-half of these are Mexican citizens. President Trump declared that there was a "crisis" of illegal immigration at the border with Mexico, and he used that crisis as a reason to begin building a

---

[7] See Giovanni Peri, Kevin Shih, and Chad Sparber, 2015, "STEM Workers, H-1B Visas, and Productivity in US Cities," *Journal of Labor Economics*, 33(S225–S255), July.

wall at the border.[8] But in fact, the apprehensions of undocumented migrants at or near U.S. border crossings did not increase under President Trump as compared to President Obama, and they decreased quite substantially as compared to Presidents Bush and Clinton. The numbers of border apprehensions are shown in Figure 5-6. For example, in 2018 there were about 400,000 apprehensions of undocumented immigrants at the border, which is slightly less than the annual number of border apprehensions under President Obama (an average of 423,000 annually during 2009–2016). Apprehensions under President Obama were much less than in the previous eight years under President George W. Bush (an annual average of 1 million during 2001–2008) and even less than under President Clinton (1.6 million in 2000, the last year of the Clinton administration).

The number of border apprehensions in the United States fell because the standard of living in Mexico rose and because the Great Recession in the United States (starting in 2008) made it less attractive to migrate. In comparison to the fall in total border apprehensions (shown in dark blue in Figure 5-6), there was an even greater fall in the number of Mexican citizens attempting to cross illegally (shown in light blue). Since 2011 there has been a growing gap between the total number of illegal crossings at the U.S.–Mexico border and the number of illegal crossings of Mexican citizens. That gap is made up in part by persons coming from *south* of Mexico—from Guatemala,

FIGURE 5-6

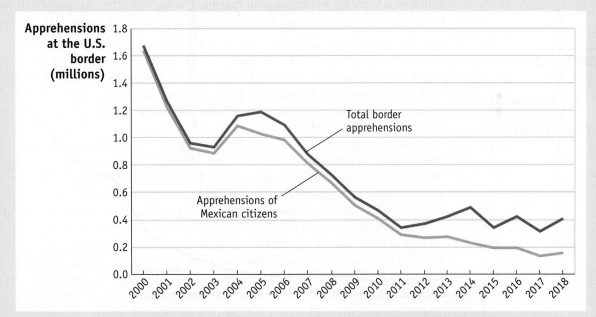

Border Apprehensions at the United States Border, 2000–2018
This figure shows the annual number of apprehensions of undocumented migrants at or near in the U.S. border from 2000 to 2018 and the number of those persons who were Mexican citizens. The number of border apprehensions fell from a high of over 1.6 million in 2000 to about 400,000 annually since 2011. Up until 2011 most of those apprehended were citizens of Mexico, but since that time there has been a growing number of migrants coming from the Northern Triangle countries of Guatemala, Honduras, and El Salvador, who travel north through Mexico and who are then apprehended at the U.S. border.

Data from: U.S. Customs and Border Patrol.

---

[8] While funding for a wall at the U.S.–Mexico border has not been approved by Congress, President Trump has cited the flow of undocumented migrants across the border as a threat to national security, and so has used funds approved for U.S. defense to begin building the wall.

Northern Triangle countries of Guatemala, Honduras, and El Salvador.

Honduras, and El Salvador, which are called the Northern Triangle—who travel north through Mexico and attempt to enter the United States (see the accompanying map).

Refugees at the U.S. Border The increasing numbers of migrants from Guatemala, Honduras, and El Salvador who attempt to cross the U.S.–Mexico border come not only because of economic hardship but also to escape violence in their home countries, and they often come as families that include children. These migrants must make the difficult choice of whether to attempt to cross the U.S. border illegally or to present themselves to customs officials as refugees, persons leaving their country because of persecution. If these migrants are judged to have credible fear of persecution, they can apply for **asylum** in the United States, and if asylum is granted, then they are permitted to stay.[9]

The number of applications for asylum filed in the United States has grown rapidly since about 2014, as shown in Figure 5-7. The high number of recent applications—exceeding 200,000 in 2019—has completed overwhelmed the ability of U.S. immigration authorities to process these applications on a timely basis, and individuals sometimes wait several years for an immigration hearing. During that time, they may be detained by immigration authorities, or, if they are released, they may be required to pay bail or

FIGURE 5-7

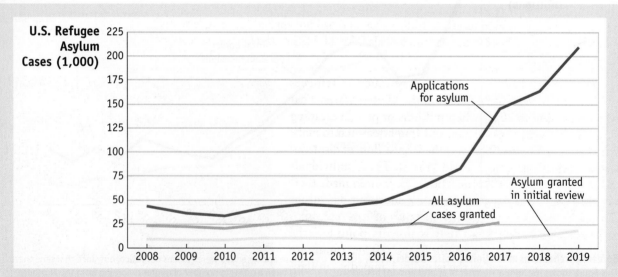

Applications for Asylum Filed and Granted, 2008–2019 This figure shows the annual number of applications for asylum from persons in the United States from 2008 to 2019. The number of applications filed has been growing rapidly since 2014 and exceeded 200,000 in 2019. The number of applications granted was around 25,000 annually up to 2017. More recent data are not available, but another data source shows that the number of asylum cases granted in the *initial review* increased from about 10,000 in 2017 to 19,000 in 2019. By either measure, the U.S. immigration system has not kept up with the requests of persons to obtain refugee status in the United States.

Data from: U.S. Department of Justice and U.S. Department of Homeland Security.

---

[9] A different category of refugee is a person who applies for this status while they are living abroad. In 2017, for example, about 50,000 persons were admitted to the United States from abroad as refugees, most of whom came from war-torn countries such as the Democratic Republic of the Congo, Iraq, and Syria.

to wear GPS ankle bracelets to monitor their location. Migrants who are discouraged from applying for asylum and who are apprehended while crossing the border illegally are also detained. In those cases, parents can be charged with criminal activity, and they have been separated from their children, who are kept in other facilities. These practices created an outcry in the United States in 2018 and led to court cases to prevent the separation of migrant parents from their children.

The number of asylum cases that were ultimately granted in the United States was about 25,000 per year up to 2017. This means that there are many people who do not receive asylum and that there is an enormous backlog of cases that have not yet been decided. While data for the number of asylum cases granted after 2017 are not available, another source of data shows the number of asylum cases that have been granted in the *initial review* (even if asylum is not granted in the initial interview, the person can be referred to Immigration Court for a further judgment). That number was about 10,000 in 2017 and increased to about 19,000 in 2019. So by either the initial or the final number of asylum cases granted, the U.S. immigration system has not kept up with the requests of persons to obtain refugee status in the United States. It is the asylum cases of persons who are seeking to come in as refugees—and not illegal immigration—that is the real crisis at the U.S. border.

President Trump took hard steps to limit this inflow of refugees to the United States. In May 2019, he threatened to impose an import tariff against Mexico unless that country posted more security personnel at its southern border with Guatemala, to slow the flow of persons entering and traveling north to the United States. In September 2019, the United States announced that persons can apply for asylum status in the United States only if they have already tried—and failed—to obtain refugee status in another country they passed through before the United States. Persons who have not already applied for refugee status would be returned to the first country they passed through on their way to the U.S. border. Under this plan, persons arriving in the United States from Guatemala who had not applied for refugee status in Mexico would be sent back to Mexico, and persons arriving from Honduras and El Salvador who had not applied for refugee status in Guatemala would be sent back to Guatemala. Not all these countries have agreed to this plan, however.[10]

Refugees Entering into Europe The inflow of refugees into Europe is even larger than into the United States. That inflow exploded in 2015, when millions of people escaping civil wars in Syria, Afghanistan, and Iraq attempted to make their way into Europe. This was the largest flow of displaced persons in Europe since World War II. These individuals and families coming from the Middle East often made their way through Turkey and then made a short but dangerous journey in makeshift boats to the islands of Kos or Lesbos in Greece, which along with Italy is an entry point into the European Union from the south. Large refugee camps are located in Greece as well as the island of Lampedusa in Italy, where these individuals and their families live while their refugee cases are being processed.

Migrants cross into Slovenia in 2015.

Greece and Italy belong to the so-called Schengen Area, which consists of 26 countries within the European Union (not including the United Kingdom or Ireland) that

---

[10] See Patrick Kingsley, "Trump Asylum Hurdle Is Tough, but Not Unique," *The New York Times, International*, September 15, 2019, p. 9. This is a controversial plan because it risks breaking the 1951 United Nations convention on refugees (signed by many countries, including the United States), which states that refugees cannot be returned to countries where they are not safe.

Kevin KAL Kallaugher, The Economist, Kaltoons.com

Remember when we thought our open internal borders would just flood us with profits?

allow persons to move freely across their borders. According to the regulations of the Schengen Area in 2015, refugees were expected to register and apply for asylum in the EU country in which they first landed. In practice, many migrants from Africa and the Middle East entering Greece and Italy did not want to register there because of the limited opportunities for local employment. Instead, these migrants sought asylum and employment in the larger and more prosperous countries of Europe. The total number of applications to these countries for asylum status, and the number of approved cases, are shown in Table 5-1 for the ten EU countries taking the largest numbers of refugees. In 2016, the total number of applications for asylum status in the European Union was 1.1 million, with more than one-half of these cases approved for resettlement in the EU. Germany took in the greatest number of refugees—over 400,000 in 2016—followed by Sweden, Italy, Austria, and France. The number of applications for and approved cases of asylum status fell in 2017 and 2018, as the flow of refugees coming from south of Europe subsided.

It is very important to realize that an application for asylum does not guarantee that asylum is granted. To receive asylum, migrants must establish that they are refugees, meaning that they face persecution in their home countries. That can be established most often for people leaving war-torn countries, but not necessarily for those leaving their home countries solely for economic reasons, that is, to seek a better life elsewhere. These individuals may not be entitled to refugee status or asylum. As EU countries began processing the many migrants that they took in during 2015, the first determination was whether these persons were entitled to refugee status, and if not, they were returned to their home countries. Although that action may seem harsh, it is taken outside of Europe, too; the United States returns those who claim refugee status but are judged to not face persecution at home, and as we just described, the United States now plans to return persons from south of Mexico

TABLE 5-1

Applications and Approved Cases of Asylum Status, Europe, 2016–2018 (thousands) This table shows the number of applications for and approved cases of asylum status in the 10 European countries with the largest number of refugees, from 2016 to 2018. In 2016, the total number of applications for asylum status in the European Union was 1.1 million, with more than one-half of these cases approved for resettlement in the EU. The number of applications for and approved cases of asylum status fell in 2017 and 2018 as the flow of refugees coming from south of Europe subsided.

	2016		2017		2018	
	Applications (1,000)	Approved (1,000)	Applications (1,000)	Approved (1,000)	Applications (1,000)	Approved (1,000)
European Union (total)	1,106	673	962	438	582	217
Austria	42	30	45	25	35	15
Belgium	25	15	24	13	19	10
France	87	29	111	33	115	33
Germany	631	434	524	262	179	76
Greece	11	3	25	10	32	15
Italy	90	35	78	32	95	31
Spain	10	7	12	4	12	3
Sweden	96	67	61	27	31	11
Switzerland	23	13	16	15	17	15
United Kingdom	31	10	28	9	29	10

Data from: Eurostat.

back to the first country they passed through if they have not applied for refugee status in that country.

Political Economy As this discussion of the United States and Europe shows, countries are often unwilling to accept those who claim to be refugees, and countries place strict limits on the inflow of migrants who enter for economic reasons. Why are countries unwilling to accept immigrants who simply wish to work there? The answer comes from the short-run, specific-factors model, which predicts that immigration lowers the wage of the workers already in the country. When these existing workers are the voting citizens, their fear of earning lower wages or losing their jobs creates a reason for the government to resist immigration. Sometimes heads of governments appeal to that fear and make opposition to immigration a defining theme of their administration. That strategy was followed by President Trump in the United States with his promise to build a wall at the U.S.–Mexico border to keep out migrants. Similar promises to keep out immigrants have been made by far-right politicians in Europe.

Still, such extreme positions appeal to only a minority of voters. According to a national poll of voters in the United States, only 14% identified themselves as "very conservative," which includes some who most oppose immigration. At the other end of the political spectrum, only 13% of voters identify themselves as "very liberal," which includes some who favor more open and even unrestricted immigration. Between these very conservative and very liberal viewpoints are the majority of people (both liberal and conservative), who support immigration policies that control the border and still have a positive view of migrants.[11]

A study supporting this more positive view of immigrants comes from the resettlement of refugees from former Yugoslavia, Somalia, Afghanistan, and Iraq into Denmark. Professors Giovanni Peri of the University of California, Davis and Mette Foged of the University of Copenhagen measured the wages earned by Danish workers over 1995–2009 in different towns, depending on whether refugees arrived there or not.[12] In towns that received refugees, the local workers did not see their wages fall; on the contrary, those wages *rose* as compared to towns that did not receive refugees. The explanation for this surprising finding is that the arriving refugees allowed local workers to shift out of manual jobs and into jobs that took advantage of their native skills (language skills, for example). In other words, rather than being substitutes for local workers, immigrants can complement them and raise their earnings. In the next section, we turn to an analysis of immigration in the long run, where we will find that the wages of local workers need not be depressed by immigration, as seen in this study of Denmark and in the Mariel boat lift discussed at the beginning of the chapter.

Effects of Immigration in the Long Run

In the long run, all factors are free to move between industries. Because it is complicated to analyze a model with three factors of production—capital, land, and labor—all of which are fully mobile between industries, we will ignore land and assume that only labor and capital are used to produce two goods: computers and shoes. The long-run model is just like the Heckscher–Ohlin model studied in Chapter 4 except that we now allow labor to move between countries. (Later in the chapter, we allow capital to move between the countries.)

---

[11] A report from the Public Religion Research Institute found that "56% of persons support restrictive immigration policies, but 89% have a positive view of immigrants" (Thomas B. Edsall, "Democrats Can Still Seize the Center," *The New York Times, Sunday Review,* November 3, 2019, p. 7).

[12] Giovanni Peri and Mette Foged, 2016, "Immigrants' Effect on Native Workers: New Analysis on Longitudinal Data," *American Economic Journal: Applied Economics,* 8(2), 1–34.

*"You seem familiar, yet somehow strange—
are you by any chance Canadian?"*

The amount of capital used in computers is K_C, and the amount of capital used in shoe production is K_S. These quantities add up to the total capital available in the economy: $K_C + K_S = \bar{K}$. Because capital is fully mobile between the two sectors in the long run, it must earn the same rental R in each. The amount of labor used to manufacture computers is L_C, and the labor used in shoe production is L_S. These amounts add up to the total labor in the economy, $L_C + L_S = \bar{L}$, and all labor earns the same wage of W in both sectors.

In our analysis, we make the realistic assumption that more labor per machine is used in shoe production than in computer production. That assumption means that shoe production is labor-intensive compared with computer production, so the labor–capital ratio in shoes is higher than it is in computers: $L_S/K_S > L_C/K_C$. Computer production, then, is capital-intensive compared with shoes, and the capital–labor ratio is higher in computers: $K_C/L_C > K_S/L_S$.

The PPF for an economy producing both shoes and computers is shown in Figure 5-8. Given the prices of both goods (determined by supply and demand in world markets), the equilibrium outputs are shown at point A, at the tangency of the PPF and world relative price line. Our goal in this section is to see how the equilibrium is affected by having an inflow of labor into Home as a result of immigration.

Box Diagram To analyze the effect of immigration, it is useful to develop a new diagram to keep track of the amount of labor and capital used in each industry. Shown as a "box diagram" in Figure 5-9, the length of the top and bottom horizontal axes is the total amount of labor $\bar{L}$ in Home, and the length of the right and left vertical axes is the total amount of capital $\bar{K}$ in Home. A point like point A in the diagram indicates that $0_S L$ units of labor and $0_S K$ units of capital are used in shoes, while $0_C L$ units of labor and $0_C K$ units of capital are used in computers. Another way to express this is that the line $0_S A$ shows the amount of labor and capital used in shoes and the line $0_C A$ shows the amount of labor and capital used in computers.

Notice that the line $0_S A$ for shoes is flatter than the line $0_C A$ for computers. We can calculate the slopes of these lines by dividing the vertical distance by the horizontal

FIGURE 5-8

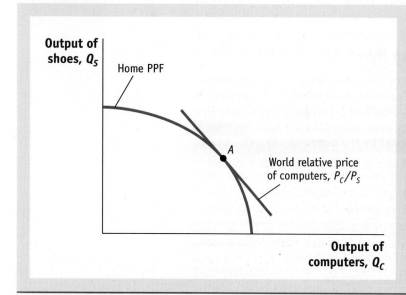

Production Possibilities Frontier Shown here is the production possibilities frontier (PPF) between two manufactured goods, computers and shoes, with initial equilibrium at point A. Domestic production takes place at point A, which is the point of tangency between the world price line and the PPF.

FIGURE 5-9

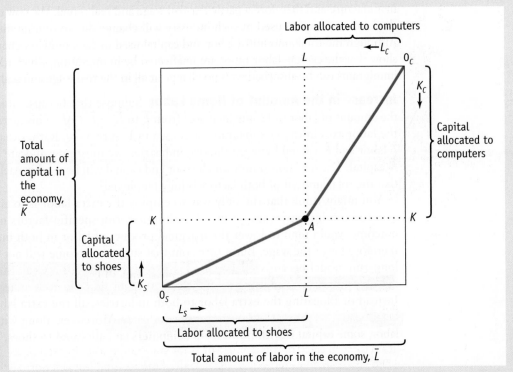

Allocation of Labor and Capital in a Box Diagram The top and bottom axes of the box diagram measure the amount of labor, $\bar{L}$, in the economy, and the side axes measure the amount of capital, $\bar{K}$. At point A, 0_SL units of labor and 0_SK units of capital are used in shoe production, and 0_CL units of labor and 0_CK units of capital are used in computers. The K/L ratios in the two industries are measured by the slopes of 0_SA and 0_CA, respectively.

distance (the rise over the run). The slope of 0_SA is $0_SK/0_SL$, the capital–labor ratio used in the shoe industry. Likewise, the slope of 0_CA is $0_CK/0_CL$, the capital–labor ratio for computers. The line 0_SA is flatter than 0_CA, indicating that the capital–labor ratio in the shoe industry is less than that in computers; that is, there are fewer units of capital per worker in the shoe industry. This is precisely the assumption that we made earlier. It is a realistic assumption given that the manufacture of computer components such as semiconductors requires highly precise and expensive equipment, which is operated by a small number of workers. Shoe production, on the other hand, requires more workers and a smaller amount of capital.

Determination of the Real Wage and Real Rental In addition to determining the amount of labor and capital used in each industry in the long run, we also need to determine the wage and rental in the economy. To do so, we use the logic introduced in Chapter 3: the wage and rental are determined by the marginal products of labor and capital, which are in turn determined by the capital–labor ratio in either industry. If there is a higher capital–labor ratio (i.e., if there are more machines per worker), then by the law of diminishing returns, the marginal product of capital and the real rental must be lower. Having more machines per worker means that the marginal product of labor (and hence the real wage) is higher because each worker is more productive. On the other hand, if there is a higher labor–capital ratio (more workers per machine), then the marginal product of labor must be lower because of diminishing returns, and hence the real wage is lower, too. In addition, having more workers per machine means that the marginal product of capital and the real rental are both higher.

The important point to remember is that each amount of labor and capital used in Figure 5-9 along line $0_S A$ corresponds to a particular capital–labor ratio for shoe manufacture and therefore a particular real wage and real rental. We now consider how the labor and capital used in each industry will change due to immigration in Home. Although the total amount of labor and capital used in each industry changes, we will show that the capital–labor ratios are unaffected by immigration, which means that the immigrants can be absorbed with no change at all in the real wage and real rental.

Increase in the Amount of Home Labor

Suppose that because of immigration, the amount of labor in Home increases from $\bar{L}$ to $\bar{L}' = \bar{L} + \Delta L$. This increase expands the labor axes in the box diagram, as shown in Figure 5-10. Rather than allocating $\bar{L}$ labor and $\bar{K}$ capital between the two industries, we must now allocate $\bar{L}'$ labor and $\bar{K}$ capital. The question is how much labor and capital will be used in each industry so that the total amount of both factors is fully employed?

You might think that the only way to employ the extra labor is to allocate more of it to both industries (as occurred in the short-run specific-factors model). This outcome would tend to lower the marginal product of labor in both industries and therefore lower the wage. But it turns out that such an outcome will not occur in the long-run model because when capital is also able to move between the industries, industry outputs will adjust to keep the capital–labor ratios in each industry constant. Instead of allocating the extra labor to both industries, all the extra labor (ΔL) will be allocated to shoes, the *labor*-intensive industry. Moreover, along with that extra labor, some capital is withdrawn from computers and allocated to shoes. To maintain

FIGURE 5-10

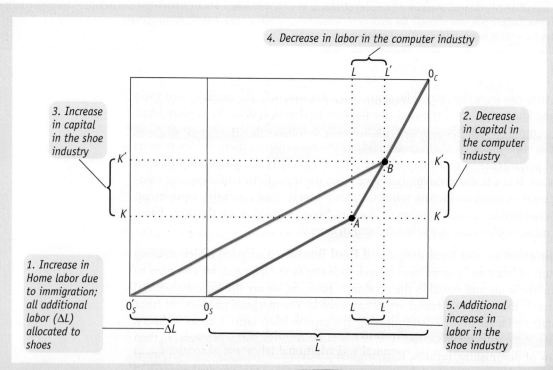

Increase in Home Labor With an increase in Home labor from $\bar{L}$ to $\bar{L} + \Delta L$, the origin for the shoe industry shifts from 0_S to $0'_S$. At point B, $0'_S L'$ units of labor and $0'_S K'$ units of capital are used in shoes, whereas $0_C L'$ units of labor and $0_C K'$ units of capital are used in computers. In the long run, industry outputs adjust so that the capital–labor ratios in each industry at point B (the slopes of $0'_S B$ and $0_C B$) are unchanged from the initial equilibrium at point A (the slopes of $0_S A$ and $0_C A$). To achieve this outcome, all new labor resulting from immigration is allocated to the shoe industry, and capital and *additional* labor are transferred from computers to shoes, keeping the capital–labor ratio in both industries unchanged.

the capital–labor ratio in the computer industry, some labor will also leave the computer industry, along with the capital, and go to the shoe industry. Because all the new workers in the shoe industry (immigrants plus former computer workers) have the same amount of capital to work with as the shoe workers prior to immigration, the capital–labor ratio in the shoe industry stays the same. *In this way, the capital–labor ratio in each industry is unchanged and the additional labor in the economy is fully employed.*

This outcome is illustrated in Figure 5-10, where the initial equilibrium is at point A. With the inflow of labor due to immigration, the labor axis expands from $\bar{L}$ to $\bar{L} + \Delta L$, and the origin for the shoe industry shifts from 0_S to $0'_S$. Consider point B as a possible new equilibrium. At this point, $0'_S L'$ units of labor and $0'_S K'$ units of capital are used in shoes, while $0_C L'$ units of labor and $0_C K'$ units of capital are used in computers. Notice that the lines $0_S A$ and $0'_S B$ are parallel and have the same slope, and similarly, the lines $0_C A$ and $0_C B$ have the same slope. The extra labor has been employed by *expanding* the amount of labor and capital used in shoes (the line $0'_S B$ is longer than $0_S A$) and *contracting* the amount of labor and capital used in computers (the line $0_C B$ is smaller than $0_C A$). That the lines have the same slope means that the capital–labor ratio used in each industry is exactly the same before and after the inflow of labor.

What has happened to the wage and rentals in the economy? Because the capital–labor ratios are unchanged in both industries, the marginal products of labor and capital are also unchanged. Therefore, the wage and rental do not change at all because of the immigration of labor! This result is very different from what happens in the short-run specific-factors model, which showed that immigration depressed the wage and raised the rental on capital and land. In the long-run model, when capital can move between industries, an inflow of labor has no impact on the wage and rental. Instead, the extra labor is employed in shoes, by combining it with capital and additional labor that has shifted out of computers. In that way, the capital–labor ratios in both industries are unchanged, as are the wage and rental.

Effect of Immigration on Industry Outputs What is the effect of immigration on the output of each industry? We have already seen from Figure 5-10 that more labor and capital are used in the labor-intensive industry (shoes), whereas less labor and capital are used in the capital-intensive industry (computers). Because the factors of production both increase or both decrease, it follows that the output of shoes expands and the output of computers contracts.

This outcome is shown in Figure 5-11, which shows the outward shift of the PPF due to the increase in the labor endowment in Home. Given the prices of computers and shoes, the initial equilibrium was at point A. At this point, the slope of the PPF equals the relative price of computers, as shown by the slope of the line tangent to the PPF. With unchanged prices for the goods, and more labor in the economy, the equilibrium moves to point B, with greater output of shoes but reduced output of computers. Notice that the slope of the PPFs at points A and B is identical because the relative price of computers is unchanged. As suggested by the diagram, the expansion in the amount of labor leads to an uneven outward shift of the PPF—it shifts out more in the direction of shoes (the labor-intensive industry) than in the direction of computers. This asymmetric shift illustrates that the new labor is employed in shoes and that this additional labor pulls capital and additional labor out of computers in the long run, to establish the new equilibrium at point B. *The finding that an increase in labor will expand one industry but contract the other holds only in the long run; in the short run, as we saw in Figure 5-4, both industries will expand.* This finding, called the **Rybczynski theorem**, shows how much the long-run model differs from the short-run model. The long-run result is named after the economist T. N. Rybczynski, who first described it.

FIGURE 5-11

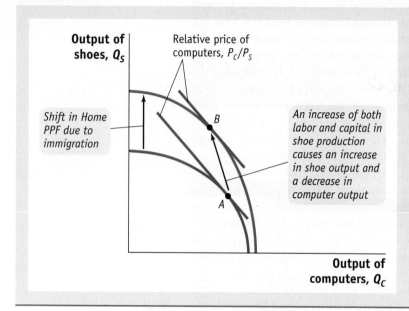

The Long-Run Effect on Industry Outputs of an Increase in Home Labor With an increase in the amount of labor in Home, the PPF shifts outward. The output of shoes increases, while the output of computers declines as the equilibrium moves from point A to B. The prices of goods have not changed, so the slopes of the PPFs at points A and B (i.e., the relative price of computers) are equal.

Rybczynski Theorem

The formal statement of the Rybczynski theorem is as follows: in the Heckscher–Ohlin model with two goods and two factors, an increase in the amount of a factor found in an economy will increase the output of the industry using that factor intensively and decrease the output of the other industry.

We have proved the Rybczynski theorem for the case of immigration, in which labor in the economy grows. As we find later in the chapter, the same theorem holds when capital in the economy grows: in this case, the industry using capital intensively expands and the other industry contracts.[13]

Effect of Immigration on Factor Prices The Rybczynski theorem, which applies to the long-run Heckscher–Ohlin model with two goods and two factors of production, states that an increase in labor will expand output in one industry but contract output in the other industry. Notice that the change in outputs in the Rybczynski theorem goes hand in hand with the previous finding that the wage and rental will not change due to an increase in labor (or capital). The reason that factor prices do not need to change is that the economy can absorb the extra amount of a factor by increasing the output of the industry using that factor intensively and reducing the output of the other industry. The finding that factor prices do not change is sometimes called the **factor price insensitivity** result.

Factor Price Insensitivity Theorem

The factor price insensitivity theorem states that: in the Heckscher–Ohlin model with two goods and two factors, an increase in the amount of a factor found in an economy can be absorbed by changing the outputs of the industries, without any change in the factor prices.

---

[13] Furthermore, the Rybczynski theorem can be used to compare the output of the same industry across two countries, where the two countries have identical technologies but differing factor endowments as in the Heckscher–Ohlin model. See Problem 8 at the end of the chapter.

The applications that follow offer evidence of changes in output that absorb new additions to the labor force, as predicted by the Rybczynski theorem, without requiring large changes in factor prices, as predicted by the factor price insensitivity result.

APPLICATION

The Effects of the Mariel Boat Lift on Industry Output in Miami

Now that we have a better understanding of long-run adjustments due to changes in factor endowments, let us return to the case of the Mariel boat lift to Miami in 1980. We know that the Cuban refugees were less skilled than the average labor force in Miami. According to the Rybczynski theorem, then, we expect some unskilled-labor–intensive industry, such as footwear or apparel, to expand. In addition, we expect that some skill-intensive industry, such as the high-tech industry, will contract. Figure 5-12 shows how this prediction lines up with the evidence from Miami and some comparison cities.[14]

Panel (a) of Figure 5-12 shows real value-added in the apparel industry for Miami and for an average of comparison cities. **Real value-added** measures the payments to labor and capital in an industry corrected for inflation. Thus, real value-added is a way to measure the output of the industry. We divide output by the population of the city to obtain real value-added per capita, which measures the output of the industry adjusted for the city size.

Panel (a) shows that the apparel industry was declining in Miami and the comparison cities before 1980. After the boat lift, the industry continued to decline but at a slower rate in Miami; the trend of output per capita for Miami has a smaller slope (and hence a smaller rate of decline in output) than that of the trend for comparison cities from 1980 onward. Notice that there is an increase in industry output in Miami from 1983 to 1984 (which may be due to new data collected that year), but even when averaging this out as the trend lines do, the industry decline in Miami is slightly slower than in the comparison cities after 1980. This graph provides some evidence of the Rybczynski theorem at work: the reduction in the apparel industry in Miami was slower than it would have been without the inflow of immigrants.

What about the second prediction of the Rybczynski theorem: Did the output of any other industry in Miami fall because of the immigration? Panel (b) of Figure 5-12 shows that the output of a group of skill-intensive industries (including motor vehicles, electronic equipment, and aircraft) fell more rapidly in Miami after 1980. These data may also provide some evidence in favor of the Rybczynski theorem. However, it also happened that with the influx of refugees, there was a flight of homeowners away from Miami, and some of these were probably high-skilled workers. So the decline in the group of skill-intensive industries, shown in panel (b), could instead be due to this population decline. The change in industry outputs in Miami provides some evidence in favor of the Rybczynski theorem. Do these changes in industry outputs in Miami also provide an adequate explanation for why wages of unskilled workers did not decline, or is there some other explanation? An alternative explanation for the finding that wages did not change comes from comparing the use of computers in Miami with national trends. Beginning in the early 1980s, computers became increasingly used in the workplace. The adoption of computers is called a "skill-biased technological change." That is, computers led to an increase in the demand for high-skilled workers and reduced the hiring of low-skilled workers. This trend occurred across the United States and in other countries.

---

[14] Figure 5-12 and the material in this application are drawn from Ethan Lewis, 2004, "How Did the Miami Labor Market Absorb the Mariel Immigrants?" Federal Reserve Bank of Philadelphia Working Paper No. 04-3.

FIGURE 5-12

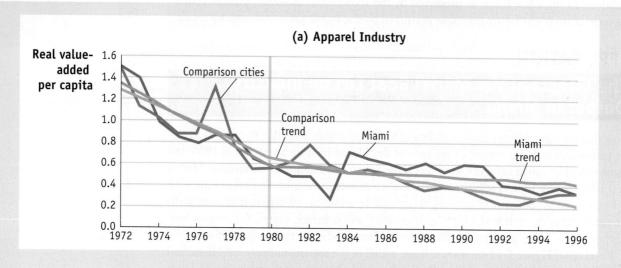

(a) Apparel Industry

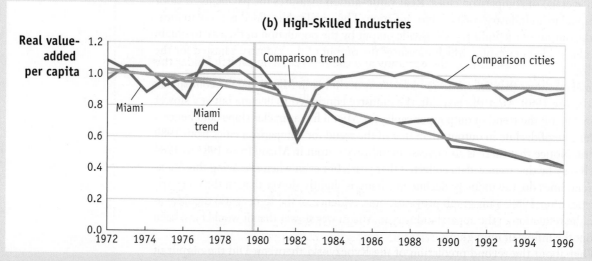

(b) High-Skilled Industries

Industry Value-Added in Miami Shown here are real value-added in the apparel industry and in high-skilled industries (measured relative to the city population), for Miami and an average of comparison cities. In panel (a), with the inflow of refugees from Cuba in 1980, real value-added in the apparel industry in Miami rose from 1983 to 1984, and the trend decline of this industry in Miami was slower (i.e., value-added did not fall as fast) after 1980 than in the comparison cities. In panel (b), real value-added in Miami in high-skilled industries fell faster after 1980 than in the comparison cities. Both these findings are consistent with the Rybczynski theorem.

Data from: Ethan Lewis, 2004, "How Did the Miami Labor Market Absorb the Mariel Immigrants?" Federal Reserve Bank of Philadelphia Working Paper No. 04–3.

In Miami, however, computers were adopted somewhat more slowly than in cities with similar industry mix and ethnic populations. One explanation for this finding is that firms in many industries, not just apparel, employed the Mariel refugees and other low-skilled workers rather than switching to computer technologies. Evidence to support this finding is that the Mariel refugees were, in fact, employed in many industries. Only about 20% worked in manufacturing (5% in apparel), and the remainder worked in service industries. The idea that the firms may have slowed the adoption of new technologies to employ the Mariel emigrants is hard to prove conclusively, however. We suggest it here as an alternative to the Rybczynski theorem to explain how the refugees could be absorbed across many industries rather than just in the industries using unskilled labor, such as apparel.

APPLICATION

The Effects of Migration on Wages

Earlier in the chapter, we pointed out that there was a U-shaped relationship between the percentage of foreign-born workers in the United States and their education levels. Figure 5-5 showed that immigrants into the United States compete primarily with workers at the lowest and highest ends of the educational levels and much less with the majority of U.S.-born workers with mid-levels of education. How has immigration into the United States affected U.S. wages in these various educational categories?

The estimated impact of immigrants on wages in the United States is reported in Table 5-2, for the period 1990–2006. Part A of Table 5-2 reports the estimated impact of the immigration on the wages of various workers, distinguished by their educational level. The first row in part A summarizes the estimates from the specific-factors model, when capital and land are kept fixed within all industries. As we discussed in an earlier application, the greatest negative impact of immigration is on native-born workers with less than 12 years of education, followed by college graduates, and then followed by high school graduates and those with some college. Overall, the average impact of immigration on U.S. wages over the period of 1990–2006 was –3.0%. That is, wages fell by 3.0%, consistent with the specific-factors model.

A different story emerges, however, if instead of keeping capital fixed, we hold constant the capital–labor ratio in the economy and the real rental on capital. Under this approach, we allow capital to grow to accommodate the inflow of immigrants, so that there is no change in the real rental. This approach is similar to the long-run model we

TABLE 5-2

Immigration and Wages in the United States This table shows the estimated effect of immigration on the wages of workers, depending on their educational level, from 1990 to 2006. Short-run estimates hold capital and land fixed, while long-run estimates allow capital to adjust so that the capital–labor ratio and real rental are constant in the economy. Part A shows the impact of immigration assuming that U.S.-born and foreign-born workers are perfect substitutes. Immigration has the greatest impact on workers with very low or very high levels of education and only a small impact on those workers with middle levels of education (12 to 15 years). The impact is even smaller in the long run, when capital adjusts to keep the real rental on capital fixed. Part B shows long-run estimates when U.S.-born and foreign-born workers in the U.S. are imperfect substitutes. In this case, immigrants compete especially strongly with other foreign-born workers by lowering their wages, and they can potentially complement the activities of U.S.-born workers.

	PERCENTAGE CHANGE IN THE WAGE OF WORKERS WITH EDUCATIONAL LEVEL				
	Less Than 12 Years	**High School Graduates**	**Some College**	**College Graduates**	**Overall Average**
Part A: Effect of Immigration on All U.S. Workers					
Method:					
Short run	–7.8	–2.2	–0.9	–4.7	–3.0
Long run	–4.7	0.9	2.2	–1.7	0.1
Part B: Long-Run Effect of Immigration, by Type of Worker					
Type of Worker:					
U.S. born	0.3	0.4	0.9	0.5	0.6
Foreign born	–4.9	–7.0	–4.0	–8.1	–6.4

Data from: Gianmarco I. P. Ottaviano and Giovanni Peri, 2012, "Rethinking the Effect of Immigration on Wages," Journal of the European Economic Association, 10(1), 152–197; and Gianmarco I. P. Ottaviano and Giovanni Peri, 2008, "Immigration and National Wages: Clarifying the Theory and the Empirics," National Bureau of Economic Research Working Paper no. 14188, Tables 7 and 8.

have discussed, except that we now distinguish several types of labor by their education levels. In the second row of part A, we see that total U.S. immigration had a negative impact on workers with the lowest and highest levels of education and a *positive* impact on the other workers (due to the growth in capital). With these new assumptions, we see that the average U.S. wage rose by 0.1% because of immigration (combined with capital growth), rather than falling by 3.0%.

The finding that the average U.S. wage is nearly constant in the long run (rising by just 0.1%) is similar to our long-run model in which wages do not change because of immigration. However, the finding that some workers gain (wages rise for the middle education levels) and others lose (wages fall for the lowest and the highest education levels) is different from our long-run model. There are two reasons for this outcome. First, as we already noted, Table 5-2 categorizes workers by different education levels. Even when the *overall* capital–labor ratio is fixed, and the real rental on capital is fixed, it is still possible for the wages of workers with certain education levels to change. Second, we can refer back to the U-shaped pattern of immigration shown in Figure 5-5, where the fraction of immigrants in the U.S. workforce is largest for the lowest and highest education levels. It is not surprising, then, that these two groups face the greatest loss in wages due to an inflow of immigrants.

We can dig a little deeper to better understand the long-run wage changes in part A. In part A, we assumed that U.S.-born workers and foreign-born workers in each education level are perfect substitutes; that is, they do the same types of jobs and have the same abilities. In reality, evidence shows that U.S. workers and immigrants often end up doing different types of jobs, even when they have similar education. In part B of Table 5-2, we build on this realistic feature by treating U.S.-born workers and foreign-born workers in each education level as imperfect substitutes. Just as the prices of goods that are imperfect substitutes (for example, different types of cell phones) can differ, the wages of U.S.-born and foreign-born workers with the same education can also differ. This modification to our assumptions leads to a substantial change in the results.

In part B of Table 5-2, we find that immigration now raises the wages of all U.S.-born workers in the long run, by 0.6% on average. That slight rise occurs because the U.S.-born and foreign-born workers are doing different jobs that can complement one another. For example, on a construction site, an immigrant worker with limited language skills can focus on physical tasks, while a U.S. worker can focus on tasks involving personal interaction. Part B shows another interesting outcome: the 1990–2006 immigration had the greatest impact on the wages of all other foreign-born workers, whose wages fell by an average of 6.4% in the long run. When we allow for imperfect substitution between U.S.-born and foreign-born workers, immigrants compete especially strongly with other foreign-born workers, and can potentially complement the activities of U.S.-born workers. Contrary to popular belief, immigrants don't necessarily lower the wages for U.S. workers with similar educational backgrounds. Instead, immigrants can raise wages for U.S. workers if the two groups are doing jobs that are complementary.

2 Movement of Capital Between Countries: Foreign Direct Investment

To continue our examination of what happens to wages and rentals when factors can move across borders, we turn now to look at how capital can move from one country to another through **foreign direct investment (FDI)**, which occurs when a firm from one country owns a company in another country. How much does the company have to own for foreign direct investment to occur? Definitions vary, but the Department of Commerce in the United States uses 10%: if a foreign company acquires 10% or more of a U.S. firm, then that is counted as an FDI inflow to the United States, and if a U.S. company acquires 10% or more of a foreign firm, then that is counted as an FDI outflow from the United States.

When a company builds a plant in a foreign country, it is sometimes called "green field FDI" (because we imagine the site for the plant starting with grass on it). When a firm buys an existing foreign plant, it is called "acquisition FDI" (or sometimes "brown-field FDI"). Having capital move from high-wage to low-wage countries to earn a higher rental is the traditional view of FDI, and the viewpoint we take in this chapter.[15]

Greenfield Investment

Our focus in this section will be on greenfield investment, that is, the building of new plants abroad. We model FDI as a movement of capital between countries, just as we modeled the movement of labor between countries. The key question we ask is: How does the movement of capital into a country affect the earnings of labor and capital there? This question is similar to the one we asked for immigration, so the earlier graphs that we developed can be modified to address FDI.

FDI in the Short Run: Specific-Factors Model

We begin by modeling FDI in the short run, using the specific-factors model. In that model, the manufacturing industry uses capital and labor and the agriculture industry uses land and labor, so as capital flows into the economy, it will be used in manufacturing. The additional capital will raise the marginal product of labor in manufacturing because workers there have more machines with which to work. Therefore, as capital flows into the economy, it will shift out the curve $P_M \cdot MPL_M$ for the manufacturing industry as shown in panel (a) of Figure 5-13.

FIGURE 5-13

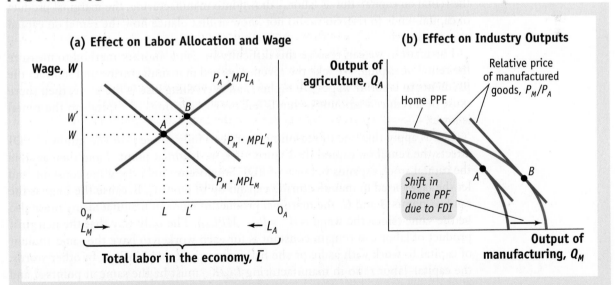

Increase in the Capital Stock in the Short Run In panel (a), an inflow of capital into the manufacturing sector shifts out the marginal product of labor curve in that sector. The equilibrium in the labor market moves from point A to B, and the wage increases from W to W'. Labor used in the manufacturing industry increases from $0_M L$ to $0_M L'$. These workers are pulled out of agriculture, so the labor used there shrinks from $0_A L$ to $0_A L'$. In panel (b), with the inflow of capital into manufacturing, and the extra labor used in that sector, the output of manufacturing increases. Because labor has been drawn out of agriculture, the output of that sector falls. These changes in outputs are shown by the outward shift of the PPF (due to the increase in capital) and the movement from point A to point B.

---

[15] As discussed in Chapter 1, there are many instances of FDI that do not fit with this traditional view.

Effect of FDI on the Wage As a result of this shift, the equilibrium wage increases, from W to W'. More workers are drawn into the manufacturing industry, and the labor used there increases from $0_M L$ to $0_M L'$. Because these workers are pulled out of agriculture, the labor used there shrinks from $0_A L$ to $0_A L'$ (measuring from right to left).

Effect of FDI on the Industry Outputs It is easy to determine the effect of an inflow of FDI on industry outputs. Because workers are pulled out of agriculture, and there is no change in the amount of land used there, output of the agriculture industry must fall. With an increase in the number of workers used in manufacturing and an increase in capital used there, the output of the manufacturing industry must rise. These changes in output are shown in panel (b) of Figure 5-13 by the outward shift of the production possibilities frontier. At constant prices for goods (i.e., the relative price lines have the same slope before and after the increase in capital), the equilibrium outputs shift from point A to point B, with more manufacturing output and less agricultural output.

Effect of FDI on the Rentals Finally, we can determine the impact of the inflow of capital on the rental earned by capital and the rental earned by land. It is easiest to start with the agriculture industry. Because fewer workers are employed there, each acre of land cannot be cultivated as intensively as before, and the marginal product of land must fall. One way to measure the rental on land T is by the value of its marginal product, $R_T = P_A \cdot MPT_A$. With the fall in the marginal product of land (MPT_A), and no change in the price of agricultural goods, the rental on land falls.

Now let us consider manufacturing, which uses more capital and more labor than before. One way to measure the rental on capital is by the value of the marginal product of capital, or $R_K = P_M \cdot MPK_M$. Using this method, however, it is difficult to determine how the rental on capital changes. As capital flows into manufacturing, the marginal product of capital falls because of diminishing returns. That effect reduces the rental on capital. But as labor is drawn into manufacturing, the marginal product of capital tends to rise. So we do not know at first glance how the rental on capital changes overall.

Fortunately, we can resolve this difficulty by using another method to measure the rental on capital. We take the revenue earned in manufacturing and subtract the payments to labor. If wages are higher, and everything else is the same, then there must be a reduced amount of funds left over as earnings of capital, so the rental is lower.

Let us apply this line of reasoning more carefully to see how the inflow of FDI affects the rental on capital. In Figure 5-14, we begin at point A and then assume the capital stock expands because of FDI. Suppose we hold the wage constant, and let the labor used in manufacturing expand up to point C. Because the wage is the same at points A and C, the marginal product of labor in manufacturing must also be the same (since the wage is $W = P_M \cdot MPL_M$). The only way that the marginal product of labor can remain constant is for each worker to have the same amount of capital to work with as he or she had before the capital inflow. In other words, the capital–labor ratio in manufacturing L_M/K_M must be the same at points A and C: the expansion of capital in manufacturing is just matched by a proportional expansion of labor into manufacturing. But if the capital–labor ratio in manufacturing is identical at points A and C, then the marginal product of capital must also be equal at these two points (because each machine has the same number of people working on it). Therefore, the rental on capital, $R_K = P_M \cdot MPK_M$, is also equal at points A and C.

Now let's see what happens as the manufacturing wage increases while holding constant the amount of capital used in that sector. The increase in the wage will

FIGURE 5-14

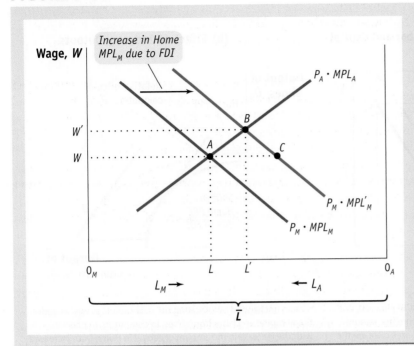

The Effect of an Increase in Capital Stock on the Rental on Capital   By carefully tracing through how the capital–labor ratio in manufacturing is affected by the movement from *A* to *C* (where wages and hence the capital–labor ratio do not change), and then the movement from *C* to *B* (where wages and the capital–labor ratio both increase), we conclude that the rental on capital is lower at point *B* than at point *A*. Therefore, the rental on capital declines when the capital stock increases through FDI.

move us up the curve $P_M \cdot MPL'_M$ from point C to point B. As the wage rises, less labor is used in manufacturing. With less labor used on each machine in manufacturing, the marginal product of capital and the rental on capital must fall. This result confirms our earlier reasoning: when wages are higher and the amount of capital used in manufacturing is the same, then the earnings of capital (i.e., its rental) must be lower. Because the rental on capital is the same at points A and C but is lower at point B than C, the overall effect of the FDI inflow is to reduce the rental on capital. We learned previously that the FDI inflow also reduces the rental on land, so both rentals fall.

FDI in the Long Run

The results of FDI in the long run, when capital and labor can move between industries, differ from those we saw in the short-run specific-factors model. To model FDI in the long run, we assume again that there are two industries—computers and shoes—both of which use two factors of production: labor and capital. Computers are capital-intensive as compared with shoes, meaning that K_C/L_C exceeds K_S/L_S.

In panel (a) of Figure 5-15, we show the initial allocation of labor and capital between the two industries at point A. The labor and capital used in the shoe industry are 0_SL and 0_SK, so this combination is measured by the line 0_SA. The labor and capital used in computers are 0_CL and 0_CK, so this combination is measured by the line 0_CA. That amount of labor and capital used in each industry produces the output of shoes and computers shown by point A on the PPF in panel (b).

Effect of FDI on Outputs and Factor Prices   An inflow of FDI causes the amount of capital in the economy to increase. That increase expands the right and left sides of the box in panel (a) of Figure 5-15 and shifts the origin up to $0'_C$. The new allocation of factors between the industries is shown at point B. Now the labor and capital used

FIGURE 5-15

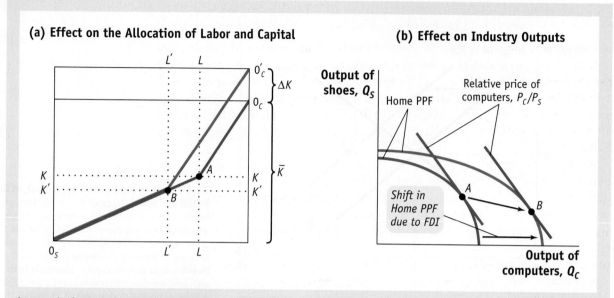

(a) Effect on the Allocation of Labor and Capital

(b) Effect on Industry Outputs

Increase in the Capital Stock in the Long Run In panel (a), the top and bottom axes of the box diagram measure the amount of labor in the economy, and the right and left axes measure the amount of capital. The initial equilibrium is at point A. When there is an inflow of capital, the equilibrium moves to point B. Similar to the box diagram for immigration (Figure 5-10), the K/L ratios remain unchanged by allocating the new capital, as well as additional capital and labor from shoes, to computers. In panel (b), with the increase in the amount of capital in Home from increased FDI, the PPF shifts outward. The output of computers increases while the output of shoes declines as the equilibrium moves from point A to B.

in the shoe industry are measured by $0_S B$, which is shorter than the line $0_S A$. Therefore, less labor and less capital are used in the production of footwear, and shoe output falls. The labor and capital used in computers are measured by $0'_C B$, which is longer than the line $0_C A$. Therefore, more labor and more capital are used in computers, and the output of that industry rises.

The change in outputs of shoes and computers is shown by the shift from point A to point B in panel (b) of Figure 5-15. In accordance with the Rybczynski theorem, the increase in capital through FDI has increased the output of the capital-intensive industry (computers) and reduced the output of the labor-intensive industry (shoes). Furthermore, this change in outputs is achieved *with no change* in the capital–labor ratios in either industry: the lines $0'_C B$ and $0_S B$ have the same slopes as $0_C A$ and $0_S A$, respectively.

Because the capital–labor ratios are unchanged in the two industries, the wage and the rental on capital are also unchanged. Each person has the same amount of capital to work with in his or her industry, and each machine has the same number of workers. The marginal products of labor and capital are unchanged in the two industries, as are the factor prices. This outcome is basically the same as that for immigration in the long run: in the long-run model, an inflow of *either* factor of production will leave factor prices unchanged.

When discussing immigration, we found cases in which wages were reduced (the short-run prediction) and other cases in which wages have been constant (the long-run prediction). What about for foreign direct investment? Does it tend to lower rentals or leave them unchanged? There are fewer studies of this question, but we next consider an important application for Singapore.

APPLICATION

The Effect of FDI on Rentals and Wages in Singapore

For many years, Singapore has encouraged foreign firms to establish subsidiaries within its borders, especially in the electronics industry. For example, many hard disks are manufactured in Singapore by foreign companies. In 2005 Singapore had the fourth-largest amount of FDI in the world (measured by stock of foreign capital found there), following China, Mexico, and Brazil, even though it is much smaller than those economies.[16] As capital in Singapore has grown, what has happened to the rental and to the wage?

One way to answer this question is to estimate the marginal product of capital in Singapore, using a production function that applies to the entire economy. The overall capital–labor ratio in Singapore grew by about 5% per year from 1970 to 1990. Because of diminishing returns, it follows that the marginal product of capital (equal to the real rental) fell, by an average of 3.4% per year as shown in part A of Table 5-3. At the same time, each worker had more capital to work with, so the marginal product of labor (equal to the real wage) grew by an average of 1.6% per year, as also shown in part A. These estimates of the falling rental and rising wage are consistent with the short-run specific-factors model.

But there is a second way to calculate a rental on capital besides using the marginal product. Under this second approach, we start with the price P_K of some capital

TABLE 5-3

Real Rental and Wages in Singapore This table shows the growth rate in the real rental and real wages in Singapore, depending on the method used to construct these factor prices. In part A, a production function approach is used to construct the factor prices, and the real rental falls over time because of the growth in capital. As a result, implied productivity growth is negative. In part B, the rental and wages are constructed from data on payments to capital and labor in Singapore, and real wages grow over time, while the real rental either grows or falls slightly. As a result, implied productivity growth is positive.

	ANNUAL GROWTH RATE (%)		
	Real Rental	Real Wages	Implied Productivity
Part A: Using Production Function and Marginal Products			
Period:			
1970–1980	−5.0	2.6	−1.5
1980–1990	−1.9	0.5	−0.7
1970–1990	−3.4	1.6	−1.1
Part B: Using Calculated Rental and Actual Wages			
Interest Rate Used and Period:			
Bank lending rate (1968–1990)	1.6	2.7	2.2
Return on equity (1971–1990)	−0.2	3.2	1.5
Earnings–price ratio (1973–1990)	−0.5	3.6	1.6

Data from: Part A from Alwyn Young, 1995, "The Tyranny of Numbers: Confronting the Statistical Realities of the East Asian Growth Experience," Quarterly Journal of Economics, 110(3), August, 641–680. Part B from Chang-Tai Hsieh, 2002, "What Explains the Industrial Revolution in East Asia? Evidence from the Factor Markets," American Economic Review, 92(3), 502–526.

[16] In 2005 China had $318 billion in foreign capital, with another $533 billion in Hong Kong; Mexico had $210 billion; Brazil $202 billion; and Singapore $189 billion, which was 7% of the total foreign capital in developing countries.

equipment. If that equipment was rented rather than purchased, what would its rental be? Let us suppose that the rental agency needs to make the same rate of return on renting the capital equipment that it would make if it invested its money in some financial asset, such as a savings account in a bank or the stock market. If it invested P_K and the asset had the interest rate of i, then it could expect to earn $P_K \cdot i$ from that asset. On the other hand, if it rents out the equipment, then that machinery also suffers wear and tear, and the rental agency needs to recover that cost, too. If d is the rate of depreciation of the capital equipment (the fraction of it that is used up each year), then to earn the same return on a financial asset as from renting out the equipment, the rental agency must receive $P_K \cdot (i + d)$. This formula is an estimate of R, the rental on capital. Dividing by an overall price index P, the real rental is

$$\frac{R}{P} = \frac{P_K}{P} \cdot (i + d)$$

In part B of Table 5-3, we show the growth rate in the real rental, computed from this formula, which depends on the interest rate used. In the first row, we use the bank lending rate for i, and the computed real rental grows by 1.6% per year. In the next rows, we use two interest rates from the stock market: the return on equity (what you would earn from investing in stocks) and the earnings–price ratio (the profits that each firm earns divided by the value of its outstanding stocks). In both these latter cases, the calculated real rental falls slightly over time, by 0.2% and 0.5% per year, much less than the fall in the real rental in part A. According to the calculated real rentals in part B, there is little evidence of a downward fall in the rentals over time.

In part B, we also show the real wage, computed from actual wages paid in Singapore. Real wages grow substantially over time—between 2.7% and 3.6% per year, depending on the exact interest rate and period used. This is not what we predicted from our long-run model, in which factor prices would be unchanged by an inflow of capital, because the capital–labor ratios are constant (so the marginal product of labor would not change). That real wages are growing in Singapore, with little change in the real rental, is an indication that there is *productivity growth* in the economy, which leads to an increase in the marginal product of labor *and* in the real wage.

We will not discuss how productivity growth is actually measured but just report the findings from the studies in Table 5-3: in part B, productivity growth is between 1.5% and 2.2% per year, depending on the period, but in part A, productivity growth is negative! The reason that productivity growth is so much higher in part B is that the average of the growth in the real wage and real rental is rising, which indicates that productivity growth has occurred. In contrast, in part A the average of the growth in the real wage and real rental is zero or negative, indicating that no productivity growth has occurred.

The idea that Singapore might have zero productivity growth contradicts what many people believe about its economy and the economies of other fast-growing Asian countries, which were thought to exhibit "miraculous" growth during this period. If productivity growth is zero or negative, then all growth is due only to capital accumulation, and FDI has no spillover benefits to the local economy. Positive productivity growth, as shown in part B, indicates that the free-market policies pursued by Singapore stimulated innovations in the manufacture of goods that have resulted in higher productivity and lower costs. This is what many economists and policy makers believe happened in Singapore, but this belief is challenged by the productivity calculations in part A. Which scenario is correct—zero or positive productivity growth for Singapore—is a source of ongoing debate in economics. Read the item **Headlines: The Myth of Asia's Miracle** for one interpretation of the growth in Singapore and elsewhere in Asia.

HEADLINES

The Myth of Asia's Miracle

A CAUTIONARY FABLE: Once upon a time, Western opinion leaders found themselves both impressed and frightened by the extraordinary growth rates achieved by a set of Eastern economies. Although those economies were still substantially poorer and smaller than those of the West, the speed with which they had transformed themselves from peasant societies into industrial power-houses, their continuing ability to achieve growth rates several times higher than the advanced nations, and their increasing ability to challenge or even surpass American and European technology in certain areas seemed to call into question the dominance not only of Western power but of

Western ideology. The leaders of those nations did not share our faith in free markets or unlimited civil liberties. They asserted with increasing self-confidence that their system was superior: societies that accepted strong, even authoritarian governments and were willing to limit individual liberties in the interest of the common good, take charge of their economics, and sacrifice short-run consumer interests for the sake of long-run growth would eventually outperform the increasingly chaotic societies of the West. And a growing minority of Western intellectuals agreed.

The gap between Western and Eastern economic performance eventually became a

political issue. The Democrats recaptured the White House under the leadership of a young, energetic new president who pledged to "get the country moving again"—a pledge that, to him and his closest advisers, meant accelerating America's economic growth to meet the Eastern challenge.

The time, of course, was the early 1960s. The dynamic young president was John F. Kennedy. The technological feats that so alarmed the West were the launch of Sputnik and the early Soviet lead in space. And the rapidly growing Eastern economies were those of the Soviet Union and its satellite nations.

Were you tricked by this fable? Did you think that the "Eastern economies" that the author, Paul Krugman, referred to in the beginning were the Asian economies? Krugman is using this rhetorical trick to suggest that the high growth of the Asian economies is not too different from the growth of the Soviet Union in the 1950s and 1960s, which was due to capital accumulation but without much productivity growth. Other economists disagree and believe that Asian growth is due in significant part to improved productivity, in addition to capital accumulation.

Source: Reprinted by permission of Foreign Affairs from "The Myth of Asia's Miracle," Paul Krugman November/December. Copyright 1994 Foreign Affairs; permission conveyed through Copyright Clearance Center, Inc.

3 Gains from Labor and Capital Flows

Foreign investment and immigration are both controversial policy issues. Most countries impose limits on FDI at some time in their development but later become open to foreign investment. Nearly all countries impose limits on the inflow of people. In the United States, controls on immigration were first established by the Quota Law of 1921, which limited the number of people arriving annually from each country of origin. The Immigration and Nationality Act Amendments of 1965 revised the country-specific limits and allowed immigration on a first-come, first-served basis, up to an annual limit, with special allowances for family members and people in certain occupations. Subsequent revisions to the immigration laws in the United States have established penalties for employers who knowingly hire undocumented immigrants, have allowed some undocumented immigrants to gain citizenship, or have tightened border controls and deported other undocumented immigrants.

Why is immigration so controversial? A glance at articles in the media will show that some groups oppose the spending of public funds on immigrants, such as for schooling, medical care, or welfare. Other groups fear the competition for jobs created by the inflow of foreign workers. We have already seen that immigration creates gains and losses for different groups, often lowering the wage for workers in similar jobs but providing benefits to firms hiring these workers.

This finding raises the important question: Does immigration provide an overall gain to the host country, not including the gains to the immigrants themselves? We presume that the immigrants are better off from higher wages in the country to which they move.[17] But what about the other workers and owners of capital and land in the host country? In the short run, we learned that workers in the host country face competition from the immigrants and receive lower wages, while owners of capital and land benefit from immigration. When we add up these various gains and losses, are there "overall gains" to the destination country, in the same way as we have found overall gains from trade? Fortunately, this answer turns out to be yes.

Immigration benefits the host country in the specific-factors model, not including the income of the immigrants themselves. If we include the immigrant earnings with Foreign income, then we find that emigration benefits the Foreign country, too. The same argument can be made for FDI. An inflow of capital benefits the host country, not including the extra earnings of foreign capital. By counting those extra earnings in Foreign income, then FDI also benefits the source country of the capital. After showing these theoretical results, we discuss how large the overall gains from immigration or FDI flows might be in practice.

Gains from Immigration

To measure the gains from immigration, we will use the specific-factors model. In Figure 5-16, we measure the *world* amount of labor on the horizontal axis, which equals $(\overline{L} + \overline{L}^*)$. The number of workers in the Home country $\overline{L}$ is measured from left (the origin 0) to right. The number of workers in Foreign $\overline{L}^*$ is measured from right (0^*) to left. Each point on the horizontal axis indicates how many workers are located

FIGURE 5-16

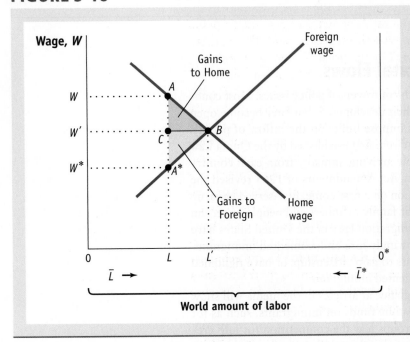

World Labor Market Initially, Home has 0^*L workers and Foreign has 0^*L workers. The Home wage is W, as determined at point A, which is higher than the Foreign wage W^* at A^*. Workers will move from Foreign to Home to receive higher wages. The equilibrium with full migration is at point B, where wages are equalized at W'. The gain to Home from migration is measured by triangle ABC, and triangle A^*BC represents the gains to Foreign.

---

[17] This ignores cases in which the immigrants regret the decision to move because of hardship in making the passage or discrimination once they arrive.

in the two countries. For example, point L indicates that $0L$ workers are located in Home, and 0^*L workers are located in the Foreign country.

Wages in Home and Abroad We already know from our discussion earlier in the chapter that as immigrants enter the Home country, the wage is reduced. In Figure 5-16, we graph this relationship as a downward-sloping line labeled "Home wage." With Home workers of $0L$ before immigration, the wage is W at point A. If Foreign workers enter and the Home labor force grows to $0L'$, then the Home wage is reduced to W' at point B. The downward-sloping "Home wage" line illustrates the inverse relationship between the number of Home workers and their wage. You can think of this line as a labor demand curve, not for a single industry, but for the economy as a whole.

Similarly, in the Foreign country, there is an inverse relationship between the numbers of workers and their wage. Before any emigration, the labor force in Foreign is 0^*L, and we show the wage at W^* at point A^*. That is lower than the Home wage of W, so some workers will want to migrate from Foreign to Home. Remembering that we measure the Foreign workers from right (0^*) to left, when the labor force abroad shrinks from 0^*L to $0^*L'$, the Foreign wages rise from W^* to W' at point B. We see that as Foreign workers leave, it benefits those left behind by raising their wages.

We will refer to point B as the **equilibrium with full migration**. At this point, the wages earned in Home and abroad are equalized at W'. It would certainly take a long time for migration to lead to complete wage equality across countries. In our discussion of emigration from the Old World to the New, we saw in Figure 5-3 that real wages in the New World were still twice as high as wages in Europe even after 40 years of large-scale migration. So the equilibrium with full migration is reached only in the very long run. The question we want to answer is whether this migration has benefited the workers (not including the immigrants), labor, and capital in the Home country. In addition, we want to know whether migration has benefited the Foreign country, including the migrants.

Gains for the Home Country To determine whether there are overall gains for Home, we need to measure the contribution of each Foreign worker to the output of one good or the other in that country. This measurement is easy to do. The marginal product of labor in either industry (multiplied by the price of shoes or computers) equals the Home wage. So the first Foreign worker to migrate has a marginal product equal to the Home wage, which is W at point A. As more Foreign workers migrate, the marginal product of labor in both Home industries falls due to diminishing returns. We can measure the immigrants' marginal product by the wage that is paid in Home, which falls from W to W' as we move down the Home wage curve from point A to B.

At the equilibrium with full migration, point B, *all* Foreign immigrants are paid the Home wage of W'. But all Foreign workers except the last one to enter had a marginal product of labor that is above W': the first Foreign worker had a marginal product of W, and the later Foreign immigrants have lower marginal products, ranging from W to W'. Therefore, their contribution to the output of goods in the Home economy *exceeds* the wage that they are paid. The first Foreign immigrant had a marginal product of W but receives the wage W', so the gain to the Home economy from having that worker is $(W' - W')$. Likewise, each immigrant to come later has a marginal product between W and W' but is still paid the wage W', so the difference between their marginal products and wages is a gain for the Home economy.

Adding the gains to the Home economy from the Foreign workers, we end up with the triangle ABC, which represents the Home gains as a result of full immigration. The reason for these gains is the law of diminishing returns: as more Foreign immigrants enter the Home workforce, their marginal products fall, and because the wage equals the marginal product of the last worker, it must be less than the marginal products of the earlier immigrants. This economic logic guarantees gains to the Home country from migration.

Gains for the Foreign Country Now consider the Foreign country. To assess the overall gains from emigration, we include the wages received by the migrants who left in calculating Foreign income. These wages are often returned to their families (see **Application: Immigrants and Their Remittances**), but even if they are not, we still incorporate the wages earned by the immigrants in our measure of Foreign income because that is where the migrants originally came from.

In the absence of any emigration, the Foreign wage is W^*, the marginal product of labor in either industry abroad (multiplied by the price of that product in Foreign). As Foreign workers emigrate, the marginal product of labor remaining in Foreign rises, and the Foreign wage rises from W^* to W' (or from points A^* to B in Figure 5-16). Each of these higher marginal products or wages—between W^* and W'—equals the drop in Foreign output (of either good) from having workers leave.

Under full migration, all Foreign migrants earn the wage W' in the Home country. Notice that this wage is *higher* than their Foreign marginal products of labor, which are between W^* and W'. The difference between the wage earned by the migrants and their Foreign marginal products equals the gain to Foreign. Adding up the gains over all Foreign emigrants, we obtain the triangle A^*BC. This gain represents the earnings of the emigrants over and above the drop in output that occurs when they leave Foreign.

APPLICATION

Immigrants and Their Remittances

Immigrants often send a substantial portion of their earnings back home, which we refer to as "remittances." The remittances flowing between major regions of the world are shown in Table 5-4 (with greater values shown in bold). Emigrants from countries in Asia and in Europe who work in those same regions send a high value of remittances back home. For example, Chinese workers return home about $4 billion each from Japan and South Korea, $3 billion from Singapore, and $2 billion from Bangladesh. Many remittances from eastern European workers working in

TABLE 5-4

Remittances Between Major Regions of the World, 2017 Shown here are the remittances sent and received by regions of the world ($ billions, with larger values in bold). Emigrants from countries in Asia and in Europe who work in those same regions send a high value of remittances back home. In addition, Europe sends a high value of remittances to Asia, and North America sends a high value of remittances to Asia and to Central and South America. The total value of remittances was $613 billion in 2017.

		Receiving Country				
		Africa	Asia	Central and South America	Europe	North America
	Africa	12.8	2.3	0.0	2.8	0.2
	Asia	21.8	**161.8**	1.1	15.4	1.3
Sending	Central and South America	0.1	1.5	9.1	5.7	2.8
Country	Europe	25.9	**46.4**	7.9	**97.2**	1.8
	North America	11.4	**73.1**	63.9	22.1	1.5
	World	**72.8**	**297.2**	**82.2**	**149.3**	8.0

western Europe are returned home. Europe also sends a high value of remittances to Asia, and North America sends a high value of remittances to Asia and to Central and South America. For example, China received about $16 billion in remittances from the United States, $4 billion from Canada, and $1 billion each from Italy, Spain, and the United Kingdom, while Mexico received $30 billion from the United States. Africa receives slightly less in remittances ($73 billion) than does Central and South America ($82 billion).

The total value of remittances was $613 billion in 2017. In that year there were about 257 million immigrant workers in the world, so the total remittances of $613 billion translate into each immigrant worker sending home approximately $2,400.

In Table 5-5, we show the remittances received by some developing countries in 2017, as compared with their net foreign aid. The countries receiving the largest amount of remittances in 2017 were India ($79 billion), Mexico ($36 billion), and the Philippines ($33 billion). For all countries except Sudan, the income sent home by emigrants is a larger source of income than official aid. Sudan was experiencing a humanitarian crisis so official aid was high. Remittances and official aid are especially important in other African countries, too.

The fact that emigrants return some of their income back home may not be enough to compensate their home countries for the loss of their labor. To calculate any gain to the home countries from the emigration of their workers, we need to include *all the earnings* of the emigrants in their home countries' income. In reality, however, emigrants do not send all of their income home, so the countries they leave can lose from their outflow.

To address this concern, Professor Jagdish Bhagwati, an Indian-born economist now at Columbia University in New York, has proposed that countries impose a "brain-drain tax" on the outflow of educated workers. The idea is to tax the earnings of people living outside the countries in which they were born and, through an organization such as the United Nations, return the proceeds from the tax to the countries that lose the most workers. In that way, countries with an outflow of educated workers would be compensated, at least in part, for the outflow. A brain-drain tax has been widely debated, but so far it has not been used in practice.

TABLE 5-5

Workers' Remittances and Net Foreign Aid, 2017 Shown here are the remittances received by various developing countries from their citizens working abroad. In nearly all cases, these remittances are much larger than the official aid received by the countries. An exception was Sudan, which was experiencing a humanitarian crisis, so aid was high.

Country	Remittances Received ($ billions)	Net Aid Received ($ billions)
Albania	1.5	0.2
Bangladesh	15.6	3.7
Colombia	6.4	0.8
Dominican Republic	6.8	0.1
Guatemala	8.5	0.4
India	78.8	3.1
Mexico	35.6	0.7
Morocco	6.9	1.9
Nigeria	22.0	3.4
Philippines	32.8	0.2
Sudan	0.4	0.8
Vietnam	15.9	2.4

Data from: World Development Indicators, The World Bank.

World Gains from Migration Combining the gains to the Home and Foreign countries, we obtain the triangular region ABA^*, the world gains from immigration. This magnitude is not too difficult to measure in practice. Turning the triangle on its side, its base equals $(W - W^*)$, the difference in the Home and Foreign wage in the absence of any migration. The height of the triangle is $(L' - L)$, the number of foreign workers that would emigrate in the equilibrium with full migration. So the area of the triangle is $\frac{1}{2}(W - W^*) \cdot (L' - L)$. To solve for the area, we need to know the difference in wages before any migration and the number of people who would emigrate.

One way to think about the world gains from migration is that they equal the *increase in world GDP due to immigration*. To understand why this is so, think about the first person to migrate from Foreign to Home. That person earns the wage W^* in Foreign, which equals his or her marginal product times the price in the industry in which he or she works. When this individual leaves Foreign, GDP in that country falls by W^*. Once he or she moves to Home, he or she earns W, which again reflects the marginal product times the industry price. So W equals the increase in Home GDP when the immigrant begins working. The difference between the Home and Foreign wages therefore equals the net increase in world GDP due to migration. By adding up this amount across all migrants, we obtain the triangular region ABA^*, the increase in world GDP and the world gains due to migration.

In practice, however, there are other costs that immigrants bear that would make the gains from immigration less than the increase in world GDP. Immigrants often face sizable moving costs, including the psychological costs of missing their families and home countries as well as monetary payments to traffickers of undocumented immigrants. These costs should be subtracted from the increase in GDP to obtain the net gains. Because all the moving costs are hard to quantify, however, in the next application we measure the net gains from immigration by the increase in Home or world GDP.

APPLICATION

Measuring the Gains from Immigration

How large are the gains from immigration? For the United States, a study by Professor George Borjas puts the net gain from immigration at about 0.1% of GDP (one-tenth of 1% of GDP). That value is obtained by using a stock of immigrants equal to 10% of the workforce in the United States and assuming that the immigrants compete for the same jobs as U.S. workers. If instead we assume the immigrants are lower-skilled on average than the U.S. population, then the low-skilled immigrants can complement the higher-skilled U.S. population, and the gains from immigration in the United States are somewhat higher, up to 0.4% of GDP. These estimates are shown in the first row of Table 5-6. The net gains to the United States in this case equal the increase in U.S. GDP.

Borjas's estimates for the U.S. gains from immigration may seem small, but lying behind these numbers is a larger shift in income from labor to capital and landowners. Labor loses from immigration, while capital and landowners gain, and the net effect of all these changes in real income is the gain in GDP that Borjas estimates. For the net gain of 0.1% of U.S. GDP due to immigration, Borjas estimates that capital would gain 2% and domestic labor would lose 1.9% of GDP. These figures lead him to conclude, "The relatively small size of the immigration surplus [that is, the gain in GDP]—particularly when compared to the very large wealth transfers caused by immigration [that is, the shift in income from labor to capital]—probably explains why the debate over immigration policy has usually focused on the potentially harmful labor market impacts rather than the overall increase in native income."

TABLE 5-6

Gains from Immigration The results from several studies of immigration are shown in this table. The second column shows the amount of immigration (as a percentage of the Home labor force), and the third column shows the increase in Home GDP or the increase in GDP of the region.

	AMOUNT OF IMMIGRATION	
	Percent of Home Labor	Increase in GDP (%)
Part A: Calculation of Home Gains		
Study used:		
Borjas (1995, 1999), U.S. gains	10	0.1–0.4
Kremer and Watt (2006), household workers	7	1.2–1.4
Peri, Shih, and Sparber (2015), STEM workers*	1.1	4.0
Part B: Calculation of Regional Gains		
Study used:		
Walmsley and Winters (2005),		
from developed to developing countries	3	0.6
Klein and Ventura (2009),		
enlargement of the European Union		
After 10 years	0.8–1.8	0.2–0.7
After 25 years	2.5–5.0	0.6–1.8
After 50 years	4.8–8.8	1.7–4.5

*STEM workers: scientists, technology professionals, engineers, and mathematicians.
Data from: George Borjas, 1995, "The Economic Benefits from Immigration," Journal of Economic Perspectives, 9(2), 3–22.
George Borjas, 1999, "The Economic Analysis of Immigration." In Orley Ashenfelter and David Card, eds., Handbook of Labor Economics, Vol. 3A (Amsterdam: North Holland), pp. 1697–1760.
Paul Klein and Gustavo Ventura, 2009, "Productivity Differences and the Dynamic Effects of Labour Movements," Journal of Monetary Economics, 56(8), November, 1059–1073.
Michael Kremer and Stanley Watt, 2006, "The Globalization of Household Production," Harvard University.
Giovanni Peri, Kevin Shih, and Chad Sparber, 2015, "STEM Workers, H-1B Visas, and Productivity in US Cities," Journal of Labor Economics, 33(S225–S255), July.
Terrie Louise Walmsley and L. Alan Winters, 2005, "Relaxing the Restrictions on the Temporary Movement of Natural Persons: A Simulation Analysis," Journal of Economic Integration, 20(4), December, 688–726.

Other calculations suggest that the overall gains from immigration could be larger than Borjas's estimates. In the second row of Table 5-6, we report figures from a study by Professors Kremer and Watt that focuses on just one type of immigrant: household workers. Foreign household workers, who are primarily female, make up 10% or more of the labor force in Bahrain, Kuwait, and Saudi Arabia, and about 7% of the labor force in Hong Kong and Singapore. The presence of these household workers often allows another member of that household—typically, a highly educated woman—to seek employment in her Home country. Thus, the immigration of low-skilled household workers allows for an increase in the high-skilled supply of individuals in Home, generating higher Home GDP as a result. It is estimated that this type of immigration, if it accounts for 7% of the workforce as in some countries, would increase Home GDP by approximately 1.2% to 1.4%.

Another larger estimate of the gains from immigration was obtained in a study by Professor Giovanni Peri and his co-authors. They measured the inflow of foreign workers to the United States who are scientists, technology professionals, engineers, or mathematicians—or STEM workers, for short. The H-1B visa program has allowed between 50,000 and 150,000 of these immigrants to enter the United States annually since 1991. Many have remained in the country as permanent residents. By 2010, foreign-born STEM workers accounted for 1.1% of the population in major cities in the United States, and accounted for 24% of the total STEM workers (foreign or U.S.-born) found in these cities. Peri and his co-authors measured the productivity gains to these cities from having this inflow of foreign talent, and they found that the gains were substantial: 10% to 20% of the productivity growth in these cities can be explained by the presence of the foreign STEM workers. These productivity gains can come from new start-up technology companies, patents for new inventions, and so on. Adding up these productivity gains over time, the presence of the foreign STEM workers accounted for a 4% increase in GDP in the United States by 2010.

In part B of Table 5-6, we report results from estimates of gains due to migration for several regions of the world. The first study, by Professors Walmsley and Winters, found that an increase in labor supply to developed countries of 3%, as a result of immigration from the developing countries, would create world gains of 0.6% of world GDP. This calculation is similar to the triangle of gains ABA^* shown in Figure 5-16. The next study, by Professors Klein and Ventura, obtains larger estimates of the world gains by modeling the differences in technology across countries. Under this approach, wealthier regions have higher productivity, so an immigrant moving there will be more productive than in Home. This productivity increase is offset somewhat by a skill loss for the immigrant (since the immigrant may not find the job for which he or she is best suited, at least initially). Nevertheless, the assumed skill loss is less than the productivity difference between countries, so immigrants are always more productive in the country to which they move.

In their 2006 study, Klein and Ventura considered the recent enlargement of the European Union (EU) from 15 countries to 25.[18] Workers from the newly added eastern European countries are, in principle, permitted to work anywhere in the EU. Klein and Ventura assumed that the original 15 EU countries are twice as productive as the newly added countries. During the first 10 years, they found that the population of those 15 EU countries increased by between 0.8% and 1.8%, and the combined GDP in the EU increased by between 0.2% and 0.7%. The range of these estimates comes from different assumptions about the skill losses of immigrants when they move, and from the psychological costs of their moving, which slow down the extent of migration. As time passed, however, more people flowed from eastern to western Europe, and GDP continued to rise. Klein and Ventura estimated that in 25 years the combined GDP of the EU will increase by between 0.6% and 1.8%, and that over 50 years, the increase in GDP would be 1.7% to 4.5%.

Gains from Foreign Direct Investment

A diagram very similar to Figure 5-16 can be used to measure the gains from FDI. In Figure 5-17, we show the world amount of capital on the horizontal axis, which equals $\overline{K} + \overline{K}^*$. The rental earned in each country is on the vertical axis. With $0K$ units of capital employed in Home (measured from left to right), the Home rental is R, determined at point A. The remaining capital 0^*K (measured from right to left) is in Foreign, and the Foreign rental is R^*, determined at point A^*.

Because the Foreign rental is higher than that in Home, capital will flow from Home to Foreign. As it enters Foreign, the additional capital will reduce the marginal product of capital and bid down the rental. Likewise, as capital leaves Home, the marginal product of capital will increase, and the Home rental will be bid up. The equilibrium with full capital flows is at point B, where rentals are equalized at R'. Similar to

---

[18] Prior to 2004, the European Union consisted of 15 countries: Belgium, France, Germany, Italy, Luxembourg, and the Netherlands (founding members in 1952); Denmark, Ireland, and the United Kingdom (added in 1973); Greece (added in 1981); Portugal and Spain (added in 1986); and Austria, Finland, and Sweden (added in 1995). On May 1, 2004, 10 more countries were added: Cyprus, the Czech Republic, Estonia, Hungary, Lithuania, Latvia, Malta, Poland, Slovakia, and Slovenia. Bulgaria and Romania were then added in 2007, and Croatia was added in 2013.

what we found in the case of immigration, the gains to Home from the capital outflow is the triangle *ABC*, while the gains to Foreign is the triangle *A*BC*, and the world gains are *A*BA*.

APPLICATION

Measuring the Gains from Foreign Direct Investment

The gains from foreign direct investment are calculated by the triangles shown in Figure 5-17. Because this calculation is complex, researchers have often asked simpler questions to get an idea of the gains from foreign direct investment. One of these questions is whether foreign firms pay *higher wages* than domestic firms operating in the same country. There is evidence in favor of this hypothesis for many countries, including China, Mexico, Portugal, Sweden, Venezuela, and the United States. But there is also a reason to be cautious about accepting these results: What if foreign firms try to establish themselves in a new country by hiring the very best workers and paying them more because they are the best? In that case, the higher wages would be evidence of high worker *quality* and would not actually indicate gains for these workers over and above what they might earn working for a domestic firm.

One recent study by Professors Bradley Setzler and Felix Tintelnot controls for the quality of workers by keeping track of the wages paid to the *same worker* when they move from working for an American firm to working for a foreign firm operating in the United States.[19] The quality of that worker does not change when they change jobs, so any difference in pay must be due to the firm they are working for.

According to this study, foreign firms operating in the United States pay wages that are 7% higher on average than when the same worker was employed in an

FIGURE 5-17

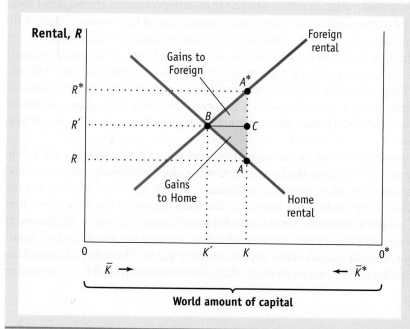

World Capital Market With 0*K* units of capital in Home, the Home rental is *R* at point *A*. The remaining capital 0*K is in Foreign, and the Foreign rental is *R** at point *A**. Capital will move from Home to Foreign to receive a higher rental. The equilibrium with full capital flows is at point *B*, where rentals are equalized at *R′*. Triangle *ABC* measures the gains to Home from the capital outflow, and triangle *A*BC* measures the gains to Foreign.

---

[19] See Bradley Setzler and Felix Tintelnot, 2020, "The Effects of Foreign Multinationals on Workers and Firms in the United States," National Bureau of Economic Research Working Paper No. 26149.

American-owned firm. There is a spread of these higher average wages from zero to 15%, depending on the nationality of the foreign firm. An exception occurs, however, for Chinese firms operating in the United States. On average, Chinese-owned firms tend to pay wages that are 4% lower than wages earned by those workers at an American firm. This study also finds that jobs created by foreign firms have positive effects on employment and wages at American-owned firms in the same city. For every one job created by a foreign-owned firm, there is an additional 0.4 jobs created in an American firm. In addition, wages are increased at American firms as foreign capital flows in, which is a gain for those workers even when they do not shift to a foreign-owned firm. That rise in wages due to an inflow of foreign capital is consistent with the short-run model as shown in Figure 5-13, panel (a).

A different source of gains provided by foreign-owned firms—which is not part of our model—occurs when those firms provide technological knowledge that spills over to domestic firms. An example comes Chile, a country that is well known for the production of grapes because of its climate and geography. In the 1970s and 1980s, Chile was one of the top grape-exporting countries but was struggling to export wine. A number of foreign firms entered Chile, mainly from Spain (which is one of the top five exporters of wine in the world), and opened facilities to produce and export wine to other South American countries and to North America. Over time, domestic Chilean firms learned the advertising methods, technology, and management used by the Spanish firms and became very successful in foreign markets. Chile has now joined Spain as one of the top five wine-exporting countries in the world.[20]

4 Conclusions

Immigration, the movement of workers between countries, potentially affects the wages in the host country in which the workers arrive. In the short-run specific-factors model, a larger supply of workers due to immigration will lower wages. Most immigrants into the United States have either the lowest or the highest amounts of education. As a result, after an inflow of labor from other countries, the wages of these two groups of workers fall in the short run. The majority of U.S. workers, those with mid-levels of education, are not affected that much by immigration. Moreover, the arrival of immigrants is beneficial to owners of capital and land in the specific-factors model. As wages are reduced in the short run, the rentals on capital and land will rise. This result helps to explain why landowners lobby for programs to allow agricultural workers to immigrate at least temporarily, and why other industries support increased immigration, such as H-1B visas for workers in the high-technology and other professional industries.

In a long-run framework, when capital can move between industries, the fall in wages will not occur. Instead, the industries that use labor intensively can expand and other industries contract, so that the immigrants become employed without any fall in wages. This change in industry outputs is the main finding of the Rybczynski theorem. The evidence from the Mariel boat lift in 1980 suggests that a readjustment of industry outputs along these lines occurred in Miami after the arrival of immigrants from Cuba: the output of the apparel industry fell by less than predicted from other cities, whereas the output of some skill-intensive industries fell by more than predicted.

---

[20] This example from the wine industry in Chile was provided by Professor Dhimitri Qirjo, SUNY Plattsburgh; in other manufacturing industries in Chile as well, domestic firms have learned from the example of foreign and domestic exporters. See Roberto Alvarez and Ricardo A. López, 2008, "Is Exporting a Source of Productivity Spillovers?" *Review of World Economics*, 144(4), 723–749.

Foreign direct investment (FDI), the movement of capital between countries, has effects analogous to immigration. In the short run, the entry of foreign capital into a country will lower the rental on capital, raise wages, and lower the rental on land. But in the long run, when capital and land can move between industries, these changes in the wage and rentals need not occur. Instead, industry outputs can adjust according to the Rybczynski theorem so that the extra capital is fully employed without any change in the wage or rentals. Evidence from Singapore suggests that foreign capital can be absorbed without a large decline in the rental or the marginal product of capital, though this is an area of ongoing debate in economics.

Both immigration and FDI create world gains as labor and capital move from countries with low marginal products to countries with high marginal products. Gains for the host country are created because the inflow of labor and capital is paid an amount that is less than its full contribution to GDP in the host country. At the same time, there are also gains to the labor and capital in the country they leave, provided that the income earned by the emigrants or capital is included in that country's welfare.

KEY POINTS

1. Holding the amount of capital and land fixed in both industries, as in the specific-factors model, immigration leads to a fall in wages. This was the case, for example, with the mass migration to the New World in the nineteenth century.

2. As wages fall because of immigration, the marginal products of the specific factors (capital and land) rise, and therefore their rentals also increase.

3. Fixing the amount of capital and land in a country is a reasonable assumption in the short run, but in the longer run, firms will move capital between industries, which will change the effect of immigration on wages and rentals.

4. In a long-run model with two goods and two factors, both of which are perfectly mobile between the industries, additional labor from immigration will be absorbed entirely by the labor-intensive industry. Furthermore, the labor-intensive industry will also absorb additional capital and labor from the capital-intensive industry, so its capital–labor ratio does not change in the long run. Because the capital–labor ratio in each industry does not change, the wage and rentals remain the same as well. This results in what is known as factor price insensitivity.

5. According to the Rybczynski theorem, immigration will lead to an increase in output in the labor-intensive industry and a decrease in the output of the capital-intensive industry. This result is different from that of the short-run specific-factors model, in which immigration leads to increased output in both industries.

6. Besides trade in goods and the movement of labor, another way that countries interact with one another is through investment. When a company owns property, plant, or equipment in another country, it is called foreign direct investment, or FDI.

7. In the short run, FDI lowers the rentals on capital and land and raises wages. In the long run, the extra capital can be absorbed in the capital-intensive industry without any change in the wage or rental.

8. According to the Rybczynski theorem, FDI will lead to an increase in the output of the capital-intensive industry and a decrease in the output of the labor-intensive industry.

9. The movement of capital and labor generates overall gains for both the source and host countries, provided that the income of the emigrants is included in the source country's welfare. Hence, there are global gains from immigration and FDI.

KEY TERMS

specific-factors model, p. 126
refugee, p. 127
asylum, p. 136

Rybczynski theorem, p. 143
factor price insensitivity, p. 144
real value-added, p. 145

foreign direct investment (FDI), p. 148
equilibrium with full
    migration, p. 157

PROBLEMS

1. **📊 Discovering Data** In this question, you will be asked to use European data to find the latest figures on refugees and asylum cases granted. The source of the data is Eurostat, at: ec.europa.eu/eurostat. Choose "Data" and "Browse statistics by theme." Under the heading "Population and social conditions," you will find "Population: . . . asylum & migration" and then an icon for "Asylum & managed migration." Under "Data" choose "main tables".

   a. How many asylum seekers are in Germany for the most recent year available? Also write down the number of asylum seekers in the most recent year available for one other country.

   b. Use the "Data" tab on the left of this webpage to learn more about the applications of asylum seekers and the decisions on those applications. What is the difference between "first instance" decisions and "final decisions" on asylum applications? Write down the numbers of these decisions for the most recent year available, in Germany and in the other country that you chose in part (a).

   c. What is a "first permit," and how many were issued in Germany and in the other country that you chose, for the most recent year available? What is the number of "all valid permits" in these two countries, and how does that compare with the population of these countries?

2. In the short-run specific-factors model, examine the impact on a small country following a natural disaster that decreases its population. Assume that land is specific to agriculture, and capital is specific to manufacturing, whereas labor is free to move between the two sectors.

   a. In a diagram similar to Figure 5-2, determine the impact of the decrease in the workforce on the output of each industry and the equilibrium wage.

   b. What happens to the rentals on capital and land?

3. How would your answer to Problem 2 change if instead we use the long-run model, with shoes and computers produced using labor and capital?

4. Consider an increase in the supply of labor due to immigration, and use the long-run model. Figure 5-10 shows the box diagram and the leftward shift of the origin for the shoe industry. Redraw this diagram but instead shift to the right the origin for computers. That is, expand the labor axis by the amount ΔL but shift it to the right

rather than to the left. With the new diagram, show how the amount of labor and capital in shoes and computers is determined, without any change in factor prices. Carefully explain what has happened to the amount of labor and capital used in each industry and to the output of each industry.

5. In the short-run specific-factors model, consider a decrease in the stock of land. For example, suppose a natural disaster decreases the quantity of arable land used for planting crops.

   a. Redraw panel (a) of Figure 5-13 starting from the initial equilibrium at point A, and show the shift in the marginal product of labor curve in each industry.

   b. What is the effect of this change in land on the quantity of labor in each industry and on the equilibrium wage?

   c. What is the effect on the rental on land and the rental on capital?

   d. Now suppose that the international community wants to help the country struck by the natural disaster and decides to do so by increasing its level of FDI. So the rest of the world increases its investment in physical capital in the stricken country. Illustrate the effect of this policy on the equilibrium wage and rentals.

6. According to part A of Table 5-2, what education level loses most (i.e., has the greatest decrease in wage) from immigration to the United States? Does this result depend on keeping the rental on capital constant? Explain why or why not.

WORK IT OUT 📖 Achieve | interactive activity

7. Suppose that computers use 4 units of capital for each worker, so that $K_C = 4 \cdot L_C$, whereas shoes use 0.2 units of capital for each worker, so that $K_S = 0.2 \cdot L_S$. There are 200 workers and 200 units of capital in the economy.

   a. Solve for the amount of labor and capital used in each industry.

   Hint: The box diagram shown in Figure 5-9 means that the amount of labor and capital used in each industry must add up to the total for the economy, so that

   $$K_C + K_S = 200 \text{ and } L_C + L_S = 200$$

   Use the facts that $K_C = 4 \cdot L_C$ and $K_S = 0.2 \cdot L_S$ to rewrite these equations as

   $$4 \cdot L_C + 0.2 \cdot L_S = 200 \text{ and } L_C + L_S = 200$$

Use these two equations to solve for L_C and L_S, and then calculate the amount of capital used in each industry using $K_C = 4 \cdot L_C$ and $K_S = 0.2 \cdot L_S$.

b. Suppose that the number of workers increases to 250 because of immigration, keeping total capital fixed at 200. Again, solve for the amount of labor and capital used in each industry. *Hint:* Redo the calculations from part (a), but using $L_C + L_S = 250$.

c. Suppose instead that the amount of capital increases to 250 due to FDI, keeping the total number of workers fixed at 200. Again solve for the amount of labor and capital used in each industry. *Hint:* Redo the calculations from part (a), using $K_C + K_S = 250$.

d. Explain how your results in parts (b) and (c) are related to the Rybczynski theorem.

Questions 8 and 9 explore the implications of the Rybczynski theorem and the factor price insensitivity result for the Heckscher–Ohlin model from Chapter 4.

8. In this question, we use the Rybczynski theorem to review the derivation of the Heckscher–Ohlin theorem.

   a. Start at the no-trade equilibrium point A on the Home PPF in Figure 4-2, panel (a). Suppose that through immigration, the amount of labor in Home grows. Draw the new PPF, and label the point B where production would occur with the same prices for goods. *Hint:* You can refer to Figure 5-11 to see the effect of immigration on the PPF.

   b. Suppose that the only difference between Foreign and Home is that Foreign has more labor. Otherwise, the technologies used to produce each good are the same across countries. Then how does the Foreign PPF compare with the new Home PPF (including immigration) that you drew in part (a)? Is point B the no-trade equilibrium in Foreign? Explain why or why not.

   c. Illustrate a new point A^* that is the no-trade equilibrium in Foreign. How do the relative no-trade prices of computers compare in Home and Foreign? Therefore, what will be the pattern of trade between the countries, and why?

9. Continuing from Problem 8, we now use the factor price insensitivity result to compare factor prices across countries in the Heckscher–Ohlin model.

   a. Illustrate the international trade equilibrium on the Home and Foreign production possibilities frontiers. *Hint:* You can refer to Figure 4-3 to see the international trade equilibrium.

   b. Suppose that the only difference between Foreign and Home is that Foreign has more labor. Otherwise, the technologies used to produce each good are the same across countries. Then, according to the factor price insensitivity result, how will the wage and rental compare in the two countries?

   c. Call the result in part (b) "factor price equalization." Is this a realistic result? *Hint:* You can refer to Figure 4-10 to see wages across countries.

   d. Based on our extension of the Heckscher–Ohlin model in Chapter 4 to allow for different productivities of factors in each country, explain why the factor price equalization result does not hold in reality.

10. Recall the formula from the application "The Effect of FDI on Rentals and Wages in Singapore." Give an intuitive explanation for this formula for the rental rate. *Hint:* Describe one side of the equation as a marginal benefit and the other as a marginal cost.

11. In Table 5-3, we show the growth in the real rental and real wages in Singapore, along with the implied productivity growth. One way to calculate the productivity growth is to take the average of the growth in the real rental and real wage. The idea is that firms can afford to pay more to labor and capital if there is productivity growth, so in that case real factor prices should be growing. But if there is no productivity growth, then the average of the growth in the real rental and real wage should be close to zero.

   To calculate the average of the growth in the real factor prices, we use the shares of GDP going to capital and labor. Specifically, we multiply the growth in the real rental by the capital share of GDP and add the growth in the real wage multiplied by the labor share of GDP. Then answer the following:

   a. For a capital-rich country like Singapore, the share of capital in GDP is about one-half and the share of labor is also one-half. Using these shares, calculate the average of the growth in the real rental and real wage shown in each row of Table 5-3. How do your answers compare with the productivity growth shown in the last column of Table 5-3?

   b. For an industrialized country like the United States, the share of capital in GDP is about one-third and the share of labor in GDP is about two-thirds. Using these shares, calculate the average of the growth in the real rental and real wage shown in each row of Table 5-3. How do your answers now compare with the productivity growth shown in the last column?

12. Figure 5-16 is a supply and demand diagram for the world labor market. Starting at points A and A^*, consider a situation in which some Foreign workers migrate to Home but not enough to reach the equilibrium with full migration (point B). As a result of the migration, the Home wage decreases from W to $W'' > W'$, and the Foreign wage increases from W^* to $W^{**} < W'$.

a. Are there gains that accrue to the Home country? If so, redraw the graph and identify the magnitude of the gains for each country. If not, say why not.

b. Are there gains that accrue to the Foreign country? If so, again show the magnitude of these gains in the diagram and also show the world gains.

6

Increasing Returns to Scale and Monopolistic Competition

Foreign trade, then, . . . [is] highly beneficial to a country, as it increases the amount and variety of the objects on which revenue may be expended.

David Ricardo, *On the Principles of Political Economy and Taxation*, Chapter 7

USMCA is a great deal for all three countries, solves the many deficiencies and mistakes in NAFTA, greatly opens markets to our farmers and manufacturers, reduces trade barriers to the U.S. and will bring all three Great Nations together in competition with the rest of the world.

President Donald Trump, October 1, 2018

Questions to Consider

1 Why do countries export and import similar goods?

2 How much do consumers benefit from having products available from many countries?

3 Do all firms gain from having access to larger markets?

In Chapter 2, we looked at data for U.S. snowboard imports and considered the reasons why the United States imports this product from so many different countries. Now we look at another sporting good that the United States imports and exports in large quantities to illustrate why a country would buy a product from other countries and sell the same product to them. In 2018 the United States imported golf clubs from 21 countries and exported them to 66 countries. In Table 6-1, we list the 12 countries that sell the most golf clubs to the United States and the 12 countries to which the United States sells the most golf clubs. The table also lists the amounts bought or sold and their average wholesale prices.

In panel (a), we see that China sells the most clubs to the United States, providing $294 million worth of golf clubs at an average price of $31 each. Next is Mexico, selling $82 million worth of clubs at an average wholesale price of $50 each. Vietnam comes next, exporting $23 million worth of clubs at an average price of $27, followed by Japan, which sells $12 million worth of golf clubs to the United States with an average price of $111. The higher average prices of golf clubs from Japan as compared with clubs from China and Vietnam most likely indicate that the clubs sold by Japan are of much higher quality. China and Vietnam have the lowest prices of the top 12 exporting countries shown in Table 6-1, though the lowest-priced golf clubs from all countries exporting to the United States come from India, which sell for only $18 each,

TABLE 6-1

U.S. Imports and Exports of Golf Clubs, 2018 This table shows the value, quantity, and average price for golf clubs imported into and exported from the United States in 2018. Many of the same countries both sell golf clubs to and buy golf clubs from the United States, illustrating what we call intra-industry trade.

(a) IMPORTS

Rank	Country	Value of Imports ($ thousands)	Quantity of Golf Clubs (thousands)	Average Price ($/club)
1	China	$293,890	9,441	$31
2	Mexico	82,312	1,644	50
3	Vietnam	22,839	833	27
4	Japan	11,709	106	111
5	Taiwan	9,960	131	76
6	Canada	528	5.2	101
7	Hong Kong	503	6.6	76
8	Thailand	168	1.9	89
9	United Kingdom	159	2.1	76
10	South Korea	67	1.5	44
11	Australia	24	0.1	162
12	Germany	16	0.3	49
13-20	Various countries	47	0.6	83
	All 20 countries	422,222	12,174	35

(b) EXPORTS

Rank	Country	Value of Exports ($ thousands)	Quantity of Golf Clubs (thousands)	Average Price ($/club)
1	Canada	$37,159	350	$106
2	Japan	32,463	196	166
3	South Korea	29,709	216	137
4	United Kingdom	8,123	57	142
5	Australia	7,351	73	101
6	Mexico	4,883	61	80
7	Hong Kong	4,063	28	144
8	Netherlands	2,507	20	126
9	Singapore	1,915	14	133
10	New Zealand	1,355	13	101
11	Argentina	1,225	11	113
12	India	1,043	9.2	113
13-64	Various countries	7,796	60	131
	All 64 countries	139,590	1,109	126

Data from: U.S. International Trade Commission Interactive Tariff and Trade DataWeb at http://dataweb.usitc.gov/.

indicating that they are of very low quality. In total, the United States imported $422 million of golf clubs in 2018.

On the export side, shown in panel (b), the top destination for U.S. clubs is Canada, followed by Japan and South Korea. Notice that all three of these countries are also among the top 12 countries selling golf clubs to the United States. The average price for U.S. exports varies between $80 and $166 per club, higher than the prices of many of the imported clubs (except for those coming from Japan, Canada and Australia), which suggests that the United States is exporting high-quality clubs.

Most of the countries that sell to the United States also buy from the United States: 7 of the top 12 selling countries shown in Table 6-1 were also among the top 12 countries buying U.S. golf clubs in 2018. Looking beyond the top 12, *all* of the 20 selling countries also bought U.S. golf clubs, even if it was only a small amount. Why does the United States export and import golf clubs to and from the same countries? The answer to this question is one of the "new" explanations for trade that we study in this chapter and the next. The Ricardian model (Chapter 2) and the Heckscher–Ohlin model (Chapter 4) explained why nations would either import or export a good, but those models do not predict the simultaneous import and export of a product, as we observe for golf clubs and many other goods.

To explain why countries import and export the same product, we need to change some assumptions made in the Ricardian and Heckscher–Ohlin models. In those models, we assumed that markets were perfectly competitive, which means there are many small producers, each producing a homogeneous (identical) product, so none of them can influence the market price for the product. As we know just from walking down the aisles in a grocery or department store, most goods are **differentiated goods**; that is, they are not identical. Based on price differences in Table 6-1, we can see that the traded golf clubs are of different types and quality. So in this chapter, we drop the assumption that the goods are homogeneous, as in perfect competition, and instead assume that goods are differentiated and allow for **imperfect competition**, in which case firms can influence the price that they charge.

The new explanation for trade explored in this chapter involves a type of imperfect competition called **monopolistic competition**, which has two key features. The first feature, just mentioned, is that the goods produced by different firms are differentiated. By offering different products, firms are able to exert some control over the price they can charge for their particular product. Because the market in which the firms operate is not a perfectly competitive one, they do not have to accept the market price, and by increasing their price, they do not lose all their business to competitors. On the other hand, because these firms are not monopolists (i.e., they are not the only firm that produces this type of product), they cannot charge prices as high as a monopolist would. When firms produce differentiated products, they retain some ability to set the price for their product, but not as much as a monopolist would have.

The second feature of monopolistic competition is **increasing returns to scale**, by which we mean that the average costs for a firm fall as more output is produced. For this reason, firms tend to specialize in the product lines that are most successful—if they sell more of those products, the average cost for the production of the successful products falls. Firms can lower their average costs by selling more in their home markets but can possibly attain even lower costs from selling more in foreign markets through exporting. So, increasing returns to scale create a reason for trade to occur even when the trading countries are similar in their technologies and factor endowments. Increasing returns to scale set the monopolistic competition trade model apart from the logic of the Ricardian and Heckscher–Ohlin models.

In this chapter, we describe a model of trade under monopolistic competition that incorporates product differentiation and increasing returns to scale. This model leads to gains from trade that are beyond those we have seen with the Ricardian or the Heckscher–Ohlin models. Under monopolistic competition, consumers gain because they have a greater variety of products—those made by home firms and those made by foreign firms—available to them. The importance of **product variety** as a source of gains from trade was recognized long ago by David Ricardo, in the first quote at the beginning of the chapter.

The monopolistic competition model helps us to understand the effects of **free-trade agreements**, in which free trade occurs among a group of countries. In this chapter, we use the Canada–U.S. Free Trade Agreement (CUSFTA) of 1989 and the North American Free Trade Agreement (NAFTA) of 1994 to illustrate the predictions of the monopolistic competition model. In 2018, the NAFTA agreement was renegotiated among the three countries and was renamed the U.S.–Mexico–Canada Agreement (USMCA), which took effect in 2020. The renegotiation of NAFTA was one of President Trump's campaign promises. As indicated in the second quotation at the start of the chapter, President Trump was dissatisfied with some aspects of NAFTA and regarded the new USMCA agreement as better. We will compare NAFTA and the USMCA to see what the differences are between them.

The final goal of the chapter is to discuss how the monopolistic competition model helps explain the trade patterns that we observe today. In our golf club example, countries specialize in different varieties of the same type of product and trade them; this type of trade is called **intra-industry trade** because it deals with imports and exports in the same industry. The monopolistic competition model explains this trade pattern and also predicts that larger countries will trade more with one another. Just as the force of gravity is strongest between two large objects, the monopolistic competition model implies that large countries (as measured by their GDP) should trade the most.[1] There is much empirical evidence to support this prediction, which is called the **gravity equation**.

1 Basics of Imperfect Competition

Monopolistic competition incorporates some aspects of a monopoly (firms have control over the prices they charge) and some aspects of perfect competition (many firms are selling). Before presenting the monopolistic competition model, it is useful to review the case of monopoly, which is a single firm selling a product. The monopoly firm faces the industry demand curve. After that, we briefly discuss the case of **duopoly**, when there are two firms selling a product. Our focus will be on the demand facing each of the two firms. Understanding what happens to demand in a duopoly will help us understand how demand is determined when there are many firms selling differentiated products, as occurs in monopolistic competition.

Monopoly Equilibrium

In Figure 6-1, the industry demand curve is shown by D. For the monopolist to sell more, the price must fall, and so the demand curve slopes downward. This fall in price means that the extra revenue earned by the monopolist from selling another unit is less than the price of that unit—the extra revenue earned equals the price charged for that unit *minus* the fall in price times the quantity sold of all earlier units. The extra revenue earned from selling one more unit is called the **marginal revenue** and is shown by the curve MR in Figure 6-1. The marginal revenue curve lies below the demand curve D because the extra revenue earned from selling another unit is less than the price.

To maximize its profit, the monopolist sells up to the point at which the marginal revenue MR earned from selling one more unit equals the **marginal cost** MC of producing one more unit. In Figure 6-1, the marginal cost curve is shown by MC. Because we have assumed, for simplicity, that marginal costs are constant, the MC curve is flat, although this does not need to be the case. To have marginal revenue equal marginal costs, the monopolist sells the quantity Q^M. To find the profit-maximizing price the

---

[1] If you have read Chapter 1, you will know that large countries do indeed trade the most, as seen in the map of world trade.

FIGURE 6-1

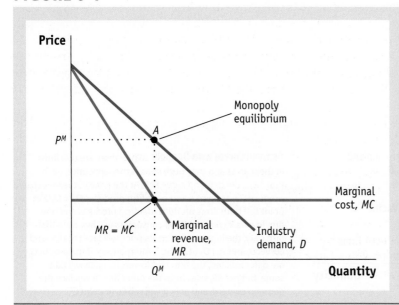

Monopoly Equilibrium   The monopolist chooses the profit-maximizing quantity, Q^M, at which marginal revenue equals marginal cost. From that quantity, we trace up to the demand curve and over to the price axis to see that the monopolist charges the price P^M. The monopoly equilibrium is at point A.

monopolist charges, we trace up from quantity Q^M to point A on the demand curve and then over to the price axis. The price charged by the monopolist P^M is the price that allows the monopolist to earn the highest profit and is therefore the monopoly equilibrium.

Demand with Duopoly

Let us compare a monopoly with a duopoly, a market structure in which two firms are selling a product. We will not solve for the duopoly equilibrium but will just study how the introduction of a second firm affects the demand facing each of the firms. Knowing how demand is affected by the introduction of a second firm helps us understand how demand is determined when there are many firms, as there are in monopolistic competition.

In Figure 6-2, the industry faces the demand curve D. If there are two firms in the industry and they charge the same price, then the demand curve facing each firm is $D/2$. For example, if both firms charged the price P_1, then the industry demand is at point A, and each firm's demand is at point B on curve $D/2$. The two firms share the market equally, each selling exactly one-half of the total market demand, $Q_2 = Q_1/2$.

If one firm charges a price different from the other firm, however, the demand facing both firms changes. Suppose that one firm charges a lower price P_2, while the other firm keeps its price at P_1. If the firms are selling the same homogeneous product, then the firm charging the lower price will get all the demand (shown by point C), which is Q_3 at the price P_2. Now suppose that the products are not homogeneous but instead are differentiated. In that case, the firm with the lower price P_2 will capture more of the market than the firm with the higher price P_1, but it will not capture the entire market. Because the products are not precisely the same (for instance, in our golf club example the higher-priced club is of better quality than the less expensive club), some consumers will still want to buy the other firm's product even though its price is higher. The firm selling at the lower price P_2 now sells the quantity Q_4, for example, at point C'.

FIGURE 6-2

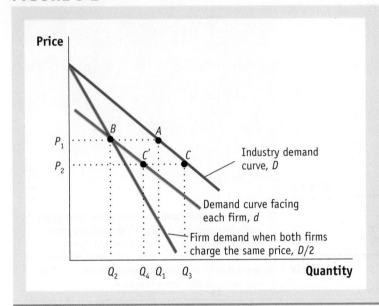

Demand Curves with Duopoly When there are two firms in the market and they both charge the same price, each firm faces the demand curve $D/2$. At the price P_1, the industry produces Q_1 at point A and each firm produces $Q_2 = Q_1/2$ at point B. If both firms produce identical products and one firm lowers its price to P_2, all consumers will buy from that firm only; the firm that lowers its price will face the demand curve, D, and sell Q_3 at point C. Alternatively, if the products are differentiated, the firm that lowers its price will take some, but not all, sales from the other firm; it will face the demand curve, d, and at P_2 it will sell Q_4 at point C'.

The demand curve d is the demand curve for the firm that lowered its price from P_1 to P_2, even though the other firm held its price at P_1. As we have illustrated, the demand curve d is *flatter* than the demand curve $D/2$. This means that each firm faces a more elastic demand curve than $D/2$: when only one firm lowers its price, it increases its quantity sold by more than when all firms lower their prices. Not only does the quantity demanded in the industry increase, but in addition, the firm that lowers its price takes away some of the quantity demanded from the other firm. In summary, the demand curve d facing each firm producing in a duopoly is more elastic than the demand curve $D/2$ each faces when the firms charge the same price.

2 Trade Under Monopolistic Competition

We begin our study of monopolistic competition by carefully stating the assumptions of the model.

Assumption 1: Each firm produces a good that is similar to but differentiated from the goods that other firms in the industry produce.

Because each firm's product is somewhat different from the goods of the other firms, a firm can raise its price without losing all its customers to other firms. Thus, each firm faces a downward-sloping demand curve for its product and has some control over the price it charges. This is different from perfect competition, in which all firms produce exactly the same product and therefore must sell at exactly the same market-determined price.

Assumption 2: There are many firms in the industry.

The discussion of duopoly demand in the previous section helps us to think about the demand curve facing a firm under monopolistic competition, when there are many firms in the industry. If the number of firms is N, then D/N is the share of demand that each firm faces when the firms are all charging the same price. When only one firm lowers its price, however, it will face a flatter demand curve d. We will begin describing the model by focusing on the demand curve *d* and later bring back the demand curve *D/N*.

The first two assumptions are about the demand facing each firm; the third assumption is about each firm's cost structure:

Assumption 3: Firms produce using a technology with increasing returns to scale.

The assumptions underlying monopolistic competition differ from our usual assumptions on firm costs by allowing for increasing returns to scale, a production technology in which the average costs of production fall as the quantity produced increases. This relationship is shown in Figure 6-3, in which average costs are labeled *AC*. The assumption that average costs fall as quantity increases means that marginal costs, labeled *MC*, must be *below* average costs. Why? Think about whether a new student coming into your class will raise or lower the class average grade. If the new student's average is below the existing class average, then when he or she enters, the class average will fall. In the same way, when *MC* is less than *AC*, then *AC* must be falling.[2]

Numerical Example As an example of the cost curves in Figure 6-3, suppose that the firm has the following cost data:

$$\text{Fixed costs} = \$100$$
$$\text{Marginal costs} = \$10 \text{ per unit}$$

Given these costs, the average costs for this firm for various quantities are as shown in Table 6-2.

Notice that as the quantity produced rises, average costs fall and eventually become close to the marginal costs of $10 per unit, as shown in Figure 6-3.

Assumption 3 means that average cost is above marginal cost. Assumption 1 means that firms have some control over the price they charge and these firms charge a price that is also above marginal cost (we learn why in a later section).

FIGURE 6-3

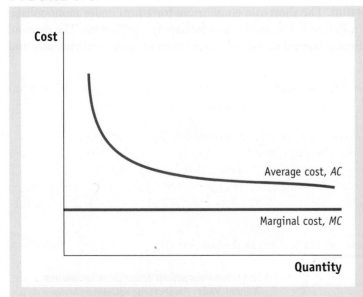

Increasing Returns to Scale This diagram shows the average cost, *AC*, and marginal cost, *MC*, of a firm. Increasing returns to scale cause average costs to fall as the quantity produced increases. Marginal cost is below average cost and is drawn as constant for simplicity.

---

[2] For simplicity, we assume that marginal costs are constant, but this need not be the case.

TABLE 6-2

Cost Information for the Firm This table illustrates increasing returns to scale, in which average costs fall as quantity rises.

Quantity Q	Variable Costs = $Q \cdot MC$ ($MC = \$10$)	Total Costs = Variable Costs + Fixed Costs ($FC = \$100$)	Average Costs = Total Costs/Quantity
10	$100	$200	$20
20	200	300	15
30	300	400	13.3
40	400	500	12.5
50	500	600	12
100	1,000	1,100	11
Large Q	$10 \cdot Q$	$10 \cdot Q + 100$	Close to 10

Whenever the price charged is above average cost, a firm earns **monopoly profit**. Our final assumption describes what happens to profits in a monopolistically competitive industry in the long run:

Assumption 4: Because firms can enter and exit the industry freely, monopoly profits are zero in the long run.

Recall that under perfect competition, we assume there are many firms in the industry and that in a long-run equilibrium each firm's profit must be zero. In monopolistic competition, there is the same requirement for a long-run equilibrium. We assume that firms can enter and exit the industry freely; this means that firms will enter as long as it is possible to make monopoly profits, and as more firms enter, the profit per firm falls. This condition leads to a long-run equilibrium in which profit for each firm is zero, just as in perfect competition!

Equilibrium Without Trade

Short-Run Equilibrium The short-run equilibrium for a firm under monopolistic competition, shown in Figure 6-4, is similar to a monopoly equilibrium. The demand curve faced by each firm is labeled d_0, the marginal revenue curve is labeled mr_0, and

FIGURE 6-4

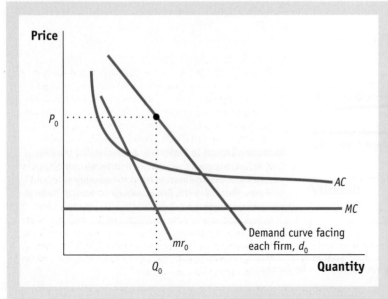

Short-Run Monopolistic Competition Equilibrium Without Trade The short-run equilibrium under monopolistic competition is the same as a monopoly equilibrium. The firm chooses to produce the quantity Q_0 at which the firm's marginal revenue, mr_0, equals its marginal cost, MC. The price charged is P_0. Because price exceeds average cost, the firm makes a monopoly profit.

the marginal cost curve of each firm is shown by MC. Each firm maximizes profit by producing Q_0, the quantity at which marginal revenue equals marginal cost. Tracing up from this quantity to the demand curve shows that the price charged by the firms is P_0. Because the price exceeds average costs at the quantity Q_0, the firm earns monopoly profit.

Long-Run Equilibrium In a monopolistically competitive market, new firms continue to enter the industry as long as they can earn monopoly profits. In the long run, the entry of new firms draws demand away from existing firms, causing demand curve d_0 to shift to the left until no firm in the industry earns positive monopoly profits (Figure 6-5). Moreover, when new firms enter and there are more product varieties available to consumers, the d_0 curve faced by each firm becomes more elastic, or flatter. We expect the d_0 curve to become more elastic as more firms enter because each product is similar to the other existing products; therefore, as the number of close substitutes increases, consumers become more price sensitive.

New firms continue to enter the industry until the price charged by each firm is on the average cost curve and monopoly profit is zero. At this point, the industry is in a long-run equilibrium, with no reason for any further entry or exit. The long-run equilibrium without trade is shown in Figure 6-5. Again, the demand curve for the firm is labeled d, with the short-run demand curve denoted d_0 and the long-run demand curve denoted d_1 (with corresponding marginal revenue curve mr_1). Marginal revenue equals marginal cost at quantity Q_1. At this quantity, all firms in the industry charge price P^A. The price P^A equals average cost at point A, where the demand curve d_1 is tangent to the average cost curve. Because the price equals average costs, the firm is earning zero monopoly profit and there is no incentive for firms to enter or exit the industry. Thus, point A is the firm's (and the industry's) long-run equilibrium without trade. Notice that the long-run equilibrium curve d_1 is to the left of and more elastic (flatter) than the short-run curve d_0.

Before we allow for international trade, we need to introduce another curve into Figure 6-5. The firm's demand curve d_1 shows the quantity demanded depending on the price charged by that firm, holding the price charged by all other firms fixed. In contrast, there is another demand curve that shows the quantity demanded from each firm when all firms in the industry charge the *same price*. This other demand curve is the total market demand D divided by the number of firms in the absence of trade N^A.

FIGURE 6-5

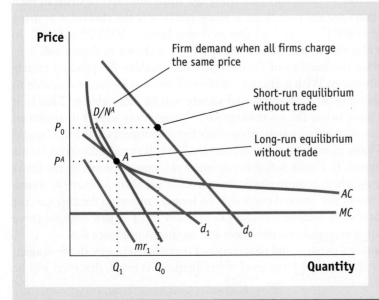

Long-Run Monopolistic Competition Equilibrium Without Trade Drawn by the possibility of making profits in the short-run equilibrium, new firms enter the industry and the firm's demand curve, d_0, shifts to the left and becomes more elastic (flatter), shown by d_1. The long-run equilibrium under monopolistic competition occurs at the quantity Q_1 where the marginal revenue curve, mr_1 (associated with demand curve d_1), equals marginal cost. At that quantity, the no-trade price, P^A, equals average costs at point A. In the long-run equilibrium, firms earn zero monopoly profits and there is no entry or exit. The quantity produced by each firm is less than in short-run equilibrium (Figure 6-4). Q_1 is less than Q_0 because new firms have entered the industry. With a greater number of firms and hence more varieties available to consumers, the demand for each variety d_1 is less than d_0. The demand curve D/N^A shows the no-trade demand when all firms charge the same price.

In Figure 6-5, we label the second demand curve as D/N^A. We omit drawing total industry demand D itself so we do not clutter the diagram.

The demand curve d_1 is flatter, or more elastic, than the demand curve D/N^A. We discussed why that is the case under duopoly (see Figure 6-2) and can review the reason again now. Starting at point A, consider a drop in the price by just one firm, which increases the quantity demanded along the d_1 curve for that firm. The demand curve d_1 is quite elastic, meaning that the drop in price leads to a large increase in the quantity purchased because customers are attracted away from other firms. If instead all firms drop their price by the same amount, along the curve D/N^A, then each firm will not attract as many customers away from other firms. When all firms drop their prices equally, then the increase in quantity demanded from each firm along the curve D/N^A is less than the increase along the firm's curve d_1. Thus, demand is less elastic along the demand curve D/N^A, which is why it is steeper than the d_1 curve. As we proceed with our analysis of opening trade under monopolistic competition, it will be helpful to keep track of both of these demand curves.

Equilibrium with Free Trade

Let us now allow for free trade between Home and Foreign in this industry. For simplicity, we assume that Home and Foreign countries are exactly the same, with the same number of consumers, the same factor endowments, the same technology and cost curves, and the same number of firms in the no-trade equilibrium. If there were no increasing returns to scale, there would be no reason at all for international trade to occur. Under the Ricardian model, for example, countries with identical technologies would not trade because their no-trade relative prices would be equal. Likewise, under the Heckscher–Ohlin model, countries with identical factor endowments would not trade because their no-trade relative prices would be the same. Under monopolistic competition, however, two identical countries will still engage in international trade because increasing returns to scale exist.

Short-Run Equilibrium with Trade We take as given the number of firms in the no-trade equilibrium in each country N^A and use this number of firms to determine the short-run equilibrium with trade. Our starting point is the long-run equilibrium without trade, as shown by point A in Figure 6-5 and reproduced in Figure 6-6. When we allow free trade between Home and Foreign, the number of consumers available to each firm doubles (because there are equal numbers of consumers in each country), as does the number of firms (because there are equal numbers of firms in each country). Because there are not only twice as many consumers but also twice as many firms, the demand curve D/N^A is the same as it was before, $2D/2N^A = D/N^A$. In other words, point A is still on the demand curve D/N^A, as shown in Figure 6-6.

Free trade doubles the number of firms, which also doubles the product varieties available to consumers. With a greater number of product varieties available to consumers, their demand for each individual variety will be more elastic. That is, if one firm drops its price below the no-trade price P^A, then it can expect to attract an even greater number of customers away from other firms. Before trade the firm would attract additional Home customers only, but after trade it will attract additional Home and Foreign consumers. In Figure 6-6, this consumer response is shown by the firm's new demand curve d_2, which is more elastic than its no-trade demand curve d_1 shown in Figure 6.5. As a result, the demand curve d_2 is no longer tangent to the average cost curve at point A but is *above* average costs for prices below P^A. The new demand curve d_2 has a corresponding marginal revenue curve mr_2, as shown in Figure 6-6.

With the new demand curve d_2 and new marginal revenue curve mr_2, the firm again needs to choose its profit-maximizing level of production. As usual, that level will be

FIGURE 6-6

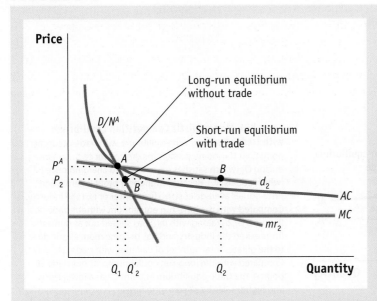

Short-Run Monopolistic Competition Equilibrium with Trade When trade is opened, the larger market makes the firm's demand curve more elastic, as shown by d_2 (with corresponding marginal revenue curve, mr_2). The firm chooses to produce the quantity Q_2 at which marginal revenue equals marginal costs; this quantity corresponds to a price of P_2. With sales of Q_2 at price P_2, the firm will make monopoly profits because price is greater than AC. When *all* firms lower their prices to P_2, however, the relevant demand curve is D/N^A, which indicates that they can sell only Q_2' at price P_2. At this short-run equilibrium (point B'), price is less than average cost and all firms incur losses. As a result, some firms are forced to exit the industry.

where marginal revenue equals marginal cost at Q_2. When we trace from Q_2 up to point B on the firm's demand curve d_2, then over to the price axis, we see that the firm will charge P_2. Because P_2 is above average cost at point B, the firm will make a positive monopoly profit. We can see clearly the firm's incentive to lower its price: at point A it earns zero monopoly profit and at point B it earns positive profit. Producing Q_2 and selling it at P_2 is the firm's profit-maximizing position.

This happy scenario for the firm is not the end of the story, however. *Every* firm in the industry (in both Home and Foreign) has the same incentive to lower its price in the hope of attracting customers away from all the other firms and earning monopoly profit. When all firms lower their prices at the same time, however, the quantity demanded from each firm increases along the demand curve D/N^A, not along d_2. Remember that the D/N^A curve shows the demand faced by each firm when all firms in the industry charge the same price. With the prices of all firms lowered to P_2, they will each sell the quantity Q_2' at point B' rather than their expected sales of Q_2 at point B. At point B', the price charged is *less than* average costs, so every firm is incurring a loss. In the short-run equilibrium with trade, firms lower their prices, expecting to make profits at point B, but end up making losses at point B'.

Point B' is not the long-run equilibrium because the losses will bankrupt some firms and cause them to exit from the industry. This exit will increase demand (both d and D/N^A) for the remaining firms and decrease the number of product varieties available to consumers. To understand where the new long-run equilibrium occurs, we turn to a new diagram.

Long-Run Equilibrium with Trade Due to the exit of firms, the number of firms remaining in each country after trade is less than it was before trade. Let us call the number of firms in each country after trade is opened N^T, where $N^T < N^A$. This reduction in the number of firms increases the share of demand facing each one, so that $D/N^T > D/N^A$. In Figure 6-7, the demand D/N^T facing each firm lies to the right of the demand D/N^A in the earlier figures. We show the long-run equilibrium with trade at point C. At point C, the demand curve d_3 facing an individual firm is tangent to the average cost curve AC. In addition, the marginal revenue curve mr_3 intersects the marginal cost curve MC.

FIGURE 6-7

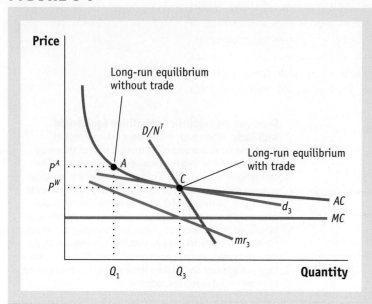

Long-Run Monopolistic Competition Equilibrium with Trade The long-run equilibrium with trade occurs at point C. At this point, profit is maximized for each firm producing Q_3 (which satisfies $mr_3 = MC$) and charging price P^W (which equals AC). Because monopoly profit is zero when price equals average cost, no firms enter or exit the industry. Compared with the long-run equilibrium without trade (Figure 6-5), d_3 (along with mr_3) has shifted out as domestic firms exited the industry and has become more elastic due to the greater total number of varieties with trade, $2N^T > N^A$. Compared with the long-run equilibrium without trade at point A, the trade equilibrium at point C has a lower price and higher sales by all surviving firms.

How does this long-run equilibrium with trade compare with the long-run equilibrium without trade? First of all, despite the exit of some firms in each country, we still expect that the world number of products, which is $2N^T$ (the number produced in each country N^T times two countries), exceeds the number of products N^A available in each country before trade, $2N^T > N^A$. It follows that the demand curve d_3 facing each firm must be more elastic than demand d_1 in the absence of trade: the availability of imported products makes consumers more price sensitive than they were before trade, so the demand curve d_3 is more elastic than demand d_1 in Figure 6-5. At free-trade equilibrium (point C), each firm still in operation charges a lower price than it did with no trade, $P^W < P^A$, and produces a higher quantity, $Q_3 > Q_1$. The drop in prices and increase in quantity for each firm go hand in hand: as the quantity produced by each surviving firm increases, average costs fall due to increasing returns to scale, and so do the prices charged by firms.

Gains from Trade The long-run equilibrium at point C has two sources of gains from trade for consumers. First, the price has fallen as compared with point A, so consumers benefit for that reason. A good way to think about this drop in the price is that it reflects increasing returns to scale, with average costs falling as the output of firms rises. The drop in average costs is a rise in productivity for these surviving firms because output can be produced more cheaply. So consumers gain from the drop in price, which is the result of the rise in productivity.

There is a second source of gains from trade to consumers. We assume that consumers obtain higher surplus when there are more product varieties available to buy; hence the increase in variety is a source of gain for consumers. Within each country, some firms exit the market after trade begins, so fewer product varieties are produced by the remaining domestic firms. However, because consumers can buy products from both Home and Foreign firms, the *total* number of varieties available with trade is greater than the number of varieties available in any one country before trade, $2N^T > N^A$. Thus, in addition to the drop in prices, there is an added consumer gain from the availability of additional product varieties.

Adjustment Costs from Trade Against these long-run gains from trade, there are short-run adjustment costs as some firms in each country shut down and exit the industry. The workers in those firms will experience a spell of unemployment as they look for new jobs. Over the long run, however, we expect these workers to find new positions, so we view these costs as temporary. We do not build these adjustment costs into the model because they are short-term, but we are still interested in how large these costs might be in practice. To compare the short-run adjustment costs with the long-run gains from trade, we next look at the evidence from Canada, Mexico, and the United States under the North American Free Trade Agreement. We will see that the predictions of the monopolistic competition model hold reasonably well in each case.

3 Free-Trade Agreements Within North America

The idea that free trade will expand the range of products available to consumers is not new—it is even mentioned by David Ricardo in the quote at the beginning of this chapter. But the ability to carefully model the effects of trade under monopolistic competition *is* new and was developed in research during the 1980s by Professors Elhanan Helpman, Paul Krugman, and the late Kelvin Lancaster. That research was not just theoretical but was used to shed light on free-trade agreements, which guarantee free trade among a group of countries. In 1989, for example, Canada and the United States entered into a free-trade agreement, called the Canada–U.S. Free Trade Agreement (CUSFTA). The potential for Canadian firms to expand their output (and enjoy lower average costs) by selling in the United States was a key factor in Canada's decision to enter into this free-trade agreement.

In this section we begin by examining the gains and adjustment costs to Canada from the CUSFTA agreement. In 1994, the agreement between Canada and the United States was extended to include Mexico, in the North American Free Trade Agreement (NAFTA). Our second goal for this section is to describe the gains and adjustment costs to Mexico and the United States from NAFTA. In 2018, the NAFTA agreement was renegotiated and renamed the U.S.–Mexico–Canada Agreement (USMCA), which took effect in 2020. The renegotiation of NAFTA was promised by President Trump to the American voters even before he was elected. Our third goal for this section is to examine how USMCA differs from the NAFTA agreement.

Gains and Adjustment Costs for Canada Under CUSFTA

Studies in Canada dating back to the 1960s predicted substantial gains from free trade with the United States because Canadian firms would expand their scale of operations to serve the larger market and lower their costs. A set of simulations based on the monopolistic competition model performed by the Canadian economist Richard Harris in the mid-1980s influenced Canadian policy makers to proceed with the free-trade agreement with the United States in 1989. Enough time has passed since then to look back and see how Canada has fared under the trade agreements with the United States, and then Mexico.

Using data from 1988 to 1996, Professor Daniel Trefler of the University of Toronto found short-run adjustment costs of 100,000 lost jobs, or 5% of manufacturing employment. Some industries that faced particularly large tariff cuts saw their employment fall by as much as 15%. These are very large declines in employment. Over time, however, these job losses were more than made up for by the creation of new jobs elsewhere in manufacturing, so there were no long-run job losses as a result of the free-trade agreement.

What about long-run gains? Trefler found a large positive effect on the productivity of firms, with productivity rising as much as 18% over eight years in the industries most affected by tariff cuts, or a compound growth rate of 2.1% per year. For manufacturing overall, productivity rose by 6%, for a compound growth rate of 0.7% per year. The difference between these two numbers, which is $2.1 - 0.7 = 1.4\%$ per year, is an estimate of how free trade with the United States affected the Canadian industries most affected by the tariff cuts over and above the impact on other industries. The productivity growth in Canada allowed for a modest rise in real earnings of 2.4% over the eight-year period for production workers, or 0.3% per year. We conclude that the prediction of the monopolistic competition model that surviving firms increase their productivity is confirmed for Canadian manufacturing. Those productivity gains led to a fall in prices for consumers and a rise in real earnings for workers, which demonstrates the first source of the gains from trade. The second source of gains from trade—increased product variety for Canadian consumers—was not measured in the study by Professor Trefler but has been estimated for the United States, as discussed later in this chapter.

Gains and Adjustment Costs for Mexico Under NAFTA

In the mid-1980s Mexican president Miguel de la Madrid embarked on a program of economic liberalization that included land reform and greater openness to foreign investment. Tariffs with the United States were as high as 100% on some goods, and there were many restrictions on the operations of foreign firms. De la Madrid believed that the economic reforms were needed to boost growth and incomes in Mexico. Joining NAFTA with the United States and Canada in 1994 was a way to ensure the permanence of the reforms already under way. Under NAFTA, Mexican tariffs on U.S. goods declined from an average of 14% in 1990 to 1% in 2001. U.S. tariffs on Mexican imports fell as well, though from levels that were much lower to begin with in most industries.

How did the fall in tariffs under NAFTA affect the Mexican economy? To answer this question, we need to keep in mind that in the years just after NAFTA began in 1994, the Mexican economy went through a financial crisis, which we discuss later in the chapter. That means the beneficial impact of NAFTA could not be seen in Mexico for some years. That delayed response to NAFTA was reinforced by the slow pace at which certain features of the free-trade agreement were implemented. On the import side, tariff reductions under NAFTA were phased in for periods as long as 15 years. Tariff cuts in the agriculture sector in Mexico had the longest phase-in period. On the export side, Mexican trucks were not allowed into the United States to deliver goods until 2011.

Productivity in Mexico As we did for Canada, let us investigate the impact of NAFTA on productivity in Mexico. In panel (a) of Figure 6-8, we show the growth in labor productivity for two types of manufacturing firms: the maquiladora plants, which are close to the border and produce almost exclusively for export to the United States, and all other nonmaquiladora manufacturing plants in Mexico.[3] The maquiladora plants should be most affected by NAFTA. In panel (b), we also show what happened to real wages and real incomes.

For the maquiladora plants in panel (a), productivity rose 45% from 1994 (when Mexico joined NAFTA) to 2003, a compound growth rate of 4.1% per year for more than nine years. For the nonmaquiladora plants, productivity rose overall by 25% from 1994 to 2003, 2.5% per year. The difference between these two numbers, which is 1.6% per year, is an estimate of the impact of NAFTA on the productivity of the maquiladora plants over and above the increase in productivity that occurred in the rest of Mexico.

---

[3] Labor productivity for the maquiladoras is real value-added per worker and for nonmaquiladoras is real output per worker. Both are taken from Gary C. Hufbauer and Jeffrey J. Schott, 2005, *NAFTA Revisited: Achievements and Challenges* (Washington, D.C.: Peterson Institute for International Economics), Table 1-9, p. 45.

FIGURE 6-8

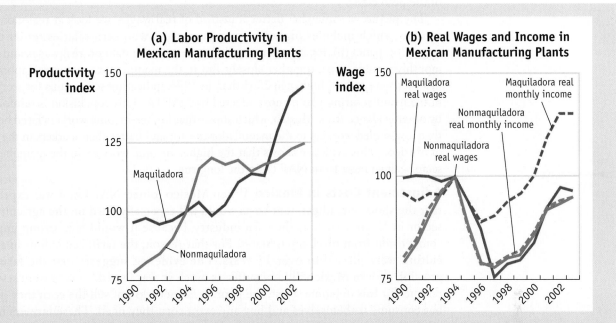

(a) Labor Productivity in Mexican Manufacturing Plants

(b) Real Wages and Income in Mexican Manufacturing Plants

Labor Productivity and Wages in Mexico Panel (a) shows labor productivity for workers in the Mexican maquiladora manufacturing plants and for workers in nonmaquiladora plants. Panel (b) shows wages and monthly income for workers in maquiladora and nonmaquiladora plants. Productivity and real monthly income grew faster in the maquiladora plants because of increased trade with the United States.

Data from: Gary C. Hufbauer and Jeffrey J. Schott, 2005, NAFTA Revisited: Achievements and Challenges *(Washington, D.C.: Peterson Institute for International Economics), p. 45.*

Real Wages and Incomes Real wages in the maquiladora and nonmaquiladora plants are shown in panel (b) of Figure 6-8. From 1994 to 1997, there was a fall of more than 20% in real wages in both sectors, despite a rise in productivity in the nonmaquiladora sector. This fall in real wages is not what we expect from the monopolistic competition model, so why did it occur?

Shortly after Mexico joined NAFTA, it suffered a financial crisis that led to a large devaluation of the peso. It would be incorrect to attribute the peso crisis to Mexico's joining NAFTA, even though both events occurred the same year. Prior to 1994 Mexico followed a fixed exchange rate policy, but in late 1994 it switched to a flexible exchange rate regime instead, and the peso devalued to much less than its former fixed value. Details about exchange rate regimes and the reasons for switching from a fixed to flexible exchange rate are covered in international macroeconomics. For now, the key idea is that when the peso's value falls, it becomes more expensive for Mexico to import goods from the United States because the peso price of imports goes up. The Mexican consumer price index also goes up, and as a result, real wages for Mexican workers fall.

The maquiladora sector, located beside the U.S. border, was more susceptible to the exchange rate change and did not experience much of a gain in productivity over that period because of the increased cost of inputs imported from the United States. Workers in both the maquiladora and nonmaquiladora sectors had to pay higher prices for imported goods, which was reflected in higher Mexican consumer prices. So the decline in real wages for workers in both sectors is similar. This decline was short-lived, however, and real wages in both sectors began to rise again in 1998. By 2003 real wages in both sectors had risen to nearly equal their value in 1994. This means that workers in Mexico did not gain or lose because of NAFTA on average: the productivity gains were not shared with workers, which is a disappointing finding, but real wages at least recovered from the effects of the peso crisis.

The picture is somewhat better if instead of real wages, we look at real monthly income, which includes higher-income employees who earn salaries rather than wages.[4] In panel (b), for the nonmaquiladora sector, the data on real wages and real monthly income move together closely. But in the maquiladora sector, real monthly incomes were indeed higher in 2003 than in 1994, indicating some gains for workers in the manufacturing plants most affected by NAFTA. This conclusion is reinforced by other evidence from Mexico, which shows that higher-income workers fared better than low-skilled workers in the maquiladora sector and better than workers in the rest of Mexico.[5] This evidence shows that the higher-income workers in the maquiladora sector gained most from NAFTA in the long run.

Adjustment Costs in Mexico   When Mexico joined NAFTA, it was expected that the short-run adjustment costs would fall especially hard on the agricultural sector in Mexico, such as the corn industry, because it would face strong import competition from the United States. For that reason, the tariff reductions in agriculture were phased in over 15 years. The evidence suggests that the farmers growing corn in Mexico did not suffer as much as was feared.[6] There were several reasons for this outcome. First, the poorest farmers do not sell the corn they grow but consume it themselves and buy any extra corn they need. These farmers benefited from cheaper import prices for corn from the United States. Second, the Mexican government was able to use subsidies to offset the reduction in income for other corn farmers. Surprisingly, the total production of corn in Mexico rose, not fell, following NAFTA.

Turning to the manufacturing sector, we should again distinguish the maquiladora from nonmaquiladora plants. For the maquiladora plants, employment grew rapidly following NAFTA, from 584,000 workers in 1994 to a peak of 1.29 million workers in 2000. After that, however, the maquiladora sector entered a downturn, due to several factors: the United States entered a recession, reducing demand for Mexican exports; China was competing for U.S. sales by exporting products similar to those sold by Mexico; and the Mexican peso became overvalued, making it difficult to export abroad. For all these reasons, employment in the maquiladora sector fell after 2000, to 1.1 million workers in 2003. It is not clear whether we should count this decline in employment as a short-run adjustment cost due to NAFTA or as a result of the adverse macroeconomic conditions in the United States and Mexico. Employment in the maquiladora sector grew after 2003 to reach nearly 2 million workers by 2007, then fell during the global financial crisis of 2008–2009 and grew again to exceed 2 million workers by 2013. Today, with rising wages in China, the maquiladora sector in Mexico is increasingly the choice of American companies that want to shift their production to a low-wage location but still remain close to home.[7]

---

[4] Wage data refer to production workers who are involved in assembly-line work and similar activities. Income data refer to all employees, including production and nonproduction workers. Monthly income includes payments from profit-sharing by firms and a Christmas bonus, which are common in Mexico.

[5] Gordon H. Hanson, 2007, "Globalization, Labor Income and Poverty in Mexico," in Ann Harrison, ed., *Globalization and Poverty* (Chicago: University of Chicago Press; Washington, D.C.: National Bureau of Economic Research [NBER]), pp. 417–452.

[6] See Margaret McMillan, Alix Peterson Zwane, and Nava Ashraf, 2007, "My Policies or Yours: Does OECD Support for Agriculture Increase Poverty in Developing Countries?" in Ann Harrison, ed., *Globalization and Poverty* (Chicago: University of Chicago Press; Washington, D.C.: NBER), pp. 183–232.

[7] See "Big maq attack: A 50-year-old export industry that provides millions of jobs has to reinvent itself quickly to stay competitive," *The Economist*, October 26, 2013. An example of an American firm choosing to open a factory in Mexico rather than China is provided in: Chris Anderson, "Mexico: The New China," *New York Times*, September 27, 2013, p. 7.

Gains and Adjustment Costs for the United States Under NAFTA

Consumers in the United States could be expected to gain from the lower prices resulting from increased trade under NAFTA. Because there is not a simple estimate of those gains, we will focus instead on the consumer gains from the expansion of *import varieties* available to consumers. That is a source of gain that is emphasized in the monopolistic competition model.

Product Variety of Imports To understand how NAFTA affected the range of products available to American consumers, Table 6-3 shows the variety of goods Mexico exported to the United States in 1990 and 2001. To interpret these numbers, start with the 1990 export variety in agriculture of 42%. That figure means that 42% of all the agricultural products the United States imported in 1990, from any country, also came from Mexico. For instance, avocados, bananas, cucumbers, and tomatoes imported from various Central or South American countries were also imported to the United States from Mexico. Measuring the variety of products Mexico exported to the United States does not take into account the *amount* that Mexico sells of each product; rather, it counts the number of different types of products Mexico sells to the United States as compared with the total *number* of products the United States imports from all countries.

From 1990 to 2001, the range of agricultural products that Mexico exported to the United States expanded from 42% to 51%. That compound growth rate of 1.9% per year is close to the average annual growth rate for export variety in all industries shown in the last column of Table 6-3, which is 2.2% per year. Export variety grew at a faster rate in the wood and paper industry (with a compound growth rate of 2.6% per year), petroleum and plastics (2.5% growth), and electronics (4.6% growth). The industries in which there has traditionally been a lot of trade between the United States and Mexico—such as machinery and transport (including autos) and textiles and garments—have slower growth in export variety because Mexico was exporting a wide range of products in these industries to the United States even before joining NAFTA.

The increase in the variety of products exported from Mexico to the United States under NAFTA is a source of gains from trade for American consumers. The United States has also imported more product varieties over time from many other countries, especially developing countries. According to one estimate, the total number of product varieties imported into the United States from 1972 to 2001—from all countries, not just Mexico—has increased by four times. Furthermore, that expansion in import variety has had the same beneficial impact on consumers as a reduction in import prices of 1.2% per year.[8] That equivalent price reduction is a measure of the gains from trade due to the expansion of varieties exported to the United States from all countries.

TABLE 6-3

Mexico's Export Variety to the United States, 1990 and 2001 This table shows the extent of variety in Mexican exports to the United States, by industry. From 1990 to 2001, export variety grew in every industry, as U.S. tariffs were reduced due to NAFTA. All figures are percentages.

	Agriculture	Textiles and Garments	Wood and Paper	Petroleum and Plastics	Mining and Metals	Machinery and Transport	Electronics	Average
1990	42	71	47	55	47	66	40	52
2001	51	83	63	73	56	76	66	67
Annual growth	1.9	1.4	2.6	2.5	1.7	1.3	4.6	2.2

Data from: Robert Feenstra and Hiau Looi Kee, 2007, "Trade Liberalization and Export Variety: A Comparison of Mexico and China," The World Economy, 30(1), 5–21.

[8] Christian Broda and David E. Weinstein, 2006, "Globalization and the Gains from Variety," *Quarterly Journal of Economics*, 121(2), May, 541–585.

Unfortunately, we do not have a separate estimate of the gains from the growth of export varieties from Mexico alone, which averages 2.2% per year from Table 6-3. Suppose we use the same 1.2% price reduction estimate for Mexico that has been found for all countries. That is, we assume that the growth in export variety from Mexico leads to the same beneficial impact on U.S. consumers as a reduction in Mexican import prices of 1.2% per year, or about one-half as much as the growth in export variety itself. In 1994, the first year of NAFTA, Mexico exported $50 billion in merchandise goods to the United States, and by 2001 this sum had grown to $131 billion. Using $90 billion as an average of these two values, a 1.2% reduction in the prices for Mexican imports would save U.S. consumers $90 billion · 1.2% = $1.1 billion per year. We will assume that all these savings are due to NAFTA, though even without NAFTA, there would likely have been some growth in export variety from Mexico.

It is crucial to realize that these consumer savings are *permanent* and that they *increase over time* as export varieties from Mexico continue to grow. Thus, in the first year of NAFTA, we estimate a gain to U.S. consumers of $1.1 billion; in the second year a gain of $2.2 billion, equivalent to a total fall in prices of 2.4%; in the third year a gain of $3.3 billion; and so on. Adding these up over the first nine years of NAFTA, the total benefit to consumers was $49.5 billion, or an average of $5.5 billion per year. In 2003, the tenth year of NAFTA, consumers would gain by $11 billion as compared with 1994. This gain will continue to grow as Mexico further increases the range of varieties exported to the United States.

Adjustment Costs in the United States Adjustment costs in the United States come as firms exit the market because of import competition and the workers employed by those firms are temporarily unemployed. One way to measure that temporary unemployment is to look at the claims under the U.S. **Trade Adjustment Assistance (TAA)** provisions. The TAA program offers assistance to workers in manufacturing who lose their jobs because of import competition. As we discussed in Chapter 3, the North American Free Trade Agreement included a special extension of TAA to workers laid off due to import competition because of NAFTA.

By looking at claims under that program, we can get an idea of the unemployment caused by NAFTA, one of the short-run costs of the agreement. From 1994 to 2002, some 525,000 workers, or about 58,000 per year, lost their jobs and were certified as adversely affected by trade or investment with Canada or Mexico under the NAFTA-TAA program.[9] As a result, these workers were entitled to additional unemployment benefits. This number is probably the most accurate estimate we have of the temporary unemployment caused by NAFTA.

How large is the displacement of 58,000 workers per year due to NAFTA? We can compare this number with overall job displacement in the United States. Over the *three* years from January 1999 to December 2001, 4 million workers were displaced, about one-third of whom were in manufacturing. So the *annual* number of workers displaced in manufacturing was 4 million · $\left(\frac{1}{3}\right)$ · $\left(\frac{1}{3}\right)$ = 444,000 workers per year. Thus, the NAFTA layoffs of 58,000 workers were about 13% of the total displacement in manufacturing, which is a substantial amount.

Other than compare the displacement caused by NAFTA with the total displacement in manufacturing, however, we can also evaluate the wages lost by displaced workers and compare this amount with the consumer gains. In Chapter 3 (see **Application: Manufacturing and Services in the United States**), we learned that about 65% of workers laid off in manufacturing during the 2015–2017 period were reemployed within three years (by January 2018). In other words, about two-thirds of

---

[9] The information in this paragraph is drawn from Gary Clyde Hufbauer and Jeffrey J. Schott, 2006, *NAFTA Revisited: Achievements and Challenges* (Washington, D.C.: Peterson Institute for International Economics), pp. 38–42, and it applies to the first 10 years of NAFTA.

workers are reemployed in less than three years; for the other third, it takes longer. To simplify the problem, suppose that the average length of unemployment for laid-off workers is three years.[10] Average yearly earnings for production workers in manufacturing were $31,000 in 2000, so each displaced worker lost $93,000 in wages (three times the workers' average annual income).[11] Total lost wages caused by displacement would be 58,000 workers displaced per year times $93,000, or $5.4 billion per year during the first nine years of NAFTA.

These private costs of $5.4 billion are nearly equal to the average welfare gains of $5.5 billion per year due to the expansion of import varieties from Mexico from 1994 to 2002, as computed previously. But the gains from increased product variety *continue and grow over time* as new imported products become available to American consumers. Recall from the previous calculation that the gains from the ongoing expansion of product varieties from Mexico were $11 billion in 2003, the tenth year of NAFTA, or twice as high as the $5.4 billion costs of adjustment. As the consumer gains continue to grow, adjustment costs due to job losses fall. Thus, the consumer gains from increased variety, when summed over years, considerably exceed the private losses from displacement. This outcome is guaranteed to occur because the gains from expanded import varieties occur *every year* that the imports are available, whereas labor displacement is a temporary phenomenon.

The calculation we have made shows that the gains to U.S. consumers from greater import variety from Mexico, when summed over time, are more than the private costs of adjustment. In practice, the actual compensation received by workers is much less than their costs of adjustment. In 2002 the NAFTA–TAA program was consolidated with the general TAA program in the United States, so there is no further record of layoffs as a result of NAFTA. Under the Trade Act of 2002, the funding for TAA was increased from $400 million to $1.2 billion per year and some other improvements to the program were made, such as providing a health-care subsidy for laid-off workers. In addition, as part of the jobs stimulus bill, called the American Recovery and Reinvestment Act, which was signed by President Obama on February 17, 2009, workers in the service sector (as well as farmers) who lose their jobs because of trade could also apply for TAA benefits. The TAA program was renewed again in 2015.

Renegotiation of NAFTA

The perception of NAFTA by President Trump was negative, as indicated by his quote at the beginning of the chapter, and some members of the U.S. public felt the same way. One reason for this sentiment is that there was a decline in manufacturing jobs in the United States in the decades since NAFTA was signed in 1994, which people sometimes attributed to that trade agreement. In fact, recent studies have argued that it is the growth in exports from China to the United States, and not any rise in Mexican exports, that explains the fall in U.S. manufacturing jobs. China joined the World Trade Organization in 2001 and was then entitled to permanently lower import tariffs in the United States, which led to the large rise in China's exports and reduced U.S. employment in manufacturing, as we discussed in Chapter 3.[12]

In Table 6-4 we show the major provisions of the U.S.–Mexico–Canada Agreement (USMCA) that are changed from the NAFTA agreement. Some of these changes have occurred in the **rules of origin** that are needed in a free-trade agreement. The rules of origin in NAFTA and USMCA specify the amount of each product that must be made in North American in order for that product to be shipped tariff-free between

---

[10] We show in Problem 5 at the end of the chapter that this assumption is accurate.
[11] We are not considering the additional losses if the new job has lower wages than earned previously.
[12] See **Application: The "China Shock" and Employment in the United States** in Chapter 3.

the United States, Mexico, and Canada. These rules are needed to prevent a product that is imported into one of these three countries from *outside* of North America—say, a French cheese being imported into Canada—from being further shipped to the United States or Mexico. These two countries might have higher import tariffs on French cheese than Canada does, so shipping that imported product from Canada would be a way to evade the higher tariffs applied by the other two countries. A free-trade area like NAFTA and USMCA only allows for free trade *of the products made within that area*, but it does not allow for free trade within the region of products imported from abroad. That is why rules of origin, specifying what products are made within the free-trade area, are needed.

The first change in USMCA as compared to NAFTA that is listed in Table 6-4 is the rules of origin for automobiles: the total North American content of an automobile must be 75% in order for that car to be shipped tariff-free between the United States, Mexico, and Canada. That percentage has been increased from 62.5% under NAFTA. In addition, 70% of all steel, aluminum, and glass used in the automobile must originate in North America, and there are specific provisions that other parts, such as the powertrain, must be made in North America. Note that while these rules of origin have been tightened from the NAFTA agreement, this change on its own does not influence *where* in North America the automobile and its parts are made.

The second change listed in Table 6-4 is that 30% of an automobile's content (which, in 2023, will rise to 40% for autos and 45% for light trucks) must be produced in North American plants where labor earns at least $16 per hour. This provision is new to the USMCA—there was nothing like it in NAFTA—and it will potentially influence the location of automobile production facilities in North America. Because $16 per hour is about three times the prevailing wage in auto manufacturing in Mexico, this provision will create some incentive to shift production out of Mexico and into the United States or Canada, so as to meet the percentage of production with wages of at least $16 per hour. Many auto workers in the United States and Canada

TABLE 6-4

A Comparison of the USMCA and NAFTA Shown here are some of the provisions of the U.S.–Mexico–Canada Agreement (USMCA) that differ from the North American Free Trade Agreement (NAFTA).

Topic	Change
Automotive production	The total North American content of an automobile must be 75%, which is increased from 62.5% under NAFTA.
Automotive wages	Thirty percent of an automobile's content (rising to 40% for autos and 45% for light trucks in 2023) must be produced in North American plants where labor earns at least $16 per hour. There was no similar provision in NAFTA.
Labor	Mexico passed new labor laws making it easier to form unions. Among other provisions, these laws give workers the rights to vote on unions and on labor contracts under secret ballots. This change strengthens Mexican labor laws as compared to NAFTA.
Dairy trade	U.S. producers will have access to about 3.6% of Canada's dairy market. There was no similar provision in NAFTA.
Internet platforms	USMCA limits the liability that Internet platforms such as Facebook and Twitter face in Mexico or Canada for third-party content that is hosted on their sites. There was no similar provision in NAFTA.
Sunset clause	The provisions of the agreement will remain in effect for 16 years, unless the three countries agree after 6 years to extend that time. There was no similar end date under NAFTA, though the U.S. president in conjunction with Congress could withdraw anytime.

Data from: "From NAFTA to USMCA: Free Trade in North America Today and Tomorrow," Livingston, https://www.livingstonintl .com/nafta/; "USMCA: Who Are the Winners and Losers of the 'New NAFTA?'" The Washington Post, October 1, 2018, https://www.washingtonpost.com/business/2018/10/01/winners-losers-usmca-trade-deal/.

earn more than that amount, especially nonproduction workers engaged in research and development, management, marketing, and other headquarters jobs. The ability of firms to shift production and nonproduction jobs across borders is called *offshoring*, a topic that we study in Chapter 7.

Another change that affects automobile production and many other manufacturing industries is the change in labor laws in Mexico, which occurred in April 2019. These changes, which were included in the USMCA negotiation, give Mexican workers the right to use secret ballots when voting whether to form a labor union, or when voting on their contracts. There is also funding provided in Mexico and other provisions to ensure that labor laws there are followed. This strengthening of labor laws in Mexico was advocated by the labor unions in the United States and was important in leading to their support of the USMCA deal.

Moving beyond manufacturing industries, President Trump was dissatisfied with the access that American farmers had for exporting dairy products to Canada. Under USMCA, American farmers will be able to export products totaling about 3.6% of the Canadian market. This provision did not exist in NAFTA, but it is not entirely new in the USMCA agreement. In fact, a similar provision that would have granted U.S. producers access to 3.25% of the Canadian dairy market had been negotiated under the Trans-Pacific Partnership (TPP). The TPP was an agreement among 12 countries in 2016, including the United States, that was negotiated under the Obama administration. President Trump pulled out of TPP shortly after being elected. Still, this dairy provision was used in the USMCA agreement.

Another industry that appears in USMCA is the Internet platforms for social media, such as Facebook and Twitter. In the United States, there are laws that prevent these platforms from being sued for the content that is uploaded by third parties. These laws are controversial, however, and are beginning to be challenged in U.S. courts. A similar law is written into USMCA, which limits the liability that Internet platforms face in Mexico or Canada for third-party content. There was no such provision in NAFTA, which began before the spread of social media.

A final provision of the USMCA that differs from NAFTA is the "sunset" provision, under which the United States, Mexico, or Canada can withdraw from the agreement. Negotiators from the United States had initially called for a very short sunset period of only 5 years. That length of time was strongly objected to by negotiators from Canada and Mexico, who argued that it did not give companies a long enough planning horizon for any investments they might make. Instead, the USMCA establishes a sunset provision of 16 years, with a further provision that the countries can meet after 6 years to determine whether to extend the agreement for *more than* the additional 10 years. There was no similar end date under NAFTA, though the U.S. president in conjunction with Congress could always withdraw from a trade agreement.

What will be the impact of the USMCA agreement as compared to NAFTA? There is disagreement on this point, even among official U.S. agencies. One report from the U.S. International Trade Commission (USITC), a government agency that is charged with implementing U.S. trade policies, finds that the USMCA will add 176,000 jobs in the entire economy.[13] Another report from the United States Trade Representative (USTR), a White House office that is charged with negotiating U.S. trade policies, argues more optimistically that USMCA will add 76,000 jobs in the automobile sector alone (this report does not make an estimate for the entire economy).[14] The USITC report agrees that more production of automobile parts may be shifted to North America to meet the new rules of origin, but it points out that this change will come at the cost of higher consumer prices for automobiles.

---

[13] See: www.usitc.gov/publications/332/pub4889.pdf?mod=article_inline.
[14] See: ustr.gov/sites/default/files/files/Press/Releases/USTR%20USMCA%20Autos%20White%20Paper.pdf.

HEADLINES

North American Trade Pact Could Cushion U.S. Economy

On December 10, 2019, the terms of the U.S.-Mexico-Canada Agreement (USMCA) were agreed to by representatives of the three countries, in a ceremony held in Mexico City. The potential impacts on the U.S. economy are discussed in this article.

The new trade agreement with Mexico and Canada won't bring an economic boom, but it could cushion the U.S. in the face of slowing global growth as it boosts some industries and removes a big source of business uncertainty. The deal, reached Tuesday [December 10, 2019], also will keep U.S. trade on track with its two largest partners. U.S. trade with Mexico and Canada topped $1 trillion through October of this year, more than double the $470 billion of trade with China.

The benefits "are not so much in what USMCA brings, but rather what it prevents," said Gregory Daco, an economist at Oxford Economics. He estimated that a U.S. withdrawal from the existing trade pact, the North American Free Trade Agreement, or Nafta, without a replacement would have dented U.S. gross domestic product by 0.5% in the first year.

The U.S. International Trade Commission, a bipartisan agency whose review is required for any trade deal, said this spring that the new North American treaty would have a positive though modest impact on growth, boosting U.S. gross domestic product by 0.35% and adding 176,000 U.S. jobs over six years after it goes into effect. "In the overall giant U.S. economy these are small changes," said Gary Clyde Hufbauer, a senior fellow at the Peterson Institute for International Economics.

President Trump made the renegotiation of Nafta—a 26-year-old trade pact between the U.S. and its immediate neighbors—a key 2016 campaign promise. And he threatened U.S. withdrawal from the agreement after he took office. Removing the withdrawal risk by passing a new agreement is the primary upside for businesses, economists say, particularly given the current backdrop of slow global economic growth, trade tensions with China and weak investment by U.S. companies.

Source: Republished with permission of The Wall Street Journal. From "North American Trade Pact Could Cushion US Economy," by Harriet Torry, December 11, 2019. Permission conveyed through Copyright Clearance Center, Inc.

The U.S.–Mexico–Canada Agreement is signed on December 10, 2019 by officials of the three countries.

In **Headlines: North American Trade Pact Could Cushion U.S. Economy**, we summarize the views of various economists on the impact of USMCA. They point out that the estimated employment effects are not that large when compared to the size of the U.S. economy. The biggest benefit of the USMCA is that it eliminates the *uncertainty* created by the prospect of pulling out of NAFTA, as President Trump threatened to do if a new deal was not agreed upon. While USMCA has strengthened some provisions of NAFTA, many other provisions of these agreements (which are hundreds of pages long) have not been changed. So the benefits that NAFTA has brought to workers and consumers in the three countries (along with the more temporary adjustment costs) can be expected to continue.

4 Intra-Industry Trade and the Gravity Equation

In the monopolistic competition model, countries both import and export diverse varieties of differentiated goods. This result differs from the Ricardian and Heckscher–Ohlin models that we studied in Chapters 2 and 4: in those models, countries either export or import a good but do not export and import the same good simultaneously. Under monopolistic competition, countries will specialize in producing different varieties of a differentiated good and will trade those varieties back and forth. As we saw from the example of golf clubs at the beginning of the chapter, this is a common trade pattern that we call intra-industry trade.

Index of Intra-Industry Trade

To develop the idea of intra-industry trade, let us return to the example of golf clubs that we discussed at the beginning of the chapter. In 2018 the United States imported $422 million in golf clubs and exported $140 million. When a country both imports and exports a good, as the United States does with golf clubs, it is an indication that some of the trade in that good is intra-industry trade. The **index of intra-industry trade** tells us what proportion of trade in each product involves both imports and exports: a high index (up to 100%) indicates that an equal amount of the good is imported and exported, whereas a low index (0%) indicates that the good is either imported or exported but not both.

The formula for the index of intra-industry trade is

$$(\text{Index of intra-industry trade}) = \frac{\text{Minimum of imports and exports}}{\frac{1}{2}(\text{Imports} + \text{exports})}$$

For golf clubs, the minimum of imports and exports is $140 million, and the average of imports and exports is $\frac{1}{2}(422 + 140) = \$281$ million. So $\frac{140}{281} = 50\%$ or one-half of the U.S. trade in golf clubs is intra-industry trade; that is, it involves both exporting and importing of golf clubs.

In Table 6-5, we show some examples of intra-industry trade in other products for the United States. Products such as whiskey and vaccines have a high index of intra-industry trade. These are examples of highly differentiated products: for whiskey and vaccines, each exporting country sells products that are different from those of other exporting countries, including the United States. Above these two items in Table 6-5 is natural gas. While natural gas is not what we normally think of as a differentiated product, it becomes differentiated once we recognize that it is imported and exported through pipelines that cross the border at different places. So it is this *geographic* differentiation that gives it the highest index of intra-industry trade in Table 6-5.

TABLE 6-5

Index of Intra-Industry Trade for the United States, 2018 Shown here are the value of imports, the value of exports, and the index of intra-industry trade for a number of products. When the value of imports is close to the value of exports, such as for natural gas, whiskey, and vaccines, then the index of intra-industry trade is highest, and when a product is mainly imported or exported (but not both), then the index of intra-industry trade is lowest.

Product	Value of Imports ($ millions)	Value of Exports ($ millions)	Index of Intra-Industry Trade (%)
Natural gas	$6,546	$4,551	82%
Whiskey	2,157	1,360	77
Vaccines	5,754	2,364	58
Telephones	273	90	50
Golf clubs	422	140	50
Mattresses	413	106	41
Apples	241	940	41
Golf carts	35	137	41
Sunglasses	1,657	399	39
Frozen orange juice	10	2	33
Small cars	106,478	17,394	28
Large passenger aircraft	4,400	187,477	5
Men's shorts	1,172	26	4

Data from: U.S. International Trade Commission, Interactive Tariff and Trade DataWeb, at dataweb.usitc.gov.

In contrast to those products, other goods such as men's shorts and large passenger aircraft have very low indexes of intra-industry trade. These goods are either mainly imported into the United States (like men's shorts) or mainly exported (like large passenger aircraft). Even though these goods are still differentiated, we can think of them as being closer to fitting the Ricardian or Heckscher–Ohlin models, in which trade is determined by comparative advantage, such as having lower relative costs in one country because of technology or resource abundance. To obtain a high index of intra-industry trade, it is necessary for the good to be differentiated *and* for costs to be similar in the Home and Foreign countries, leading to both imports and exports.

The Gravity Equation

The index of intra-industry trade measures the degree of intra-industry trade for a product but does not tell us anything about the total amount of trade. To explain the value of trade, we need a different equation, called the "gravity equation." This equation was given its name by Dutch economist and Nobel laureate Jan Tinbergen. Tinbergen was trained in physics, so he thought about the trade between countries as similar to the force of gravity between objects: Newton's universal law of gravitation states that objects with larger mass, or that are closer to each other, have a greater gravitational pull between them. Tinbergen's gravity equation for trade states that countries with larger GDPs, or that are closer to each other, have more trade between them. Both these equations can be explained simply—even if you have never studied physics, you will be able to grasp their meanings. The point is that just as the force of gravity is strongest between large objects, the monopolistic competition model predicts that large countries (as measured by their GDP) should trade the most with one another. There is much empirical evidence to support this prediction, as we will show.

Newton's Universal Law of Gravitation
Suppose that two objects each have mass M_1 and M_2 and are located distance d apart. According to Newton's universal law of gravitation, the force of gravity F_g between these two objects is

$$F_g = G \cdot \frac{M_1 \cdot M_2}{d^2}$$

where G is a constant that tells us the magnitude of this relationship. The larger each object is, or the closer they are to each other, the greater is the force of gravity between them.

The Gravity Equation in Trade
The equation proposed by Tinbergen to explain trade between countries is similar to Newton's law of gravity, except that instead of the mass of two objects, we use the GDP of two countries, and instead of predicting the force of gravity, we are predicting the amount of trade between them. The gravity equation in trade is

$$\text{Trade} = B \cdot \frac{GDP_1 \cdot GDP_2}{dist^n}$$

where Trade is the amount of trade (measured by imports, exports, or their average) between two countries, GDP_1 and GDP_2 are their gross domestic products, and *dist* is the distance between them. Notice that we use the exponent n on distance, $dist^n$, rather than $dist^2$ as in Newton's law of gravity, because we are not sure of the precise relationship between distance and trade. The B in front of the gravity equation is a constant that indicates the relationship between the "gravity term" (i.e., $GDP_1 \cdot GDP_2/dist^n$) and Trade. It can also be interpreted as summarizing the effects of all factors (other than size and distance) that influence the amount of trade between two countries; such factors include tariffs (which would lower the amount of trade and reduce B), sharing a common border (which would increase trade and raise B), and so on.

According to the gravity equation, the larger the countries are (as measured by their GDP), or the closer they are to each other, the greater is the amount of trade between them. This connection among economic size, distance, and trade is an implication of the monopolistic competition model that we have studied in this chapter. The monopolistic competition model implies that larger countries trade the most for two reasons: larger countries export more because they produce more product varieties, and they import more because their demand is higher. Therefore, larger countries trade more in both exports and imports.

Deriving the Gravity Equation To explain more carefully why the gravity equation holds in the monopolistic competition model, we can work through some algebra using the GDPs of the various countries. Start with the GDP of Country 1, GDP_1. Each of the goods produced in Country 1 is a differentiated product, so they are not the same as the varieties produced in other countries. Every other country will demand the goods of Country 1 (because they are different from their home-produced goods), and the amount of their demand will depend on two factors: (1) the relative size of the importing country (larger countries demand more), and (2) the distance between the two countries (being farther away leads to higher transportation costs and less trade).

To measure the relative size of each importing country, we use its share of world GDP. Specifically, we define Country 2's share of world GDP as $Share_2 = GDP_2/GDP_W$. To measure the transportation costs involved in trade, we use distance raised to a power, or $dist^n$. Using these definitions, exports from Country 1 to Country 2 will equal the goods available in Country 1 (GDP_1), times the relative size of Country 2 ($Share_2$), divided by the transportation costs between them ($dist^n$), so that

$$\text{Trade} = \frac{GDP_1 \cdot Share_2}{dist^n} = \left(\frac{1}{GDP_W} \right) \frac{GDP_1 \cdot GDP_2}{dist^n}$$

This equation for the trade between Countries 1 and 2 looks similar to the gravity equation, especially if we think of the term ($1/GDP_W$) as the constant term B. We see from this equation that the trade between two countries will be proportional to their relative sizes, measured by the product of their GDPs (the greater the size of the countries, the larger is trade), and inversely proportional to the distance between them (the smaller the distance, the larger is trade). The following application explores how well the gravity equation works in practice.

APPLICATION

The Gravity Equation for Canada and the United States

We can apply the gravity equation to trade between any pair of countries, or even to trade between the provinces or states of one country and another. Panel (a) of Figure 6-9 shows data collected on the value of trade between Canadian provinces and U.S. states in 1993. On the horizontal axis, we show the gravity term:

$$\text{Gravity term} = \frac{GDP_1 \cdot GDP_2}{dist^{1.25}}$$

where GDP_1 is the gross domestic product of a U.S. state (in billions of U.S. dollars), GDP_2 is the gross domestic product of a Canadian province (in billions of U.S. dollars), and $dist$ is the distance between them (in miles). We use the exponent 1.25 on the distance term because other research studies have shown that it describes the relationship between distance and trade value quite well. The horizontal axis is plotted as a logarithmic scale, with values from 0.001 to 100. A higher value along the horizontal axis indicates either a large GDP for the trading province and state or a smaller distance between them.

FIGURE 6-9

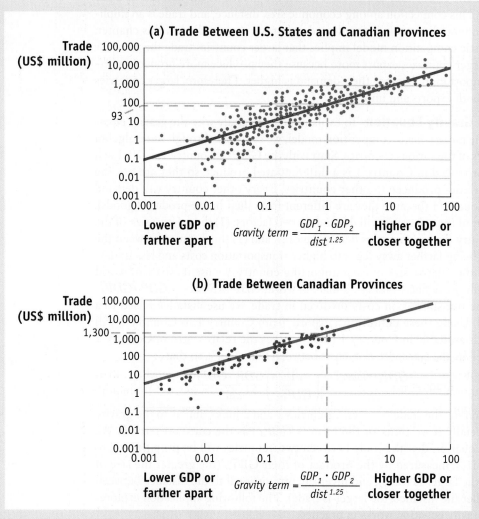

(a) Trade Between U.S. States and Canadian Provinces

Trade (US$ million)

$$\text{Gravity term} = \frac{GDP_1 \cdot GDP_2}{dist^{1.25}}$$

Lower GDP or farther apart   Higher GDP or closer together

(b) Trade Between Canadian Provinces

Trade (US$ million)

$$\text{Gravity term} = \frac{GDP_1 \cdot GDP_2}{dist^{1.25}}$$

Lower GDP or farther apart   Higher GDP or closer together

Gravity Equation for the United States and Canada, 1993 Plotted in these figures are the dollar value of exports in 1993 and the gravity term (plotted in log scale). Panel (a) shows these variables for trade between 10 Canadian provinces and 30 U.S. states. When the gravity term is 1, for example, the amount of trade between a province and state is $93 million. Panel (b) shows these variables for trade between 10 Canadian provinces. When the gravity term is 1, the amount of trade between the provinces is $1.3 billion, 14 times larger than between a province and a state. These graphs illustrate two important points: there is a positive relationship between country size (as measured by GDP) and trade volume, and there is much more trade within Canada than between Canada and the United States.

Data from: Author's calculations using data from James A. Anderson and Eric van Wincoop, 2003, "Gravity with Gravitas: A Solution to the Border Puzzle," American Economic Review, 170–192.

The vertical axis in Figure 6-9 shows the 1993 value of exports (in millions of U.S. dollars) between a Canadian province and U.S. state or between a U.S. state and Canadian province; this is the value of trade for the province–state pair. That axis is also plotted as a logarithmic scale, with values from $0.001 million (or $1,000) to $100,000 million (or $100 billion) in trade. There are 30 states and 10 provinces included in the study, so there are a total of 600 possible trade flows between them (though some of those flows are zero, indicating that no exporting takes place). Each of the points in panel (a) represents the trade flow and gravity term between one state and one province.

We can see from the set of points in panel (a) that states and provinces with a higher gravity term between them (measured on the horizontal axis) also tend to have more trade (measured on the vertical axis). That strong, positive relationship shown by the set of points in panel (a) demonstrates that the gravity equation holds well empirically.

Panel (a) also shows the "best fit" straight line through the set of points, which has the following equation:

$$\text{Trade} = 93 \frac{GDP_1 \cdot GDP_2}{dist^{1.25}}$$

The constant term $B = 93$ gives the best fit to this gravity equation for Canadian provinces and U.S. states. When the gravity term equals 1, as illustrated in panel (a), then the predicted amount of trade between that state and province is $93 million. The closest example to this point is Alberta and New Jersey. In 1993 there were $94 million in exports from Alberta to New Jersey, and they had a gravity term of approximately 1.

Trade Within Canada Because the gravity equation works well at predicting international trade between provinces and states in different countries, it should also work well at predicting trade *within* a country, or *intra-national* trade. To explore this idea, panel (b) of Figure 6-9 graphs the value of exports (in millions of U.S. dollars) between any two Canadian provinces, along with the gravity term for those provinces. The scale of the axes in panel (b) is the same as in panel (a). From panel (b), we again see that there is a strong, positive relationship between the gravity term between two provinces (measured on the horizontal axis) and their trade (measured on the vertical axis). The "best fit" straight line through the set of points has the following equation:

$$\text{Trade} = 1,300 \frac{GDP_1 \cdot GDP_2}{dist^{1.25}}$$

That is, the constant term $B = 1,300$ gives the best fit to this gravity equation for Canadian provinces. When the gravity term equals 1, as illustrated in panel (b), then the predicted amount of trade between two provinces is $1,300 million, or $1.3 billion. The closest example to this combination is between British Columbia and Alberta: in 1993 their gravity term was approximately 1.3, and British Columbia exported $1.4 billion worth of goods to Alberta.

Comparing the gravity equation for international trade between Canada and the United States with the gravity equation for intra-national trade in Canada, the constant term for Canadian trade is much bigger—1,300 as compared with 93. Taking the ratio of these two constant terms $(1,300/93 = 14)$, we find that on average there is 14 times more trade *within* Canada than occurs across the border! That number is even higher if we consider an earlier year, 1988, just before Canada and the United States signed their Free Trade Agreement in 1989. In 1988 intra-national trade within Canada was 22 times higher than international trade between Canada and the United States.[15] Even though that ratio fell from 1988 to 1993 because of the free-trade agreement between Canada and the United States, it is still remarkable that there is so much more trade *within* Canada than across the border, or more generally, so much more intra-national than international trade.

The finding that trade across borders is less than trade within countries reflects all the barriers to trade that occur between countries. Factors that make it easier or more difficult to trade goods between countries are often called **border effects**, and they include the following:

- Taxes imposed when imported goods enter into a country, called **tariffs**

- Limits on the number of items allowed to cross the border, called **quotas**

- Other administrative rules and regulations affecting trade, including the time required for goods to clear customs

---

[15] That calculation comes from John McCallum, 1995, "National Borders Matter," *American Economic Review*, 615–623. The 1993 data used in Figure 6-9 derive from James A. Anderson and Eric van Wincoop, 2003, "Gravity with Gravitas: A Solution to the Border Puzzle," *American Economic Review*, 170–192.

- Geographic factors such as whether the countries share a border
- Cultural factors, such as whether the countries have a common language that might make trade easier

In the gravity equation, all the factors that influence the amount of trade are reflected in the constant B. As we have seen, the value of this constant differs for trade within a country versus trade between countries. In later chapters, we explore in detail the consequences of tariffs, quotas, and other barriers to trade. The lesson from the gravity equation is that such barriers to trade can potentially have a large impact on the amount of international trade as compared with intra-national trade.

5 Conclusions

When firms have differentiated products and increasing returns to scale, the potential exists for gains from trade above and beyond those that we studied in earlier chapters under perfect competition. We have demonstrated these additional gains using a model of monopolistic competition. In this model, trade will occur even between countries that are identical because the potential to sell in a larger market will induce firms to lower their prices below those charged in the absence of trade. When all firms lower their prices, however, some firms are no longer profitable and exit the market. The remaining firms expand their output, lowering their average costs through increasing returns to scale. The reduction in average costs lowers the prices charged by firms, creating gains for consumers in the importing country. In addition, because each firm produces a differentiated product, trade between countries allows for the importing of product varieties that are different from those produced domestically, creating a second source of gains for consumers.

When some firms have to exit the market, short-run adjustment costs arise within this model because of worker displacement. Using examples from Canada, Mexico, and the United States, we have argued that the short-run adjustment costs are less than the long-run gains. Regional trade agreements like NAFTA and the U.S.–Mexico–Canada Agreement (USMCA) are a good application of the monopolistic competition model. Another application is the "gravity equation," which states that countries that are larger or closer to one another will trade more. That prediction is supported by looking at data on trade between countries. Research has also shown that trade within countries is even larger than trade between countries.

KEY POINTS

1. The monopolistic competition model assumes differentiated products, many firms, and increasing returns to scale. Firms enter whenever there are profits to be earned, so profits are zero in the long-run equilibrium.

2. When trade opens between two countries, the demand curve faced by each firm becomes more elastic, as consumers have more choices and become more price sensitive. Firms then lower their prices in an attempt to capture consumers from their competitors and obtain profits. When all firms do so, however, some firms incur losses and are forced to leave the market.

3. Introducing international trade under monopolistic competition leads to additional gains from trade for

two reasons: (i) lower prices as firms expand their output and lower their average costs, and (ii) additional imported product varieties available to consumers. There are also short-run adjustment costs, such as unemployment, as some firms exit the market.

4. The assumption of differentiated goods helps us to understand why countries often import and export varieties of the same type of good. That outcome occurs with the model of monopolistic competition.

5. The gravity equation states that countries with higher GDP, or that are close, will trade more. In addition, research has shown that there is more trade within countries than between countries.

PROBLEMS

1. **Discovering Data**

   a. Of two products, rice and paintings, which do you expect to have a higher index of intra-industry trade? Why?

   b. Access the U.S. TradeStats Express website at tse.export.gov/tse/tsehome.aspx. Click on "National Trade Data" and then "Global Patterns of U.S. Merchandise Trade." Under the "Product" section click the "Change" button under "item" to choose the HS classification system. Then change the item to rice (HS 1006) and obtain the export and import values. Do the same for paintings (HS 9701); then calculate the intra-industry trade index for rice and paintings in a recent year. Do your calculations confirm your expectation from part (a)? If your answers did not confirm your expectation, explain why not.

2. Explain how increasing returns to scale in production can be a basis for trade.

3. Starting from the long-run equilibrium without trade in the monopolistic competition model, as illustrated in Figure 6-5, consider what happens when the Home country begins trading with two other identical countries. Because the countries are all the same, the number of consumers in the world is three times larger than in a single country, and the number of firms in the world is three times larger than in a single country.

   a. Compared with the no-trade equilibrium, how much does industry demand D increase? How much does the number of firms (or product varieties) increase? Does the demand curve D/N^A still apply after the opening of trade? Explain why or why not.

   b. Does the d_1 curve shift or pivot due to the opening of trade? Explain why or why not.

   c. Compare your answer to (b) with the case in which Home trades with only one other identical country. Specifically, compare the elasticity of the demand curve d_1 in the two cases.

   d. Illustrate the long-run equilibrium with trade, and compare it with the long-run equilibrium when Home trades with only one other identical country.

4. Starting from the long-run trade equilibrium in the monopolistic competition model, as illustrated in Figure 6-7, consider what happens when industry demand D increases. For instance, suppose that this is the market for cars, and lower gasoline prices generate higher demand D.

   a. Redraw Figure 6-7 for the Home market and show the shift in the D/N^T curve and the new short-run equilibrium.

   b. From the new short-run equilibrium, is there exit or entry of firms, and why?

   c. Describe where the new long-run equilibrium occurs, and explain what has happened to the number of firms and the prices they charge.

5. In the section "Gains and Adjustment Costs for the United States Under NAFTA," we calculated the lost wages of workers displaced because of NAFTA. Prior experience in the manufacturing sector shows that about two-thirds of these workers obtain new jobs within three years. One way to think about that reemployment process is that one-third of workers find jobs in the first year, and another one-third of remaining unemployed workers find a job each subsequent year. Using this approach, in the table that follows, we show that one-third of workers get a job in the first year (column 2), leaving two-thirds of workers unemployed (column 4). In the second year, another $\left(\frac{1}{3}\right) \cdot \left(\frac{2}{3}\right) = \frac{2}{9}$ of workers get

a job (column 2), so that $\left(\frac{1}{3}\right)+\left(\frac{2}{9}\right)=\frac{5}{9}$ of the workers are employed (column 3). That leaves $1-\frac{5}{9}=\frac{4}{9}$ of the workers unemployed (column 4) at the end of the second year.

Year	Fraction Finding Job	Total Fraction Employed	Total Fraction Unemployed
1	$\frac{1}{3}$	$\frac{1}{3}$	$1-\frac{1}{3}=\frac{2}{3}$
2	$\frac{1}{3}\cdot\frac{2}{3}=\frac{2}{9}$	$\frac{1}{3}+\frac{2}{3}=\frac{5}{9}$	$1-\frac{5}{9}=\frac{4}{9}$
3	$\frac{1}{3}\cdot\frac{4}{9}=\frac{4}{27}$		
4			
5			
6	$\frac{1}{3}\cdot\left(\frac{2}{3}\right)^{Year-1}$		

a. Fill in two more rows of the table using the same approach as for the first two rows.

b. Notice that the fraction of workers finding a job each year (column 2) has the formula

$$\text{Fraction finding job} = \tfrac{1}{3}\cdot\left(\tfrac{2}{3}\right)^{Year-1}$$

Using this formula, fill in six more values for the fraction of workers finding a job (column 2), up to year 10.

c. To calculate the average spell of unemployment, we take the fraction of workers finding jobs (column 2), multiply it by the years of unemployment (column 1), and add up the result over all the rows. By adding up over 10 rows, calculate what the average spell of unemployment is. What do you expect to get when adding up over 20 rows?

d. Compare your answer to (c) with the average three-year spell of unemployment of 65% mentioned earlier in the chapter. Was that number accurate?

6. What evidence is there that Canada was better off than before under the Canada–U.S. Free-Trade Agreement (CUSFTA) that started in 1989? What evidence is there of adjustment costs under this agreement?

7. In what way will the U.S.–Mexico–Canada Agreement (USMCA) benefit labor unions in the United States as compared with the NAFTA agreement?

8. Our derivation of the gravity equation from the monopolistic competition model used the following logic:

(i) Each country produces different varieties of each product.

(ii) Each country demands all of the product varieties that every other country produces.

(iii) Thus, large countries demand more imports from other countries.

The gravity equation relationship does not hold in the Heckscher–Ohlin model. Explain how the logic of the gravity equation breaks down in the Heckscher–Ohlin model; that is, which of the statements just listed is no longer true in the Heckscher–Ohlin model?

9. In the analysis of the gravity equation, explain why trade within a country was found to be greater than trade between countries.

WORK IT OUT   ≋ Achieve | interactive activity

10. The United States, Japan, and China are among the world's largest producers. To answer the following questions, assume that their markets are monopolistically competitive, and use the gravity equation with $B = 93$ and $n = 1.25$.

	Real GDP in 2017 ($ billions)	Distance from the United States (miles)
China	18,396	7,245
Japan	5,107	6,314
United States	18,219	—

a. Using the gravity equation, compare the expected level of trade between the United States and Japan and between the United States and China.

b. The distance between Beijing and Tokyo is 1,302 miles. Would you expect more trade between China and Japan or between China and the United States? Explain what variable (i.e., country size or distance) drives your result.

7

Offshoring of Goods and Services

One facet of increased services trade is the increased use of offshore outsourcing in which a company relocates labor-intensive service-industry functions to another country. . . . When a good or service is produced more cheaply abroad, it makes more sense to import it than to make or provide it domestically.

Economic Report of the President, 2004, p. 229

Increasing numbers of Americans . . . perceive offshoring . . . as an actual or potential threat to their jobs or to their wages even if they hold onto their jobs.

Jagdish Bhagwati and Alan S. Blinder, 2007, *Offshoring of American Jobs*

Questions to Consider

1 Why do some firms shift parts of their production to other countries?

2 Who can gain when firms shift their production abroad?

3 Do countries gain overall when their firms offshore to other countries?

You may have flown on the newest commercial aircraft produced by Boeing, the 787 Dreamliner, which is distinguished by its soft "mood" lighting that changes from lavender to orange to green. The aircraft not only promises greater comfort for passengers, but also saves money in its operation because it is built from light, more fuel-efficient materials. This aircraft is assembled in Boeing's plant in Everett, Washington, which employs about 1,000 people. But the components for the 787 are manufactured in many hundreds of other companies located all over the world. For example, sections of the fuselage are built in Japan, in Italy, and by another American company in Charleston, South Carolina; the wings are built in Japan, Korea, and Australia; the engine and landing gear are built in the United Kingdom; the passenger doors are built in France, and so on.

Aircraft are only one example of products that are assembled using components made in many countries. Much smaller products, such as the iPhone or the Barbie doll, are assembled using parts that are produced all over the world, too. The provision of a service or the production of various parts of a good in different countries that are then used or assembled into a final good in another location is called **foreign outsourcing** or, more simply, **offshoring**. We will not worry about the subtle distinction between these two terms in this chapter (see **Side Bar: "Foreign Outsourcing" Versus "Offshoring"**); we'll use "offshoring" because it is most commonly used by economists.

The parts of a Boeing 787 come from many countries

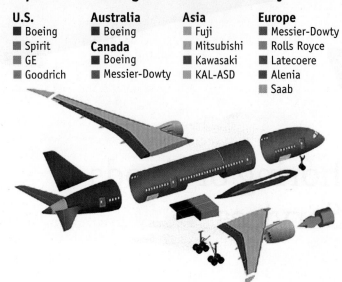

U.S.	Australia	Asia	Europe
■ Boeing	■ Boeing	■ Fuji	■ Messier-Dowty
■ Spirit	**Canada**	■ Mitsubishi	■ Rolls Royce
■ GE	■ Boeing	■ Kawasaki	■ Latecoere
■ Goodrich	■ Messier-Dowty	■ KAL-ASD	■ Alenia
			■ Saab

Offshoring is a type of international trade that differs from the type of trade analyzed with the Ricardian and Heckscher–Ohlin models; the goods traded in those models were final goods. Offshoring is trade in *intermediate inputs*, which can sometimes cross borders several times before being incorporated into a final good that can be sold domestically or abroad. Offshoring is a relatively new phenomenon in world trade.[1] The amount of world trade relative to the GDPs of countries was high even in

SIDE BAR

"Foreign Outsourcing" Versus "Offshoring"

In discussions of foreign outsourcing, we often hear the term "offshoring." The quote from the *Economic Report of the President* at the beginning of the chapter used the term "offshore outsourcing." Is there a difference between "foreign outsourcing" and "offshoring"?

The term "offshoring" is sometimes used to refer to a company that moves some of its operations overseas but retains ownership of those operations. In other words, the company moves some operations offshore but does not move production outside of its own firm. Intel, for example, produces microchips in China and Costa Rica using subsidiaries that it owns. Intel has engaged in foreign direct investment (FDI) to establish these offshore subsidiaries.

Mattel, on the other hand, arranges for the production of the Barbie doll in several different countries. Unlike Intel, however, Mattel does not actually own the firms in those countries. Furthermore, Mattel lets these

firms purchase their inputs (like the hair and cloth for the dolls) from whichever sources are most economical. Mattel is engaging in foreign outsourcing because it contracts with these foreign firms but has not engaged in any FDI.

Dell is an intermediate case. Dell assembles its computers overseas in firms it does not own, so it is outsourcing rather than offshoring the assembly. However, Dell exercises careful control over the inputs (such as computer parts) that these overseas firms use. Dell outsources the assembly but monitors the overseas firms closely to ensure the high quality of the computers being assembled.

In this chapter, we will not worry about the distinction between "offshoring" and "foreign outsourcing"; we'll use the term "offshoring" whenever the components of a good or service are produced in several countries, regardless of who owns the plants that provide the components or services.

---

[1] There is also the concept of *domestic outsourcing*, which occurs when a company decides to shift some of its production activities from one location to another within the same country. In this text, outsourcing always means *foreign outsourcing*.

the late nineteenth and early twentieth centuries. But it is unlikely that a good would have crossed borders multiple times at several stages of production because the costs of transportation and communication were too high. Today, however, these costs have fallen so much that it is now economical to combine the labor and capital resources of several countries to produce a good or service. Indeed, if you have ever called for help with your laptop, chances are that you have spoken with someone at a call center in India, which shows just how low the costs of communication have become!

Is offshoring different from the type of trade examined in the Ricardian and Heckscher–Ohlin models? From one point of view, the answer is no. Offshoring allows a company to purchase inexpensive goods or services abroad, just as consumers can purchase lower-priced goods from abroad in the Ricardian and Heckscher–Ohlin models. This is what the quote from the *Economic Report of the President* at the beginning of the chapter suggests: with offshoring we import those goods and services that are cheaper to produce abroad. From another point of view, however, offshoring is different. Companies now have the opportunity to send *a portion* of their activities to other countries. The jobs associated with those activities leave the United States, and by paying lower wages abroad, U.S. firms lower their costs and pass on these savings to consumers. Offshoring results in lower prices but changes the mix of jobs located in the United States. Higher-skilled workers in the United States, engaged in activities such as marketing and research, will be combined with less-skilled workers abroad, engaged in assembling products. In a sense, offshoring is similar to immigration in that U.S. firms are able to employ foreign workers, even though those workers do not have to leave their home countries.

The first goal of this chapter is to examine in detail the phenomenon of offshoring and describe the ways in which it differs from trade in final products. We discuss how offshoring affects the demand for high-skilled and low-skilled labor and the wages paid to those workers. Since the early 1980s, there has been a significant change in the pattern of wage payments in the United States and other countries—the wages of skilled workers have been rising relative to those of less-skilled workers. We examine whether this change in relative wages is the result of offshoring or whether there are other explanations for it. We also describe the new phenomena of **job polarization**, which occurs when employment grows in occupations that pay the highest wages and in those that pay the lowest wages, but declines in occupations that pay mid-level wages.

A second goal of the chapter is to discuss the gains from offshoring. We argue that offshoring creates gains from trade, similar to those seen from the trade of final goods in the Ricardian or Heckscher–Ohlin models. But having overall gains from trade for a country does not necessarily mean that every person in the country gains. As the second quote at the beginning of the chapter shows, many workers are fearful that their jobs and wages are threatened by offshoring. We focus attention on how offshoring affects the wages and the employment of different types of workers.

A third goal of the chapter is to describe some of the newest trends in offshoring. In its production of aircraft, Boeing has learned to reduce the number of suppliers that it relies on from many thousands to several hundred, thereby lowering the costs of communication along its global supply chain. Mexico is an attractive offshoring location to U.S. companies because the costs of face-to-face communication are lower when compared with offshore firms that are farther away. Some U.S. companies are choosing to move back closer to the United States because the low costs of communication allow them to make quick changes to design and production, in what is called **onshoring**. As companies continue to seek the most efficient means and locations to produce goods, they must balance the lower wages found abroad with the benefits of being closer to home, and that balance changes continually over time.

1 A Model of Offshoring

To develop a model of offshoring, we need to identify all the activities involved in producing and marketing a good or service. These activities are illustrated in Figure 7-1. Panel (a) describes the activities in the order in which they are performed (starting with research and development [R&D] and ending with marketing and after-sales service). For instance, in producing a television, the design and engineering are developed first; components such as wiring, casing, and screens are manufactured next; and finally the television is assembled into its final version and sold to consumers.

For the purpose of building a model of offshoring, however, it is more useful to line up the activities according to the ratio of high-skilled/low-skilled labor used, as in panel (b). We start with the less-skilled activities, such as the manufacture and assembly of simple components (like the case or the electric cord for the television), then move to more-complex components (like the screen). Next are the supporting service activities such as accounting, order processing, and product service (sometimes called "back-office" activities because the customer does not see them). Finally, we come to activities that use more-skilled labor, such as marketing and sales ("front-office" activities), and those that use the most-skilled labor such as R&D.

Value Chain of Activities

The whole set of activities that we have illustrated in Figures 7-1(a) and 7-1(b) is sometimes called the **value chain** for the product, with each activity adding more value to the combined product. All these activities do not need to be done in one

FIGURE 7-1

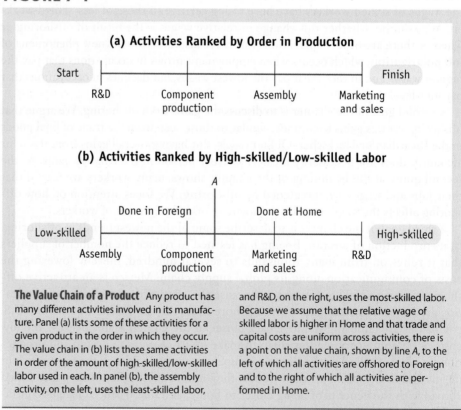

The Value Chain of a Product Any product has many different activities involved in its manufacture. Panel (a) lists some of these activities for a given product in the order in which they occur. The value chain in (b) lists these same activities in order of the amount of high-skilled/low-skilled labor used in each. In panel (b), the assembly activity, on the left, uses the least-skilled labor, and R&D, on the right, uses the most-skilled labor. Because we assume that the relative wage of skilled labor is higher in Home and that trade and capital costs are uniform across activities, there is a point on the value chain, shown by line *A*, to the left of which all activities are offshored to Foreign and to the right of which all activities are performed in Home.

country—a firm can transfer some of these activities abroad by offshoring them when it is more economical to do so. By lining up the activities in terms of the relative amount of skilled labor they require, we can predict which activities are likely to be transferred abroad. This prediction depends on two assumptions, which follow.

Assumption 1: Because low-skilled workers in Foreign earn very low wages, the *relative* wage of low-skilled labor to high-skilled labor is lower in Foreign than it is in Home. Let W_L be the wage of low-skilled labor in Home and W_H the wage of high-skilled labor. Similarly, let W_L^* and W_H^* be the wages of low-skilled and high-skilled workers in Foreign. Our first assumption is that Foreign wages are less than those in Home, $W_L^* < W_L$ and $W_H^* < W_H$, and also that the *relative wage* of low-skilled labor to high-skilled labor is lower in Foreign than in Home, so that $W_L^*/W_H^* < W_L/W_H$. This assumption on the relative wage is realistic because low-skilled labor in developing countries earns very low wages. For example, low-skilled labor might earn $1 per hour (or less) in a developing country, as compared with a minimum wage of $12 per hour in California. High-skilled labor in developing countries also receives lower wages than in developed countries, but that difference is not so great: managers in developing countries might earn one-half as much as in the United States or Europe. For example, say that managers earn $100 per hour in Home and $50 per hour in Foreign. Then the relative wage W_L^*/W_H^* in Foreign (a developing country) is $1/$50 = 0.02, which is less than the relative wage W_L/W_H in Home (a developed country) of $12/$100 = 0.12.

The reciprocal of these ratios is the wage of high-skilled labor relative to low-skilled labor, or the **relative wage of skilled workers**. Another way of stating our assumption is that the relative wage of skilled workers in Foreign, which in our example is $W_H^*/W_L^* = $50/$1 = 50$, is *higher* than the relative wage of skilled workers in Home, which is $W_H/W_L = $100/$12 = 8.3$.

Assumption 2: The costs of capital and trade apply *uniformly* across all the activities in the value chain. As the firm considers sending some activities abroad, it knows that it will lower its labor costs because wages in Foreign are lower. However, the firm must also take into account the extra costs of doing business in Foreign, which can be of two types.

1. The firm may have to pay higher capital costs because of higher expenses to build a factory or higher prices for utilities such as electricity and fuel.

2. The firm may have to pay higher trade costs. Trade costs are the extra costs incurred for transportation and communication (which will be especially high if Foreign is still developing infrastructure such as roads, ports, and telecommunication networks), and from tariffs if Foreign imposes taxes on imported goods (such as component parts) when they come into the country.

Higher capital and trade costs in Foreign can prevent a Home firm from offshoring all its activities abroad. In making the decision of what to offshore, the Home firm will balance the savings from lower wages against the extra costs of capital and trade.

Our second assumption is that these extra costs apply *uniformly* across all the activities in the value chain; that is, these extra costs add, say, 10% to each and every component of operation in Foreign as compared with Home. Unlike our assumption about relative wages in Home and Foreign, this assumption is a bit unrealistic. For instance, the extra costs of transportation versus those of communication are quite different in countries such as China and India; good roads for transport have developed slowly, while communications technology has developed rapidly. As a result, technology in telephones is advanced in those countries, so cell phones are often cheaper there than in the United States and Europe. In this case, the higher infrastructure costs will affect the activities that rely on transportation more than activities that rely on communication.

Slicing the Value Chain

Now suppose that the Home firm with the value chain in Figure 7-1(b) considers transferring some of these activities from Home to Foreign. Which activities will be transferred? Based on our assumptions that $W_L^*/W_H^* < W_L/W_H$ and that the extra costs of capital and trade apply uniformly, it makes sense for the firm to send abroad the activities that are the least skilled-labor-intensive and keep in Home the activities that are the most skilled-labor-intensive. Looking at Figure 7-1, all activities to the left of the vertical line A might be done in Foreign, for example, whereas those activities to the right of the vertical line will be done in Home. We can refer to this transfer of activities as "slicing the value chain."[2]

Activities to the left of line A are sent abroad because the cost savings from paying lower wages in Foreign are greatest for activities that require less-skilled labor. Because the extra costs of capital and trade are uniform across activities, the cost savings on wages are most important in determining which activities to transfer and which to keep in Home.

Relative Demand for Skilled Labor Across the Value Chain Now that we know the division of activities between Home and Foreign, we can graph the demand and supply for labor in each country, as illustrated in Figure 7-2. For Home, we add up the quantities demanded for high-skilled labor H and low-skilled labor L for all the activities to the right of line A in Figure 7-1(b). On the horizontal axes in Figure 7-2, we measure the **relative employment of skilled workers**, the ratio of the number of high-skilled workers employed to the number of low-skilled workers employed, H/L. On the vertical axes, we measure the relative wage W_H/W_L, the ratio of high-skilled wages to low-skilled wages. In panel (a) we graph the relative employment for skilled labor in Home H/L against the relative wage W_H/W_L. The relative demand curve for skilled labor slopes downward because a higher relative wage for skilled labor would cause Home firms to substitute less-skilled labor in some activities. For example, if the relative wage of skilled labor increases, Home firms might hire high school rather than college graduates as salespeople and then train them on the job. This substitution causes the relative employment of high-skilled labor H/L to fall.

In Foreign, we add up the demand for high-skilled labor H^* and for low-skilled labor L^* for all the activities to the left of line A in Figure 7-1(b). Panel (b) in Figure 7-2 graphs the relative demand for skilled labor in Foreign H^*/L^* against the relative wage W_H^*/W_L^*. Again, this curve slopes downward because a higher relative wage for skilled labor would cause Foreign firms to substitute less-skilled labor in some activities.

In each country, we can add a relative supply curve to the diagram. This curve slopes upward because a higher relative wage for skilled labor causes more-skilled individuals to enter this industry. For instance, if the high-skilled wage increases relative to the low-skilled wage in either country, then individuals will invest more in schooling to equip themselves with the skills necessary to earn the higher relative wage and the high-skilled relative employment in Home and Foreign will increase.

The intersection of the relative demand and relative supply curves, at points A and A^*, gives the equilibrium relative wage of skilled labor in this industry in each country, W_H/W_L and W_H^*/W_L^*, and the equilibrium relative employment of skilled labor, H/L and H^*/L^*. Starting at these points, next we study how the equilibria change as Home offshores more activities to Foreign.

---

[2] This term is drawn from Paul Krugman, 1995, "Growing World Trade: Causes and Consequences," *Brookings Papers on Economic Activity*, 1.

FIGURE 7-2

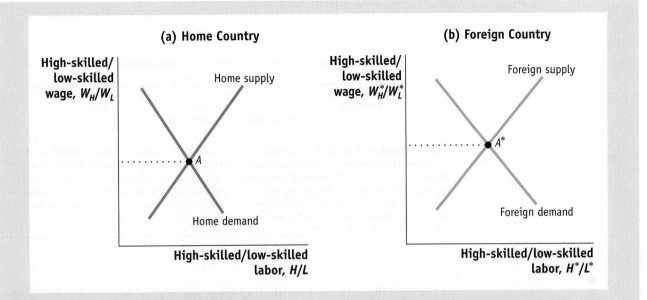

(a) Home Country

(b) Foreign Country

Relative Demand and Supply for High-Skilled/Low-Skilled Labor Panel (a) shows how the relative demand and supply for skilled labor in Home, H/L, depends on the relative wage, W_H/W_L. The equilibrium relative wage in Home is determined at A where relative Home demand and supply are equal. Panel (b) shows how the relative demand and supply for skilled labor in Foreign, H^*/L^*, depends on the relative wage, W_H^*/W_L^*. The Foreign equilibrium is at point A^*.

Changes in Foreign Costs and in Offshoring

Suppose that the costs of capital or trade in Foreign fall. For example, the North American Free Trade Agreement (NAFTA) in 1994 and the U.S.-Mexico-Canada Agreement (USMCA) in 2020 lowered tariffs (part of trade costs) charged on goods crossing the U.S.–Mexico border. This fall in trade costs made it easier for U.S. firms to offshore to Mexico. Even before NAFTA, Mexico had liberalized the rules concerning foreign ownership of capital there, thereby lowering the cost of capital for U.S. firms. Similarly, in 1991, India eliminated many regulations that had been hindering foreign investment, and it also reduced the cost of communication. Before 1991 it was difficult for a new business to start, or even to secure a phone or fax line in India; after 1991 the regulations on domestic- and foreign-owned business were simplified, and communication technology improved dramatically with cell phones and fiber-optic cables. These policy changes made India more attractive to foreign investors and firms interested in offshoring.

Effect on Home Relative Labor Demand and Relative Wage When the costs of capital or trade decline in Foreign, it becomes desirable to shift more activities in the value chain from Home to Foreign. Figure 7-3 illustrates this change with the shift of the dividing line from A to B. The activities between A and B, which used to be done in Home, are now done in Foreign. As an example, consider the transfer of television production from the United States to Mexico. As U.S. firms first shifted manufacturing to Mexico, the chassis of the televisions were constructed there. Later on, electronic circuits were constructed in Mexico, and later still the picture tubes were manufactured there.[3]

---

[3] Martin Kenney and Richard Florida, 1994, "Japanese Maquiladoras: Production Organization and Global Commodity Chains," *World Development*, 22(1), 27–44.

FIGURE 7-3

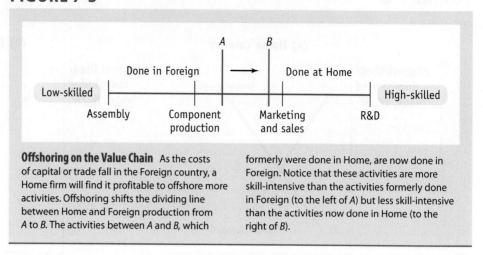

Offshoring on the Value Chain As the costs of capital or trade fall in the Foreign country, a Home firm will find it profitable to offshore more activities. Offshoring shifts the dividing line between Home and Foreign production from *A* to *B*. The activities between *A* and *B*, which formerly were done in Home, are now done in Foreign. Notice that these activities are more skill-intensive than the activities formerly done in Foreign (to the left of *A*) but less skill-intensive than the activities now done in Home (to the right of *B*).

How does this increase in offshoring affect the relative demand for skilled labor in each country? First consider the Home country. Notice that the activities no longer performed in Home (i.e., those between *A* and *B*) are *less* skill-intensive than the activities still done there (those to the right of *B*). This means that the activities now done in Home are more skill-intensive, on average, than the activities formerly done in Home. For this reason, the relative demand for skilled labor in Home will increase, and the Home demand curve will shift to the right, as shown in Figure 7-4, panel (a). Note that this diagram does not show the *absolute* quantity of labor demanded, which we expect would fall for both high-skilled and low-skilled labor when there is more offshoring; instead, we are graphing the *relative* demand for high-skilled/low-skilled labor, which increases because the activities still done in Home are more skill-intensive than before the decrease in trade and capital costs. With the increase in the relative demand for skilled labor, the equilibrium will shift from point *A* to point *B* in Home; that is, the relative wage of skilled labor will increase because of offshoring.

Effect on Foreign Relative Labor Demand and Relative Wage Now let's look at what happens in Foreign when Home offshores more of its production activities to Foreign. How will offshoring affect the relative demand for labor and relative wage in Foreign? As we saw in Figure 7-3, the activities that are newly offshored to Foreign (those between *A* and *B*) are *more* skill-intensive than the activities that were initially offshored to Foreign (those to the left of *A*). This means that the range of activities now done in Foreign is more skill-intensive, on average, than the set of activities formerly done there. For this reason, the relative demand for skilled labor in Foreign also increases, and the Foreign demand curve shifts to the right, as shown in panel (b) of Figure 7-4. With this increase in the relative demand for skilled labor, the equilibrium shifts from point A^* to point B^*. As a result of Home's increased offshoring to Foreign, then, the relative wage of skilled labor increases in Foreign. The conclusion from our model is that *both* countries experience an increase in the relative wage of skilled labor because of increased offshoring.

It might seem surprising that a shift of activities from one country to the other can increase the relative demand for skilled labor in *both* countries. An example drawn from your classroom experience might help you to understand how this can happen. Suppose you have a friend who is majoring in physics but is finding

FIGURE 7-4

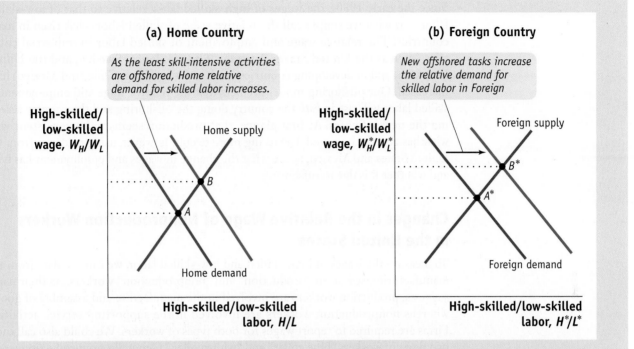

(a) Home Country

As the least skill-intensive activities are offshored, Home relative demand for skilled labor increases.

High-skilled/low-skilled wage, W_H/W_L

Home supply

B

A

Home demand

High-skilled/low-skilled labor, H/L

(b) Foreign Country

New offshored tasks increase the relative demand for skilled labor in Foreign

High-skilled/low-skilled wage, W_H^*/W_L^*

Foreign supply

B^*

A^*

Foreign demand

High-skilled/low-skilled labor, H*/L*

Change in the Relative Demand for Skilled Labor With greater off-shoring from Home to Foreign, some of the activities requiring less skill that were formerly done in Home are now done abroad. It follows that the relative demand for skilled labor in Home increases and the relative wage rises from point *A* to point *B*. The relative demand for skilled labor in Foreign also increases because the activities shifted to Foreign are more skill-intensive than those formerly done there. It follows that the relative wage for skilled labor in Foreign also rises, from point A^* to point B^*.

it difficult: she is scoring below average in a physics class that she is taking. So you invite her to join you in an economics class, and it turns out that your friend has a knack for economics: she scores above average in that class. How does your friend's transfer from physics to economics affect the class averages? Because she was performing below average in the physics class, when she leaves the class, her departure raises the class average (computed now using the students still there, not including her). Because your friend performs better than average in the economics class, her arrival raises the class average there, too (computed using everyone, including your friend). Thus, your friend's move from one class to another raises the average in both classes.

This result is just like the logic of the offshoring model: *As activities in the middle of the value chain are shifted by offshoring from Home to Foreign, they raise the relative demand for skilled labor in both countries because these activities are the least skill-intensive of those formerly done in Home but the most skill-intensive of tasks done in Foreign.* That is why the relative demand for skilled labor increases in both countries, along with the relative wage of skilled labor. This result is one of the most important predictions from our offshoring model, and it would not occur in our earlier models of trade, such as the Heckscher–Ohlin model.[4] We now turn to evidence from the United States and Mexico to see whether this prediction is borne out.

---

[4] The Heckscher–Ohlin model tells us that the factor prices in the two countries will move toward equality when they open trade. So the wage relative to the capital rental will move in different directions in the two countries due to the opening of trade, not in the same direction.

2 Explaining Changes in Wages and Employment

Since the early 1980s, the wages of high-skilled labor relative to that of low-skilled labor—or what we simply call the relative wage of skilled labor—has risen in many countries. The relative wage and employment of skilled labor in industrial countries (such as the United States, Australia, Canada, Japan, Sweden, and the United Kingdom) and in developing countries (such as Hong Kong, Chile, and Mexico) have increased. Our offshoring model predicts that the relative wage and employment of skilled labor will rise in *both* the country doing the offshoring and the country receiving the new activities. At first glance, that prediction seems to be consistent with what has actually occurred. Let us dig more deeply, however, using evidence from the United States and Mexico, to see what the change in wages and employment has been and whether it is due to offshoring.

Changes in the Relative Wage of Nonproduction Workers in the United States

To measure the wages of high-skilled and low-skilled labor, we can use data from the manufacturing sector on "production" and "nonproduction" workers. As their name suggests, production workers are involved in the manufacture and assembly of goods, whereas nonproduction workers are involved in the supporting service activities. Firms are required to report wages for both types of workers. We could also call these two types of workers "blue collar" and "white collar." Generally, nonproduction workers require more education, and so we will categorize these workers as "high-skilled," whereas production workers are categorized here as "low-skilled" workers.[5]

Figure 7-5 shows the average annual wages of nonproduction workers divided by the average annual wages of production workers in U.S. manufacturing, from 1958 to 2014.[6] We refer to this ratio of wages as the **relative wage of nonproduction workers**, and it is analogous to the ratio of high-skilled to low-skilled wages, or W_H/W_L in our model. We see that the relative wage of nonproduction workers moved erratically from 1958 to 1967, and that from 1968 to about 1982, the relative wage was on a downward trend. It is generally accepted that the relative wage fell during this period because of an increase in the supply of college graduates and skilled workers who moved into nonproduction jobs. The increase in supply brought down the nonproduction wage, so the relative wage also fell. Starting in 1982, however, this trend reversed itself and the relative wage of nonproduction workers rose steadily until 2000, then fell until 2004, after which it rose again through 2014.

Changes in Relative Employment of Nonproduction Workers Figure 7-6 shows the number of nonproduction workers employed in U.S. manufacturing divided by the number of production workers employed, from 1958 to 2014. We refer to this ratio of employment as the **relative employment of nonproduction workers** and it is analogous to the ratio of high-skilled to low-skilled labor, or H/L in our model. In Figure 7-6 we see that there was a steady increase in the relative employment of nonproduction workers employed in U.S. manufacturing until about 1992. Such a trend indicates that firms were hiring fewer production, or low-skilled workers, relative to nonproduction workers. During the 1990s the ratio of nonproduction to production workers fell until 1998, after which relative employment rose again erratically.

---

[5] This distinction is far from perfect, however. Nonproduction workers include clerical and custodial staff, for example, who may be less skilled than some production workers.

[6] More recent years for these data are not available.

FIGURE 7-5

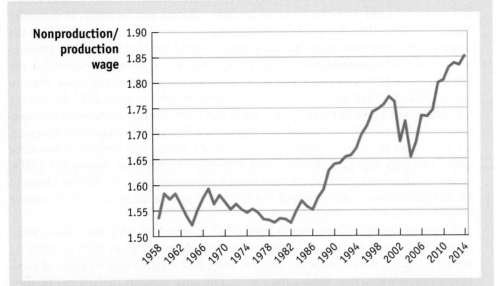

Relative Wage of Nonproduction Workers, U.S. Manufacturing This diagram shows the average wage of nonproduction workers divided by the average wage of production workers in U.S. manufacturing. This relative wage of nonproduction workers moved erratically during the 1960s and 1970s, although showing some downward trend. This trend reversed itself beginning in the early 1980s, as the relative wage of nonproduction workers increased until 2000. It then fell until 2004, and rose again through 2014.

Data from: Annual Survey of Manufactures and National Bureau of Economic Research (NBER) productivity database, updated from U.S. Bureau of the Census.

FIGURE 7-6

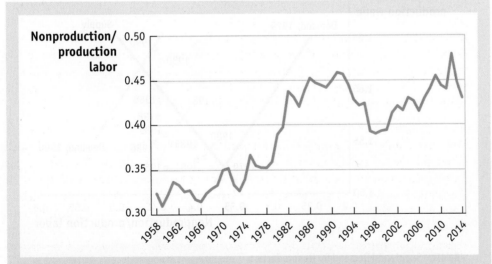

Relative Employment of Nonproduction Workers, U.S. Manufacturing This diagram shows the number of nonproduction workers employed in U.S. manufacturing divided by the number of production workers employed. There was a steady increase in the relative employment of nonproduction workers employed in U.S. manufacturing until the early 1990s. That trend indicates that firms were hiring fewer production workers relative to nonproduction workers. During the 1990s there was a fall in the relative employment of nonproduction workers until 1998, after which relative employment rose again erratically.

Data from: Annual Survey of Manufactures and NBER productivity database, updated from U.S. Bureau of the Census.

The increase in the relative supply of college graduates from 1968 to 1982 is consistent with the reduction in the relative wage of nonproduction workers, as shown in Figure 7-5, and with the increase in their relative employment, as shown in Figure 7-6. After 1982, however, the story changes. We would normally think that the rising relative wage of nonproduction workers should have led to a shift in employment *away* from nonproduction workers, but it did not: As shown in Figure 7-6, the relative employment of nonproduction workers continued to rise from 1980 to about 1992, then fell until 1998, and rose again erratically until 2012. So during the 1980s, and again in recent years, there has been both an increase in the relative wage of nonproduction workers *and* an increase in their relative employment. How can both the relative wage and the relative employment increase at the same time? The only explanation consistent with these facts is that during the 1980s, and again in recent years, there has been an *outward shift* in the relative demand for nonproduction workers, which led to a simultaneous increase in their relative employment *and* in their wages.

This conclusion is illustrated in Figure 7-7, in which we plot the relative wage of nonproduction workers and their relative employment from 1979 to 1990. As we have already noted, both the relative wage and relative employment of nonproduction workers rose during the 1980s. The only way this pattern can be consistent with a supply and demand diagram is if the relative demand for skilled labor increases, shifting up the curve from Demand, 1979 to Demand, 1990. This increased demand would lead to an increase in the relative wage for skilled labor *and* an increase in its relative employment, the pattern seen in the data for the United States.

FIGURE 7-7

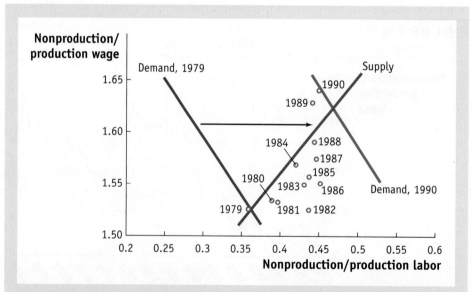

Relative Supply and Demand for Nonproduction Workers in the 1980s This diagram shows the wage of nonproduction workers relative to the wage of production workers on the vertical axis, and on the horizontal axis the employment of nonproduction workers relative to the employment of production workers. Both the relative wage and the relative employment of nonproduction workers rose in U.S. manufacturing during the 1980s, indicating that the relative demand for skilled workers must have increased, shifting the relative demand curve to the right.

Data from: The data used in constructing this graph are from the Annual Survey of Manufactures and from the NBER productivity database, updated from U.S. Bureau of the Census.

Explanations What factors can lead to an increase in the relative demand for skilled labor? One explanation is offshoring. An increase in demand for high-skilled workers, at the expense of low-skilled workers, can arise from offshoring, as shown by the rightward shift in the relative demand for skilled labor in Figure 7-4(a). The evidence from the manufacturing sector in the United States is strongly consistent with our model of offshoring.

There is, however, a second possible explanation for the increase in the relative demand for skilled workers in the United States. In the 1980s, personal computers began to appear in the workplace. The addition of computers (or other high-tech equipment) in the workplace can increase the demand for skilled workers to operate them. The shift in relative demand toward skilled workers because of the use of high-tech equipment is called **skill-biased technological change**. Given these two potential explanations for the same observation, how can we determine which of these factors was most responsible for the actual change in wages?

Answering this question has been the topic of many research studies in economics. The approach that most authors have taken is to measure skill-biased technological change and offshoring in terms of some underlying variables. For skill-biased technological change, we can look at changes in the amount of computers and other high-technology equipment used in manufacturing industries. For offshoring, we can look at changes in the quantity of imports of intermediate inputs used in manufacturing industries. By studying how the use of high-tech equipment and the imports of intermediate inputs have grown and comparing this with the wage movements in industries, we can determine each factor's contribution to explaining the wage movements.

The result from these studies is that *both* offshoring and skill-biased technological change are important explanations of the increase in the relative demand for nonproduction workers in U.S. manufacturing. There is some debate as to which of these factors is *most* important, and the results are mixed. According to some studies, skilled-biased technological change is the dominant factor explaining the increase in the relative demand for nonproduction workers and also the increase in their relative wage. But other studies have also found an important role for offshoring, and these studies suggest that offshoring can explain roughly the same amount of the shift in relative demand, and increase in the relative wage, that is explained by skill-biased technological change.[7]

Taken together, however, these two factors can explain only about 50% of the increase in the relative wage of nonproduction workers during the 1980s. Some other factor must be at work that led firms to lay off some of their production workers and shift relative demand toward nonproduction workers. One other factor that may account for this shift away from production workers was the very deep recession that occurred in the United States from 1980 to 1982. Production workers were laid off during the recession, but as the economy improved after 1982, firms found other ways to do the activities that these production workers used to do. Those other ways included installing high-tech equipment or shifting some of those activities overseas, as our model predicts.

Changes in the Relative Wage of Nonproduction Workers in Mexico

Our model of offshoring predicts that the relative wage of skilled labor will rise in *both* countries. We have already seen (in Figure 7-5) that the relative wage of nonproduction workers rises in the United States. But what happens in Mexico?

---

[7] See Robert C. Feenstra and Gordon H. Hanson, 1999, "The Impact of Outsourcing and High-Technology Capital on Wages: Estimates for the United States, 1979–1990," *Quarterly Journal of Economics*, 114(3), 907–940.

FIGURE 7-8

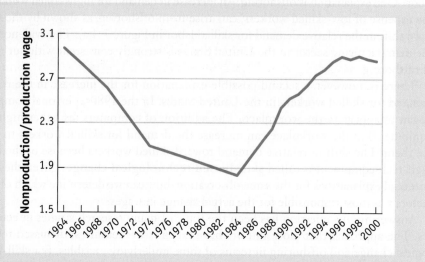

Relative Wage of Nonproduction Workers, Mexico Manufacturing This diagram shows the average wage of nonproduction workers divided by the average wage of production workers in the manufacturing sector of Mexico. After declining during the 1960s and 1970s, this relative wage of nonproduction workers began to move upward in the mid-1980s, at the same time that the relative wage was increasing in the United States (see Figure 7-5). The relative wage in Mexico continued to rise until 1996, two years after NAFTA began, and then leveled out.

Data from: Robert C. Feenstra and Gordon H. Hanson, May 1997, "Foreign Direct Investment and Relative Wages: Evidence from Mexico's Maquiladoras," Journal of International Economics, 4, 371–393 ; and Gerardo Esquivel and José Antonio Rodríguez-López, 2003, "Technology, Trade, and Wage Inequality in Mexico Before and After NAFTA," Journal of Development Economics, 72, 543– 565.

In Figure 7-8, we show the relative wage of nonproduction workers in Mexico from 1964 to 2000. The data used in Figure 7-8 come from the census of industries in Mexico, which occurred infrequently, so there are only a few turning points in the graph in the early years. We can see that the relative wage of nonproduction workers fell from 1964 to 1984, then rose until 1996, leveling out thereafter. The fall in the relative wage from 1964 to 1984 is similar to the pattern in the United States and probably occurred because of a similar increased supply of skilled labor in the workforce. More important, the rise in the relative wage from 1984 to 1996 is also similar to what happened in the United States and illustrates the prediction of our model of offshoring: that relative wages move in the *same* direction in both countries.

The leveling off of the relative wage of nonproduction workers in Mexico occurred in 1996, two years after the North American Free Trade Agreement (NAFTA) established free trade between the United States, Canada, and Mexico. The tariff reductions on imports from Mexico to the United States began in 1994 and were phased in over the next 10 years. Tariffs on imports from the United States and other countries into Mexico had been reduced much earlier, however—right around the 1984 turning point that we see in Figure 7-8. According to one study:[8]

> In 1985, in the midst of the debt crisis and as a result of the collapse of the oil price, Mexico initiated an important process of trade liberalization. In that year, Mexico implemented a considerable unilateral reduction in trade barriers and announced its intention to participate in the General Agreement on Tariffs and Trade (GATT).

---

[8] Gerardo Esquivel and José Antonio Rodríguez-López, 2003, "Technology, Trade, and Wage Inequality in Mexico Before and After NAFTA," *Journal of Development Economics*, 72, 546–547.

The average tariff charged by Mexico fell from 23.5% in 1985 to 11.0% in 1988, and the range of goods subject to tariffs was reduced. After 1985, Mexico also became much more open to the establishment of manufacturing plants by foreign (especially American) firms.

Summing up, the changes in relative wages in the United States and Mexico match each other during the period from 1964 to 1984 (with relative wages falling) and during the period from 1984 to 1996 (with relative wages rising in both countries). Offshoring from the United States to Mexico rose from 1984 to 1996, so the rise in relative wages matches our prediction from the model of offshoring.

Job Polarization in the United States

In the preceding sections, we developed a model of offshoring that predicted an increase in the relative wage and relative employment of nonproduction workers. We have seen that this prediction matches well the evidence for the United States during the 1980s, when the nonproduction relative wage and relative employment both rose. Figures 7-5 and 7-6 show a tendency for the relative wage and relative employment of nonproduction workers to rise since that time, too, though with some declines in the relative wage and relative employment in certain years. To carefully explain the trends that have occurred since the 1980s, we need to expand our offshoring model with new concepts.

Average Wages in Occupations Figure 7-9 shows how the decade of the 1980s differs from later periods. The horizontal axis plots information on the average wages earned in 326 occupations in the United States from 1979 to 2007. We divide these occupations into 100 groups of about three occupations each. The first group is the three occupations that earn the lowest average wages, the next group earns the next-lowest average wages, and so forth, up to the top group that earns the highest

FIGURE 7-9

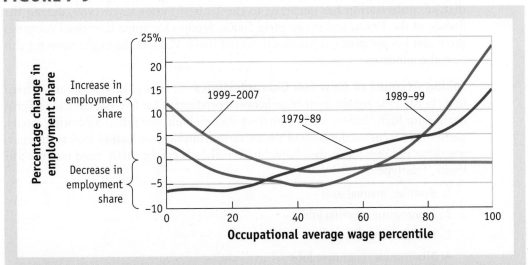

Change in Employment Shares by Occupational Wage Percentile The horizontal axis in this diagram organizes 326 U.S. occupations from the percentile of occupations paying the lowest average wages (on the left) to the percentile paying the highest wages (on the right). For each of these wage percentiles, we plot the *change* in the employment share of workers in those occupations for the periods 1979–89, 1989–99, and 1999–2007. From 1989–99 and 1999–2007, the occupations with the lowest wages and with the highest wages had increasing employment shares, whereas the occupations in the middle had falling employment shares.

From: David H. Autor, 2010, "The Polarization of Job Opportunities in the U.S. Labor Market: Implications for Employment and Earnings," Center for American Progress and the Hamilton Project, April 2010.

average wages. Each of these groups is called an "occupational average wage percentile." Within each of these wage percentiles, we calculate what share of total employment the workers in those occupations represent (not shown on graph), and then calculate how that share of employment has *changed* over time (measured on the vertical axis). We plot the *change* in the share of employment for three periods: 1979–89, 1989–99, and 1999–2007.

Looking first at the line for 1979–89, we see that occupations with the lowest average wages (on the left of Figure 7-9) experienced about a 6% fall in their employment share during this period, whereas the occupations with the highest wages (on the right) experienced about a 15% rise in their employment share. The line for 1979–89 slopes upward steadily, which means that occupations with higher average wages attracted more workers over that decade. This upward slope matches what we have already learned for the United States during the 1980s: there was a relative increase in demand for high-skilled workers, who earned higher wages. That increase in demand for higher-skilled workers could have come from offshoring or from the introduction of computers and other high-technology equipment, which were used more by higher-skilled workers.

Now let us turn to the later decades of 1989–99 and 1999–2007. Rather than rising steadily, you can see that the line for 1989–99 falls and then rises, while the line for 1999–2007 falls and then stays quite flat. In both cases, the employment share of the occupations earning the *lowest* average wages (on the far left of Figure 7-9) *increased*. In contrast, the employment share of the occupations earning wages in the middle (such as those between 40 and 60 on the horizontal axis) fell. The employment share of occupations earning the highest wages (between 80 and 100) increased tremendously during 1989–99, but changed very little in the later period, 1999–2007.

Economists call the phenomenon shown in Figure 7-9 job polarization, which occurs when the employment shares of jobs with the lowest wages and jobs with the highest wages increase, while the employment share of jobs with wages in the middle falls. Put simply, job polarization means that there are more jobs with high wages or low wages, and fewer jobs with wages in the middle. Figure 7-9 shows that job polarization has occurred in the United States since 1989, during the decade of the 1990s, and in the early 2000s. Studies for some European countries show that job polarization has also occurred there. What is the explanation for this new phenomenon?

Taking Account of New Job Characteristics To answer this question, we need to go beyond the simple distinction between production (or low-skilled) and nonproduction (or high-skilled) workers that we used to build our initial offshoring model. Rather than focus on the skills of the *workers* themselves, we instead look at the characteristics of the *jobs* that they hold. Specifically, *jobs* can be categorized into the following four types:

1. Routine, manual jobs

2. Nonroutine, manual jobs

3. Routine, cognitive jobs

4. Nonroutine, cognitive jobs

One job characteristic involves the amount of physical and mental ability required by the job. Production workers typically work in *manual* jobs, meaning jobs that involve physical activity, exertion, strength, mechanical ability, and dexterity. Nonproduction workers are more likely to be in jobs that involve less physical activity but more attention to writing and numerical skills and face-to-face communication with others, or what we call *cognitive* skills. Thus, one way to classify jobs is according to this characteristic of "manual" versus "cognitive" jobs. This classification fits with the distinction between production workers, who work at manual jobs, and nonproduction workers, who work at cognitive jobs.

A second important job characteristic is whether it is "routine" or "nonroutine." A person performing a *routine job* must follow a series of rules or actions. Examples of manual, routine jobs are assembly-line workers, forklift operators, construction workers, and mechanics. Cognitive jobs can also be routine: for example, secretaries, bookkeepers, filing clerks, and bank tellers. Although the ability to do routine jobs may be learned from on-the-job training, the actions taken in the job can also be described in a manual. That makes it possible to replace routine jobs with high-tech equipment (such prefabricating parts of buildings rather than constructing them on site) or to offshore these jobs to another country where wages are lower (such as when assembly is done in a plant abroad). Call centers are another example of a cognitive, routine job: workers at call centers answer questions over the phone and rely on a large manual of answers to perform their jobs, so these jobs can be replaced with a computerized answering service or offshored.

On the other hand, *nonroutine jobs* cannot be described by a set of rules or actions, and rely more on the worker's adaptation to various situations that can arise. The need for adaptability makes it much more difficult to automate or offshore nonroutine jobs. Examples of manual, nonroutine jobs include personal care (e.g., manicures, haircuts), health-care support, and building and grounds maintenance. These are among the lowest-paying jobs. Examples of cognitive, nonroutine jobs include public relations professionals, managers, and research and development (R&D) engineers and scientists. These jobs are often highly paid. Thus, nonroutine jobs can be either low-paying or high-paying, but in either case it is difficult to replace these jobs by computers or by offshoring.

Figure 7-10 classifies occupations into these four groups (nonroutine manual, routine manual, routine cognitive, and nonroutine cognitive) as shown in the horizontal axis. For each group, we use our previous data to calculate the growth in employment accounted for by workers in those occupations for the three periods that are plotted. The results for each period are shown by the bars in Figure 7-10.

For the period 1983–2000, the lowest employment growth was in nonroutine manual and routine manual jobs, which are the first two types of occupations on the left in

FIGURE 7-10

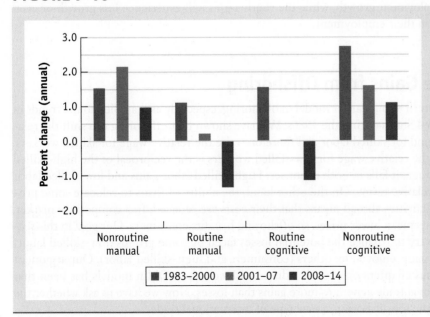

Growth in Employment by Type of Occupation
The horizontal axis in this diagram arranges occupations into four groups: nonroutine manual jobs; routine manual jobs; routine cognitive jobs; and nonroutine cognitive jobs. For each of these groups, we plot the growth rate of employment over the periods 1983–2000 (red bars), 2001–07 (green bars), and 2008–14 (purple bars).

Data from: Robert G. Valletta, Federal Reserve Bank of San Francisco's Economic Letter, "Higher Education, Wages, and Polarization" (2015-02) January 12, 2015. The opinions expressed in this article do not necessarily reflect the views of the management of the Federal Reserve Bank of San Francisco or of the Board of Governors of the Federal Reserve System. Economic Letter available at the following: http://www.frbsf .org/economic-research/publications/economicletter/2015 /january/wages-education-college-labor-earnings-income/.

Figure 7-10. Those manual jobs are shown by the first two red bars and had employment growth between 1% and 1.5% per year during this period. Routine cognitive jobs are shown by the third red bar, and had employment growth of slightly more than 1.5% per year. Nonroutine cognitive jobs are shown by the fourth red bar, and had the most rapid employment growth, more than 2.5% per year. As we move from left to right in Figure 7-10, the red bars show declining and then rising employment growth, which roughly matches the red line shown in Figure 7-9 for the period 1989–99, which sloped down at first and then rose steadily upward. So during the 1980s and 1990s, these diagrams confirm that the higher-paying jobs (those on the right in Figure 7-9) had the greatest employment growth and that these were nonroutine cognitive jobs (on the right in Figure 7-10), such as public relations professionals, managers, and R&D scientists.

From 2001 to 2007 (green bars), the employment growth in the low-paying non-routine manual jobs (the first green bar on the left in Figure 7-10) is much greater than the employment growth in routine manual jobs and routine cognitive jobs (the next two green bars). Indeed, during this period there was practically no growth at all in the routine jobs of either kind, but there was growth in low-paying nonroutine manual jobs and in high-paying nonroutine cognitive jobs. This growth in employment of the lowest-paying and highest-paying jobs illustrates the polarization of the labor market.

The most recent period, 2008–14 (purple bars), includes the global financial crisis and the Great Recession of 2008–09. In this final period, employment fell in manual and cognitive routine jobs (which usually pay mid-level wages), but rose in nonroutine jobs (both low-paying manual and high-paying cognitive). This period further illustrates the polarization of the labor market.

The explanation for these trends is that the routine jobs are more susceptible to offshoring (as they are moved to another country) or to being replaced by computers and other machines (what we have earlier in the chapter called *skilled-biased technological change*). In the 1980s, offshoring and skilled-biased technological change seemed to mainly affect production workers, as those activities were moved overseas or replaced by computers. But since the 1990s offshoring has had a greater impact on *nonproduction* workers employed in cognitive but routine occupations; this is the offshoring of *service* activities. We will give many examples of the trade in and the offshoring of service activities later in the chapter. We can expect that the nonroutine jobs—whether they are manual or cognitive—will continue to experience employment growth, while the routine jobs will experience less growth or even declines in their employment.

3 The Gains from Offshoring

Let us return to our earlier model of offshoring, especially as it applied to the trends in the United States during the 1980s. We have shown that offshoring can shift the relative demand for skilled labor and therefore raise the relative wage for skilled workers. Because the relative wage for low-skilled workers is the reciprocal of the high-skilled relative wage, it falls in both countries. High-skilled labor gains and low-skilled labor loses in relative terms. On the other hand, the ability of firms to relocate some production activities abroad means that their costs are reduced. In a competitive market, lower costs mean lower prices, so offshoring benefits consumers. Our goal in this section is to try to balance the potential losses faced by some groups (low-skilled labor) with the gains enjoyed by others (consumers and high-skilled labor). Our argument in previous chapters on the Ricardian and Heckscher–Ohlin models has been that international trade generates more gains than losses. Now we have to ask whether the same is true for offshoring, a new type of international trade.

One answer to this question comes from a surprising source. The Nobel laureate Paul Samuelson has been among the foremost proponents of global free trade, but in 2004 he had the following to say about the gains from foreign outsourcing:[9]

> Most noneconomists are fearful when an emerging China or India, helped by their still low real wages, outsourcing and miracle export-led developments, cause layoffs from good American jobs. This is a hot issue now, and in the coming decade, it will not go away. Prominent and competent mainstream economists enter in the debate to educate and correct warm-hearted protestors who are against globalization. Here is a fair paraphrase of the argumentation that has been used. . . .
>
> Yes, good jobs may be lost here in the short run. But still total U.S. net national product *must, by the economic laws of comparative advantage, be raised in the long run (and in China, too)*. The gains of the winners from free trade, properly measured, work out to exceed the losses of the losers. . . . Correct economic law recognizes that some American groups can be hurt by dynamic free trade. But correct economic law vindicates the word "creative" destruction by its proof that the gains of the American winners are big enough to more than compensate the losers.

Does this paraphrase by Samuelson sound familiar? You can find passages much like it in this chapter and earlier ones, saying that the gains from trade exceed the losses. But listen to what Samuelson says next:

> The last paragraph can be only an innuendo. For it is dead wrong about [the] *necessary* surplus of winnings over losings.

So Samuelson seems to be saying that the winnings for those who gain from trade *do not necessarily* exceed the losses for those who lose. How can this be? His last statement seems to contradict much of what we have learned in this book. Or does it?

Simplified Offshoring Model

To understand Samuelson's comments, we can use a simplified version of the offshoring model we have developed in this chapter. Instead of having many activities involved in the production of a good, suppose that there are only *two* activities: components production and research and development (R&D). Each of these activities uses high-skilled and low-skilled labor, but we assume that components production uses low-skilled labor intensively and that R&D uses high-skilled labor intensively. As in our earlier model, we assume that capital costs are equal in the two activities and do not discuss this factor. Our goal is to compare a no-trade equilibrium with an offshoring trade equilibrium, to determine whether there are overall gains from trade.

Suppose that the firm has a certain amount of high-skilled (H) and low-skilled (L) labor to devote to components and R&D. It is free to move these workers between the two activities. For example, scientists can be used in the research lab or can instead be used to determine the best method to produce components; similarly, workers who are assembling components can instead assist with the construction of full-scale models in the research lab. Given the amount of high-skilled and low-skilled labor used in total, we can graph a production possibilities frontier (PPF) for the firm between components and R&D activities, as shown in Figure 7-11. This PPF looks just like the PPF for a country, except that now we apply it to a single firm. Points on the PPF,

---

[9] Paul Samuelson, 2004, "Where Ricardo and Mill Rebut and Confirm Arguments of Mainstream Economists Supporting Globalization," *Journal of Economic Perspectives*, 18(3), 135–146.

FIGURE 7-11

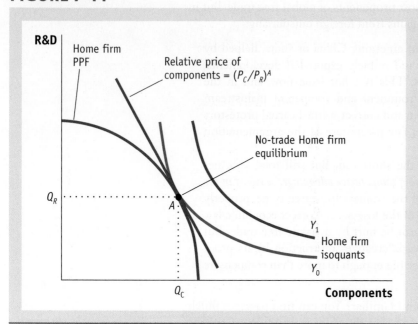

No-Trade Equilibrium for the Home Firm The PPF shows the combinations of components and R&D that can be produced by a firm with a given amount of labor and capital. In the absence of offshoring, the firm produces at A, using quantity Q_C of components and Q_R of R&D to produce amount Y_0 of the final good. The line tangent to the isoquant at point A measures the value that the firm puts on components relative to R&D, or their relative price, $(P_C/P_R)^A$. Amount Y_1 of the final good cannot be produced in the absence of offshoring because it lies outside the firm's PPF.

such as A, correspond to differing amounts of high-skilled and low-skilled labor used in the components and R&D activities. Moving left from point A to another point on the PPF, for example, would involve shifting some high-skilled and low-skilled labor from the production of components into the R&D lab.

Production in the Absence of Offshoring

Now that we have the PPF for the firm, we can analyze an equilibrium for the firm, just as we have previously done for an entire economy. Suppose initially that the firm cannot engage in offshoring of its activities. This assumption means that the component production and R&D done in Home are used to manufacture a final product in Home: it cannot assemble any components in Foreign, and likewise, it cannot send any of its R&D results abroad to be used in a factory in Foreign.

The two production activities are used to produce a final good. To determine how much of the final good is produced, we can use **isoquants**. An isoquant is similar to a consumer's indifference curve, except that instead of utility, it illustrates the production of the firm; it is a curve along which the firm's output is constant despite changing combinations of inputs. Two of these isoquants are labeled as Y_0 and Y_1 in Figure 7-11. The quantity of the final good Y_0 can be produced using the quantity Q_C of components and the quantity Q_R of R&D, shown at point A in the figure. Notice that the isoquant Y_0 is tangent to the PPF at point A, which indicates that this isoquant is the highest amount of the final good that can be produced using any combination of components and R&D on the PPF. The quantity of the final good Y_1 cannot be produced in the absence of offshoring because it lies outside the PPF. Thus, point A describes the quantity of components and R&D that the firm chooses in the absence of offshoring, or what we will call the "no-trade" or "autarky" equilibrium for short.

Tangent to the no-trade equilibrium A in Figure 7-11, we draw a line with the slope of the isoquant at point A. The slope of the isoquant measures the value, or price, that the firm puts on components relative to R&D. We can think of these prices as internal to the firm, reflecting the marginal costs of production of the two activities.

An automobile company, for example, would be able to compute the extra labor and other inputs needed to produce some components of a car and that would be its internal price of components P_C. Similarly, it could compute the marginal cost of developing one more prototype of a new vehicle, which is the internal price of R&D or P_R. The slope of the price line tangent to point A is the price of components relative to the price of R&D, $(P_C/P_R)^A$, in the absence of offshoring.[10]

Equilibrium with Offshoring Now suppose that the firm can import and export its production activities through offshoring. For example, some of the components can be manufactured in a Foreign plant and then imported by Home's firm. Alternatively, some R&D done in Home can be exported to a Foreign plant and used there. In either case, the quantity of the final good is no longer constrained by the Home PPF. Just as in the Ricardian and Heckscher–Ohlin models, in which a higher level of utility (indifference curve) can be obtained if countries specialize and trade with each other, here a higher level of production (isoquant) is possible by trading intermediate activities.

We refer to the relative price of the two activities that the Home firm has available through offshoring as the world relative price or $(P_C/P_R)^{W1}$. Let us assume that the world relative price of components is cheaper than Home's no-trade relative price, $(P_C/P_R)^{W1} < (P_C/P_R)^A$. That assumption means the Home firm can import components at a lower relative price than it can produce them itself. The assumption that $(P_C/P_R)^{W1} < (P_C/P_R)^A$ is similar to the assumption we made in the earlier offshoring model, that the relative wage of low-skilled labor is lower in Foreign, $W_L^*/W_H^* < W_L/W_H$. With a lower relative wage of low-skilled labor in Foreign, the components assembly will also be cheaper in Foreign. It follows that Home will want to offshore components, which are cheaper to produce abroad, while the Home firm will export R&D (i.e., offshoring it to Foreign firms), which is cheaper to produce in Home.

The Home equilibrium with offshoring is illustrated in Figure 7-12. The world relative price of components is tangent to the PPF at point B. Notice that the world relative price line is *flatter* than the no-trade relative price line in Home. The flattening of the price line reflects the lower world relative price of components as compared with their no-trade relative price in Home. As a result of this fall in the relative price of components, the Home firm undertakes more R&D and less component production, moving from point A to point B on its PPF.

Starting at point B on its PPF, the Home firm now exports R&D and imports components, moving along the relative price line to point C. Therefore, through offshoring the firm is able to move off of its PPF to point C. At that point, the isoquant labeled Y_1 is tangent to the world price line, indicating that the maximum amount of the final good Y_1 is being produced. Notice that this production of the final good exceeds the amount Y_0 that the Home firm produced in the absence of offshoring.

Gains from Offshoring Within the Firm The increase in the amount of the final good produced—from Y_0 to Y_1—is a measure of the gains from trade to the Home firm through offshoring. Using the same total amount of high-skilled and low-skilled labor in Home as before, the company is able to produce more of the final good through its ability to offshore components and R&D. Because more of the final good is produced with the same overall amount of high-skilled and low-skilled labor available in Home, the Home company is more productive. Its costs of production fall, and we expect that the price of its final product also falls. The gains for this company are therefore spread to consumers, too.

---

[10] Recall that the slope of a price line is the relative price of the good on the horizontal axis, which is Components in Figure 7-11.

FIGURE 7-12

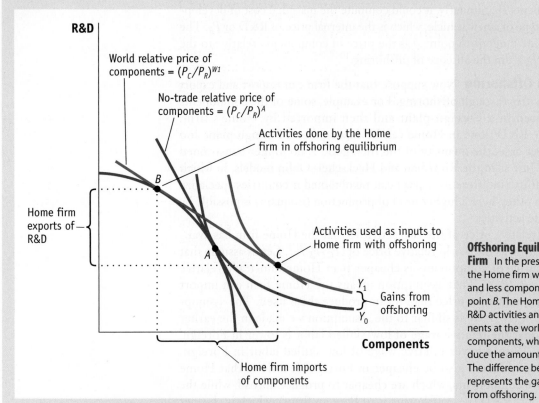

Offshoring Equilibrium for the Home Firm In the presence of offshoring, the Home firm will do more R&D and less component production, at point B. The Home firm then exports R&D activities and imports components at the world relative price of components, which allows it to produce the amount Y_1 of the final good. The difference between Y_0 and Y_1 represents the gains to the Home firm from offshoring.

For these reasons, we agree with the quote about offshoring at the beginning of the chapter: "When a good or service is produced more cheaply abroad, it makes more sense to import it than to make or provide it domestically." In our example, component production is cheaper in Foreign than in Home, so Home imports components from Foreign. There are overall gains from offshoring. That is our first conclusion: *when comparing a no-trade situation to the equilibrium with offshoring, and assuming that the world relative price differs from that in Home, there are always gains from offshoring.*

The idea that there are gains to firms from offshoring is corroborated by a 2005 study of the offshoring of material inputs and services by U.S. manufacturing firms in the 1990s.[11] Over the eight years from 1992 to 2000, that study found that the off-shoring of service activities—like back-office operations—can explain between 11% and 13% of the total increase in productivity within the U.S. manufacturing sector. In addition, the offshoring of material inputs explains between 3% and 6% of the increase in manufacturing productivity. Combining these effects, offshoring explains between 15% and 20% of overall productivity growth in the manufacturing sector, a substantial gain for U.S. firms and for consumers who pay lower prices.

To see how this conclusion is related to the earlier quotation from Samuelson, we need to introduce one more feature into our discussion. Rather than just comparing the no-trade and offshoring equilibria in our model, we need to also consider the impact of offshoring on a country's *terms of trade*.

---

[11] Mary Amiti and Shang-Jin Wei, 2005, "Service Offshoring, Productivity, and Employment: Evidence from the United States," International Monetary Fund, IMF Working Paper 05/238; and 2006, "Service Offshoring and Productivity: Evidence from the United States," National Bureau of Economic Research (NBER) Working Paper No. 11926.

Terms of Trade

As explained in Chapters 2 and 3, the terms of trade equal the price of a country's exports divided by the price of its imports. In the example we are discussing, the Home terms of trade are $(P_R/P_C)^{W1}$, because Home is exporting R&D and importing components. A rise in the terms of trade indicates that a country is obtaining a higher price for its exports or paying a lower price for its imports, both of which benefit the country. Conversely, a fall in the terms of trade harms a country because it is paying more for its imports or selling its exports for less.

In his paper, Samuelson contrasts two cases. In the first, the Foreign country improves its productivity in the good that it exports (components), thereby lowering the price of components; in the second, the Foreign country improves its productivity in the good that Home exports (R&D services), thereby lowering *that* price. These two cases lead to very different implications for the terms of trade and Home gains, so we consider each in turn.

Fall in the Price of Components Turning to Figure 7-13, let the Home country start at the equilibrium with offshoring shown by points B and C. From that situation, suppose there is a *fall* in the relative price of component production. That price might fall, for instance, if the Foreign country improves its productivity in components, thereby lowering the price paid by Home for this service. Because components are being imported by Home, a fall in their price is a *rise* in the Home terms of trade, to $(P_R/P_C)^{W2}$. Let us trace how this change in the terms of trade will affect the Home equilibrium.

FIGURE 7-13

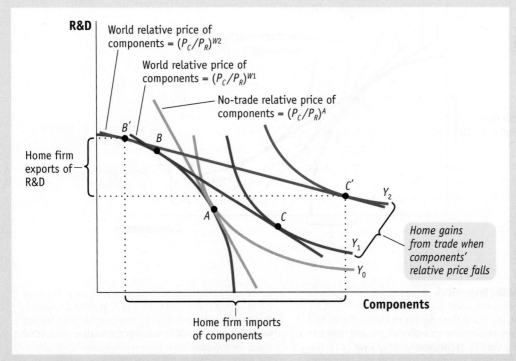

Fall in the Price of Components If the relative price of components falls from $(P_C/P_R)^{W1}$ to $(P_C/P_R)^{W2}$, then the Home firm will do even more R&D and less components production, at point B' rather than B. The increase in the terms of trade allows the Home firm to produce output Y_2 at point C', and the gains from trade are higher than in the initial offshoring equilibrium (points B and C).

Because of the fall in the relative price of components, the world price line shown in Figure 7-13 becomes *flatter*. Production will shift to point B', and by exporting R&D and importing components along the world price line, the firm ends up at point C'. Production of the final good at point C' is Y_2, which exceeds the production Y_1 in the initial equilibrium with offshoring.[12] Thus, the Home firm enjoys *greater* gains from offshoring when the price of components falls. This is the first case considered by Samuelson, and it reinforces our conclusions that offshoring leads to overall gains.

Fall in the Price of R&D We also need to consider the second case identified by Samuelson, and that is when there is a fall in the price of R&D services rather than components. This is what Samuelson has in mind when he argues that offshoring might allow developing countries, such as India, to gain a comparative advantage in those activities in which the United States formerly had comparative advantage. As Indian companies like Wipro (an information technology and services company headquartered in Bangalore) engage in more R&D activities, they are directly competing with American companies exporting the same services. So this competition can lower the world price of R&D services.

In Figure 7-14, we reproduce Figure 7-12, including the Home no-trade equilibrium at point A and the Home production point B with offshoring. Starting at point B, a fall in the world relative price of R&D will lead to a *steeper* price line (because the

FIGURE 7-14

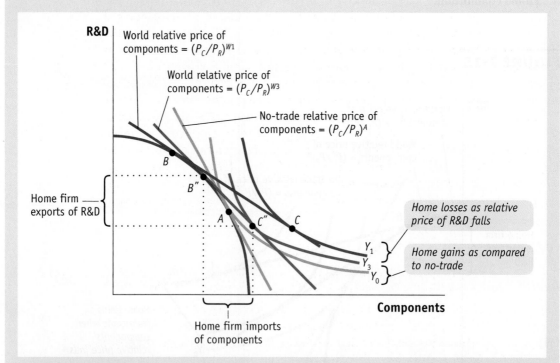

A Fall in the Price of R&D A fall in the relative price of R&D makes the world price line steeper, $(P_C/P_R)^{W3}$. As a result, the Home firm reduces its R&D activities and increases its components activities, moving from B to B'' along the PPF. At the new world relative price, the Home firm faces a terms-of-trade loss and can no longer export each unit of R&D for as many components as it could in the initial offshoring equilibrium. The final good output is reduced from Y_1 to Y_3 at point C''. Notice that the final good output, Y_3, is still higher than output without trade, Y_0. After the fall in the relative price of R&D, there are still gains from trade relative to no trade (point A) but losses relative to the initial offshoring equilibrium (points B and C).

---

[12] Notice that the fall in the relative price of components leads to an increase in the amount of components imported but that the amount of R&D exported from Home does not necessarily increase. You are asked to explore this case further in Problem 8 at the end of the chapter.

slope of the price line is the world relative price of components, which increases when P_R *falls*). At the new price $(P_C/P_R)^{W3}$, Home shifts production to point B'' and, by exporting R&D and importing components, moves to point C''. Notice that final output has *fallen* from Y_1 to Y_3. Therefore, the fall in the price of R&D services leads to losses for the Home firm. To explain where the losses are coming from, notice that Home is exporting R&D and importing components in the initial offshoring equilibrium (points B and C), so its terms of trade are the price of R&D divided by the price of components (P_R/P_C). With the fall in the price of R&D, Home's terms of trade have *worsened*, and so Home is worse off compared with its initial offshoring equilibrium. Samuelson's point is that the United States *could* be worse off if China or India became more competitive in, and lowered the prices of, the products that the United States itself is exporting, such as R&D services. This is theoretically correct. Although it may be surprising to think of the United States being in this position, the idea that a country will suffer when its terms of trade fall is familiar to us from developing-country examples (such as the Prebisch–Singer hypothesis) in earlier chapters.

Furthermore, notice that final output of Y_3 is still higher than Y_0, the no-offshoring output. *Therefore, there are still Home gains from offshoring at C'' as compared with the no-trade equilibrium at A.* It follows that Home can never be worse off with trade as compared with no trade. Samuelson's point is that a country is worse off when its terms of trade fall, even though it is still better off than in the absence of trade. With the fall in the terms of trade, some factors of production will lose and others will gain, but in this case the gains of the winners are not enough to compensate the losses of the losers. Our simple model of offshoring illustrates Samuelson's point.

The offshoring that occurred from the United States in the 1980s often concerned manufacturing activities. But since the 1990s, the focus has frequently been on the offshoring of **business services** to foreign countries. Business services are activities such as accounting, auditing, human resources, order processing, telemarketing, and after-sales service, like getting help with your computer. When these activities are routine (i.e., they can be codified and described in manuals), then the activities are increasingly being transferred abroad. Firms in the United States are transferring these activities to India, for example, where the wages of educated workers are much lower than in the United States. This is the sort of competition that Samuelson had in mind when he spoke of China and India improving their productivity and comparative advantage in activities that the United States already exports. The next application discusses the magnitude of service exports and also the changes in their prices.

APPLICATION

U.S. Terms of Trade and Service Exports

Because Samuelson's argument is a theoretical one, the next step is to examine the evidence for the United States. If the United States has been facing competition in R&D and the other skill-intensive activities that we export, then we would expect the terms of trade to fall. Conversely, if the United States has been offshoring in manufacturing, then the opportunity to import lower-priced intermediate inputs should lead to a rise in the terms of trade.

Merchandise Prices To evaluate these ideas, we make use of data on the terms of trade for the United States. In Figure 7-15, we first show the terms of trade for the United States for merchandise goods (excluding petroleum), which is the gold line.[13]

---

[13] Merchandise goods include agriculture, mining, and manufacturing. We have excluded petroleum because its world price is determined by conditions such as shortages and wars and thus behaves quite differently from the prices of other merchandise goods.

FIGURE 7-15

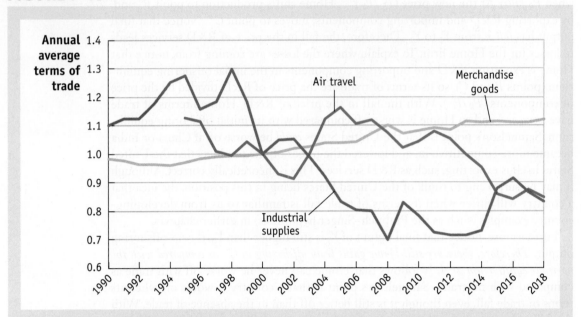

Terms of Trade for the United States, 1990–2018 Shown here are the U.S. terms of trade for merchandise goods (excluding petroleum), industrial supplies, and air travel services. The terms of trade for merchandise goods fell slightly from 1990 to 1994 and then rose to 2008, with a dip in 2009 and rising thereafter. The terms of trade for industrial supplies rose erratically up to 1998, then declined to 2008 and rose erratically again after that. The terms of trade for air travel services was volatile, falling from 1995 to 2002, rising until 2005, and falling thereafter. In sum, the terms of trade for industrial supplies and air travel showed significant periods of decline that are not reflected in the overall terms of trade for merchandise goods.
Data from: Bureau of Labor Statistics.

The terms of trade for goods fell slightly from 1990 to 1994 but then rose to 2008, with a dip in 2009 and rising thereafter. The overall improvement in the merchandise terms of trade shows that we are able to import intermediate inputs (and also import final goods) at lower prices over time. This rise in the terms of trade means that there are increasing gains from trade in merchandise goods for the United States. To explore this idea more carefully, though, we should also consider the terms of trade in particular sectors.

Industrial Supply Prices In Figure 7-15 we show the terms of trade for industrial supplies (the green line), which includes construction materials, chemicals, and other industrial materials. Those terms of trade rose erratically up to 1998, then had a long decline until 2008, and rose erratically again after that. The decline from 1998 to 2008 is evidence that the United States paid *higher* import prices for industrial supplies (or lower export prices, since the terms of trade equal the price of exports divided by the price of imports). That rise in import prices for industrial supplies from 1998 to 2008 most likely reflected the construction boom in China during those years, which increased the price of imported construction materials. That boom was interrupted by the global financial crisis that started in 2008.

The rising import prices—or falling terms of trade—in industrial materials shown in Figure 7-15 contrast with the rising overall terms of trade in merchandise goods. Because the merchandise terms of trade are calculated over all goods (except petroleum) that the United States exports and imports, its movements are quite smooth. When we focus on a particular category of goods, like industrial supplies, however, we see that the terms of trade declined from 1998 to 2008. Thus, the optimistic view that the United States has rising overall terms of trade is offset somewhat by the contrary evidence from the industrial supplies sector.

Service Prices For trade in services, such as finance, insurance, and R&D, it is very difficult to measure prices in international trade. These services are tailored to the buyer, and, as a result, there are not standardized prices. For this reason, we do not have an overall measure of the terms of trade in services. There is one type of service, however, for which it is relatively easy to collect international prices: air travel. The terms of trade in air travel equal the price that foreigners pay for travel on U.S. airlines (a service export) divided by the price that Americans pay on foreign airlines (a service import). In Figure 7-15, we also show the U.S. terms of trade in air travel since 1995 (the blue line).

The terms of trade in air travel are quite volatile, falling from 1995 to 2002, rising until 2005, and falling again erratically thereafter. For this one category of services, the decline in the terms of trade since 2005 indicates that export prices are falling or import prices are rising, an outcome that is contrary to the result we found for overall merchandise goods. Just as we found for industrial supplies, the declining terms of trade for air travel since 2005 indicate a loss for the United States. Once again, the optimistic view that the terms of trade are improving for the United States is not confirmed when we examine a particular sector like air travel. Rather, the falling terms of trade that Samuelson is concerned about seem to have occurred for the United States in some sectors, but not for overall merchandise trade.

Service Trade What about other traded services? Although standard prices are not available, data on the *amount* of service exports and imports for the United States are collected annually. These data are shown in Table 7-1 for 2018. The United States runs a substantial surplus in services trade, with exports of $806 billion and imports of $544 billion. In most categories of services the exports exceed imports, and that difference is largest in management and consulting services; education (which is exported when a foreign student studies in the United States); financial services; travel; and charges for the use of intellectual property (which include royalties and license fees that are collected from foreign firms when they use U.S. patents and trademarks, or are paid by U.S. firms to foreign firms when they use foreign patents).

TABLE 7-1

U.S. Trade in Services, 2018 ($ millions) This table shows U.S. exports and imports in the major categories of services trade for 2018.

	Exports	Imports
Telecommunications, computer, and information services	$43,196	$34,618
Management and consulting services	86,868	47,612
R&D and testing services	42,555	34,618
Operational leasing	6,843	2,321
Technical, trade-related, and other business services	36,439	29,644
Total business, professional, and technical services	$215,861	148,813
Education	44,715	6,511
Financial services	112,015	21,545
Insurance services	17,466	53,420
Telecommunications	9,354	7,341
Total other private services	183,550	88,817
Travel	214,680	144,463
Passenger fares	41,465	42,043
Other transportation	5,149	3,860
Use of intellectual property	128,748	56,117
Total private services	$805,745	$544,347

Data from: U.S. Bureau of Economic Analysis.

FIGURE 7-16

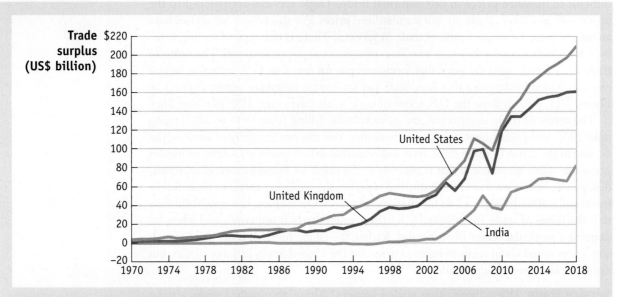

Trade Surplus in Business Services This figure shows the combined trade surplus in computer and information services, insurance, and financial services for the United States, the United Kingdom, and India from 1970 to 2018. The U.S. surplus in these categories of services has been growing since about 1985, with an occasional dip, and is close to and sometimes exceeds the trade surplus of the United Kingdom, its chief competitor. Since about 2010 the surplus of the United States has climbed ahead of that for the United Kingdom. India's surplus began growing around 2002 and is based entirely on its exports of computer and information services.

Data from: World Bank World Development Indicators.

The fact that exports exceed imports in many categories in Table 7-1 means that the United States has a comparative advantage in traded services. Indeed, the U.S. surplus in business, professional, and technical services is among the highest in the world, similar to that of the United Kingdom and higher than that of Hong Kong and India. London is a world financial center and competes with New York and other U.S. cities, which explains the high trade surplus of the United Kingdom, whereas Hong Kong is a regional hub for transportation and offshoring to China. The combined trade balance in computer and information services, insurance, and financial services for the United States, the United Kingdom, and India since 1970 is graphed in Figure 7-16.

Since about 2010 the surplus of the United States has climbed ahead of that for the United Kingdom. India's surplus began growing around 2002 and is based entirely on its exports of computer and information services. In 2018 the combined U.S. surplus in computers, insurance, and financial services ($210 billion) was two and one-half times larger than that of India ($83 billion), and also higher than that of the United Kingdom ($162 billion).

What will these surpluses look like a decade or two from now? It is difficult to project, but notice in Figure 7-16 that in 2002, as the Indian surplus began growing, the U.S. surplus dipped to become more similar to that of the United Kingdom. The Indian trade surplus is entirely due to its exports of computer and information services—a category in which the United States also has strong net exports. So even though the Indian trade surplus is still much smaller than that of the United States, it appears to pose a competitive challenge to the United States. It is at least possible that in a decade or two from now, India's overall surplus in service exports could catch up to that of the United States. Only time will tell whether the United States will eventually face the same type of competition from India in its service exports that it has already faced for many years from the United Kingdom.

4 The Future of Offshoring and You

We have covered a lot of ground in this chapter, starting with the changes that have occurred during the 1980s to labor demand in the United States and in many other countries. Those changes favored nonproduction workers, who were more skilled and who benefited from the introduction of computers that they could work with. Along with the introduction of new information technology there were improvements in communication technology, too, which facilitated the ability of firms to offshore some of their production activities to other countries. Nonproduction workers also benefited from offshoring during the 1980s, at least in relative terms as compared with the wages of production workers.

But since the 1990s, the changes in labor demand have become more complex because of job polarization. Not all nonproduction workers have gained: instead, only those workers engaged in nonroutine occupations have been able to withstand the combined forces of computers and offshoring. Routine service activities performed by nonproduction workers, such as secretaries, bookkeepers, filing clerks, and bank tellers, have been increasingly replaced by machines or by workers overseas. It is important to remember that nonroutine occupations also extend to production workers if they are employed in occupations such as personal care, health-care support, and building and grounds maintenance that cannot be done over the Internet. So those nonroutine occupations and the production workers employed in those jobs have had growing employment.

What does the job polarization mean for you? It means that you should strive to be in a career that is not routine, but where your own special talents and creativity can come to the forefront. Such a career can be in many different occupations, because there is always scope to go beyond the routine and work at a job that cannot be easily taken over by machines or by others.

A good example to illustrate this point is the offshoring of medical services. The transcription of doctors' notes from spoken to written form was one of the first service activities offshored to India. Since then, other types of medical services have also been offshored, and a *New York Times* article in 2003 identified the reading of X-rays—or radiology—as the next area that could shift overseas: "It turns out that even American radiologists, with their years of training and annual salaries of $250,000 or more, worry about their jobs moving to countries with lower wages, in much the same way that garment knitters, blast-furnace operators and data-entry clerks do. . . . Radiology may just be the start of patient care performed overseas."[14]

It has been found, however, that the types of radiology jobs that can potentially be transferred overseas are very limited.[15] Radiology is a high-paying profession precisely because the reading of X-rays is difficult and takes years of training and practice to perfect. X-rays are normally analyzed in the same hospital in which the patient is being treated. In a few specific cases, such as the reading of mammograms for breast cancer, it is possible that the work can be outsourced (i.e., performed outside the hospital), either domestically or offshore. Firms known as "nighthawks" already provide some outsourcing services to hospitals, principally during nighttime hours. Nighthawk firms are headquartered in the United States but have radiologists at offshore sites, including Australia, Israel, Spain, and India. These nighttime services allow smaller hospitals that cannot afford a full-time night radiologist to obtain readings during evening hours, and allow the nighthawk firms to keep their radiologists fully employed by combining the demand from multiple hospitals.

---

[14] Andrew Pollack, "Who's Reading Your X-Ray?" *New York Times*, November 16, 2003, section 3, pp. 1, 9.
[15] The material in the following paragraphs is drawn from Frank Levy and Ari Goelman, "Offshoring and Radiology," presented at the Brookings Institute Trade Forum May 12–13, 2005.

The offshoring to nighthawk firms is a natural response to the round-the-clock demand for hospital services but less-than-full-time demand for radiologists on-site. Often these nighttime services are used only for preliminary reads, allowing the immediate treatment of patients; the X-ray image is then read again by the staff radiologist in the United States the next day. That is, in many cases, the services being outsourced are not directly competing for the daytime jobs but, instead, are complements to these U.S. jobs.

Radiology is under no imminent threat from outsourcing because the profession involves decisions that cannot be codified in written rules. Much of the radiologist's knowledge is gained from reading countless X-rays with complex images and shadows, and the ability to recognize patterns cannot easily be passed on to another person or firm. It follows that the work cannot be offshored except in the case of the nighttime activities of nighthawk firms, which actually work in conjunction with the daytime activities in major hospitals.

In every profession there will always be jobs that cannot be performed by someone who is not on-site. For many of the service activities listed in Table 7-1, the United States will continue to have comparative advantage even while facing foreign competition. In many manufacturing industries, the United States will continue to maintain some activities at home, such as R&D and marketing.

Indeed, as discussed in **Headlines: American Factories Demand White-Collar Education for Blue-Collar Work**, it is expected that within three years, the majority of jobs in manufacturing in the United States will be filled by college graduates. These

HEADLINES

American Factories Demand White-Collar Education for Blue-Collar Work

It is expected that within three years the majority of jobs in manufacturing in the United States will be filled by college graduates. This article discusses the experience of one firm—Pioneer Service—that uses computer-aided equipment run by skilled workers to make parts for aerospace customers as well as Tesla and other luxury car manufacturers.

College-educated workers are taking over the American factory floor. New manufacturing jobs that require more advanced skills are driving up the education level of factory workers who in past generations could get by without higher education....

Within the next three years, American manufacturers are, for the first time, on track to employ more college graduates than workers with a high-school education or less, part of a shift towards automation that has increased factory output, opened the door to more women and reduced prospects for lower-skilled workers. "You used to do stuff by hand," said Erik Hurst, an economics professor at the University of Chicago.

"Now, we need workers who can manage the machines."

U.S. manufacturers have added more than a million jobs since the recession, with the growth going to men and women with degrees.... Over the same time, manufacturers employed fewer people with at most a high-school diploma. Employment in manufacturing jobs that require the most complex problem-solving skills, such as industrial engineers, grew 10% between 2012 and 2018; jobs requiring the least declined [by] 3%....

At Pioneer Service Inc., a machine shop in the Chicago suburb of Addison, Ill., employees in polo shirts and jeans, some with advanced degrees, code commands for robots making complex aerospace

components on a hushed factory floor. That is a far cry from work at Pioneer in the 1990s, when employees had to wear company uniforms to shield their clothes from the grease flying off the 1960s-era manual machines used to make parts for heating-and-cooling systems. Pioneer employs 40 people, the same number in 2012. Only a handful of them are from the time when simple metal parts were machined by hand. "Now, it's more tech," said Aneesa Muthana, Pioneer's president and co-owner. "There has to be more skill." Pioneer, which makes parts for Tesla vehicles and other luxury cars, had its highest revenue last year, Ms. Muthana said. The company's success mirrors that of other manufacturers that survived the financial crisis.

Source: Reproduced with permission of The Wall Street Journal. *From "American Factories Demand White-Collar Education for Blue-Collar Work," by Austen Hefford, December 9, 2019. Permission conveyed through Copyright Clearance, Center, Inc.*

skilled employees are working with computer-aided equipment on the factory floor to produce goods in very different ways from the past. So the concepts of skill-biased technical change and automation that we discussed earlier in the chapter do not necessarily lead to a loss in jobs, but can lead to a gain in jobs for high-skilled workers. That tendency to bring jobs back to the United States is reinforced by rising wages in China and by the fact that companies are sometimes finding that communication with overseas suppliers can be slow and costly.

So whether you are thinking about the offshoring of jobs, or the polarization of the labor market, or your own prospects for employment after graduation, do not be discouraged. Even when some activities are being offshored or automated, other jobs remain or come back to the United States. The experience of firms like Pioneer Service shows that there are many ways for jobs to be created in the United States, and for entrepreneurs like Aneesa Muthana to prosper. You also can use your imagination, skills, and education to create goods and services that people will buy and that will make life better.

5 Conclusions

In this chapter, we have studied a type of trade that is becoming increasingly important: offshoring, by which we mean the shifting of some production activities to another country, while other production activities are kept in Home. Rather than trading final goods, like wheat for cloth as in the Ricardian model of Chapter 2, or computers for shoes as in the Heckscher–Ohlin model of Chapter 4, with offshoring each good can be produced in stages in several countries and then assembled in a final location.

In the model of offshoring we presented, because low-skilled labor is relatively cheap abroad, it makes sense for Home to offshore to the Foreign country those activities that are less skill-intensive, while keeping in Home those activities that are more skill-intensive. "Slicing" the value chain in this way is consistent with the idea of comparative advantage, because each country is engaged in the activities for which its labor is relatively cheaper. From *both* the Home and Foreign point of view, the ratio of high-skilled to low-skilled labor employed in value chain activities goes up. A major finding of this chapter, then, is that an increase in offshoring will raise the relative demand (and hence relative wage) for skilled labor in *both* countries.

This prediction of the offshoring model is confirmed by examining evidence for nonproduction (high-skilled) and production (low-skilled) workers in the United States during the 1980s. In that decade, both the wage and the employment of nonproduction workers relative to production workers increased. That finding is consistent with an increase in the relative demand for nonproduction workers, which was caused by a combination of skilled-biased technological change and offshoring of production activities. During the 1990s, the relative wage of nonproduction workers continued to increase, but the relative employment of nonproduction workers fell. We have argued that these changes were consistent with the polarization of the job market that has occurred since 1990.

Polarization of the job market means that there is employment growth for high-paying and low-paying jobs, but less growth or even declines in jobs with mid-level wages. The explanation for this phenomenon is that routine jobs—whether they are manual or cognitive—can be replaced by computers and by offshoring. These jobs pay mid-level wages and have had the lowest employment growth since 1990. There has been more offshoring of *service* activities since that time, too, so that nonproduction workers engaged in routine cognitive jobs have also faced a decline in employment. These jobs do not pay as much as managers and R&D engineers engaged in nonroutine cognitive jobs, so without these lower-paid workers, the *average* wage of nonproduction workers goes up while their employment falls. This pattern matches the trends for the 1990s. Since 2000, job polarization has continued to occur.

We have also examined whether offshoring leads to overall gains for the economy. In a simplified model in which there are only two activities, we found that a fall in the world price of the low-skill-intensive input will lead to gains to the Home firm from offshoring. In contrast, a fall in the price of the skilled labor-intensive input will lead to losses to the Home firm, as compared with the prior trade equilibrium. Such a price change is a terms-of-trade loss for Home, leading to losses from the lower relative price of exports. So even though Home gains overall from offshoring (producing at least as much as it would in a no-offshoring equilibrium), it is still the case that competition in the input being exported by Home will make it worse off.

We have also explored the offshoring of service activities. Offshoring from the United States to Mexico consists mainly of low-skilled production jobs, whereas offshoring from the United States to India consists of higher-skilled jobs performed by college-educated Indians. This type of offshoring has been made possible by information and communication technologies (such as the Internet and fiber-optic cables) and has allowed cities like Bangalore, India, to establish service centers for U.S. companies. These facilities not only answer questions from customers in the United States and worldwide, but they also engage in accounting and finance, writing software, R&D, and many other skilled business services.

The fact that it is not only *possible* to shift these activities to India but *economical* to do so shows how new technologies make possible patterns of international trade that would have been unimaginable a decade ago. Such changes show "globalization" at work. But the evidence from job polarization shows us that there is still growing demand and employment in nonroutine jobs in the United States. For yourself, try to choose an occupation in which your own special skills and interests mean that you cannot be easily replaced—that is where you can expect to thrive.

KEY POINTS

The provision of a service or the production of various parts of a good in different countries for assembly into a final good in another location is called foreign outsourcing or offshoring.

1. We can apply the same ideas that we developed for trade in final goods among countries to the trade of intermediate offshored activities. For instance, if low-skilled labor is relatively inexpensive in the Foreign country, then the activities that are least skill-intensive will be offshored there, and Home will engage in the activities that are more skill-intensive.

2. We can also predict what happens to relative wages of skilled labor when there is a change in trading costs and more offshoring. Our model predicts that the relative demand for skilled labor increases in both countries. This result helps to explain the observation that the relative wage of nonproduction/production workers increased both in the United States and in Mexico during the 1980s.

3. During the 1990s and into the 2000s, the changes in labor demand in the United States and other countries became more complex due to the phenomenon of job polarization. Employment has increased for both low-paying and high-paying jobs but has fallen for jobs with mid-level wages. The explanation for these changes is that nonproduction jobs that are routine are more likely to be offshored or replaced by computers, and these jobs pay mid-level wages.

4. In an overall sense, there are gains from offshoring, because the specialization of countries in different production activities allows firms in both countries to produce a greater output of final goods. That increase in output represents a productivity gain due to offshoring trade. But the extent of gain is reduced when Foreign exports more of the same good that Home is exporting.

5. With service offshoring, it is possible that a country like India will have rising productivity in activities in which the United States has comparative advantage, such as R&D. Rising productivity in India would lead to a fall in the price of R&D, which is a terms-of-trade loss for the United States. For that reason, the United States could lose due to service offshoring, though it still gains as compared with a situation of no offshoring at all.

KEY TERMS

foreign outsourcing, p. 199
offshoring, p. 199
job polarization, p. 201
onshoring, p. 201
value chain, p. 202

relative wage of skilled workers, p. 203
relative employment of skilled
  workers, p. 204
relative wage of nonproduction
  workers, p. 208

relative employment of nonproduction workers, p. 208
skill-biased technological change, p. 211
isoquants, p. 218
business services, p. 223

PROBLEMS

1. **Discovering Data** What type of occupation would you like to pursue after graduation? To see what is available, go to the Bureau of Labor Statistics website at: http://www.bls.gov/ooh/.

   a. Find four occupations that you think fit the four categories shown in the horizontal axis of Figure 7-10: nonroutine manual jobs; routine manual jobs; routine cognitive jobs; and nonroutine cognitive jobs. For each occupation, what is the growth in employment in the United States, and how does it compare with the employment growth since 2008 shown in Figure 7-10?

   b. Choose an occupation that you would most like to pursue, and explain why you wish to pursue it. What is the employment growth for that occupation?

WORK IT OUT ✻ Achieve | interactive activity

2. Consider an offshoring model in which the hours of labor used in four activities in the United States and Mexico are as in the table that follows.

   Note that labor hours in Mexico are four times those in the United States, reflecting Mexico's lower productivity. Also note that the ratio of high-skilled to low-skilled labor used in each activity increases as we move to the right, from 1/6 in assembly, to 10/1 in R&D. Suppose that the wage of U.S. low-skilled workers is $10 per hour and that of high-skilled workers is $25 per hour, and that the wage of Mexican low-skilled workers is $1 per hour and that of high-skilled workers is $5 per hour (these values are made up to be convenient, not realistic). Also suppose that the trade costs are 25%, 30%, or 50%, which means that an additional 25%, 30%, or 50% is added to the costs of offshoring to Mexico.

Hours of Labor Used in Each Activity (per unit of output):

	Assembly	Component Production	Office Services	R&D
Low-skilled labor	Mexico: 24	Mexico: 16	Mexico: 16	Mexico: 4
	U.S.: 6	U.S.: 4	U.S.: 4	U.S.: 1
High-skilled labor	Mexico: 4	Mexico: 4	Mexico: 8	Mexico: 40
	U.S.: 1	U.S.: 1	U.S.: 2	U.S.: 10
High-skilled/low-skilled ratio	1/6	1/4	1/2	10/1

   a. Fill in the blank cells in the following table by computing the costs of production of each activity in each country (two cells are filled in for you):

	Assembly	Component Production	Office Services	R&D
Mexico	$44			
United States				
Imported by United States from Mexico, Trade Costs = 20%				
Imported by United States from Mexico, Trade Costs = 30%	$57.2			
Imported by United States from Mexico, Trade Costs = 50%				

   b. With trade costs of 50%, where is the value chain sliced? That is, which activities are cheaper to import from Mexico and which are cheaper to produce in the United States?

   c. With trade costs of 30%, and then 20%, where is the value chain sliced?

3. Consider an offshoring model just like that shown in Figure 7-1, in which the relative wage of low-skilled labor to high-skilled labor is lower in Foreign than in Home and the costs of capital and trade are uniform across production activities.

   a. Suppose that Home uniformly increases the tariff level it applies to imports of all goods and services from Foreign. How does this affect the slicing of the value chain?

   b. Draw relative labor supply and demand diagrams for Home and Foreign showing the effect of this change. What happens to the relative wage in each country?

   c. Suppose instead that the Home country requires that low-skilled labor in Foreign be paid a minimum wage that is higher than its current wage (but still less than what low-skilled labor earns at Home). How does this affect the slicing of the value chain, and what happens to the relative demand for skilled labor in each country?

   d. Continuing from part (c), suppose that the minimum wage for low-skilled labor in Foreign is high enough that the relative wage of low-skilled/high-skilled labor in Foreign *exceeds* that in Home. Under these circumstances, what goods on the value chain will Home choose to offshore to Foreign?

4. Consider a U.S. firm's production of automobiles, including research and development and component production.

   a. Starting from a no-trade equilibrium in a PPF diagram, illustrate the gains from offshoring if the United States has a comparative advantage in component production.

   b. Now suppose that advances in engineering abroad decrease the relative price of research and development. Illustrate this change on your diagram and state the implications for production in the United States.

   c. Does the U.S. firm gain from advances in research and development abroad? Explain why or why not.

5. Consider the model of a firm that produces final goods using R&D and components as inputs, with cost data as follows:

Components: Total costs of production = $P_C \cdot Q_C = 200$
Earnings of high-skilled labor = $W_H \cdot H_C = 20$
Earnings of low-skilled labor = $W_L \cdot L_C = 80$

Earnings of capital = $R \cdot K_C = 100$
Share of total costs paid to high-skilled labor = $20/200 = 10\%$
Share of total costs paid to low-skilled labor = $80/200 = 40\%$

R&D: Total costs of R&D = $P_R \cdot Q_R = 200$
Earnings of high-skilled labor = $W_H \cdot H_R = 80$
Earnings of low-skilled labor = $W_L \cdot L_R = 20$
Earnings of capital = $R \cdot K_R = 100$
Share of total costs paid to high-skilled labor = $80/200 = 40\%$
Share of total costs paid to low-skilled labor = $20/200 = 10\%$

   a. In which factor(s) is components intensive? In which factor(s) is R&D intensive?

   b. Suppose that due to the opening of trade, the price of components falls by $\Delta P_C/P_C = -10\%$, while the price of R&D remains unchanged, $\Delta P_R/P_R = 0$. Using the hint below, calculate the change in the wage of skilled and low-skilled labor.

Hint: We follow a procedure similar to that used in Chapter 4 when calculating the change in factor prices in the Heckscher–Ohlin model.

First, write the total costs in each activity as consisting of the payments to labor and capital:

$P_C \cdot Q_C = R \cdot K_C + W_H \cdot H_C + W_L \cdot L_C,$
for components

$P_R \cdot Q_R = R \cdot K_R + W_H \cdot H_R + W_L \cdot L_R,$
for R&D

Because we assume that 50% of costs in either components or R&D is always paid to capital, then $R \cdot K_C = 0.5(P_C \cdot Q_C)$ and $R \cdot K_R = 0.5(P_R \cdot Q_R)$, so we can rewrite the above two equations as

$0.5(P_C \cdot Q_C) = W_H \cdot H_C + W_L \cdot L_C,$ for components
$0.5(P_R \cdot Q_R) = W_H \cdot H_R + W_L \cdot L_R,$ for R&D

Taking the change in these equations:

$0.5(\Delta P_C \cdot Q_C) = \Delta W_H \cdot H_C + \Delta W_L \cdot L_C,$
for components

$0.5(\Delta P_R \cdot Q_R) = \Delta W_H \cdot H_R + \Delta W_L \cdot L_R,$
for R&D

Dividing the equations by $(\Delta P_C \cdot Q_C)$ and $(\Delta P_R \cdot Q_R)$, respectively, we can rewrite the equations as

$$0.5\left[\frac{\Delta P_C}{P_C}\right] = \left(\frac{\Delta W_H}{W_H}\right)\left(\frac{W_H \cdot H_C}{P_C \cdot Q_C}\right) + \left(\frac{\Delta W_L}{W_L}\right)\left(\frac{W_L \cdot H_C}{P_C \cdot Q_C}\right)$$

for components

$$0.5\left[\frac{\Delta P_R}{P_R}\right]=\left(\frac{\Delta W_H}{W_H}\right)\left(\frac{W_H\cdot H_R}{P_R\cdot Q_R}\right)+\left(\frac{\Delta W_L}{W_L}\right)\left(\frac{W_L\cdot H_R}{P_R\cdot Q_R}\right)$$

for R&D

Use the cost shares and price change data in these formulas to get

$$-5\%=\left(\frac{\Delta W_H}{W_H}\right)\left(\frac{20}{200}\right)+\left(\frac{\Delta W_L}{W_L}\right)\left(\frac{80}{200}\right)$$

for components

$$0=\left(\frac{\Delta W_H}{W_H}\right)\left(\frac{80}{200}\right)+\left(\frac{\Delta W_L}{W_L}\right)\left(\frac{20}{200}\right)$$

for R&D

Now solve these two equations for the change in the high-skilled wage ($\Delta W_H/W_H$), and the change in the low-skilled wage ($\Delta W_L/W_L$).

c. What has happened to the *relative wage* of high-skilled/low-skilled labor? Does this match the predictions of the offshoring model in this chapter?

6. Consider the model of a firm that produces final goods using R&D and components as inputs, with cost data as follows:

Components: Total costs of production = $P_C\cdot Q_C=200$

Earnings of high-skilled labor = $W_H\cdot H_C=50$

Earnings of low-skilled labor = $W_L\cdot L_C=50$

Earnings of capital = $R\cdot K_C=100$

Share of total costs paid to high-skilled labor = 50/200 = 25%

Share of total costs paid to low-skilled labor = 50/200 = 25%

R&D: Total costs of R&D = $P_R\cdot Q_R=200$

Earnings of high-skilled labor = $W_H\cdot H_R=60$

Earnings of low-skilled labor = $W_L\cdot L_R=40$

Earnings of capital = $R\cdot K_R=100$

Share of total costs paid to high-skilled labor = 60/200 = 30%

Share of total costs paid to low-skilled labor = 40/200 = 20%

a. In which factor(s) is components intensive? In which factor(s) is research intensive?

b. Suppose that due to the opening of trade, the relative price of R&D increases, $\Delta P_R/P_R=10\%$, whereas the price of components stays unchanged, $\Delta P_C/P_C=0$. Calculate the change in the wages of high-skilled and low-skilled labor.

c. What has happened to the *relative wage* of high-skilled/low-skilled labor? How does this result compare to Problem 5, and explain why it is similar or different.

7. The quote from the 2004 *Economic Report of the President* at the beginning of the chapter generated a lot of controversy that year. The chairman of the Council of Economic Advisers, N. Gregory Mankiw, made the following additional comments in a speech while presenting the report: "Outsourcing is just a new way of doing international trade. More things are tradable than were tradable in the past, and that's a good thing."

Those statements quickly led to reactions from both Democratic and Republican members of Congress. Tom Daschle, then the Democratic Senate minority leader, said, "If this is the administration's position, they owe an apology to every worker in America." Dennis Hastert, then Republican Speaker of the House, said, "Outsourcing can be a problem for American workers and the American economy." John Kerry, the 2004 Democratic presidential candidate, referred to businesses that offshored as "Benedict Arnold corporations." In response, Mankiw clarified his earlier comments: "My lack of clarity left the wrong impression that I praised the loss of U.S. jobs."

You might feel that these statements just represented a squabble between politicians trying to score points during a presidential campaign. Statements about outsourcing and offshoring are made during many presidential campaigns, including in 2016 when Donald Trump said that he's "never eating another Oreo again" because its parent company is "closing a factory in Chicago and they're moving to Mexico." With all this media attention, it is worth trying to sort out who gains and who loses from offshoring.

a. Why does Mankiw say that "outsourcing is a good thing"? Who is it good for in the United States? Are there overall gains for the United States? Explain with a diagram.

b. Later in this chapter, Paul Samuelson is quoted as saying that there is no "necessary surplus of winnings over losings" due to offshoring.

Use Figure 7-14 to carefully explain why Samuelson says this.

c. Go online to find out whether Nabisco still produces Oreo cookies in the United States, whether jobs are being moved to Mexico, and why.

8. In Figure 7-13, we saw that a fall in the relative price of components leads to an increase in the amount of components imported but that the amount of R&D exported from Home does not necessarily increase. To explore this further, complete the following:

a. Let the relative price of components continue to fall in Figure 7-13, and show in a graph what happens to the equilibrium point on the isoquant for the final good.

b. Now draw another graph that has the relative price of components on the vertical axis and the imports of components on the horizontal axis. Start at the no-trade relative price of components, where imports are zero. Then label the various world relative prices of components on the vertical axis, and graph the quantity of imports at each price. Can we be sure that the import demand curve slopes downward?

c. Now draw a new graph that has the relative price of R&D on the vertical axis and the exports of R&D on the horizontal axis. Start at the no-trade relative price of R&D, where exports are zero. Then label the various world relative prices of R&D on the vertical axis, and graph the quantity of exports at each price. When the relative price of R&D is high enough, what do you notice about the export supply curve?

9. Why might it be relatively easier for a developing country like India to export service activities through offshoring than to participate in the global economy by producing manufacturing components?

10. It is widely noted that even though China is the favored destination for manufacturing offshoring, it is far behind India in the business of offshored services. What differences between these two countries might account for this observation?

11. Chinese hourly manufacturing wages have increased by more than 10% per year on average since 2001, which is much higher than wage growth in developed or other developing countries. How will this wage growth in China affect its ability to serve as an offshoring location? If China itself starts to offshore, what countries will it choose as a destination?

8

Import Tariffs and Quotas Under Perfect Competition

I would tax China on products coming in. I would do a tariff, yes—and . . . the tax should be 45 percent.

Donald J. Trump, Republican candidate for president, January 5, 2016

Over a thousand Americans are working today because we stopped a surge in Chinese tires.

President Barack Obama, referring to a tariff on Chinese tires, January 24, 2012

I take this action to give our domestic steel industry an opportunity to adjust to surges in foreign imports, recognizing the harm from 50 years of foreign government intervention in the global steel market, which has resulted in bankruptcies, serious dislocation, and job loss.

President George W. Bush, announcing a tariff on imported steel, March 5, 2002

Questions to Consider

1 Why do governments sometimes apply a tariff on imported goods?

2 Why does the World Trade Organization try to reduce the use of tariffs?

3 If the quantity of imports is restricted by a quota, how is that different from using a tariff?

It was once proposed that the United States should apply a tariff against the imports from a certain Asian country. When that idea became public, the government of the Asian country cut back on its purchases of U.S. Treasury bills, which are a type of bond. That decrease in demand for U.S. Treasury bills—like a decrease in demand for any product—led to a fall in their price. Because U.S. Treasury bills always pay the same total amount when they mature, a fall in their price means that the effective interest rate being earned on the bond goes up. That rise in the interest rate on Treasury bills led to an increase in interest rates in all other U.S. markets. So in this case, just the *proposal* of an import tariff had adverse macroeconomic effects in the United States.

Does this story sound familiar to you? Perhaps you are thinking of the import tariffs on China that were imposed under President Trump during 2018–19. In 2016, when he was still the Republican candidate for president, Mr. Trump had already decided that he would apply tariffs against imports from China, as indicated in the first quote at the beginning of the chapter. That announcement did not have any impact on the markets at the time, however, probably because it was not expected to occur. In fact, the story we have described above *did happen*, but it was much earlier, in 1995, when Bill Clinton was president. At that time the United States considered putting an **import tariff**—a tax on imported goods—on luxury cars imported from Japan. As a result, Japan reduced its purchases of U.S. Treasury bills and U.S. interest rates

235

went up. Following that temporary rise in interest rates, the American and Japanese governments negotiated over the proposed tariff, and the tariff on luxury cars from Japan was never actually implemented.

While President Clinton was persuaded to not apply the tariff on luxury cars from Japan, President Trump was not restrained in the same way. As we described in Chapter 1 (see **The U.S.–China Trade War**), the United States raised tariffs against Chinese imports multiple times during 2018–19, and China responded by raising its tariffs on U.S. imports. The U.S. stock market often fell as tariffs were increased during this trade war, though it recovered afterwards. A "phase one" truce to this trade war was announced on December 13, 2019, which prevented higher tariffs (planned for two days later) from being imposed by the United States. Interestingly, on that date the markets did not respond much to the announcement of the truce, perhaps because the details had not been fully worked out. While this truce prevented new tariffs from being imposed, it only partially removed the existing tariffs between the two countries.

These contrasting stories from the administrations of Presidents Clinton and Trump illustrate several important points. First, all recent U.S. presidents have used tariffs, as indicated by the quotes from Presidents Obama and George W. Bush at the beginning of the chapter.[1] But President Trump applied tariffs on *more products* than his predecessors. These products included washing machines, solar panels, steel and aluminum, and a very wide range of other products imported from China. Second, using import tariffs against trading partners can often lead to some form of retaliation by those partners. It is unusual for that retaliation to have a macroeconomic impact, as in the example from President Clinton; more typically, the retaliation takes the form of the trade partner applying tariffs of its own, as China did in response to U.S. tariffs during the trade war of 2018–19.

Third, as we will learn in this chapter, the president is not free to apply just any tariff. We begin this chapter by discussing the international rules that govern the use of tariffs; the international body that governs these rules (the World Trade Organization, WTO); and the WTO's precursor, the General Agreement on Tariffs and Trade (GATT). These institutions set the framework for the application of tariffs, and country governments typically adopt their own trade laws that mirror the GATT and WTO rules. Most of the U.S. tariffs that we have mentioned so far were justified by some provision of U.S. trade law, as we explain.

A fourth lesson of this chapter is that import tariffs are sometimes used for political and not economic reasons. The **political economy** of tariffs is illustrated by the following examples:

- During the 2000 presidential campaign, George W. Bush promised that he would implement a tariff on imports of steel. That promise was also made for political purposes: it helped Bush secure votes in Pennsylvania, West Virginia, and Ohio, states that produce large amounts of steel.

- In 2009, President Barack Obama approved a 35% tariff on the import of tires from China, which was in place until 2012. That tariff was seen as a victory for the United Steelworkers, the union that represents American tire workers. By approving this tariff, it is believed that President Obama won additional support from the labor movement for the Affordable Care Act that was approved in Congress later that year.

This chapter is the first of several that focus on **trade policy**, government actions meant to influence the amount of international trade. Examples of trade policy include the use of import tariffs (taxes on imports), **import quotas** (quantity limits on

---

[1] While President Clinton did not impose the tariff on Japanese luxury cars, he applied tariffs on imported steel products in 1993.

imports), and **export subsidies** (meaning that the exporter of a good receives a higher price than the buyer pays). In this chapter, we begin our investigation of trade policies by focusing on the effects of tariffs and quotas in a perfectly competitive industry. In the next chapter, we continue by discussing the use of import tariffs and quotas when the industry is imperfectly competitive.

This chapter examines first the most commonly used trade policy, the tariff. We explain the reasons why countries apply tariffs and the effects of these tariffs on the producers and consumers in the importing and exporting countries. We show that import tariffs typically lead to welfare losses for "small" importing countries, by which we mean countries that are too small to affect world prices. Following that, we examine the situation for a "large" importing country, meaning a country that is a large enough buyer for its tariff to affect world prices. In that case, we find that the importing country can possibly gain by applying a tariff, but only at the expense of the exporting countries.

The chapter then examines the use of an import quota, which is a limit on the quantity of a good that can be imported from a foreign country. Past examples of import quotas in the United States include limits on the imports of agricultural goods, automobiles, and steel. More recently, the United States and Europe imposed temporary quotas on the import of textile and apparel products from China. We note that, like a tariff, an import quota often imposes a cost on the importing country. Furthermore, we argue that the cost of quotas can sometimes be even greater than the cost of tariffs. For that reason, the use of quotas has been greatly reduced under the WTO, though they are still used.

Throughout this chapter, we assume that firms are perfectly competitive. That is, each firm produces a homogeneous good and is small compared with the market, which comprises many firms. Under perfect competition, each firm is a price taker in its market. In the next chapter, we learn that tariffs and quotas have different effects in imperfectly competitive markets.

1 A Brief History of the World Trade Organization

As we discussed in Chapter 1, during the period between World War I and World War II, unusually high tariffs between countries reduced the volume of world trade. When peace was reestablished following World War II, representatives of the Allied countries met on several occasions to discuss the rebuilding of Europe and issues such as high trade barriers and unstable exchange rates. One of these conferences, held in Bretton Woods, New Hampshire, in July 1944, established the International Monetary Fund (IMF) and the International Bank for Reconstruction and Development, later known as the World Bank. A second conference held at the Palais des Nations, in Geneva, Switzerland, in 1947 established the General Agreement on Tariffs and Trade (GATT), the purpose of which was to reduce barriers to international trade between nations.[2]

Under the GATT, countries met periodically for negotiations, called "rounds," to lower trade restrictions between countries. Each round is named for the country in which the meeting took place. The Uruguay Round of negotiations, which lasted from 1986 to 1994, established the World Trade Organization (WTO) on January 1, 1995. The WTO is a greatly expanded version of the GATT. It keeps most of the GATT's earlier provisions but adds rules that govern an expanded set of global interactions (including trade in services and intellectual property protection) through binding agreements. The most recent round of WTO negotiations, the Doha Round, began in Doha, Qatar, in November 2001.

---

[2] A history of the GATT is provided in Douglas A. Irwin, Petros C. Mavroidis, and Alan O. Sykes, 2008, *The Genesis of the GATT* (New York: Cambridge University Press).

Although the goal of the WTO is to keep tariffs low, it allows countries to charge a higher tariff on a specific import under some conditions. In **Side Bar: Key Provisions of the GATT**, we show some of the articles of the GATT that still govern trade in the WTO. Some of the main provisions are as follows:

1. A nation must extend the same tariffs to all trading partners that are WTO members. Article I of the GATT, the "most favored nation" clause, states that every country belonging to the WTO must be treated the same: if a country imposes low tariffs on one trading partner, then those low tariffs must be extended to every other trading partner belonging to the WTO.[3]

2. Tariffs may be imposed in response to unfair trade practices such as **dumping**. As we discuss in the next chapter, "dumping" is defined as the sale of export goods in another country at a price less than that charged at home, or alternatively, at a price less than costs of production and shipping. Article VI of the GATT states that an importing country may impose a tariff on goods dumped into its country by a foreign exporter.

3. Countries should not limit the quantity of goods and services that they import. Article XI states that countries should not maintain quotas against imports. We discuss exceptions to this rule later in this chapter.

4. Countries should declare export subsidies provided to particular firms, sectors, or industries. Article XVI deals with export subsidies, benefits such as tax breaks or other incentives for firms that produce goods specifically for export. The article states that countries should notify each other of the extent of subsidies and discuss the possibility of eliminating them. In WTO negotiations since 2005, the elimination of export subsidies in agricultural has been proposed, as we discuss in Chapter 10.

5. Countries can temporarily raise tariffs for certain products. Article XIX, called the **safeguard provision** or the **escape clause**, is a focus in this chapter. Article XIX lists the conditions under which a country can temporarily raise tariffs on particular products. It states that a country can apply a tariff when it imports "any product . . . in such increased quantities and under such conditions as to cause or threaten serious injury to domestic producers." In other words, the importing country can temporarily raise the tariff when domestic producers are suffering due to import competition.

    The steel tariff of 2002 is an example of a tariff that was applied by the United States under Article XIX of the GATT. European governments strenuously objected to the steel tariff, however, and filed a complaint against the United States with the WTO. A panel at the WTO ruled in favor of the European countries. This ruling entitled them to retaliate against the United States by putting tariffs of their own on some $2.2 billion worth of U.S. exports. This pressure from Europe, along with pressure from companies in the United States that had been purchasing the cheaper imported steel, led President Bush to remove the steel tariff in December 2003. Later in the chapter, we discuss the steel tariff imposed by President Bush in more detail, and look at the more recent steel tariff imposed by President Trump.

6. Article XXI of the GATT, which allows for "security exceptions," enables countries to take policy actions that they feel are needed for national security. Although it is controversial to use this exception to justify the application of tariffs, President Trump justified the use of tariffs on steel and aluminum imports by claiming a "security exception."

---

[3] In the United States, the granting of most favored nation trade status to a country is now called "normal trade relations" because most countries now belong to the WTO and enjoy that status.

7. **Regional trade agreements** are permitted under Article XXIV of the GATT. The GATT recognizes the ability of blocs of countries to form two types of regional trade agreements: (i) **free-trade areas**, in which a group of countries voluntarily agree to remove trade barriers between themselves, and (ii) **customs unions**, which are free-trade areas in which the countries also adopt identical tariffs between themselves and the rest of the world. We discuss regional trade agreements in Chapter 11.

SIDE BAR

Key Provisions of the GATT

ARTICLE I
General Most-Favoured-Nation Treatment

1. With respect to customs duties . . . and with respect to all rules and formalities in connection with importation and exportation . . . any advantage, favour, privilege or immunity granted by any contracting party to any product originating in or destined for any other country shall be accorded immediately and unconditionally to the like product originating in or destined for the territories of all other contracting parties. . . .

ARTICLE VI
Anti-Dumping and Countervailing Duties

1. The contracting parties recognize that dumping, by which products of one country are introduced into the commerce of another country at less than the normal value of the products, is to be condemned if it causes or threatens material injury to an established industry. . . . [A] product is to be considered . . . less than its normal value, if the price of the product exported from one country to another

   a. is less than the comparable price . . . for the like product when destined for consumption in the exporting country, or,

   b. in the absence of such domestic price, is less than either

      i) the highest comparable price for the like product for export to any third country in the ordinary course of trade, or

      ii) the cost of production of the product in the country of origin plus a reasonable addition for selling cost and profit. . . .

ARTICLE XI
General Elimination of Quantitative Restrictions

1. No prohibitions or restrictions other than duties, taxes or other charges, whether made effective through quotas, import or export licenses or other measures, shall be instituted or maintained by any contracting party on the importation of any product of the territory of any other contracting party or on the exportation or sale for export of any product destined for the territory of any other contracting party. . . .

ARTICLE XVI
Subsidies

1. If any contracting party grants or maintains any subsidy, including any form of income or price support, which operates directly or indirectly to increase exports of any product from, or to reduce imports of any product into, its territory, it shall notify the contracting parties in writing of the extent and nature of the subsidization. In any case in which it is determined that serious prejudice to the interests of any other contracting party is caused or threatened by any such subsidization, the contracting party granting the subsidy shall, upon request, discuss with the other contracting party . . . the possibility of limiting the subsidization.

ARTICLE XIX
Emergency Action on Imports of Particular Products

1. a. If, as a result of unforeseen developments and of the effect of the obligations incurred by a contracting party under this Agreement, including tariff concessions, any product is being imported into the territory of that contracting party in such increased quantities and under such conditions as to cause or threaten serious injury to domestic producers in that territory of like or directly competitive products, the contracting party shall be free, in respect of such product, and to the extent and for such time as may be necessary to prevent or remedy such injury, to suspend the obligation in whole or in part or to withdraw or modify the concession.

ARTICLE XXI

Nothing in this agreement shall be construed . . .

b. to prevent any contracting party from taking any action which it considers necessary for the protection of its essential security interests. . . .

ARTICLE XXIV
Territorial Application—Frontier Traffic—Customs Unions and Free-Trade Areas

4. The contracting parties recognize the desirability of increasing freedom of trade by the development, through voluntary agreements, of closer integration between the economies of the countries party to such agreements. They also recognize that the purpose of a customs union or of a free-trade area should be to facilitate trade between the constituent territories and not to raise barriers to the trade of other contracting parties with such territories.

5. Accordingly, the provisions of this Agreement shall not prevent [the formation of customs unions and free-trade areas, provided that]:

   a. . . . the duties [with outside parties] shall not on the whole be higher or more restrictive than the general incidence of the duties . . . prior to the formation. . . .

Information from: http://www.wto.org/english/docs_e/legal_e/gatt47_01_e.htm#article.

2 The Gains from Trade

In earlier chapters, we demonstrated the gains from trade using a production possibilities frontier and indifference curves. We now instead demonstrate the gains from trade using Home's demand and supply curves, together with the concepts of **consumer surplus** and **producer surplus**. You may already be familiar with these concepts from an earlier economics course, but we provide a brief review here.

Consumer and Producer Surplus

Suppose that home consumers have the demand curve D in panel (a) of Figure 8-1 and face the price of P_1. Then total demand is D_1 units. For the last unit purchased, the consumer buying it values that unit at close to its purchase price of P_1, so they obtain little or no surplus over the purchase price. But for all the earlier units purchased (from 0 to D_1 units), the consumers valued the product at higher than its purchase price: the consumers' willingness to pay for the product equals the height of the demand curve. For example, the person buying unit D_2 would have been willing to pay the price of P_2, which is the height of the demand curve at that quantity. Therefore, that individual obtains the surplus of $(P_2 - P_1)$ from being able to purchase the good at the price P_1.

For each unit purchased before D_1, the value that the consumer places on the product exceeds the purchase price of P_1. Adding up the surplus obtained on each unit purchased, from 0 to D_1, we can measure consumer surplus (CS) as the shaded region below the demand curve and above the price P_1. This region measures the satisfaction that consumers receive from the purchased quantity D_1, over and above the amount $P_1 \cdot D_1$ that they have paid.

Panel (b) of Figure 8-1 illustrates producer surplus. This panel shows the supply curve of an industry; the height of the curve represents the firm's marginal cost at each level of production. At the price of P_1, the industry will supply S_1. For the last

FIGURE 8-1

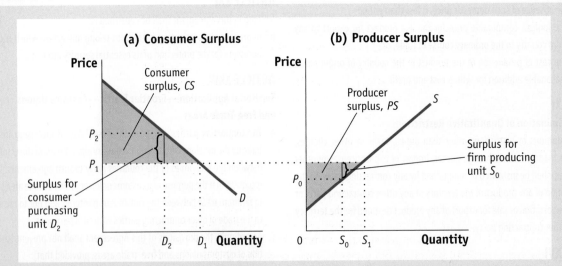

(a) Consumer Surplus

(b) Producer Surplus

Consumer and Producer Surplus In panel (a), the consumer surplus from purchasing quantity D_1 at price P_1 is the area below the demand curve and above that price. The consumer who purchases unit D_2 is willing to pay price P_2 but only pays P_1. The difference is the consumer surplus and represents the satisfaction of consumers over and above the amount paid. In panel (b), the producer surplus from supplying the quantity S_1 at the price P_1 is the area above the supply curve and below that price. The supplier who supplies unit S_0 has marginal costs of P_0 but sells it for P_1. The difference is the producer surplus and represents the return to fixed factors of production in the industry.

unit supplied, the price P_1 equals the marginal cost of production for the firm supplying that unit. But for all earlier units supplied (from 0 to S_1 units), the firms were able to produce those units at a marginal cost *less than* the price P_1. For example, the firm supplying unit S_0 could produce it with a marginal cost of P_0, which is the height of the supply curve at that quantity. Therefore, that firm obtains the producer surplus of $(P_1 - P_0)$ from being able to sell the good at the price P_1.

For each unit sold before S_1, the marginal cost to the firm is less than the sale price of P_1. Adding up the producer surplus obtained for each unit sold, from 0 to S_1, we obtain producer surplus (*PS*) as the shaded region in panel (b) above the supply curve and below the price of P_1. It is tempting to think of producer surplus as the profits of firms, because for all units before S_1, the marginal cost of production is less than the sale price of P_1. But a more accurate definition of producer surplus is that it equals the return to fixed factors of production in the industry. That is, producer surplus is the difference between the sales revenue $P_1 \cdot S_1$ and the total variable costs of production (i.e., wages paid to labor and the costs of intermediate inputs). If there are fixed factors such as capital or land in the industry, as in the specific-factors model we studied in Chapter 3, then producer surplus equals the returns to these fixed factors of production. We might still loosely refer to this return as the "profit" earned in the industry, but it is important to understand that producer surplus is not *monopoly profit*, because we are assuming perfect competition (i.e., zero monopoly profits) throughout this chapter.[4]

Home Welfare

To examine the effects of trade on a country's welfare, we consider once again a world composed of two countries, Home and Foreign, with each country consisting of producers and consumers. Total Home welfare can be measured by adding up consumer and producer surplus. As you would expect, the greater the total amount of Home welfare, the better off are the consumers and producers overall in the economy. To measure the gains from trade, we will compare Home welfare in no-trade and free-trade situations.

No Trade In panel (a) of Figure 8-2, we combine the Home demand and supply curves in a single diagram. The no-trade equilibrium occurs at the autarky price of P^A, where the quantity demanded equals the quantity supplied, of Q_0. Consumer surplus is the region above the price of P^A and below the demand curve, which is labeled as *CS* in panel (a) and also shown as area a in panel (b). Producer surplus is the area below the price of P^A and above the supply curve, which is labeled as *PS* in panel (a) and also shown as area $(b + c)$ in panel (b). So the sum of consumer surplus and producer surplus is the area between the demand and supply curves, or $CS + PS$ = area $(a + b + c)$. That area equals Home's welfare in the market for this good in the absence of international trade.

Free Trade for a Small Country Now suppose that Home can engage in international trade for this good. As we have discussed in earlier chapters, the world price P^W is determined by the intersection of supply and demand in the world market. Generally, there will be many countries buying and selling on the world market. We will suppose that the Home country is a **small country**, by which we mean that it is small in comparison with all the other countries buying and selling this product. For that reason, Home will be a *price taker* in the world market: it faces the fixed world price of P^W, and its own level of demand and supply for this product has no influence

---

[4] Recall from Chapter 6 that under imperfect competition, firms can influence the price of their goods and hence earn positive monopoly profits.

FIGURE 8-2

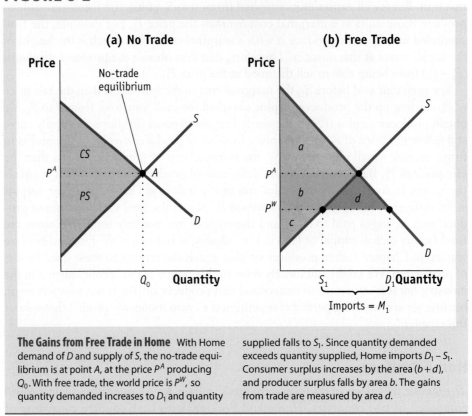

The Gains from Free Trade in Home With Home demand of D and supply of S, the no-trade equilibrium is at point A, at the price P^A producing Q_0. With free trade, the world price is P^W, so quantity demanded increases to D_1 and quantity supplied falls to S_1. Since quantity demanded exceeds quantity supplied, Home imports $D_1 - S_1$. Consumer surplus increases by the area $(b + d)$, and producer surplus falls by area b. The gains from trade are measured by area d.

on the world price. In panel (b) of Figure 8-2, we assume that the world price P^W is below the Home no-trade price of P^A. At the lower price, Home demand will increase from Q_0 under no trade to D_1, and Home supply will decrease from Q_0 under no trade to S_1. The difference between D_1 and S_1 is *imports* of the good, or $M_1 = D_1 - S_1$. Because the world price P^W is below the no-trade price of P^A, the Home country is an importer of the product at the world price. If, instead, P^W were above P^A, then Home would be an exporter of the product at the world price.

Gains from Trade Now that we have established the free-trade equilibrium at price P^W, it is easy to measure Home welfare as the sum of consumer and producer surplus with trade, and compare it with the no-trade situation. In panel (b) of Figure 8-2, Home consumer surplus at the price P^W equals the area $(a + b + d)$, which is the area below the demand curve and above the price P^W. In the absence of trade, consumer surplus was the area a, so the drop in price from P^A to P^W has increased consumer surplus by the amount $(b + d)$. Home consumers clearly gain from the drop in price.

Home firms, on the other hand, suffer a decrease in producer surplus from the drop in price. In panel (b), Home producer surplus at the price P^W equals the area c, which is the area above the supply curve and below the price P^W. In the absence of trade, producer surplus was the area $(b + c)$, so the drop in price from P^A to P^W has decreased producer surplus by the amount b. Home firms clearly lose from the drop in price.

Comparing the gains of consumers, $(b + d)$, with the losses of producers, area b, we see that consumers gain more than the producers lose, which indicates that total Home welfare (the sum of consumer surplus and producer surplus) has gone up.

We can calculate the total change in Home welfare due to the opening of trade by adding the changes in consumer surplus and producer surplus:

Rise in consumer surplus:	$+(b + d)$
Fall in producer surplus:	$-b$
Net effect on Home's welfare:	**$+d$**

The area d is a measure of the *gains from trade* for the importing country due to free trade in this good. It is similar to the gains from trade that we have identified in earlier chapters using the production possibilities frontier and indifference curves, but it is easier to measure: the triangle d has a base equal to free-trade imports $M_1 = D_1 - S_1$, and a height that is the drop in price, $P^A - P^W$, so the gains from trade equal the area of the triangle, $\frac{1}{2} \cdot (P^A - P^W) \cdot M_1$. Of course, with many goods being imported, we would need to add up the areas of the triangles for each good and take into account the net gains on the export side to determine the overall gains from trade for a country. Because gains are positive for each individual good, after summing all imported and exported goods, the gains from trade are still positive.

Home Import Demand Curve

Before introducing a tariff, we use Figure 8-3 to derive the **import demand curve**, which shows the relationship between the world price of a good and the quantity of imports demanded by Home consumers. We first derived this curve in Chapter 2, for the Ricardian model. We now briefly review the derivation of the import demand curve before analyzing the effect of an import tariff on prices and welfare.

In panel (a) of Figure 8-3, we again show the downward-sloping demand curve (D) and the upward-sloping supply curve (S) for Home. The no-trade equilibrium is at point A, which determines Home's no-trade equilibrium price P^A and its no-trade

FIGURE 8-3

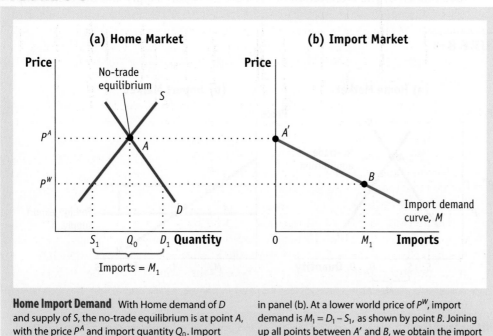

Home Import Demand With Home demand of D and supply of S, the no-trade equilibrium is at point A, with the price P^A and import quantity Q_0. Import demand at this price is zero, as shown by the point A' in panel (b). At a lower world price of P^W, import demand is $M_1 = D_1 - S_1$, as shown by point B. Joining up all points between A' and B, we obtain the import demand curve, M.

equilibrium quantity of Q_0. Because quantity demanded equals quantity supplied, there are zero imports of this product. Zero imports is shown as point A' in panel (b).

Now suppose the world price is at P^W, below the no-trade price of P^A. At the price of P^W, the quantity demanded in Home is D_1, but the quantity supplied by Home suppliers is only S_1. Therefore, the quantity imported is $M_1 = D_1 - S_1$, as shown by the point B in panel (b). Joining points A' and B, we obtain the downward-sloping import demand curve M.

Notice that the import demand curve applies for all prices below the no-trade price of P^A in Figure 8-3. Having lower prices leads to greater Home demand and less Home supply and, therefore, positive imports. What happens if the world price is *above* the no-trade price? In that case, the higher price would lead to greater Home supply and less Home demand, so Home would become an exporter of the product.

3 Import Tariffs for a Small Country

We can now use this supply and demand framework to show what happens when a small country imposes a tariff. As we have already explained, an importing country is "small" if its tariff does not have any effect on the world price of the good on which the tariff is applied. As we will see, the Home price of the good will increase due to the tariff. Because the tariff (which is a tax) is applied at the border, the price charged to Home's consumers will increase by the amount of the tariff.

Free Trade for a Small Country

In Figure 8-4, we again show the free-trade equilibrium for the Home country. In panel (b), the Foreign export supply curve X^* is horizontal at the world price P^W. The horizontal export supply curve means that Home can import any amount at the price P^W without having an impact on that price. The free-trade equilibrium is determined by the intersection of the Foreign export supply and the Home import

FIGURE 8-4

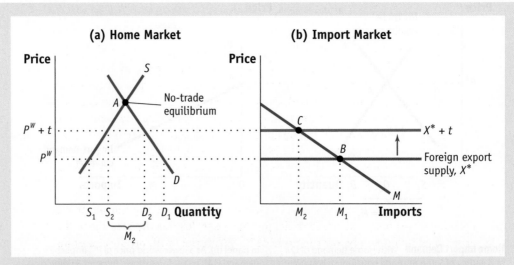

Tariff for a Small Country Applying a tariff of t dollars will increase the import price from P^W to $P^W + t$. The domestic price of that good also rises to $P^W + t$. This price rise leads to an increase in Home supply from S_1 to S_2, and a decrease in Home demand from D_1 to D_2, in panel (a). Imports fall due to the tariff, from M_1 to M_2 in panel (b). As a result, the equilibrium shifts from point B to C.

demand curves, which is point B in panel (b), at the world price P^W. At that price, Home demand is D_1 and Home supply is S_1, shown in panel (a). Imports at the world price P^W are then just the difference between demand and supply, or $M_1 = D_1 - S_1$.

Effect of the Tariff

With the import tariff of t dollars, the export supply curve facing the Home country shifts up by exactly that amount, reflecting the higher price that must be paid to import the good. The shift in the Foreign export supply curve is analogous to the shift in domestic supply caused by a sales tax, as you may have seen in earlier economics courses; it reflects an effective increase in the costs of the firm. In panel (b) of Figure 8-4, the export supply curve shifts up to $X^* + t$. The intersection of the post-tariff export supply curve and the import demand curve now occurs at the price of $P^W + t$ and the import quantity of M_2. The import tariff has reduced the amount imported, from M_1 under free trade to M_2 under the tariff, because of its higher price.

We assume that the imported product is identical to the domestic alternative that is available. For example, if the imported product is a women's cruiser bicycle, then the Home demand curve D in panel (a) is the demand for women's cruisers, and the Home supply curve is the supply of women's cruisers. When the import price rises to $P^W + t$, then we expect that the Home price for locally produced bicycles will rise by the same amount. This is because at the higher import price of $P^W + t$, the quantity of cruisers demanded in Home falls from its free-trade quantity of D_1 to D_2. At the same time, the higher price will encourage Home's firms to increase the quantity of cruisers they supply from the free-trade quantity of S_1 to S_2. As firms increase the quantity they produce, however, the marginal costs of production rise. The Home supply curve (S) reflects these marginal costs, so the Home price will rise along the supply curve until Home firms are supplying the quantity S_2, at a marginal cost just equal to the import price of $P^W + t$. Since marginal costs equal $P^W + t$, the price charged by Home firms will also equal $P^W + t$, and the domestic price will equal the import price.

Summing up, Home demand at the new price is D_2, Home supply is S_2, and the difference between these are Home imports of $M_2 = D_2 - S_2$. Foreign exporters still receive the "net-of-tariff" price (i.e., the Home price minus the tariff) of P^W, but Home consumers pay the higher price $P^W + t$. We now investigate how the rise in the Home price from P^W to $P^W + t$ affects consumer surplus, producer surplus, and overall Home welfare.

Effect of the Tariff on Consumer Surplus In Figure 8-5, we again show the effect of the tariff of t dollars, which is to increase the price of the imported and domestic good from P^W to $P^W + t$. Under free trade, consumer surplus in panel (a) was the area under the demand curve and above P^W. With the tariff, consumers now pay the higher price, $P^W + t$, and their surplus is the area under the demand curve and above the price $P^W + t$. The fall in consumer surplus due to the tariff is the area between the two prices and to the left of Home's demand, which is $(a + b + c + d)$ in panel (a) of Figure 8-5. This area is the amount that consumers lose due to the higher price caused by the tariff.

Effect of the Tariff on Producer Surplus We can also trace the impact of the tariff on producer surplus. Under free trade, producer surplus was the area above the supply curve in panel (a) and below the price of P_W. With the tariff, producer surplus is the area above the supply curve and below the price $P_W + t$: since the tariff increases the Home price, firms are able to sell more goods at a higher price, thus increasing their surplus. We can illustrate this rise in producer surplus as the amount between the two prices and to the left of Home supply, which is labeled as a in panel (a). This area is the amount that Home firms gain because of the higher price caused by the tariff.

FIGURE 8-5

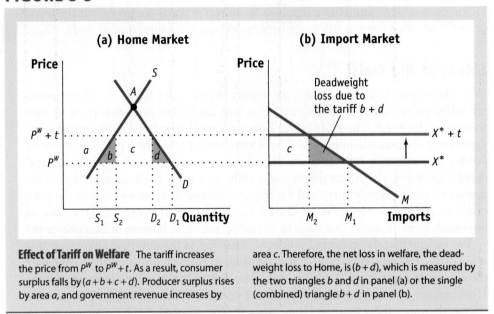

Effect of Tariff on Welfare The tariff increases the price from P^W to $P^W + t$. As a result, consumer surplus falls by $(a + b + c + d)$. Producer surplus rises by area a, and government revenue increases by area c. Therefore, the net loss in welfare, the deadweight loss to Home, is $(b + d)$, which is measured by the two triangles b and d in panel (a) or the single (combined) triangle $b + d$ in panel (b).

As we have just explained, the rise in producer surplus should be thought of as an increase in the return to fixed factors (capital or land) in the industry. Sometimes we even think of labor as a partially fixed factor because the skills learned in one industry cannot necessarily be transferred to other industries. In that case, it is reasonable to think that the increase in Home producer surplus can also benefit Home's workers in the import-competing industry, along with capital and land, but this benefit comes at the expense of consumer surplus.

Effect of the Tariff on Government Revenue In addition to affecting consumers and producers, the tariff also affects government revenue. The amount of revenue collected is the tariff t times the quantity of imports $(D_2 - S_2)$. In Figure 8-5, panel (a), this revenue is shown by the area c. The collection of revenue is a gain for the government in the importing country.

Overall Effect of the Tariff on Welfare We are now in a position to summarize the impact of the tariff on the welfare of the Home importing country, which is the sum of producer surplus, consumer surplus, and government revenues. Thus, our approach is to *add up* these impacts to obtain a net effect. In adding up the losses of consumers and the gains of producers, one dollar of consumer surplus is the same as one dollar of producer surplus or government revenue. In other words, we do not care whether the consumers facing higher prices are poor or rich, and do not care whether the specific factors in the industry (capital, land, and possibly labor) earn a lot or a little. Under this approach, transferring one dollar from consumer to producer surplus will have no impact on overall welfare: the decrease in consumer surplus will cancel out the increase in producer surplus.

You may object to this method of evaluating overall welfare, and feel that a dollar taken away from a poor consumer and given to a rich producer represents a net loss of overall welfare, rather than zero effect, as in our approach. We should be careful in evaluating the impact of tariffs on different income groups in the society, especially for poor countries or countries with a high degree of inequality among income groups. But for now we ignore this concern and simply add up consumer surplus, producer surplus, and government revenue. Keep in mind that under this approach we are just evaluating the *efficiency* of tariffs and not their effect on equity (i.e., how fair the tariff is to one group versus another).

The overall impact of the tariff in the small country can be summarized as follows:

Fall in consumer surplus:	$-(a + b + c + d)$
Rise in producer surplus:	$+a$
Rise in government revenue:	$+c$
Net effect on Home's welfare:	$-(b + d)$

In Figure 8-5(b), the triangle $(b + d)$ is the *net welfare loss* in a small importing country due to the tariff. We sometimes refer to this area as a **deadweight loss**, meaning that it is not offset by a gain elsewhere in the economy. Notice that in panel (a) the area a, which is a gain for producers, just cancels out that portion of the consumer surplus loss; the area a is effectively a transfer from consumers to producers via the higher domestic prices induced by the tariff. Likewise, area c, the gain in government revenue, also cancels out that portion of the consumer surplus loss; this is a transfer from consumers to the government. Thus, the area $(b + d)$ is the remaining loss for consumers that is not offset by a gain elsewhere. This deadweight loss is measured by the two triangles, b and d, in panel (a), or by the combined triangle $(b + d)$ in panel (b). The two triangles b and d of deadweight loss can each be given a precise interpretation, as follows.

Production Loss Notice that the base of triangle b is the net increase in Home supply due to the tariff, from S_1 to S_2. The height of this triangle is the increase in marginal costs due to the increase in supply. The unit S_1 was produced at a marginal cost equal to P^W, which is the free-trade price, but every unit above that amount is produced with higher marginal costs. The fact that marginal costs exceed the world price means that this country is producing the good inefficiently: it would be cheaper to import it rather than produce the extra quantity at home. The area of triangle b equals the increase in marginal costs for the extra units produced and can be interpreted as the **production loss** (or the *efficiency loss*) for the economy due to producing at marginal costs above the world price. Notice that the production loss is only a portion of the overall deadweight loss, which is $(b + d)$ in Figure 8-5.

Consumption Loss The triangle d in panel (a) (the other part of the deadweight loss) can also be given a precise interpretation. Because of the tariff and the price increase from P^W to $P^W + t$, the quantity consumed in Home is reduced from D_1 to D_2. The area of the triangle d can be interpreted as the drop in consumer surplus for those individuals who are no longer able to consume the units between D_1 and D_2 because of the higher price. We refer to this drop in consumer surplus as the **consumption loss** for the economy.

APPLICATION

U.S. Tariffs on Steel, 2002–03

We can use our small-country model to calculate a rough estimate of how costly the 2002–03 U.S. steel tariffs were in terms of welfare. Although the United States may not be a small country when it comes to its influence on import and export prices, it is a good starting point for our analysis, and we will examine the large-country case in the next section. For now, we stay with our small-country model and illustrate the deadweight loss due to the U.S. steel tariff that was imposed by President George W. Bush from March 2002 to December 2003. In the next application, we examine the tariffs on steel and other products that were applied by President Trump during 2018–19, especially on imports from China.

Steel Tariff Used by President Bush When he was running for the presidency in 2000, George W. Bush made a campaign pledge to implement tariffs on imports of steel. After he was elected, President Bush directed the U.S. International Trade Commission (ITC) to initiate a Section 201 investigation into the steel industry. As summarized in **Side Bar: Provisions of U.S. Trade Law**, Section 201 allows for the use of tariffs to assist a domestic industry that is suffering "serious injury" due to rising imports. These tariffs are referred to as a *safeguard* against the rising imports. Section 201 of U.S. trade law is similar to Article XIX of the GATT (see **Side Bar: Key Provisions of the GATT**).

After investigating, the ITC determined that the steel industry met the conditions of Section 201, and so it recommended that tariffs be put in place. The tariffs recommended by the ITC varied across products, ranging from 10% to 20% for the first year, as shown in Table 8-1, and then falling over time until they were eliminated after three years.

TABLE 8-1

U.S. ITC Recommended and Actual Tariffs for Steel Shown here are the tariffs recommended by the U.S. International Trade Commission for steel imports in 2002, and the actual tariffs that were applied in 2002.

Product Category	Tariff Recommended by the U.S. ITC (for 2002, %)	Actual U.S. Tariff (used in 2002, %)
Carbon and Alloy Flat Products		
Slab	20	30
Flat products	20	30
Tin mill products	U*	30
Carbon and Alloy Long Products		
Hot-rolled bar	20	30
Cold-finished bar	20	30
Rebar	10	15
Carbon and Alloy Tubular Products		
Tubular products	?**	15
Alloy fittings and flanges	13	13
Stainless and Tool Steel Products		
Stainless steel bar	15	15
Stainless steel rod	?**	15
Stainless steel wire	U*	8

*Uncertain—the ITC was divided on whether a tariff should be used.

**A specific recommendation was not made by the U.S. ITC.

Data from: Robert Read, 2005, "The Political Economy of Trade Protection: The Determinants and Welfare Impact of the 2002 U.S. Emergency Steel Safeguard Measures," The World Economy, 1119–1137.

The ITC decision on steel was based on several factors.[5] First, imports had been rising and prices were falling in the steel industry from 1998 to early 2001, leading to substantial losses for U.S. firms. Those losses, along with falling investment and employment, met the condition of "serious injury" as required by Section 201. An explanation given

---

[5] We focus here on the ITC conclusions for flat-rolled carbon steel, from U.S. International Trade Commission, 2001, Steel: Investigation No. TA-201-73, Volume I, Publication 3479, Washington, D.C.

SIDE BAR

Provisions of U.S. Trade Law

The Trade Expansion Act of 1962 and the Trade Act of 1974 describe conditions under which the United States can apply tariffs. Three sections of these acts have been used to justify recent U.S. tariffs. The first of these, Section 201, allows for the use of a safeguard tariff and is similar to Article XIX of the GATT; the second provision, Section 232, allows for tariffs to protect national security, as mentioned in Article XXI of the GATT; and the third provision, Section 301, allows for the use of tariffs whenever the United States feels that its trading partners are taking actions that are disadvantageous to U.S. commerce.

Section 201 (of the Trade Act of 1974): Safeguard Tariff

This section allows the president to impose temporary duties and other trade measures if the U.S. International Trade Commission (ITC) determines that a surge in imports is *a substantial cause or threat of serious injury to a U.S.*

industry. The term "substantial cause" means a cause that is *important and not less than any other cause.*

Section 232 (of the Trade Expansion Act of 1962): National Security

This section allows the president to adjust imports by using tariffs or quotas if the Department of Commerce finds that certain products are imported in such quantities or under circumstances that *threaten to impair U.S. national security.*

Section 301 (of the Trade Act of 1974): Trade Agreements

This section allows the United States Trade Representative (USTR) to suspend trade agreement concessions or impose import restrictions if it determines that a U.S. trading partner *is violating trade agreement commitments or engaging in discriminatory or unreasonable practices that burden or restrict U.S. commerce.*

Information from: Congressional Research Service, Trump Administration Tariff Actions (Sections 201, 232, and 301): Frequently Asked Questions, February 22, 2019, https://www.everycrsreport.com/reports /R45529.html.

---

by the ITC for the falling import prices was that the U.S. dollar appreciated substantially prior to 2001: as the dollar rises in value, foreign currencies become cheaper and so do imported products such as steel, as occurred during this period. To meet the criterion of Section 201 and Article XIX, rising imports need to be a "substantial cause" of serious injury, which is defined as "a cause which is important and not less than any other cause." Sometimes another cause of injury to U.S. firms can be a domestic recession, but that was not the case in the years preceding 2001, when demand for steel products was rising.[6]

President Bush accepted the recommendation of the ITC but applied even higher tariffs, ranging from 8% to 30%, as shown in Table 8-1, with 30% tariffs applied to the most commonly used steel products (such as flat-rolled steel sheets and steel slab). Initially, the tariffs were meant to be in place for three years and to decline over time. Knowing that U.S. trading partners would be upset by this action, President Bush exempted some countries from the tariffs on steel. The countries exempted included Canada, Mexico, Jordan, and Israel, all of which have free-trade agreements with the United States, and 100 small developing countries that were exporting only a very small amount of steel to the United States.

Deadweight Loss Due to the Steel Tariff To measure the deadweight loss due to the tariffs levied on steel, we need to estimate the area of the triangle $b + d$ in Figure 8-5(b). The base of this triangle is the change in imports due to the tariffs, or $\Delta M = M_1 - M_2$. The height of the triangle is the increase in the domestic price due to the tariff, or $\Delta P = t$. So the deadweight loss equals

$$DWL = \frac{1}{2} \cdot t \cdot \Delta M$$

It is convenient to measure the deadweight loss relative to the value of imports, which is $P^W \cdot M$. We will also use the percentage tariff, which is t/P^W, and the percentage change in the quantity of imports, which is $\%\Delta M = \Delta M/M$. The deadweight loss relative to the value of imports can then be rewritten as

$$\frac{DWL}{P^W \cdot M} = \frac{1}{2} \cdot \frac{t \cdot \Delta M}{P^W \cdot M} = \frac{1}{2} \cdot \left(\frac{t}{P^W}\right) \cdot \%\Delta M$$

---

[6] A short recession began in the United States in March 2001 and ended eight months later, in November 2001.

For the tariffs on steel, the most commonly used products had a tariff of 30%, so that is the percentage increase in the price: $t/P^W = 0.3$. It turns out that the quantity of steel imports also fell by 30% the first year after the tariff was imposed, so that $\%\Delta M = 0.3$. Therefore, the deadweight loss is

$$\frac{DWL}{P^W \cdot M} = \frac{1}{2}(0.3 \cdot 0.3) = 0.045, \text{ or } 4.5\% \text{ of the import value}$$

The value of steel imports that were affected by the tariff was about $4.7 billion in the year prior to March 2002 and $3.5 billion in the year after March 2002, so average imports over the two years were $(4.7 + 3.5) = \$4.1$ billion (these values do not include the tariffs).[7]

If we apply the deadweight loss of 4.5% to the average import value of $4.1 billion, then the dollar magnitude of deadweight loss is $0.045 \cdot 4.1$ billion = $185 million. As we discussed earlier, this deadweight loss reflects the net annual loss to the United States from applying the tariff. If you are a steelworker, then you might think that the price of $185 million is money well spent to protect your job, at least temporarily. On the other hand, if you are a consumer of steel, then you will probably object to the higher prices and deadweight loss. In fact, many of the U.S. firms that purchase steel—such as firms producing automobiles—objected to the tariffs and encouraged President Bush to end them early. But the biggest objections to the tariffs came from exporting countries whose firms were affected by the tariffs, especially the European countries.

Response of the European Countries   The tariffs on steel most heavily affected Europe, Japan, and South Korea, along with some developing countries (Brazil, India, Turkey, Moldova, Romania, Thailand, and Venezuela) that were exporting a significant amount of steel to the United States. These countries objected to the restriction on their ability to sell steel to the United States.

The countries in the European Union (EU) therefore took action by bringing the case to the WTO. They were joined by Brazil, China, Japan, South Korea, New Zealand, Norway, and Switzerland. The WTO has a formal **dispute settlement procedure** under which countries that believe that the WTO rules have not been followed can bring their complaint and have it evaluated. The WTO evaluated this case and, in early November 2003, ruled that the United States had failed to sufficiently prove that its steel industry had been harmed by a sudden increase in imports and therefore did not have the right to impose safeguard tariffs.

The WTO ruling was made on legal grounds: that the United States had essentially failed to prove its case (i.e., its eligibility for Article XIX protection).[8] But there are also economic grounds for doubting the wisdom of the safeguard tariffs in the first place. Even if we accept that there might be an argument on equity or fairness grounds for temporarily protecting an industry facing import competition, it is hard to argue that such protection should occur because of a change in exchange rates. The U.S. dollar appreciated for much of the 1990s, including the period before 2001 on which the ITC focused, leading to much lower prices for imported steel. But the appreciation of the dollar also lowered the prices for *all other* import products, so many other industries in the United States faced import competition, too. On fairness grounds, there is no special reason to single out the steel industry for protection.

The WTO ruling entitled the European Union and other countries to retaliate against the United States by imposing tariffs of their own against U.S. exports. The European

---

[7] The drop in imports of 30% corresponds to a fall in import value of $1.2 billion (since $1.2/4.1 \approx 0.30$, or 30%).

[8] One of the legal reasons for the WTO ruling was that imports of flat-rolled steel into the United States had fallen from 1998 to 2001, so this product did not meet the requirement that imports had to be increasing to receive Article XIX protection. The imports of other steel products had been rising, however.

countries quickly began to draw up a list of products—totaling some $2.2 billion in U.S. exports—against which they would apply tariffs. The European countries naturally picked products that would have the greatest negative impact on the United States, such as oranges from Florida, where Jeb Bush, the president's brother, was governor.

The threat of tariffs being imposed on these products led President Bush to reconsider the U.S. tariffs on steel. On December 5, 2003, he announced that they would be suspended after being in place for only 19 months rather than the three years as initially planned. This chain of events illustrates how the use of tariffs by an importer can easily lead to a response by exporters and a **tariff war**. The elimination of the steel tariffs by President Bush avoided such a retaliatory tariff war.

APPLICATION

U.S. and Foreign Tariffs Under President Trump, 2018–19

The previous application about the tariff applied by President Bush on imports of steel during 2002–03 taught us several lessons: how Section 201 of U.S. trade law is applied, how to calculate the deadweight loss of a tariff, and how foreign countries can sometimes retaliate by threatening to apply tariffs of their own against U.S. exports. These lessons will be helpful as we examine the tariffs that were applied during 2018–19 by the administration of President Trump.

Tariffs Applied by President Trump   In panel (a) of Table 8-2, we list the tariffs that were implemented by President Trump. First was a tariff on imports of washing machines, in a Section 201 case brought by the American producer Whirlpool. The ITC found that this case met the conditions of Section 201, and tariffs were applied for three years. Tariffs in the first year, 2018, were 20% on the first 1.2 million imported washing machines (rising to 50% for imports above 1.2 million), with slightly lower tariffs in the next two years. Interestingly, this 20% tariff did not lead to a simple 20% increase in the prices of imported and home-produced washing machines, as expected from our small-country model (see Figure 8-5). According to one study, sellers in the United States tried to "disguise" the price increases by spreading them over washing machines and dryers, which are often bought together: the prices of both appliances rose by 11.5%, which is $86 per washing machine and $92 per dryer.[9]

Multiplying these price increases for washers and dryers by the average number of each sold in 2017 and 2018 gives a *loss in consumer surplus* of $1.55 billion. That is the area $(a + b + c + d)$ in Figure 8-5 panel (a). Very little of that consumer surplus loss was offset by tariff revenue collected, which is area c: from February 2018 to January 2019, only $82 million was collected in tariff revenue. What about the producer surplus gain, area a? Because the retail prices of both washers and dryers increased, and many of the dryers are imported, a substantial portion of the producer surplus gain a actually went to *foreign exporters* of the dryers (who increased their prices but did not face any tariff). That portion is therefore a loss for the United States, which should be added to the deadweight loss to obtain the "net loss" for the United States. We do not attempt to make a more detailed calculation, but we expect that a substantial part of the consumer loss of $1.55 billion is a net loss for the United States.

---

[9] See Aaron B. Flaaen, Ali Hortaçsu, and Felix Tintelnot, 2019, "The Production Relocation and Price Effects of U.S. Trade Policy: The Case of Washing Machines," National Bureau of Economic Research Working Paper No. 25767.

TABLE 8-2

U.S. and Foreign Tariffs, 2018–19 Panel (a) of this table shows the tariffs applied on U.S. imports by the administration of President Trump during 2018–19. Panel (b) shows the tariffs applied on U.S. exports by foreign countries in retaliation for the U.S. import tariffs.

(a) Tariffs on U.S. Imports

Product or Country	2017 Tariff (%)	First Date of Tariff*	2018 or 2019 Tariff** (%)	Trade Law
Washing machines	1.3	February 7, 2018	20–50	Section 201
Solar panels	0	February 7, 2018	30	Section 201
Steel	0	March–June, 2018	25	Section 232
Aluminum	2	March–June, 2018	12	Section 232
China (many products)	1.2–3.4	July 2018–October 2019	13.4–26.2	Section 301

(b) Retaliatory Tariffs on U.S. Exports

Retaliating Country	2017 Tariff (%)	First Date of Tariff*	2018 or 2019** Tariff (%)	In Response to U.S. Tariffs on
China	7.8	April 2018–October 2019	22.7	Steel, aluminum, other products
Mexico	9.6	June 5, 2018	28	Steel, aluminum
Turkey	9.7	June 21, 2018	31.8	Steel, aluminum
European Union	3.9	June 22, 2018	29.2	Steel, aluminum
Canada	2.1	July 1, 2018	20.2	Steel, aluminum
Russia	5.2	August 6, 2018	36.8	Steel, aluminum
India	n.a.	June 15, 2019	10–70	Steel, aluminum

n.a. = not available.

* When a range of dates is shown (except for China), then the tariff was increased on various countries at different dates. For China, the U.S. tariffs in panel (a) were increased by 10% or by 25% on various products at different dates, and the Chinese retaliatory tariffs in panel (b) were increased by differing amounts on various products at different dates.

** The 2018 tariff is reported, except for those products where the tariff was increased in 2019. When a range of values is shown, then various products had different tariffs.

Data from: Modified from Pablo D. Fajgelbaum, Pinelopi K. Goldberg, Patrick J. Kennedy, and Amit K. Khandelwal, February 2020, "The Return to Protectionism," Quarterly Journal of Economics, 135(1), 1–55.

The second case of tariffs shown in Table 8-2 is for imported solar panels. That Section 201 case was brought by the American firms Suniva and SolarWorld, and followed from earlier tariffs applied on this product applied under President Obama. We describe those tariffs in the following chapter.

The next cases listed in Table 8-2 are for imports of steel and aluminum. For these products, President Trump did not rely on Section 201 to justify the tariffs but instead turned to a little-used provision of U.S. trade law: Section 232, which deals with national security. National security is mentioned in Article XXI of the GATT (see **Side Bar: Key Provisions of the GATT**), but that provision is meant to apply in times of war or to restrict trade in war materials. The United States provides a broader justification in Section 232 that is used to assist industries that are judged to be essential for national security. Section 232 does not have the requirements of Section 201, that imports are increasing or that they are a "substantial cause of serious injury," but only that they are essential for national security. This provision of U.S. trade law has rarely been used rarely: there were only nine cases before the Trump administration in which the Department of Commerce recommended some action, and only six of those cases were a trade action (the most recent being in 1986). For steel and aluminum imports in 2018, the tariff increases from 2017 to 2018 were 25% and 10%, respectively, with only a few countries exempted from the tariffs.[10]

---

[10] Argentina, Brazil, and South Korea were exempted from the tariffs on steel and aluminum because they agreed to limit their exports of those products to the United States by a specified quota amount, and Australia received an exemption without a quota. American companies were permitted to apply for exclusions from paying the tariffs on specific types of imported steel if they could show that those products were not available from U.S. firms.

Tariffs Applied by Foreign Countries Because Section 232 of U.S. trade law is not well justified under the GATT or WTO, U.S. trading partners objected strongly to the tariffs on steel and aluminum, and they retaliated by applying tariffs on U.S. exports. In panel (b) of Table 8-2, we list the countries that retaliated against the United States and the average tariffs that they imposed in 2018. China was the first to retaliate, followed by Mexico, Turkey, the European Union, Canada, Russia, and finally India. In contrast to the *threatened* retaliation against the United States due to the steel tariff of 2002, during 2018–19 there was *actual* retaliation by these countries. Nevertheless, this retaliation did not lead the United States to remove the tariffs on steel and aluminum.

The value of U.S. exports that were targeted for these retaliatory tariffs was similar to the value of U.S. imports of steel and aluminum that were sent from each country; that is, the foreign tariffs applied to a similar amount of trade as the U.S. tariffs. It is surprising that Canada and Mexico are included in this list of retaliating countries because they both have a free-trade agreement (NAFTA) with the United States. Canada is the largest and Mexico is the fourth-largest exporter of steel to the United States. The steel and aluminum tariffs were initially imposed against these countries, but they were later removed in anticipation of gaining approval for the new U.S.-Mexico-Canada free-trade agreement (USMCA, discussed in Chapter 6).

Last but not least, the final U.S. tariffs listed in Table 8-2 are those applied against China between July 2018 and October 2019, in the U.S.–China Trade War that we described in Chapter 1. To apply these tariffs, the administration of President Trump appealed to Section 301 of U.S. trade law, which allows the United States to apply tariffs whenever it feels that a trading partner is "violating trade agreement commitments or engaging in discriminatory or unreasonable practices that burden or restrict U.S. commerce." This is the easiest to apply of the provisions of U.S. trade law that we have reviewed (see **Side Bar: Provisions of U.S. Trade Law**). The United States cited the fact that China requires American companies locating there to share their technology with Chinese partners as justification for the Section 301 tariffs.

The U.S. tariffs first applied on varying amounts of Chinese imports from July 2018 to October 2019 (and continuing after that) were between 10% and 25%, and by December 2019 they were applied to nearly all imports from China. That country responded with tariffs that targeted a somewhat smaller value of U.S. exports, covering about two-thirds of its purchases by December 2019. A "phase one" truce to this trade war was announced on December 13, 2019, that prevented higher tariffs (planned for two days later) from being imposed by the United States. While this truce prevented new tariffs from being imposed, it only partially removed the existing tariffs between the two countries.

Costs of the Trump Tariffs What are the welfare costs to the United States from the long list of U.S. tariffs in Table 8-2? We report the estimates from one study that confirms the assumption that the United States is a "small country."[11] This study finds that a tariff of a given percentage, applied to a particular product, tended to increase the U.S. import prices at the border by the same percentage, as is shown in Figure 8-5. The study first calculates the impact of the 2018 tariffs, which included those on washing machines, solar panels, and steel and aluminum, along with the initial 10% tariffs that were applied on $200 billion of U.S. imports from China in September 2018. Those results are then extended to incorporate the increase in the tariff on Chinese imports to 25% in June 2019.

Both the 2018 and the extended 2018–19 results are shown in Table 8-3. This study did not attempt to estimate the producer surplus gain from the tariffs because this

[11] See Mary Amiti, Stephen J. Redding, and David Weinstein, "The Impact of the 2018 Trade War on U.S. Prices and Welfare," *Journal of Economic Perspectives*, 33(4), 187–210.

TABLE 8-3

Welfare Impact of 2018 and 2019 U.S. Tariffs Panel (a) shows the welfare impact of the 2018 U.S. tariffs, which included those on washing machines, solar panels, steel and aluminum, and the initial 10% tariffs that were applied on $200 billion of U.S. imports from China in September 2018. Panel (b) extends those results to include the increase in the U.S. tariffs on China during 2019.

(a) IMPACT OF TARIFFS ON U.S. IMPORTS APPLIED IN 2018

	(1) Consumer Loss from Higher Import Prices	(2) Tariff Revenue	(3) Deadweight Loss
Annual cost ($ billions)	52.8	36.0	16.8
Annual cost per household ($)	414	282	132

(b) IMPACT OF TARIFFS ON U.S. IMPORTS APPLIED IN 2018–19

	(1) Consumer Loss from Higher Import Prices	(2) Tariff Revenue	(3) Deadweight Loss
Annual cost ($ billions)	106	26.9	79.1
Annual cost per household ($)	831	211	620

Note: Per household numbers are calculated based on 127.6 million households in the United States in 2018.

Data from: Mary Amiti, Stephen J. Redding, and David E. Weinstein, "New China Tariffs Increase Costs to U.S. Households," Federal Reserve Bank of New York Liberty Street Economics (blog), May 23, 2019, https://libertystreeteconomics.newyorkfed.org/2019/05/new-china-tariffs-increase-costs-to-us-households.html.

calculation is difficult, as we have already noted for the tariff on washing machines.[12] Rather, it reports the portion of the consumer surplus loss that is caused by the higher import prices, as measured by the reduced area under the *import* demand curve, area $c + (b + d)$ in Figure 8-5, panel (b). Column (1) of panel (a) in Table 8-3 indicates that the consumer loss was $52.8 billion in 2018. To put that number in perspective, we can divide by the number of households in the United States (127.6 million) to get $414 per household. That is a substantial amount: for comparison, the U.S. income tax reform of 2017 was predicted to save the average U.S. household $1,610, so one-quarter of that would be lost to consumers from the 2018 U.S. tariffs.

In column (2) of panel (a) in Table 8-3, we also report the tariff revenue collected in 2018 (area c in Figure 8-5). By subtracting this tariff revenue from the consumer cost, we obtain an estimate of the deadweight loss due to the tariffs, which is area $(b + d)$. The deadweight loss due to the 2018 tariffs was $16.8 billion, or $132 per household, as reported in column (3).

In panel (b) of Table 8-3, the results are extended to allow for the higher tariffs on China in 2019. As the tariff is raised in Figure 8-5, panel (b), you can see that it is quite possible for the amount of tariff revenue (the area c) to fall, because the higher tariff is applied to a smaller amount of imports. That is what occurred when the tariff on imports from China was raised from 10% to 25%: some of those goods were instead purchased from countries such as Vietnam. As a result, the average annual tariff revenue shown in panel (b) for 2018–19 fell to $26.9 billion in column (2), or $211 per household. But the

---

[12] This study focused on wholesale prices at the border, so it did not pick up the subtle response in the retail prices of washing machines and dryers, as discussed earlier, which both increased by 11.5% when the tariff on washing machines increased by 20%. Some of the producer surplus gain for dryers is actually a loss for the United State, since it goes to foreign firms exporting that product to the United States.

deadweight loss increases as the tariff goes up. The annual deadweight loss in 2018–19 is calculated as $79.1 billion in column (3), or $620 per household. Summing the deadweight loss and the tariff revenue, we obtain $106 billion, or $831 per household in the United States. Now the loss to consumers from tariff revenue and the deadweight loss amounts to *one-half* of the tax savings from the 2017 income tax reform (and the total consumer surplus loss, if we included area *a* in Figure 8-5, would be higher still).

It is important to realize that this study of the costs of the Trump tariffs did not incorporate the costs that resulted from the retaliation by foreign countries that raised tariffs on U.S. exports. Later in the chapter, we discuss another study that incorporates those costs from retaliation.

APPLICATION

The Political Economy of Tariffs

Our finding that a tariff always leads to deadweight losses for a small importing country explains why most economists oppose the use of tariffs. In the previous application, we showed that recent U.S. tariffs have a high deadweight loss resulting in high costs to consumers. Why, then, do the United States—and many other countries—use tariffs as part of their trade policies?

One important reason that tariffs are used even though they have a deadweight loss is politics. The tariff benefits Home producers, as we have seen, so if the government cares more about producer surplus than consumer surplus, it might decide to use the tariff despite the deadweight loss and consumer costs. Indeed, the benefits to producers (and their workers) are typically more concentrated on specific firms and states than the costs to consumers, which are spread nationwide. This is our interpretation of the tariff that President George W. Bush granted to the steel industry from 2002 to 2003: its benefits were concentrated in the steel-producing states of Pennsylvania, West Virginia, and Ohio, and its costs to consumers—in this case, steel-using industries—were spread more thinly and widely across the entire country.

The same argument—that the consumer costs of a tariff are spread thinly over many consumers—was used to justify the tariffs on steel and aluminum that were imposed by President Trump. When the tariff on steel was first announced in March 2018, U.S. Secretary of Commerce Wilbur Ross showed a can of Campbell's Soup on a television interview and said that the price of the can of soup would go up less than one cent:[13]

> What I'd like to do, though, is to emphasize again the limited impact [from the steel tariffs]. This is a can of Campbell's Soup. In the can of Campbell's Soup, there's about 2.6 cents, 2.6 pennies, worth of steel. So if that goes up by 25 percent, that's about six-tenths of 1 cent on the price of a can of Campbell's Soup. Well, I just bought this can today at a 7-Eleven down here, and the price was $1.99. So who in the world is going be bothered by six-tenths of a cent?

There is an important element of truth in what Secretary Ross said. Import tariffs hurt the purchasers of the import product (or in this case, the buyers of the can of soup), but those costs are often spread thinly over many consumers. In contrast, the gains from protecting Home firms from competition (in this case, the gains to U.S. steel producers) are focused on a specific industry. So the industry asking for protection from imports has greater political power to persuade the government to use the tariffs.

[13] Interview on CNBC, March 2, 2018, https://www.cnbc.com/2018/03/02/wilbur-ross-tariffs-are-nbd-but-campbells-says-cans-will-cost-more.html.

What about when the consumer costs get larger, as we have found for the high consumer costs of the 2018–19 tariffs? Interestingly, it appears that President Trump tried to minimize the apparent impact of these tariffs on consumers by focusing the tariffs on *intermediate inputs* used by firms. The tariffs on steel and aluminum, for example, would still end up raising prices for households, but this increase would be spread over a great number of products (including Campbell's Soup), so those higher prices would not be so apparent. The same tactic was used in the tariffs applied against China, which were focused almost exclusively on imported intermediate inputs, and not on consumer goods. Nearly all of the China tariffs applied from July 2018 to October 2019 were on imported intermediate inputs, and it was only the very last round of these tariffs—due to be imposed on December 15, 2019—that would have hit consumer goods like toys and electronics, whose prices would have increased for holiday shoppers. But as we have discussed, on December 13, 2019, an agreement was reached to not apply those tariffs and to reduce a portion of the earlier tariffs. This "truce' in the U.S.–China trade war helped to protect consumers from price increases that would have been the most apparent.[14]

4 Import Tariffs for a Large Country

Under the small-country assumption that we have used so far, we know for sure that the deadweight loss is positive; that is, the importing country is always harmed by the tariff. The small-country assumption means that the world price P^W is unchanged by the tariff applied by the importing country. If we consider a large enough importing country or a **large country**, however, then we might expect that its tariff will change the world price. In that case, the welfare for a large importing country can be improved by a tariff, as we now show.

Foreign Export Supply

If the Home country is large, then we can no longer assume that it faces a Foreign export supply curve X^* that is horizontal at the given world price P^W. Instead, we need to derive the Foreign export supply curve using the Foreign market demand and supply curves. In panel (a) of Figure 8-6, we show the demand curve D^* and supply curve S^* for Foreign. These intersect at the point A^*, with a no-trade equilibrium price of P^{A^*}. Because Foreign demand equals supply at that price, Foreign exports are zero, which we show by point $A^{*'}$ in panel (b), where we graph Foreign exports against their price.

Now suppose the world price P^W is above the Foreign no-trade price of P^{A^*}. At the price of P^W, the Foreign quantity demanded is lower, at D_1^* in panel (a), but the quantity supplied by Foreign firms is larger, at S_1^*. Because Foreign supply exceeds demand, Foreign will export the amount $X_1^* = S_1^* - D_1^*$ at the price of P^W, as shown by the point B^* in panel (b). Drawing a line through points $A^{*'}$ and B^*, we obtain the upward-sloping Foreign export supply curve X^*.

We can then combine the Foreign export supply curve X^* and Home import demand curve M, which is also shown in panel (b). They intersect at the price P^W, the world equilibrium price. Notice that the Home import demand curve starts at the no-trade price P^A on the price axis, whereas the Foreign export supply curve starts at the price P^{A^*}. As we have drawn them, the Foreign no-trade price is lower, $P^{A^*} < P^A$.

---

[14] See Chad Bown, "The Trade War Will Catch Up to Trump." *The Atlantic: Ideas*, September 10, 2019, https://www.theatlantic.com/ideas/archive/2019/09/trump-trade-war-muted/597676/.

FIGURE 8-6

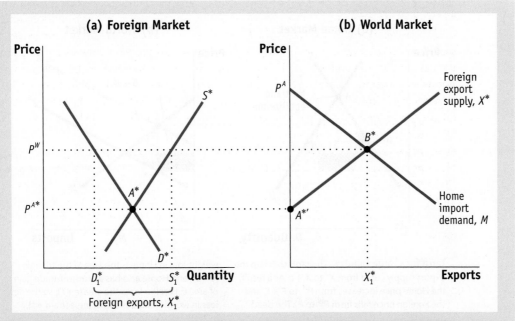

(a) Foreign Market

(b) World Market

Foreign Export Supply In panel (a), with Foreign demand of D^* and Foreign supply of S^*, the no-trade equilibrium in Foreign is at point A^*, with the price of P^{A^*}. At this price, the Foreign market is in equilibrium and Foreign exports are zero—point A^* in panel (a) and point $A^{*'}$ in panel (b), respectively. When the world price P^W is higher than the Foreign no-trade price, the quantity supplied by Foreign, S_1^*, exceeds the quantity demanded by Foreign, D_1^*, and Foreign exports $X_1^* = S_1^* - D_1^*$. In panel (b), joining up points $A^{*'}$ and B^*, we obtain the upward-sloping export supply curve X^*. With the Home import demand of M, the world equilibrium is at point B^*, with the price P^W.

In Chapter 2 through Chapter 5 of this book, a country with comparative advantage in a good would have a lower no-trade relative price and would become an exporter when trade was opened. Likewise, in panel (b), Foreign exports the good since its no-trade price P^{A^*} is lower than the world price, and Home imports the good since its no-trade price P^A is higher than the world price. So the world equilibrium illustrated in panel (b) is similar to that in some of the trade models presented in earlier chapters.

Effect of the Tariff

In panel (b) of Figure 8-7, we repeat the Home import demand curve M and Foreign export supply curve X^*, with the world equilibrium at B^*. When Home applies a tariff of t dollars, the cost to Foreign producers of supplying the Home market is t more than it was before. Because of this increase in costs, the Foreign export supply curve shifts up by exactly the amount of the tariff, as shown in panel (b) with the shift from X^* to $X^* + t$. The $X^* + t$ curve intersects import demand M at point C, which establishes the Home price (including the tariff) paid by consumers. On the other hand, the Foreign exporters receive the net-of-tariff price, which is directly below the point C by exactly the amount t, at point C^*. Let us call the price received by Foreign exporters P^*, at point C^*, which is the new world price.

The important feature of the new equilibrium is that the price Home pays for its imports, $P^* + t$, rises by *less than* the amount of the tariff t as compared with the initial world price P^W. The reason that the Home price rises by *less than* the full amount of the tariff is that the price received by Foreign exporters, P^*, has fallen as compared

FIGURE 8-7

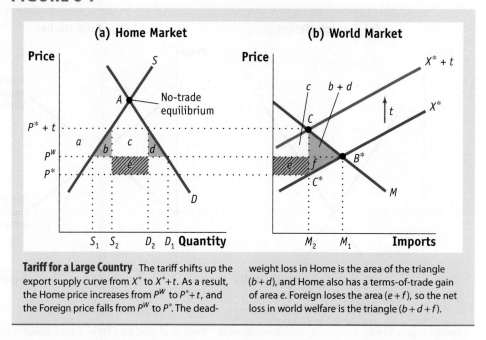

Tariff for a Large Country The tariff shifts up the export supply curve from X^* to X^*+t. As a result, the Home price increases from P^W to P^*+t, and the Foreign price falls from P^W to P^*. The dead-weight loss in Home is the area of the triangle $(b+d)$, and Home also has a terms-of-trade gain of area e. Foreign loses the area $(e+f)$, so the net loss in world welfare is the triangle $(b+d+f)$.

with the initial world price P^W. So Foreign producers are essentially "absorbing" a part of the tariff, by lowering their price from P^W (in the initial free-trade equilibrium) to P^* (after the tariff).

In sum, we can interpret the tariff as driving a wedge between what Home consumers pay and what Foreign producers receive, with the difference (of t) going to the Home government. As is the case with many taxes, the amount of the tariff (t) is shared by both consumers and producers.

Terms of Trade In Chapter 2, we defined the **terms of trade** for a country as the ratio of export prices to import prices. Generally, an improvement in the terms of trade indicates a gain for a country because it is either receiving more for its exports or paying less for its imports. To measure the Home terms of trade, we want to use the net-of-tariff import price P^* (received by Foreign firms) since that is the total amount transferred from Home to Foreign for each import. Because this price has fallen (from its initial world price of P^W), it follows that the Home terms of trade have increased. We might expect, therefore, that the Home country gains from the tariff in terms of Home welfare. To determine whether that is the case, we need to analyze the impact on the welfare of Home consumers, producers, and government revenue, which we do in Figure 8-7.

Home's Welfare In panel (a), the Home consumer price increases from P^W to P^*+t, which makes consumers worse off. The drop in consumer surplus is represented by the area between these two prices and to the left of the demand curve D, which is shown by $(a+b+c+d)$. At the same time, the price received by Home firms rises from P^W to P^*+t, making Home firms better off. The increase in producer surplus equals the area between these two prices and to the left of the supply curve S, which is the amount a. Finally, we also need to keep track of the changes in government revenue. Revenue collected from the tariff equals the amount of the tariff (t) times the new amount of imports, which is $M_2 = D_2 - S_2$. Therefore, government revenue equals the area $(c+e)$ in panel (a).

By summing the change in consumer surplus, producer surplus, and government revenue, we obtain the overall impact of the tariff in the large country, as follows:

Fall in consumer surplus:	$-(a+b+c+d)$
Rise in producer surplus:	$+a$
Rise in government revenue:	$+(c+e)$

Net effect on Home's welfare: $+e-(b+d)$

The triangle $(b+d)$ is the deadweight loss due to the tariff (just as it is for a small country). But for the large country, there is also a source of gain—the area e—that offsets this deadweight loss. If e exceeds $(b+d)$, then Home is better off due to the tariff; if e is less than $(b+d)$, then Home is worse off.

Notice that the area e is a rectangle whose height is the fall in the price that Foreign exporters receive, the difference between P^W and P^*. The base of this rectangle equals the quantity of imports, M_2. Multiplying the drop in the import price by the quantity of imports to obtain the area e, we obtain a precise measure of the **terms-of-trade gain** for the importer. If this terms-of-trade gain exceeds the deadweight loss of the tariff, which is $(b+d)$, then Home gains from the tariff.

Thus, we see that a large importer might gain by the application of a tariff. We can add this to our list of reasons why countries use tariffs, in addition to their being a source of government revenue or a tool for political purposes. However, for the large country, any net gain from the tariff comes at the expense of the Foreign exporters, as we show next.

Foreign and World Welfare Although Home might gain from the tariff, Foreign, the exporting country, definitely loses. In panel (b) of Figure 8-7, the Foreign loss is measured by the area $(e+f)$. We should think of $(e+f)$ as the loss in Foreign producer surplus from selling fewer goods to Home at a lower price. Notice that the area e is the terms-of-trade gain for Home but an equivalent terms-of-trade loss for Foreign; Home's gain comes at the expense of Foreign. In addition, the large-country tariff incurs an extra deadweight loss of f in Foreign, so the combined total outweighs the benefits to Home. For this reason, we sometimes call a tariff imposed by a large country a "beggar thy neighbor" tariff.

Adding together the change in Home's welfare and Foreign's welfare, the area e cancels out and we are left with a *net loss* in world welfare of $(b+d+f)$, the triangle in panel (b). This area is a deadweight loss for the world. The terms-of-trade gain that Home has extracted from the Foreign country by using a tariff comes at the expense of the Foreign exporters, and in addition, there is an added world deadweight loss. The fact that the large-country tariff leads to a world deadweight loss is another reason that most economists oppose the use of tariffs.

Optimal Tariff for a Large Importing Country We have found that a large importer might gain by the application of tariffs, but have yet to determine what level of tariff a country should apply in order to maximize welfare. It turns out there is a shortcut method we can use to evaluate the effect of the tariff on the welfare of a large importing country. The shortcut method uses the concept of the **optimal tariff**.

The optimal tariff is defined as the tariff that leads to the maximum increase in welfare for the importing country. For a large importing country, a small tariff initially increases welfare because the terms-of-trade gain exceeds the deadweight loss. That is, the area of the rectangle e in panel (a) of Figure 8-7 exceeds the area of the triangle $(b+d)$ in panel (b) when the tariff is small enough. The reason for this is that both the height and base of the triangle $(b+d)$ shrink to zero when the tariff is very small, so the area of the triangle is very small indeed; but for the rectangle e, only the height shrinks to zero when the tariff is small, so the area of the rectangle exceeds that of the triangle.

FIGURE 8-8

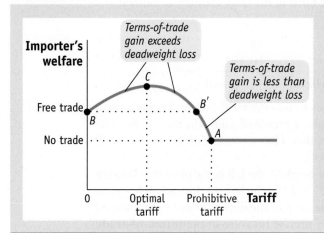

Tariffs and Welfare for a Large Country For a large importing country, a tariff initially increases the importer's welfare because the terms-of-trade gain exceeds the deadweight loss. So the importer's welfare rises from point B. Welfare continues to rise until the tariff is at its optimal level (point C). After that, welfare falls. If the tariff is too large (greater than at B), then welfare will fall below the free-trade level. For a prohibitive tariff, with no imports at all, the importer's welfare will be at the no-trade level, at point A.

By this mathematical reasoning, the Home gains are positive—$e > (b + d)$—when the Home tariff is sufficiently small.

In Figure 8-8, we graph Home welfare against the level of the tariff. Free trade is at point B, where the tariff is zero. A small increase in the tariff, as we have just noted, leads to an *increase* in Home welfare (because the terms-of-trade gain exceeds the deadweight loss). Therefore, starting at point B, the graph of Home welfare must be upward-sloping. But what if the tariff is very large? If the tariff is too large, then welfare will fall *below* the free-trade level of welfare. For example, with a prohibitive tariff so high that no imports are purchased at all, then the importer's welfare will be at the no-trade level, shown by point A. So while the graph of welfare must be increasing for a small tariff from point B, as the tariff increases, welfare eventually falls past the free-trade level at point B' to the no-trade welfare at point A.

Given that points B and A are both on the graph of the importer's welfare (for free trade and no trade, respectively) and that welfare must be rising after point B, it follows that there must be a highest point of welfare, shown by point C. At this point, the importer's welfare is highest because the difference between the terms-of-trade gain and deadweight loss is maximized. We will call the tariff at that point the "optimal tariff." For increases in the tariff beyond its optimal level (i.e., between points C and A), the importer's welfare falls because the deadweight loss due to the tariff overwhelms the terms-of-trade gain. But whenever the tariff is below its optimal level, between points B and C, then welfare is higher than its free-trade level because the terms-of-trade gain exceeds the deadweight loss.

Optimal Tariff Formula It turns out that there is a simple formula for the optimal tariff. The formula depends on the elasticity of Foreign export supply, which we call E_X^*. Recall that the elasticity of any supply curve is the percentage increase in supply caused by a percentage increase in price. Likewise, the elasticity of the Foreign export supply curve is the percentage change in the quantity exported in response to a percentage change in the world price of the export. If the export supply curve is very steep, then there is little response of the quantity supplied, and so the elasticity E_X^* is low. Conversely, if the export supply curve is very flat, there is a large response of the quantity supplied due to a change in the world price, and so E_X^* is high. Recall also that a small importing country faces a perfectly horizontal, or perfectly elastic, Foreign export supply curve, which means that the elasticity of Foreign's export supply is infinite.

Using the elasticity of Foreign export supply, the optimal tariff equals

$$\text{optimal tariff} = \frac{1}{E_X^*}$$

That is, the optimal tariff (measured as a percentage) equals the inverse of the elasticity of Foreign export supply. For a small importing country, the elasticity of Foreign export supply is infinite, and so the optimal tariff is zero. That result makes sense, since any tariff higher than zero leads to a deadweight loss for the importer (and no terms-of-trade gain), so the best tariff to choose is zero, or free trade.

For a large importing country however, the Foreign export supply is less than infinite, and we can use this formula to compute the optimal tariff. As the elasticity of Foreign export supply decreases (which means that the Foreign export supply curve is steeper), the optimal tariff is higher. The reason for this result is that with a steep Foreign export supply curve, Foreign exporters will lower their price more in response to the tariff.[15] For instance, if E_X^* decreases from 3 to 2, then the optimal tariff increases from $\frac{1}{3} = 33\%$ to $\frac{1}{2} = 50\%$, reflecting the fact that Foreign producers are willing to lower their prices more, taking on a larger share of the tariff burden. In that case, the Home country obtains a larger terms-of-trade increase and hence the optimal level of the tariff is higher.

APPLICATION

U.S. Tariffs on Steel Once Again

Let us return to the U.S. tariff on steel, and reevaluate the effect on U.S. welfare in the large-country case. The calculation of the deadweight loss that we did earlier in the applications (see the applications **U.S. Tariffs on Steel, 2002–03** and **U.S. and Foreign Tariffs Under President Trump, 2018–19**) assumed that the United States was a small country, facing fixed world prices for steel. In that case, the 30% tariff on some steel products used by President Bush was fully reflected in U.S. prices, which would rise by 30%, and similarly for the 25% tariff used by President Trump. But what if the import prices for steel in the United States did not rise by the full amount of the tariff? If the United States is a large enough importer of steel, then the Foreign export price will fall and the U.S. import price will rise by less than the tariff. It is then possible that the United States gained from the tariff.

To determine whether the United States gained from the tariff on steel products, we can compute the deadweight loss (area $b + d$) and the terms-of-trade gain (area e) for each imported steel product using the optimum tariff formula.

Optimal Tariffs for Steel Let us apply this formula to the U.S. steel tariffs to see how the tariffs applied compare with the theoretical optimal tariff. In Table 8-4, we show various steel products in column (1) along with their respective elasticities of export supply to the United States in column (2). By taking the inverse of each export supply elasticity, we obtain the optimal tariff in column (3). For example, alloy steel flat-rolled products (the first item) have a low export supply elasticity, 0.27, so they have a very high optimal tariff of $1/0.27 = 3.7 = 370\%$. In contrast, iron and nonalloy steel flat-rolled products (the last item) have a very high export supply elasticity of 750, so the optimal tariff is $1/750 \approx 0\%$. Products between these have optimal tariffs ranging from 1% to 125%.

---

[15] See Problem 4 at the end of the chapter, where you will show that steeper export supply leads Foreign to absorb more of the tariff.

TABLE 8-4

Optimal Tariffs for Steel Products This table shows optimal tariffs for steel products, calculated with the elasticity formula, as compared to actual tariffs used on U.S. steel imports in 2002–03 and in 2018–19.

	(1)	(2)	(3)	(4)	(5)
Product Category		**Elasticity of Export Supply**	**Optimal Tariff (%)**	**Actual Tariff (%) 2002–03**	**Actual Tariff (%) 2018–19**
Alloy steel flat-rolled products		0.27	370	30	25
Iron and steel rails and railway track		0.80	125	0	25
Iron and steel bars, rods, angles, shapes		0.80	125	15–30	25
Ferrous waste and scrap		17	6	0	25
Iron and steel tubes, pipes, and fittings		90	1	13–15	25
Iron and nonalloy steel flat-rolled products		750	0	0	25

Data from: Elasticities of export supply provided by Christian Broda and David Weinstein, May 2006, "Globalization and the Gains from Variety," Quarterly Journal of Economics, *121(2), 541–585.*

In column (4) of Table 8-4, we show the actual tariffs that were applied to these products under President Bush in 2002–03, and in column (5), we show the actual tariff applied under President Trump in 2018–19. For alloy steel flat-rolled products (the first item), the actual tariff under President Bush was 30% and under President Trump was 25%, both of which are far below the optimal tariff. That means the terms-of-trade gain for that product was higher than the deadweight loss: the tariff is on the portion of the welfare graph between *B* and *C* in Figure 8-8, and U.S. welfare is above its free-trade level. The same holds for iron and steel bars, rods, angles, and shapes, for which the tariffs of 15% to 30% under President Bush, or 25% under President Trump, are again less than their optimal level, so the United States obtains a terms-of-trade gain that exceeds the deadweight loss.

For iron and steel tubes, pipes, and fittings, however, the U.S. tariffs were 13% to 15% under President Bush and 25% under President Trump, but the optimal tariff for that product was only 1%. Because of the very high elasticity of export supply, the United States had practically no effect on the world price: the United States was nearly like a small country for that product. So the deadweight loss for that product exceeded the terms-of-trade gain, and the United States lost by applying a tariff in 2002–03 and in 2018–19.

To summarize, for the three product categories in Table 8-4 to which the United States applied tariffs in 2002–03, in two products the terms-of-trade gain exceeded the deadweight loss, so U.S. welfare rose due to the tariff, but in a third case the deadweight loss was larger, so U.S. welfare fell due to the tariff. Likewise for the tariff of 25% in 2018–19, in the first three products listed in Table 8-4 the terms-of-trade gain exceeded the deadweight loss, so U.S. welfare rose due to the tariff, but in the last two products the deadweight loss was larger, so U.S. welfare fell.[16] The first three products illustrate the large-country case for tariffs, in which the welfare of the importer can rise because of a tariff, whereas the last two products illustrate the small-country case, in which the importer loses from the tariff.

---

[16] For the fourth product listed in Table 8-4, ferrous waste and scrap, the optimal tariff is 6% in column (3) and the actual tariff under President Trump is 25% in column (5). In this case it is uncertain whether the deadweight loss from the tariff is greater or less than the terms of trade gain, so we do not know whether U.S. welfare rose or fell due to the tariff.

From the information given in Table 8-4, we do not know whether the United States gained or lost overall from the steel tariffs: that calculation would require adding up the gains and losses due to the tariff over all imported steel products, which we have not done. But we should keep in mind that any rise in U.S. welfare comes at the expense of exporting countries. Even if there was an overall terms-of-trade gain for the United States when adding up across all steel products, that gain would be at the expense of all the foreign countries exporting steel to the United States. As we have already discussed, in 2002–03 many steel exporters objected to the U.S. tariffs at the WTO and threatened to apply *retaliatory* tariffs of their own against U.S. exports. In 2018–19, China and other countries actually imposed retaliatory tariffs on U.S. exports. We now turn to an assessment of what the costs from those retaliatory tariffs were for the United States.

APPLICATION

U.S. and Foreign Tariffs Under President Trump Once Again

In the previous application, we saw that the United States should be treated as a small country—with a nearly flat (or perfectly elastic) foreign supply curve of exports—in some steel products, but with an upward-sloping foreign supply curve of exports in other steel products. This mixed result makes it hard to judge whether to treat the United States as a small country or a large country *overall*. Here, we turn to another research study that provides some guidance.

We have emphasized that the large-country argument for tariffs depends on what happens to the terms of trade, the ratio of export prices to import prices. To measure the Home terms of trade, we want to use the net-of-tariff import price P^* (received by Foreign firms) because that is the total amount transferred from Home to Foreign for each import. But what export price should we use? So far, we have just been treating the Home price of exports as constant, under the assumption that these Home *export* prices do not change due to the Home *import* tariff. But now we must drop that assumption, for two reasons.

First, the foreign retaliatory tariffs applied against the United States in 2018–19, listed in Table 8-2, panel (b), should be expected to lower U.S. export prices. To explain why, we go back to Figure 8-7. Think of the Home market—shown in panel (a)—as China or the European Union, and the Foreign country—with the upward sloping export supply curve X^* in panel (b)—as the United States. A tariff applied by China or the European Union against the United States lowers the world price from P^W to P^*. That world price is earned by U.S. exporting firms, which we are treating as the Foreign country. So this fall in U.S. export prices leads to a *fall* in the terms of trade and, therefore, a welfare loss for the United States.

There is also a second reason that we need to drop the assumption that U.S. export prices are constant, but this reason leads to the conclusion that the U.S. terms of trade might *rise*. To explain this second reason, start with the increase in U.S. import tariffs. Treating the United States as a large Home country (Figure 8-7), the price for Home firms goes up and they expand their output. Now go beyond this diagram and think about what happens in the labor market. As the price for Home firms goes up, they can expand their output only by hiring labor away from other industries, and that will result in an *increase in wages*. These wages are paid by firms in the import industries (who are expanding their output due to the tariff), but over time, the same wages have to be paid in export industries, too. As wages go up in the export industries, those firms will have to increase the prices that they charge. So by this logic, the *increase in wages will lead to a rise in export price and a rise in the U.S. terms of trade*. This rise in the terms of trade is different from what we show in Figure 8-7, where it comes from a fall in the price P^* of imports, and instead it occurs because of a rise in export prices. Despite this difference, the rise in export prices still leads to a rise in the terms of trade, which is a welfare gain. This linkage between increasing import tariffs and the rise in export prices is an example of a **general equilibrium effect**, because it is relies on the interaction between three markets (imports, the labor market, and exports).

To sum up, there are two reasons why U.S. export prices will change because of the rise in U.S. import tariffs, and they work in opposite directions: if retaliatory tariffs are applied by foreign countries, then U.S. export prices will fall; but as wages increase and spread from import to export industries, U.S. export prices will rise. Which one of these effects dominates? A detailed study of the U.S. and foreign retaliatory tariffs applied during 2018 and their effects on the prices of U.S. imports and exports finds that the *positive* influence of rising wages on export prices dominates, so that the U.S. terms of trade improve because of this general equilibrium effect. Nevertheless, this improvement in the terms of trade is *not enough* to compensate for the deadweight losses from the tariffs, so that the United States still loses overall.[17]

The results from this study are shown in Table 8-5. In contrast to our earlier discussion of the study that treated the United States as a small country (see **Application: U.S. and Foreign Tariffs Under President Trump, 2018–19**), this study treats the United States as a large country—with terms-of-trade effects—by allowing its export prices to change. But similar to that earlier study, we once again ignore the changes in producer surplus within the United States. In Table 8-5 we first report the portion of the consumer surplus loss that is caused by the higher import prices, as measured by the reduced area under the *import* demand curve, area $c + (b + d)$ in Figure 8-7, panel (b). That amount equals $68.8 billion in column (1) of Table 8-5, which is similar to the consumer loss of $52.8 billion shown in column (1) of Table 8-3, panel (a). The $52.8 billion loss comes from a different study but otherwise measures the same consumer cost due to rising import prices. Dividing the consumer cost of $68.8 billion by the number of households in the United States, we obtain $539 as the consumer cost per household. Again, this is similar to the consumer cost per household of $414 in Table 8-3, panel (a), which is obtained from a different study.

Next, in column (2) of Table 8-5, we list the $39.4 billion in tariff revenue collected during 2018 (area c in Figure 8-7). Then in column (3) we report the terms-of-trade gain

TABLE 8-5

Welfare Impact of 2018 U.S. and Foreign Tariffs, with Terms-of-Trade Effects This table shows the welfare impact of the 2018 tariffs on U.S. imports and of the foreign retaliatory tariffs on U.S. exports. These estimates treat the United States as a large country because it can influence *export* prices. U.S. export prices fall when foreign countries apply tariffs on those exports, but they rise when wages in the economy increase. Because the second effect is stronger than the first, the U.S. terms of trade rise. The net loss for the United States equals the consumer loss minus the tariff revenue collected plus the terms-of-trade gain.

	(1) Consumer Loss from Higher Import Prices	(2) Tariff Revenue	(3) Terms-of-Trade Gain	(4) Net Loss
Annual cost ($ billions)	68.8	39.4	21.6	7.8
Annual cost per household ($ billions)	539	309	169	61

Note: Per household numbers are calculated based on 127.6 million households in the United States in 2018.

Data from: Pablo D. Fajgelbaum, Pinelopi K. Goldberg, Patrick J. Kennedy, and Amit K. Khandelwal, February 2020, "The Return to Protectionism," Quarterly Journal of Economics, 135(1), 1–55.

[17] See Pablo D. Fajgelbaum, Pinelopi K Goldberg, Patrick J. Kennedy, and Amit K. Khandelwal, February 2020, "The Return to Protectionism," *Quarterly Journal of Economics*, 135(1), 1–55.

due to the rising export prices, which equaled $21.6 billion in 2018. By subtracting the tariff revenue gain and the terms-of-trade gain from the consumer loss, we obtain the *net loss* for the United States shown in column (4), which is $7.8 billion or $61 per household. This amount is much smaller than the total consumer loss from higher import prices shown in column (1), because the United States gained in its terms of trade and in tariff revenue. But the United States *still lost overall* from the 2018 tariffs because it faced retaliation from foreign counties that applied tariffs on U.S. exports. Those retaliatory tariffs prevented the United States from gaining from its own import tariffs applied during 2018 under President Trump.

5 Import Quotas

On January 1, 2005, China was poised to become the world's largest exporter of textiles and apparel. On that date, a system of worldwide import quotas known as the **Multifibre Arrangement (MFA)** was abolished. Import quotas are a restriction on the amount of a particular good that one country can purchase from another country. Under the MFA, begun in 1974, import quotas restricted the amount of nearly every textile and apparel product that was imported to Canada, the European countries, and the United States. These countries limited their textile imports to protect their own domestic firms producing those products. With the end of the MFA, China was ready to enjoy greatly increased exports—but this did not occur. The threat of import competition from China led the United States and Europe to negotiate *new* temporary import quotas with China, as we discuss in this section.

Besides the MFA, there are many other examples of import quotas. For example, since 1993 Europe had a quota on the imports of bananas that allowed for a greater number of bananas to enter from its former colonies in Africa than from Latin America. In 2005 that quota was simplified and converted into a tariff, even though that tariff still discriminated among countries based on their colonial past. Then, in 2009, Europe agreed to reduce the tariff on Latin American bananas, effectively bringing to an end this "banana war," which had lasted for more than 15 years. Another example is the quota on U.S. imports of cars from Japan, which began in 1981 and lasted through much of the 1980s. That quota limited the U.S. imports of Japanese cars to about 2 million vehicles per year, as we discuss in more detail below.

In this section, we explain how quotas affect the importing and exporting countries and examine the differences between quotas and tariffs. Like a tariff, an import quota often imposes a welfare cost on the importing country. But we will find that quotas can often lead to higher welfare losses for the importer than tariffs.

Import Quota in a Small Country

Applying an import quota for a small country is similar to applying a tariff, so we can use the graphs developed earlier in the chapter to analyze quotas, too.

Free-Trade Equilibrium In panel (a) of Figure 8-9, we show the demand curve D and supply curve S for Home. At the free-trade world price of P^W, Home quantity demanded is D_1 and quantity supplied is S_1, so imports are $M_1 = D_1 - S_1$. The import demand curve $M = D - S$ is shown in panel (b). The assumption that the Home country is small means that the fixed world price P^W is not affected by the import quota, so under free trade, the Foreign export supply curve X^* is a horizontal line at the world price P^W. The Home import demand curve M and Foreign export supply curve X^* intersect at point B, resulting in the free-trade level of imports, M_1.

FIGURE 8-9

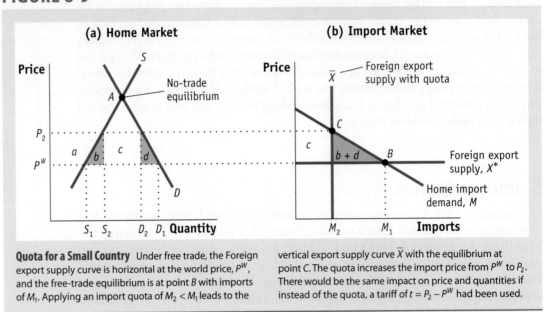

(a) Home Market

(b) Import Market

Quota for a Small Country Under free trade, the Foreign export supply curve is horizontal at the world price, P^W, and the free-trade equilibrium is at point B with imports of M_1. Applying an import quota of $M_2 < M_1$ leads to the vertical export supply curve $\overline{X}$ with the equilibrium at point C. The quota increases the import price from P^W to P_2. There would be the same impact on price and quantities if instead of the quota, a tariff of $t = P_2 - P^W$ had been used.

Effect of the Quota Now suppose that an import quota of $M_2 < M_1$ is imposed, meaning that the quantity imported cannot exceed this amount. This quota effectively establishes a vertical export supply curve labeled as $\overline{X}$ in panel (b), which fixes the import quantity at M_2. The vertical export supply curve now intersects import demand at point C, which establishes the Home price of P_2. In panel (a), the price of P_2 leads firms to increase the quantity supplied to S_2 and consumers to decrease their quantity demanded to D_2.

The import quota therefore leads to an increase in the Home price and a reduction in Home imports, just like a tariff. Furthermore, notice that there would be an equivalent effect on the import price and quantity if instead of the quota, the government had imposed an import tariff of $t = P_2 - P^W$. That is, the tariff of $t = P_2 - P^W$ would raise the Home price to P_2 and reduce imports to the level M_2. We conclude that for every level of the import quota, there is an **equivalent import tariff** that would lead to the same price and quantity of imports in Home.[18]

Effect on Welfare As we have shown, the quota leads to an increase in the Home price. The rise in the price for consumers leads to a fall in consumer surplus. That fall is measured by the area between the prices P_2 and P^W and to the left of the demand curve, which is the area $(a + b + c + d)$ in panel (a) of Figure 8-9. On the other hand, the increase in the price facing Home producers leads to a gain in producer surplus. That gain is measured by the area between the prices P_2 and P^W and to the left of the supply curve, which is the area a in Figure 8-9(a). These two welfare effects are the same as would occur under a tariff.

The quota and tariff differ, however, in terms of area c, which would be collected as government revenue under a tariff. Under the quota, this area equals the difference between the domestic price P_2 and the world price P^W, times the quantity of imports M_2. Therefore, whoever is actually importing the good will be able to earn the difference between the world price P^W and the higher Home price P_2 by selling the imports in the Home market. We call the difference between these two prices the

[18] As we show in the next chapter, this conclusion depends on our assumption of perfect competition and does not hold without that assumption.

rent associated with the quota, and hence the area *c* represents the total **quota rents**. There are four possible ways that these quota rents can be allocated:

1. Giving the Quota to Home Firms First, **quota licenses** (i.e., permits to import the quantity allowed under the quota system) can be given to Home firms, which are then able to import at the world price P^W *and sell locally at P_2*, earning the difference between these as rents. An example of this is the dairy industry in the United States, in which U.S. producers of cheese receive licenses to import from abroad. With home firms earning the rents *c*, the net effect of the quota on Home welfare is

Fall in consumer surplus:	$-(a + b + c + d)$
Rise in producer surplus:	$+a$
Quota rents earned in Home:	$+c$
Net effect on Home's welfare:	$-(b + d)$

We see from this calculation that the net effect on Home welfare is a loss of amount $(b + d)$. That loss is the same as what we found in Section 3 of this chapter for the loss of a tariff in a small country. As in that section, we still refer to $(b + d)$ as a deadweight loss.

2. Rent Seeking One complication of simply giving valuable quota licenses to Home firms is that these firms may engage in some kind of inefficient activities to obtain them. For example, suppose that Home firms are producing batteries and import the chemical needed as an input. If licenses for the imported chemicals are allocated in proportion to each firm's production of batteries in the previous years, then the Home firms will likely produce more batteries than they can sell (and at lower quality) *just to obtain the import licenses for the following year*. Alternatively, firms might engage in bribery or other lobbying activities to obtain the licenses. These kinds of inefficient activities done to obtain quota licenses are called **rent seeking**. It has been suggested that the waste of resources devoted to rent-seeking activities could be as large as the value of rents themselves so that the area *c* would be wasted rather than accrue to Home firms. If rent seeking occurs, the welfare loss due to the quota would be

Fall in consumer surplus:	$-(a + b + c + d)$
Rise in producer surplus:	$+a$
Net effect on Home's welfare:	$-(b + c + d)$

The waste of resources due to rent seeking leads to a fall in Home welfare of $(b + c + d)$, which is larger than that for a tariff. It is often thought that rent seeking is more severe in some developing countries where rules are not well enforced and officials are willing to take bribes in exchange for the licenses.

3. Auctioning the Quota A third possibility for allocating the rents that come from the quota is for the government of the importing country to auction off the quota licenses. This occurred in Australia and New Zealand during the 1980s. In Australia, the auctions covered imports of textiles, apparel, footwear, and motor vehicles. The quota auctions used for imports of textiles and apparel in Australia were an alternative to the Multifibre Arrangement (MFA). Auctions of import quotas have also been proposed in the United States but have never actually occurred.[19] In a well-organized, competitive auction, the revenue collected should exactly equal the value of the rents, so that area *c* would be earned by the Home government. Using the auction method to allocate quota rents, the net loss in domestic welfare due to the quota becomes

---

[19] The proposals to auction import quotas in the United States were made during the 1980s; see C. Fred Bergsten, 1987, *Auction Quotas and United States Trade Policy* (Washington, D.C.: Peterson Institute for International Economics). Government auctions have occurred in the United States for bandwidth in radio frequencies and also for offshore oil drilling.

Fall in consumer surplus:	$-(a+b+c+d)$
Rise in producer surplus:	$+a$
Auction revenue earned in Home:	$+c$
Net effect on Home welfare:	$-(b+d)$

The net effect on Home welfare in this case is the deadweight loss of $(b+d)$, which is once again the same loss as incurred from a tariff.

4. "Voluntary" Export Restraint The final possibility for allocating quota rents is for the government of the importing country to give authority for implementing the quota to the government of the *exporting* country. Because the exporting country allocates the quota among its own producers, this is sometimes called a **"voluntary" export restraint (VER)**, or a **"voluntary" restraint agreement (VRA)**. In the 1980s the United States used this type of arrangement to restrict Japanese automobile imports. In that case, Japan's Ministry of International Trade and Industry (MITI), a government agency that implements Japan's trade policies, told each Japanese auto manufacturer how much it could export to the United States. In this case, the quota rents are earned by foreign producers, so the loss in Home welfare equals

Fall in consumer surplus:	$-(a+b+c+d)$
Rise in producer surplus:	$+a$
Net effect on Home's welfare:	$-(b+c+d)$

The VER gives a higher net loss $(b+c+d)$ for the importer than does a tariff because the quota rents are earned by foreign exporters. This result raises the question of why VERs are used at all. One answer is that when the quota rents are given to firms in the exporting country, that country is much less likely to retaliate by adopting import tariffs or quotas of its own. In other words, the transfer of quota rents to the exporter becomes a way to avoid a tariff or quota war.

Costs of Import Quotas in the United States Table 8-6 presents some estimates of the home deadweight losses, along with the quota rents, for major U.S. quotas in the years around 1985. In all cases except dairy, the rents were earned by foreign exporters. We discuss the case of automobiles in the next chapter, for which the quota rents earned by foreigners range from $2 billion to $8 billion. Textiles and apparel also had very large quota rents and U.S. deadweight losses (about $5 billion each)

TABLE 8-6

Annual Cost of U.S. Import Protection ($ billions) Shown here are estimates of the deadweight losses and quota rents due to U.S. import quotas in the 1980s, for the years around 1985. Many of these quotas are no longer in place today.

	U.S. Deadweight Loss (area $b+d$)	Quota Rents (area c)
Automobiles	0.2–1.2	2.2–7.9
Dairy	1.4	0.25*
Steel	0.1–0.3	0.7–2.0
Sugar	0.1	0.4–1.3
Textiles and apparel	4.9–5.9	4.0–6.1
Import tariffs	1.2–3.4	0
Total	7.9–12.3	7.3–17.3

*In dairy the quota rents are earned by U.S. importers and so are not included in the total.

Data from: Robert Feenstra, Summer 1992, "How Costly Is Protectionism?" Journal of Economic Perspectives, 159–178.

under the MFA. In addition, the MFA imposed large losses on the exporting countries, due to rent-seeking activities by exporters to obtain the quota permits. Adding up the costs shown in Table 8-6, the total U.S. deadweight loss from these quotas was in the range of $8 billion to $12 billion annually in the mid-1980s, whereas the quota rents transferred to foreigners were another $7 billion to $17 billion annually.

Some, but not all, of these costs for the United States are no longer relevant today. The quota in automobiles ceased being applied after 1987 because Japanese producers built plants in the United States and therefore reduced their imports. The quotas in the steel industry were replaced by the safeguard tariffs that President Bush temporarily imposed from 2002 to 2003. But the quotas used in sugar remain. Finally, while the MFA expired on January 1, 2005, it was replaced by a new set of quotas with China that were in place until 2008. There were continuing losses for the United States due to quotas in the textile and apparel industries, as we discuss in the next application.

APPLICATION

China and the Multifibre Arrangement

One of the founding principles of GATT was that countries should not use quotas to restrict imports (see Article XI of **Side Bar: Key Provisions of the GATT**). The Multifibre Arrangement (MFA), organized under the auspices of the GATT in 1974, was a major exception to that principle and allowed the industrial countries to restrict imports of textile and apparel products from the developing countries. Importing countries could join the MFA and arrange quotas bilaterally (i.e., after negotiating with exporters) or unilaterally (on their own). In practice, the import quotas established under the MFA were very detailed and specified the amount of each textile and apparel product that each developing country could sell to countries such as Canada, Europe, and the United States.

Although the amount of the quotas was occasionally revised upward, it did not keep up with the increasing ability of new supplying countries to sell. Under the Uruguay Round of WTO negotiations held from 1986 to 1994, developing countries were able to negotiate an end to this system of import quotas. The MFA expired on January 1, 2005. The biggest potential supplier of textile and apparel products was China, so the expiration of the MFA meant that China could export as much as it wanted to other countries—or so it thought. The potential for a huge increase in exports from China posed a problem for many other countries. Some developing countries expected that rising exports from China would compete with their own export of apparel items, on which many workers depended for their livelihood. The large producers in importing countries were also concerned with the potential rise in Chinese exports because it could lead to the loss of jobs for their own workers in textiles and apparel.

Growth in Exports from China Immediately after January 1, 2005, exports of textiles and apparel from China grew rapidly. For example, exports of Chinese tights and pantyhose to the European Union increased by 2,000% in January and February, as compared with a year earlier; imports of pullovers and jerseys from China jumped nearly 1,000%; and imports of trousers more than tripled. Overall in 2005, China's textile and apparel imports to the United States rose by more than 40% as compared with the year before, as shown in Figure 8-10, where we include the top 20 exporters to the U.S. market.[20] In panel (a), we show the change in the value of textile and apparel imports from each country. The surge of imports from China came

---

[20] Figure 8-10 and the welfare estimates in the following paragraphs are from James Harrigan and Geoffrey Barrows, 2009, "Testing the Theory of Trade Policy: Evidence from the Abrupt End of the Multifibre Arrangement," *The Review of Economics and Statistics*, 91(2), 282–294.

FIGURE 8-10

(a) Change in the Value of Exports

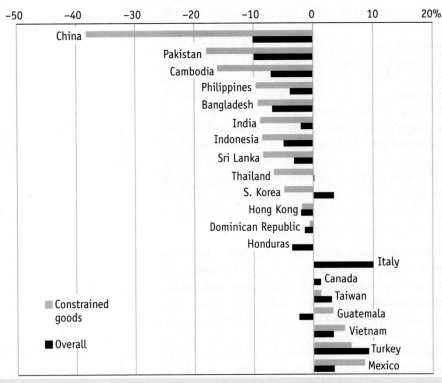

(b) Change in the Price of Exports

Changes in Clothing and Textile Exports to the United States after the MFA, 2004–05 After the expiration of the Multifibre Arrangement (MFA), the value of clothing and textile exports from China rose dramatically, as shown in panel (a). This reflects the surge in the quantity of exports that were formerly constrained under the MFA as well as a shift to Chinese exports from other, higher-cost producers such as Hong Kong, Taiwan, and South Korea. In panel (b), we see that the prices of goods constrained by the MFA typically fell by more than the average change in export prices after the MFA's expiry. This is exactly what our theory of quotas predicts: the removal of quotas lowers import prices for consumers.

Data from: James Harrigan and Geoffrey Barrows, 2009, "Testing the Theory of Trade Policy: Evidence from the Abrupt End of the Multifibre Arrangement," Review of Economics and Statistics, 91(2), 282–294.

at the expense of some higher-cost exporters, such as South Korea, Hong Kong, and Taiwan, whose exports to the United States declined by 10% to 20%.

In panel (b) of Figure 8-10, we show the percentage change in the prices of textiles and apparel products from each country, depending on whether the products were "constrained goods," subject to the MFA quota before January 1, 2005. China has the largest drop in prices from 2004 to 2005, 38% in the "constrained goods" categories. Many other countries also experienced a substantial fall in their prices due to the end of the MFA quota: 18% for Pakistan; 16% for Cambodia; and 8% to 9% for the Philippines, Bangladesh, India, Indonesia, and Sri Lanka. A drop in price due to the removal of the import quota is exactly what we predict from the theory, as we move from the price P_2 in Figure 8-9 to the free-trade price P^W. Surprisingly, a few countries in Figure 8-10 show increases in their prices, such as Mexico. However, less than 1% of Mexico's sales of textiles and apparel to the United States were constrained by the quota, so that price increase does not appear to be due to the removal of the MFA.

Welfare Cost of MFA Given the drop in prices in 2005 from countries selling to the United States, it is possible to estimate the welfare loss due to the MFA. The United States did not auction the quota licenses for textiles and apparel, so the quota rents were earned by foreign exporting firms. That means the welfare loss for the United States due to the MFA is the area $(b + c + d)$ in Figure 8-9. Using the price drops from 2004 to 2005, that area is estimated to be in the range of $6.5 billion to $16.2 billion in 2005.[21] The simple average of these estimates is $11.4 billion as the total cost to the United States. To put that welfare loss in perspective, there were 111 million households in the United States in 2005, and the typical household spent about $1,400 on apparel. Dividing the loss of $11.4 billion by the 111 million households, we obtain about $100 per household, or 7% of their annual spending on apparel as the welfare cost of the MFA.[22]

Import Quality Besides the overall decline in prices, there was also an interesting pattern to the price drops: the prices of textile and apparel products dropped the most (in percentage terms) for the lower-priced items. So, an inexpensive T-shirt coming from China and priced at $1 had a price drop of more than 38% (more than 38¢), whereas a more expensive item priced at $10 experienced a price drop of less than 38% (less than $3.80). As a result, U.S. demand shifted toward the lower-priced items imported from China: there was "quality downgrading" in the exports from China.

To understand why this quality downgrading occurred, it is easiest to think about the problem in reverse: when a quota like the MFA is applied, what is the effect on quality? The MFA, like most other quotas, was applied to the *quantity* of the import sent to each country: it was applied to yards of cloth, or number of shirts, or dozens of pairs of socks, and so on. Faced with a quota of that type, the exporting firm would have an incentive to *upgrade* the type of cloth, shirts, or socks that it sells, since selling a higher value for the same quantity will still meet the quota limitation. So when the MFA starts, we expect to see "quality upgrading" in the exports for each country. By the same logic, when the MFA was removed, there was "quality downgrading" in the exports from China to the United States and exports from other countries, too.

Reaction of the United States and Europe The surge in exports from China to the United States and Europe was short-lived, however. The European Union

---

[21] Notice that this range of estimates for 2005 is comparable to (but wider than) the range of estimates for the welfare costs of textiles and apparel in Table 8-6, which is $8.9 billion to $12 billion for 1985, obtained by adding up the deadweight loss and the quota rents.

[22] In comparison, there were 737,000 U.S. workers in the textile and apparel industries in 2004, with an average annual salary of $31,500. If we divide the total loss of $11.4 billion by all these workers, we obtain about $15,500 per job protected in the U.S. industry, or about one-half of the annual salary of each worker.

threatened to impose new quotas on Chinese exports, and in response, China agreed on June 11, 2005, to "voluntary" export restraints that would limit its growth of textile exports to about 10% per year through the end of 2008. For the United States, the ability to negotiate a new system of quotas with China had been guaranteed by a special agreement with China when it joined the WTO in 2001. Under this agreement, China was limited to a 7.5% annual growth in its textile exports to the United States, from 2005 to 2008. This temporary quota expired at the end of 2008, at which time we might have expected the U.S. textile and apparel industry to renew its call for quota protection once again. But because of the worldwide recession, Chinese exports in this industry were much lower in 2009 than they had been in earlier years. For that reason, China indicated that it would not accept any further limitation on its ability to export textile and apparel products to the United States and to Europe, and both these quotas expired.

6 Conclusions

A tariff on imports is the most commonly used trade policy tool. In this chapter, we have studied the effect of tariffs on consumers and producers in both importing and exporting countries. We have looked at several different cases. First, we assumed that the importing country is so small that it does not affect the world price of the imported good. In that case, the price faced by consumers and producers in the importing country will rise by the full amount of the tariff. With a rise in the consumer price, there is a drop in consumer surplus; and with a rise in the producer price, there is a gain in producer surplus. In addition, the government collects revenue from the tariff. When we add together all these effects—the drop in consumer surplus, gain in producer surplus, and government revenue collected—we still get a *net loss* for the importing country. We have referred to that loss as the deadweight loss resulting from the tariff.

The fact that a small importing country always has a net loss from a tariff explains why most economists oppose the use of tariffs. Still, this result leaves open the question of why tariffs are used. One reason that tariffs are used, despite their deadweight loss, is that they are an easy way for governments to raise revenue, especially in developing countries. A second reason is politics: the government might care more about protecting firms than avoiding losses for consumers. A third reason is that the small-country assumption may not hold in practice: countries may be large enough importers of a product that a tariff will affect its world price. In this large-country case, the decrease in imports demanded due to the tariff causes foreign exporters to lower their prices. Of course, consumer and producer prices in the importing country still go up, since these prices include the tariff, but they rise by less than the full amount of the tariff. We have shown that if we add up the drop in consumer surplus, gain in producer surplus, and government revenue collected, it is possible for a small tariff to generate welfare gains for the importing country.

Still, any gain for the importer in this large-country case comes at the expense of the foreign exporters. For that reason, the use of a tariff in the large-country case is sometimes called a "beggar thy neighbor" policy. We have found that the drop in the exporter's welfare due to the tariff is greater than the gain in the importer's welfare. Therefore, the world loses overall because of the tariff. This is another reason that most economists oppose the use of tariffs.

In addition to an import tariff, we have also studied import quotas, which restrict the quantity of imports into a country. The WTO has tried to limit the use of import quotas and has been somewhat successful. For example, the Multifibre Arrangement (MFA) was a complex system of quotas intended to restrict the import of textiles and apparel into many industrialized countries. It was supposed to end on January 1, 2005, but both the United States and the European Union then established new quotas against imports of textiles and apparel from China, which expired at the end of 2008. The United States continues to have a quota on imports of sugar, and up until very recently, the European Union had a quota and then a discriminatory tariff on imports of bananas (that "banana war" has now ended). These are some of the best-known import quotas, and there are other examples, too.

Under perfect competition, the effect of applying an import quota is similar to the effect of applying an import tariff: they both lead to an increase in the domestic price in the importing country, with a loss for consumers and a gain for producers. One difference, however, is that under a tariff the government in the importing country collects revenue, whereas under a quota, whoever is able to bring in the import earns the difference between the domestic and world prices, called "quota rents." For example, if firms in the importing country have the licenses to bring in imports, then they earn the quota rents. Alternatively, if resources are wasted by firms trying to capture these rents, then there is an additional deadweight loss. It is more common, however, for the foreign exporters to earn the quota rents, as occurs under a "voluntary" export restraint, administered by the foreign government. A fourth possibility is that the government in the importing country auctions the quota licenses, in which case it earns the equivalent of the quota rents as auction revenue; this case is identical to the tariff in its welfare outcome.

KEY POINTS

1. The government of a country can use laws and regulations, called "trade policies," to affect international trade flows. An import tariff, which is a tax at the border, is the most commonly used trade policy.

2. The rules governing trade policies in most countries are outlined by the General Agreement on Tariffs and Trade (GATT), an international legal convention adopted after World War II to promote increased international trade. Since 1995 the new name for the GATT is the World Trade Organization (WTO).

3. In a small country, the quantity of imports demanded is assumed to be very small compared with the total world market. For this reason, the importer faces a fixed world price. In that case, the price faced by consumers and producers in the importing country will rise by the full amount of the tariff.

4. The use of a tariff by a small importing country always leads to a net loss in welfare. We call that loss the "deadweight loss."

5. In a large country, the decrease in imports demanded due to the tariff causes foreign exporters to lower their prices. Consumer and producer prices in the importing country still go up, since these prices include the tariff, but they rise by less than the full amount of the tariff (since the exporter price falls).

6. The use of a tariff for a large country can lead to a net gain in welfare because the price charged by the exporter has fallen; this is a terms-of-trade gain for the importer.

7. The "optimal tariff" is the tariff amount that maximizes welfare for the importer. For a small country, the optimal tariff is zero since any tariff leads to a net loss. For a large country, however, the optimal tariff is positive.

8. The formula for the optimal tariff states that it depends inversely on the foreign export supply elasticity. If the foreign export supply elasticity is high, then the optimal tariff is low, but if the foreign export supply elasticity is low, then the optimal tariff is high.

9. Import quotas restrict the quantity of a particular import, thereby increasing the domestic price, increasing domestic production, and creating a benefit for those who are allowed to import the quantity allotted. These benefits are called "quota rents."

10. Assuming perfectly competitive markets for goods, quotas are similar to tariffs since the restriction in the amount imported leads to a higher domestic price. However, the welfare implications of quotas are different from those of tariffs depending on who earns the quota rents. These rents might be earned by firms in the importing country (if they have the licenses to import the good), or by firms in the exporting country (if the foreign government administers the quota), or by the government in the importing country (if it auctions off the quota licenses). The last case is most similar to a tariff, since the importing government earns the revenue.

KEY TERMS

import tariff, p. 235
political economy, p. 236
trade policy, p. 236
import quota, p. 236
export subsidy, p. 237
dumping, p. 238
safeguard provision, p. 238
escape clause, p. 238
regional trade agreements, p. 239
free-trade areas, p. 239
customs unions, p. 239
consumer surplus, p. 240

producer surplus, p. 240
small country, p. 241
import demand curve, p. 243
deadweight loss, p. 247
production loss, p. 247
consumption loss, p. 247
dispute settlement procedure,
  p. 250
tariff war, p. 251
large country, p. 256
terms of trade, p. 258
terms-of-trade gain, p. 259

optimal tariff, p. 259
general equilibrium effect, p. 264
Multifibre Arrangement (MFA),
  p. 265
equivalent import tariff, p. 266
quota rents, p. 267
quota licenses, p. 267
rent seeking, p. 267
"voluntary" export restraint (VER),
  p. 268
"voluntary" restraint agreement
  (VRA), p. 268

PROBLEMS

1. **📶 Discovering Data** At the opening of this chapter, we referred to the events of May 1995, when the United States considered putting tariffs on imports of luxury cars from Japan. Specifically, on May 16, 1995, U.S. Trade Representative Mickey Kantor announced that the United States would impose trade sanctions against Japan, targeting 13 Japanese import vehicles for 100% tariffs valued at $5.9 billion annually. Those targeted vehicles included all Lexus models and several Acura and Infiniti models. To determine how U.S. interest rates reacted to this announcement, use the FRED database at: https://research.stlouisfed.org/fred2/.

   a. Search for "Interest rate on US treasury bills," and choose the 3-Month Treasury Bill: Secondary Market Rate, and Weekly (which you will find under "other formats"). Adjust the graph to see what happened to the interest rate in the week including May 16, 1995. How does this movement in the interest rate compare with neighboring weeks?

   b. What type of retaliation by the government of Japan for the proposed tariff can explain this change in interest rates?

   c. About one month later, President Clinton announced that the two countries had reached an agreement, which ended the threat of the tariffs being imposed. What happened to the interest rates during the month of June?

2. The following questions refer to **Side Bar: Key Provisions of the GATT.**

   a. If the United States applies a tariff to a particular product (e.g., steel) imported from one country, what is the implication for its steel tariffs applied to all other countries according to the "most favored nation" principle?

   b. Is Article XXIV an exception to most favored nation treatment? Explain why or why not.

   c. Under the GATT articles, instead of a tariff, can a country impose a quota (quantitative restriction) on the number of goods imported? What is an exception to this rule that was discussed in this chapter?

3. Consider a small country applying a tariff t to imports of a good like that represented in Figure 8-5.

   a. Suppose that the country decides to reduce its tariff to t'. Redraw the graphs for the Home and import markets and illustrate this change. What happens to the quantity and price of goods produced in Home? What happens to the quantity of imports?

   b. Are there gains or losses to domestic consumer surplus due to the reduction in tariff? Are there gains or losses to domestic producer surplus due to the reduction in tariff? How is government revenue affected by the policy change? Illustrate these on your graphs.

   c. What is the overall gain or loss in welfare due to the policy change?

4. Consider a large country applying a tariff t to imports of a good like that represented in Figure 8-7.

   a. How does the export supply curve in panel (b) compare with that in the small-country case? Explain why these are different.

   b. Explain how the tariff affects the price paid by consumers in the *importing* country and the price received by producers in the *exporting* country. Use graphs to illustrate how the prices are affected if (i) the export supply curve is very elastic (flat) or (ii) the export supply curve is inelastic (steep).

5. Consider a large country applying a tariff t to imports of a good like that represented in Figure 8-7. How does the size of the terms-of-trade gain compare with the size of the deadweight loss when (i) the tariff is very small and (ii) the tariff is very large? Use graphs to illustrate your answer.

6. a. If the foreign export supply is perfectly elastic, what is the optimal tariff Home should apply to increase welfare? Explain.

   b. If the foreign export supply is less than perfectly elastic, what is the formula for the optimal tariff Home should apply to increase welfare?

   c. What happens to Home's welfare if it applies a tariff higher than the optimal tariff?

WORK IT OUT   Achieve | interactive activity

7. Rank the following in ascending order of Home welfare and justify your answers. If two items are equivalent, indicate this accordingly.

   a. Tariff of t in a small country corresponding to the quantity of imports M

   b. Tariff of t in a large country corresponding to the same quantity of imports M

   c. Tariff of t' in a large country corresponding to the quantity of imports $M' > M$

8. Rank the following in ascending order of Home welfare and justify your answers. If two items are equivalent, indicate this accordingly.

   a. Tariff of t in a small country corresponding to the quantity of imports M

   b. Quota with the same imports M in a small country, with quota licenses distributed to Home firms and no rent seeking

   c. Quota of M in a small country with quota licenses auctioned to Home firms

   d. Quota of M in a small country with the quota given to the exporting firms

   e. Quota of M in a small country with quota licenses distributed to rent-seeking Home firms

9. Why did President George W. Bush suspend the U.S. tariffs on steel 17 months ahead of schedule?

10. What provision of U.S. trade law was used by President Trump to apply a tariff on steel and aluminum? What provision of U.S. trade was used to justify the tariffs on goods imported from China? Do these provisions make it easier or harder to apply a tariff than Section 201?

11. Suppose Home is a small country. Use the graphs below to answer the questions.

(a) Home Market

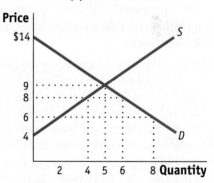

(b) Import Market

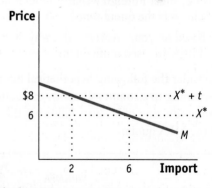

   a. Calculate Home consumer surplus and producer surplus in the absence of trade.

   b. Now suppose that Home engages in trade and faces the world price, $P^W = \$6$. Determine the consumer and producer surplus under free trade. Does Home benefit from trade? Explain.

   c. Concerned about the welfare of the local producers, the Home government imposes a tariff in the amount of $2 (i.e., $t = \$2$). Determine the net effect of the tariff on the Home economy.

12. Refer to the graphs in Problem 11. Suppose that instead of a tariff, Home applies an import quota limiting the amount Foreign can sell to 2 units.

   a. Determine the net effect of the import quota on the Home economy if the quota licenses are allocated to local producers.

   b. Calculate the net effect of the import quota on Home welfare if the quota rents are earned by Foreign exporters.

   c. How do your answers to parts (a) and (b) compare with part (c) of Problem 11?

13. Consider a small country applying a tariff t as in Figure 8-5. Instead of a tariff on *all* units imported, however, we will suppose that the tariff applies only to imports *in excess* of some quota amount M' (which is less than the total imports). This is called a "tariff-rate quota" (TRQ) and is commonly used on agricultural goods, including sugar imports into the United States.

   a. Redraw Figure 8-5, introducing the quota amount M'. Remember that the tariff applies only to imports *in excess* of this amount. With this in mind, what is the rectangle of tariff revenue collected? What is the rectangle of quota rents? Explain briefly what quota rents mean in this scenario.

   b. How does the use of a TRQ rather than a tariff at the same rate affect Home welfare? How does the TRQ, as compared with a tariff at the same rate, affect Foreign welfare? Does it depend on who gets the quota rents?

   c. Based on your answer to (b), why do you think TRQs are used quite often?

14. Consider the following hypothetical information pertaining to a country's imports, consumption, and production of T-shirts following the removal of the MFA quota:

	With MFA	Without MFA (Free Trade)
World price ($/shirt)	2.00	2.00
Domestic price ($/shirt)	3.00	2.00
Domestic consumption (million shirts/year)	200	250
Domestic production (million shirts/year)	150	100
Imports (million shirts/year)	50	150

   a. Graph the effects of the quota removal on domestic consumption and production.

   b. Determine the gain in consumer surplus from the removal of the quota.

   c. Determine the loss in producer surplus from the removal of the quota.

   d. Calculate the quota rents that were earned under the quota.

   e. Determine how much the country has gained from removal of the quota.

15. Suppose that a producer in China is constrained by the MFA to sell a certain number of shirts, regardless of the type of shirt. For a T-shirt selling for $2.00 under free trade, the MFA quota leads to an increase in price to $3.00. For a dress shirt selling for $10.00, the MFA will also lead to an increase in price.

	With MFA	Without MFA (Free Trade)
Domestic price of T-shirt ($/shirt)	3.00	2.00
Domestic price of dress shirt ($/shirt)	?	10.00

   a. Suppose that the MFA leads to an increase in the price of dress shirts from $10 to $12. Will the producer be willing to export both T-shirts and dress shirts? (Remember that only a fixed number of shirts can be exported, but of any type.) Explain why or why not.

   b. For the producer to be willing to sell *both* T-shirts and dress shirts, what must be the price of dress shirts under the MFA?

   c. Based on your answer to part (b), calculate the price of dress shirts *relative* to T-shirts before and after the MFA. What has happened to the relative price due to the MFA?

   d. Based on your answer to part (c), what will happen to the relative demand in the United States for dress shirts versus T-shirts from this producer due to the MFA?

   e. Thinking now of the total export bundle of this producer, does the MFA lead to quality upgrading or downgrading? How about the removal of the MFA?

9

Import Tariffs and Quotas Under Imperfect Competition

Today I have signed into law H.R. 644, the Trade Facilitation and Trade Enforcement Act of 2015, an Act that is an important milestone to the overall U.S. trade agenda and that will help our workers and businesses to compete fairly with the rest of the world.

President Barack Obama, February 24, 2016

If the case of heavyweight motorcycles is to be considered the only successful escape-clause [tariff], it is because it caused little harm and it helped Harley-Davidson get a bank loan so it could diversify.

John Suomela, chief economist, U.S. International Trade Commission, 1993[1]

Questions to Consider

1 Can governments use trade policy to give home firms a strategic advantage in their markets?

2 Why would foreign firms dump their products by exporting them at a price below their costs?

3 Is there an argument for using infant industry protection, and has it worked in practice?

In a recent survey of economists, 87% agreed with the statement "tariffs and import quotas usually reduce general economic welfare."[2] It is no exaggeration to say that this belief has been a guiding principle of the international institutions established to govern the world economy since World War II, especially the World Trade Organization. That belief is the message from Chapter 8, which showed that the application of tariffs and quotas will reduce welfare for a small country. We also found that although a large country might gain from the application of a tariff, any such gain would come at the expense of its trading partners, so the *world* as a whole would still lose. It follows there is really no good economic argument for the use of tariffs or quotas, though as we discussed in Chapter 8, they are sometimes used for political reasons to help a candidate obtain votes or campaign contributions from a particular industry or region of the country.

Still, you might wonder if that is really the whole story. As we discussed in Chapter 1, from 1860 to 1900 the United States had average tariff rates that fluctuated between 20% and 50%. Similarly, countries that industrialized after World War II, such as Japan, South Korea, and Taiwan, started with high tariffs and quotas that were eliminated only slowly and incompletely. More recently, China had very high tariffs before

---

[1] Cited in Douglas A. Irwin, 2002, *Free Trade under Fire* (Princeton, NJ: Princeton University Press), pp. 136–137.
[2] Robert Whaples and Jac C. Heckelman, 2005, "Public Choice Economics: Where Is There Consensus?" *American Economist*, 49(1), 66–78.

it joined the World Trade Organization in 2001, and it still applies tariffs on some imports that are well above those in the United States or Europe.

These observations can lead us to wonder if there are any arguments in favor of tariffs that are missing from our treatment in Chapter 8, which dealt with tariffs under perfect competition. Do the effects of trade policies differ when an industry is young and there are only a small number of producers, so markets are imperfectly competitive? In mature industries with only a small number of producers, can a government help these firms gain an advantage in international markets? We explore the answers to these questions in this chapter and the next.

These questions received a lot of attention from trade economists in the 1980s, in a body of research that became known as **strategic trade policy**. The idea of strategic trade policy was that government trade policies could give a strategic advantage to Home firms in imperfectly competitive markets that would enable them to compete more effectively with Foreign firms. Initially, the economists writing in this area thought that their research would challenge the idea that free trade is best for a country. As more research was done, however, supporters of strategic trade policy theory realized that the new arguments were limited in their scope: in some cases, the use of tariffs or quotas would backfire and harm the Home country, and in other cases, their use would give results similar to the large-country case we analyzed in the previous chapter. We will give examples of both outcomes.

When countries use strategic trade policies to try to give advantage to their own firms, other countries trading with them often regard these policies as "unfair" and may respond to these policies in some way. This is the idea behind the first quotation at the beginning of the chapter from President Barack Obama, who announced in 2016 the enactment of the bipartisan bill called the Trade Facilitation and Trade Enforcement Act of 2015. The goal of that bill was to reinforce trade policies directed against countries that are thought to be competing unfairly in the U.S. market. In Chapter 8 we described several U.S. trade laws that allowed recent tariffs to be applied by the United States (especially against China) in industries such as washing machines and steel. In this chapter we discuss other examples of tariffs, including those imposed by the United States and the European Union against imports of solar panels from China.

To explore strategic trade policy, we need to abandon the assumption that markets are perfectly competitive, an assumption that was central to the treatment of tariffs and quotas in Chapter 8. Instead, we need to allow for imperfect competition, which we defined in Chapter 6 as the market conditions that exist when firms have influence over the price that they charge and can charge a price above marginal costs for their goods. Recall that imperfect competition can arise when there is a small number of producers, as in a monopoly or oligopoly, or if products are differentiated from one another, as we assumed in our model of monopolistic competition in Chapter 6. In this chapter, we use the extreme case of a single producer—a Home or Foreign monopoly—to see how tariffs and quotas affect prices, trade, and welfare. In practice, imperfectly competitive industries often have more than one firm, but focusing on the monopoly case will give us the clearest sense of how the effects of these policy tools differ from those under perfect competition.

We begin by analyzing the effects of tariffs and quotas under the assumption of a Home monopoly. In the perfectly competitive framework of Chapter 8, quotas and tariffs had an equivalent impact on Home prices. In imperfectly competitive markets, however, these two trade policy instruments have *different* effects on Home prices, so the choice of which, if any, trade policy to implement must take these different effects into account.

The second case we analyze is a Foreign monopoly that exports to the Home market. We analyze the effect of an import tariff applied by the Home country and find that the tariff has effects similar to those in the large-country case under perfect competition (described in Chapter 8) in which the Home country can potentially gain from the tariff. A specific example of a Foreign monopolist is the Foreign **discriminating monopoly**, which charges a lower price to Home than to firms in its own local market and is therefore **dumping** its product into the Home market. A tariff applied against a Foreign discriminating monopoly is called an **antidumping duty**. Because of the special way in which antidumping duties are applied, they are unlikely to result in gains for the Home country and instead result in losses.

The final case we analyze is an **infant industry** at Home, by which we mean an industry that is too young to have achieved its lowest costs. Often these industries comprise a small number of firms. In our analysis, we assume there is only one firm, so it is again a case of Home monopoly. The special feature of this Home firm is that it cannot compete effectively under free trade, because the world price is below its minimum cost of production today, so the firm makes a loss. But by increasing its output today, the firm will learn how to produce its output more efficiently, and therefore have lower costs in the future, so that it can compete profitably at the world price. One way to achieve this end is for the government to step in and offer assistance—such as with a tariff—that will help the firm to survive long enough to achieve lower, world-competitive costs. This policy is called an "infant industry tariff."

Although we include the infant industry tariff argument in this chapter on strategic trade policy, it is actually a much older argument, dating back to the writings of John Stuart Mill (1806–1873). We will give several examples of potential infant industries, including the computer industry in Brazil, which was protected from import competition from 1977 to the early 1990s. We also analyze the tariff used in the 1980s to protect Harley-Davidson motorcycles in the United States, and tariffs and quotas used in the automotive industry in China. The key policy question for an infant industry is whether a government should impose a temporary tariff today to protect infant industry from competition, thereby keeping it in business long enough for it to learn how to achieve lower costs (and thus competitive prices) in the future.

1 Tariffs and Quotas with Home Monopoly

To illustrate the effect of tariffs and quotas under imperfect competition, we start with the example of a Home monopolist—a single firm selling a homogeneous good. In this case, free trade introduces many more firms selling the same good into the Home market, which eliminates the monopolist's ability to charge a price higher than its marginal cost (the free-trade equilibrium results in a perfectly competitive Home market). As we will show, tariffs and quotas affect this trade equilibrium differently because of their impact on the Home monopoly's **market power**, the extent to which a firm can set its price. With a tariff, the Home monopolist still competes against a large number of importers and so its market power is limited. With an import quota, on the other hand, once the quota limit is reached, the monopolist is the only producer able to sell in the Home market; hence, the Home monopolist can exercise its market power once again. This section describes the Home equilibrium with and without trade and explains this difference between tariffs and quotas.

No-Trade Equilibrium

We begin by showing in Figure 9-1 the no-trade equilibrium with a Home monopoly. The Home demand curve is shown by D, and because it is downward-sloping, as the monopolist sells more, the price will fall. This fall in price means that the extra

FIGURE 9-1

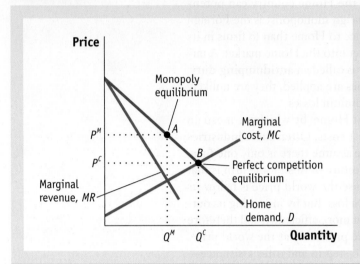

No-Trade Equilibrium In the absence of international trade, the monopoly equilibrium at Home occurs at the quantity Q^M, where marginal revenue equals marginal cost. From that quantity, we trace up to the demand curve at point A, and across to the vertical axis to find that the price charged is P^M. Under perfect competition, the industry supply curve is the MC curve, so the no-trade equilibrium would occur where demand equals supply (point B), at the quantity Q^C and the price P^C.

revenue earned by the monopolist from selling one more unit is less than the price: the extra revenue earned equals the price charged for that unit *minus* the fall in price times the quantity sold of all earlier units. The extra revenue earned from selling one more unit, the **marginal revenue**, is shown by curve MR in Figure 9-1.

To maximize its profits, the monopolist produces at the point where the marginal revenue MR earned from selling one more unit equals the marginal cost MC of producing one more unit. As shown in Figure 9-1, the monopolist produces quantity Q^M. Tracing up from Q^M to point A on the demand curve and then over to the price axis, the price charged by the monopolist is P^M. This price enables the monopolist to earn the highest profits and is the monopoly equilibrium in the absence of international trade.

Comparison with Perfect Competition We can contrast the monopoly equilibrium with the perfect competition equilibrium in the absence of trade. Instead of a single firm, suppose there are many firms in the industry. We assume that all these firms combined have the same cost conditions as the monopolist, so the industry marginal cost is identical to the monopolist's marginal cost curve of MC. Because a perfectly competitive industry will produce where price equals marginal cost, the MC curve is also the industry supply curve. The no-trade equilibrium under perfect competition occurs where supply equals demand (the quantity Q^C and the price P^C). The competitive price P^C is less than the monopoly price P^M, and the competitive quantity Q^C *is* higher than the monopoly quantity Q^M. This comparison shows that in the absence of trade, the monopolist restricts its quantity sold to increase the market price. Under free trade, however, the monopolist cannot limit quantity and raise price, as we investigate next.

Free-Trade Equilibrium

Suppose now that Home engages in international trade. We will treat Home as a "small country," which means that it faces the fixed world price of P^W. In Figure 9-2, we draw a horizontal line at that price and label it as X^*, the Foreign export supply curve. At that price, Foreign will supply any quantity of imports (because Home is a small country, the Foreign export supply is perfectly elastic). Likewise, the Home monopolist can sell as much as it desires at the price of P^W (because it is able to

FIGURE 9-2

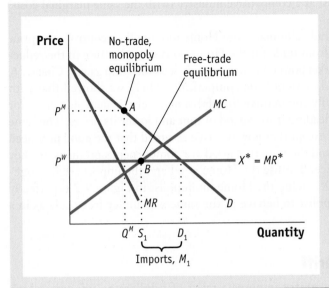

Home Monopoly's Free-Trade Equilibrium Under free trade at the fixed world price P^W, Home faces Foreign export supply of X^* at that price. Because the Home firm cannot raise its price above P^W without losing all its customers to imports, X^* is now also the demand curve faced by the Home monopolist. Because the price is fixed, the marginal revenue MR^* is the same as the demand curve. Profits are maximized at point B, where marginal revenue equals marginal costs. The Home firm supplies S_1, and Home consumers demand D_1. The difference between these is imports, $M_1 = D_1 - S_1$. Because the Home monopoly now sets its price at marginal cost, the same free-trade equilibrium holds under perfect competition.

export at the world price) but cannot charge any more than that price at Home. If it charged a higher price, Home consumers would import the product instead. Therefore, the Foreign supply curve of X^* is *also* the new demand curve facing the Home monopolist: the original no-trade Home demand of D no longer applies to the monopolist.

Because this new demand curve facing the Home monopolist is horizontal, the Home firm's new marginal revenue curve is the same as the demand curve, so $X^* = MR^*$. To understand why this is so, remember that marginal revenue equals the price earned from selling one more unit *minus* the fall in price times the quantity sold of all earlier units. For a horizontal demand curve, there is no fall in price from selling more because additional units sell for P^W, the same price for which the earlier units sell. Thus, marginal revenue is the price earned from selling another unit, P^W. Therefore, the demand curve X^* facing the Home monopolist is identical to the marginal revenue curve: the no-trade marginal revenue of MR no longer applies.

To maximize profits under the new free-trade market conditions, the monopolist will set marginal revenue equal to marginal cost (point B in Figure 9-2) and will supply S_1 at the price P^W. At the price P^W, Home consumers demand D_1, which is more than the Home supply of S_1. The difference between demand and supply is Home imports under free trade, or $M_1 = D_1 - S_1$.

Comparison with Perfect Competition

Let us once again compare this monopoly equilibrium with the perfect competition equilibrium, now with free trade. As before, we assume that the cost conditions facing the competitive firms are the same as those facing the monopolist, so the industry supply curve under perfect competition is equal to the monopolist's marginal cost curve of MC. With free trade and perfect competition, the industry will supply the quantity S_1, where the price P^W equals marginal cost, and consumers will demand the quantity D_1 at the price P^W. Under free trade for a small country, then, a Home monopolist produces the same quantity and charges the same price as a perfectly competitive industry. The reason for this result is that free trade for a small country eliminates the monopolist's control over price—that is, its market power. It faces a horizontal demand curve, equal to marginal revenue, at the world price of P^W. Because the monopolist has no control over the market price, it behaves just as a competitive industry (with the same marginal costs) would behave.

This finding that free trade eliminates the Home monopolist's control over price is an extra source of gains from trade for the Home consumers because of the reduction in the monopolist's market power. We have already seen this extra gain in Chapter 6, in which we first discussed monopolistic competition. There we showed that with free trade, a monopolistically competitive firm faces more-elastic demand curves for its differentiated product, leading it to expand output and lower its prices. The same result holds in Figure 9-2, except that now we have assumed that the good produced by the Home monopolist and the imported good are homogeneous products, so they sell at exactly the same price. Because the Home good and the import are homogeneous, the demand curve X^* facing the Home monopolist in Figure 9-2 is perfectly elastic, leading the monopolist to behave in the same way under free trade as in a competitive industry.

Effect of a Home Tariff

Now suppose the Home country imposes a tariff of t dollars on imports, which increases the Home price from P^W to $P^W + t$. In Figure 9-3, the effect of the tariff is to raise the Foreign export supply curve from X^* to $X^* + t$. The Home firm can sell as much as it desires at the price of $P^W + t$ but cannot charge any more than that price. If it did, the Home consumers would import the product. Thus, the Foreign supply curve of $X^* + t$ is also the new demand curve facing the Home monopolist.

Because this new demand curve is horizontal, the new marginal revenue curve is once again the same as the demand curve, so $MR^* = X^* + t$. The reasoning for this result is similar to the reasoning under free trade: with a horizontal demand curve, there is no fall in price from selling more, so the Home firm can sell as much as it desires at the price of $P^W + t$. So the demand curve $X^* + t$ facing the Home monopolist is identical to its marginal revenue curve.

FIGURE 9-3

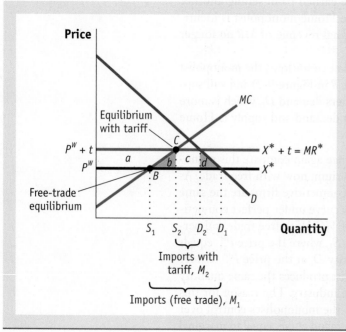

Tariff with Home Monopoly Initially, under free trade at the fixed world price P^W, the monopolist faces the horizontal demand curve (and marginal revenue curve) X^*, and profits are maximized at point B. When a tariff t is imposed, the export supply curve shifts up since Foreign firms must charge $P^W + t$ in the Home market to earn P^W. This allows the Home monopolist to increase its domestic price to $P^W + t$, but no higher, since otherwise it would lose all its customers to imports. The result is fewer imports, M_2, because Home supply S increases and Home demand D decreases. The deadweight loss of the tariff is measured by the area $(b + d)$. This result is the same as would have been obtained under perfect competition because the Home monopolist is still charging a price equal to its marginal cost.

To maximize profits, the monopolist will once again set marginal revenue equal to marginal costs, which occurs at point C in Figure 9-3, with the price $P^W + t$ and supply of S_2. At the price $P^W + t$, Home consumers demand D_2, which is more than Home supply of S_2. The difference between demand and supply is Home imports, $M_2 = D_2 - S_2$. The effect of the tariff on the Home monopolist relative to the free-trade equilibrium is to raise its production from S_1 to S_2 and its price from P^W to $P^W + t$. The supply increase in combination with a decrease in Home demand reduces imports from M_1 to M_2.

Comparison with Perfect Competition Let us compare this monopoly equilibrium with the tariff to what would happen under perfect competition. The tariff-inclusive price facing a perfectly competitive industry is $P^W + t$, the same price faced by the monopolist. Assuming that the industry supply curve under perfect competition is the same as the monopolist's marginal cost MC, the competitive equilibrium is where price equals marginal cost, which is once again at the quantity S_2 and the price $P^W + t$. So with a tariff, a Home monopolist produces the same quantity and charges the same price as would a perfectly competitive industry. This result is similar to the result we found under free trade. This similarity occurs because the tariff still limits the monopolist's ability to raise its price: it can raise the price to $P^W + t$ but no higher because otherwise consumers will import the product. Because the monopolist has limited control over its price, it behaves in the same way a competitive industry would when facing the tariff.

Home Loss Due to the Tariff Because the tariff and free-trade equilibria are the same for a Home monopoly and a perfectly competitive industry, the deadweight loss from the tariff is also the same. As we learned in Chapter 8, the deadweight loss under perfect competition is found by taking the total fall in consumer surplus due to the rise in price from P^W to $P^W + t$, adding the gain in producer surplus from the rise in price, and then adding the increase in government revenue due to the tariff. Summing all these components shows a net welfare loss of $(b + d)$:

Fall in consumer surplus:	$-(a + b + c + d)$
Rise in producer surplus:	$+a$
Rise in government revenue:	$+c$
Net effect on Home's welfare:	$-(b + d)$

Under Home monopoly, the deadweight loss from the tariff is the same. Home consumers still have the loss of $(a + b + c + d)$ because of the rise in price, while the Home monopolist gains the amount a in profits because of the rise in price. With the government collecting area c in tariff revenue, the deadweight loss is still area $(b + d)$.

Effect of a Home Quota

Let us now contrast the tariff with an import quota imposed by the Home government. As we now show, the quota results in a higher price for Home consumers, and therefore a larger Home loss, than would a tariff imposed on the same equilibrium quantity of imports. The reason for the higher costs is that the quota creates a "sheltered" market for the Home firm, allowing it to exercise its monopoly power, which leads to higher prices than under a tariff. Economists and policy makers are well aware of this additional drawback to quotas, which is why the World Trade Organization has encouraged countries to replace many quotas with tariffs.

To show the difference between the quota and tariff with a Home monopoly, we use Figure 9-4, in which the free-trade equilibrium is at point B and the tariff equilibrium is at point C (the same points that appear in Figure 9-3). Now suppose that instead of the tariff, a quota is applied. We choose the quota so that it equals

FIGURE 9-4

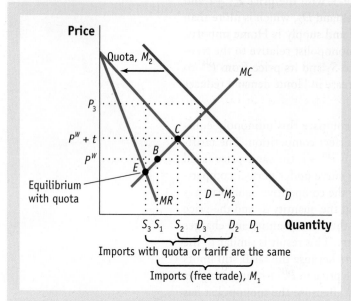

Effect of Quota with Home Monopoly Under free trade, the Home monopolist produces at point B and charges the world price of P^W. With a tariff of t, the monopolist produces at point C and charges the price of $P^W + t$. Imports under the tariff are $M_2 = D_2 - S_2$. Under a quota of M_2, the demand curve shifts to the left by that amount, resulting in the demand $D - M_2$ faced by the Home monopolist. That is, after M_2 units are imported, the monopolist is the only firm able to sell at Home, and so it can choose a price anywhere along the demand curve $D - M_2$. The marginal revenue curve corresponding to $D - M_2$ is MR, and so with a quota, the Home monopolist produces at point E, where MR equals MC. The price charged at point E is $P_3 > P^W + t$, so the quota leads to a higher Home price than the tariff.

the imports under the tariff, which are M_2. Since imports are fixed at that level, the effective demand curve facing the Home monopolist is the demand curve D *minus* the amount M_2. We label this effective demand curve $D - M_2$. Unlike the situation under the tariff, the monopolist now retains the ability to influence its price: it can choose the optimal price and quantity along $D - M_2$. We graph the marginal revenue curve MR for the effective demand curve $D - M_2$. The profit-maximizing position for the monopolist is where marginal revenue equals marginal cost, at point E, with price P_3 and supply S_3.

Let us now compare the tariff equilibrium, at point C, with the quota equilibrium, at point E. It will definitely be the case that the price charged under the quota is higher, $P_3 > P^W + t$. The higher price under the quota reflects the ability of the monopolist to raise its price once the quota amount has been imported. The higher price occurs even though the quota equilibrium *has the same level of imports as the tariff*, M_2. Therefore, the effects of a tariff and a quota are no longer equivalent as they were under perfect competition: the quota enables a monopolist to exercise its market power and raise its price.

What about the quantity produced by the monopolist? Because the price is higher under the quota, the monopolist will definitely produce a lower quantity under the quota, $S_3 < S_2$. What is more surprising, however, is that it is even possible that the quota could lead to a fall in output as compared with free trade: in Figure 9-4, we have shown $S_3 < S_1$. This is not a necessary result, however, and instead we could have drawn the MR curve so that $S_3 > S_1$. It is surprising that the case $S_3 < S_1$ is even possible because it suggests that workers in the industry would *fail to be protected* by the quota; that is, employment could fall because of the reduction in output under the quota. We see, then, that the quota can have undesirable effects as compared with a tariff when the Home industry is a monopoly.

Home Loss Due to the Quota Our finding that Home prices are higher with a quota than with a tariff means that Home consumers suffer a greater fall in surplus because of the quota. On the other hand, the Home monopolist earns higher profit from the quota because its price is higher. We will not make a detailed calculation of the deadweight loss from the quota with Home monopoly because it is complicated. We can say, however, that the deadweight loss will always be *higher* for a quota than for a tariff because the Home monopolist will always charge a higher price. That higher price benefits the monopolist but harms Home consumers and creates an extra deadweight loss because of the exercise of monopoly power.

Furthermore, the fact that the Home monopolist is charging a higher price also increases the quota rents, which we defined in the previous chapter as the ability to import goods at the world price and sell them at the higher Home price (in our example, this is the difference between P_3 and P^W times the amount of imports M_2). In the case of Home monopoly, the quota rents are greater than government revenue would be under a tariff. Recall that quota rents are often given to Foreign countries in the case of "voluntary" export restraints, when the government of the exporting country implements the quota, or else quota rents can even be wasted completely when rent-seeking activities occur. In either of these cases, the increase in quota rents adds to Home's losses if the rents are given away or wasted.

In the following application, we examine a quota used in the United States during the 1980s to restrict imports of Japanese cars. Because the car industry has a small number of producers, it is imperfectly competitive. So our predictions from the case of monopoly discussed previously can serve as a guide for what we expect in the case of Home oligopoly.

APPLICATION

U.S. Imports of Japanese Automobiles

A well-known case of a "voluntary" export restraint (VER) for the United States occurred during the 1980s, when the United States limited the imports of cars from Japan. To understand why this VER was put into place, recall that during the early 1980s, the United States suffered a deep recession. That recession led to less spending on durable goods (such as automobiles), and as a result, unemployment in the auto industry rose sharply.

In 1980 the United Automobile Workers and Ford Motor Company applied to the International Trade Commission (ITC) for protection under Article XIX of the General Agreement on Tariffs and Trade (GATT) and Section 201 of U.S. trade laws. As described in Chapter 8 (see **Side Bar: Provisions of U.S. Trade Law**), Section 201 protection can be given when increased imports are a "substantial cause of serious injury to the domestic industry," where "substantial cause" must be "not less than any other cause." In fact, the ITC determined that the U.S. recession was a more important cause of injury to the auto industry than increased imports. Accordingly, it did not recommend that the auto industry receive protection.

With this negative determination, several members of Congress from states with auto plants continued to pursue import limits by other means. In April 1981 Senators John Danforth from Missouri and Lloyd Bentsen from Texas introduced a bill in the U.S. Senate to restrict imports. Clearly aware of this pending legislation, the Japanese government announced on May 1 that it would "voluntarily" limit Japan's export of automobiles to the U.S. market. For the period April 1981 to March 1982, this limit was set at 1.83 million autos. After March 1984 the limit was raised to 2.02 million and then to 2.51 million vehicles annually. By 1988 imports fell *below* the VER limit because Japanese companies began assembling cars in the United States.

We are interested in whether American producers were able to exercise their monopoly power and raise their prices under the quota restriction. We are also interested in how much import prices increased. To measure the increase in import prices, we need to take into account a side effect of the 1980 quota: it led to an increase in the features of

FIGURE 9-5

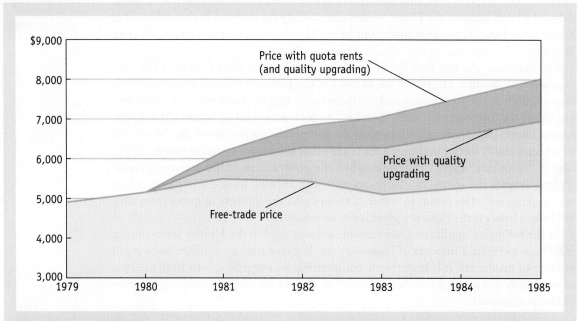

Prices of Japanese Car Imports Under the "voluntary" export restraint (VER) on Japanese car imports, the average price rose from $5,150 to $8,050 between 1980 and 1985. Of that $2,900 increase, $1,100 was the result of quota rent increases earned by Japanese producers. Another $1,650 was the result of quality improvements in the Japanese cars, which became heavier and wider, with improved horsepower, transmissions, and so on. The remaining $150 is the amount that import prices would have risen under free trade.

Japanese cars being sold in the United States such as size, weight, horsepower, and so on, or what we call an increase in quality.[3] The overall increase in auto import prices during the 1980s needs to be broken up into the increases due to (1) the quality upgrading of Japanese cars; (2) the "pure" increase in price because of the quota, which equals the quota rents; and (3) any price increase that would have occurred anyway, even if the auto industry had not been subject to protection.

Price and Quality of Imports The impact of the VER on the price of Japanese cars is shown in Figure 9-5. Under the VER on Japanese car imports, the average price rose from $5,150 to $8,050 between 1980 and 1985. Of that $2,900 increase, $1,100 was the result of quota rents earned by Japanese producers in 1984 and 1985. Another $1,650 was from quality improvements in the Japanese cars, which became heavier and wider, with improved horsepower, transmissions, and so on. The remaining $150 is the amount that import prices would have risen under free trade.

Quota Rents If we multiply the quota rents of $1,100 per car by the imports of about 2 million cars, we obtain total estimated rents of $2.2 billion, which is the lower estimate of the annual cost of quota rents for automobiles. The upper estimate of $7.9 billion comes from also including the increase in price for European cars sold in the United States. Although European cars were not restricted by a quota, they did experience a significant increase in price during the quota period; that increase was due to the reduced competition from Japanese producers.

The Japanese firms benefited from the quota rents that they received. In fact, their stock prices *rose* during the VER period, though only after it became clear that the

---

[3] The previous chapter discusses the quality effect of a U.S. import quota on Chinese textile and apparel exports to the United States.

FIGURE 9-6

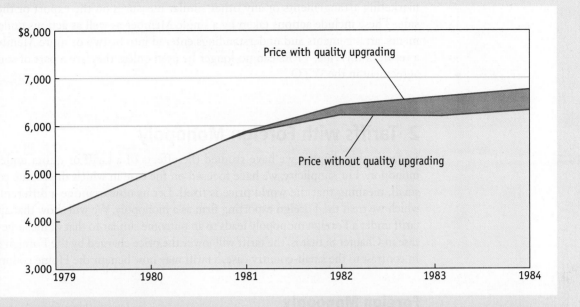

Prices of American Small Cars Under the VER on Japanese car imports, the average price of U.S. cars rose very rapidly when the quota was first imposed: from $4,200 in 1979 to $6,000 in 1981, or a 43% increase over two years. Only a very small part of that increase was explained by quality improvements, and in the later years of the quota, U.S. quality did not rise by as much as it did in the Japanese imports.

Japanese Ministry of International Trade and Industry would administer the quotas to each producer (so that the Japanese firms would capture the rents). Moreover, because each producer was given a certain number of cars it could export to the United States, but no limit on the value of the cars, producers had a strong incentive to export more expensive models. That explains the quality upgrading that occurred during the quota, which was when Japanese producers started exporting more luxurious cars to the United States.

Price of U.S. Cars What happened to the prices of American small cars during this period? Under the VER on Japanese car imports, the average price of U.S. cars rose very rapidly when the quota was first imposed: from $4,200 in 1979 to $6,000 in 1981, a 43% increase over two years. That price increase was due to the exercise of market power by the U.S. producers, who were sheltered by the quota on their Japanese competitors. Only a small part of that price increase was explained by quality improvements, since the quality of U.S. cars did not rise by as much as the quality of Japanese imports, as seen in Figure 9-6. So the American producers were able to benefit from the quota by raising their prices, and the Japanese firms also benefited by combining a price increase with an improvement in quality. The fact that both the Japanese and U.S. firms were able to increase their prices substantially indicates that the policy was very costly to U.S. consumers.

The GATT and WTO The VER that the United States negotiated with Japan in automobiles was outside of the GATT framework: because this export restraint was enforced by the Japanese rather than the United States, it did not necessarily violate Article XI of the GATT, which states that countries should not use quotas to restrict imports. Other countries used VERs during the 1980s and early 1990s to restrict imports in products such as automobiles and steel. All these cases were exploiting a loophole in the GATT agreement whereby a quota enforced by the *exporter* was not a violation of the GATT. This loophole was closed when the World Trade

Organization (WTO) was established in 1995. Part of the WTO agreement states that "a Member shall not seek, take or maintain any voluntary export restraints, orderly marketing arrangements or any other similar measures on the export or the import side. These include actions taken by a single Member as well as actions under agreements, arrangements and understandings entered into by two or more Members."[4] As a result of this rule, VERs can no longer be used unless they are a part of some other agreement in the WTO.[5]

2 Tariffs with Foreign Monopoly

So far in this chapter, we have studied the effects of a tariff or quota under Home monopoly. For simplicity, we have focused on the case in which the Home country is small, meaning that the world price is fixed. Let us now examine a different case, in which we treat the Foreign exporting firm as a monopoly. We will show that applying a tariff under a Foreign monopoly leads to an outcome similar to that of the large-country case in Chapter 8; that is, the tariff will lower the price charged by the Foreign exporter. In contrast to the small-country case, a tariff may now benefit the Home country.

Foreign Monopoly

To focus our attention on the Foreign monopolist selling to the Home market, we will assume that there is no competing Home firm, so the Home demand D in Figure 9-7 is supplied entirely by exports from the Foreign monopolist. This assumption is not very realistic because normally a tariff is being considered when there is also a Home firm. But ignoring the Home firm will simplify our analysis while still helping us to understand the effect of an imperfectly competitive Foreign exporter.

Free-Trade Equilibrium In addition to the Home demand of D in Figure 9-7, we also show Home marginal revenue of MR. Under free trade, the Foreign monopolist maximizes profits in its export market where Home marginal revenue MR equals Foreign marginal cost MC^*, at point A in Figure 9-7. It exports the amount X_1 to the Home market and charges the price of P_1.

Effect of a Tariff on Home Price If the Home country applies an import tariff of t dollars, then the marginal cost for the exporter to sell in the Home market increases to $MC^* + t$. With the increase in marginal costs, the new intersection with marginal revenue occurs at point B in Figure 9-7, and the import price rises to P_2.

Under the case we have drawn in Figure 9-7, where the MR curve is steeper than the demand curve, the increase in price from P_1 to P_2 is *less than* the amount of the tariff t. In other words, the vertical rise along the MR curve caused by the tariff (the vertical distance from point A to B, which is the tariff amount) corresponds to a smaller vertical rise moving along the demand curve (the difference between P_1 and P_2). In this case, the net-of-tariff price received by the Foreign exporter, which is $P_3 = P_2 - t$, has *fallen* from its previous level of P_1 because the price rises by less than the tariff. Because the Home country is paying a lower net-of-tariff price P_3 for its import, it has experienced a terms-of-trade gain as a result of the tariff.

The effect of the tariff applied against a Foreign monopolist is similar to the effect of a tariff imposed by a large country (analyzed in Chapter 8). There we found that a

---

[4] From Article 11, "Prohibition and Elimination of Certain Measures," of the WTO Agreement on Safeguards.
[5] An example is the quota in textiles that the United States negotiated with China in 2005, which was allowed under the provisions of China's entry into the WTO, as discussed in the previous chapter.

FIGURE 9-7

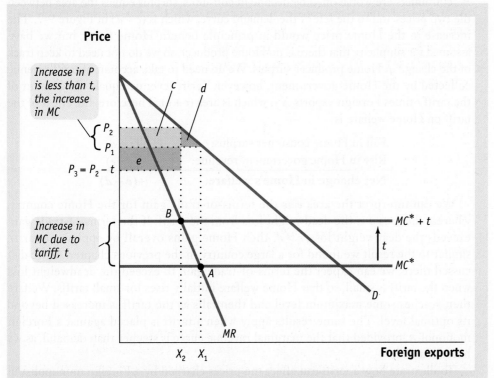

Tariff with a Foreign Monopoly Under free trade, the Foreign monopolist charges prices P_1 and exports X_1, where marginal revenue MR equals marginal cost MC^*. When an antidumping duty of t is applied, the firm's marginal cost rises to $MC^* + t$, so the exports fall to X_2 and the Home price rises to P_2. The decrease in consumer surplus is shown by the area $c + d$, of which c is collected as a portion of tax revenues. The net-of-tariff price that the Foreign exporter receives falls to $P_3 = P_2 - t$. Because the net-of-tariff price has fallen, the Home country has a terms-of-trade gain, area e. Thus, the total welfare change depends on the size of the terms-of-trade gain e relative to the deadweight loss d.

tariff would lower the price charged by Foreign firms because the quantity of exports decreased, so Foreign marginal costs also fell. Now that we have assumed a Foreign monopoly, we get the same result but for a different reason. The marginal costs of the monopolist are constant at MC^* in Figure 9-7, or $MC^* + t$ including the tariff. The rise in marginal costs from the tariff leads to an increase in the tariff-inclusive Home price as the quantity of Home imports falls, but the monopolist chooses to increase the Home price by *less than* the full amount of the tariff. In that way, the quantity exported to Home does not fall by as much as it would if the Foreign firm increased its price by the full amount of the tariff. So, the Foreign firm is making a strategic decision to absorb part of the tariff itself (by lowering its price from P_1 to P_3) and pass through only a portion of the tariff to the Home price (which rises from P_1 to P_2).

Summary To preserve its sales to Home, the Foreign monopolist chooses to increase the Home price by less than the amount of the tariff. This result depends on having MR steeper than D, as shown in Figure 9-7. It is not necessarily the case that MR is steeper than D for all demand curves, but this is usually how we draw them. In the case of a straight-line demand curve such as the one drawn in Figure 9-7, for example, the marginal revenue curve is exactly twice as steep as the demand curve.[6] In this case, the Home import price rises by exactly half of the tariff amount, and the Foreign export price falls by exactly half of the tariff amount.

---

[6] You are asked to show this result in Problem 7 at the end of the chapter.

Effect of the Tariff on Home Welfare With the rise in the Home price from P_1 to P_2, consumers are worse off. The decline in consumer surplus equals the area between the two prices and to the left of the demand curve, which is $(c + d)$ in Figure 9-7. The increase in the Home price would in principle benefit Home firms, but we have assumed for simplicity that there is no Home producer, so we do not need to keep track of the change in Home producer surplus. We do need to take account of tariff revenue collected by the Home government, however. Tariff revenue equals the amount of the tariff t times Foreign exports X_2, which is area $(c + e)$. Therefore, the effect of the tariff on Home welfare is

Fall in Home consumer surplus:	$-(c + d)$
Rise in Home government revenue:	$+(c + e)$
Net change in Home's welfare:	**$+(e - d)$**

We can interpret the area e as the terms-of-trade gain for the Home country, whereas the area d is the deadweight loss from the tariff. If the terms-of-trade gain exceeds the deadweight loss, $e > d$, then Home gains overall by applying a tariff, similar to the result we found for a large country in the previous chapter. As we discussed there, we can expect the terms-of-trade gain to exceed the deadweight loss when the tariff is small, so that Home welfare initially rises for small tariffs. Welfare then reaches some maximum level and then falls as the tariff is increased beyond its optimal level. The same results apply when a tariff is placed against a Foreign monopolist, provided that the marginal revenue curve is steeper than demand, as we have assumed.

To illustrate how a tariff can affect the prices charged by a Foreign monopolist in practice, we once again use the automobile industry as an example. Because there are a small number of firms in that industry, it is realistic to expect them to respond to a tariff in the way that a Foreign monopolist would.

APPLICATION

Import Tariffs on Japanese Trucks

We have found that in the case of a Foreign monopolist, Home will experience a terms-of-trade gain from a small tariff. The reason for this gain is that the Foreign firm will lower its net-of-tariff price to avoid too large an increase in the price paid by consumers in the importing country. To what extent do Foreign exporters actually behave that way?

To answer this question, we can look at the effects of the 25% tariff on imported Japanese compact trucks imposed by the United States in the early 1980s and still in place today. The history of how this tariff came to be applied is an interesting story. Recall from the application earlier in the chapter that in 1980 the United Automobile Workers and Ford Motor Company applied for a tariff under Article XIX of the GATT and Section 201 of U.S. trade law. They were turned down for the tariff, however, because the International Trade Commission determined that the U.S. recession was a more important cause of injury in the auto industry than growing imports. For cars, the "voluntary" export restraint (VER) with Japan was pursued. But for compact trucks imported from Japan, it turned out that another form of protection was available.

At that time, most compact trucks from Japan were imported as cab/chassis with some final assembly needed. These were classified as "parts of trucks," which carried a tariff rate of only 4%. But another category of truck—"complete or unfinished trucks"—faced a tariff rate of 25%. That unusually high tariff was a result of the "chicken war" between the United States and West Germany in 1962. At that time, Germany joined the European Economic Community (EEC) and was required to adjust its external tariffs to match those of the other EEC countries. This adjustment resulted in an increase in its tariff on imported U.S. poultry. In retaliation, the United States increased its tariffs on trucks and other products, so the 25% tariff on trucks became a permanent item in the U.S. tariff code.

That tariff created an irresistible opportunity to reclassify the Japanese imports and obtain a substantial increase in the tariff, which is exactly what the U.S. Customs Service did with prodding from the U.S. Congress. Effective August 21, 1980, imported cab/chassis "parts" were reclassified as "complete or unfinished" trucks. This reclassification raised the tariff rate on all Japanese trucks from 4% to 25%, which remains in effect today.

How did Japanese exporters respond to the tariff? According to one estimate, the tariff on trucks was only *partially* reflected in U.S. prices: of the 21% increase, only 12% (or about 60% of the increase) was passed through to U.S. consumer prices; the other 9% (or about 40% of the increase) was absorbed by Japanese producers.[7] Therefore, this tariff led to a terms-of-trade gain for the United States, as predicted by our theory: for a straight-line demand curve (as in Figure 9-7), marginal revenue is twice as steep, and the tariff will lead to an increase in the Home import price that is equal to the decrease in the Foreign export price.[8] The evidence for Japanese trucks is not too different from what we predict in that straight-line case.

Notice that the terms-of-trade gain from the tariff applied on a Foreign monopolist is similar to the terms-of-trade gain from a tariff applied by a "large" country, as we discussed in the previous chapter. In both cases, the Foreign firm or industry absorbs part of the tariff by lowering its price, which means that the Home price rises by less than the full amount of the tariff. If the terms-of-trade gain, measured by the area e in Figure 9-7 exceed the deadweight loss d, then the Home country gains from the tariff. This is our first example of strategic trade policy that leads to a potential gain for Home.

In principle, this potential gain arises from the tariff that the United States has applied on imports of compact trucks, and that is still in place today. But some economists feel that this tariff has the undesirable side effect of encouraging the U.S. automobile industry to focus on the sales of trucks, since compact trucks have higher prices because of the tariff.[9] That strategy by U.S. producers can work when gasoline price are low, so consumers are willing to buy trucks. At times of high prices, however, consumers instead want fuel-efficient cars, which have not been the focus of the American industry. So high fuel prices can lead to a surge in imports and fewer domestic sales, exactly what happened after the oil price increase of 1979 and again in 2008, just before the financial crisis. Some industry experts believe that these factors contributed to the losses faced by the American industry during the financial crisis, as explained in **Headlines: The Chickens Have Come Home to Roost**.

---

[7] Robert Feenstra, 1989, "Symmetric Pass-Through of Tariffs and Exchange Rates Under Imperfect Competition: An Empirical Test," *Journal of International Economics*, 27(1/2), 25–45.
[8] You are asked to derive this relationship numerically in Problem 7 at the end of the chapter.
[9] Larger trucks and SUVs imported into the United States do not have this tariff.

HEADLINES

The Chickens Have Come Home to Roost

This article discusses the history of the 25% tariff that still applies to U.S. imports of lightweight trucks. The author argues that this tariff caused some of the difficulties in the U.S. automobile industry today.

Although we call them the big three automobile companies, they have basically specialized in building trucks. This left them utterly unable to respond when high gas prices shifted the market towards hybrids and more fuel efficient cars.

One reason is that Americans like to drive SUVs, minivans and small trucks when gasoline costs $1.50 to $2.00 a gallon. But another is that the profit margins have been much higher on trucks and vans because the US protects its domestic market with a twenty-five percent tariff. By contrast, the import tariff on regular automobiles is just 2.5 percent and US duties from tariffs on all imported goods are just one percent of the overall value of merchandise imports. Since many of the inputs used to assemble trucks are not subject to tariffs anywhere near 25 percent—US tariffs on all goods average only 3.5 percent—the effective protection and subsidy equivalent of this policy has been huge.

It is no wonder much of the initial foray by Japanese transplants to the US involved setting up trucks assembly plants, no wonder that Automakers only put three doors on SUVs so they can qualify as vans and no wonder that Detroit is so opposed to the US-Korea Free Trade Agreement that would eventually allow trucks built in Korea Duty-Free access to the US market.

What accounts for this distinctive treatment of trucks? An accident of history that shows how hard it is for the government to withdraw favors even when they have no sound policy justification.

It all comes down to the long forgotten chicken wars of the 1960s. In 1962, when implementing the European Common Market, the Community denied access to US chicken producers. In response after being unable to resolve the issue diplomatically, the US responded with retaliatory tariffs that included a twenty five

percent tariffs on trucks that was aimed at the German Volkswagen Combi-Bus that was enjoying brisk sales in the US.

Since the trade (GATT) rules required that retaliation be applied on a nondiscriminatory basis, the tariffs were levied on all truck-type vehicles imported from all countries and have never been removed. Over time, the Germans stopped building these vehicles and today the tariffs are mainly paid on trucks coming from Asia. The tariffs have bred bad habits, steering Detroit away from building high-quality automobiles towards trucks and trucklike cars that have suddenly fallen into disfavor.

If Congress wants an explanation for why the big three have been so uncompetitive it should look first at the disguised largess it has been providing them with for years. It has taken a long time—nearly 47 years—but it seems that eventually the chickens have finally come home to roost.

Source: Robert Lawrence, guest blogger on Dani Rodrik's weblog, posted May 4, 2009. http://www.rodrik.typepad.com/dani_rodriks_weblog/2009/05/the-chickens-have-come-home-to-roost.html.

3 Dumping

With imperfect competition, firms can charge *different* prices across countries and will do so whenever that pricing strategy is profitable. Recall that we define imperfect competition as the firm's ability to influence the price of its product. With international trade, we extend this idea: not only can firms charge a price that is higher than their marginal cost, they can also choose to charge different prices in their domestic market than in their export market. This pricing strategy is called **price discrimination** because the firm is able to choose how much different groups of customers pay. To discriminate in international trade, there must be some reason that consumers in the high-price market cannot import directly from the low-cost market; for example, that reason could be transportation costs or tariffs between the markets.

Dumping occurs when a foreign firm sells a product abroad at a price that is either less than the price it charges in its local market, or less than its average cost to produce the product. Dumping is common in international trade, even though the rules of the World Trade Organization (WTO) discourage this activity. Under the rules of the WTO, an importing country is entitled to apply a tariff any time a foreign firm dumps its product on a local market. Such a tariff is called an antidumping duty. We study antidumping duties in detail in the next section. In this section, we want to ask the more general question: Why do firms dump at all? It might appear at first glance that selling abroad at prices less than local prices or less than the average costs of production must be unprofitable. Is that really the case? It turns out the answer is no. It can be profitable to sell at low prices abroad, even at prices lower than average cost.

Discriminating Monopoly To illustrate how dumping can be profitable, we use the example of a Foreign monopolist selling both to its local market and exporting to Home. As described previously, we assume that the monopolist is able to charge different prices in the two markets; this market structure is sometimes called a discriminating monopoly. The diagram for a Foreign discriminating monopoly is shown in Figure 9-8. The local demand curve for the monopolist is D^*, with marginal revenue MR^*. We draw these curves as downward-sloping for the monopolist because to induce additional consumers to buy its product, the monopolist lowers its price (downward-sloping D^*), which decreases the revenue received from each additional unit sold (downward-sloping MR^*).

In the export market, however, the Foreign firm will face competition from other firms selling to the Home market. Because of this competition, the firm's demand curve in the export market will be more elastic; that is, it will lose more customers by raising prices than it would in its local market. If it faces enough competition in its export market, the Foreign monopolist's export demand curve will be horizontal at the price P, meaning that it cannot charge more than the competitive market price. If the price for exports is fixed at P, selling more units does not depress the price or the extra revenue earned for each unit exported. Therefore, the marginal revenue for exports equals the price, which is labeled as P in Figure 9-8.

Equilibrium Condition We can now determine the profit-maximizing level of production for the Foreign monopolist, as well as its prices in each market. For the discriminating monopoly, profits are maximized when the following condition holds:

$$MR = MR^* = MC^*$$

This equation looks similar to the condition for profit maximization for a single-market monopolist, which is marginal revenue equals marginal cost, except that now the marginal revenues should also be equal in the two markets.

We illustrate this equilibrium condition in Figure 9-8. If the Foreign firm produces quantity Q_1, at point B, then the marginal cost of the last unit equals the export marginal revenue MR. But not all of the supply Q_1 is exported; some is sold locally. The amount sold locally is determined by the equality of the firm's local marginal revenue MR^* with its export marginal revenue MR (at point C), *and* the equality of its local marginal cost MC^* with MR (at point B). All three variables equal P, though the firm charges the price P^* (by tracing up the Foreign demand curve) to its local consumers. Choosing these prices, the profit-maximization equation just given is satisfied, and the discriminating monopolist is maximizing profits across both markets.

The Profitability of Dumping The Foreign firm charges P^* to sell quantity Q_2 in its local market (from Q_2, we go up to the local demand curve D^* and across to the price). The local price exceeds the price P charged in the export market. Because the Foreign firm is selling the same product at a lower price to the export market, it is dumping its product into the export market.

What about the comparison of its export price with average costs? At total production of Q_1 at point B, the firm's average costs are read off the average cost curve above that point, so average costs equal AC_1, lower than the local price P^* but higher than the export price P. Because average costs AC_1 are above the export price P, the firm is

FIGURE 9-8

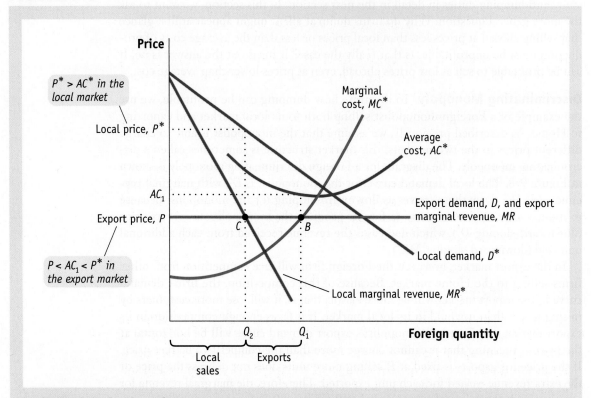

Foreign Discriminating Monopoly The Foreign monopoly faces different demand curves and charges different prices in its local and export markets. Locally, its demand curve is D^* with marginal revenue MR^*. Abroad, its demand curve is horizontal at the export price, P, which is also its marginal revenue of MR. To maximize profits, the Foreign monopolist chooses to produce the quantity Q_1 at point B, where local marginal cost equals marginal revenue in the export market, $MC^* = MR$. The quantity sold in the local market, Q_2 (at point C), is determined where local marginal revenue equals export marginal revenue, $MR^* = MR$. The Foreign monopolist sells Q_2 to its local market at P^*, and $Q_1 - Q_2$ to its export market at P. Because $P < P^*$ (or alternatively $P < AC_1$), the firm is dumping.

also dumping according to this cost comparison. But we will argue that the Foreign firm still earns positive profits from exporting its good at the low price of P. To see why that is the case, we turn to a numerical example.

Numerical Example of Dumping

Suppose the Foreign firm has the following cost and demand data:

$$
\begin{aligned}
\text{Fixed costs} &= \$100 \\
\text{Marginal costs} &= \$10 \text{ per unit} \\
\text{Local price} &= \$25 \\
\text{Local quantity} &= 10 \\
\text{Export price} &= \$15 \\
\text{Export quantity} &= 10
\end{aligned}
$$

The profits earned from selling in its local market are

$$\underbrace{(\$25 \cdot 10)}_{\text{Revenue}} - \underbrace{\$10 \cdot 10}_{\substack{\text{Variable} \\ \text{cost}}} - \underbrace{\$100}_{\substack{\text{Fixed} \\ \text{cost}}} = \underbrace{\$50}_{\text{Profits}}$$

Notice that the average costs for the firms are

$$\text{Average costs} = \frac{\$200}{10} = \$20$$

Now suppose that this firm sells an additional 10 units abroad, at the price of $15, which is less than its average cost of production. It is *still* worthwhile to sell these extra units because profits become

$$\underbrace{(\$25 \cdot 10 + \$15 \cdot 10)}_{\text{Revenue}} - \underbrace{\$10 \cdot 20}_{\substack{\text{Variable} \\ \text{cost}}} - \underbrace{\$100}_{\substack{\text{Fixed} \\ \text{cost}}} = \underbrace{\$100}_{\text{Profits}}$$

Profits have increased because the extra units are sold at $15 but produced at a *marginal cost* of $10, which is less than the price received in the export market. Therefore, each unit exported will increase profits by the difference between the price and marginal costs. Thus, even though the export price is less than average costs, profits still rise from dumping in the export market.

Policy Response to Dumping

In the previous section, we learned that dumping is not unusual: a Foreign monopolist that discriminates between its local and export markets by charging different prices in each can end up charging a lower price in its export market. Furthermore, the price it charges in its export market might be less than its average cost of production and still be profitable. Our interest now is in understanding the policy response in the Home importing country.

Antidumping Duties

Under the rules of the WTO, an importing country is entitled to apply a tariff—called an antidumping duty—any time that a foreign firm is dumping its product. An imported product is being dumped if its price is below the price that the exporter charges in its own local market; if the exporter's local price is not available, then dumping is determined by comparing the import price with (1) a price charged for the product in a third market, or (2) the exporter's average costs of production.[10] If one of these criteria is satisfied, then the exporting firm is dumping and the importing country can respond with antidumping duty. The amount of the antidumping duty is calculated as the difference between the exporter's local price and the "dumped" price in the importing country.

There are many examples of countries applying antidumping duties. Every year, there are dozens (and in some years hundreds) of antidumping cases brought by U.S. companies against foreign countries. In addition, there are dozens (and in some cases hundreds) of antidumping cases brought by foreign countries against companies exporting from the United States.[11] The large number of these antidumping cases contrasts with the small number of cases under Sections 201, 232, and 301 of U.S. trade law that we discussed in Chapter 8 (in **Side Bar: Provisions of U.S. Trade Law**). On average, there is only one safeguard tariff case (Section 201) brought every year in the United States that leads to tariffs being applied. Likewise, only a small number of national defense or trade agreement cases (Sections 232 or 301) occur each year, though the administration of President Trump used these cases more

---

[10] See Article VI of the GATT in **Side Bar: Key Provisions of the GATT** in Chapter 8.
[11] See end-of-chapter Problem 1 to learn more about the number of antidumping cases.

often. Therefore, the number of antidumping cases brought by companies within the United States, or applied against companies exporting from the United States, vastly exceed the number of cases in which tariffs are used under Sections 201, 232, or 301. There were about 1,200 antidumping cases filed from 1980 to 2011, and in more than one-half of these cases, antidumping duties were levied.

To understand why so many antidumping cases are used in the United States, we can briefly review the rule for these cases. To have antidumping duties applied, a case must first go to the U.S. Department of Commerce, which rules on whether imports are selling domestically at "less than fair value": that is, below the price in their own market or below the average cost of making them. These rulings were positive in about 90% of cases. The case is then brought before the International Trade Commission, which must rule on whether imports have caused "material injury" to the domestic industry (defined as "harm that is not inconsequential, immaterial, or unimportant"). This criterion is much easier to meet than the "substantial cause of serious injury" provision for a safeguard (Section 201) tariff, and as a result, the ITC more frequently rules in favor of antidumping duties. Furthermore, the application of antidumping duties does not require the additional approval of the U.S. president, as does the safeguard tariff.

In the following application, we discuss one specific example of antidumping duties applied by the United States and the European Union on the imports of solar panels from China.

APPLICATION

United States and European Duties on Solar Panels from China

Since November 2012, the United States has applied antidumping duties on the imports of solar panels from China, which were renewed in 2018. In December 2013, the European Union also applied tariffs against Chinese solar panels, but these expired in 2018 and were not renewed.

Dumping in the United States In October 2011, seven U.S. companies led by SolarWorld Industries America, based in Hillsboro, Oregon, filed a trade case against Chinese exporters of photovoltaic cells, or solar panels. These U.S. companies argued that the Chinese firms were dumping solar panels into the United States—that is, they were exporting them at less than the costs of production—and also that these firms were receiving substantial export subsidies from the Chinese government. These twin claims of dumping and of export subsidies triggered several investigations by the U.S. Department of Commerce and the International Trade Commission (ITC) to determine the U.S. response.

The ITC completed its first investigation in December 2011, and it made a preliminary finding that the U.S. companies bringing the trade case had been harmed—or "materially injured"—by the U.S. imports of solar panels from China. From 2009 to 2011, imports of solar panels from China increased by four times, and their value grew from $640 million to more than $3 billion. During this period, several American solar panel producers went bankrupt, so it was not surprising that the ITC found material injury due to imports.

Following the ITC's investigation, the U.S. Department of Commerce held two inquiries during 2012 to determine the extent of dumping and the extent of Chinese export subsidies. It is particularly difficult to determine the extent of dumping when the exporting firm is based in a nonmarket economy like China because it is hard to determine the market-based costs of the firms. To address this difficulty, the Department of

Commerce looked at the costs of production in another exporting country—Thailand—and used those costs to estimate what market-based costs in China would be.[12] In a preliminary ruling in May 2012, and a later ruling in October 2012, the Department of Commerce found that a group of affiliated producers, all owned by Suntech Power Holdings Co. Ltd., were selling in the United States at prices 32% below costs, and that a second group of producers were selling at 18% below costs. The 32% and 18% gaps included an export subsidy of about 11%. Because there was an additional export subsidy of 4% to 6% paid to the Chinese producers that was not reflected in the 32% and 18% gaps between costs and prices, tariffs of 36% were recommended for the first group of producers, and tariffs of 24% were recommended for the second group.

In November 2012, the ITC made a final determination of material injury to the U.S. solar panel industry, and the tariffs went into effect. Not all American producers supported these tariffs, however, because they raised costs for firms such as SolarCity Corporation, which finances and installs rooftop solar systems. These firms are the consumers of the imported solar panels, and they face higher prices as a result of the tariffs. In addition to the antidumping duties, another tariff—called a **countervailing duty**—was applied against imports of solar panels from China. A countervailing duty is used when the foreign government subsidizes its own exporting firms so that they can charge lower prices for their exports. (We examine export subsidies in Chapter 10.)

To avoid these antidumping and countervailing duties, China moved some of its production to Taiwan. As a result, new U.S. antidumping duties were enacted in 2014 that applied to solar panels made in China and to those made in Taiwan. Then China moved its production facilities to other countries, primarily to Malaysia, as well as Singapore, Germany, and South Korea. This meant that the antidumping duties targeting China were no longer effective, and solar panel imports grew rapidly while prices in the United States fell.

In 2017, SolarWorld America joined Suniva, a Chinese-owned company operating in the United States, in again applying for tariff protection. Instead of seeking antidumping tariffs against specific countries, however, the companies applied for safeguard (Section 201) tariff protection, which would apply to solar panel imports from all countries. There was intense opposition to these tariffs from U.S. companies that install solar panels onto buildings, because these companies would face U.S. higher prices for solar panels due to the tariffs. Despite this opposition, the International Trade Commission ruled in favor of these Section 201 tariffs on the grounds that imports of solar panels had risen substantially, their prices had fallen, and many U.S. companies producing solar panels were going bankrupt from the low-priced imports.

President Trump approved the tariffs on solar panels in February 2018, which started at 30% but will decline over four years and expire in 2022. The tariffs came too late, however, to benefit the two companies that initiated the Section 201 case. Suniva declared bankruptcy in 2017, and SolarWorld Germany, the parent company of SolarWorld America, declared bankruptcy in 2018. Another U.S. company called SunPower then purchased SolarWorld America and planned to operate the plant in Hillsboro, Oregon, to produce solar panels.[13]

Dumping in the European Union Procedures for applying antidumping and countervailing duties similar to those used in the United States also apply in the European Union (EU). But the decision to apply duties in the EU is more complicated

---

[12] The Chinese industry instead wanted the Department of Commerce to use the costs of producing solar panels in India as an estimate of what the market-based Chinese costs would be. Because the costs in India are presumably lower than costs in Thailand, it would be less likely that the Chinese exporters would be found to be dumping.

[13] In 2019, SunPower announced that the Hillsboro plant was for sale but that it intends to lease back a portion of the space to continue with some production. See Mike Rogoway, "SunPower Puts Hillsboro Factory Up for Sale but Says It Will Keep Operating," *The Oregonian*, May 16, 2019.

because the *same* import duties are used for *all* countries in the EU, and these duties are determined by the European Commission, located in Brussels. The decision's complexity arises because the governments of the EU countries do not always agree on whether a duty should be applied. This was the case in 2013, when the government of Germany opposed the proposed duties on imports of solar panels because it was discussing other trade agreements with the Chinese government at that time. Nevertheless, the majority of EU country governments supported antidumping and countervailing duties against imports of solar panels from China, and they went into effect in December 2013.

The EU duties applied in 2013 were supposed to last for only two years. But in 2015, the European Commission determined that Chinese manufacturers were getting around the duties by shipping solar cells through Taiwan and Malaysia. As a result, new duties were put in place in 2015 that applied to Chinese companies shipping through those countries. The antidumping duties against solar panels imported into the European Union expired in 2018 and were not renewed. The EU instead allowed for free trade on imports of solar panels.

Strategic Trade Policy? The purpose of an antidumping duty is to raise the price of the dumped good in the importing Home country, thereby protecting the domestic producers of that good. There are two reasons for the Home government to use this policy. The first reason is that Foreign firms are acting like discriminating monopolists, as we discussed above. Then, because we are dealing with dumping by a Foreign monopolist, we might expect that the antidumping duty, which is a tariff, will lead to a terms-of-trade gain for the Home country. That is, we might expect that the Foreign monopolist will absorb part of the tariff by lowering its own price, as was illustrated in Figure 9-7. It follows that the rise in the consumer price in the importing country is less than the full amount of the tariff, as was illustrated in the application dealing with Japanese compact trucks.

Does the application of antidumping duties lead to a terms-of-trade gain for the Home country, making this another example of strategic trade policy that can potentially benefit the Home country? In fact, the answer to this question is often "no," because the antidumping provisions of U.S. trade law are *overused*. These provisions create a much greater cost for consumers and a larger welfare loss than does the less frequent application of tariffs under Sections 201, 232, or 301 of U.S. trade law. To understand why they are overused and why they create a large welfare loss, we need to explain how antidumping duties are calculated.

Calculation of Antidumping Duty The amount of an antidumping duty is calculated based on the Foreign firm's local price. If its local price is $10 (after converting from Foreign's currency to U.S. dollars), and its export price to the Home market is $6, then the antidumping tariff is calculated as the difference between these prices, $4 in our example. This method of calculating the tariff creates an incentive for the Foreign firm to *raise* its export price even before the tariff is applied so that the duty will be lower. If the Foreign firm charges an export price of $8 instead of $4 but maintains its local price of $10, then the antidumping tariff will be only $2. Even better, the Foreign firm could charge $10 in its export market (the same as its local price) and avoid the antidumping tariff altogether!

Thus, the calculation of an antidumping duty creates a strong incentive for Foreign firms to *raise* their export prices to reduce or avoid the duty. This increase in the import price results in a terms-of-trade *loss* for the Home country. Such an increase in the import price is illustrated in Figure 9-9 as the rise from price P_1 to P_2. This price increase leads to a gain for Home firms of area a, but a loss for Home consumers of area $(a + b + c + d)$. There is no revenue collected when the duty is not imposed, so the net loss for the Home country is area $(b + c + d)$. This loss is higher than the

FIGURE 9-9

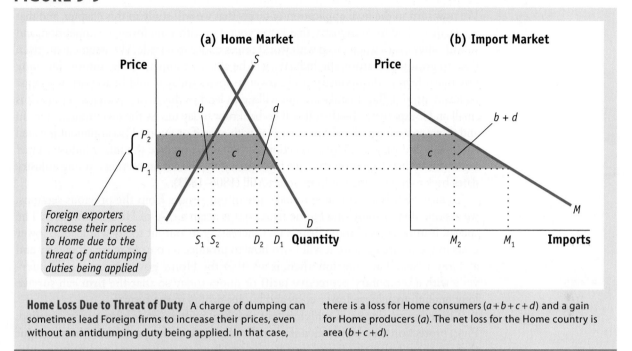

(a) Home Market

(b) Import Market

Foreign exporters increase their prices to Home due to the threat of antidumping duties being applied

Home Loss Due to Threat of Duty A charge of dumping can sometimes lead Foreign firms to increase their prices, even without an antidumping duty being applied. In that case, there is a loss for Home consumers $(a+b+c+d)$ and a gain for Home producers (a). The net loss for the Home country is area $(b+c+d)$.

deadweight loss from a tariff (which is area $b + d$) and illustrates the extra costs associated with the threat of an antidumping duty.

Furthermore, the fact that Foreign firms will raise their prices to reduce the potential duty gives Home firms an incentive to charge Foreign firms with dumping, even if none is occurring: just the *threat* of an antidumping duty is enough to cause Foreign firms to raise their prices and reduce competition in the Home market for that good. In fact, evidence shows that Foreign firms often change their prices and *increase* the price charged in the importing country when an antidumping case is filed, even before an antidumping tariff is applied.

This line of reasoning explains why Home firms are willing to file antidumping cases so often: filing a case can influence Foreign firms to raise their prices in the Home market (so as to avoid a dumping duty), which helps the Home firms by reducing competition. But that benefit to the Home firms comes at a high cost to Home consumers.

While politicians often regard the antidumping provisions of trade law as essential to create a "fair" playing field for firms (see the quotation from President Obama as the beginning of the chapter), economists regard antidumping provisions as very costly to consumers and to overall welfare in the importing country. According to one estimate, the annual cost to the United States from its antidumping policies is equivalent to the deadweight loss of a 6% uniform tariff applied across all imports, which is about the size of the average U.S. tariff in 2019, so that antidumping policies have nearly the same cost as all other U.S. tariffs put together.[14]

---

[14] The 6% cost of U.S. antidumping policy comes from Kim Ruhl, 2012, "Antidumping in the Aggregate," New York University Stern School of Business, and the 6% average U.S. tariff in 2019 comes from Figure 1-4 in Chapter 1. Actually, the deadweight loss from a *uniform* 6% tariff will be somewhat less than the loss from the *average* 6% U.S. tariff in 2019, because the U.S. tariffs are much higher on some products and against some countries, like China.

4 Infant Industry Protection

We now turn to the final application of tariffs that we will study in this chapter, and that is a tariff applied to an industry that is too young to withstand foreign competition, and so will suffer losses when faced with world prices under free trade. We assume that, given time to grow and mature, the industry will be able to compete in the future. The only way that a firm in this industry could cover its losses today would be to borrow against its future profits. But if banks are not willing to lend to this firm—perhaps because it is small and inexperienced—then it will go bankrupt today unless the government steps in and offers some form of assistance, such as with a tariff or quota. This argument is called the "infant industry case" for protection. Although we include the infant industry tariff argument in this chapter on strategic trade policy, the idea of protecting a young industry dates back to the writings of John Stuart Mill (1806–1873).

To analyze this argument and make use of our results from the previous sections, we assume there is only one Home firm, so it is again a case of Home monopoly. The special feature of this Home firm is that increasing its output today will lead to lower costs in the future because it will learn how to produce its output more efficiently and at a lower cost. The question, then, is whether the Home government should intervene with a temporary protective tariff or quota today so that the firm can survive long enough to achieve lower costs and higher profits in the future.

There are two cases in which infant industry protection is potentially justified. First, protection may be justified if a tariff today leads to an increase in Home output that, in turn, helps the firm learn better production techniques and reduce costs in the future. This is different from increasing returns to scale as discussed in Chapter 6. With increasing returns to scale, lower costs arise from producing farther down along a decreasing average cost curve; while a tariff might boost Home production and lower costs, removing the tariff would reduce production to its initial level and still leave the firm uncompetitive at world prices. For infant industry protection to be justified, the firm's learning must *shift down* the entire average cost curve to the point where it is competitive at world prices in the future, even without the tariff.

If the firm's costs are going to fall in the future, then why doesn't it simply borrow today to cover its losses and pay back the loan from future profits? Why does it need import protection to offset its current losses? The answer was already hinted at above: banks may be unwilling to lend to this firm because they don't know with certainty that the firm will achieve lower costs and be profitable enough in the future to repay the loan. In such a situation, a tariff or quota offsets an imperfection in the market for borrowing and lending (the capital market). What is most essential for the infant industry argument to be valid is not imperfect competition (a single Home firm), but rather, this imperfection in the Home capital market.

A second case in which import protection is potentially justified is when a tariff in one period leads to an increase in output and reductions in future costs *for other firms in the industry*, or even for firms in other industries. This type of **externality** occurs when firms learn from each other's successes. For instance, consider the high-tech semiconductor industry. Each firm innovates its products at a different pace, and when one firm has a technological breakthrough, other firms benefit by being able to copy the newly developed knowledge. In the semiconductor industry, it is not unusual for firms to mimic the successful innovations of other firms and benefit from a **knowledge spillover**. In the presence of spillovers, the infant industry tariff promotes a positive externality: an increase in output for one firm lowers the costs for everyone. Because firms learn from one another, each firm on its own does not have much incentive to invest in learning by increasing its production today. In this case, a tariff is needed to offset this externality by increasing production, allowing for these spillovers to occur among firms so that there are cost reductions.

As both of these cases show, the infant industry argument supporting tariffs or quotas depends on the existence of some form of **market failure**. In our first example, the market does not provide loans to the firm to allow it to avoid bankruptcy; in the second, the firm may find it difficult to protect its intellectual knowledge through patents, which would enable it to be compensated for the spillover of knowledge to others. These market failures create a potential role for government policy. In practice, however, it can be very difficult for a government to correct market failure. If the capital market will not provide loans to a firm because it doesn't think the firm will be profitable in the future, then why would the government have better information about that firm's future prospects? Likewise, in the case of a spillover of knowledge to other firms, we cannot expect the government to know the extent of spillovers. Thus, we should be skeptical about the ability of government to distinguish the industries that deserve infant industry protection from those that do not.

Furthermore, even if either of the two conditions we have identified to potentially justify infant industry protection holds, these market failures do not guarantee that the protection will be worthwhile—we still need to compare the future benefits of protection (which are positive) with its costs today (the deadweight losses). So while some form of market failure is a *prerequisite* condition for infant industry protection to be justified, we will identify two further conditions below that must be satisfied for the protection to be successful. With these warnings in mind, let's look at how infant industry protection can work.

Free-Trade Equilibrium

In panel (a) of Figure 9-10, we show the situation a Home firm faces today, and in panel (b) we show its situation in the future. We assume that the Home country is small and therefore faces a fixed world price. As discussed earlier in the chapter, even a

FIGURE 9-10

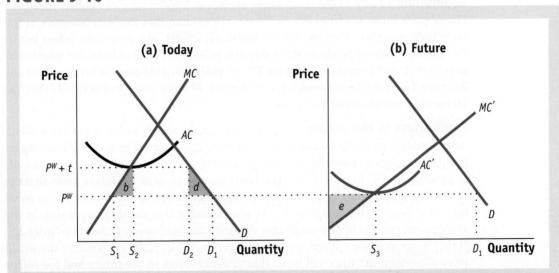

Infant Industry Protection In the situation today (panel a), the industry would produce S_1, the quantity at which $MC = P^W$. Because P^W is less than average costs at S_1, the industry would incur losses at the world price of P^W and would be forced to shut down. A tariff increases the price from P^W to $P^W + t$, allowing the industry to produce at S_2 (and survive) with the net loss in welfare of $(b+d)$. In panel (b), producing S_2 today allows the average cost curve to fall through learning to AC'. In the future, the firm can produce the quantity S_3 at the price P^W without tariff protection and earn producer surplus of e.

Home monopolist will behave in the same manner as a perfectly competitive industry under free trade, assuming that they have the same marginal costs. We also assume that any increase in the firm's output today leads to a reduction in costs in the future (i.e., a downward shift in the firm's average cost curve).

Equilibrium Today With free trade today, the Home firm faces the world price of P^W (which, you will recall from earlier in this chapter, is also its marginal revenue curve) and will produce to the point at which its marginal cost of production equals P^W. The Home firm therefore supplies the quantity S_1. To verify that S_1 is actually the Home supply, however, we need to check that profits are not negative at this quantity. To do so, we compare the firm's average costs with the price. The average cost curve is shown as AC in panel (a), and at the supply of S_1, average costs are much higher than the price P^W. That means the Home firm is suffering losses and would shut down today instead of producing S_1.

Tariff Equilibrium

To prevent the firm from shutting down, the Home government could apply an import tariff or quota to raise the Home price. Provided that the Home firm increases its output in response to this higher price, we assume that this increased size allows the firm to learn better production techniques so that its future costs are reduced. Given the choice of an import tariff or quota to achieve this goal, the Home government should definitely choose the tariff. The reason is that when a Home monopolist is faced with a quota rather than a tariff, it will produce *less* output under the quota so that it can further raise its price. The decrease in output leads to additional deadweight loss today, as discussed earlier in the chapter. Furthermore, because we have assumed that the firm's learning depends on how much it produces and output is lower under the quota, there would be less learning and a smaller reduction in future costs under a quota than a tariff. For both reasons, a tariff is a better policy than a quota when the goal is to nurture an infant industry.

Equilibrium Today If the government applies an import tariff of t dollars today, the Home price increases from P^W to $P^W + t$. We assume that the government sets the tariff high enough so that the new Home price, $P^W + t$, just covers the infant industry's average costs of production. At this new price, the firm produces the quantity S_2 in panel (a). As illustrated, the price $P^W + t$ exactly equals average costs, AC, at the quantity S_2, so the firm is making zero profits. Making zero profits means that the Home firm will continue to operate.

Equilibrium in the Future With the firm producing S_2 today, it can learn about better production methods and lower its costs in the future. The effect of learning on production costs is shown by the downward shift of the average cost curve from AC in panel (a) to AC' in panel (b).[15] The lower average costs in the future mean that the firm can produce quantity S_3 without tariff protection at the world price P^W in panel (b) and still cover its average costs. We are assuming that the downward shift in the average cost curve is large enough that the firm can avoid losses at the world price P^W. If that is not the case—if the average cost curve AC' in panel (b) is above the world price P^W—then the firm will be unable to avoid losses in the future and the infant industry protection will not be successful. But if the temporary tariff today allows the firm to operate in the future without the tariff, then the infant industry protection has satisfied the *first condition* to be judged successful.

---

[15] The marginal cost curve might also shift down, from MC in panel (a) to MC' in panel (b), although that shift is not essential to our argument.

Effect of the Tariff on Welfare The application of the tariff today leads to a deadweight loss, and in panel (a), the deadweight loss is measured by the triangles $(b + d)$. But we also need to count the gain from having the firm operating in the future. In panel (b) of Figure 9-10, the producer surplus earned in the future by the firm is shown by the region e. We should think of the region e as the present value (i.e., the discounted sum over time) of the firm's future producer surplus; it is this amount that would be forgone if the firm shut down today. The *second condition* for the infant industry protection to be successful is that the deadweight loss $(b + d)$ when the tariff is used should be less than the area e, which is present value of the firm's future producer surplus when it no longer needs the tariff.

For the tariff to be successful, it needs to satisfy both conditions: the firm has to be able to produce without losses and without needing the tariff in the future; and the future gains in producer surplus need to exceed the current deadweight loss from the tariff. To evaluate the second criterion, we need to compare the future gain of e with the deadweight loss today of $(b + d)$. If e exceeds $(b + d)$, then the infant industry protection has been worthwhile, but if e is less than $(b + d)$, then the costs of protection today do not justify the future benefits. The challenge for government policy is to try to distinguish worthwhile cases (those for which future benefits exceed present costs) from those cases that are not worthwhile. In the application that follows, we will see whether the governments of China, Brazil, and the United States have been able to distinguish between these cases.

APPLICATION

Examples of Infant Industry Protection

There are many examples of infant industry protection in practice, and we will consider three: (1) a complete ban on imports imposed from 1977 to the early 1990s to protect the computer industry in Brazil; (2) a U.S. tariff imposed to protect Harley-Davidson motorcycles in the United States during the 1980s; and (3) tariffs and quotas imposed to protect the automobile industry in China, which were reduced when China joined the World Trade Organization in 2001.

Computers in Brazil

There are many cases in which infant industry protection has not been successful. One well-known case involves the computer industry in Brazil. In 1977 the Brazilian government began a program to protect domestic firms involved in the production of personal computers (PCs). It was thought that achieving national autonomy in the computer industry was essential for strategic military reasons. Not only were imports of PCs banned, but domestic firms also had to buy from local suppliers whenever possible and foreign producers of PCs were not allowed to operate in Brazil.

The Brazilian ban on imports lasted from 1977 to the early 1990s. This was a period of rapid innovation in PC production worldwide, with large drops in the cost of computing power. In Figure 9-11, we show the effective price of computing power in the United States and Brazil between 1982 and 1992, which fell very rapidly in both countries. The price we are graphing is "effective" because it is not just the retail price of a new PC but a price index that reflects the improvements over time in the PC's speed of calculations, storage capacity, and so on.

Prices in Brazil Brazilian firms were adept at reverse engineering the IBM PCs being sold from the United States. But the reverse engineering took time, and the fact that Brazilian firms were required to use local suppliers for many parts within the computers added to the costs of production. We can see from Figure 9-11 that Brazil

FIGURE 9-11

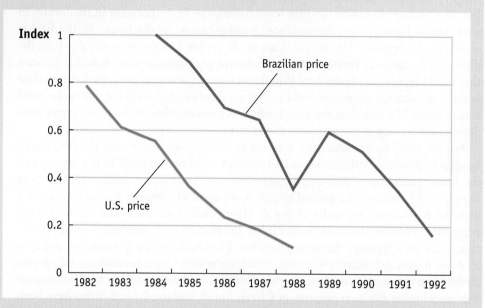

Computer Prices in the United States and Brazil, 1982–92 This diagram shows the effective price of computer power in the United States and Brazil. Both prices fell very rapidly because of technological improvements, but the drop in the U.S. price exceeded that of the Brazilian price. The difference between the two prices is a measure of the technology gap between Brazil and the United States in the production of personal computers.

Data from: Eduardo Luzio and Shane Greenstein, November 1995, "Measuring the Performance of a Protected Infant Industry: The Case of Brazilian Microcomputers," Review of Economics and Statistics, 77(4), 622–633.

never achieved low prices at the same time as in the United States. By 1992, for example, the effective price in Brazil had just reached the price that had been achieved in the United States five years earlier, in 1987. The persistent gap between the prices in Brazil and the United States means that Brazil was never able to produce computers at competitive prices without tariff protection. This fact alone means that the infant industry protection was not successful.

Consumer and Producer Surplus In Table 9-1, we show the welfare calculation for Brazil, as well as other details of the PC industry. Local sales peaked at about $750 million in 1986, and the following year, the Brazilian prices rose to within 20% of those in the United States. But that is as close as the Brazilian industry ever got to world prices. In 1984 prices in Brazil were nearly double those in the United States, which led to a producer surplus gain of $29 million but a consumer surplus loss in Brazil of $80 million. The net loss was therefore $80 million − $29 million = $51 million, which was 0.02% of Brazilian gross domestic product (GDP) that year. By 1986 the net loss had grown to $164 million, or 0.06% of GDP. This net loss was the deadweight loss from the tariff during the years it was in place. The industry was never able to produce in the absence of tariffs, so there are no future gains (like area *e* in Figure 9-10) that we can count against those losses.

Other Losses The higher prices in Brazil imposed costs on Brazilian industries that relied on computers in manufacturing, as well as on individual users, and they became increasingly dissatisfied with the government's policy. During his campaign in 1990, President Fernando Collor de Mello promised to abolish the infant industry protection for personal computers, which he did immediately after he was elected.

TABLE 9-1

Brazilian Computer Industry This table shows the effects of the government ban on imports of personal computers into Brazil.

Year	Sales ($ millions)	Brazil/U.S. Price (%)	Producer Surplus Gain ($ millions)	Consumer Surplus Loss ($ millions)	Net Loss ($ millions)	Net Loss (% of GDP)
1984	$126	189%	$29	$80	$51	0.02%
1985	384	159	70	179	109	0.04
1986	746	143	113	277	164	0.06
1987	644	119	50	112	62	0.02
1988	279	127	29	68	39	0.01

Data from: Eduardo Luzio and Shane Greenstein, November 1995, "Measuring the Performance of a Protected Infant Industry: The Case of Brazilian Microcomputers," Review of Economics and Statistics, 77(4), 622–633.

A number of reasons have been given for the failure of this policy to develop an efficient industry in Brazil: imported materials such as silicon chips were expensive to obtain, as were domestically produced parts that local firms were required to use; in addition, local regulations limited the entry of new firms into the industry. Whatever the reasons, this case illustrates how difficult it is to successfully nurture an infant industry and how difficult it is for the government to know whether temporary protection will allow an industry to survive in the future.

U.S. Tariff on Heavyweight Motorcycles

Harley-Davidson does not really fit the usual description of an "infant" industry: the first plant opened in 1903 in Milwaukee, Wisconsin, and it was owned and operated by William Harley and the three Davidson brothers. Until the late 1970s it did not face intense import competition from Japanese producers; but by the early 1980s, Harley-Davidson was on the verge of bankruptcy. Even though it had been around since 1903, Harley-Davidson had many of the characteristics we associate with an infant industry: the inability to compete at the international price today and (as we will see) the potential for lower costs in the future. By including this case in our discussion of infant industries, we are able to make a precise calculation of the effect of the tariffs on consumers and producers to determine whether the infant industry protection was successful.

In 1983 Harley-Davidson, the legendary U.S.-based motorcycle manufacturer, was in trouble. It was suffering losses due to a long period of lagging productivity combined with intense competition from Japanese producers. Two of these producers, Honda and Kawasaki, not only had plants in the United States but also exported Japan-made goods to the United States. Two other Japanese producers, Suzuki and Yamaha, produced and exported their products from Japan. In the early 1980s these four Japanese firms were engaged in a global price war that spilled over into the U.S. market, and inventories of imported heavyweight cycles rose dramatically in the United States. Facing this intense import competition, Harley-Davidson applied to the International Trade Commission (ITC) for Section 201 protection.

As required by law, the ITC engaged in a study to determine the source of injury to the industry, which in this case was identified as heavyweight (more than 700 cc) motorcycles. Among other factors, it studied the buildup of inventories by Japanese producers in the United States. The ITC determined that there was more than nine months' worth of inventory of Japanese motorcycles already in the United States, which could depress the prices of heavyweight cycles and threaten bankruptcy for Harley-Davidson. As a result, the ITC recommended to President Ronald Reagan that import protection be placed on imports of heavyweight motorcycles. This case is interesting because it is one of the few times that the *threat* of injury by imports has been used as a justification for tariffs under Section 201 of U.S. trade law.

President Reagan approved the recommendation from the ITC, and tariffs were imposed on imports of heavyweight motorcycles. These tariffs were initially very high, but they declined over five years. The initial tariff, imposed on April 16, 1983, was 45%; it then fell annually to 35%, 20%, 15%, and 10% and was scheduled to end in April 1988. In fact, Harley-Davidson petitioned the ITC to end the tariff one year early, after the 15% rate expired in 1987, by which time it had cut costs and introduced new and very popular products so that profitability had been restored. Amid great fanfare, President Reagan visited the Harley-Davidson plant in Milwaukee, Wisconsin, and declared that the tariff had been a successful case of protection.

President Ronald Reagan visits the Harley-Davidson plant.

Calculation of Deadweight Loss Was the tariff on heavyweight motorcycles really successful? To answer this, we need to compare the deadweight loss of the tariff with the future gain in producer surplus. In our discussion of the steel tariff in the previous chapter, we derived a formula for the deadweight loss from using a tariff, and now we apply the 45% tariff and the 17% fall in imports for 1983 from Table 9-2:

$$\frac{DWL}{P^W \cdot M} = \frac{1}{2} \cdot \frac{t \cdot \Delta M}{P^W \cdot M} = \frac{1}{2} \cdot (0.45 \cdot 0.17) = 0.038, \text{ or } 3.8\%.$$

We can calculate the average import sales from 1982 to 1983 as $(452 + 410)/2 =$ \$431 million. Multiplying the percentage loss by average imports, we obtain the deadweight loss in 1983 of $0.038 \cdot 431 = $ \$16.3 million. That deadweight loss is reported in the last column of Table 9-2, along with the loss for each following year. Adding up these deadweight losses, we obtain a total loss of \$112.5 million over the four years that the tariff was used.[16]

Future Gain in Producer Surplus To judge whether the tariff was effective, we need to compare the deadweight loss of \$112.5 million with the *future* gain in producer surplus (area *e* in Figure 9-10). How can we assess these future gains? We can use a technique that economists favor: we can evaluate the future gains in producer surplus by examining the stock market value of the firm around the time that the tariff was removed.

During the time that the tariff was in place, the management of Harley-Davidson reduced costs through several methods: implementing a "just-in-time" inventory system, which means producing inventory on demand rather than having excess amounts in warehouses; reducing the workforce (and its wages); and implementing "quality circles," groups of assembly workers who volunteer to meet together to discuss workplace improvements, along with a "statistical operator control system" that allowed employees to evaluate the quality of their output. Many of these production techniques were copied from Japanese firms. The company also introduced a new engine. These changes allowed Harley-Davidson to transform losses during the period from 1981 to 1982 into profits for 1983 and in following years.

In July 1986 Harley-Davidson became a public corporation and issued stock on the American Stock Exchange: 2 million shares at \$11 per share, for a total offering

---

[16] This calculation is not quite accurate because we have used the calendar years 1983 to 1986 rather than the 12 months from April of each year to March of the next year, during which the tariff was effective.

TABLE 9-2

U.S. Imports of Heavyweight Motorcycles This table shows the effects of the tariff on imports of heavyweight motorcycles in the United States.

Year	Import Sales ($ millions)	Import Quantity	% Fall in Imports (from 1982)	Tariff (%)	Net Loss/Average Sales (%)	Deadweight Loss ($ millions)
1982	$452	164,000				
1983	410	139,000	17%	45%	3.8%	$16.3
1984	179	80,000	69	35	12.1	38.4
1985	191	72,000	78	20	7.8	25.2
1986	152	43,000	116	15	8.7	26.4
January–March, 1987	59	14,000	98	15	7.3	6.3
Total, 1983–87						112.5

Data from: Heavy Weight Motorcycles. Report to the President on Investigation No. TA-203-17, under Section 203 of the Trade Act of 1974. U.S. International Trade Commission, June 1987, and author's calculations.

of $22 million. It also issued debt of $70 million, which was to be repaid from future profits. In June 1987 it issued stock again: 1.23 million shares at $16.50 per share, for a total offering of $20.3 million. The sum of these stock and debt issues is $112.3 million, which we can interpret as the present discounted value of the producer surplus of the firm. This estimate of area *e* is nearly equal to the consumer surplus loss, $112.5 million, in Table 9-2. Within a month after the second stock offering, however, the stock price rose from $16.50 to $19 per share. Using that price to evaluate the outstanding stock of 3.23 million, we obtain a stock value of $61 million, plus $70 million in repaid debt, to obtain $131 million as the future producer surplus.

By this calculation, the future gain in producer surplus from tariff protection to Harley-Davidson ($131 million) exceeds the deadweight loss of the tariff ($112.5 million). Furthermore, since 1987 Harley-Davidson has become an even more successful company. Its sales and profits have grown every year, and many model changes have been introduced, so it is now the Japanese companies that copy Harley-Davidson. By March 2005 Harley-Davidson had actually surpassed General Motors in its stock market value: $17.7 billion versus $16.2 billion. Both of these companies suffered losses during the financial crisis of 2008 and 2009, but Harley-Davidson continued to operate as usual whereas General Motors declared bankruptcy on June 1, 2009, and required a government bailout. Since that time General Motors has recovered, and at the end of 2019 it had a stock market value of $53 billion, while Harley-Davidson had a stock market value of $6 billion.

Was Protection Successful? Does this calculation mean that the infant industry protection was successful? A complete answer to that question involves knowing what would have happened if the tariff had *not* been put in place. When we say that infant industry protection is successful if the area *e* of future producer surplus gain ($131 million) exceeds the deadweight loss ($112.5 million), we are assuming that the firm would not have survived at all without the tariff protection. That assumption may be true for Harley-Davidson. It is well documented that Harley-Davidson was on the brink of bankruptcy from 1982 to 1983. Citibank had decided that it would not extend more loans to cover Harley's losses, and Harley found alternative financing on December 31, 1985, just one week before filing for bankruptcy.[17] If the tariff saved the company, then this was clearly a case of successful infant industry protection.

---

[17] See Peter C. Reid, 1990, *Made Well in America: Lessons from Harley-Davidson on Being the Best* (New York: McGraw-Hill).

On the other hand, even if Harley-Davidson had not received the tariff and had filed for bankruptcy, it might still have emerged to prosper again. Bankruptcy does not mean that a firm stops producing; it just means that the firm's assets are used to repay all possible debts. Even if Harley-Davidson had gone bankrupt without the tariff, some or all of the future gains in producer surplus might have been realized. So we cannot be certain whether the turnaround of Harley-Davidson required the use of the tariff.[18]

Despite all these uncertainties, it still appears that the tariff on heavyweight motorcycles bought Harley-Davidson some breathing room. This is the view expressed by the chief economist at the ITC at that time, in the quotation at the beginning of the chapter: "If the case of heavyweight motorcycles is to be considered the only successful escape-clause [tariff], it is because it caused little harm and it helped Harley-Davidson get a bank loan so it could diversify."[19] We agree with this assessment that the harm caused by the tariff was small compared with the potential benefits of avoiding bankruptcy, which allowed Harley-Davidson to become the very successful company that it is today.

Protecting the Automobile Industry in China

The final example of infant industry protection that we discuss involves the automobile industry in China. In 2009, China overtook the United States as the largest automobile market in the world (measured by domestic sales plus imports). Strong competition among foreign firms located in China, local producers, and import sales have resulted in new models and falling prices so that the Chinese middle class can now afford to buy automobiles. In 2009, there were more than 13 million vehicles sold in China, as compared with 10.4 million cars and light trucks sold in the United States. By 2017 there were 28 million new cars sold in China, 10 million more than made in the United States and nearly double the European Union sales.

Growth in automotive production and sales has been particularly strong since 2001, when China joined the World Trade Organization (WTO). With its accession to the WTO, China agreed to reduce its tariffs on foreign autos, which were as high as 260% in the early 1980s, then fell to 80% to 100% by 1996, to 25% by 2006, and to 15% today. China has loosened its import quotas, as well. Those tariffs and quotas, in addition to restrictions at the province and city level on what types of cars could be sold, had limited China's imports and put a damper on the auto industry in that country. Prices were high and foreign producers were reluctant to sell their newest models to China. That situation has changed dramatically. Now, foreign firms scramble to compete in China with their latest designs and are even making plans to export cars from China. Is the Chinese automobile industry a successful case of infant industry protection? Are the benefits gained by the current production and export of cars greater than the costs of the tariffs and quotas imposed in the past? To answer this, we begin by briefly describing the history of the Chinese auto industry.

Production in China Beginning in the early 1980s, China permitted a number of joint ventures between foreign firms and local Chinese partners. The first of these in 1983 was Beijing Jeep, which was a joint venture between American Motors Corporation (AMC—later acquired by Chrysler Corporation) and a local firm in Beijing. The following year, Germany's Volkswagen signed a 25-year contract to make passenger cars in Shanghai, and France's Peugeot agreed to another passenger car project to make vehicles in Guangzhou.

---

[18] The chairman of Harley-Davidson stated in 1987 that the tariff had not actually helped the company that much because the Japanese producers were able to downsize some of their motorcycles to 699 cc engine size, and thereby avoid the tariff (*Wall Street Journal*, March 20, 1987, p. 39).

[19] John Suomela, chief economist at the U.S. International Trade Commission, as cited in Douglas A. Irwin, 2002, *Free Trade Under Fire* (Princeton, N.J.: Princeton University Press), pp. 136–137.

Although joint venture agreements provided a window for foreign manufacturers to tap the China market, there were limits on their participation. Foreign manufacturers could not own a majority stake in a manufacturing plant—Volkswagen's venture took the maximum of 50% foreign ownership. The Chinese also kept control of distribution networks for the jointly produced automobiles. These various regulations, combined with high tariff duties, helped at least some of the new joint ventures achieve success. Volkswagen's Shanghai plant was by far the winner under these rules, and it produced more than 200,000 vehicles per year by the late 1990s, more than twice as many as any other plant. Volkswagen's success was also aided by some Shanghai municipal efforts. Various restrictions on engine size, as well as incentives offered to city taxi companies that bought Volkswagens, helped ensure that only Volkswagen's models could be sold in the Shanghai market; essentially, the Shanghai Volkswagen plant had a local monopoly.

Cost to Consumers The tariffs and quotas used in China kept imports fairly low throughout the 1990s, ranging from a high of 222,000 cars imported in 1993 to a low of 27,500 imports in 1998; 160,000 cars were imported in 2005. Since tariffs were in the range of 80% to 100% by 1996, import prices were approximately doubled because of the tariffs. But the quotas imposed on auto imports probably had at least as great an impact on prices of imports *and* domestically produced cars. Our analysis earlier in the chapter showed that quotas have a particularly large impact on domestic prices when the Home firm is a monopoly. That situation applied to Volkswagen's joint venture in Shanghai, which enjoyed a local monopoly on the sales of its vehicles.

The effect of this local monopoly was to substantially increase prices in the Shanghai market. In Figure 9-12, we show the estimated markups of price over marginal costs for autos sold in China from 1995 to 2001, by various producers. The markups for Shanghai

FIGURE 9-12

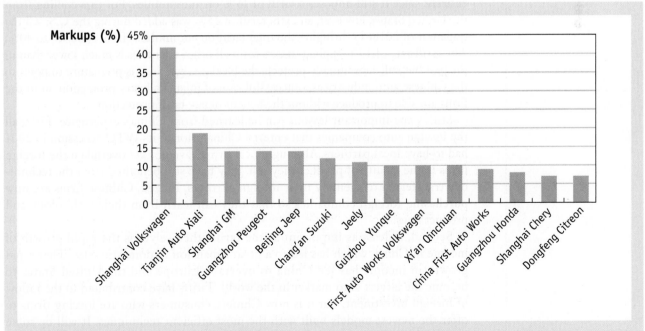

Automobile Markups by Firms in China, 1995–2001 This diagram shows the percentage markups (price over marginal cost) applied to automobiles sold in China from 1995 to 2001, by various producers. The highest markup was charged by Shanghai Volkswagen, which had a local monopoly in Shanghai.

Data from: Haiyan Deng, 2010, "Market Structure and Pricing Strategy of China's Automobile Industry," Journal of Industrial Economics, 58(4), 818–845.

Volkswagen are the highest, reaching a high of 54% in 1998 and then falling to 28% in 2001, for an average of 42% for the period from 1995 to 2001. In comparison, the average markup charged by Tianjin Auto was 19%, and the average markup charged by Shanghai GM was 14%. All the other producers shown in Figure 9-12 have even lower markups.

From this evidence, it is clear that Shanghai Volkswagen was able to substantially raise its prices because of the monopoly power granted by the local government. Furthermore, the Jetta and Audi models produced by Shanghai Volkswagen during the 1990s were outdated models. That plant had the highest production through 2001, despite its high prices and outdated models, so a large number of consumers in the Shanghai area and beyond bore the costs of that local protection. This example illustrates how a Home monopoly can gain from protection at the expense of consumers. The example also illustrates how protection can stifle the incentive for firms to introduce the newest models and production techniques.

Foreign Production in China The local monopoly held by Shanghai Volkswagen has been eroded by the entry of foreign firms into the Chinese market. General Motors first entered the Chinese market in 1999 in a joint venture with Shanghai Automotive, and in 2009 it opened two new plants in Shanghai, at a cost of $1.5 billion and $2.5 billion. In 2018, General Motors produced 3.6 million vehicles in China, which is its largest retail market. Ford has seven plants in China, the most recent of which opened in Harbin in 2017. The Korean producer Hyundai likewise opened a new plant in 2017, which is its eighth factory in China. Tesla has a plant in Shanghai, called the Gigafactory 3, to produce its electric cars, and it made its first delivery of a Chinese-built Tesla in December 2019. German auto companies other than Volkswagen and Japanese companies also have numerous plants in China.

Infant Industry Protection? For the tariffs and quotas used in China to be justified as infant industry protection, they should lead to a large enough drop in future costs so that the protection is no longer needed. China has not reached that point entirely, since it still imposes a tariff of 15% on automobiles. For cars coming from the United States, however, an extra tariff of 25% was added during the U.S.–China trade war of 2018–19, bringing the total tariff on automobiles from America to 40%. The tariff rate of 15% applied to cars from all other countries is much lower than in the past but still substantially protects the local market. So it is premature to point to the Chinese auto industry as a successful case of infant industry protection, until the firms are able to produce without the benefit of any tariff protection.

Still, some important lessons can be learned from China's experience. First, all the foreign auto companies that entered China prior to its WTO accession in 2001 had to have local partners. Although local firms have not yet overtaken the foreign firms in the quality of product they sell, they have still benefited from the technology transferred to them by their foreign partners. Indeed, Chinese firms are now purchasing foreign companies so that they can learn from their technology and product lines.

Second, at least as important as the tariffs themselves is the rapid growth of income in China, which has led to a great expansion in domestic sales. That rapid growth in income has led China to overtake Europe and the United States to become the largest auto market in the world. Tariffs have contributed to the inflow of foreign investment, but it is now Chinese consumers who are forcing firms to offer the newest models built with the most efficient techniques. It will be some years before we know whether Chinese firms will learn enough from their foreign partners to produce models that are highly desired by customers in China and around the world.

5 Conclusions

In Chapter 8, we discussed the use of import tariffs and quotas under perfect competition and highlighted the difference between the small-country and large-country cases. With perfect competition, a small importing country loses from a tariff (because it cannot affect world prices), but the large importing country can potentially gain from a tariff (because the tariff depresses the world price). Import quotas have effects similar to those of import tariffs under perfect competition, so we often refer to quotas and tariffs as "equivalent."

We can contrast the results obtained under perfect competition with the results we learned in this chapter, in which we assume imperfect competition—either Home or Foreign monopoly. Under Home monopoly, the effects of a tariff and quota are very different. With a tariff, the Home monopolist can increase its price by the amount of the tariff (as would a competitive industry) but cannot exercise its monopoly power. With an import quota, however, the Home firm is able to charge a higher price than it could with a tariff because it enjoys a "sheltered" market. So the import quota leads to higher costs for Home consumers than the tariff, and these two policies are no longer "equivalent" as they are under perfect competition.

Under Foreign monopoly, the results are similar to those of the large-country case analyzed in Chapter 8: the tariff leads to a fall in the price received by the Foreign monopolist, so the price paid by Home consumers rises by *less than* the full amount of the tariff. The tariff is shared between an increase in the Home price and a decrease in the Foreign price, and the Home importer obtains a terms-of-trade gain. For small tariffs, the terms-of-trade gain exceeds the deadweight loss, and the Home country gains from the tariff. So this is a case in which the use of a tariff as strategic trade policy can benefit the Home country, but at the expense of the Foreign firm.

A specific example of a tariff applied against a Foreign monopoly occurs when the Foreign firm is a discriminating monopoly and dumps its output into Home at a lower price than it charges in its own local market. When dumping occurs, the importing country is permitted by WTO rules to respond with a tariff, which is called an anti-dumping duty. In principle, we might expect Home to gain from the duty because the Foreign firm will lower its price (as occurs for a tariff applied against a Foreign monopolist). But we have argued that Home gains from the antidumping duty are unlikely to arise because of special features in the way these duties are applied. Instead, the expected outcome from antidumping duties is that Foreign exporters raise prices even when a duty is *not* applied, leading to Home losses. Because of these losses, the use of antidumping duties as strategic trade policy is not effective.

Another topic discussed in this chapter is the infant industry case for protection. We studied three industries as examples of infant industry protection: computers in Brazil, Harley-Davidson motorcycles in the United States, and automobiles in China. For computers in Brazil, the ban on imports during the 1980s was not successful because the industry was never able to learn enough from the world leaders to reach the same level of efficiency and competitive prices. In addition to the industry being competitive at world prices, successful infant industry protection requires that the cost of temporary protection is less than the gains from having the industry continue (without that protection). The tariff given to protect Harley-Davidson motorcycles in the United States during the 1980s was successful because Harley-Davidson survived and became very profitable: its producer surplus gains in 1986 just exceeded the cost of the temporary tariff protection. A final case that we considered was automobile production in China, which has grown rapidly and overtaken production in Europe and the United States. But that industry is still protected by a 15% tariff, so it is too early to judge whether this will be a successful case of infant industry protection.

KEY POINTS

1. Free trade will lead a Home monopoly in a small country to act in the same way as a perfectly competitive industry and charge a price equal to marginal cost. Therefore, competition from imports eliminates the monopoly power of the Home firm.

2. Quotas are not equivalent to tariffs when the Home firm is a monopolist. Because a quota limits the number of imports, the Home monopolist can charge higher prices than under a tariff, which results in greater costs to consumers.

3. When a tariff is applied against a Foreign monopolist, the results are similar to those of the large-country case analyzed in the previous chapter: the Foreign monopolist increases the price in the importing country by less than the full amount of the tariff and allows its own net-of-tariff price to fall. Hence, the tariff is shared between an increase in the Home price and a decrease in the Foreign price, a terms-of-trade gain for Home.

4. Dumping is the practice of a Foreign firm exporting goods at a price that is below its own domestic price or below its average cost of production. If the price charged for the exported good is above the firm's marginal cost, then dumping is profitable. We expect to observe dumping when the Foreign firm is acting like a discriminating monopolist.

5. Countries respond to dumping by imposing antidumping duties on imports. Antidumping duties are calculated as the difference between a Foreign firm's local price (or average costs) and its export price. To reduce or avoid the antidumping duties, Foreign firms can raise their export prices. That increase in price is a terms-of-trade loss for the importer and occurs because the Foreign firm can influence the duty.

6. In the United States and other countries, the use of antidumping tariffs far exceeds the use of tariffs under Section 201 and other trade laws. It is easy for domestic firms to bring a charge of dumping, and in many cases upholding the charge results in an increase in foreign prices and a decrease in competition for the domestic firm. The excessive use of antidumping cases also invites other countries to respond with their own charges of dumping.

7. An infant industry is a firm that requires protection to compete at world prices today. When a government applies a temporary tariff, it expects that costs for the firm or the industry overall will fall due to learning, thereby allowing it to compete at world prices in the future.

KEY TERMS

PROBLEMS

1. **Discovering Data** Figures A, B, and C (see the next page) are taken from Chad Bown: "The Pattern of Antidumping and Other Types of Contingent Protection" (World Bank, PREM Notes No. 144, October 21, 2009), and updated at https://datacatalog.worldbank.org/dataset /temporary-trade-barriers-database-including -global-antidumping-database.

   a. Figure A shows the number of newly initiated trade remedy investigations, including safeguard (SG, which are Section 201 tariffs), China

   safeguard (CSG, which was a special provision of U.S. trade law after China joined the WTO in 2001, allowing for a safeguard tariff against imports from China), antidumping (AD), and countervailing duty (CVD) (a countervailing duty is used when foreign firms receive a subsidy from their government, and then the CVD prevents them from charging lower prices in the importing country). Each bar shows the number of new cases in each quarter of the year (Q1, Q2, etc.) for 2007 through Q1 of 2012. The number of cases is graphed separately for developing countries and developed countries. What

FIGURE A

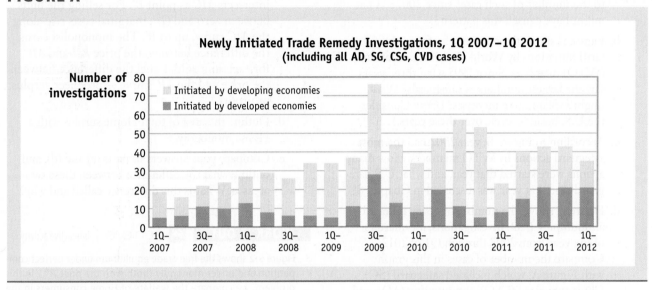

Newly Initiated Trade Remedy Investigations, 1Q 2007–1Q 2012
(including all AD, SG, CSG, CVD cases)

FIGURE B

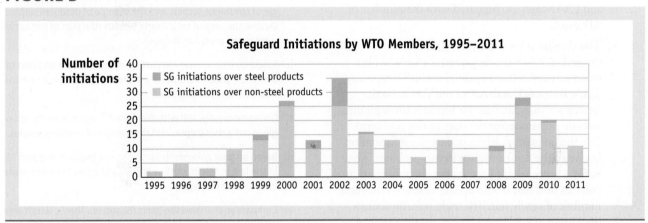

Safeguard Initiations by WTO Members, 1995–2011

FIGURE C

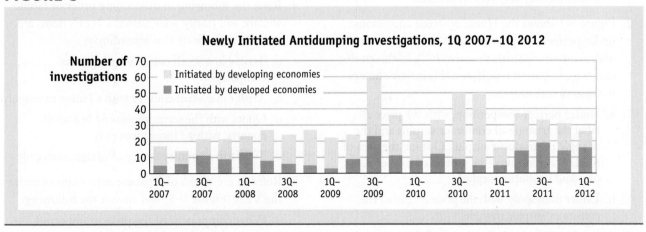

Newly Initiated Antidumping Investigations, 1Q 2007–1Q 2012

Data from: Chad P. Bown, 2009, "The Pattern of Antidumping and Other Types of Contingent Protection," World Bank, PREM Notes No. 144, 21 October. Updated from Chad P. Bown, 2012, "Global Antidumping Database," available at http://econ.worldbank.org/ttdb/.

does this graph tell us about what has happened to the number of such cases since 2007? What might have caused this pattern?

b. Figure B shows the number of safeguard (SG) tariff initiations by World Trade Organization (WTO) members. Since 1995 what three years saw the largest numbers of safeguards? What might explain these increases? (*Hint:* Consider the U.S. business cycle over these years.)

c. According to Figure B, year 2002 had the most safeguard actions by WTO members. How many actions were started that year, and what U.S. safeguard case that year was discussed in Chapter 8?

d. Figure C shows the number of newly initiated antidumping (AD) investigations, for quarters of the year from 2007 through Q1 of 2012. Compare the number of cases in this graph with Figure A, which included safeguard (SG), China safeguard (CSG), antidumping (AD), and countervailing duty (CVD) cases. What can you conclude about the total number of SG, CSG, and CVD cases as compared with the number of AD cases?

e. The data used for Figures A, B, and C run through 2011 or the first quarter of 2012. This information has been updated at the "Temporary Trade Barriers Database" of the World Bank. Search for that database (or locate it through the website mentioned at the start of this problem). Use the links provided to update the information in one of the figures shown in this problem. That is, for a more recent year, report any information you can find that would update either: (i) the total number of newly initiated trade remedy actions (including SG, AD, and CVD); (ii) the number of safeguard (SG) actions; (iii) the number of antidumping (AD) actions; or (iv) the number of countervailing duty (CVD) actions.

2. Figure 9-1 shows the Home no-trade equilibrium under perfect competition (with the price P^C) and under monopoly (with the price P^M). In this problem, we compare the welfare of Home consumers in these two situations.

a. Under perfect competition, with the price P^C, label the triangle of consumer surplus and the triangle of producer surplus. Outline the area of total Home surplus (the sum of consumer surplus and producer surplus).

b. Under monopoly, with the price P^M, label the consumer surplus triangle.

c. Producer surplus is the same as the profits earned by the monopolist. To measure this, label

the point in Figure 9-1 where the *MR* curve intersects *MC* as point *B′*. For selling the units between zero and Q^M, marginal costs rise along the *MC* curve, up to *B′*. The monopolist earns the difference between the price P^M and *MC* for each unit sold. Label the difference between the price and the *MC* curve as producer surplus, or profits.

d. Outline the area of total Home surplus with a Home monopoly.

e. Compare your answers to parts (a) and (d), and outline what the difference between these two areas is. What is this difference called and why?

WORK IT OUT   ✿ Achieve | interactive activity

3. Figure 9-2 shows the free-trade equilibrium under perfect competition and under monopoly (both with the price P^W). In this problem, we compare the welfare of Home consumers in the no-trade situation and under free trade.

a. Under perfect competition, with the price P^W, label the triangle of consumer surplus and the triangle of producer surplus. Outline the area of total Home surplus (the sum of consumer surplus and producer surplus).

b. Based on your answers to part (a) in this problem and part (a) of the last problem, outline the area of gains from free trade under perfect competition.

c. Under monopoly, still with the price P^W, again label the triangle of consumer surplus and the triangle of producer surplus.

d. Based on your answers to part (c) in this problem and part (d) in the last problem, outline the area of gains from free trade under Home monopoly.

e. Compare your answers to parts (b) and (d). That is, which area of gains from trade is higher and why?

4. Rank the following in descending order of Home welfare and justify your answers. If two items are equivalent, indicate this accordingly.

a. Tariff *t* in a small country with perfect competition

b. Tariff *t* in a small country with a Home monopoly

c. Quota with the same imports *M* in a small country, with a Home monopoly

d. Tariff *t* in a country facing a Foreign monopoly

5. Refer to the prices of Japanese auto imports under the VER (Figure 9-5) and answer the following:

a. What component of the price of imported automobiles from Japan rose the most over the period 1980 to 1985?

b. Sketch how Figures 9-5 and 9-6 might have looked if the United States had applied a tariff to Japanese auto imports instead of the VER (with the same level of imports). In words, discuss how the import prices and U.S. prices might have compared under a tariff and the VER.

c. Which policy—a tariff or the VER—would have been least costly to U.S. consumers?

6. In this problem, we analyze the effects of an import quota applied by a country facing a Foreign monopolist. In Figure 9-7, suppose that the Home country applies an import quota of X_2, meaning that the Foreign firm cannot sell any more than that amount.

a. To achieve export sales of X_2, what is the highest price that the Foreign firm can charge?

b. At the price you have identified in part (a), what is the Home consumer surplus?

c. Compare the consumer surplus you identify in part (b) with the consumer surplus under free trade. Therefore, outline in Figure 9-7 the Home losses due to the quota. *Hint:* Remember that there is no Home firm, so you do not need to take into account Home producer surplus or tariff revenue. Assume that quota rents go to Foreign firms.

d. Based on your answer to (c), which has the greater loss to the Home country—a tariff or a quota, leading to the same level of sales X_2 by the Foreign firm?

7. Suppose that the demand curve for a good is represented by the straight line

$$P = 20 - 2Q$$

Fill in the missing information in the following chart:

Quantity	Price	Total Revenue	Marginal Revenue
0			NA
1			
2			
3			
4			
5			
6			
7			
8			
9			
10			

a. Draw a graph containing both the demand curve and marginal revenue curve.

b. Is the marginal revenue curve a straight line as well? What is the slope of the marginal revenue curve? How does that slope compare with that of the demand curve?

c. Does the marginal revenue curve contain negative values over the specified range of quantities? Explain why or why not.

8. Consider the case of a Foreign monopoly with no Home production, shown in Figure 9-7. Starting from free trade at point A, consider a $5 tariff applied by the Home government.

a. If the demand curve is linear, as in Problem 7, what is the shape of the marginal revenue curve?

b. How much does the tariff-inclusive Home price increase because of the tariff, and how much does the net-of-tariff price received by the Foreign firm fall?

c. Discuss the welfare effects of implementing the tariff. Use a graph to illustrate under what conditions, if any, there is an increase in Home welfare.

9. Suppose the Home firm is considering whether to enter the Foreign market. Assume that the Home firm has the following costs and demand:

Fixed costs	= $400
Marginal costs	= $15 per unit
Local price	= $30
Local quantity	= 40
Export price	= $20
Export quantity	= 20

a. Calculate the firm's total costs from selling only in the local market.

b. What is the firm's average cost from selling only in the local market?

c. Calculate the firm's profit from selling only in the local market.

d. Should the Home firm enter the Foreign market? Briefly explain why.

e. Calculate the firm's profit from selling to both markets.

f. Is the Home firm dumping? Briefly explain.

10. Suppose that in response to a *threatened* antidumping duty of t, the Foreign monopoly raises its price by the amount t.

a. Illustrate the losses for the Home country.

b. How do these losses compare with the losses from a safeguard tariff of the amount t, applied by the Home country against the Foreign monopolist?

c. In view of your answers to (a) and (b), why are antidumping cases filed so often?

11. Why is it necessary to use a market failure to justify the use of infant industry protection?

12. What is a positive externality? Explain the argument of knowledge spillovers as a potential reason for infant industry protection.

13. If infant industry protection is justified, would it be better for the Home country to use a tariff or a quota, and why?

10

Export Policies in Resource-Based and High-Technology Industries

The decision you have taken today on export competition is truly extraordinary; it is the WTO's [World Trade Organization's] most significant outcome on agriculture.

Robêrto Azevedo, Director General of the WTO, December 2015

The details [on agricultural subsidies] we announced today ensure farmers will not stand alone in facing unjustified retaliatory tariffs while President Trump continues working to solidify better and stronger trade deals around the globe.

Sonny Perdue, United States Secretary of Agriculture, July 25, 2019

The Middle East has its oil, China has rare earth.

Deng Xiaoping, architect of China's economic reforms, Southern Tour of China, January 1992

Questions to Consider

1 Why do countries subsidize their farmers?

2 Can countries control the export of their rare natural resources?

3 Why do countries subsidize their high-tech exports?

Since the founding of the World Trade Organization in 1995, ministerial meetings of its member countries have been held every two years. A frequent topic at these meetings, and one of the most contentious, is the government subsidies that many countries give to their agricultural sector. The attempt to dismantle these subsidies leads to fierce resistance at the WTO meetings, including the 2005 meeting in Hong Kong, which was marked by large-scale protests. Groups such as farmers from India and South Korea and fishermen from the Philippines objected to the impact that agricultural reforms would have on reducing subsidies, thereby threatening their livelihoods. Despite this opposition, at the Hong Kong meeting the member countries of the WTO made the first plans to eliminate agricultural subsidies, and these were followed by concrete commitments at the 2015 meeting held in Nairobi, Kenya. The director general of the WTO, Robêrto Azevedo, hailed the 2015 commitments as "truly extraordinary," as seen in the first quote at the beginning of this chapter.

Police fight rioters outside the World Trade Organization's meeting in Hong Kong, 2005. The protesters included South Korean farmers worried about rice imports.

The agreement to eliminate agricultural subsidies played a key role in the Doha Round of WTO tariff negotiations. These negotiations began in 2001 in the city of Doha, Qatar, and continued with meetings every several years including those in Hong Kong in 2005 and in Nairobi, Kenya, in 2015. The Doha Round was intended to benefit developing countries, but many of the issues addressed by the member countries of the WTO were too hard to resolve. Only the agreement to eliminate agricultural subsidies was achieved, first at the 2005 WTO meeting and later at the 2015 meeting. While some progress has been made toward that goal, there have also been setbacks. In July 2019, the United States increased its subsidies to farmers, as referred to in the second quote at the beginning of the chapter. Those subsidies were intended to compensate farmers for lost U.S. farm exports due to retaliatory tariffs imposed by the United States' trading partners during 2018–19. The increased use of agricultural subsidies in the United States conflicts with the WTO's commitment to eliminate such subsidies.

Why is it so difficult for countries to eliminate agricultural subsidies? The main reason is politics. Farmers in South Korea, along with those in Japan, Europe, and the United States, benefit from an intricate system of **import tariffs** (taxes on imports) and **export subsidies** (payments to exporters) that keeps prices for their crops high. Raising the incomes of farmers in these countries is often a political goal. But high prices in those countries can *lower* prices in the rest of the world, as we will explain. The lower world price hurts farmers in land-rich developing countries such as Brazil, India, China, and some African nations by making it harder for them to export their own agricultural products. On the other hand, the lower world prices benefit consumers in land-poor developing countries that must import agricultural products. Consumers in those countries would be hurt if prices ended up rising as a result of agricultural reforms in the WTO. That agricultural reforms have these conflicting effects on different groups explains why it is so difficult to eliminate the subsidies.

The first goal of this chapter is to explain the impact of agricultural subsidies on prices and the welfare of different groups. Export subsidies are not the only kind of policy that governments use to influence trade in resource-based industries. The second goal of this chapter is to explain the effect of two other export policies. To raise government revenue, some countries impose export tariffs, which are taxes applied by the exporting country when a good leaves the country.[1] Argentina, for example, charges export tariffs on many agricultural and resource exports. In 2019, the tariffs were increased to 30% on soybeans, soy oil, and soymeal, to 12% on wheat, and to 9% on beef. Another policy sometimes used is an export quota, a restriction on the amount that producers are allowed to export. China, for example, applied quotas on firms exporting "rare earth" minerals in 2011 and 2012. China has significant deposits of these minerals (as indicated by the final quote at the beginning of the chapter), which are valuable because they are used in many high-tech products.[2] Because the export quota limited the amount that was exported, Chinese firms enjoyed a substantial increase in the price they received for their exports.

The third goal of the chapter is to examine how governments can strategically use export subsidies to bolster high-technology companies and industries. A difference

---

[1] In the United States, export tariffs are prohibited by Clause 5 of the U.S. Constitution.

[2] There are 17 rare earth minerals, consisting of the 15 lanthanides along with yttrium and scandium. Lanthanum, for example, is used in batteries and lighting, and neodymium is used in making permanent magnets, which are found in high-tech products ranging from smartphones to hybrid cars to wind turbines.

between agricultural production and high-tech production is that we usually think of agriculture as a perfectly competitive industry (many producers, each of which has no control over the price of their products), whereas many high-tech industries are imperfectly competitive (a small number of producers that have some control over the price of their products). Large commercial aircraft, for example, are built by only two worldwide producers: Airbus in Europe and Boeing in the United States. Both of these producers receive generous government subsidies because legislators often believe that subsidies to high-tech industries will raise those industries' profits and benefit the country. Export subsidies often lead to political friction between the countries that use them, however. We assess whether the "strategic" use of subsidies in high-tech industries is beneficial to the countries using those policies.

1 WTO Goals on Agricultural Subsidies

In Table 10-1, we describe the goals established at the Hong Kong meeting of the WTO in December 2005. Since that time, some of these goals have been implemented by the WTO, but the broader development goals of the Doha Round were not achieved.

Agricultural Export Subsidies

An export subsidy is payment to firms for every unit exported (either a fixed amount or a fraction of the sales price). Governments give subsidies to encourage domestic firms to produce more in particular industries. As shown in Table 10-1, the member

TABLE 10-1

Goals Made at the Hong Kong WTO Meeting, December 2005 This table shows the goals that were set at the 2005 WTO meeting in Hong Kong, which had as its major focus the subsidies on agricultural products. This meeting was part of the Doha Round of WTO negotiations. Some of these goals have been achieved since 2005.

Issue	Goals Made in Hong Kong (2005)	Unresolved Issues in Hong Kong (2005)
Agricultural export subsidies	Abolition by end of 2013, with a "substantial part" scrapped before 2011, and parallel elimination of indirect subsidies.	Must agree [on] value of indirect subsidies and detailed phase-out programs.
Domestic farm supports	Agreement to classify WTO members in three bands based on their level of domestic farm support (top—European Union, middle—United States and Japan, bottom—everyone else).	Must agree [on] size of subsidy reduction and rules to stop countries from shifting trade-distorting subsidies into categories sheltered from deep cuts.
Agricultural tariffs	Agreement on four tiers (different for rich and poor countries) and on a mechanism allowing poor nations to raise duties to counter import surges.	Must decide size of tariff cuts and number and treatment of "sensitive" and "special" products.
Cotton Agreement	Agreement to eliminate export subsidies in 2006 and grant unrestricted access for cotton exports from West African producers and other least developed countries (LDCs).	United States will have the "objective" of cutting its $4 billion subsidies to cotton growers further and faster than the still-to-be-agreed-upon overall reduction for domestic farm supports.

Information from: Guy de Jonquières, "Tentative Steps Forward Seen as Better Than None at All," Financial Times, December 19, 2005, p. 2.

countries of the WTO made a goal of abolishing all export subsidies in agriculture by the end of 2013. While some progress was made toward the goal, as we discuss below for cotton and for sugar beets, the member countries of the WTO established new deadlines at a 2015 meeting in Nairobi, Kenya. At that 2015 meeting it was agreed that developed countries should immediately eliminate their export subsidies in agriculture, while developed countries had until 2018 to end their export subsidies. Later, those deadlines were extended: developed countries were given until 2020 to eliminate export subsidies. The deadline for developing countries was extended to 2023 and that for the least developed countries was extended to 2030.

Indirect Subsidies Included in the Hong Kong export subsidy agreement was the parallel elimination of **indirect subsidies** to agriculture, including food aid from developed countries to poor countries and other exports by state-sponsored trading companies in advanced countries. Europe has already eliminated its food aid subsidies and argues that *cash aid* to poor countries is much more effective; the United States continues to export agricultural commodities as aid. Later in the chapter, we explore the argument made by the European Union (EU) that cash aid is more effective than food aid in assisting developing countries.

Domestic Farm Supports Also discussed in the Hong Kong agreement were **domestic farm supports**, which refer to any assistance given to farmers, even if it is not directly tied to exports. Such domestic assistance programs can still have an indirect effect on exports by lowering the costs (hence augmenting the competitiveness) of domestic products. The Hong Kong agreement was a first step toward classifying the extent of such programs in each country, and the EU was classified as having the highest supports. The EU has historically maintained a system of agricultural subsidies known as the **Common Agricultural Policy (CAP)**, which subsidizes farmers in order to raise their incomes. The CAP payments have been reduced in light of the 2005 and 2015 WTO agreements. To see the extent of these reductions, we discuss one specific crop: sugar beets.

Subsidies to Sugar Beets In 2003, the CAP paid European farmers up to 50 euros per ton of harvested sugar beets, which was five times the world market price. Because of the subsidy, European farmers could afford to sell the sugar made from their sugar beets at a much lower price than the world market price, but with a higher price received by farmers when the 50 euros per ton subsidy was included. As a result, the sugar beet subsidy made the EU a leading supplier of sugar worldwide, even though countries in tropical climates such as Brazil and India have a natural comparative advantage in producing sugar through growing sugarcane.

With pressure from the 2005 Hong Kong WTO meeting, in 2006 there was a major reform in the policy for sugar beets in the EU. The prices received by farmers were allowed to fall by as much as 40% from their previous level. A number of farmers could no longer operate profitably and left the sector. The total cultivated areas fell from 2.2 million hectares in 2005 to 1.3 million hectares in 2015, a decline of 40%. For those farmers remaining, the CAP payments provided to them were not based on the difference between local and world prices, but instead were based on the reduction in prices from their previous level. So the CAP payments would partially compensate farmers for their lost income but would not act as an export subsidy. Financial incentives were also provided to sugar factories to encourage factory closure. The goal of all these reforms was to reduce the production of sugar beets in the EU, thereby allowing developing countries to supply more sugar to the world market.

Cotton Subsidies Export subsidies in cotton received special attention at the Hong Kong meeting because that crop, which is exported by many low-income African countries (especially Benin, Burkina Faso, Chad, and Mali), has been highly subsidized in the United States. The United States historically paid cotton farmers to grow more cotton and then subsidized agribusiness and manufacturers to buy the American cotton, so both the production *and* the sale of cotton received subsidies. Cotton subsidies were the subject of a WTO case brought by Brazil against the United States in 2002. In 2005, the WTO ruled that the U.S. subsidies in cotton violated WTO rules and needed to be reduced, and that ruling was upheld in 2009 after a series of appeals by the United States.

As a result of this pressure from both the WTO and from domestic groups who feel that agricultural subsidies are too costly, the United States has significantly reformed its subsidies to cotton growers. In the 2014 Farm Bill of the United States, all direct payments to exporters based on the difference between U.S. and non-U.S. prices are eliminated. These payments were judged to act like export subsidies, and they were replaced by a program that acts instead like a form of crop insurance. Farmers have to pay a premium to participate in this program. Those farmers then receive a payment if there is a fall in prices from the time of planting to when they harvest their crops. They can use this insurance against a price decline to help them obtain bank loans when planting their crops. The total expenditures by the U.S. government under this program are supposed to be covered from the premiums paid by farmers. This type of insurance, which does not distinguish between domestic production and exports, is permitted under WTO rules.

These two cases—of cotton in the United States and sugar beets in the EU—show how pressure from WTO members can lead to beneficial policy reforms. The path toward achieving the WTO commitments is not always straight, however, and setbacks occur. In 2017, the EU continued its reform of policies in sugar beets by dismantling the system of production quotas. These quotas had limited the amount grown by each farmer, in an attempt to raise the market price. When the production quotas were eliminated, there was a substantial increase in supply and a collapse of prices for sugar beets. As a result, eleven EU countries introduced new subsidy payments to sugar beet farmers.[3] In the United States, new subsidies to farmers (not just in cotton) were introduced in 2018 and used again in 2019, to compensate for the retaliatory tariffs applied against U.S. agricultural exports, as we will describe later in the chapter. So in both cases, the WTO commitments to eliminate subsidies in agriculture were set aside to assist farmers facing special difficulty.

Other Matters from the Hong Kong WTO Meeting

In addition to the elimination of the subsidies themselves, other issues related to export subsidies were discussed at the 2005 Hong Kong meeting. One of these issues was the use of tariffs as a response to other countries' use of subsidies.

Tariffs in Agriculture Export subsidies applied by large countries depress world prices, as we will explain in this chapter. As a result, exporting countries can expect tariffs to be imposed on the subsidized products when they are imported by other countries. At the 2005 Hong Kong meeting, importing countries wanted a "special safeguard mechanism" that could be applied to all other agricultural products. Under this mechanism, tariffs could be temporarily raised whenever imports suddenly rose or their prices suddenly fell. This provision was agreed to 10 years later, at the 2015 Nairobi meeting, when the developing countries won the right to impose such a special safeguard mechanism.

---

[3] These countries were Croatia, Czech Republic, Finland, Greece, Hungary, Italy, Lithuania, Poland, Romania, Spain, and Slovakia.

2 Export Subsidies in a Small Home Country

Having seen the importance of agricultural subsidies at the WTO meetings, we now describe the effect of export subsidies on prices, exports, and welfare. We begin with a small country called Home that faces a fixed world price for its exports. Following that, we see how the outcomes differ when Home is large enough to affect world prices.

Consider a small country exporting sugar. The Home no-trade equilibrium is at point A in Figure 10–1. With free trade, Home faces the world price of sugar P^W. In panel (a) of Figure 10–1, the quantity supplied in Home at that price is S_1 and the quantity demanded is D_1 tons of sugar. Because quantity demanded is less than quantity supplied, the Home country exports $X_1 = S_1 - D_1$ tons under free trade. That quantity of exports is shown as point B in panel (b) corresponding to the free-trade price of P^W. By determining the level of exports at other prices, we can trace out the Home export supply curve X.

Impact of an Export Subsidy

Now suppose that because the government wishes to boost the exports of the domestic sugar producers, each ton of sugar exported receives a subsidy of s dollars from the government. Panel (a) of Figure 10-1 traces the effect of this subsidy on the domestic

FIGURE 10-1

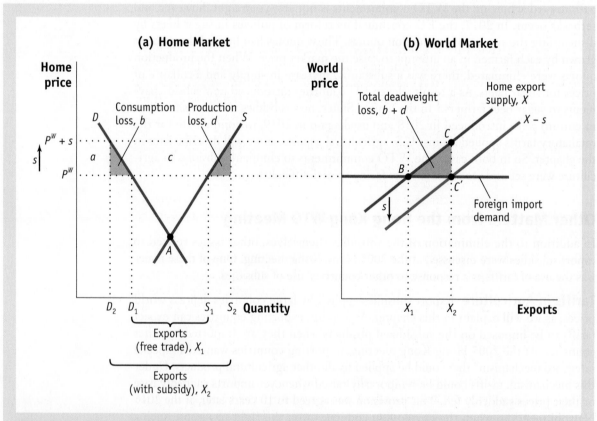

Export Subsidy for a Small Country Applying a subsidy of s dollars per unit exported will increase the price that Home exporters receive from P^W to $P^W + s$. As a result, the domestic price of the similar good will also rise by that amount. This price rise leads to an increase in Home quantity supplied from S_1 to S_2 and a decrease in Home quantity demanded from D_1 to D_2, in panel (a). Exports rise as a result of the subsidy, from X_1 to X_2 in panel (b). The Home export supply curve shifts down by exactly the amount of the subsidy since the marginal cost of a unit of exports decreases by exactly s. As in the case of a tariff, the deadweight loss as a result of the subsidy is the triangle $(b+d)$, the sum of consumption loss b and production loss d.

economy. With an export subsidy of s dollars per ton, exporters will receive $P^W + s$ for each ton exported rather than the lower free-trade price P^W. Because they are allowed to export any amount they want at the subsidized price, the Home firms will not accept a price less than $P^W + s$ for their domestic sales: if the domestic price was less than $P^W + s$, the firms would just export all their sugar at the higher price. Thus, the domestic price for sugar must rise to $P^W + s$ so that it equals the export price received by Home firms.

Notice that with the domestic sugar price rising to $P^W + s$, Home consumers could in principle *import* sugar at the price of P^W rather than buy it from local firms. To prevent imports from coming into the country, we assume that the Home government has imposed an import tariff equal to (or higher than) the amount of the export subsidy. This is a realistic assumption. Many subsidized agricultural products that are exported are also protected by an import tariff to prevent consumers from buying at lower world prices. We see that the combined effect of the export subsidy and import tariff is to raise the price paid by Home consumers and received by Home firms.

With the price rising to $P^W + s$, the quantity supplied in Home increases to S_2, while the quantity demanded falls to D_2 in panel (a). Therefore, Home exports increase to $X_2 = S_2 - D_2$. The change in the quantity of exports can be thought of in two ways as reflected by points C and C' in panel (b). On one hand, if we were to measure the Home price P^W on the vertical axis, point C is on the original Home export supply curve X: that is, the rise in Home price has resulted in a *movement along* Home's initial supply curve from point B to C since the quantity of exports has increased with the Home price.

On the other hand, with the vertical axis of panel (b) measuring the world price and given our small-country assumption that the world price is fixed at P^W, the increase in exports from X_1 to X_2 because of the subsidy can be interpreted as a *shift* of the domestic export supply curve to $X - s$, which includes point C'. Recall from Chapter 8 that the export supply curve shifts by precisely the amount of the tariff. Here, because the export subsidy is like a negative tariff, the Home export supply curve shifts down by exactly the amount s. In other words, the subsidy allows firms to sell their goods to the world market at a price exactly s dollars lower *at any point* on the export supply curve; thus, the export supply curve shifts down. According to our small-country assumption, Home is a price taker in the world market and thus always sells abroad at the world price P^W; the only difference is that with the subsidy, Home exports higher quantities.

Summary From the domestic perspective, the export subsidy increases both the price and quantity of exports, a movement along the domestic export supply curve. From the world perspective, the export subsidy results in an increase in export supply and, given an unchanged world price (because of the small-country assumption), the export supply curve shifts down by the amount of the subsidy s. As was the case with a tariff, the subsidy has driven a wedge between what domestic exporters receive ($P^W + s$ at point C) and what importers abroad pay (P^W at point C').

Impact of the Subsidy on Home Welfare Our next step is to determine the impact of the subsidy on the welfare of the exporting country. The rise in Home price lowers consumer surplus by the amount $(a + b)$ in panel (a). That is the area between the two prices (P^W and $P^W + s$) and underneath the demand curve D. On the other hand, the price increase raises producer surplus by the amount $(a + b + c)$, the area between the two prices (P^W and $P^W + s$) and above the supply curve S. Finally, we need to determine the effect on government revenue. The export subsidy costs the government s per unit exported, or $s \cdot X_2$ in total. That revenue cost is shown by the area $(b + c + d)$.

Adding up the impact on consumers, producers, and government revenue, the overall impact of the export subsidy is

Fall in consumer surplus:	$-(a+b)$
Rise in producer surplus:	$+(a+b+c)$
Fall in government revenue:	$-(b+c+d)$
Net effect on Home's welfare:	$-(b+d)$

The triangle $(b+d)$ in panel (b) is the net loss or **deadweight loss** due to the subsidy in a small country. The result that an export subsidy leads to a deadweight loss for the exporter is similar to the result that a tariff leads to a deadweight loss for an importing country. As with a tariff, the areas b and d can be given precise interpretations. The triangle d equals the increase in marginal costs for the extra units produced because of the subsidy and can be interpreted as the **production loss** or the *efficiency loss* for the economy. The area of the triangle b can be interpreted as the drop in consumer surplus for those individuals no longer consuming the units between D_1 and D_2, which we call the **consumption loss** for the economy. The combination of the production and consumption losses is the deadweight loss for the exporting country.

3 Export Subsidies in a Large Home Country

Now suppose that the Home country is a large enough seller on international markets that its subsidy affects the world price of the sugar (e.g., this occurs with European sugar subsidies and U.S. cotton subsidies). This large-country case is illustrated in Figure 10-2. In panel (b), we draw the Foreign import demand curve M^*

FIGURE 10-2

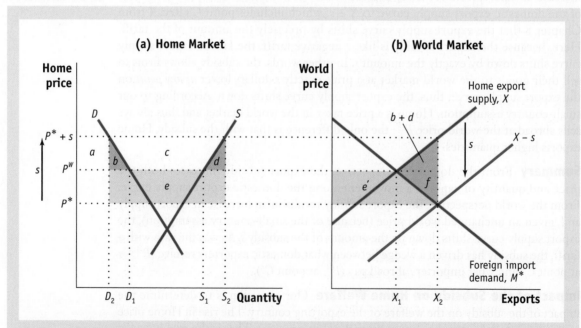

Export Subsidy for a Large Country Panel (a) shows the effects of the subsidy in Home. The Home price increases from P^W to P^*+s, Home quantity demanded decreases from D_1 to D_2, and Home quantity supplied increases from S_1 to S_2. The deadweight loss for Home is the area of triangle $(b+d)$, but Home also has a terms-of-trade loss of area e. In the world market, the Home subsidy shifts out the export supply curve from X to $X-s$ in panel (b). As in the small-country case, the export supply curve shifts down by the amount of the subsidy, reflecting the lower marginal cost of exports. As a result, the world price falls from P^W to P^*. The Foreign country gains the consumer surplus area e', so the world deadweight loss due to the subsidy is the area $(b+d+f)$. The extra deadweight loss f arises because only a portion of the Home terms-of-trade loss is a Foreign gain.

as downward-sloping because changes in the amount exported, as will occur when Home applies a subsidy, now affect the world price.

Under free trade, the Home and world price is P^W. At this price, Home exports $X_1 = S_1 - D_1$, and the world export market is in equilibrium at the intersection of Home export supply X and Foreign import demand M^*. Home and Foreign consumers pay the same price for the good, P^W, which is the world price.

Effect of the Subsidy

Suppose that Home applies a subsidy of s dollars per ton of sugar exported. As we found for the small country, a subsidy to Home export production is shown as a downward shift of the Home export supply curve in panel (b) by the amount s; the vertical distance between the original export supply curve X and the new export supply curve $X - s$ is precisely the amount of the subsidy s. The new intersection of Home export supply, $X - s$, and Foreign import demand M^* corresponds to a new world price of P^*, decreased from the free-trade world price P^W, and a Home price $P^* + s$, increased from the free-trade price P^W. Furthermore, the equilibrium with the subsidy now occurs at the export quantity X_2 in panel (b), increased from X_1.

In Chapter 2, we defined the **terms of trade** for a country as the ratio of export prices to import prices. Generally, a fall in the terms of trade indicates a loss for a country because it is either receiving less for exports or paying more for imports. We have found that with the export subsidy, Foreign consumers pay a lower price for Home exports, which is therefore a fall in the Home terms of trade but a gain in the Foreign terms of trade. We should expect, therefore, that the Home country will suffer an overall loss because of the subsidy but that Foreign consumers will gain. To confirm these effects, let's investigate the impact of the subsidy on Home and Foreign welfare.

Home Welfare In panel (a) of Figure 10-2, the increase in the Home price from P^W to $P^* + s$ reduces consumer surplus by the amount $(a + b)$. In addition, the increase in the price benefits Home firms, and producer surplus rises by the amount $(a + b + c)$. We also need to take into account the cost of the subsidy. Because the amount of the subsidy is s, and the amount of Home exports (after the subsidy) is $X_2 = S_2 - D_2$, it follows that the revenue cost of the subsidy to the government is the area $(b + c + d + e)$, which equals $s \cdot X_2$ (the government pays s for every unit exported). Therefore, the overall impact of the subsidy in the large country can be summarized as follows:

Fall in consumer surplus:	$-(a + b)$
Rise in producer surplus:	$+(a + b + c)$
Fall in government revenue:	$-(b + c + d + e)$
Net effect on Home's welfare:	$-(b + d + e)$

In the world market, panel (b), the triangle $(b + d)$ is the deadweight loss due to the subsidy, just as it is for a small country. For the large country, however, there is an extra source of loss, the area e, which is the terms-of-trade loss to Home: $e = e' + f$ in panel (b). When we analyze Foreign and world welfare, it will be useful to divide the Home terms-of-trade loss into two sections, e' and f, but from Home's perspective, the terms-of-trade welfare loss is just their sum, area e. This loss is the decrease in export revenue because the world price has fallen to P^*; Home loses the difference between P^W and P^* on each of X_2 units exported. So a large country loses even more from a subsidy than a small country because of the reduction in the world price of its exported good.

Foreign and World Welfare While Home definitely loses from the subsidy, the Foreign importing country definitely gains. Panel (b) of Figure 10-2 illustrates the consumer surplus benefit to Foreign of the Home subsidy; the price of Foreign imports decreases and Foreign's terms of trade improve. The change in consumer surplus for Foreign is area e', the area below its import demand curve M^* and between the free-trade world price P^W and the new world price (with subsidy) P^*.

When we combine the total Home consumption and production losses $(b + d)$ plus the Home terms-of-trade loss e, and subtract the Foreign terms-of-trade gain e', there is an overall deadweight loss for the world, which is measured by the area $(b + d + f)$ in panel (b). The area f is the additional world deadweight loss due to the subsidy, which arises because the terms-of-trade loss in Home is not completely offset by a terms-of-trade gain in Foreign.

Because there is a transfer of terms of trade from Home to Foreign, the export subsidy might seem like a good policy tool for large wealthy countries seeking to give aid to poorer countries. However, this turns out not to be the case. The deadweight loss f means that using the export subsidy to increase Home production and send the excess exported goods overseas (as was the case for food aid, discussed earlier as an example of an indirect subsidy) is an inefficient way to transfer gains from trade among countries. It would be more efficient to simply give cash aid in the amount of the Home terms-of-trade loss to poor importers, a policy approach that, because it does not change the free-trade levels of production and consumption in either country, would avoid the deadweight loss $(b + d + f)$ associated with the subsidy. This argument is made by the European countries, which, several years ago, eliminated transfers of food as a form of aid and switched to cash payments. The United States has now agreed to make the same policy change, as discussed in the following application.

APPLICATION

Who Gains and Who Loses?

Now that we have studied the effect of export subsidies on world prices and trade volume in theory, we return to the agreement to eliminate export subsidies that was reached at the 2015 Nairobi meeting of the WTO and ask: Which countries will gain and which will lose when export subsidies (including the "indirect" subsidies like food aid) are eliminated?

Gains The obvious gainers from this action will be current agricultural exporters in developing countries such as Brazil, Argentina, Indonesia, and Thailand, along with potential exporters such as India and China. These countries will gain from the rise in world prices as agricultural subsidies by the industrialized countries—especially Europe and the United States—are eliminated. These countries will gain even more when and if an agreement is reached on the elimination of agricultural tariffs in the industrial countries, including Japan and South Korea, that protect crops such as rice. Both of these actions will also benefit the industrial countries themselves, which suffer both a deadweight loss *and* a terms-of-trade loss from the combination of export subsidies and import tariffs in agriculture. Farmers in the industrial countries who lose the subsidies will be worse off, and the government might choose to offset that loss with some type of adjustment assistance. In the United States and Europe, however, it is often the largest farmers who benefit the most from subsidy programs, and they may be better able to adjust to the elimination of subsidies (through switching to other crops) than small farmers.

Losses Which countries will lose from the elimination of export subsidies? To the extent that the elimination of export subsidies leads to higher world prices, as we expect from our analysis (in Figure 10-2, the price would rise from P^* to P^W), then the food-importing countries, typically the poorer non–food-producing countries, will lose. This theoretical result is confirmed by several empirical studies. One study

FIGURE 10-3

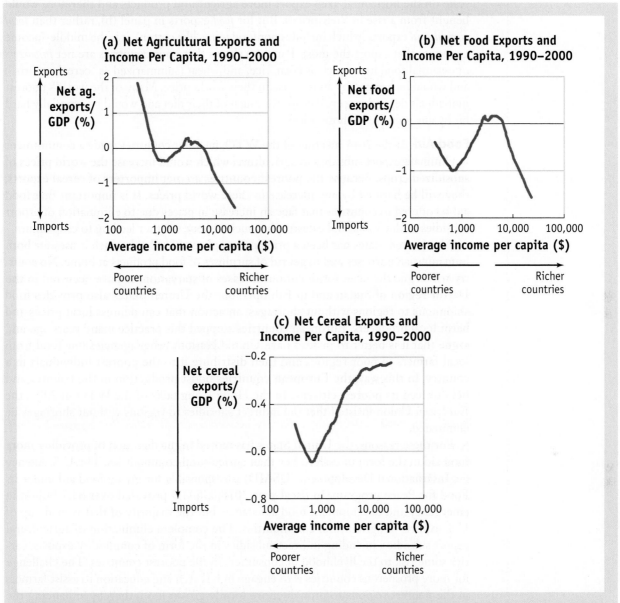

(a) Net Agricultural Exports and Income Per Capita, 1990–2000

(b) Net Food Exports and Income Per Capita, 1990–2000

(c) Net Cereal Exports and Income Per Capita, 1990–2000

Agriculture, Food, and Cereal Exports Panel (a) shows net agricultural exports graphed against countries' income per capita. The poorer countries export more agricultural products overall and would thus benefit from a rise in the prices due to the removal of subsidies. On the other hand, panel (b) shows that it is middle-income countries that export the most food. Panel (c) shows that poor countries are net *importers* of essential food items (cereals) such as corn, rice, and wheat and would be harmed by an increase in their world price.

Data from: Margaret McMillan, Alix Peterson Zwane, and Nava Ashraf, 2007, "My Policies or Yours: Have OECD Agricultural Policies Affected Incomes in Developing Countries?" In Ann Harrison, Globalization and Poverty (Chicago: University of Chicago Press and NBER), pp. 183–232.

found that the existing pattern of agricultural supports (tariffs and subsidies) raises the per capita income of two-thirds of 77 developing nations, including most of the poorest countries, such as Burundi and Zambia.[4] This result is illustrated in Figure 10-3. Panel (a) shows net agricultural exports graphed against countries' income per capita

---

[4] Margaret McMillan, Alix Peterson Zwane, and Nava Ashraf, 2007, "My Policies or Yours: Have OECD Agricultural Policies Affected Incomes in Developing Countries?" in *Globalization and Poverty*, ed. Ann Harrison [Chicago: University of Chicago Press and National Bureau of Economic Research (NBER)], pp. 183–232.

over the period 1990 to 2000. The poorer countries (i.e., those lower on the income scale on the horizontal axis) export more agricultural products and therefore would benefit from a rise in their prices. But for *food* exports in panel (b), rather than *total agricultural* exports (which includes nonfood items like cotton), it is the middle-income countries that export the most. Panel (c) shows that poor countries are net *importers* of essential food items such as corn, rice, and wheat (summarized as "cereal exports") and would be harmed by an increase in their world price. Many of the world's poorest individuals depend on cereal crops for much of their diet and would be especially hard hit by any increase in those prices.

Food Aid At the 2015 meeting of the WTO, member countries made a commitment to eliminate export subsidies in agriculture, which would increase the world prices of subsidized crops. Because the poorest countries are net importers of cereal exports, they will be harmed by any increase in these world prices. It is important that food aid be offered to countries that face an increase in prices due to elimination of export subsidies or due to natural catastrophes such as poor weather leading to crop failure.

The United States has been a principal supplier of food aid, which it uses for both humanitarian purposes and to get rid of surpluses of food products at home. No country will argue the need for donations in cases of starvation, as have occurred in the Darfur region of Sudan and in Ethiopia, but the United States also provides food shipments to regions without shortages, an action that can depress local prices and harm local producers. European countries stopped this practice many years ago and argue that it is better to instead have United Nations relief agencies buy food from local farmers in poor regions and then distribute it to the poorest individuals in a country. In this way, the European countries boost production in the country and help to feed its poorest citizens. In the Hong Kong talks of the WTO in 2005, the European Union insisted that the indirect subsidies to regions without shortages be eliminated.

For these reasons, the United States has moved in the direction of providing more food aid in the form of cash rather than agricultural commodities. The U.S. Agency for International Development (USAID) is responsible for giving food aid under its Food for Peace program. In fiscal year 2018, USAID provided over $3.7 billion in emergency and development food assistance, but the majority of that is made up of U.S. exports of agricultural commodities. The complete elimination of agricultural export subsidies, including indirect subsidies in the form of commodity exports, carries some risk to the livelihood of consumers in the poorest countries. The challenge for more prosperous countries is to engage in research and education to assist farmers in the poorest regions to provide more locally grown food, thereby enhancing the food security in those countries.

4 Production Subsidies

The goals reached in Hong Kong in 2005 distinguish between export subsidies in agriculture—which will be eliminated according to the 2015 agreement—and all other forms of domestic support that increase production (e.g., tax incentives and other types of subsidies). These other forms of agricultural support are expected to have less impact on exports than direct subsidies. Therefore, there is less impact on other countries from having domestic support programs as compared with export subsidies. To illustrate this idea, let's examine the impact of a "production subsidy" in agriculture for both a small and a large country.

Suppose the government provides a subsidy of *s* dollars for *every unit* (e.g., ton of sugar in our example) that a Home firm produces. This is a **production subsidy** because it is a subsidy to every unit produced and not just to units that are exported.

There are several ways that a government can implement such a subsidy. The government might guarantee a minimum price to the farmer, for example, and make up the difference between the minimum price and any lower price for which the farmer sells. Alternatively, the government might provide subsidies to users of the crop to purchase it, thus increasing demand and raising market prices; this would act like a subsidy to every unit produced. As mentioned earlier, the United States has used both methods to support its cotton growers.

These policies all fall under Article XVI of the GATT (see **Side Bar: Key Provisions of the GATT** in Chapter 8). Article XVI states that partner countries should be notified of the extent of such subsidies, and when possible, they should be limited. In Hong Kong, the WTO members further agreed to classify countries according to the extent of such subsidies, with the European Union classified as having a high level of production subsidies, the United States and Japan having a middle level, and all other countries having low subsidies (see Table 10-1). No further resolution has been reached about the timing and extent of future cuts in these production subsidies.

Effect of a Production Subsidy in a Small Home Country

To illustrate the effect of a production subsidy, we begin with a small country that faces a fixed world price of P^W. In Figure 10-4, panel (a), the production subsidy of s increases the price received by Home producers to $P^W + s$ and increases Home's quantity supplied from S_1 to S_2. The quantity *demanded* in Home does not change, however, because producers *continue to charge the world price* in Home. This is the case (in contrast to the export subsidy) because Home producers receive a subsidy regardless

FIGURE 10-4

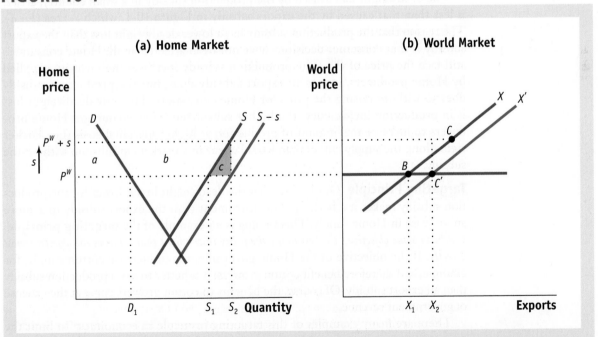

Production Subsidy for a Small Country In panel (a), applying a production subsidy of s dollars per unit produced will increase the price that Home firms receive from P^W to $P^W + s$. This price rise leads to an increase in Home quantity supplied from S_1 to S_2. The consumer price in Home is not affected because the production subsidy does not distinguish between items sold in Home or exported (firms therefore continue to charge the world price in Home), so the quantity demanded stays at D_1. The deadweight loss of the subsidy for a small country is the area c. In panel (b), exports rise as a result of the production subsidy, from X_1 to X_2, though the increase in exports is less than for the export subsidy because, for the production subsidy, quantity demanded does not change in Home.

of whom they sell to (domestic consumers or Foreign consumers through exporting). So with a production subsidy, Home producers charge the world price to Foreign consumers and receive the extra subsidy from the government and likewise charge the world price to Home consumers, and again receive the extra subsidy. In contrast, for an export subsidy, Home firms receive the subsidy *only* for export sales and not for domestic sales.

Because the price for Home consumers with the production subsidy is still P^W, there is no change in the quantity demanded in Home, which remains at D_1. In panel (b), we see that the production subsidy increases the quantity of exports from $X_1 = S_1 - D_1$ to $X_2 = S_2 - D_1$. Because demand is not affected, the production subsidy increases exports by less than an export subsidy would. That result occurs because the quantity demanded decreases with an export subsidy due to higher Home prices, leading to greater Home exports. In contrast, with the production subsidy, the quantity demanded in Home is unchanged, so exports do not rise as much.

Home Welfare   With the increase in the price received by Home producers, from P_W to $P_W + s$, there is a corresponding rise in producer surplus of the amount $(a + b)$ in panel (a). The government revenue cost of the subsidy is the entire area $(a + b + c)$, which equals the amount of the subsidy s, times Home production S_2. So the overall impact of the production subsidy is

Change in consumer surplus:	*none* (because demand is not affected)
Rise in producer surplus:	$+(a + b)$
Fall in government revenue:	$-(a + b + c)$
Net effect on Home's welfare:	$-c$

The deadweight loss caused by the production subsidy in a small country, area c, is less than that caused by the export subsidy in Figure 10-1, which is area $(b + d)$. The reason that the production subsidy has a lower deadweight loss than the export subsidy is that consumer decisions have not been affected at all: Home consumers still face the price of P^W. The production subsidy increases the quantity supplied by Home producers, just as an export subsidy does, but the production subsidy does so without raising the price for Home consumers. The only deadweight loss is in production inefficiency: the higher subsidized price encourages Home producers to increase the amount of production at higher marginal costs (i.e., farther right along the supply curve) than would occur in a market equilibrium without the subsidy.

Targeting Principle   Our finding that the deadweight loss is lower for the production subsidy makes it a better policy instrument than the export subsidy to achieve an increase in Home supply. This finding is an example of the **targeting principle**: *to achieve some objective, it is best to use the policy instrument that achieves the objective most directly*. If the objective of the Home government is to increase cotton supply, for example, and therefore benefit cotton growers, it is better to use a production subsidy than an export subsidy. Of course, the benefits to cotton growers come at the expense of government revenue.

There are many examples of this targeting principle in economics. To limit the consumption of cigarettes and improve public health, the best policy is a tax on cigarette purchases, as many countries use. To reduce pollution from automobiles, the best policy would be a tax on gasoline, the magnitude of which is much higher in Europe than in the United States. And, to use an example from this book, to compensate people for losses from international trade, it is better to provide trade adjustment assistance directly (discussed in Chapter 3) to those affected than to impose an import tariff or quota.

Effect of the Production Subsidy in a Large Home Country

We will not draw the large-country case in detail but will use Figure 10-4 to briefly explain the effects of a production subsidy on prices, exports, and welfare. When the price for Home producers rises from P^W to $P^W + s$, the quantity of the exported good supplied increases from S_1 to S_2. Because demand has not changed, exports increase by exactly the same amount as the quantity supplied by domestic producers. We show that increase in exports by the outward shift of the export supply curve, from X to X' in panel (b). As mentioned previously, the rise in the quantity of exports due to the production subsidy, from point B to C' in Figure 10-4, is *less than* the increase in the quantity of exports for the export subsidy, from point B to C' shown in Figure 10-1. With the export subsidy, the price for Home producers *and* consumers rose to $P^W + s$, so exports increased because of both the rise in quantity supplied and the drop in quantity demanded. As a result, the export subsidy shifted down the Home export supply curve by exactly the amount s in Figure 10-1. In contrast, with a production subsidy, exports rise only because Home quantity supplied increases so that export supply shifts down by an amount less than s in Figure 10-4.

If we drew a downward-sloping Foreign import demand curve in panel (b), then the increase in supply as a result of the production subsidy would lower the world price. But that drop in world price would be *less than* the drop that occurred with the export subsidy because the increase in exports under the production subsidy is less.

Summary Production subsidies in agriculture still lower world prices, but they lower prices by less than export subsidies. For this reason, the WTO is less concerned with eliminating production subsidies and other forms of domestic support for agriculture. Export subsidies are supposed to be entirely eliminated over time, but certain production subsidies can remain provided that they are not too large and do not impact exports. In practice, the WTO members are entitled to question the use of agricultural subsidies in other countries, especially newly enacted subsidies, to determine whether they meet WTO commitments. A recent example of this questioning occurred for the new agricultural subsidies that the United States introduced in 2018–19. As explained in the next application, those subsidies were used in response to foreign retaliatory tariffs applied against U.S. farm exports.

APPLICATION

The Political Economy of U.S. Agricultural Subsidies, 2018–19

As we described in Chapter 8, in 2018–19 the United States imposed import tariffs on a number of products and against many countries (see **Application: U.S. and Foreign Tariffs Under President Trump, 2018–19**). In many cases, foreign countries retaliated by applying tariffs of their own against U.S. exports, and some of these foreign tariffs were applied against U.S. agricultural products. For example, China applied tariffs against major U.S. agricultural exports like pork and soybeans, and against more minor exports like whiskey and cranberries. Those products are grown and made in states represented by leading Republican legislators, and the Chinese government hoped that the farmers in those states would bring political pressure to end the U.S. tariffs that led to foreign retaliation. Canada, Mexico, and the EU also applied tariffs against U.S. exports of whiskey, Mexico applied tariffs against U.S. exports of pork, and the EU further applied a tariff against U.S. exports of Harley-Davidson motorcycles. In 2018, foreign tariffs were applied against $121 billion of U.S. exports, or 6.1% of total U.S. exports.

Retaliatory Tariffs and the 2016 Election Several research studies have considered the impact of the retaliatory tariffs on voting outcomes in the United States. One study shows that they systematically impacted counties in the United States that voted in 2016 for President Trump rather than his Democratic challenger Hillary Clinton.[5] To determine this impact, the researchers started with the list of all products that were subject to foreign retaliatory tariffs. Each product was traced to the areas of the country where it is grown (for agricultural goods) or manufactured. Then the results were summarized over the counties that were won by each of the two candidates, Trump and Clinton, in 2016.

Using this approach, the study found that 4.2% of exports were affected by foreign tariffs in counties where Hillary Clinton won, and 8.1% of exports were affected by foreign tariffs in counties where Donald Trump won. In other words, counties where the majority of people voted Republican have *twice as many* exports (on average) that are subject to foreign tariffs. In the 2020 election, the study predicted, it can be expected that individuals in those counties, having realized that exports are falling due to the foreign tariffs, might decide to switch their vote from Republican to Democratic in the hopes of reducing the U.S. and foreign tariffs. To determine whether this has happened in the past, we can look at the results from the 2018 midterm elections.

Retaliatory Tariffs and the 2018 Election In the midterm election of 2018 the president was not elected, but 35 out of 100 seats in the U.S. Senate and all 435 seats in the U.S. House of Representatives were up for election. In the Senate, the Republican Party gained two seats, while in the House of Representatives the Democratic Party gained 41 seats. Those gains gave the Democratic Party the majority of seats in the House of Representatives.

A second research study investigates whether the pattern of voting in each district was influenced by foreign retaliatory tariffs.[6] The results from this second study indicate that the retaliatory tariffs led to a switch from a Republican to a Democratic representative in *five* (out of 435) districts. These five cases were all in "swing" districts where the Republican candidate previously won by only a small majority. In 2018, a Democratic candidate was elected instead, and because these were also districts that were the hardest hit by retaliatory tariffs, it follows that foreign tariffs were one reason for the switch from Republican to Democratic in those districts.[7]

U.S. Agricultural Subsidies Because many of the counties targeted by foreign tariffs are in rural areas, the administration of President Trump provided new agricultural subsidies in 2018 and 2019 to offset the losses experienced by farmers. The subsidies granted in 2018 totaled $12 billion and were allocated to farmers growing soybeans, sorghum, corn, wheat, and several other crops affected by the foreign tariffs. A further $16 billion was provided in 2019.

In our discussion about the impact of foreign tariffs on voting in "swing" districts in 2018, that research study accounted for the impact of *both* foreign tariffs and the offsetting impact of the agricultural subsidies that were provided. While foreign tariffs

[5] Joseph Parilla and Max Bouchet, October 2018, *Which US Communities Are Most Affected by Chinese, EU, and NAFTA Retaliatory Tariffs?* (Washington, D.C.: Brookings Institution Press).

[6] Emily J. Blanchard, Chad P. Bown, and David Chor, 2019, "Did Trump's Trade War Impact the 2018 Election?" NBER Working Paper No. w26434, with summary at: voxeu.org/article /trump-s-trade-war-cost-republicans-congressional-seats-2018-midterm-elections.

[7] Another cause for swing voters to switch from Republican to Democratic representative would be their concern for continuing health care (which would be more likely to be preserved under Democratic representatives). This research study finds that concerns about health care account for a switch from a Republican to a Democratic candidate in another *eight* districts.

can lead some individuals to vote Democratic rather than Republican, the subsidies provided to farmers by the Republican administration can offset this change in voting behavior. Taking *both* effects into account, it is estimated that five extra districts switched from Republican to Democratic in 2018. Without the agricultural subsidies, probably more districts would have switched, but that number cannot be accurately estimated.

Response in the WTO The new agricultural subsidies provided by the United States work against its commitments at the WTO to reduce agricultural subsidies. As described in **Headlines: Trump's $16 Billion Farm Bailout Criticized at WTO**, the EU, China, and five other members of the WTO questioned whether these new subsidies are permitted under U.S. obligations to limit its subsidies. This article mentions several criteria that are used to determine whether subsidies are permitted. One criterion is whether the new subsidies "unduly influence planting decisions." This influence on planting decisions has been explained in Figure 10-4, which shows that a production subsidy leads to an increase in production from S_1 to S_2. The WTO wants to minimize this production increase in order to minimize its impact on exports and on world prices. Another criterion mentioned at the end of the article is that total expenditures of the United States on "trade-distorting" agricultural subsidies should not exceed $19 billion per year. The United States has agreed to limit its expenditures on subsidies that affect trade, as have other members of the WTO. The United States and other WTO members are expected to stay within these limitations on their agricultural subsidies.

HEADLINES

Trump's $16 Billion Farm Bailout Criticized at WTO

This article describes the reaction at the WTO to the 2019 announcement that the United States would subsidize its farmers to compensate for the retaliatory tariffs that they were facing. A number of WTO members questioned whether these subsidies were permitted under U.S. obligations under the WTO to limit its subsidies.

The European Union joined China and five other World Trade Organization members in criticizing the Trump administration's $16 billion assistance program for U.S. farmers, indicating the bailout may violate international rules. The U.S. Department of Agriculture's latest farmer assistance program could exceed America's WTO subsidy commitments and unduly influence U.S. planting decisions. . . .

Last month the USDA said it authorized as much as $16 billion in agriculture assistance programs in order to respond to the "impacts of unjustified retaliatory duties on U.S. agricultural goods." The U.S. administration said last year that it would deliver as much as $12 billion to farmers after Beijing retaliated against U.S. agricultural products. . . . Over the past two years some of America's largest trading partners have leveled tariffs on billions of dollars worth of agricultural goods to retaliate against President Donald Trump's duties on steel, aluminum and other goods. . . .

The EU asked the U.S. for details on the timing and eligibility criteria for the U.S. subsidies and questioned whether the U.S. measures would qualify as WTO-permitted subsidies or subsidies that distort international trade. China went a step further and alleged that the U.S. program would exceed America's WTO limits for trade-distorting subsidies if current prices and volumes remain stable. It could be possible for the U.S. to craft its agricultural purchasing program in a way that adheres to WTO rules as long as the U.S. subsidies don't exceed America's WTO commitment to cap trade-distorting subsidies at $19 billion per year.

5 Export Tariffs

Export and production subsidies are not the only policies that countries use to influence trade in certain products. Some countries apply **export tariffs**—which are taxes applied by the exporting country when a good leaves the country. As we saw in the introduction to this chapter, Argentina applies export tariffs on many of its agricultural products. Mozambique charges a tariff on exports of diamonds, and Thailand charges a tariff on exports of teak wood. The main purpose of these export tariffs is to raise revenue for the government; farmers and other companies do not benefit from the export tariffs because they pay the tax.

In this section we look at how export tariffs affect the overall welfare of the exporting country, taking into account the effects on consumers, producers, and government revenue. We start with the case of a small exporting country facing fixed world prices. Following that, we look at how the outcome differs when the country is large enough to affect world prices.

Impact of an Export Tariff in a Small Country

Consider a small country (like Argentina) that exports soybeans. The Home no-trade equilibrium is shown at point A in panel (a) of Figure 10-5. With free trade, Home

FIGURE 10-5

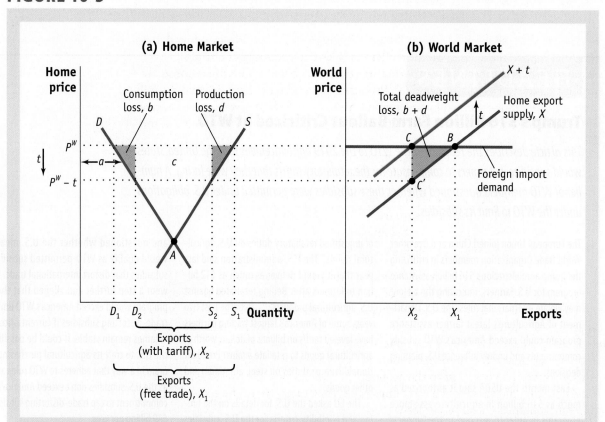

Export Tariff for a Small Country Applying an export tariff of t pesos per unit exported will decrease the price that Home exporters receive from P^W to $P^W - t$. As a result, the domestic price of the similar good will also fall by that amount. This price fall leads to a decrease in Home quantity supplied from S_1 to S_2, and an increase in Home quantity demanded from D_1 to D_2, in panel (a). Exports fall due to the tariff, from X_1 to X_2 in panel (b). The Home export supply curve shifts up by the amount of the tariff in panel (b) since the marginal cost of a unit of exports increases by exactly t. The deadweight loss due to the subsidy is the triangle $(b + d)$, the sum of the consumption loss b and production loss d.

faces a world price of soybeans of P^W pesos (we are using the currency of Argentina). At that price, the quantity supplied in Home is S_1 and the quantity demanded is D_1 in panel (a), so Home will export soybeans. The quantity of exports is $X_1 = S_1 - D_1$, which is shown by point B in panel (b). So far, the free-trade equilibrium in Figure 10-5 is the same as that in Figure 10-1, which showed the impact of an export subsidy. But the two figures will change when we consider the effects of an export tariff.

Now suppose that the government applies a tariff of t pesos to the exports of soybeans. Instead of receiving the world price of P^W, producers will instead receive the price of $P^W - t$ for their exports, because the government collects t pesos. If the price they receive in Home is any higher than this amount, then producers will sell only in the Home market and not export at all. As a result there will be an oversupply in Home and the local price will fall. Thus, in equilibrium, the Home price must also fall to equal the export price of $P^W - t$.

With the price falling to $P^W - t$, the quantity supplied in Home falls to S_2, and the quantity demanded increases to D_2 in panel (a). Therefore, Home exports fall to $X_2 = S_2 - D_2$. The change in the quantity of exports can be thought of as a leftward, or upward, shift of the export supply curve in panel (b), where we measure the world price rather than the Home price on the vertical axis. The export supply curve shifts up by the amount of the tariff t. This result is analogous to what happened when we introduced a subsidy in Figure 10-1. In that case, the export supply curve fell by the amount of the subsidy s.

The new intersection of supply and demand in the world market is at point C in panel (b), with exports of X_2. Alternatively, on the original export supply curve X, exports of X_2 occur at the point C' and the domestic price of $P^W - t$.

Impact of the Export Tariff on Small-Country Welfare
We can now determine the impact of the tariff on the welfare of the small exporting country. Since the Home price falls because of the export tariff, consumers benefit. The rise in consumer surplus is shown by area a in panel (a). Producers are worse off, however, and the fall in producer surplus is shown by the amount $(a + b + c + d)$. The government collects revenue from the export tariff, and the amount of revenue equals the amount of the tariff t times exports of X_2, area c.

Adding up the impact on consumers, producers, and government revenue, the overall impact of the export tariff on the welfare of a small exporting country is

Rise in consumer surplus:	$+a$
Fall in producer surplus:	$-(a + b + c + d)$
Rise in government revenue:	$+c$
Net effect on Home's welfare:	$-(b + d)$

To sum up, the export tariff for a small country has a deadweight loss of $(b + d)$. (This outcome is similar to the results of the import tariff that we studied in Chapter 8 and the export subsidy we studied earlier in this chapter.) That loss can be broken up into two components. The triangle b in panel (a) is the consumption loss for the economy. It occurs because as consumers increase their quantity from D_1 to D_2, the amount that they value these extra units varies between P^W and $P^W - t$, along their demand curve. The true cost to the economy of these extra units consumed is always P^W. Therefore, the value of the extra units is less than their cost to the economy, indicating that there is a deadweight loss.

Triangle d is the production loss to the economy. It occurs because as producers reduce their quantity from S_1 to S_2, the marginal cost of supplying those units varies between P^W and $P^W - t$, along their supply curve. But the true value to the economy of these extra units consumed is always P^W, because that is the price at which they could be exported without the tariff. Therefore, the value of the forgone units exceeds their cost to the economy, indicating again that there is a deadweight loss.

Impact of an Export Tariff in a Large Country

We have shown that the export tariff in a small country leads to a decline in overall welfare. Despite that, some governments—especially in developing countries—find that export tariffs are a convenient way to raise revenue, because it is very easy to apply the tax at border stations as goods leave the country. The fact that the economy overall suffers a loss does not prevent governments from using this policy.

What happens in a large exporting country? Does an export tariff still produce an overall loss? Recall from Chapter 8 that an import tariff in a large country would lead to an overall *gain* rather than a loss, provided that the tariff is not too high. This gain arises because the import tariff reduces demand for the imported product, and therefore lowers its price, which leads to a terms-of-trade gain. In this section, we see that an export tariff also leads to a terms-of-trade gain. That result occurs because an export tariff reduces the amount supplied to the world market, and therefore increases the price of the export product, which is a terms-of-trade gain.

Figure 10-6 illustrates the effect of an export tariff for a large country. Under free trade the price of soybeans is P^W, which is at the intersection of Home export supply X and Foreign import demand M^* in panel (b). When the government applies a tariff of t pesos to soybean exports, the Home export supply curve shifts up by exactly the amount of the tariff from X to $X + t$. The new intersection of the Home export supply curve and the Foreign import demand curve occurs at point C, and the world price has risen from P^W to P^*.

The price P^* is paid by Foreign buyers of soybeans and includes the export tariff. The Foreign import demand curve M^* is downward-sloping rather than horizontal as it was in Figure 10-5 for a small country. Because the Foreign import demand curve slopes downward, the price P^* is greater than P^W but not by as much as the tariff t,

FIGURE 10-6

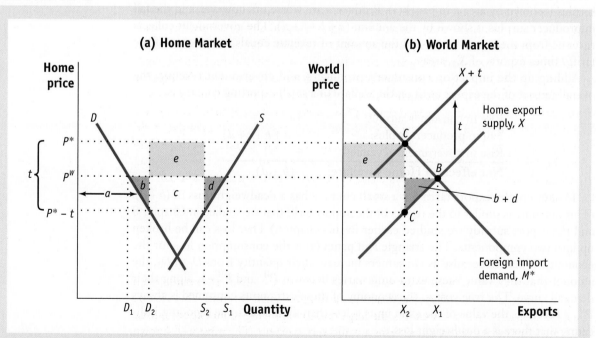

Export Tariff for a Large Country   The tariff shifts up the export supply curve from X to $X + t$, in panel (b). As a result, the world price increases from P^W to P^*. But this increase in the world price is less than the upward shift in export supply of t. It follows that the Home price decreases from P^W to $P^* - t$, in panel (a). Home quantity demanded increases from D_1 to D_2, and Home quantity supplied decreases from S_1 to S_2. The deadweight loss for Home is the area of triangle $(b + d)$. Because world price rises from P^W to P^*, Home also has a terms-of-trade gain of area e.

which equals the upward shift in the export supply curve. Home receives price $P^* - t$, which is measured net of the export tariff. Because P^* has risen above P^W by less than the amount t, it follows that $P^* - t$ falls below P^W, as shown in panel (a).

Impact of the Export Tariff on Large-Country Welfare We can now determine the impact of the tariff on the welfare of the large exporting country. Home consumers and producers faced the price of P^W under free trade, but face the lower price of $P^* - t$ once the tariff is applied. The rise in consumer surplus is shown by area a in panel (a), and the fall in producer surplus is shown by area $(a + b + c + d)$. The revenue the government collects from the export tariff equals the amount of the tariff t times exports of X_2, by area $(c + e)$.

Adding up the impacts on consumers, producers, and government revenue, the overall impact of the export tariff on the welfare of a large exporting country is

Rise in consumer surplus:	$+a$
Fall in producer surplus:	$-(a + b + c + d)$
Rise in government revenue:	$+(c + e)$
Net effect on Home's welfare:	$e - (b + d)$

Compared with the effect of an export tariff for a small country, we find that the net effect on large-country Home welfare can be positive rather than negative, as long as $e > (b + d)$. The amount $(b + d)$ is still the deadweight loss; area e is the *terms-of-trade gain* due to the export tariff. In either panel of Figure 10-6, this terms-of-trade gain is measured by the rise in the price paid by Foreign purchasers of soybeans, from P^W to P^*, multiplied by the amount of exports X_2. This terms-of-trade gain is the "extra" money that Home receives from exporting soybeans at a higher price. If the terms-of-trade gain exceeds the deadweight loss, then the Home country gains overall from applying the tariff.

To sum up, the effect of an export tariff is most similar to that of an import tariff because it leads to a terms-of-trade gain. In Chapter 8 we argued that for an import tariff that is not too high, the terms-of-trade gain e would always exceed the deadweight loss $(b + d)$. That argument applies here, too, so that for export tariffs that are not too high, the terms-of-trade gain e exceeds the deadweight loss and Home country gains. In Chapter 8 we stressed that this terms-of-trade gain came at the expense of the Foreign country, which earns a lower price for the product it sells under an import tariff. Similarly, the Foreign country loses under an export tariff because it is paying a higher price for the product it is buying. So, just as we called an import tariff a "beggar thy neighbor" policy, the same idea applies to export tariffs because they harm the Foreign country. These results are the opposite of those we found for an export subsidy, which for a large Home country always leads to a terms-of-trade loss for Home and a benefit for Foreign buyers.

6 Export Quotas

The finding that a large country can gain from an export tariff gives a government an added reason to use this policy, in addition to earning the tariff revenue. There is one other export policy that also benefits the large country applying it: an **export quota**, which is a limit on the amount that firms are allowed to export. The most well-known system of export quotas in the world today is the system used by the Organization of Petroleum Exporting Countries (OPEC), which includes six countries in the Middle East, four in Africa, and two in South America. OPEC sets limits on the amount of oil that can be exported by each country, and by limiting oil exports in this way, it keeps world petroleum prices high. Those high prices benefit not only OPEC's member countries, but also other oil-exporting countries that do not belong to OPEC. (At the same time, the high prices clearly harm oil-importing countries.) The oil companies themselves benefit from the export quotas because they earn the higher prices. Thus, the export quota is different from an export tariff (which is, in effect, a tax on firms that lowers their producer surplus).

We can use Figure 10-7 to illustrate the effect of an export quota. This figure is similar to Figure 10-6 because it deals with a large exporting country. Initially under free trade, the world trade price occurs at the intersection of Home export supply X and Foreign import demand M^*, at point B in panel (b) with exports of X_1. Now suppose that the Home country imposes a quota that limits its exports to the quantity $\overline{X}$, with $\overline{X} < X_1$. We can think of the export supply curve as a vertical line at the amount $\overline{X}$. A vertical line at $\overline{X}$ would intersect Foreign import demand at point C, leading to a higher world price of $P_2^* > P^W$.

That higher world price is earned by the Home producers. But because they export less ($\overline{X}$ rather than the free-trade amount X_1), they sell more locally. Local sales can be found by subtracting exports of $\overline{X}$ from the Home supply curve in panel (a), shifting the remaining Home supply left to the curve labeled $S - \overline{X}$. The intersection of this remaining Home supply with Home demand occurs at the price P_2 in panel (a), which is lower than the initial world price of P^W. As we found for the export tariff in Figure 10-6, the fall in the Home price leads to an increase in Home demand from D_1 to D_2. That quantity is the amount that Home firms supply to the local market. The *total* amount supplied by Home firms is $D_2 + \overline{X} = S_2$, which has fallen in relation to the free-trade supply of S_1. So we see that a side-effect of the export quota is to limit the total sales of Home firms.

FIGURE 10-7

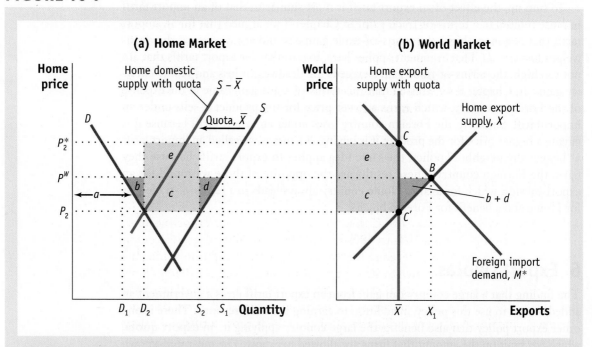

Export Quota for a Large Country The export quota leads to a vertical export supply curve above the quantity $\overline{X}$ in panel (b). As a result, the world price increases from P^W to P_2^*. Because Home firms can export only the amount $\overline{X}$, the remaining home supply curve shifts left by that amount, as shown by $S - \overline{X}$.

This remaining Home supply intersects Home demand at the price P_2 in panel (a), which is lower than the initial world price of P^W. This increase in the world price is less than the upward shift in export supply of t. The deadweight loss for Home is the area of triangle $(b+d)$, while Home firms earn the quota rents of area $c+e$.

Let's compare the welfare effects of the export quota with those of the export tariff. Home consumers gain the same amount of consumer surplus a due to lower domestic prices. The change in producer surplus is more complicated. If producers earned the lower price of P_2 on *all* their quantity sold, as they do with the export tariff, then they would lose $(a + b + c + d)$ in producer surplus. But under the export quota they also earn rents of $(c + e)$ on their export sales, which offsets the loss in producer surplus. These rents equal the difference between the Home and world prices, $P_2^* - P_2$, times the amount exported $\overline{X}$. A portion of these rents—the area e—is the rise in the world price times the amount exported, or the terms-of-trade gain for the exporter; the remaining amount of rents—the area c—offsets some of the loss in producer surplus. The government does not collect any revenue under the export quota, because the firms themselves earn rents from the higher export prices.

The overall impact of the export quota is

Rise in consumer surplus:	$+a$
Fall in producer surplus:	$-(a + b + c + d)$
Rise in rents earned by producers:	$+(c + e)$
Rise in government revenue:	0
Net effect on Home's welfare:	$e - (b + d)$

To summarize, the overall effect of the export quota on the Home country welfare is the same as the export tariff, with a net effect on welfare of $e - (b + d)$. If this amount is positive, then Home gains from the export quota. The effects of the quota on Home firms and the government differ from those of the tariff. Under the export tariff the Home government earns revenue of $(c + e)$, while under the export quota that amount is earned instead as quota rents by Home firms.

This conclusion is the same as the one we reached in Chapter 8, when we examined the ways that import quotas can be allocated. One of those ways was by using a "voluntary" export restraint (VER), which is put in place by the exporting country rather than the importing country. The VER and the export quota are the same idea with different names. In both cases, the restriction on exports raises the world price. Firms in the exporting country can sell at that higher world price, so they earn the quota rents, with no effect on government revenue. In the following application, we look at how China used export quotas to limit its export of some mineral products.

APPLICATION

Chinese Export Policies in Mineral Products

Like many developing countries, China uses a wide variety of export policies. Export tariffs ranging from 10% to 40% are applied to steel products, for example, which create a source of revenue for the government. In addition, China has applied both tariffs and quotas to its exports of mineral products. The policies that China has applied to mineral exports have attracted international attention recently, since some of these minerals are essential to the production of goods in other countries. As we saw in Figures 10-6 and 10-7, export tariffs and export quotas both increase the world price, making it more expensive for other countries to obtain a product and at the same time benefiting the exporting country with a terms-of-trade gain.

In 2009, the United States, the EU, and Mexico filed a case against China at the World Trade Organization (WTO), charging that the export tariffs and export quotas that China applied on bauxite, zinc, yellow phosphorus, and six other industrial minerals distorted the pattern of international trade.[8] Export restrictions of this type are banned under Article XI of the General Agreement on Tariffs and Trade (see **Side Bar: Key Provisions of the GATT**, Chapter 8). When China joined the WTO in 2001, it was required to eliminate its export restrictions, including those on minerals. But an exception to Article XI states that this rule does not apply to "export prohibitions or restrictions temporarily applied to prevent or relieve critical shortages of foodstuffs or other products essential to the exporting contracting party." For example, a country facing a food shortage can restrict its food exports to keep the food at home. In its response to this 2009 case, China claimed that this exception applied to its exports of industrial minerals; China was restricting its exports of the minerals because they were needed by Chinese industries using these products (such as the solar panel industry), and also because the export quota would limit the total amount sold of these precious resources and leave more in the ground for future use. But in July 2011, the WTO ruled that this exception did not apply to China's exports of these products and that it must remove its export restrictions on industrial minerals. China filed an appeal, but the WTO reaffirmed the ruling again in January 2012.

This legal battle at the WTO was closely watched around the world, because shortly after the case was filed in 2009, China also started applying export quotas to other mineral products: **rare earth** minerals, such as lanthanum (used in batteries and lighting) and neodymium (used in making permanent magnets, which are found in high-tech products ranging from smartphones to hybrid cars to wind turbines). At that time, China controlled more than 95% of the world production and exports of these minerals. The export quotas applied by China contributed to a rise in the world prices of these products. For example, the price of lanthanum went from $6 per kilogram in 2009 to $60 in 2010, to $151 in 2011, and then back down to $36 in 2012.

In Figure 10-8, we show the value, average price, and quantity of Chinese exports in three categories of rare earth minerals over the period from 2007 to 2015. Panel (a) shows the value of exports in billions of dollars, panel (b) shows the average price in dollars per kilogram, and panel (c) shows the quantity exported in millions of kilograms. For all three categories of rare earth minerals, the average export price rose dramatically in 2011, while the quantity exported fell in 2011 and 2012 because of the limits imposed by the Chinese export quota. For two of the categories (scandium and yttrium, and cerium compounds), the price rise was enough to lead to much greater export value despite the lower quantity, indicating that the demand is highly inelastic, at least in the short run (within a year). Figure 10-8 shows how a country can gain by applying an export quota: the export value went up, so Chinese firms earned more despite the reduced quantity of exports.

In Figure 10-8, the price and export value fell in 2012 even though the quantity exported remained low (because of the continued export quota). That price fall was caused by mines being opened in other countries: the high world prices in 2011 made it profitable for Australia to open a new mine, and the United States reopened a mine in the Mojave Desert that had closed a decade earlier for environmental reasons. The U.S. mine includes deposits of light rare earth elements, such as neodymium (needed to make permanent magnets in hard drives) and europium (needed for fluorescent light bulbs and TV screens), as well as the heavy rare elements terbium, yttrium, and dysprosium (which are needed to manufacture wind turbines and solar cells).[9] These new sources of supply led to the price drop in 2012.

---

[8] The six other minerals are coke, fluorspar, magnesium, manganese, silicon carbide, and silicon metal. The information in this paragraph and the next is drawn from Keith Bradsher, "In Victory for the West, W.T.O. Orders China to Stop Export Taxes on Minerals," *New York Times*, January 30, 2012, and "Rare Earth Trade Case Against China May Be Too Late," *New York Times*, March 13, 2012.

[9] See Kyle Wiens, "A Visit to the Only American Mine for Rare Earth Metals," *The Atlantic*, February 21, 2012, electronic edition.

FIGURE 10-8

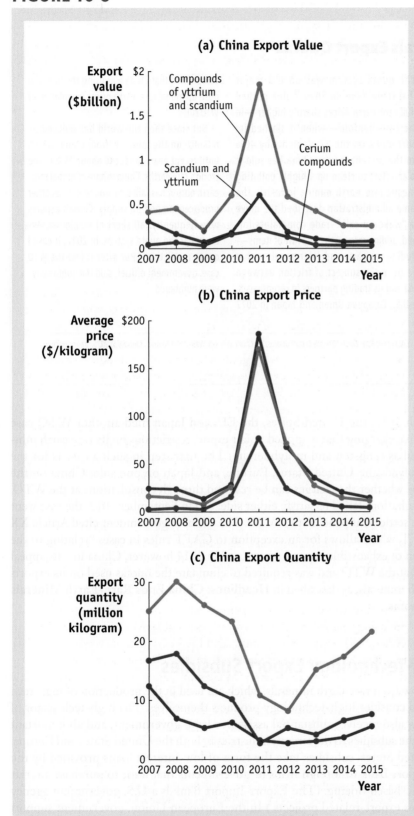

(a) China Export Value

(b) China Export Price

(c) China Export Quantity

China Exports of Rare Earth Minerals, 2007–15
Panel (a) shows the value of Chinese exports
(in $ billion) for three categories of rare earth
minerals over the period 2007–15. Panel (b) shows
the average price for each category (in dollars
per kilogram), and panel (c) shows the quantity
exported (in millions of kilograms). For all three
categories of rare earth minerals, the average
export price rose dramatically in 2011 while the
quantity fell in 2011 and 2012 because of the
Chinese export quota. For two of the categories
(scandium and yttrium, and cerium compounds),
the price rise was enough to lead to much greater
export value despite the lower quantity.

Data from: China Customs Statistics, 2007–15.

HEADLINES

China Ends Rare-Earth Minerals Export Quotas

China has dropped decade-old quotas limiting exports of strategically important minerals that sparked a global trade dispute and led some countries to reduce their reliance on Chinese supplies. The shift comes after Beijing lost a dispute at the World Trade Organization in 2013. But the policy also proved to be of little value for Beijing as many countries found other sources for the materials known as rare earths, which are widely used in high-technology industries such as smartphones and missile systems. "The change is likely because of the pressure from the WTO decision," said Frank Tang, an analyst at investment bank North Square Blue Oak. "China is saying that as a WTO member, it'll have to abide by WTO rules."

The quota system was once a major global trade issue. In 2010, China pushed global rare-earth prices sharply higher—in some cases tenfold—when it slashed its export quota on the 17 elements by 40% from the preceding year. China has said it was an effort to clean up a highly polluting domestic rare-earth mining industry. The Obama administration described the move as a "wake-up call." Trade complaints followed, adding rare earths to a raft of items—including car parts and solar panels—that have been the subject of friction between China and its trading partners in recent years. The U.S., European Union and Japan in 2012

complained that China was using the quota to push up global rare-earth prices in violation of WTO rules.

But since then the world has reduced its reliance on the minerals from China, which until recent years produced about 93% of the world's rare earths. China's share of global rare-earth output has fallen to around 86% as other producers amped up supply. China's exports now frequently fall short of maximum levels under the quota system. In 2012, it eased quota restrictions. But after it lost the WTO case, government officials said the quota's days were numbered.

Source: Republished with permission of Dow Jones & Company, Inc. From "China Ends Rare-Earth Minerals Export Quotas," by Chuin-Wei Yap, Wall Street Journal, January 5, 2015, online edition. Permission conveyed through Copyright Clearance Center, Inc.

In March 2012, the United States, the EU, and Japan filed another WTO case against China, charging that it applied unfair export restrictions on its rare earth minerals, as well as tungsten and molybdenum. The first step in such a case is for the parties involved (the United States, Europe, and Japan on one side; China on the other) to see whether the charges can be resolved through consultations at the WTO. Those consultations failed to satisfy either side, and in September 2012, the case went to a dispute settlement panel at the WTO. The Chinese government cited Article XX of the GATT, which allows for an exception to GATT rules in cases "relating to the conservation of exhaustible natural resources." In 2014 however, China lost its appeal of that case at the WTO and was required to eliminate the quotas used on its exports of rare earth minerals, as described in **Headlines: China Ends Rare-Earth Minerals Export Quotas**.

7 High-Technology Export Subsidies

We turn now from rare earth minerals, which are used in the production of high-tech products, to consider high-technology products themselves. The high-tech sector of an economy also receives substantial assistance from government, and an important example is the subsidies to the aircraft industries in both the United States and Europe. In the United States, subsidies take the form of low-interest loans provided by the Export-Import Bank to foreign firms or governments that want to purchase aircraft from Seattle-based Boeing. (The Export-Import Bank is a U.S. government agency that finances export-related projects.) In the European Union, government support for research and development and other subsidies are given to Airbus, which produces parts and assembles its finished products in a number of European countries. In Japan and South Korea, direct subsidies have been given to high-tech manufacturing firms that achieve certain targets for increasing their export sales. High-tech subsidies are given by many other countries, too.

Why do governments support their high-technology industries? In the case of agricultural products, subsidies are instituted primarily because of the political clout of those industries. Although politics plays a role in subsidies for high-tech industries, governments also subsidize these industries because they may create benefits that spill over to other firms in the economy. That is, governments believe that high-tech industry produces a positive **externality**. This argument for a subsidy is similar to the infant industry argument used to justify protective tariffs (see Chapter 9), except that the protection is applied to an export industry rather than an import-competing industry.

"Strategic" Use of High-Tech Export Subsidies

In addition to the spillover argument for export subsidies, governments and industries also argue that export subsidies might give a **strategic advantage** to export firms that are competing with a small number of rivals in international markets. By a strategic advantage, we mean that the subsidized industry can compete more effectively with its rivals on the world market. Think of the aircraft industry, which currently has just two producers of large, wide-bodied airplanes: Boeing in the United States and Airbus in Europe. Each of these firms receives some type of subsidy from its government. If high-tech subsidies allow firms to compete more effectively and earn more profits in international markets, and if the extra profits are more than the amount of the subsidy, then the exporting country will obtain an overall benefit from the export subsidy, similar to the benefit that comes from a large country applying a tariff.

To examine whether countries can use their subsidies strategically, we use the assumption of **imperfect competition**. We already used this assumption in Chapter 9, in which we considered the cases of Home monopoly and Foreign monopoly. Now we allow for two firms in the market, which is called a **duopoly**. In that case, each firm can set the price and quantity of its output (and hence maximize its profits) based on the price and quantity decisions of the other firm. When a government uses subsidies to affect this interaction between firms and to increase the profits of its own domestic firm, the government is said to be acting strategically. In this section, we examine the effects of strategic export subsidies to determine whether profits of the exporting firm will rise enough to offset the cost of the subsidy to the government.

Because we now assume that certain high-tech industries operate in imperfectly competitive markets, we need to use a different set of tools to model their supply decisions than we have used thus far in this chapter. To capture the strategic decision making of two firms, we use **game theory**, the modeling of strategic interactions (games) between firms as they choose actions that will maximize their returns. The main goal in this section is to model the strategic interaction of high-tech firms in Home and Foreign, and then to see the impact of export subsidies on their respective decisions and payoffs.

To examine the effect of an export subsidy, we start with the free-trade situation, before any subsidies are in place. Suppose there are two firms that are competing for sales of a new type of aircraft. For example, one of the newest aircraft that Airbus sells is the double-decker A380, which Boeing has no plans to copy. One of the newest aircraft that Boeing sells is the smaller 787 Dreamliner, and Airbus has developed a similar model called the A350 (discussed later in the chapter). For convenience, we focus on the decision of each firm to produce a relatively new aircraft that competes with the other firm for sales to the rest of the world. By ignoring sales to firms in their own countries, we will not have to keep track of consumer surplus in the United States or Europe. Instead, the measure of welfare for these countries will depend only on the profits earned by Boeing or Airbus from their sales to the rest of the world.

FIGURE 10-9

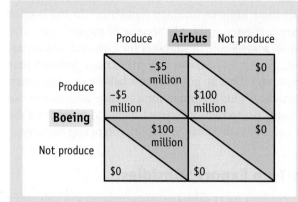

Payoff Matrix Between Two Firms The lower-left number in each quadrant shows the profits of Boeing, and the upper-right number shows the profits of Airbus. Each firm must decide whether to produce a new type of aircraft. A Nash equilibrium occurs when each firm is making its best decision, given the action of the other. For this pattern of payoffs, there are two Nash equilibria, in the upper-right and lower-left quadrants, where one firm produces and the other does not.

Payoff Matrix In Figure 10-9, we show a **payoff matrix** for Boeing and Airbus, each of which has to decide whether to produce the new aircraft. Each quadrant of the matrix shows the profits earned by Boeing in the lower-left corner and the profits of Airbus in the upper-right corner. When both firms produce (upper-left quadrant), their prices are reduced through competition, and they both end up making negative profits (i.e., losses) of $5 million.[10]

If Airbus produces the new aircraft and Boeing does not (lower-left quadrant), then Boeing earns nothing, whereas Airbus, the only supplier, earns high profits of $100 million. Conversely, if Boeing produces and Airbus does not (upper-right quadrant), Airbus earns nothing, and Boeing, now the only supplier, earns high profits of $100 million. Finally, if both firms choose to not produce (lower-right quadrant), then they both earn profits of 0.

Nash Equilibrium With the pattern of payoffs shown in Figure 10-9, we want to determine what the outcome of this game between the two firms will be. At first glance, this seems like a difficult problem. It is hard for each firm to decide what to do without knowing whether the other firm is going to produce. To solve this problem, we use the concept of the Nash equilibrium, named after John Nash, a winner of the Nobel Prize in economics.[11]

The idea of a **Nash equilibrium** is that each firm must make its own best decision, taking as given each possible action of the rival firm. When each firm is acting that way, the outcome of the game is a Nash equilibrium. That is, the action of each player is the best possible response to the action of the other player.

Best Strategy for Boeing To determine the Nash equilibrium, we proceed by checking each quadrant of the payoff matrix. Let us look at Boeing's possible strategies, starting with the case in which its rival, Airbus, chooses to produce. If Boeing knows that Airbus will produce, then Boeing needs to decide whether to produce. If Boeing produces, then it earns –$5 million (in the upper-left quadrant); if Boeing does not produce, then it earns 0 (in the lower-left quadrant). Therefore, if Airbus produces, then Boeing is better off *not* producing. This finding proves that having both firms produce is not a Nash equilibrium. Boeing would never stay in production, since it prefers to drop out of the market whenever Airbus produces.

---

[10] The numbers we are using in the payoff matrix are made up for convenience, but they illustrate the idea of competition between the firms for the sale of a new aircraft.

[11] The book and movie *A Beautiful Mind* describes the career of John Nash.

Best Strategy for Airbus Let's continue with the case in which Boeing does not produce but Airbus does (lower-left quadrant of Figure 10-9). Is this the best strategy for Airbus? To check this, suppose that Airbus chooses instead to not produce. That would move us from the lower-left quadrant to the lower-right quadrant in Figure 10-9, meaning that Airbus's profits fall from $100 million to 0. This outcome is worse for Airbus, so it would not change its decision: it would still choose to produce. We conclude that the decision illustrated in the lower-left quadrant, with Airbus producing and Boeing not producing, is a Nash equilibrium because each firm is making its best decision given what the other is doing. When Airbus produces, then Boeing's best response is to not produce, and when Boeing does not produce, then Airbus's best response is to produce. There is no reason for either firm to change its behavior from the Nash equilibrium.

Multiple Equilibria Is it possible to find more than one Nash equilibrium? To check for this, we need to check the other quadrants in Figure 10-9. Let us try the case in the upper-right quadrant, where Boeing produces but Airbus does not. Consider Airbus making the decision to produce or not, given that Boeing produces, or Boeing making the decision to produce or not, given that Airbus does not produce. Using the same logic we have already gone through, you can confirm that neither firm would want to change the decision it has made as seen in the upper-right quadrant: if either firm changed its choice, its profits would fall. If Boeing decides not to produce, then its profits fall to 0 (from the upper-right to the lower-right quadrant), whereas if Airbus decides to produce, its profits fall to –$5 million (from the upper-right to the upper-left quadrant). So we conclude that the upper-right quadrant, with Boeing producing and Airbus not producing, is *also* a Nash equilibrium. When Boeing produces, then Airbus's best response is to not produce, and when Airbus does not produce, then Boeing's best response is to produce. Finally, by applying the same logic to the other quadrants, we can confirm that there are no more Nash equilibria.

When there are two Nash equilibria, there must be some force from outside the model that determines in which equilibrium we are. An example of one such force is the **first mover advantage**, which means that one firm is able to decide whether to produce before the other firm. If Boeing had this advantage, it would choose to produce, and Airbus, as the second mover, would not produce, so we would be in the upper-right quadrant. Let us suppose that is the Nash equilibrium from which we start. Because Airbus is not producing, it is making zero profits. In this situation, the government in Europe might want to try to change the Nash equilibrium so that Airbus would instead earn positive profits. That is, by providing subsidies to Airbus, we want to determine whether the payoffs in the matrix change such that the Nash equilibrium also changes.

The type of subsidy we consider in our model is a cash payment to Airbus. In practice, however, subsidies are of many kinds: Boeing has benefited from U.S. military contracts, where the research and development (R&D) done for those contracts has been used in its civilian aircraft, too. Airbus, on the other hand, has benefited from direct R&D subsidies to defray the "launch costs" of getting a new aircraft off the ground. Both companies have benefited from low-cost loans provided by their governments to purchasers of aircraft. Later in the chapter, we examine in more detail actual export subsidies that are used in the aircraft industry.

Effect of a Subsidy to Airbus

Suppose the European governments provide a subsidy of $25 million to Airbus. With this subsidy in place, Airbus's profits will increase by $25 million when it produces. In Figure 10-10, we add that amount to the payoffs for Airbus and check to see whether

FIGURE 10-10

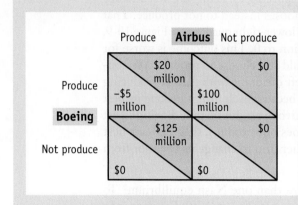

Payoff Matrix with Foreign Subsidy When the European governments provide a subsidy of $25 million to Airbus, its profits increase by that much when it produces a new aircraft. Now there is only one Nash equilibrium, in the lower-left quadrant, with Airbus producing but Boeing not producing. The profits for Airbus have increased from 0 to $125 million, while the subsidy cost only $25 million, so there is a net gain of $100 million in European welfare.

the Nash equilibria have changed. Recall that the free-trade Nash equilibria occur when one firm produces and the other does not.

Best Strategy for Airbus Let us start with the free-trade Nash equilibrium in which Boeing produces but Airbus does not (upper-right quadrant) and see whether it changes when Airbus receives a government subsidy. After the subsidy, that option is no longer a Nash equilibrium: if Boeing is producing, then Airbus is now better off by *also* producing because then it receives a $25 million subsidy from the government. With the subsidy, it will now earn $20 million ($5 million in negative profits plus the $25 million subsidy) even when Boeing produces. Recall that in the original situation, if Boeing produced, then Airbus would not choose to produce because otherwise it would lose $5 million. With the subsidy, Airbus now earns $20 million by producing instead of losing $5 million.

Best Strategy for Boeing Is this new position a Nash equilibrium? To answer that, we need to see whether Boeing would still be making the right decision given that Airbus is producing. When Airbus produces, Boeing loses $5 million when it produces (upper-left quadrant) but loses nothing when it does not produce (lower-left quadrant). Therefore, Boeing will want to drop out of the market. Once Boeing makes the decision not to produce, Airbus's decision doesn't change. It still chooses to produce, but its payoff increases dramatically from $20 million to $125 million, and we move to the lower-left quadrant, with Airbus producing and Boeing not.

Nash Equilibrium You can readily check that the lower-left quadrant is a unique Nash equilibrium: each firm is making its best decision, given the action of the other. Furthermore, it is the *only* Nash equilibrium. The effect of the European governments' subsidy has been to shift the equilibrium from having Boeing as the only producer (where we started, in the upper-right quadrant) to having Airbus as the only producer (in the lower-left quadrant).

European Welfare The European subsidy has had a big impact on the equilibrium of the game being played between the two firms. But can we necessarily conclude that Europe is better off? To evaluate that, we need to add up the welfare of the various parties involved, much as we did earlier in the chapter.

The calculation of European welfare is simplified, however, because of our assumption that production is for export to the rest of the world. From Europe's point of view, we do not need to worry about the effect of the subsidy on consumer surplus in its own market. The only two items left to evaluate, then, are the profits for Airbus from its sales to the rest of the world and the cost of the subsidy to the European government.

Airbus's profits have increased from 0 (when it was not producing but Boeing was) to $125 million (now that Airbus is producing but Boeing is not). The revenue cost of the subsidy to Europe is $25 million. Therefore, the net effect of the subsidy on European welfare is

Rise in producer surplus:	+125
Fall in government revenue:	−25
Net effect on European welfare:	**+100**

In this case, the subsidy led to a net gain in European welfare because the increase in profits for Airbus is more than the cost of the subsidy.[12]

Subsidy with Cost Advantage for Boeing

Our finding that the subsidy can raise European welfare depends, however, on the numbers we assumed so far. Let us now consider another case in which Boeing has a cost advantage over Airbus. In this case, we assume that the cost advantage is the result not of U.S. subsidies but of U.S. comparative advantage in aircraft production.

When Boeing has a cost advantage in aircraft production, the payoff matrix is as shown in Figure 10-11. Boeing earns profits of $5 million when both firms produce and profits of $125 million when Airbus does not produce. There is now only one Nash equilibrium, and it is in the upper-right quadrant in which Boeing produces and Airbus does not. The alternative free-trade Nash equilibrium in Figure 10-9 (in which Airbus produces and Boeing does not) is no longer a Nash equilibrium because, with the cost advantage we are now assuming Boeing has, even if Airbus chooses to produce, it is better for Boeing to produce and earn profits of $5 million than not produce and earn 0 profits.

Now suppose, once again, that the European governments provide a $25 million subsidy to Airbus. We add that amount to the payoffs of Airbus when it produces (still assuming that Boeing has a cost advantage over Airbus), as shown in Figure 10-12.

Best Strategy for Airbus Let's see how the subsidy has affected the previous Nash equilibrium in which Boeing produces and Airbus does not (upper-right quadrant). Given that Boeing produces, the decision to not produce is no longer the best one for

FIGURE 10-11

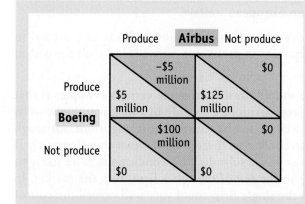

Another Payoff Matrix, with Boeing Cost Advantage If Boeing has a cost advantage in the production of aircraft, the payoffs are as shown here. Boeing earns profits of $5 million when both firms are producing, and profits of $125 million when Airbus does not produce. Now there is only one Nash equilibrium, in the upper-right quadrant, where Boeing produces and Airbus does not.

[12] Notice that if the initial equilibrium was one in which Airbus produced and Boeing did not, then the only effect of the subsidy would be to make this equilibrium unique; it would not change the decision of either firm. Moreover, the effect on total European welfare would be zero because the subsidy would be just a transfer from the European government to Airbus.

FIGURE 10-12

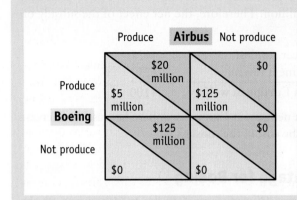

Produce **Airbus** Not produce

Produce

Boeing

Not produce

	Produce	Not produce
Produce	$20 million / $5 million	$0 / $125 million
Not produce	$125 million / $0	$0 / $0

Another Payoff Matrix with Foreign Subsidy When the European governments provide a subsidy of $25 million to Airbus, its profits increase by that much when it produces. Now the only Nash equilibrium is in the upper-left quadrant, where both firms produce. The profits for Airbus have increased from 0 to $20 million, but the subsidy costs $25 million, so there is a net loss of $5 million in European welfare.

Airbus: with the subsidy now in place and Boeing producing, Airbus's best decision is to produce and to earn profits of $20 million (upper-left quadrant) rather than 0.

Best Strategy for Boeing Is this new position a Nash equilibrium? Once again, we need to check to see whether, given Airbus's new postsubsidy decision to produce, Boeing is still making the right decision. Given that Airbus produces, then Boeing earns profits of $5 million when it produces and 0 when it does not. Therefore, Boeing will stay in the market, and we have proved that having both firms produce is a Nash equilibrium.

European Welfare Once Again When Boeing has a cost advantage, the European subsidy allows Airbus to enter the market, but it *has not* resulted in the exit of Boeing as it did in the earlier no-cost-advantage scenario. Let us evaluate the effect on European welfare under these circumstances.

Airbus's profits have increased from 0 (when it was not producing, but Boeing was) to $20 million (now that both firms are producing). The revenue cost of the subsidy to Europe is still $25 million. Therefore, the net effect of the subsidy on European welfare is

Rise in producer profits:	+20
Fall in government revenue:	−25
Net effect on European welfare:	−5

When Boeing has a cost advantage, then, the subsidy leads to a *net loss* in European welfare because the increase in profits for Airbus is less than the cost of the subsidy.

Summary The lesson that we should draw from these various examples is that under conditions of imperfect competition, a subsidy by one government to its exporting firm might increase welfare for its nation, but it might not. Although profits for the exporting firm certainly rise, there is an increase in welfare only if profits rise by more than the cost of the subsidy. This condition is more likely to be satisfied if the subsidy leads to the *exit* of the other firm from the market. In that case, the profits earned by the single firm could very well exceed the cost of the subsidy. When both firms remain in the market after the subsidy, however, it is unlikely that the increase in profits for the subsidized firm will exceed the subsidy cost. In the following application, we are especially interested in whether subsidies in the aircraft industry have kept one firm out of a market segment in which another produces.

APPLICATION

WTO Controversies Due to Subsidies in Commercial Aircraft

In the large passenger aircraft industry, there have been just three competitors: Boeing and McDonnell-Douglas in the United States and Airbus in Europe. The former two companies merged on August 1, 1997, so the industry effectively became a duopoly. The United States and Europe have used various types of subsidies to support their respective firms. First, there are indirect subsidies that arise because in the production of civilian and military aircraft, the research and development (R&D) for the military versions effectively subsidize R&D for the civilian aircraft. These indirect subsidies have benefited both McDonnell-Douglas and Boeing in the United States. Second, the government might directly subsidize the R&D costs of a new aircraft, as Europe subsidizes R&D at Airbus. Third, the government can subsidize the interest rates that aircraft buyers pay when they borrow money to purchase aircraft. Europe and the United States both provide such low-interest loans, for instance, through the Export-Import Bank in the United States, as mentioned previously.

1992 Agreement Recognizing that these subsidies are ultimately costly, in 1992 the United States and the European Community reached an agreement to limit them. The main features of this agreement are summarized in Table 10-2. Development subsidies are limited to 33% of the total development costs of a new aircraft, and it is expected that the aircraft manufacturers will repay these subsidies at the government interest rate. In addition, the agreement limits indirect (military) subsidies to not more than 4% of any firm's annual sales, prohibits production subsidies, and limits the ability of government agencies to subsidize the interest rate on purchases of aircraft. According to one estimate, this agreement reduced subsidies

TABLE 10-2

Provisions of the 1992 Agreement Between the United States and the European Community on Trade in Civil Aircraft This table shows the major provisions of a 1992 agreement between the United States and Europe that limited the subsidies provided to the development and production of civilian aircraft.

Aircraft Covered
- All aircraft of 100 seats or larger are subject to the provisions of the agreement.

Direct Support Levels
- Funds advanced by governments for aircraft development may not exceed 33% of total development costs and are to be provided only to programs in which there is a reasonable expectation of recoupment within 17 years.

Interest Rates
- Airbus will repay the first 25% of total development costs at the government cost of borrowing within 17 years of first disbursement; the remaining 8% will be repaid at the government cost of borrowing plus 1% within 17 years of first disbursement.

Indirect Supports
- Both sides agree that indirect (i.e., military) supports should neither confer unfair advantage on manufacturers of civil aircraft nor lead to distortions in international trade in such aircraft.
- Identifiable benefits from indirect support are limited to 3% of the value of industry-wide turnover in each signatory and 4% of the value of each firm's annual sales. Benefits will primarily be calculated as cost reductions in the development of a civil aircraft program realized from technology acquired through government R&D programs.

Production Supports
- No further production subsidies are allowed.

Excerpted from: Laura D'Andrea Tyson, 1992, Who's Bashing Whom? Trade Conflict in High Technology Industries (Washington, D.C.: Peterson Institute for International Economics).

by between 7.5% and 12.5% of the costs of production. As a result of the reduction in subsidies, prices for aircraft rose by somewhere between 3.1% and 8.8%. This agreement between the United States and Europe benefited the countries' governments because they no longer had to spend the money on the subsidies, and most likely also benefited the aircraft companies because prices rose, but the higher prices led to welfare losses for the purchasing countries.

Dreamliner's first take-off on December 15, 2009.

Airbus 350's first take-off on June 15, 2013.

The Superjumbo and the Dreamliner Airbus and Boeing have each claimed that the terms of the 1992 Agreement have been violated in the development of their newest commercial aircraft. For Airbus that aircraft is the double-decker A380, which is even larger than the Boeing 747 and competes directly with the 747 in long flights. Making commercial flights since 2007, this "superjumbo" aircraft carries up to 555 passengers and consists of two passenger decks for its entire length. The expenditures to develop the A380 are estimated to have been $12 billion, one-third of which the governments of France, Germany, the Netherlands, Belgium, Spain, Finland, and the United Kingdom are expected to pay. The European governments provided some $3.5 billion in low-interest loans to cover development costs. Boeing did not produce a new model to compete with the A380. Instead, it modified its 747 jumbo jet model to compete with the A380, and it focused its R&D on its new 787 Dreamliner, a midsized (250-passenger) wide-bodied aircraft. Boeing received subsidies in the form of tax breaks from the state of Washington, where its headquarters and production facilities are located. In 2005 both the United States and the EU filed countercomplaints at the World Trade Organization (WTO) regarding illegal subsidies by the other party to their respective aircraft producers. The EU was accused of subsidizing the A380, while the United States was accused of subsidizing Boeing's 787 Dreamliner.

Over the years, the WTO has ruled in favor of both companies, finding that the EU gave up to $18 billion in subsidized financing to Airbus, while the United States gave up to $4 billion in subsidized financing to Boeing. Both governments then requested that they be permitted to apply "countermeasures" against the other countries, which means that they can apply tariffs against products imported from those countries in retaliation for the subsidies. In 2018 the WTO ruled in favor of the United States, and one year later, the WTO determined the "countermeasures" that the United States could apply. As described in **Headlines: U.S. to Impose Tariffs on EU Goods After WTO's Airbus Ruling**, those countermeasures consist of U.S. tariffs on $7.5 billion in imported goods from the EU. The United States applied these new tariffs in October 2019. But there is still a pending WTO decision on countermeasures that the EU can apply against the United States based on its subsidies to Boeing. Once that decision is made, then it is expected that the EU will apply tariffs of its own against U.S. exports.

National Welfare Did the development subsidies provided by the European governments to the Airbus A380 increase their national welfare? From the theory presented previously, that outcome is more likely to happen if Airbus is the only firm producing in that market. And such is the case, because Boeing did not try to produce a double-decker aircraft to compete with the A380, but modified its 747 jumbo jet model to compete with it. That means that *both* producers were competing with each other in the market for long-haul flights in wide-body aircraft — the A380 and the 747. This is the scenario in Figure 10-12, where each firm has produced an aircraft that competes with the other's aircraft. Our theory predicts that subsidies

HEADLINES

U.S. to Impose Tariffs on EU Goods After WTO's Airbus Ruling

The WTO has determined that the EU and the United States have provided subsidies to Airbus and to Boeing, respectively, beyond those permitted by the 1992 Agreement. The United States responded in October 2019 with tariffs against EU imports, and it is expected that the EU will respond with tariffs against U.S. exports when the WTO finalizes that case.

The U.S. plans to swiftly impose tariffs on $7.5 billion in aircraft, food products and other goods from the European Union after the World Trade Organization authorized the levies Wednesday [October 2, 2019], citing the EU's subsidies to Airbus. The new duties represent the most significant trade action against the EU since the Trump administration hit the bloc with steel and aluminum duties last year, and could further sour relations between allies that have long sought to resolve trade disputes without resorting to tariffs. . . .

The Office of the U.S. Trade Representative said it would impose the tariffs starting Oct. 18, with 10% levies on jetliners and 25% duties on other products including Irish and Scotch whiskies, cheeses and hand tools. The U.S. was authorized to impose tariffs of up to 100% on $7.5 billion of goods by the WTO in what has been a 15-year battle over support programs for Airbus and U.S. aerospace rival Boeing. The latter had pushed for a 100% duty on Airbus jets.

The global trade regulator had already determined that both aircraft makers received illegal government subsidies, with the case against the Airbus subsidies moving through the WTO system first. . . .

The WTO is set to rule on Boeing's subsidies early next year, at which point the EU will be authorized to strike back with tariffs of its own. . . . "If somebody is imposing tariffs on our aviation companies, we will do exactly the same," European Commission President Jean-Claude Juncker said Wednesday evening in Brussels at an event held by the American Chamber of Commerce to the European Union. . . . Europe could consider imposing tariffs before pursuing a broader settlement and even before the WTO rules on its case against Boeing, according to EU diplomats.

Excerpted from: Republished with permission of Dow Jones & Company, Inc. From "U.S. to Impose Tariffs on EU Goods after WTO's Airbus Ruling," by Emre Peker and Josh Zumbrun, Wall Street Journal, October 2, 2019. Permission conveyed through Copyright Clearance Center, Inc.

are unlikely to be in the national interest when both firms compete with each other in the same market. This means that it is unlikely that EU national welfare increased from the subsidies provided to Airbus for the A380.

This prediction from our theory—that subsidies are unlikely to be in the national interest when both firms remain in the market—is borne out by the experience of Airbus. In February 2019, Airbus announced that it would stop production of the A380 in 2021 due to a lack of future orders, just 14 years after the aircraft had its first commercial flight.[13] Furthermore, Airbus indicated that it was unlikely to repay the remaining loans that it received from the EU for the development of the A380. As of 2019, the 747 had been flying for 50 years, but Boeing has only a small number of orders left for this aircraft. So both firms could stop production at roughly the same time (though the existing A380 and 747 planes will be flying for many years). When their production stops, the two firms will no longer be competing for sales of large wide-body aircraft. Future competition between these firms will be over the production and sales of midsize wide-body aircraft, such as the Dreamliner and the A350 from Airbus.

---

[13] See Sylvia Pfeifer, "Airbus Signals Tough Stance on Repaying Loans for A380," *Financial Times*, March 9, 2019, p. 10.

8 Conclusions

Countries use export subsidies in a wide range of industries, including agriculture, mining, and high technology. For agriculture, the underlying motivation for the export subsidies is to prop up food prices, thereby raising the real incomes of farmers. This motivation was also discussed at the end of Chapter 3 using the specific-factors model. In this chapter, we use supply and demand curves to analyze the effect of export subsidies, but we obtain the same result as in the specific-factors model: export subsidies raise prices for producers, thereby increasing their real income (in the specific-factors model) and their producer surplus (using supply curves).

Shifting income toward farmers comes with a cost to consumers, however, because of the higher food prices in the exporting country. When we add up the loss in consumer surplus, the gain in producer surplus, and the revenue cost of the subsidy, we obtain a net loss for the exporting country as a result of the subsidy. This deadweight loss is similar to that from a tariff in a small country. On the other hand, for a large country, an import tariff and an export subsidy have different welfare implications. Both policies lead to a rise in domestic prices (of either the import good or the export good) and a fall in world prices. For an export subsidy, however, the fall in world prices is a terms-of-trade loss for the exporting country. This means that applying an export subsidy in a large exporting country leads to even greater losses than applying it to a small country: there is no possibility of gain, as we found for a large-country import tariff.

The losses arising from an export subsidy, for either a small or a large country, are less severe when we instead consider production subsidies. A production subsidy provides a farmer with an extra payment for every unit produced, regardless of whether it is sold at home or abroad. So consumer prices do not change from their world level. Since consumer prices are not affected, exports increase only because domestic supply increases. In other words, the excess supply in response to production subsidies will indirectly spill over into international markets but production subsidies do not exclusively subsidize those exports (as export subsidies do). For these reasons, the losses arising from production subsidies in an exporting country are less severe than the losses arising from export subsidies.

The losses experienced by an exporting country due to subsidies are reversed when countries instead use export tariffs, as occurs for some natural resource products. With export tariffs in a large country, the exporter obtains a terms-of-trade gain through restricting supply of its exports and driving up the world price. This terms-of-trade gain comes at the expense of its trade partners who are buying the products, so like an import tariff, an export tariff is a "beggar thy neighbor" policy.

The losses experienced by an exporting country due to subsidies also change when we consider high-technology industries, operating under imperfect competition. In this chapter, we examined an international duopoly (two firms) producing a good for sale in the rest of the world: Boeing and Airbus, competing for sales of a new aircraft. We showed that it is *possible* for an export subsidy to lead to gains for the exporting country, by increasing the profits earned by the exporting firms by more than the cost of the subsidy. But that result often requires the subsidy to force the other firm out of the market, which does not necessarily occur. In this case, if both firms stay in the market and are subsidized by their governments, then it is unlikely that the subsidies are in the national interest of either the United States or the European Union; instead, the countries purchasing the aircraft gain because of the lower price, while the United States and Europe lose as a result of the costs of the subsidies.

KEY POINTS

1. An export subsidy leads to a fall in welfare for a small exporting country facing a fixed world price. The drop in welfare is a deadweight loss and is composed of a consumption and production loss, similar to an import tariff for a small country.

2. In the large-country case, an export subsidy lowers the price of that product in the rest of the world. The decrease in the export price is a terms-of-trade loss for the exporting country. Therefore, the welfare of the exporters decreases because of both the deadweight loss of the subsidy and the terms-of-trade loss. This is in contrast to the effects of an import tariff in the large-country case, which generates a terms-of-trade gain for the importing country.

3. Export subsidies applied by a large country create a benefit for importing countries in the rest of the world, by lowering their import prices. Therefore, the removal of these subsidy programs has an adverse effect on those countries. In fact, many of the poorest countries are net food importers that will face higher prices as agricultural subsidies in the European Union and the United States are removed.

4. Production subsidies to domestic producers also have the effect of increasing domestic production. However, consumers are unaffected by these subsidies. As a result, the deadweight loss of a production subsidy is less than that for an equal export subsidy, and the terms-of-trade loss is also smaller.

5. An export tariff or quota applied by a large country creates a terms-of-trade gain for these countries, by raising the price of their export product. In addition, the export tariff or quota creates a deadweight loss. If the terms-of-trade gain exceeds the deadweight loss, then the exporting country gains overall.

6. It is common for countries to provide subsidies to their high-technology industries because governments believe that these subsidies can create a strategic advantage for their firms on international markets. Because these industries often have only a few global competitors, we use game theory (the study of strategic interactions) to determine how firms make their decisions under imperfect competition.

7. A Nash equilibrium is a situation in which each player is making the best response to the action of the other player. In a game with multiple Nash equilibria, the outcome can depend on an external factor, such as the ability of one player to make the first move.

8. Export subsidies can affect the Nash equilibrium of a game by altering the profits of the firms. If a subsidy increases the profits to a firm by more than the subsidy cost, then it is worthwhile for a government to undertake the subsidy. As we have seen, though, subsidies are not always worthwhile unless they can induce the competing firm to exit the market altogether, which may not occur.

KEY TERMS

import tariff, p. 318
export subsidy, p. 318
indirect subsidies, p. 320
domestic farm supports, p. 320
Common Agricultural Policy (CAP), p. 320
deadweight loss, p. 324
production loss, p. 324

consumption loss, p. 324
terms of trade, p. 325
production subsidy, p. 328
targeting principle, p. 330
export tariff, p. 334
export quota, p. 337
rare earths, p. 340
externality, p. 343

strategic advantage, p. 343
imperfect competition, p. 343
duopoly, p. 343
game theory, p. 343
payoff matrix, p. 344
Nash equilibrium, p. 344
first mover advantage, p. 345

PROBLEMS

1. **📊 Discovering Data** In Figure 10-8 we showed the value of Chinese exports of rare earth minerals, along with their average price and quantity sold, in three categories of exports. The source for the data in Figure 10-8 is the *China Customs Statistics*. In this problem, you will check the value of imports of rare earth minerals for the United States. To answer this question, you can access the Trade Stats Express database at the International Trade

Administration, U.S. Department of Commerce. (If you are using this textbook in another country, you should try to answer this question using the customs statistics for your own country.)

a. Start at the webpage *www.trade.gov*, and choose "Import Statistics" to find the "National Trade Data." Choose "Product Profiles of U.S. Merchandise Trade with a Selected Market." Select China as a "Trade Partner," and select "Imports." Change the "Item" to the Harmonized System (HS) codes. Choose the HS code 28, and display the U.S. imports from China within this HS code. You will find two 4-digit HS codes that include RARE_EARTH within their names. What are these codes? Graph the value of U.S. imports in each of these codes for 2008–18. What do you notice about the graphs during the key period 2010–12? What has happened to these imports in recent years?

b. Subtract the U.S. imports for these two HS codes from the *total* imports within HS 28 (as shown at the top of the display), and call this the *remaining imports*. Then graph the remaining imports over 2008–18. How does the shape of this graph compare with those in part (a)?

c. Now inspect the value of imports for all other 4-digit HS codes within this category of HS 28. Are there any other codes that show a marked increase during 2011, with a reduction after that? What are these other codes? By inspection of their names, could these other codes include rare earth minerals?

2. Describe the impact of each of the following goals from the Hong Kong WTO meeting on (i) domestic prices and welfare of the country taking the action and (ii) world prices and welfare for the partner countries.

a. Elimination of agriculture export subsidies

b. Reduction of agricultural import tariffs

WORK IT OUT   ≋ Achieve | interactive activity

3. Consider a large country with export subsidies in place for agriculture. Suppose the country changes its policy and decides to cut its subsidies in half.

a. Are there gains or losses to the large country, or is it ambiguous? What is the impact on domestic prices for agriculture and on the world price?

b. Suppose a small food-importing country abroad responds to the lowered subsidies by lowering its tariffs on agriculture by the same amount. Are there gains or losses to the small country, or is it ambiguous? Explain.

c. Suppose a large food-importing country abroad reciprocates by lowering its tariffs on agricultural goods by the same amount. Are there gains or losses to this large country, or is it ambiguous? Explain.

---

4. Suppose Home is a small exporter of wheat. At the world price of $100 per ton, Home growers export 20 tons. Now suppose the Home government decides to support its domestic producer with an export subsidy of $40 per ton. Use the following figure to answer these questions.

a. What is the quantity exported under free trade and with the export subsidy?

b. Calculate the effect of the export subsidy on consumer surplus, producer surplus, and government revenue.

c. Calculate the overall net effect of the export subsidy on Home welfare.

5. Refer to Problem 4. Rather than a small exporter of wheat, suppose that Home is a large country. Continue to assume that the free-trade world price is $100 per ton and that the Home government provides the domestic producer with an export subsidy in the amount of $40 per ton. Because of the export subsidy, the local price increases to $120, while the foreign market price declines to $80 per ton. Use the following figure to answer these questions.

a. Relative to the small-country case, why does the new domestic price increase by less than the amount of the subsidy?

b. Calculate the effect of the export subsidy on consumer surplus, producer surplus, and government revenue.

c. Calculate the overall net effect of the export subsidy on Home welfare. Is the large country better or worse off as compared to the small country with the export subsidy? Explain.

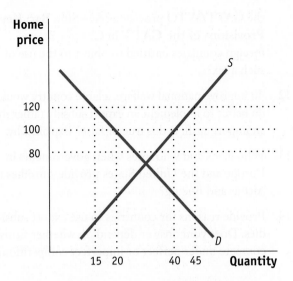

6. Refer to Problem 4. Suppose Home is a small exporter of wheat. At the world price of $100 per ton, Home growers export 20 tons. But rather than an export subsidy, suppose the Home government provides its domestic producer with a production subsidy of $40 per ton. Use the following figure to answer these questions.

   a. What is the quantity exported with the production subsidy?

   b. Calculate the effect of the production subsidy on consumer surplus, producer surplus, and government revenue.

   c. Calculate the overall net effect of the production subsidy on Home welfare. Is the cost of the production subsidy more or less than the cost of the export subsidy for the small country? Explain.

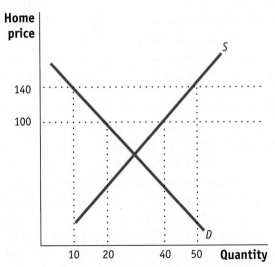

7. Explain why the WTO is more concerned with the use of direct export subsidies than production subsidies in achieving the same level of domestic support.

8. Boeing and Airbus are the world's only major producers of large wide-bodied aircrafts. But the increasing cost of fuel and the changing demand in the airline industry increases the need for smaller regional jets. Suppose that both firms must decide whether they will produce a smaller plane. We will assume that Boeing has a slight cost advantage over Airbus in both large and small planes, as shown in the payoff matrix that follows (in millions of U.S. dollars). Assume that each producer chooses to produce only large, only small, or no planes at all.

   a. What is the Nash equilibrium of this game?

   b. Are there multiple equilibria? If so, explain why. *Hint:* Guess at an equilibrium and then check whether either firm would want to change its action, given the action of the other firm. Remember that Boeing can change only its own action, which means moving up or down a column, and Airbus can change only its own action, which means moving back or forth on a row.

		Airbus		
		Large planes	Small planes	Not produce
Boeing	Large planes	−5 / 10	125 / 115	0 / 115
	Small planes	100 / 150	0 / 15	0 / 150
	Not produce	100 / 0	125 / 0	0 / 0

9. Refer to Problem 8. Now suppose the European government wants Airbus to be the sole producer in the lucrative small-aircraft market. Then answer the following:

   a. What is the minimum amount of subsidy that Airbus must receive when it produces small aircraft to ensure that outcome as the unique Nash equilibrium?

   b. Is it worthwhile for the European government to undertake this subsidy?

10. Here we examine the effects of domestic sales taxes on the market for exports, as an example of the "targeting principle." For example, in the domestic market, there are heavy taxes on the purchase

of cigarettes. Meanwhile, the United States has several very large cigarette companies that export their products abroad.

a. What is the effect of the sales tax on the quantity of cigarette exports from the United States? *Hint:* Your answer should parallel the case of production subsidies but for a consumption tax instead.

b. How does the change in exports, if any, due to the sales tax compare with the effect of an export subsidy on cigarettes?

11. Refer to Problem 10. Based on your answer there, would foreign countries have a reason to object to the use of a sales tax on cigarettes by the United States? Based on your knowledge of the GATT/WTO provisions (see **Side Bar: Key Provisions of the GATT** in Chapter 8), are foreign countries entitled to object to the use of such a tax?

12. To improve national welfare, a large country would do better to implement an export subsidy rather than an import tariff. Is this true or false? Explain why.

13. Who gains and who loses when governments in Europe and the United States provide subsidies to Airbus and Boeing?

14. Provide reasons for countries to use export subsidies. Does your answer depend on whether firms compete under perfect or imperfect competition?

11

International Agreements on Trade and the Environment

Our house is on fire. I am here to say, our house is on fire. . . . I don't want you to be hopeful. I want you to panic. I want you to feel the fear I feel every day. And then I want you to act.

> Greta Thunberg, World Economic Forum, Davos, Switzerland, January 25, 2019

Our house is still on fire. Your inaction is fueling the flames by the hour. We are still telling you to panic, and to act as if you loved your children above all else.

> Greta Thunberg, World Economic Forum, Davos, Switzerland, January 21, 2020

On day one I will immediately rejoin the Paris climate accord.

> Vice President Joe Biden, campaign video viewed April 15, 2020

Questions to Consider

1 Why is the World Trade Organization needed?

2 Do *all* countries gain when a regional free-trade area is formed?

3 Does international trade help or harm the environment?

Every year since 1927, *Time* magazine in America has chosen a "Person of the Year" to feature on its cover. In 2019, that honor went to Greta Thunberg, a 16-year-old from Sweden who is the youngest person to be chosen. Along with her photo was a description of her journey from skipping school every Friday and standing in front of the Swedish parliament with a sign proclaiming "Skolstrejk för Klimatet" (School Strike for Climate), to giving addresses at the World Economic Forum and at the United Nations (see the quotes at the beginning of the chapter). Because of her initial protest, Greta is credited with starting the mass strike of September 20, 2019, when 40 million people around the globe protested the lack of progress to arrest global climate change.

Despite strong displays of public opinion like the September 2019 strike, international agreements to limit global climate change are difficult to maintain. A high point came in 2015, when close to 200 countries adopted what is called the **Paris Agreement** (also known as the Paris Accord), a resolution to limit the increase in global temperature. This type of resolution requires the cooperation of many country governments over many years, and that has not always been obtained. In Europe, the

Greta Thunberg on a "School Strike for Climate" outside the Swedish parliament.

JONATHAN NACKSTRAND/AFP/Getty Images

357

Farmers in the Netherlands block a highway to protest environmental regulations.

high-income countries are united in adopting measures to limit emissions of carbon dioxide and other greenhouse gases. But there have been strong protests from some groups in those countries. Farmers in the Netherlands, for example, used their tractors to block major highways in October 2019 to protest regulations that would limit nitrous oxide emissions from agriculture. In some of the middle-income countries of Europe, such as the Czech Republic, Estonia, Hungary, and Poland, the governments have not been able to agree on or implement such environmental policies.[1]

In the United States, the extent of concern about climate change depends partly on political sympathies. A recent survey by the Pew Charitable Trust found that the percentage of the U.S. population that considers climate change a "major threat" rose from 40% in 2013 to 57% in 2019, but that rise is most pronounced among Democrats.[2] In 2019 debates, former Vice President Joe Biden and all the other candidates for the Democratic nomination for president expressed the importance of addressing climate change. In contrast, President Trump decided to pull the United States out of the Paris Agreement in 2017, which President Obama had previously agreed to in 2015. President Trump is not the first Republican president to decline to enter into a multilateral agreement on climate change, as we explain later in the chapter.

The same problems that arise when trying to reach international agreement on climate change also occur with international agreements about international trade. The World Trade Organization (WTO) was established in 2001, building on the General Agreement on Trade and Tariffs from 1947, to encourage countries to reduce tariffs and allow for freer international flows of goods and services. But recently, the WTO has also not been able to make progress toward that goal. The latest set of discussions at the WTO is called the Doha Round because it began in Doha, Qatar, in 2001. The Doha Round was intended to be the "development round," meaning that it was directed at the needs of developing countries. But many of the issues addressed in this attempted agreement were too hard to resolve. As we explained in the previous chapter, the trade ministers of all 164 WTO countries who met in Nairobi, Kenya, in 2015 failed to reaffirm the Doha Round, effectively ending those discussions.

The goal of this chapter is to examine why international agreements like those negotiated under the WTO and those negotiated for environmental reasons like the Paris Agreement are needed and why they do not have support from all countries. We begin by reviewing the reasons why international agreements dealing with tariffs are needed. As we discussed in Chapter 8, large countries can influence the price they pay for imports by applying an import tariff: the tariff increases the import price for consumers in the large country but lowers the price received by foreign exporting firms. The reduction in the price received by exporters is a **terms-of-trade gain** for the importing country. In this chapter, we show that when two or more countries apply tariffs against one another in an attempt to capture this terms-of-trade gain, they all end up losing. Because the terms-of-trade gain for one country is canceled by the use of a tariff by another country, both countries suffer as a result of the tariffs.

---

[1] See Stephen Pope, "Climate Change Divides Europe," *Forbes*, July 7, 2019.
[2] For Democratic-leaning participants in the survey, the share saying that climate change is a major threat rose from 58% in 2013 to 84% in 2019. But among Republican-leaning participants, the share rose from 22% in 2013 to 27% in 2019. See: www.pewresearch.org/fact-tank/2019/08/28/u-s-concern-about-climate-change-is-rising-but-mainly-among-democrats/.

International agreements to reduce tariffs and move toward free trade can avoid such losses. These international agreements take several forms. The WTO is a **multilateral trade agreement** involving many countries, with agreement to lower tariffs between all the members. Smaller **regional trade agreements** involve several countries, often located near one another. The U.S.-Mexico-Canada Agreement (USMCA) of 2020 (which replaced the North American Free Trade Agreement, or NAFTA) and the European Union (EU) are both examples of regional trade agreements. Africa formed a Continental Free Trade Area (AfCFTA) in 2018; the EU entered into an economic partnership agreement with Japan in 2019; and the United States has ambitions to enter into a trade agreement with the EU. All of these proposed free-trade areas are to some degree a response to the failure of the Doha Round of WTO negotiations, and they show that sometimes it is necessary to negotiate with a smaller group of countries. We discuss the effects of these regional trade agreements both on the countries included in the agreement and on the countries left out.

We also discuss international agreements on the environment. Rulings at the WTO have an indirect impact on the environment, but other international agreements, such as the Paris Agreement in 2015, have a more direct impact. The Paris Agreement is intended to reduce carbon dioxide emissions worldwide and therefore slow global warming. We argue that for "global" pollutants such as carbon dioxide, countries do not fully recognize or take into account the environmental costs of their economic activity. We need international agreements to ensure that countries recognize these environmental costs. These international agreements (such as the Green Deal in the EU) are reinforced by the commitments made by individual countries and regions.

1 Multilateral Trade Agreements

When countries seek to reduce trade barriers among themselves, they enter into a **trade agreement**—a pact to reduce or eliminate trade restrictions. Multilateral trade agreements occur among a large set of countries, such as the members of the WTO, that have negotiated many "rounds" of trade agreements. Under the **most favored nation principle** of the WTO, the lower tariffs agreed to in multilateral negotiations must be extended *equally* to all WTO members (see Article I in **Side Bar: Key Provisions of the GATT** in Chapter 8). Countries joining the WTO enjoy the low tariffs extended to all member countries but must also agree to lower their own tariffs.

The goal of this section is to demonstrate the logic of multilateral agreements. For simplicity, we assume that there are only two countries in the world that enter into an agreement; however, the theoretical results that we obtain also apply when there are many countries. The important feature of multilateral agreements is that no countries are *left out* of the agreement.

The Logic of Multilateral Trade Agreements

Before we begin our analysis of the effects of multilateral trade agreements, let's review the effects of tariffs imposed by large countries under perfect competition.

Tariffs for a Large Country In Figure 11-1, we show the effects of a large-country (Home) tariff, repeated from Chapter 8. We previously found that a tariff leads to a deadweight loss for Home, which is the sum of consumption and production losses, area $(b + d)$ in Figure 11-1. In addition, the tariff leads to a terms-of-trade gain for Home, area e, which equals the reduction in Foreign price due to the tariff, $(P^W - P^*)$, multiplied by the amount of Home imports under the tariff, $(D_2 - S_2)$. If Home applies an optimal tariff, then its terms-of-trade gain exceeds its deadweight loss,

FIGURE 11-1

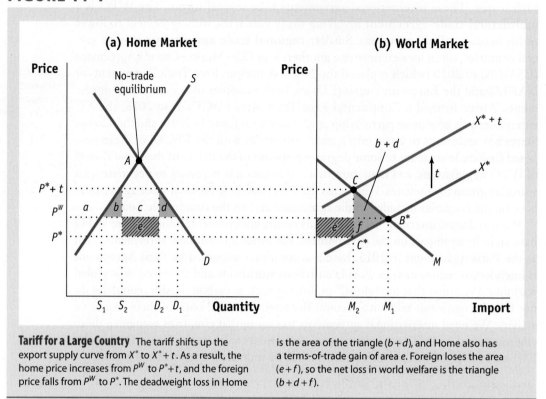

(a) Home Market

Price

No-trade
equilibrium

S

A

$P^* + t$

P^W a   b   c   d

P^* e

D

S_1 S_2 D_2 D_1 **Quantity**

(b) World Market

Price

$X^* + t$

b + d

X^*

C

t

B^*

e   f

C^*

M

M_2 M_1 **Import**

Tariff for a Large Country The tariff shifts up the export supply curve from X^* to $X^* + t$. As a result, the home price increases from P^W to $P^* + t$, and the foreign price falls from P^W to P^*. The deadweight loss in Home is the area of the triangle $(b + d)$, and Home also has a terms-of-trade gain of area e. Foreign loses the area $(e + f)$, so the net loss in world welfare is the triangle $(b + d + f)$.

so that $e > (b + d)$. Panel (b) shows that for the rest of the world (which in our two-country case is just Foreign), the tariff leads to a deadweight loss f from producing an inefficiently low level of exports relative to free trade, and a terms-of-trade loss e due to the reduction in its export prices. That is, the Home terms-of-trade gain comes at the expense of an equal terms-of-trade loss e for Foreign, plus a Foreign deadweight loss f.

Payoff Matrix This quick review of the welfare effects of a large-country tariff under perfect competition can be used to derive some new results. Although our earlier analysis indicated that it is optimal for large countries to impose small positive tariffs, that rationale ignored the strategic interaction among *multiple* large countries. If every country imposes even a small positive tariff, is it still optimal behavior for each country individually? We can use game theory to model the strategic choice of whether to apply a tariff, and use a payoff matrix to determine the Nash equilibrium outcome for each country's tariff level. A Nash equilibrium occurs when each player is taking the action that is the best response to the action of the other player (i.e., yielding the highest payoff).

In Figure 11-2, we show a payoff matrix between the Home and Foreign countries (both large), each of which has to decide whether to impose a tariff against the other country. Each quadrant of the matrix includes Home's payoff in the lower-left corner and Foreign's payoff in the upper-right corner. We will start with a situation of free trade and then measure the change in welfare for Home or Foreign by applying a tariff. For convenience, we will also assume that the two countries are exactly the same size, so their payoffs are symmetric.

Free Trade When both countries do not impose tariffs, we are in a free-trade situation, shown in the upper-left quadrant. For convenience, let us write the payoffs

FIGURE 11-2

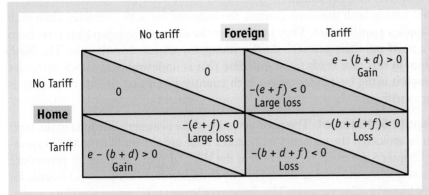

Payoffs in a Tariff Game This payoff matrix shows the welfare of the home and foreign countries as compared with free trade (upper-left quadrant in which neither country applies a tariff). Welfare depends on whether one or both countries apply a tariff. The structure of payoffs is similar to the "prisoner's dilemma" because both countries suffer a loss when they both apply tariffs, and yet this is the unique Nash equilibrium.

for the two countries under free trade as zero, which means that we will measure the payoffs in any other situation as *relative to* free trade.

Tariffs First, suppose that Home imposes a tariff but Foreign does not. Then the Home payoff as compared with free trade is $e - (b + d)$ (which is positive for an optimal tariff), and the Foreign payoff is $-(e + f)$, the terms-of-trade and deadweight losses described previously. These payoffs are shown in the lower-left quadrant of the matrix. Now suppose that Foreign imposes a tariff but Home does not. Because we have assumed that the Home and Foreign countries are the same size, they have the same potential payoffs from using a tariff. Under these circumstances, the Foreign payoff from its own tariff is $e - (b + d) > 0$, and the Home payoff is the loss $-(e + f) < 0$. These two payoffs are shown in the upper-right quadrant of the matrix.

Finally, suppose that *both* countries impose optimal tariffs and that the tariffs are the same size. Then the terms-of-trade gain that each country gets from its own tariff is canceled out by the terms-of-trade loss it suffers because of the other country's tariff. In that case, neither country gets any terms-of-trade gain but both countries still suffer a deadweight loss. That deadweight loss is $(b + d)$ from each country's own tariffs plus area f, the deadweight loss from the other country's tariff. The total deadweight loss for each country is $-(b + d + f) < 0$, as shown in the lower-right quadrant of the matrix.

Prisoner's Dilemma

The pattern of payoffs in Figure 11-2 has a special structure called the **prisoner's dilemma**. The "prisoner's dilemma" refers to a game in which two accomplices are caught for a crime that they committed, and each has to decide whether to confess. They are kept in separate cells, so they cannot communicate with each other. If one confesses and the other does not, then the person confessing will get a much lighter jail sentence and is better off than taking the chance of being found guilty in a trial. But if they both confess, then they both go to jail for the full sentence. This is like the pattern in Figure 11-2, in which each country acting on its own has an incentive to apply a tariff, but if they both apply tariffs, they will both be worse off.

Nash Equilibrium The only Nash equilibrium in Figure 11-2 is for both countries to apply a tariff (lower-right quadrant). Starting at that point, if either country eliminates its tariff, then it loses $(e + f)$ as compared with free trade, rather than $(b + d + f)$. Because we know that $e > (b + d)$ for an optimal tariff, it follows that each country acting on its own is worse off by moving to free trade (i.e., removing its tariff). That is, the loss $(e + f)$ is greater than the loss $(b + d + f)$. As a result, the Nash equilibrium is for both countries to apply a tariff.

But, like having both prisoners confess, the outcome for both countries when each country applies a tariff is bad. They both suffer the deadweight losses that arise from their own tariff and their partner's tariff, without any terms-of-trade gain. The Nash equilibrium in this case leads to an outcome that is undesirable for both countries even though it is the best outcome for each country given that the other country is imposing a tariff.

WTO Dispute Settlement The poor outcome of the prisoner's dilemma in the tariff game can be avoided if the countries enter into a trade agreement like the WTO agreement. In Chapter 8, for example, we saw how the WTO **dispute settlement procedure** came into play when the steel tariffs applied by President Bush became problematic for the United States' trading partners. The dispute settlement mechanism acts like a mediation procedure to settle differences between countries. The EU filed a case at the WTO objecting to these tariffs, and it was ruled that the tariffs did not meet the criteria for a safeguard tariff. As a result, the WTO ruled that European countries could *retaliate* by imposing tariffs of their own against U.S. exports. The threat of these tariffs led President Bush to eliminate the steel tariffs ahead of schedule, and the outcome moved both countries from potentially applying tariffs to both countries having zero tariffs.

Thus, the WTO mechanism eliminated the prisoner's dilemma by providing an incentive to remove tariffs; the outcome was in the preferred upper-left quadrant of the payoff matrix in Figure 11-2, rather than the original Nash equilibrium in the lower-right quadrant. The same logic comes into play when countries agree to join the WTO. They are required to reduce their own tariffs, but in return, they are also assured of receiving lower tariffs from other WTO members. That assurance enables countries to mutually reduce their tariffs and move closer to free trade.

Sometimes the trade issues being discussed between countries are too difficult to allow them to escape the prisoner's dilemma, however. In Figure 11-2 we assumed that the gains and losses associated with an optimal tariff are the same for both countries: they both gain $e - (b + d)$ when they apply their own optimal tariff, but lose $-(e + f)$ when the other country applies its optimal tariff. Thus, when both countries apply their tariffs, each ends up with a loss of $-(b + d + f)$ (lower-right quadrant). In contrast, when no tariffs are applied, both countries are better off (upper-left quadrant).

In the real world, countries may not agree that the payoffs for themselves and other countries are similar in size, or even what these payoffs actually are. In the Doha Round of negotiations under the WTO, for example, one issue that could not be resolved concerned open trade in service industries, such as banking and insurance. The developed countries would like to export those services, but developing countries fear that establishing foreign banks in their countries will result in the demise of their own local banks. Another issue was patent protection for medicinal drugs, which is desired by firms in the developed countries but increases the cost of these drugs in the developing world. In both these cases, the gains to the developed countries were too lopsided to allow a deal to be made with the developing countries.

The United States and the WTO The administration of President Trump was skeptical of the dispute settlement procedure of the WTO. In 2018 and 2019, the United States used several provisions of trade law to apply tariffs that had been used only infrequently in that way (see Chapter 8). Through the WTO, many countries objected to the United States' imposition of these tariffs. Even before the WTO ruled on these cases, foreign countries responded by applying tariffs against U.S. exports (see **Application: U.S. and Foreign Tariffs Under President Trump, 2018–19** in Chapter 8). Since December 10, 2019, the WTO has not been able to issue rulings in any dispute settlement cases because several judges who hear those cases have finished

HEADLINES

The World Trade Organization Is Faltering. The US Can't Fix It Alone.

This op-ed is written by the Senate Finance Committee chairman Chuck Grassley (Republican) and Ranking Member Ron Wyden (Democrat). They express concern with the dispute settlement procedure of the World Trade Organization and believe that this procedure can be improved through cooperation with other countries.

Today, the WTO is where nations negotiate the rules for international trade and resolve disputes that arise when a trading partner believes the rules aren't being followed. This trading system has been critical to helping reduce global poverty rates, which have shrunk even while the global population has expanded. We support the WTO's mission, but we are growing frustrated that the institution is not fully and effectively performing its intended functions. . . .

[W]hile the WTO serves as a forum to settle disputes among its members, we have serious concerns about the degree to which the system is working. The Appellate Body—the quasi-judicial review forum used to take a second look into dispute decisions—has long strayed off course from its original form and function. Our concerns about systemic and procedural problems with the Appellate Body are not new, nor are they partisan. US presidents on both sides of the aisle have taken issue with Appellate Body members addressing issues that were not raised by the parties involved in the dispute, taking longer than 90 days to decide appeals, and creating new rights and obligations for WTO members—all against the terms of the Dispute Settlement Understanding.

We see great value in having an institution like the Appellate Body that ensures dispute panels faithfully apply the rules to which we all agreed. However, the Appellate Body also needs to operate as the members agreed. . . . Undoubtedly, there is a lot of work to do to fix these problems. The United States has long been a leader on these issues, but we can't do it alone. The United States, Japan and the European Union have been discussing WTO reforms. Partnerships like this are essential to showing member states who consistently break the rules that their actions won't be tolerated. We encourage and welcome others to join us in these efforts.

Source: Excerpted from Chuck Grassley and Ron Wyden, "The World Trade Organization Is Faltering. The US Can't Fix It Alone," October 10, 2019, www.grassley.senate.gov/news/commentary/grassley-wyden-op-ed-world-trade-organization-faltering-us-can-t-fix-it-alone.

their terms and the United States blocked the appointment of any new judges. So the ability of the WTO to resolve differences between countries, and therefore avoid the prisoner's dilemma outcome, has been greatly diminished.

In **Headlines: The World Trade Organization Is Faltering. The US Can't Fix It Alone**, we explain why some politicians in the United States are dissatisfied with the actions of the WTO. The article is written by the Senate Finance Committee chairman Chuck Grassley (a Republican) and Ranking Member Ron Wyden (a Democrat), who point out that the dispute settlement procedure takes too long[3] and that the WTO sometimes creates "new rights and obligations for WTO members" that are not part of the WTO agreement. They explain that this criticism of the WTO dispute settlement procedure has come from a number of U.S. presidents and that it will require the cooperation of other countries in the WTO to be resolved.

The End of the Trade War?

We have shown that a tariff game between two countries has the structure of a prisoner's dilemma: the Nash equilibrium, where both countries apply their optimal tariffs, leads to a poor outcome for both. The 2018–19 trade war between the United States and China was brought to a (temporary) resolution by a "phase one"

---

[3] The WTO rulings on the countercharges of Boeing and Airbus against each other, discussed in Chapter 9, took more than 15 years to be finalized.

agreement on January 15, 2020. That agreement still left in place the higher tariffs between the United States and China on many goods, however. The United States imposed high tariffs on other foreign countries, too. This situation illustrates an undesirable prisoner's dilemma outcome for all countries.

Why did the United States and its trading partners find themselves in this situation? There are two reasons. First, the United States was skeptical of the WTO's ability to reach fair and timely decisions when there are disagreements between it and other countries. So rather than letting the WTO arrange a mutual reduction in tariffs (as occurred in the steel industry under President Bush), the administration of President Trump decided to pursue agreements with foreign countries (particularly with China) on its own.

The second reason that the United States maintained high tariffs against China and other countries is that it was pursuing *different objectives* than lowering tariffs. These objectives can be seen in the "phase one" agreement with China. Under this agreement, the existing tariffs between the countries were not raised or lowered, but China agreed to take other actions. For example, China agreed to enforce intellectual property laws more vigorously, which would prevent Chinese firms from copying American and other foreign products and technology. In addition, China agreed to allow foreign firms to establish plants there without needing local partners. This means that foreign firms would not have to share their technology with local partners. Both of these issues were of concern to American businesses and to the administration of President Trump at the start of the trade war with China. Resolving these issues can be viewed as a success of the phase one agreement. Still, China was taking steps to reform its intellectual property and foreign investment laws before the trade war, so the value of these extra commitments is not as great as it might seem.

Managed Trade The most important provision in the phase one agreement was China's commitment to purchase $200 billion more exports from the United States by the end of 2021 than it had purchased in 2017, before the trade war began. Achieving this increase will require that China nearly double its imports from the United States by the end of 2021.[4] Specifying the amount that a country must purchase from another is called **managed trade**.

Economists do not believe that consumers or countries can be persuaded to purchase more than they really want from a given country, something that would need to happen for managed trade to work. China could purchase the extra $200 billion from the United States only if those exports had started growing by about 20% per year from 2017. Due to the trade war, however, Chinese purchases of U.S. goods actually *fell* by $20 billion between 2017 and 2019, and the coronavirus pandemic in 2020 caused imports from the United States to fall even more. It is unrealistic to expect that China will be able to reach the goal of purchasing $200 billion more from the United States by the end of 2021. Attempting to achieve this goal would mean that China must buy less from other countries, a shift that would lead to strong objections at the WTO because it would not reflect normal trade patterns.

At the time of writing, it is not known whether China's target of purchasing $200 billion more from the United States by the end of 2021 will still be in effect, and if it is not reached, what the penalty for China would be. President Trump did not

---

[4] China bought about $185 billion of exports from the United States in 2017, but only $134 billion of those purchases were in sectors that are covered by the phase one agreement. China agreed to increase its purchases of U.S. exports in those specific sectors by $76.7 billion in 2020 and by $123.3 billion in 2021 as compared to 2017. This increase of $123.3 billion in 2021 would bring total China purchases in those sectors to about $257 billion, nearly twice as much as in 2017. See Chad Bown, "Unappreciated Hazards of the US-China Phase One Deal," Peterson Institute for International Economics, January 21, 2020, from which the information in this paragraph and the next is drawn.

lower the tariffs on China under the phase one agreement in an attempt to ensure compliance with the terms of the agreement, but with the coronavirus pandemic it seems possible that the target could be pushed into the future. This uncertainty over future tariffs creates uncertainty for firms not only in China, but also in the United States. In turn, this uncertainty limits investment, which can reduce GDP growth in both countries. The managed trade commitment of phase one is not the approach to increasing trade favored by most economists. They believe the best way to increase trade between two countries is to mutually reduce tariffs, without tying that reduction to a specific increase in the amount of trade.

2 Regional Trade Agreements

Now that we have discussed multilateral agreements, we turn to regional trade agreements that occur between smaller groups of countries. When entering into a regional trade agreement, countries agree to eliminate tariffs among themselves but do not reduce tariffs against the countries left out of the agreement. For example, the United States has many regional trade agreements, including those with Israel, Jordan, Chile, a number of countries in Central and South America, and South Korea. In South America, the countries of Argentina, Brazil, Paraguay, Uruguay, and Venezuela belong to a free-trade area called Mercosur. In fact, there are more than 200 free-trade agreements worldwide, which some economists feel threaten the WTO as the major forum for multilateral trade liberalization.

One of the newest and largest regional trade agreements in the world is the **Comprehensive and Progressive Agreement for Trans-Pacific Partnership (CP-TPP)**. This agreement was accepted in January 2018 and establishes a free-trade area among 11 countries that border the Pacific Ocean: Australia, Brunei, Canada, Chile, Japan, Malaysia, Mexico, New Zealand, Peru, Singapore, and Vietnam. This free-trade area originally included the United States, and it was an important part of President Obama's broader foreign policy agenda, which focused on Asia. The **Trans-Pacific Partnership** (TPP), as it was originally called, was signed by those 11 countries and the United States in February 2016, and it allowed two years for the trade agreement to be ratified by all the countries. However, the TPP was opposed by many politicians in the United States. In fact, all four Democratic candidates for the presidential nomination in 2015–16 opposed the TPP because, among other objections, they felt it did not sufficiently address labor and environmental issues. The TPP was never ratified in the United States, and in January 2017 President Trump withdrew from the agreement.

Under regional trade agreements, several countries eliminate tariffs among themselves but maintain tariffs against countries outside the region. Such regional trade agreements are permitted under Article XXIV of the GATT, which states that countries can enter into such agreements provided they do not jointly increase their tariffs against outside countries. (See **Side Bar: Key Provisions of the GATT** in Chapter 8.) Although they are authorized by the GATT, regional trade agreements contradict the most favored nation principle, which states that every country belonging to the GATT/WTO should be treated equally. The countries included in a regional trade agreement are treated better (because they face zero tariffs) than the countries excluded. For this reason, regional trade agreements are sometimes called **preferential trade agreements**, to emphasize that the member countries are favored over other countries. Despite this violation of the most favored nation principle, regional trade agreements are permitted because it is thought that the removal of trade barriers among expanding groups of countries is one way to achieve freer trade worldwide.

Characteristics of Regional Trade Agreements

Regional trade agreements can be classified into two basic types: free-trade areas and customs unions.

Free-Trade Area A **free-trade area** is a group of countries that agree to eliminate tariffs (and other barriers to trade) among themselves while keeping whatever tariffs they formerly had with the rest of the world. In 1989 Canada entered into a free-trade agreement with the United States known as the Canada–U.S. Free Trade Agreement. Under this agreement, tariffs between the two countries were eliminated over the next decade. In 1994, Canada and the United States entered into an agreement with Mexico called the North American Free Trade Agreement (NAFTA). NAFTA created free trade among all three countries. Each of these countries still has its own tariffs with all other countries of the world. As we learned in Chapter 6, in 2020 NAFTA was replaced by the U.S.–Mexico–Canada Agreement (USMCA).

Customs Union A **customs union** is similar to a free-trade area, except that in addition to eliminating tariffs among countries in the union, the countries within a customs union also agree to a *common* schedule of tariffs with each country outside the union. Examples of customs unions include the countries in the EU and the signatory countries of Mercosur in South America. All countries in the EU have identical tariffs with respect to each outside country; the same holds for the countries in Mercosur. When a new country enters a customs union, it must adjust the tariffs that it levies against countries outside the customs union to match the tariffs levied by all countries already within the customs union. Likewise, when a country leaves a customs union, its government is free to adjust its tariff levels with its trading partners. In 2020, for example, the United Kingdom (U.K.) left the EU in what is called **Brexit**. The U.K. intends to keep a free-trade area (meaning zero tariffs) with the countries of Europe, but it will have to negotiate tariffs with all other foreign countries.

Rules of Origin The fact that the countries in a free-trade area do not have common tariffs for outside countries, as do countries within a customs union, leads to an obvious problem with free-trade areas: if Botswana, for example, wants to sell a good to Canada, what would prevent it from first exporting the good to the United States or Mexico, whichever has the lowest tariff, and then shipping it to Canada? The answer is that free-trade areas have complex **rules of origin** that specify what type of goods can be shipped duty-free within the free-trade area.

A good entering Mexico from Botswana, for example, is not granted duty-free access to the United States or Canada unless that good is first incorporated into another product in Mexico, giving the new product enough "North American content" to qualify for duty-free access. So Botswana or any other outside country cannot just choose the lowest-tariff country through which to enter North America. Rather, products can be shipped duty-free between countries only if most of their production occurred within North America. To determine whether this criterion has been satisfied, the rules of origin must specify—for each and every product—how much of its production (as determined by value-added or the use of some key inputs) took place in North America. When NAFTA was replaced by the USMCA, the rules of origin for automobiles to be shipped duty-free between Mexico, the United States, and Canada were tightened. Under the USMCA, the total North American content of an automobile must be 75% for that car to be shipped tariff-free between the United States, Mexico, and Canada. That percentage was increased from 62.5% under NAFTA.

Notice that these rules are not needed in a customs union because in that case the tariffs on outside members are the same for all countries in the union: there is no incentive to import a good into the lowest-tariff country. So why don't countries just create a customs union, making the rules of origin irrelevant? The answer is that modifying the tariffs applied against an outside country is a politically sensitive issue. The United States, for example, might want a higher tariff on textiles than Canada or Mexico, and Mexico might want a higher tariff on corn. The USMCA allows each of these three countries to have its own tariffs for each commodity on outside countries. So despite the complexity of rules of origin, they allow countries to enter into a free-trade agreement without modifying their tariffs on outside countries.

APPLICATION

Brexit and Rules of Origin

In 2016, the citizens of the United Kingdom voted in favor of leaving the European Union (EU), in what is called Brexit. It was very difficult for the government of the United Kingdom to prepare a plan for how that separation would take place. Prime Minister Theresa May tried to negotiate the terms of withdrawal, but she was unsuccessful and lost her position as prime minister in July 2019. She was replaced by Prime Minister Boris Johnson, who vowed to leave the EU by October 31, 2019. The United Kingdom was not able to leave the EU under this strict deadline, which was extended to January 31, 2020. After that date, the United Kingdom will have eleven months, to December 31, 2020, to work out the details of withdrawal with the European Commission, which governs the EU.

Why has it been so difficult to design a plan for the United Kingdom to leave the EU? To answer this, it is essential to understand the geography of the British Isles. The United Kingdom consists of Great Britain (England, Scotland, and Wales) and also Northern Ireland. When the United Kingdom leaves the EU, these countries will still be in a free-trade area. Not included as part of the United Kingdom is the Republic of Ireland, which is an independent country located on the same island as Northern Ireland (see map). The citizens of Northern Ireland and the Republic of Ireland have endured decades of bitter fighting. They are now at peace under the Belfast Agreement (also known as the Good Friday Agreement) of April 10, 1998. With this peace, there is great political sensitivity to avoid any hard border between Northern Ireland and the Republic of Ireland, even though they are different countries.

Before the United Kingdom left the EU, Northern Ireland (as part of the United Kingdom) and the Republic of Ireland were both in the EU. Because the EU is a customs union, all countries in the EU have the same tariffs on outside countries, as well as zero tariffs for shipments within the EU. That meant that Northern Ireland and the Republic of Ireland had the same import tariffs. When the United Kingdom leaves the EU, however, Northern Ireland will also leave the EU. Furthermore, the United Kingdom will be free to establish new tariffs with other countries, which means that Northern Ireland and the Republic of Ireland will impose different import tariffs on goods from other countries.

The United Kingdom would still like to be in a free-trade area with the EU, meaning zero tariffs with all EU countries, including the Republic of Ireland. But if Northern Ireland and the Republic of Ireland have different import tariffs, what is to prevent a good from, say, Canada that is bound for Scotland from being imported into *either* Northern Ireland or the Republic of Ireland, depending on which has the lowest tariff, and then shipped over to Scotland? The answer is rules of origin: a good that is imported from Canada into the Republic of Ireland *cannot* be shipped duty-free to Northern Ireland or to Scotland, because it would not have been made in the free-trade area consisting of the United Kingdom and the EU.

To enforce these rules of origin means that there must also be borders to ensure that only goods made *within* the free-trade area consisting of the United Kingdom and the EU can pass across those borders duty-free. This leads to the most difficult

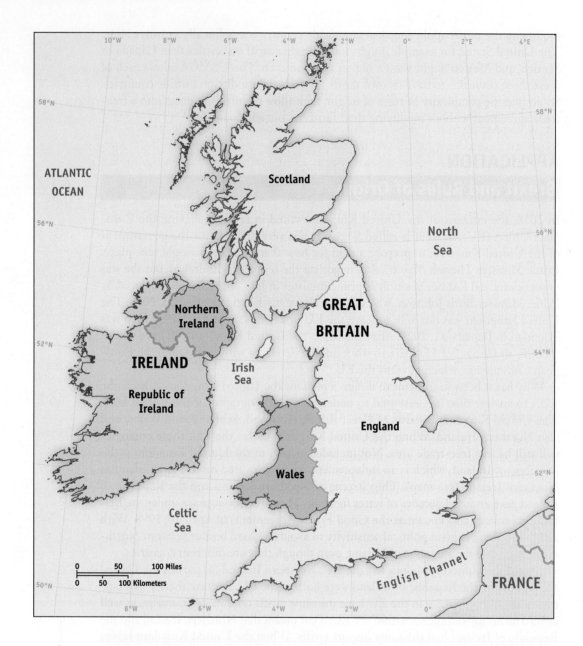

problem: will there be a customs border between Northern Ireland (which is in the United Kingdom) and the Republic of Ireland (which is in the EU), to check that only locally made products from the free-trade area are crossing duty-free? As we have already explained, all parties want to avoid a hard border between Northern Ireland and the Republic of Ireland. How then will it be possible to check that the rules of origin are satisfied?

The answer proposed by Prime Minister Boris Johnson is to establish a *customs border* in the Irish Sea, the body of water separating the island of Ireland from Great Britain. Goods shipped between the island of Ireland and Great Britain will have to satisfy rules of origin in order to be accepted duty-free. This customs border will create an inconvenience for citizens going from Northern Ireland to Great Britain, which are after all in the same country! But that inconvenience is judged to be better than establishing a customs border between Northern Ireland and the Republic of Ireland. This difficult issue of where to put the customs border separating the Republic of Ireland from the United Kingdom is one reason why Brexit has been so hard and taken so long to achieve.

Trade Creation and Trade Diversion

Now that we have covered the various provisions found in regional trade agreements, we turn to their main economic effects. When a regional trade agreement is formed and trade increases between member countries, the increase in trade can be of two types. The first type of trade increase, **trade creation**, occurs when a member country imports a product from another member country that formerly it produced for itself. In this case, there is a gain in consumer surplus for the importing country (by importing greater amounts of goods at lower prices) and a gain in producer surplus for the exporting country (from increased sales). These gains from trade are analogous to those that occur from the opening of trade in the Ricardian or Heckscher–Ohlin models. No other country inside or outside the trade agreement is affected because the product was not traded before. Therefore, trade creation brings welfare gains for both countries involved.

The second reason for trade to increase within a regional agreement is **trade diversion**, which occurs when a member country imports a product from another member country that it formerly imported *from a country outside of the new trade region*. In this case, the diversion of trade away from the country outside of the region will bring a loss in producer surplus in that country, because of its reduced export sales. So the country outside the union with reduced exports loses. What is more surprising is that trade diversion can even bring losses to the countries inside the free-trade area. A numerical example will illustrate how this can occur.

Numerical Example of Trade Creation and Diversion

To illustrate the potential for trade diversion, we use an example from USMCA, in which the United States might import auto parts from Mexico that it formerly imported from Asia.[5] Let us keep track of the gains and losses for the countries involved. Asia will lose export sales to North America, so it suffers a loss in producer surplus in its exporting industry. Mexico gains producer surplus by selling the auto parts. The problem with this outcome is that Mexico is not the most efficient (lowest-cost) producer of auto parts: we know that Asia is more efficient because that is where the United States initially purchased its auto parts. Because the United States is importing from a less efficient producer, there is some potential loss for the United States due to trade diversion. We can determine whether this is indeed the case by numerically analyzing the cases of trade creation and trade diversion.

Suppose that the costs to the United States of importing an auto part from Mexico or from Asia are as shown in Table 11-1. The rightmost columns show the total costs of the part under free trade (zero tariff), a 10% tariff, and a 20% tariff. Under free trade, the auto part can be produced in Mexico for $20 or in Asia for $19. Thus, Asia is the most efficient producer. If the United States purchased the part from an American supplier, it would cost $22, as shown in the last row of the table. With a tariff of 10%, the costs of importing from Mexico or Asia are increased to $22 and $20.90, respectively. Similarly, a 20% tariff would increase the cost of importing to $24 and $22.80, respectively. Under USMCA, however, the cost of importing from Mexico is $20 regardless of the tariff.

With the data shown in Table 11-1, we can examine the effect of USMCA on each country's welfare. First, suppose that the tariff applied by the United States is 20%, as shown in the last column. Before USMCA, it would have cost $24 to import the auto

---

[5] The largest exporters of auto parts to the United States are Canada, China, Mexico, and Japan. Until 2011, Japan exported a greater value of auto parts to the United States than did China, but since that time China has overtaken Japan as the largest Asian exporter to the United States.

TABLE 11-1

Cost of Importing an Automobile Part This table shows the cost to the United States of purchasing an automobile part from various source countries, with and without tariffs. If there is a 20% tariff on all countries, then it would be cheapest for the United States to buy the auto part from itself (for $22). But when the tariff is eliminated on Mexico after USMCA, then the United States would instead buy from that country (for $20), which illustrates the idea of trade creation. If instead we start with a 10% tariff on all countries, then it would be cheapest for the United States to buy from Asia (for $20.90). When the tariff on Mexico is eliminated under USMCA, then the United States would instead buy there (for $20), illustrating the idea of trade diversion.

	U.S. Tariff		
	0%	10%	20%
From Mexico, before USMCA	$20	$22	$24
From Asia, before USMCA	$19	$20.90	$22.80
From Mexico, after USMCA	$20	$20	$20
From Asia, after USMCA	$19	$20.90	$22.80
From the United States	$22	$22	$22

part from Mexico, $22.80 to import it from Asia, and $22 to produce it locally in the United States. Before USMCA, then, producing the part in the United States for $22 is the cheapest option. With the tariff of 20%, therefore, there are no imports of this auto part into the United States.

Trade Creation When Mexico joins USMCA, it pays no tariff to the United States, whereas Asia continues to have a 20% tariff applied against it. After USMCA, the United States will import the part from Mexico for $20 because the price is less than the U.S. cost of $22. Therefore, all the auto parts will be imported from Mexico. This is an example of trade creation. The United States clearly gains from the lower cost of the auto part; Mexico gains from being able to export to the United States; and Asia neither gains nor loses, because it never sold the auto part to the United States to begin with.

Trade Diversion Now suppose instead that the U.S. tariff on auto parts is 10% (the middle column of Table 11-1). Before USMCA, the United States can import the auto part from Mexico for $22 or from Asia for $20.90. It still costs $22 to produce the part at home. In this case, the least-cost option is for the United States to import the auto part from Asia. When Mexico joins USMCA, however, this outcome changes. It will cost $20 to import the auto part from Mexico duty-free, $20.90 to import it from Asia subject to the 10% tariff, and $22 to produce it at home. The least-cost option is to import the auto part from Mexico. Because of the establishment of USMCA, the United States *switches* the source of its imports from Asia to Mexico, an example of trade diversion.

Producer surplus in Asia falls because it loses its export sales to the United States, whereas producer surplus in Mexico rises. What about the United States? Before USMCA, it imported from Asia at a price of $20.90, of which 10% (or $1.90 per unit) consisted of the tariff. The net-of-tariff price that Asia received for the auto parts was $19. After USMCA the United States instead imports from Mexico, at the price of $20, but it does not collect any tariff revenue at all. So the United States gains 90¢ on each unit from paying a lower price, but it also loses $1.90 in tariff revenue from not purchasing from Asia. From this example, it seems that importing the auto part from Mexico is not a very good idea for the United States because it no longer collects tariff revenue. To determine the overall impact on U.S. welfare, we can analyze the same example in a graph.

Trade Diversion in a Graph

In Figure 11-3, we show the free-trade price of the auto part from Asia as P_{Asia}, and the free-trade export supply curve from Asia as the horizontal line labeled S_{Asia}. By treating this price as fixed, we are supposing that the United States is a small country relative to the potential supply from Asia. Inclusive of the tariff, the cost of imported parts from Asia becomes $P_{Asia} + t$, and the supply curve is $S_{Asia} + t$. The free-trade supply from Mexico is shown as the upward-sloping curve labeled S_{Mex}; inclusive of the tariff, the supply curve is $S_{Mex} + t$.

Before USMCA, both Mexico and Asia face the same tariff of t. So the equilibrium imports occur at point A, where the quantity imported is Q_1 and the tariff-inclusive price to the United States is $P_{Asia} + t$. Of the total imports Q_1, the amount Q_2 comes from Mexico at point B, since under perfect competition these imports have the same tariff-inclusive price as those from Asia. Thus, tariff revenue is collected on imports from both Mexico and Asia, so the total tariff revenue is the area $(a + b + c + d)$ in Figure 11-3.

After Mexico joins USMCA, it is able to sell to the United States duty-free. In that case, the relevant supply curve is S_{Mex}, and imports from Mexico expand to Q_3 at point C. Notice that the price charged by Mexico at point C still equals the tariff-inclusive price from Asia, which is $P_{Asia} + t$, even though Mexican imports do not have any tariff. Mexico charges that price because its marginal costs have risen along its supply curve, so even though the tariff has been removed, the price of its imports to the United States has not changed.

Because the imports from Mexico enter the United States duty-free, the United States loses tariff revenue of $t \cdot Q_3$, which is the area $(a + b + c)$ in Figure 11-3. The

FIGURE 11-3

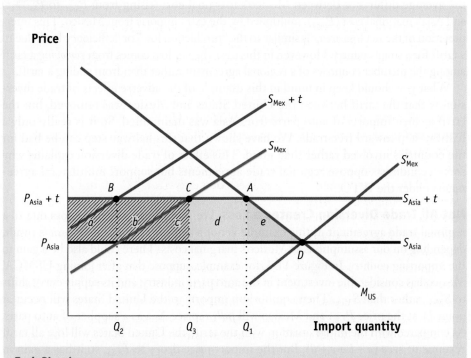

Trade Diversion With Mexico and Asia facing the same tariff of t for sales into the United States, the equilibrium is at A with the quantity Q_2 exported by Mexico and the remainder exported by Asia at a price of $P_{Asia} + t$. U.S. tariff revenue is the area $(a + b + c + d)$. Eliminating the tariff with Mexico under USMCA leads to an expansion of Mexican exports to Q_3. The United States loses the tariff revenue $(a + b + c)$, which is the U.S. loss as a result of trade diversion from Asia to Mexico.

price of imports into the United States has not changed, so the United States is worse off due to USMCA by the loss in its tariff revenue. Mexico is better off because of the increase in its producer surplus from charging the price $P_{Asia} + t$, without paying any tariff on its expanded amount of exports. Mexico's producer surplus rises by $(a + b)$, the area to the left of the supply curve S_{Mex}. If we add together the changes in U.S. and Mexican welfare, the combined change in their welfare is

Loss in U.S. tariff revenue:	$-(a + b + c)$
Gain in Mexico's producer surplus:	$+(a + b)$
Combined effect due to USMCA:	$-c$

So we see that the combined welfare of the United States and Mexico actually *falls* as a result of USMCA. This is a very counterintuitive result because we normally expect that countries will be better off when they move toward free trade. Instead, in this example, we see that one of the countries within the regional agreement is worse off (the United States), and so much so that its fall in welfare exceeds the gains for Mexico, so that their combined welfare falls!

Interpretation of the Loss This is one of the few instances in this textbook in which a country's movement toward free trade makes that country worse off. What is the reason for this result? Asia is the most efficient producer of auto parts in this example for units $Q_3 - Q_2$: its marginal costs equal P_{Asia} (not including the tariff). By diverting production to Mexico, the marginal costs of Mexico's extra exports to the United States rise from P_{Asia} (which is the marginal cost at quantity Q_2, not including the tariff) to $P_{Asia} + t$ (which is Mexico's marginal cost at quantity Q_3). Therefore, the United States necessarily loses from trade diversion, and by more than Mexico's gain.

The combined loss to the United States and Mexico of area c can be interpreted as the average difference between Mexico's marginal cost (rising from P_{Asia} to $P_{Asia} + t$) and Asia's marginal cost (P_{Asia}), multiplied by the extra imports from Mexico. This interpretation of the net loss area c is similar to the "production loss" or "efficiency loss" due to a tariff for a small country. However, in this case, the net loss comes from *removing* a tariff among the member countries of a regional agreement rather than from adding a tariff.

What you should keep in mind in this example of the adverse effects of trade diversion is that the tariff between the United States and Mexico was removed, but the tariff against imports of auto parts from Asia was maintained. So it is really only a halfway step toward free trade. We have shown that this halfway step can be bad for the countries involved rather than good. This effect of trade diversion explains why some economists oppose regional trade agreements but support multilateral agreements under the WTO.

Not All Trade Diversion Creates a Loss We should stress that the loss due to a regional trade agreement in this example is not a *necessary* result, but a *possible* result, depending on our assumptions of Mexico's marginal costs. There could also be a gain to the importing country. In Figure 11-3, for example, suppose that after joining USMCA, Mexico has considerable investment in the auto parts industry, and its supply curve shifts to S'_{Mex} rather than S_{Mex}. Then equilibrium imports to the United States will occur at point D, at the price P_{Asia}, and Mexico will *fully* replace Asia as a supplier of auto parts. As compared with the initial situation with the tariff, the United States will lose all tariff revenue of area $(a + b + c + d)$. But the import price drops to P_{Asia}, so it has a gain in consumer surplus of area $(a + b + c + d + e)$. Therefore, the net change in U.S. welfare is

Gain in consumer surplus:	$+(a + b + c + d + e)$
Loss in tariff revenue:	$-(a + b + c + d)$
Net effect on U.S. welfare:	$+e$

The United States experiences a net gain in consumer surplus in this case, and Mexico's producer surplus rises because it is exporting more.

This case combines elements of trade diversion (Mexico has replaced Asia) and trade creation (Mexico is exporting more to the United States than total U.S. imports before USMCA). Thus, we conclude that USMCA and other regional trade agreements have the potential to create gains among their members, *but only if the amount of trade creation exceeds the amount of trade diversion*. In the following application we look at what happened to Canada and the United States when free trade opened between them, to see whether the extent of trade creation for Canada exceeded the amount of trade diversion.

APPLICATION

Trade Creation and Diversion for Canada

In 1989, Canada formed a free-trade agreement with the United States and, five years later, entered into the North American Free Trade Agreement with the United States and Mexico. Research by Professor Daniel Trefler at the University of Toronto has analyzed the effect of these free-trade agreements on Canadian manufacturing industries. As summarized in Chapter 6, initially there was unemployment in Canada, but that was a short-term result. A decade after the free-trade agreement with the United States, employment in Canadian manufacturing had recovered and that sector also enjoyed a boom in productivity.

In his research, Trefler also estimated the amount of trade creation versus trade diversion for Canada in its trade with the United States. He found that the reduction in Canadian tariffs on U.S. goods increased imports of those goods by 54%. This increase was trade creation. However, since Canada was now buying more tariff-free goods from the United States, those tariff reductions reduced Canadian imports from the rest of the world by 40% (trade diversion). To compare these amounts, keep in mind that imports from the United States make up 80% of all Canadian imports, whereas imports from the rest of the world make up the remaining 20%. So the 54% increase in imports from the United States should be multiplied (or weighted) by its 80% share in overall Canadian imports to get the amount of trade creation. Likewise, the 40% reduction in imports from the rest of the world should be multiplied by its 20% share in Canadian imports to get trade diversion. Taking the difference between the trade created and diverted, we obtain

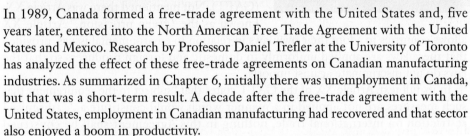

$$\underbrace{80\%}_{\substack{\text{Share of} \\ \text{U.S. imports}}} \times \underbrace{54\%}_{\substack{\text{Increase in} \\ \text{U.S. imports}}} - \underbrace{20\%}_{\substack{\text{Share of} \\ \text{other imports}}} \times \underbrace{40\%}_{\substack{\text{Decrease in} \\ \text{other imports}}} \approx 35\% > 0$$

Because this calculation gives a positive number, Trefler concludes that trade creation exceeded trade diversion when Canada and the United States entered into the free-trade agreement. Therefore, Canada definitely gained from the free-trade agreement with the United States.

3 International Agreements on the Environment

Meetings of the WTO have been frequently marked by protesters, like those shown in the photo from the 1999 Seattle meetings, who were concerned about how WTO rulings affect the environment. The WTO does not directly address environmental issues; other international agreements, called **multilateral environmental agreements**, deal specifically with the environment. There are some 200 multilateral environmental agreements, including the Convention on International Trade in Endangered Species and the Montreal Protocol on Substances that Deplete the

Protestors dressed as turtles at the 1999 meeting of the World Trade Organization in Seattle.

Ozone Layer (which has eliminated the use of chlorofluorocarbons that deplete the ozone layer). But the WTO still indirectly affects the environment, as the protesters in Seattle were well aware, so we'll begin by clarifying the role of the GATT and WTO in environmental issues.

Environmental Issues in the GATT and WTO

In an earlier chapter (see **Side Bar: Key Provisions of the GATT** in Chapter 8), we summarized some of the founding articles of the General Agreement on Tariffs and Trade (GATT). Not mentioned there was Article XX, known as the "green provision." Article XX allows countries to adopt their own laws in relation to environmental issues, provided that these laws are applied uniformly to domestic and foreign producers so that the laws do not discriminate against imports.

In its full text, Article XX of the GATT states that "subject to the requirement that such measures are not applied in a manner which would constitute a . . . disguised restriction on international trade, nothing in this Agreement shall be construed to prevent the adoption or enforcement by any contracting party of measures: . . . (b) necessary to protect human, animal or plant life or health; . . . (g) relating to the conservation of exhaustible natural resources if such measures are made effective in conjunction with restrictions on domestic production or consumption."

If the provisions of the GATT and WTO permit countries to apply their own environmental regulations, why were people dressed as turtles and dolphins protesting WTO rulings at the 1999 Seattle meetings? To understand the concerns of these protesters, we need to dig into the details of some specific GATT/WTO cases, summarized in Table 11-2.[6]

Tuna–Dolphin Case In 1991, before the WTO was formed, Mexico brought a GATT case against the United States. The reason for the case was that the United States had banned imports of tuna from Mexico because Mexican fishermen did not catch tuna using nets that safeguarded against the accidental capture of dolphins. The U.S. Marine Mammal Protection Act requires that U.S. tuna fishermen use nets that are safe for dolphins, and by Article XX(g) of the GATT, the United States reasoned that the same requirement could be extended to Mexican fishermen. But the U.S. ban on imports of tuna from Mexico ran afoul of the GATT.

GATT concluded that the United States could not ban the import of tuna because the United States applied the import restriction to the *production process method* and not the product itself. The idea that the production process could not be a basis for a trade restriction was a principle of GATT that was upheld in this case. In addition, the GATT panel ruled that "GATT rules did not allow one country to take trade action for the purpose of attempting to enforce its own domestic laws in another country—even to protect animal health or exhaustible natural resources." Both of these conclusions were a blow to environmentalists interested in protecting the dolphins, and this is the reason that some of the Seattle protesters were dressed as dolphins.

---

[6] These cases are drawn from Jeffrey A. Frankel, November 2003, "The Environment and Globalization," NBER Working Paper No. 10090. Environmental cases are summarized on the WTO webpage at www.wto.org/English/tratop_e/envir_e/edis00_e.htm.

TABLE 11-2

Environmental Cases at the GATT and WTO This table shows the outcome of environmental cases ruled upon by the General Agreement on Tariffs and Trade (GATT) and the World Trade Organization (WTO).

Case	Issue	Outcome
Tuna–Dolphin In 1991 Mexico appealed to the GATT against a U.S. ban on Mexican tuna imports.	The United States put a ban on imports of tuna from Mexico that were not caught with nets that were safe for dolphins (as required in the United States under the Marine Mammal Protection Act).	In 1992 the GATT ruled in favor of Mexico that the U.S. import ban violated GATT rules. But the strong consumer response led to the use of safe nets and to the labeling of imported tuna as "dolphin safe."
Shrimp–Turtle In 1996 India, Malaysia, Pakistan, and Thailand appealed to the WTO against a U.S. ban on shrimp imports.	The United States put a ban on imports of shrimp from India, Malaysia, Pakistan, and Thailand that were not caught with nets safe for sea turtles (as required in the United States under the Species Act).	In 1998 the WTO ruled in favor of India, Malaysia, Pakistan, and Thailand that the U.S. import ban violated WTO rules. But the United States could still require these exporting countries to use turtle-safe nets, provided that adequate notice and consultation were pursued.
Gasoline In 1994 Venezuela and Brazil appealed to the GATT against a U.S. ban on gasoline imports.	The United States put a ban on imports of gasoline from Venezuela and Brazil because the gas exceeded the maximum amount allowed of a smog-causing chemical (under the U.S. Clean Air Act).	In 1996 the WTO ruled in favor of Venezuela and Brazil that the U.S. import restriction violated equal treatment of domestic and foreign producers. The United States adjusted the rules to be consistent with the WTO and still pursued its own clean air goals.
Biotech Food In 2003 the United States appealed to the WTO that Europe was keeping out genetically modified food and crops.	Since 1998 no imports of genetically modified food or crops had been approved in the EU.	In 2006 the WTO ruled that the European actions violated the principle that import restrictions must be based on "scientific risk assessments." But labeling and consumer concerns in Europe have nonetheless limited such imports.

Data from: Updated from Jeffrey A. Frankel, 2005, "The Environment and Globalization," in Globalization: What's New, *ed. Michael Weinstein (New York: Columbia University Press), pp. 129–169. Reprinted in R. Stavins, ed., 2005,* Economics of the Environment *(New York: W. W. Norton), pp. 361–398.*

Even though the GATT panel ruled in favor of Mexico and against the United States in this case, the strong consumer response led to the dolphins being protected. Interested parties in the United States and Mexico worked out a system of labeling that now appears on cans of tuna in the United States, declaring the product to be "dolphin safe." Since 1990 the major companies have sold only this dolphin-friendly product from Mexico, and the labeling procedure was found to be consistent with GATT. So despite the initial ruling against the United States, the outcome of this case has had the desired effect of protecting dolphins in Mexican waters (in addition to the protection they already received in U.S. waters).

Shrimp–Turtle Case In 1996, just after the WTO was formed, a second closely related case arose involving shrimp and sea turtles. In this case, India, Malaysia, Pakistan, and Thailand appealed to the WTO against a U.S. ban on shrimp imports. The United States had banned imports of shrimp from these countries because they were not caught with nets that were safe for sea turtles, as required in the United States under the Endangered Species Act of 1987. Again, by Article XX(g) of the GATT, the United States reasoned that the same requirement could be extended against fishermen from these Asian countries.

Although this case has a number of similarities to the earlier tuna–dolphin case, the outcome at the WTO was different. The WTO still ruled against the United States, but in this case it *did not rule* against the principle that one country could restrict imports based on the production process method used in another country. On the contrary, the WTO ruled that the United States was consistently applying its laws to American and Asian producers in requiring that turtle-safe nets be used. The problem with the U.S. import ban was that it was applied without due notice and consultation with the exporting countries involved, which did not allow the countries sufficient time to employ turtle-safe devices. In other words, the WTO ruling against the United States was on narrow, technical grounds and not on the principle of protecting endangered species in foreign waters.

In many ways, this WTO ruling was more favorable to environmentalists than the earlier tuna–dolphin ruling at the GATT. The WTO panel explicitly recognized that "the conservation of exhaustible natural resources" referred to in Article XX(g) applies to living resources, especially if they are threatened with extinction. After the United States allowed more flexibility in its regulations and made good-faith efforts to develop an agreement with the Asian producers, the laws requiring the use of turtle-safe nets for exporters were found to be consistent with the WTO in a 2001 ruling.

Gasoline from Venezuela and Brazil A third GATT/WTO case that involves environmental issues was brought against the United States by Venezuela and Brazil in 1994. The United States had restricted imports of gasoline from these countries because the gas did not meet the requirements of the U.S. Clean Air Act (which mandates a maximum amount of certain smog-causing chemicals). In this case, the WTO ruled in 1996 that the United States violated the principle that national and foreign producers should be treated equally. The issue was that refineries in the United States were given a three-year grace period to meet the Clean Air Act goals, whereas that grace period was not extended to refineries abroad. So the U.S. import restriction discriminated against the refineries in Venezuela and Brazil.

This gasoline case is often seen as a loss for environmentalists, but economists would argue that U.S. regulations were in fact acting like "disguised protection" against the import of Venezuelan gasoline. From the perspective of promoting free trade and treating foreign producers fairly, the WTO was correct in ruling against the United States. The United States was not blocked by the WTO in pursuing clean air goals, but it had to modify its requirements so that they were applied equally to U.S. and foreign producers.

Biotech Food in Europe A final case concerns whether food that has been genetically modified can be imported into Europe. In 2003 the United States (joined by Argentina and Canada) appealed to the WTO that the EU was keeping out genetically modified food and crops. Since 1998 no such imports had been approved in the EU, though it denied that there was any "moratorium" on these imports. Rather, Europe claimed that it needed more time to study the health effects of genetically modified organisms and was not approving such imports for precautionary reasons.

The WTO ruled in 2006 that the European actions violated the principle that import restrictions must be based on "scientific risk assessments." That is, countries cannot keep out imports based on precautionary reasons but must have some scientific evidence to back up the import restriction. Despite this ruling, the EU can use consumer labeling to allow the buyers to decide whether to purchase foods that have been genetically modified. As in our earlier discussion of the labeling of U.S. tuna imports from Mexico, it is expected that the labeling of genetically modified organisms in Europe will allow consumers to exert their power by limiting purchases of these foods if they so choose. Since 2006, Europe has approved the import of about 50 genetically modified food products, most for animal feed imports.

Summary of GATT/WTO Cases The cases in Table 11-2 show that WTO rulings have not adversely affected the environment: in the tuna–dolphin case, the reaction of consumers in the United States was enough to ensure that dolphin-safe nets were used in Mexico; in the shrimp–turtle case, the WTO did not object to the principle of requiring foreign countries to use the same turtle-friendly nets as do the U.S. companies; in the gasoline case, the imports from Venezuela and Brazil had to meet the requirements of the Clean Air Act, after the same grace period given to U.S. firms; and in the case of biotech foods, labeling in Europe is expected to limit such imports if consumers so choose.

These outcomes have led some observers to conclude that even though environmentalists have lost some specific cases at the WTO, they have gained the upper hand in ensuring that environmental concerns are respected: environmentalists may have lost some battles, but they have won the war! This conclusion does not mean that environmental concerns can now be dropped. On the contrary, the lobbying activity of environmental groups, including the costumed protesters at the Seattle meetings, has been important in shifting public opinion and WTO rulings in directions that support the environment, and such lobbying activities should continue to be pursued.

Does Trade Help or Harm the Environment?

Having clarified the role of the WTO in resolving specific cases brought between particular countries, let us turn to the more general question of whether trade helps or harms the environment. Many of the protesters at the 1999 WTO meetings in Seattle believed that trade is bad for the environment, and that is why they demonstrated. The cases we reviewed above show that these protests can lead to increased regard for environmental protection in WTO decisions. But these cases do not answer the question of whether free trade is good or bad for the environment. To address that question, we need to introduce the idea of externalities.

Externalities An **externality** occurs when one person's production or consumption of a good affects another person. Externalities can be positive (such as when one firm's research and development [R&D] discoveries are used by other firms) or negative (such as when the production of a good leads to pollution). Closely related to the concept of externalities is the idea of **market failure**, which means that the positive or negative effects of the externality on other people are not paid for. For example, when the discovery of one firm is freely copied by another firm, there is a failure of the second firm to pay for the knowledge; and when a firm freely pollutes, there is a failure of that firm to pay penalties for the adverse effects of the pollution or to clean up that pollution.

In your intermediate microeconomics course, you learned that externalities can lead to outcomes that are not desirable from a social point of view. For example, if discoveries can be freely copied, then a firm will invest too little in its R&D; and if pollution is not penalized, then a firm will pollute too much. The solution in both cases is to add some government regulations that essentially create a "price" for the cost or benefit of the externality. To encourage firms to undertake R&D, for example, nearly all governments support a patent system that allows the inventor of a new product to earn profits (which is the "price" received) from its sales without fear of being copied, at least for some period. The ability of firms to patent their discoveries encourages more R&D, which is socially beneficial. To combat pollution, many countries regulate the emissions of their industries and assess fines (which is the "price" paid to pollute) when these regulations are disregarded. These regulations lead to less pollution, which is again socially beneficial. These examples show how government action can improve the outcomes in the presence of externalities.

Externalities and Trade When we introduce international trade, we focus on understanding how trade interacts with externality: does trade lead to more of a negative externality, making the outcome worse, or offset it, making the outcome better? If it is too difficult to directly control the externality, perhaps because it requires coordinated action on the part of many governments, then there might be an argument to take action by controlling the amount of trade instead. As we will now show, there are some cases in which having more trade raises the externality and lowers welfare, but

FIGURE 11-4

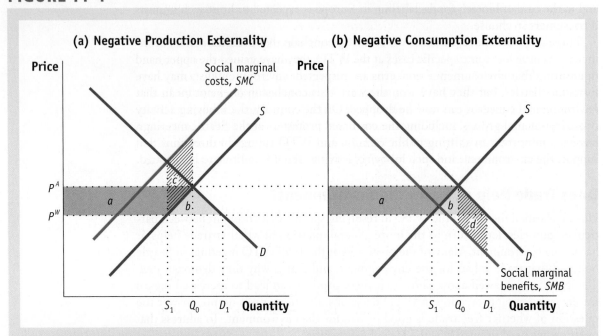

(a) Negative Production Externality

Price

Social marginal costs, *SMC*

P^A

P^W

a

c

b

S

D

S_1 Q_0 D_1 **Quantity**

(b) Negative Consumption Externality

Price

P^A

P^W

a

b

d

S

D

Social marginal benefits, *SMB*

S_1 Q_0 D_1 **Quantity**

Externalities and the Gains from Trade Panel (a) illustrates a negative production externality, which means that the social marginal cost curve, *SMC*, lies above the private marginal cost (supply) curve *S*. With free trade, the price falls from P^A to P^W and home supply falls from Q_0 to S_1. As a result, the social cost of the externality is reduced by area *c*, which measures a social gain that is additional to the private gains from trade, area *b*. Panel (b) illustrates a negative

consumption externality, which means that the social marginal benefits, *SMB*, lie below the private marginal benefit (demand) curve *D*. The vertical distance between the *SMB* and *D* curve, times the quantity consumed, reflects the social cost of the externality. With free trade Home demand increases from Q_0 to D_1. As a result, the social cost of the externality increases by area *d*. That area is a social cost that offsets the private gains from trade, area *b*.

there are other cases in which having more trade reduces the externality and increases welfare. The answer to the question "Does free trade help or harm the environment?" is that it all depends and either case is possible.

To show that either case is possible, we use Figure 11-4. In panels (a) and (b) we show the Home demand curve *D* and supply curve *S* for an industry. (You can ignore the curves *SMC* and *SMB* for now.) In the absence of international trade, the autarky (no-trade) price is at P^A, and the quantities demanded and supplied are equal at Q_0. With international trade, we assume that the world price is fixed at the level P^W, less than the autarky price. The quantity demanded rises to D_1 and the quantity supplied falls to S_1, and the difference between them equals imports of $M_1 = D_1 - S_1$.

It is easy to determine the gains to this country from opening trade. With the fall in price from P^A to P^W, consumer surplus rises by the area *a* (in red) + *b* (in green) and producer surplus falls by the area *a*. The combined effect on consumers and producers (what we call the *private* gains from trade) is area *b*. That outcome is the same as the outcome we saw in Figure 8-2. When we introduce externalities into the picture, however, this conclusion will change.

Negative Production Externality The supply curve *S* shown in both panels of Figure 11-4 represents the marginal costs of production for firms, or what we call "private" marginal costs. When there is an externality, then the true marginal costs for society, the "social" marginal costs, differ from the private marginal costs. When there is a negative production externality such as pollution, then the social marginal costs are higher than the private marginal costs, because the pollution is imposing an extra cost on society. This extra cost of pollution for each unit of quantity produced is measured by the vertical distance between the social marginal cost curve, labeled by *SMC* in panel (a), and the private marginal cost curve, *S*.

When trade is opened, we have already argued that the quantity supplied by the Home industry falls from Q_0 to S_1. This *fall* in production *reduces* the social cost of pollution. We can measure the reduction in the social cost by the fall in production times the distance between the *SMC* and *S* curves. In other words, the shaded area *c* in panel (a) is the reduction in the social cost of pollution. This reduced social cost should be counted as a gain. This social cost gain is added to the private gains from trade (area *b*), so the total gains from trade in this case is the amount $(b + c)$. When there is a negative production externality in Home, then, free trade reduces the externality as compared with autarky and leads to additional social gains.

If we change our assumptions, however, the opening of trade will not necessarily lead to an additional gain. There are a number of cases in which the external cost increases instead of falling, a change that leads to social losses. For example, suppose production externality is positive instead of negative, as would be the case if the industry is engaged in R&D that has spillover benefits for another industry. If the industry doing research has reduced its output because of import competition, then the spillover benefits to the other industry will fall and there will be a social loss rather than a social gain. We studied such a case in Chapter 9, where we said that such a loss might justify an "infant industry" tariff to offset it.

Even when the production externality is negative, as shown in panel (a), we might not end up with *world* gains from trade when we take into account the Foreign country, too. The reduction in supply in Home and the accompanying reduction in the external cost might be offset by an *increase* in supply in Foreign and an *increase* in social external cost there. With pollution, for example, we need to consider whether the reduction in pollution in Home due to lower local supply is really a social gain if the Foreign country experiences an increase in pollution due to its additional exports.

Negative Consumption Externality In addition to the externality that can arise from production, it is possible that the consumption of a good leads to an externality. An example is the consumption of automobiles that use gasoline, and therefore create carbon monoxide, which contributes to smog and carbon dioxide, which then contribute to global climate change. Negative consumption externalities like these mean that the true, social benefit of consuming the good, measured by curve *SMB*, is less than the private benefit from consumption as measured by curve *D*, which shows the price that consumers are willing to pay. For example, in panel (b) of Figure 11-4 consumers are willing to pay the price P^W to consume the amount D_1. That the *SMB* curve lies *below* the demand curve *D* indicates that the social value of consuming D_1 is less than P^W. The vertical distance between the *SMB* and *D* curve, times the quantity consumed, reflects the *social cost* of the externality.

With free trade, the quantity demanded rises from Q_0 to D_1. This rise in consumption increases the social cost of pollution. We can measure the increase in the social cost by the rise in the quantity consumed times the distance between the *SMB* and demand curves. So the shaded area *d* in panel (b) is the increase in the social cost of pollution. This increase in the social cost is a loss for the country, which should be counted against the private gains from trade, area *b*. If $b > d$ then the country still gains from trade, but if $b < d$ then the country loses from trade overall, because the increase in the social cost of the externality overwhelms the private gains.

A particular type of negative consumption externality occurs when people have free access to the same resource that they all desire. A historical example comes from the idea of people grazing their animals on a plot of land they all have access to, called the "commons." Because none of the individuals own the land, there is an incentive to keep letting more animals graze there until the grass is depleted. This outcome is called the **tragedy of the commons**. It is an example of a negative consumption externality: the private marginal cost of letting another animal onto the common is zero, but the social marginal cost of positive because the grass is being used.

In the next sections, we look at a series of examples that illustrate both production and consumption externalities, and the idea that free trade can either harm or help the environment.

Trade in Fish Because of overharvesting, many species of fish are no longer commercially viable and, in some extreme cases, are close to extinction. Examples include the Atlantic cod, tuna in the Mediterranean, and sturgeon in European and Asian waters. According to one scientific study, 29% of fish and seafood species have collapsed; that is, their catch declined by 90% or more between 1950 and 2003. The same authors, writing in 2009, found that the "exploitation rates" of some species had fallen, but that "63% of assessed fish stocks worldwide still require rebuilding, and even lower exploitation rates are needed to reverse the collapse of vulnerable species."[7]

In terms of Figure 11-4, the tragedy of the commons illustrates a negative consumption externality that arises because a resource (the fish) is limited. International trade increases the demand for the limited good and therefore worsens the consumption externality, as shown in panel (b). When it is not possible to control the externality directly by limiting the amount of the resource being consumed, then nations should act to restrict the amount of trade.

The fundamental cause of the overharvesting of fish is not that the resource is traded internationally but that it is treated as common property by the people who are harvesting it. If instead there was a system of international rules that assigned property rights to the fish and limited the harvest of each nation, then the overharvesting could be avoided. One country acting on its own does not have enough incentive to control its fish harvest if other countries do not also enact controls. In the absence of international controls, international trade will make the overfishing problem in the global fishing industry worse.

International agreements for fish and other endangered species are arranged through the Convention on International Trade in Endangered Species (CITES). According to information at www.cites.org, CITES has protected 5,000 species of animals and 29,000 species of plants against overexploitation through international trade.

Trade in Buffalo The fish trade is not the only case in which international trade has interacted with the tragedy of the commons and resulted in the near extinction of a species. An historical case from America occurred with the slaughter of the Great Plains buffalo in a 10-year period from 1870 to 1880. Various reasons are often given for the slaughter: the railroad allowed hunters to reach the Great Plains easier; the buffalo were killed by the U.S. military in its fight against Native Americans; and climate change on the Great Plains—a wet period up to the 1850s followed by 30 years of drought—combined with overhunting by Native Americans. But recent research has uncovered a new reason that dominates all others for the slaughter of the buffalo: an invention in London circa 1871 that allowed the buffalo hides to be tanned for industrial use (such as for belts), creating a huge demand from Europe for the hides.[8] As a result, the price of hides increased in America, and the vast majority of untanned hides were exported to Europe for use in industry.

---

[7] Juliet Eilperin, November 3, 2006, "World's Fish Supply Running Out, Researchers Warn," *Washington Post*, p. A01, citing Boris Worm et al., 2009, "Rebuilding Global Fisheries," *Science*, 325, 578–585.
[8] See M. Scott Taylor, March 2011, "Buffalo Hunt: International Trade and the Virtual Extinction of the North American Bison," *American Economic Review*, 101(70), 3162–3195.

FIGURE 11-5

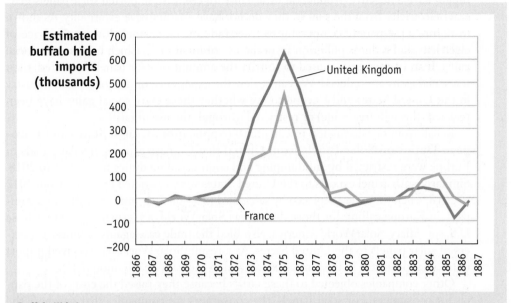

Buffalo Hide Imports This figure shows estimates of the imports to the United Kingdom and France of buffalo hides from the United States. The amount of imports into these countries (in excess of imports to Canada) was small or negative before 1871, but then grew rapidly and peaked in 1875. That year the United Kingdom and France combined imported more than 1 million hides and over the entire period from 1871 to 1878 imported some 3.5 million hides. Much of this trade volume can be attributed to an invention in London in 1871 that allowed buffalo hides to be tanned for industrial use.

Data from: M. Scott Taylor, March 2011, "Buffalo Hunt: International Trade and the Virtual Extinction of the North American Bison," American Economic Review, *101(70), 3162–3195.*

Estimates of the import of untanned hides from the United States to the United Kingdom and France are shown in Figure 11-5. These estimates come from comparing import demand in the United Kingdom and France with demand in Canada, where the invention allowing buffalo hides to be tanned for industrial use was not known. We are therefore looking at the *extra* demand in the United Kingdom and France after the invention was put to use. We can see from Figure 11-5 that the amount of imports into these countries (in excess of imports into Canada) was small or negative before 1871, but then grew rapidly and peaked in 1875. That year the United Kingdom and France combined imported more than 1 million hides and, over the entire period from 1871 to 1878, imported some 3.5 million hides, which can plausibly account for the slaughter of the entire Great Plains herd. A further slight increase in imports in the 1880s likely reflects hides from the northern herd of buffalo in the United States.

Figure 11-5 shows convincingly that international trade, combined with the innovation in tanning technology in London and the absence of any property rights over the buffalo, was responsible for the slaughter of the buffalo. That is a sad result of market forces and one that we want to avoid today through agreements such as CITES. We now turn to a different example of trade policy cases being discussed in the world today that have environmental implications: trade in solar panels.

Trade in Solar Panels In contrast to the overharvesting of fish and the slaughter of the buffalo, international trade in solar panels can bring added social gains. In terms of Figure 11-4 panel (a), think of the good being demanded and supplied as the generation of electricity. About two-thirds of electricity generated in the United States is from fossil fuels (coal, natural gas, and petroleum), all of which contribute to greenhouse gases, which contribute to global climate change. Thus, those sources of supply have a negative production externality. In contrast, imported solar panels generate electricity from the sun, so they do not have any negative externality. As shown in Figure 11-4 panel (a), opening to free trade in solar panels lowers the price of electricity and reduces pollution from the use of fossil fuels, which brings extra social gains. If an import tariff is used to restrict the amount of solar panels imported, then the social gains are reduced. We can review the experience of the solar panel industry in the United States and Europe to see whether these extra social gains have been realized (through free trade) or restricted (through the use of tariffs).

Recall from our discussion in Chapter 9 (**Application: United States and European Duties on Solar Panels from China**) that Chinese exports of solar panels to Europe were restricted by antidumping and countervailing duties from 2013 to 2018. Similarly, solar panel exports to the United States were restricted by duties from 2012 to 2018, when they were replaced by safeguard (Section 201) import tariffs. The company in Europe calling for those duties was SolarWorld, a German company whose U.S. subsidiary, SolarWorld America, also filed the trade case against Chinese exporters of solar panels to the United States. As a result, SolarWorld has received import duties that protect it in the United States and in the European Union (EU).

Other companies objected to these tariffs because they raised the costs of the panels for consumers. For solar panels, the consumers are companies that purchase the solar panels and install them on homes and businesses. One of the biggest of these companies in the United States is SolarCity Corporation, which opposed the use of antidumping and countervailing duties because those duties would raise the prices on the solar panels that it purchases.

Likewise in Europe, the added costs to consumers were recognized, and the EU ended its tariff protection in 2018. The decision to not renew tariffs was meant to promote the more widespread use of solar panels in Europe, as that continent strives for increased reliance on renewable energy sources. The elimination of tariffs in the EU, allowing for greater imports of solar panels, is in keeping with the added social benefits from these imports as seen in Figure 11-4, panel (a). The additional social benefit comes from the reduction in the social costs of using fossil fuels to generate electricity. Unlike the United States, which opted for the continued use of import tariffs in 2018, the EU decided that it will assist consumers and the companies installing solar panels by allowing the European price to fall to the low world price.

A U.S. Infant Industry? The tariff on solar panels that was renewed in the United States in 2018 was intended to benefit SolarWorld America, a global manufacturer of solar panels located in the United States. In 2018, however, its German parent firm went bankrupt and SolarWorld America sold its production facilities.[9] This import tariff, then, did not have its intended effect to protect SolarWorld. Instead, the tariff has raised the price of solar panels for consumers and shifted demand toward other fossil fuel-based sources of electricity, with their added social cost.

Despite this negative social impact from the tariff on solar panels, the tariff may have inadvertently helped the environmental cause in another way. SolarCity, the company that *bought* solar panels and that opposed U.S. import duties, now produces solar panels for itself. SolarCity was founded by Elon Musk, who also founded the car company Tesla, and in 2016 the two companies merged. That same year, SolarCity was building the largest factory in North America to produce solar cells, at the site of a former Republic Steel factory in Buffalo, New York. SolarCity reportedly received $750 million in subsidies from the state of New York to convert

---

[9] In Chapter 9 we described that SolarWorld America was purchased by another U.S. company, SunPower, which intends to produce a reduced amount of solar panels.

that old factory to its new use. The factory in Buffalo, called the Tesla Gigafactory 2 (Tesla factory Gigafactory 1 produces batteries in Nevada), began producing solar cells in 2017. In 2018, it was announced that the Gigafactory 2 would begin producing solar roofs.

SolarCity may have been helped in the short term by the tariff that was intended to protect the now-bankrupt SolarWorld. If this tariff is *temporary*, then it could be an example of the effective use of an infant industry tariff (discussed in Chapter 9). In 2014, SolarCity purchased a smaller company, Silevo, which had developed a new and more efficient technology for making solar panels. The new technology that was developed by Silevo resulted in lower production costs for solar panels. These lower costs would be reflected in the downward shift in the average cost curve needed for infant industry protection to be effective (see Figure 9-10 in Chapter 9). The infant industry argument also requires that the tariff is temporary, meaning that SolarCity will be able to produce solar panels and solar roofs at full scale in the Gigafactory 2 even without subsidies or tariff protection. In that case, consumers of solar panels will benefit from low world prices, and Gigafactory 2 will be an important source of domestic supply, potentially lowering prices even further.

International Agreements on Pollution

Pollution is a by-product of many manufacturing activities. The tragedy of the commons applies to pollution, too, because companies and countries can treat the air and water as a common-property resource, allowing pollutants to enter it without regard for where these pollutants end up. Pollution is an international issue because it often crosses borders in the water or atmosphere. We use the term "global pollutants" for substances that cross country borders. Examples include chlorofluorocarbons (CFCs), which result in a depletion of the ozone layer in the atmosphere, and carbon dioxide (CO_2), which contributes to global warming. In contrast, we use the term "local pollutants" for substances that, for the most part, stay within a country. An example is smog, which is caused by the carbon monoxide in factory emissions and automobile exhaust.

Global Pollutants For global pollutants, a prisoner's dilemma similar to that illustrated in Figure 11-2 for tariffs again applies. Because the pollution crosses international borders, each country does not face the full cost of its own pollution. It follows that there is little incentive to regulate global pollutants. In the absence of regulation, however, countries will end up with the bad outcome of having too much global pollution, so international agreements are needed to control the amount.

Payoff Matrix To make this argument more carefully, in Figure 11-6 we show the payoff matrix for two countries, each of which decides whether to regulate the emissions of a pollutant. The regulations could take the form of limits on how much of the pollutant an industry can emit, which means that the industry must install special equipment to reduce its emissions, at its own expense. Each quadrant of the matrix includes Home's payoff in the lower-left corner and Foreign's payoff in the upper-right corner. We start with a situation of regulation and then measure the change in welfare for Home or Foreign when there are no pollution regulations (or when pollution regulations are not enforced).

Starting in the upper-left cell, when both countries regulate emissions of the pollutant, consumers are better off as compared with no regulations, while producers are worse off because of the expense of the regulations. If one country—say, Home—decides to not regulate, then its producers will gain because they no longer have to install the extra equipment to reduce emissions, but, because of the extra pollution, consumers in Home and Foreign will lose if regulations are not used. The outcome is

FIGURE 11-6

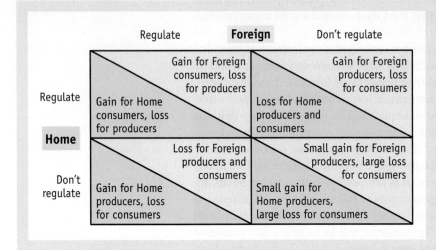

Payoffs in an Environmental Game This payoff matrix shows the gains and losses for home and foreign countries, depending on whether they adopt environmental regulations. If governments weigh producer surplus more than consumer surplus, then the structure of payoffs is similar to the prisoner's dilemma because the Nash equilibrium is to have both countries not adopt regulations. That outcome can occur with "global" pollutants.

similar if Foreign decides to not regulate: its producers gain, and consumers in both countries lose. Finally, if neither country regulates, then there is a large loss for consumers from the extra pollution and a small gain for producers due to the cost savings from not installing the equipment (this gain is small because neither producer is subject to the regulations, so competition can eliminate most of their gains).

Nash Equilibrium Let us use the structure of payoffs in Figure 11-6 to determine the Nash equilibrium. Start in the upper-left quadrant, where both countries regulate their pollution emissions. If either country deviates from this position and does not regulate, it will experience a gain for producers and a loss for consumers. If pollution is local, then the country might realize that the costs to consumers outweigh the gains to producers. That is why the Environmental Protection Agency (EPA) in the United States regulates the pollution from factories and from cars: the gains to consumers from reducing pollution outweigh the costs to producers.

In the case of global pollution, however, this calculation changes. If a country's pollution crosses international borders, as with CO_2 emissions, then the perceived gains to a country's *own* consumers from regulating the pollution may be less than the costs to producers. In that case, neither country will want to stay in the regulated quadrant in the upper left of Figure 11-6 and will have an incentive to *not* regulate its global pollution. Given that one country does not regulate its global pollution, the other country will have an even greater incentive to not regulate: if Home does not regulate in Figure 11-6 so that we are in the bottom row, then Foreign's best decision will likely be to not regulate either because the additional loss to its consumers will be offset by a gain to producers.[10]

Thus, the payoffs shown in Figure 11-6 can lead us to a situation in which neither country regulates pollution, in the lower-right quadrant, despite the large losses to consumers. That outcome is similar to the prisoner's dilemma that we discussed for the tariff game (Figure 11-2): both countries can end up with a bad outcome (with high tariffs or high pollution), even though they are individually making their best decisions. Just like the tariff game, multilateral agreements are needed to ensure that countries end up instead in the upper-left quadrant, with both countries regulating the global pollution.

---

[10] In the problems at the end of the chapter, you are asked to work through examples using specific numbers for the gains and losses in Figure 11-6, to determine the Nash equilibrium.

Multilateral Agreements One example of an international agreement is the Montreal Protocol on Substances that Deplete the Ozone Layer, which has successfully eliminated the use of CFCs. In that case, the scientific evidence showing that CFCs were creating a "hole" in the ozone layer above Australia and New Zealand was conclusive. In addition, the CFCs that were used in refrigerators, air conditioners, and other appliances could be replaced with alternative chemicals at relatively low cost. So it was not that difficult to get all countries to agree to phase out the use of CFCs, which began in 1989 and has already reduced the damage to the ozone layer.

A more difficult case is that of global warming, which is caused by gases (CO_2, methane, and ozone) in the atmosphere trapping the sun's radiation and making the earth warmer. Because these gases are released by the mining and burning of fossil fuels (oil, natural gas, and coal), any attempt to slow the rate of global warming will require widespread change for nearly all countries. Multilateral agreements to address global warming began with a 1992 United Nations treaty and then continued with the 1997 agreement called the Kyoto Protocol and with the 2015 Paris Agreement. These international agreements are reinforced by commitments in regions and countries, such as the **Green Deal** in the EU. These international and national commitments are discussed in our final application.

APPLICATION

The Kyoto Protocol, the Paris Agreement, and the Green Deal

In December 1997, representatives from many nations met in Kyoto, Japan, to discuss nonbinding targets for reducing emissions of greenhouse gases. The principal greenhouse gas is CO_2, which is released by cars, factories, home heating, the generation of electricity through coal plants, and basically nearly every activity that involves combustion. CO_2 creates a "greenhouse" effect, whereby heat is trapped inside the atmosphere, slightly increasing the earth's temperature. Even small increases in temperature can have dramatic consequences through the melting of ice caps, which raises the level of oceans; changes weather patterns; affects agriculture, tourism, and other economic activities; endangers species; and may have even worse consequences.

The **Kyoto Protocol** built on the United Nations' 1992 treaty on climate change, which was ratified by 189 countries, including the United States. Five years later, in 1997, the Kyoto Protocol established specific targets for reduction in greenhouse gas emissions: the industrial countries should cut their emissions of greenhouse gases by a collective 5.2% less than their 1990 levels (which is estimated to be a reduction of 29% from what 2010 levels were predicted to occur without the agreement). Targets for individual countries include an 8% reduction for the EU, 7% for the United States, 6% for Japan, 0% for Russia, and permitted increases for Australia and Iceland. In addition, a market for emissions targets was established so that Russia, for example, could sell its credits to other countries if it produced less than its 1990 level of greenhouse gases.

More than 160 countries ratified this agreement, including about 40 industrial countries. Russia ratified the treaty in November 2004, bringing the amount of greenhouse gases accounted for by the members to more than 55% of the world total. The treaty then took effect three months later, in February 2005. The United States did not ratify this treaty, however, and it was the only large industrial country to not join the effort. Why did the United States refuse to join? There were three reasons given at the time to explain why:[11] (1) although the evidence toward global warming

---

[11] These reasons are all mentioned in a speech given by President George W. Bush to the United Nations in 2001. See "In the President's Words: 'A Leadership Role on the Issue of Climate Change,'" *New York Times*, June 12, 2001, electronic edition.

is strong, we still do not understand all the consequences of policy actions; (2) the United States is the largest emitter of greenhouse gases and meeting the Kyoto targets would negatively affect its economy; and (3) Kyoto failed to include the developing countries, especially China and India.

The first point has become less plausible over time, as the evidence and consequences of global warming become more apparent. The second point also turns out to be no longer true: although the United States was the largest emitter of CO_2 until 2005 (because of its very large economy), China has been the largest emitter since then. In addition, it turns out that the costs to the United States of reducing its emissions are less than what was believed at one time. *The United States significantly reduced its CO_2 emissions after 2007, so that emissions in 2012 were less than those from 15 years earlier, the time of the 1997 Kyoto meeting.* Since 2012 the CO_2 emissions from the United States have fluctuated up and down; the average over 2017–18 was about the same as in 2012, and emissions are predicted to decrease in the future. What has caused this reduction in CO_2 emissions in the United States? The two principal sources were: (1) the Great Recession, which slowed economic growth and CO_2 emissions, and (2) the low price of natural gas, which was used instead of coal to generate electricity. The low price of natural gas was due to increased supplies, starting in 2005, from fracking. The term **fracking** (a shortened version of "hydraulic fracturing") refers to a process for releasing oil and gas by injecting fluids into underground fissures to force them open and release the gas. Fracking is controversial because the fluids used to achieve this process are polluting water supplies near the fracking sites, and because opening the fissures leads to localized earthquakes. Despite this controversy, the natural gas released by fracking is much cleaner to burn than oil or coal. For this reason, the increased use of fracking in the United States has contributed to reduced CO_2 emissions.

The third point—that the Kyoto Protocol left out developing countries such as China and India—is perhaps the major reason why the United States did not ratify the treaty. Just as in the prisoner's dilemma game illustrated in Figure 11-6, if one player does not regulate its emissions, then there is less incentive for the other player to regulate. Since the time of the Kyoto Protocol, however, pollution in China has become worse and the income of its citizens has grown, so there is greater social demand to adopt cleaner technologies. One month before the Paris talks in December 2015, President Barack Obama and President Xi Jinping of China jointly announced that they would develop national plans to reduce CO_2 emissions. President Obama committed that the United States would emit 26% to 28% less carbon in 2025 than it did in 2005, and President Xi pledged that China's emissions would peak in 2030 or earlier, and decline thereafter. These announcements made the prospects for a multilateral agreement at the Paris talks much more likely.

The main goal of the Paris Agreement is to limit the emissions of greenhouse gases so that the global average temperature does not rise by more 2 degrees Celsius (3.6 degrees Fahrenheit) above preindustrial levels, while aiming for the more stringent target of not more than a 1.5 degree increase. Unlike the Kyoto Protocol, which had specific targets for reduction in greenhouse gas emissions for industrial counties only, the limits to emissions in the Paris Agreement apply to all countries and are voluntary. The language in the Paris Agreement actually makes it an *extension* of the 1992 United Nations treaty on climate change, which was endorsed by the United States. Technically speaking, then, the Paris Agreement is an extension of the 1992 treaty and not a new agreement, so a vote in the U.S. congress is not needed. In September 2016, President Obama ratified the Paris Agreement by executive order and U.S. membership started on November 4, 2016.

Less than one year later, on June 1, 2017, President Trump indicated that the United States would withdraw from the agreement, citing the negative impact on the U.S. economy. Under the terms of the Paris Agreement, a country cannot withdraw earlier than three years from when it joined, so the formal notice of the U.S. withdrawal was on November 4, 2019, and the withdrawal becomes effective one year later, on November 4, 2020. By coincidence, that is one day after the U.S. presidential election on November 3, 2020. At the time of writing, it is not known whether President Trump will be reelected, in which case it can be expected that the U.S. withdrawal will proceed, or whether the Democratic candidate and former Vice President Joe Biden will be elected, in which case it can be expected that the U.S. withdrawal from the Paris Agreement will be canceled (if elected, Joe Biden has pledged to rejoin the Paris Agreement on the first day of his administration, as indicated by the quote at the beginning of the chapter).

The goals of the Paris Agreement are reinforced by other commitments in regions and countries, such as the Green Deal in the EU. Under this plan the EU intends to be "carbon neutral" by the year 2050, which means that it will withdraw as much CO_2 from the atmosphere as it adds to it.[12] While some buildings and villages today are carbon-neutral, this goal has never been attempted on such a massive scale. Achieving this goal will require a great investment in renewable energy sources (like solar and wind). Firms in Europe will have to adopt new production methods that release less carbon, and that are probably more expensive. Because goods imported from outside the EU will not necessarily be produced using such "clean" production methods, the EU is considering applying a **carbon tariff** on imports, which means that the amount of carbon emitted in the production of imports will be taxed as the imports enter EU countries. Such carbon tariffs will be difficult to implement because the carbon emitted by every good will have to be assessed. Carbon tariffs will also face objections from the exporting countries. The United States has warned the EU that it will not accept such carbon tariffs, and that it will respond with tariffs of its own against the EU.

In the United States, a Green New Deal was proposed by Representative Alexandria Ocasio-Cortez (a Democrat from New York), who was elected in 2018. Like the EU plan, this proposal was to make the United States carbon-neutral. It has not made headway in the U.S. Congress, however. Less ambitious provisions have been adopted in individual states, such as California. A 2017 bill in California requires that companies perform a "life cycle assessment" on the materials that they purchase (such as steel), which means measuring the carbon emissions in the manufacture of those materials. Only materials that are below a maximum level of emissions can be used in construction.

As explained in **Headlines: California Law Aims to Tackle Imported Emissions**, this California law will make it difficult to import steel from countries like China, as was used to build the new San Francisco Bay Bridge. Most of the steel in China is produced in blast furnaces that emit much more carbon per ton of steel produced than more modern methods. For that reason, it is unlikely that the Chinese steel will meet the California standards. It is possible that this standard will be objected to at the WTO, because it acts as a type of trade restriction that is based on the *production process* for construction materials like steel. As we discussed earlier in environmental cases like the Shrimp–Turtle Case (see Table 11-2), the WTO is becoming somewhat more accepting of such standards, provided that they treat imported and domestically produced goods equally.

---

[12] Trees withdraw CO_2 from the atmosphere, as do the oceans. Carbon neutrality for the EU might be calculated by including "carbon offsets," which means that carrying out tree planting or other carbon-reducing activities abroad that are paid for by the EU can count toward its goal.

HEADLINES

California Law Aims to Tackle Imported Emissions

As of 2019, California companies bidding for public construction projects must do a "life cycle assessment" of the materials purchased for each project. This assessment requires that companies identify all the sources of carbon emissions in the manufacturing of the materials. Only materials that are below a maximum level of emissions can be used in construction.

The Buy Clean California Act was inspired by a controversy over the construction of a new portion of the San Francisco Bay Bridge. The state chose to purchase steel from a carbon-intensive Chinese mill to minimize costs, despite also receiving bids from cleaner mills in Oregon and California. The new law applies to steel, glass and insulation purchased by the state of California. It requires that state agencies take climate change into account in their planning and investment decisions, and employ full lifecycle cost accounting to evaluate and compare infrastructure investments and alternatives. The law requires that the California Department of General Services set a maximum acceptable emissions intensity for each material.

After 1 July, 2019, companies bidding for projects with the state of California will have to submit robust life-cycle assessments of the materials used in the projects and ensure that they meet the new standards. California-based companies that manufacture steel and other construction materials are currently covered under the state's emission trading system. Heavy energy users deemed at risk of competition from companies abroad with lower energy prices are currently given 15% of their tradable permits for free, as a way of trying to avoid carbon leakage. This bill will likely greatly benefit domestic industries by creating a market barrier for high-carbon-intensive foreign competitors.

The new San Francisco Bay Bridge is shown on the left, before the demolition of the old bridge on the right.

Justin Sullivan/Getty Images

The emissions embodied in construction materials, such as steel and glass, can vary greatly depending on how they are manufactured and how the energy used in the manufacturing process is generated. For example, steel produced through the use of arc furnaces can be much less energy intensive than steel produced in traditional blast furnaces. Countries such as China that rely primarily on coal for electricity generation will tend to produce materials with higher embodied carbon emissions than regions such as the EU or US with cleaner generation mixes.

Does this mean that the law will effectively ban the use of Chinese steel and other building materials in California? In the short term, this will likely be the case, as few if any existing Chinese manufacturers would meet the standards that the state will likely set. However, the law seeks to incentivize manufacturers globally to embrace lower-carbon approaches in order to gain access to the California market. . . . How the new law will interact with World Trade Organization regulations around the restriction of trade based on processes or production methods is still something of an open question. In general, carbon-related tariffs will pass muster as long as they are not tailored to discriminate against specific countries.

Source: Excerpted from Carbonbrief, October 18, 2017, www.carbonbrief.org/california-new-law-aims-tackle-imported-emissions.

4 Conclusions

Throughout this book, we have referred to international agreements on trade, including multilateral agreements such as the GATT and WTO, and regional agreements such as USMCA and the EU. In this chapter, we have explored the rationale for these agreements more carefully, and discussed areas other than trade (such as the environment) that these agreements encompass.

The first issue we addressed is why international agreements are needed at all. The answer is that there are strong temptations for countries to use tariffs for their own benefit, or to avoid adopting environmental regulations, as occurs when countries do not face the costs of their own global pollutants. In these situations, countries have an incentive to use tariffs or not regulate, but when all countries act in this manner, they end up losing: the outcome can be high tariffs or high pollution. This outcome can occur because the countries are in a "prisoner's dilemma" in which the Nash equilibrium leads both parties to act in ways that seem right taken on their own but result in a poor outcome (i.e., both use tariffs or pollute). International agreements are needed to avoid these bad equilibria and restore a free-trade or low-pollution outcome.

A second issue we have addressed is that *halfway* steps toward the complete use of markets (as with complete free trade) can also have bad results. We found that such an outcome was a possibility with regional trade agreements, also called "preferential trade agreements," if the amount of trade diversion caused by the agreement is more than the amount of trade creation. Because preferential trade agreements provide zero tariffs only to the countries included in the agreement but maintain tariffs against all outside countries, they are a halfway step toward free trade. Countries that are not members of the agreement are worse off from being excluded. We have also shown that such agreements *might* make the member countries worse off, too, because the lowest-cost producers can be excluded from the agreement.

Another case in which a halfway step toward open markets can make countries worse off is with the overharvesting of resources. We have argued that in the absence of property rights for an exhaustible resource such as fish, opening countries to free trade can lead to even more harvesting of the resource, sometimes to the point of near extinction or extinction. That outcome is bad for the exporting country, at least, and illustrates a negative externality in consumption. So free trade *in the absence of well-defined property rights* can lead to losses. Economists think of this case as opening one market (i.e., free trade between countries) without having a properly functioning market for the resource (no property rights). Viewed in that way, the overharvesting of an exhaustible resource is similar to trade diversion in a regional trade agreement, since the trade agreement also opens one market (i.e., free trade between member countries) without having complete free trade (tariffs are applied against the nonmember countries). Both overharvesting and trade diversion are bad outcomes that arise in settings in which markets are not functioning properly.

In the solar industry, the United States and the EU have until recently applied antidumping and countervailing duties on these imports from China. These tariffs have an added social cost because they raise the price of using solar panels and shift demand toward the production of electricity using fossil fuels. The EU recognized this added social cost and eliminated tariffs on solar panels in 2018, but the United States did not. One firm in the United States, SolarCity, has lowered its production costs through new technology. If this company is profitable after the U.S. tariffs on solar panels are removed, then it may be an example of successful infant industry protection.

Actions by individuals to improve the environment are also important. The Swedish teenager Greta Thunberg is a striking recent example of these actions, as are protests at WTO meetings, which *have* made a difference: although environmentalists have lost some battles at the WTO, some observers believe they have won the war, because the WTO is more willing to take into account environmental concerns in its rulings. International agreements that directly affect the environment are also needed, such as the Paris Agreement of 2015. These international agreements are reinforced by the commitments made in regions and countries, such as the Green Deal in the EU and the Buy Clean California Act.

KEY POINTS

1. There are two primary types of free-trade agreements: multilateral and regional. Multilateral agreements are negotiated among large groups of countries (such as all countries in the WTO) to reduce trade barriers among them, whereas regional agreements operate among a smaller group of countries, often in the same region.

2. Under perfect competition, we can analyze the benefits of multilateral agreements by considering the Nash equilibrium of a two-country game in which the countries are deciding whether to apply a tariff. The unique Nash equilibrium for two large countries is to apply tariffs against each other, which is an example of a "prisoner's dilemma." By using an agreement to remove tariffs, both countries become better off by eliminating the deadweight losses of the tariffs.

3. Regional trade agreements are also known as preferential trade agreements, because they give preferential treatment (i.e., free trade) to the countries included within the agreement, but maintain tariffs against outside countries. There are two types of regional trade agreements: free-trade areas (such as USMCA) and customs unions (such as the EU).

4. The welfare gains and losses that arise from regional trade agreements are more complex than those that arise from multilateral trade agreements because only the countries included within the agreement have zero tariffs, while tariffs are maintained against the countries outside the agreement. Under a free-trade area, the countries within the regional trade agreement each have their own tariffs against outside countries, whereas under a customs union, the countries within the regional trade agreement have the same tariffs against outside countries.

5. Trade creation occurs when a country within a regional agreement imports a product from another member country that formerly it produced for itself. In this case, there is a welfare gain for both the buying and the selling country.

6. Trade diversion occurs when a member country imports a product from another member country that it formerly imported from a country outside of the new trade region. Trade diversion leads to losses for the former exporting country and possibly for the importing country and the new trading region as a whole.

7. The WTO does not deal directly with the environment, but environmental issues come up as the WTO is asked to rule on specific cases. A review of these cases shows that the WTO has become friendlier to environmental considerations in its rulings.

8. In the presence of externalities, international trade might make a negative externality worse, bringing a social cost that offsets the private gains from trade. International trade can also reduce a negative externality, leading to a social gain that is in addition to the private gains from trade. From this logic and from real-world examples, we conclude that free trade can help or hurt the environment.

9. International agreements on the environment are needed for the same reasons that agreements on tariffs are needed—to avoid a prisoner's dilemma type of outcome, which is bad for all countries. The Kyoto Protocol agreed to in 1997, and implemented in 2005, had only limited success because the United States did not agree to participate, and developing countries such as China and India were excluded. The Paris Agreement of nearly 200 countries in 2015 originally included the United States, but it later withdrew.

KEY TERMS

Paris Agreement, p. 357
terms-of-trade gain, p. 358
multilateral trade agreement, p. 359
regional trade agreement, p. 359
trade agreement, p. 359
most favored nation principle, p. 359
prisoner's dilemma, p. 361
dispute settlement procedure, p. 362
managed trade, p. 364

Comprehensive and Progressive Agreement for Trans-Pacific Partnership, p. 365
Trans-Pacific Partnership, p. 365
preferential trade agreements, p. 365
free-trade area, p. 366
customs union, p. 366
Brexit, p. 366
rules of origin, p. 366
trade creation, p. 369

trade diversion, p. 369
multilateral environmental agreements, p. 373
externality, p. 377
market failure, p. 377
tragedy of the commons, p. 380
Green Deal, p. 385
Kyoto Protocol, p. 385
fracking, p. 386
carbon tariff, p. 387

PROBLEMS

1. **Discovering Data** Listen to the podcast #116 called Fish Subsidies: What's the Catch? at tradetalkspodcast .com, and answer the following questions:

    a. How long have negotiations about fish subsidies been taking place in the WTO, and what is the date by which these negotiations should be concluded?

    b. What are the two features of fishing that make it a tragedy of the commons?

    c. What country catches the most fish? Does this country take any actions to limit the catch?

    d. What are EEZs, and why do they differ from fishing on the high seas?

    e. What is IUU fishing? What is one problem that negotiators run into when trying to limit subsidies on IUU fishing?

    f. In order to limit subsidies on legal fishing, some countries favor a list approach, which would specify lists of subsidies that are permitted and that are not permitted. Describe how the proposals from the following countries differ from this list approach: the United States; China; and India.

2. a. How is a customs union different from a free-trade area? Provide examples of each.

    b. Why do some economists prefer multilateral trade agreements over regional trade agreements?

3. Figure 11-2 shows the tariff game between Home and Foreign, both large countries.

    a. Redraw the payoff matrix for a game between a large and small country.

    b. What is/are the Nash equilibrium/equilibria, assuming that the large country applies an optimal tariff?

    c. What does your answer to (b) tell you about the role of the WTO in a situation like this?

WORK IT OUT ⚞ Achieve | interactive activity

4. Consider the following variation of Table 11-1 for the U.S. semi-conductor market:

	U.S. Tariff		
	0%	8%	16%
From Canada, before USMCA	$45	$W	$52.2
From Asia, before USMCA	$40	$X	$Y
From Canada, after USMCA	$43	$Z	$Z
From Asia, after USMCA	$40	$X	$Y
From the United States	$46	$46	$46

a. Fill in the values for W, X, Y, and Z.

b. Suppose that before USMCA, the United States had a 16% tariff on imported semiconductors. Which country supplied the U.S. market? Is it the lowest-cost producer?

c. After USMCA, who supplies the U.S. market? Has either trade creation or diversion occurred because of USMCA? Explain.

d. Now suppose that before USMCA, the United States had an 8% tariff on imported semiconductors. Then repeat parts (b) and (c).

e. In addition to the assumptions made in (d), consider the effect of an increase in high-technology investment in Canada due to USMCA, allowing Canadian firms to develop better technology. As a result, *three years after the initiation of USMCA*, Canadian firms can begin to sell their products to the United States for $40. What happens to the U.S. trade pattern three years after USMCA? Has either trade creation or diversion occurred because of USMCA? Explain.

5. Assume that Thailand and India are potential trading partners of China. Thailand is a member of ASEAN but India is not. Suppose the import price of textiles from India (P_{India}) is 50 per unit under free trade and is subject to a 20% tariff. As of January 1, 2010, China and Thailand entered into the China–ASEAN free-trade area, eliminating tariffs on Thai imports. Use the following figure to answer the questions:

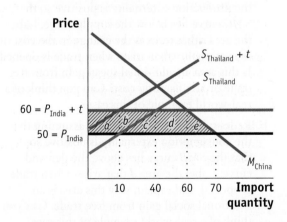

a. Before the China–ASEAN free-trade area, how much does China import from each trading partner? What is the import price? Calculate the tariff revenue.

b. After the China–ASEAN free-trade area, how much does China import from each trade partner? What is the import price? What is the total tariff revenue of China?

c. Based on your answer to part (b), what is the impact of the China–ASEAN free-trade area on the welfare of China?

d. What is the effect of the China–ASEAN free-trade area on the welfare of Thailand and India?

e. The China–ASEAN agreement may lead to a similar one between China and India. How would this affect China's imports from each country? What would be the effect on welfare in China, Thailand, and India if such an agreement were signed?

6. Redraw the graph of trade diversion (Figure 11-3) with the S'_{Mex} curve intersecting the M_{US} curve *between* points A and D.

a. When the United States and Mexico join USMCA, who supplies auto parts to the United States? Does the United States import a larger quantity of auto parts after USMCA; that is, does trade creation occur?

b. What is the change in government revenue compared with before USMCA?

c. Is the United States better off for joining USMCA?

7. Using Table 11-2, explain why environmentalists have "lost the battle but won the war" in their dealings with the WTO. Refer to specific WTO cases in your answer.

8. Refer to Figure 11-4 when answering this question.

a. Redraw Figure 11-4, panel (a), assuming that the production externality is positive so that the *SMC* curve lies below the supply curve. Label the area c that reflects the change in the cost of the externality that arises when trade is opened. Is this area an additional social gain from free trade or an offsetting cost? Can you think of a real-world example of this case?

b. Redraw Figure 11-4, panel (b), assuming that the consumption externality is positive so that the *SMB* curve lies above the demand curve. Label the area d that arises when trade is opened, and explain why this area is an additional social gain from free trade. Can you think of a real-world example of this case?

9. Refer to the following variations of the payoff matrix for the environmental game shown in Figure 11-6. In this problem, a number is assigned to represent the welfare level of each outcome for Home and Foreign.

a. First, consider the case of global pollution in which the government puts more weight on producer profits than consumer well-being when calculating welfare (this is so since a portion of consumer costs is borne by the other country). How can you tell that the government favors producers over consumers from the following payoff matrix? What is the Nash equilibrium for this environmental game? Is it a prisoner's dilemma? Briefly explain.

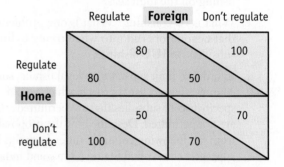

b. Next, consider the case of local pollution in which the government puts more weight on consumer well-being than producer profits when calculating welfare. How can you tell that the government favors consumers over producers from the following payoff matrix? What is the Nash equilibrium for this environmental game? Is it a prisoner's dilemma? Briefly explain.

Regulate   **Foreign**   Don't regulate

	Regulate	Don't regulate
Regulate	70 / 70	70 / 50
Don't regulate	50 / 70	50 / 50

Home

Index

Note: Page numbers followed by f indicate figures; those followed by n indicate footnotes; those followed by t indicate tables; key terms are in **boldface** type.

A

Abercrombie and Fitch, 18
Absolute advantage, 34
  in apparel and textiles, of United States, 39–42, 40f, 42t
  international trade equilibrium and, 46–47
  in wheat, of United States, 41, 42t
Abundance in a factor, 103–105
Abundance in an effective factor, 106
Acemoglu, Daron, 61, 77n
Adjustment costs
  long-run free-trade equilibrium and, 180–181
  in Mexico, NAFTA and, 184
  in United States, NAFTA and, 186–187
AfCFTA. *See* African Continental Free Trade Area (AfCFTA)
Affordable Care Act, 236
Afghanistan, emigration from, 137, 139
Africa. *See also specific countries*
  cotton production of, 320–321
  emigration from, 2, 20–21, 127
  migration to, 20
  remittances sent to, 159
  snowboard exports of, 31, 32t
  trade of, 10
African Continental Free Trade Area (AfCFTA), 359
Agricultural subsidies, 319t, 319–321
  to cotton, 320–321
  domestic farm supports and, 320
  indirect, 320
  political economy of, 331–333
  to sugar beets, 320
AI. *See* Artificial intelligence (AI)
Airbus, export subsidies and, 343–351
Aircraft industry, high-technology export subsidies in
  to Airbus, effect of, 345–347, 346f

with cost advantage for Boeing, 347f, 347–348, 348f
  strategic use of, 343–345
  WTO controversies due to, 349t, 349–351
Airline travel, COVID-19 and, 2
Alvarez, Roberto, 164n
AMC. *See* American Motors Corporation (AMC)
American Factory (documentary), 25–26
American Giant, 95
American Motors Corporation (AMC), 308
American Recovery and Reinvestment Act, 187
Americas. *See also* Central America; Latin America; North America; South America; *specific countries*
  trade within, 9
Amiti, Mary, 220n, 253n
Anderson, James A., 195n
Annan, Kofi, 1, 3, 10
Antidumping duties, 279, 295–299
  calculation of, 298–299, 299f
Apparel
  China's comparative advantage in, 41–42, 42t
  Chinese, tariff on, 237
  manufacture of, factor intensity and, 95
  MFA and, 265, 269–272
  U.S. absolute advantage in, 39–42, 40f, 42t
Apple, 18
Argentina
  exemption from Trump tariffs, 252n
  export subsidies and, 326
  export tariffs of, 334
  immigration to, 130
  in Mercosur, 365
  trade/GDP ratio for, 11t, 12
Artificial intelligence (AI), factor intensity and, 95–96
Ashraf, Nava, 184n, 327n
Asia. *See also specific countries*
  emigration from, 2, 20–21
  factors of production of, 92
  foreign direct investment in, 23
  migration to, 20
  remittances sent to, 158, 159
  trade flows of, 8t, 9

Asylum, refugees applying for, 136f, 136–137, 138
Auctioning quota licenses, 267–268
Australia
  auctioning of quota licenses in, 267
  in CT-TPP, 365
  hole in ozone layer over, 385
  immigration to, 130
  Kyoto Protocol and, 385
  snowboard exports of, 31, 32t, 33
  trade/GDP ratio for, 12, 13f, 16
  trade of, 10
  wages in, 130
Austria
  immigration to, 138
  labor migration and, 20
  snowboard exports of, 31, 32t, 33, 34
  trade/GDP ratio for, 11t
Autarky, 67
Autarky equilibrium, 38n
Automobile industry
  Chinese, infant industry protection for, 308–310, 309f
  foreign direct investment in, 22, 23, 24–26
  rules of origin under USMCA and, 188–189
Autor, David, 77n
Azerbaijan, exports of, 10
Azevedo, Robêrto, 317n

B

Bahrain, household workers in, 161
Balanced trade, 35
Bananas, European quota on, 265
Bangladesh, remittances sent to, 158
Barbie doll manufacture, 199, 200
Barrows, Geoffrey, 269n, 270n
Beijing Jeep, 308
Bentsen, Lloyd, 285
Bergsten, C. Fred, 267n
Bernanke, Ben, 1, 9
Bernhofen, Daniel M., 67n
Bernstein, Aaron, 95n
Bersin, Alan, 125
Bhagwati, Jagdish, 159, 199
Biden, Joe, 357, 358
Bilateral trade balance, 4

Biotech food case, brought to WTO, 375t, 376
Blanchard, Emily J., 332n
Blinder, Alan S., 199
BMW, 25
Boeing, 199, 201
  export subsidies and, 343–351
Bolivia, gains from trade and, 61–62
Border effects, 176
Borjas, George, 160
Bouchet, Max, 332n
Bown, Chad, 256n, 332n, 364n
Bradsher, Keith, 340n
  in Mercosur, 365
Brazil
  ban on computer imports in, 303–305, 304f, 305t
  coffee imports from, 85–87, 86f
  cotton subsidies and, 321
  exemption from Trump tariffs, 252n
  export subsidies and, 326
  foreign direct investment in, 153n
  gasoline case brought against United States by, 375t, 376
  sugar production of, 320
  trade/GDP ratio for, 11t, 12, 68t, 69
Bretton Woods conference, 237
Brexit, 8n, 21, 366, 367–368
Broda, Christian, 185n, 262
Brown, John C., 67n
Brunei, in CT-TPP, 365
Buffalo trade, 380–381, 381f
Burger King, 23–24
Burlington Industries, 41
Bush, George W., 235, 236, 385n
  immigration policy of, 135
  tariffs under, 238, 247–249, 248t, 255, 362
Business services, 223
BYD, 26

C

Canada
  in CT-TPP, 365
  CUSFTA and, 171–172, 181–182, 366
  exemption from Bush steel tariff, 249
  factor endowment of, 105
  factors of production of, 92
  golf club imports of, 170